THE ROUGH GUIDE TO

İstanbul

written and researched by

Terry Richardson

with additional contributions by

Zoë Smith

D0104958

ROUGH GUIDES

roughguides.com

Contents

Introduction to
İstanbul

İstanbul is unique. The only city in the world to straddle two continents and to have played capital to consecutive Christian and Islamic empires, its location, at the crossroads of Europe and Asia, has helped it shape the region's history for over 2500 years. Built on seven hills, the city (in its former guise of Constantinople) was the centre of the Byzantine Christian world from the fourth to the fifteenth centuries AD – the formidable six-kilometre-long land walls, the imposing bulk of the church of Aya Sofya, and the delicate frescoes in the Kariye Museum are just some of the wonderful remnants of this period. The Ottomans, who famously conquered the city in 1453, have left an even more impressive legacy, and it is the domes and minarets of their many mosques that dominate the skyline of the old city, endowing it with the "oriental" exoticism that so enthrals Western visitors.

With a **population** estimated at seventeen million and rising, İstanbul is a metropolis going on megalopolis, a teeming, vibrant urban centre that can make other European cities seem dull in comparison. A city this size may seem an anomaly in a country where half the populace still work the fields in remote villages, but in many ways booming İstanbul is Turkey. It may have been stripped of its capital status back in 1923, but İstanbul exerts a powerful, almost mystical hold on the psyche of the nation, and remains, in the minds of all Turks, the country's foremost city, its cultural, economic and intellectual heart.

No one could deny that İstanbul has its concerns. A city whose population has increased at least twelvefold since the establishment of the Turkish Republic in 1923 is bound to have suffered from such **rapid urban growth**. Traffic congestion, pollution, rising crime rates, water shortages and earthquakes are just some of the problems successive İstanbul mayors have had to deal with.

Despite the problems, however, there's a buzz and confidence to İstanbul that makes everything and anything seem possible. **Foreign investment** has poured in over the last decade, particularly from the Gulf States, once-rampant inflation is down to single digits,

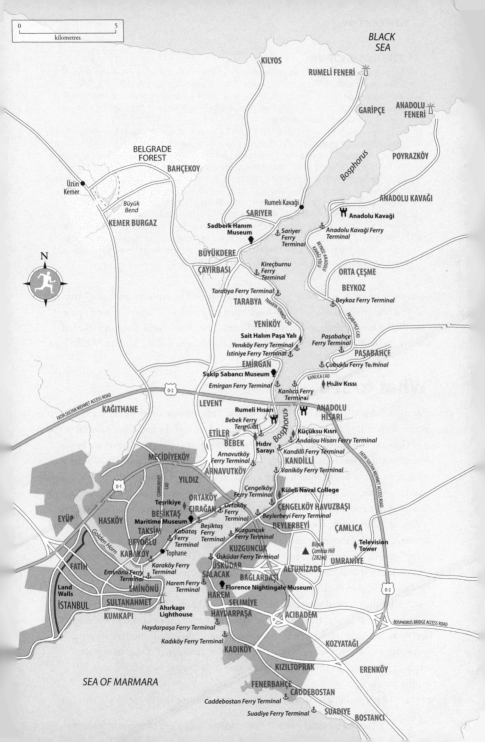

THE BOSPHORUS

Geographically, historically and strategically, the Bosphorus, the thirty-kilometre-long strait connecting the Black Sea with the Aegean (via the Sea of Marmara and the Dardanelles) and dividing Europe from Asia, is one of the world's crucial waterways. With a medley of tankers, ferries and fishing boats weaving their way up, down or across its glittering blue waters, it is also one of its most visually stunning.

The river derives its name ("Ford of the Cow") from one version of a **Greek myth** in which Zeus seduces the beautiful Io. Zeus's jealous wife, Hera, suspects the lovers, so Zeus turns the unfortunate Io into a cow to disguise her. Pursued by an angry horsefly, Io swims the straits to flee her tormentor. Were Io to attempt her escape today, she'd most likely be mown down by one of the eighty thousand or so ships that pass through each year, a consequence of the 1936 Montreaux Convention, in which Turkey was bound to allow free passage, despite the obvious dangers of so much shipping using such a narrow strait (a mere 700m at its narrowest). In ancient times, ships laden with Scythian grain from the Black Sea hinterland sailed through en route to the bread-hungry citizens of Pericles's Athens. Today, Russian tankers filled with oil and liquefied gas ply the same route into the Mediterranean and fuel-starved Europe, helping make the Bosphorus the second busiest waterway in the world – so busy there are plans to build a mega-canal, a second Bosphorus, to alleviate the problem (see p.153).

tourism is booming and the city is home to the İstanbul Biennial, an established arts festival of worldwide importance. It's little wonder that support for EU accession is dropping; İstanbullus know that their vital metropolis can, if necessary, stand alone and take full advantage of its unique position between Christian Europe and the Muslim Middle East.

What to see

For most visitors, İstanbul is a city of two halves: the **old city**, superbly sited on a triangular peninsula pointing across the Bosphorus towards Asia, and the lively districts of Beyoğlu and Galata on the other side of the Golden Horn. Most of the major sights are in the former, within a remarkably compact area that's easily explored on foot. At its heart is the historic district of **Sultanahmet**, an area of twisting, cobbled lanes, overhung by quaint old wooden houses, and studded with landmark buildings from the powerful Byzantine and Ottoman empires: the **Aya Sofya**, the **Hippodrome**, **Topkapı Palace** and the **Blue Mosque**.

West of Sultanahmet, the university district of **Beyazit** is dominated by the **Grand Bazaar**, an exotic "shopping centre" that has been doing business for over five hundred years; while to the north, nudging up to the waters of the Golden Horn, lie bustling **Sirkeci** and **Eminönü**, the former famous for its grandiloquent station, eastern terminus of the *Orient Express*, the latter for the olfactory delights of the Ottoman-era **Spice Bazaar**.

The atmospheric **northwest quarter** boasts the wonderful Byzantine church of St Saviour in the Chora, now the **Kariye Museum**, and, a little beyond it, the mighty **land walls** of Theodosius. It's in the backstreets here, particularly around the ultra-orthodox **Fatih** district, where visitors will find the "traditional" İstanbul of young women garbed in headscarves and skull-capped men sipping sweet black tea while waiting for the next call to prayer. Across the Golden Horn lies the old "European" quarter of **Beyoğlu**, an area of graceful nineteenth-century apartment blocks that has

become the nerve centre of a booming arts, cultural and nightlife scene, focused on İstanbul's major shopping street, **İstiklal Caddesi**.

Recent improvements in the transport infrastructure, notably the tram and funicular railway, mean it's relatively quick and easy to get from one sightseeing area to another – even the far-flung sites in **Asian İstanbul** are well linked to the old city, Beyoğlu and Galata by ferry. The ferry ride alone makes a trip across worthwhile, with the nightlife of **Kadıköy** and the Ottoman architecture of **Üsküdar** the major attractions.

North of the city centre, the Bosphorus is lined on either side with swish villages-cum-suburbs; these can be explored by bus but are best seen from the decks of the **Bosphorus Cruise**, which zigzags between Europe and Asia as it heads up the strait to the pretty fishing village of Anadolu Kavağı. Under an hour's boat ride south of İstanbul, out in the Sea of Marmara, the charming **Princes' Islands**, with their horse-drawn carriages, *fin-de-siècle* wooden villas, pine forests and beaches, have long provided a summer retreat from the bustle of the city – and are cheap and quick to reach by ferry.

There's plenty to see **outside the city**, too: **Edirne**, a former Ottoman capital; legendary **Troy**; the World War I battlefields of **Gallipoli**; "Green" **Bursa**, draped across the slopes of towering Uludağ; and the laidback, rural retreat that is lakeside **İznik**.

When to go

İstanbul and its environs have a relatively damp **climate**, with hot, humid summers and cool, rainy winters with occasional snowfalls. The city is at its best in May and June, then again in September and October, months that offer the perfect combination of dry, warm weather and long daylight hours. July and August can be sweltering in the daytime, especially from midday to mid-afternoon, though by way of compensation the night-time dining and drinking at the city's numerous pavement and rooftop bars and restaurants is a delight. In January, February and even into March, it can be very chilly, with winds whipping down the Bosphorus from the Black Sea and fog rolling in from both the strait and the Sea of Marmara, though periods of bright, sunny weather punctuate the grey, and the city takes on an ethereal beauty in the snow.

THE ORIENT EXPRESS

Immortalized in Graham Greene's *Stamboul Train* and Agatha Christie's *Murder on the Orient Express*, the train that linked Paris and Vienna with İstanbul became a metaphor for style, opulence and, of course, intrigue. The eastern terminus for the *Orient Express* was Sirkeci Station, opened with great fanfare in 1888, right in the heart of imperial İstanbul. Designed by Prussian architect August Jachmund, it was an oriental fantasy, with a Parisian-style dome, minaret-like turrets and Moghul-influenced windows.

The *Orient Express* connected Europe with the capital of the Ottoman Empire, but across the Bosphorus in Asia another temple to travel arose: Haydarpaşa. Completed in 1908, this German-built station, a monumental, mock-castle structure with stunning views back across the water to the domes and minarets of the old city, is even more splendid than Sirkeci. The station was part of imperialist Germany's great scheme to link Berlin and the Persian Gulf by rail – a grand plan that never quite reached fruition.

Author Picks

Most unusual building Take a ferry up the Golden Horn to see the gleaming, gilded nineteenth-century church of St Stephen of the Bulgars, cast in prefabricated panels in distant Vienna and erected on a prime waterfront site. See p.98

On your bike The busy streets of the metropolis are a nightmare for cyclists, so head out to one of the traffic-free Princes' Islands in the Sea of Marmara, the nearest a half-hour sea-bus ride away. Hire a bike and shake off the city grime among pine-scented hills and wave-lapped shores. See pp.158–165

Least-known Byzantine mosaics Virtually every visitor admires the Aya Sofya's glittering mosaics, and most the stunning collection in the Kariye Museum. Just as impressive are those in the side chapel of the former Church of Theotokos Pammakaristos, attached to the Fethiye Camii in the seldom-visited district of Fatih. See p.91

Best walk A walk alongside the mighty land walls of Theodosius is one of the most satisfying outings in the city. Churches, mosques, traditional houses – even the remnants of a palace – dot the line of the fortifications that stretch over six kilometres between the Sea of Marmara and the Golden Horn. See pp.100–107

Eat out in Asia The twenty-minute ferry ride across the Bosphorus (see p.26), from Europe to Asia, costs a bargain 1.75TL. While you're there, enjoy a meal at one of the city's best restaurants, Kadıköy's *Çiya Sofrası* (see p.191), or the traditional *lokanta Kanaat* in Üsküdar.

Hookah havens Trying out a hookah or waterpipe is on the "to do" list of many visitors. The best-known location is Tophane (see box, p.115) but for a toke with a stunning view try the *Ağa Kapısı* café (see p.180) or *Kallavi* (see p.183). For Ottoman atmosphere head to the *Erenler Çay Bahçesi* (see p.180).

Our author recommendations don't end here. We've flagged up our favourite places – a perfectly sited hotel, an atmospheric café, a special restaurant – throughout the Guide, highlighted with the ★ symbol.

21

things not to miss

It's not possible to see everything İstanbul has to offer in one trip – and we don't suggest you try. What follows is a selection of the city's highlights, including spectacular architecture, outstanding museums and culinary treats. All entries have a page reference to take you straight into the Guide, where you can find out more. Coloured numbers refer to chapters in the Guide section.

2

1 AYA SOFYA
Page 43

The most important Byzantine building in the world – as the Hagia Sophia or "Church of the Divine Wisdom", it was the heart of eastern Christendom for close on a millennium.

2 YEREBATAN SARNIÇI
Page 59

It's hard to believe that something so prosaic as an underground cistern could be so fascinating, but combine Roman engineering and craftsmanship with contemporary lighting and you get one of the city's most impressive remains.

3 DESSERT TIME
Page 180

Join the sweet-toothed Turks and tuck into some *baklava*, preferably accompanied by real Turkish Maraş ice cream, in the famous *Karaköy Güllüoğlu* (see p.183).

3

5

 6

9 **MEYHANE CULTURE**
Page 178

No visit to İstanbul is complete without a no-holds-barred night out at a lively *meyhane* (tavern).

10 **SELIMIYE CAMII, EDIRNE**
Page 270

The dome of this sixteenth-century mosque appears to float effortlessly above the faithful praying below.

11 **HIPPODROME**
Page 59

The arena of the Roman, then the Byzantine city, the Hippodrome is now an open park area still boasting the Egyptian Obelisk.

12 **DOLMABAHÇE PALACE**
Page 131

The late-Ottoman Dolmabahçe Palace in Beşiktaş dominates the Bosphorus waterfront.

13 **THE ARCHEOLOGY MUSEUM**
Page 56

Discover İstanbul's fascinating history in this superb museum.

14 **TOPKAPI PALACE**
Page 47

The symbolic and political centre of an empire that stretched from the Balkans to Arabia and the Russian steppes to North Africa.

18

19

20

TRAM ON ISTIKLAL CADDESI

Basics

Getting there

Flights to İstanbul from the UK and Ireland take between three and a little over four hours depending on your starting point. Only two carriers fly direct from the US and Canada, so most North Americans reach İstanbul via a European gateway airport. Many travellers from Australia and New Zealand use a Round-the-World (RTW) ticket that includes the city, but there are direct flights from South Africa. Note that there are two international airports in İstanbul (see p.21).

Making an early booking, being flexible and (especially if flying from the US) avoiding weekend flights are the keys to getting the best deal regardless of season. There's not necessarily a big difference in price between summer and winter, though as most people tend to visit İstanbul in the warmer months (April–Oct), seat demand is consequently higher and prices tend to jump alarmingly unless you book very early. Christmas and New Year, Easter and other school holidays, not to mention Turkish national and religious holidays, also see hikes in seat prices.

Travelling overland by train or car from Britain or elsewhere in Europe is still feasible, but it will take far longer than flying and almost certainly cost more.

Flights from the UK and Ireland

Two **budget airlines** fly to İstanbul. Pegasus (Wflypgs.com) offer one-way flights to both Atatürk and Sabiha Gökçen international airports. In winter (Nov–March) prices from Stansted start as low as £52, rising up to £200 for late, summer-season bookings. easyJet (Weasyjet.com) fly from Luton year-round to Sabiha Gökçen starting at £30, and rising to £250 for late, summer-period bookings; from April to November they also fly from Gatwick for similar prices.

Scheduled flights, particularly if you book early and/or look out for promotional offers, can be very good value and often leave at more sociable hours. However, many of the cheaper, shorter-duration fares have advance-purchase and/or minimum-stay requirements, and severe restrictions on date changes or refunds.

The widest choice of scheduled flights from the UK is with the Turkish national carrier, Turkish Airlines (THY; Wturkishairlines.com). THY links London Heathrow with İstanbul at least three times daily, and there are also daily flights from Manchester to İstanbul. London to İstanbul costs £210 to £550 depending on how far in advance you book; fares from Manchester are around £20 higher. British Airways (Wbritishairways.com) has three daily services from London Heathrow to İstanbul (from around £215 in July & Aug). Flights from Manchester (at least 3 daily) cost around £300 in summer but entail a change at Heathrow, sometimes requiring a coach transfer from Gatwick.

From Belfast, there are year-round daily scheduled services with British Airways, involving a stop in London or Manchester, but prices are high (in excess of £330 in July & Aug). From Dublin, there is now a direct daily flight with Turkish Airlines, starting at €340. Probably the cheapest option is to use a budget carrier from either Dublin or Belfast into Gatwick, then continue with easyJet or Pegasus on to İstanbul.

Flights from North America

The cheapest way to reach İstanbul from North America is to pick up a bargain transatlantic fare to Europe, then arrange the final İstanbul-bound leg of the journey yourself (for onward flights from the UK, see opposite).

Turkish Airlines (THY; Wturkishairlines.com) and Delta Airlines (Wdelta.com) are the only carriers flying direct year-round **from the US**. THY operate twice daily flights (once daily in winter) from New York (JFK), several weekly from Los Angeles and Washington DC and once daily out of Chicago, while Delta fly out of JFK daily in the summer and several weekly in the winter. United Airlines (Wunited.com) generally has the cheapest stopping fares, via Frankfurt. European carriers, such as British Airways (Wbritishairways.com), Air France (Wairfrance.com), KLM (Wklm.com), Alitalia (Walitalia.com) and Swiss (Wswiss.com), route through **European hubs** such as London, Paris, Frankfurt, Milan and Zürich, with the best choice probably being Lufthansa (Wlufthansa.com) via Frankfurt.

One-month **fares** out of New York start from US$735 in winter and up to US$1800 in peak season for a direct flight with THY, $550–2100 with Delta. From LA prices range between $880 and $2300.

There is only one direct flight **from Canada** to Turkey, with THY flying between Toronto and İstanbul several times a week; fares start from Can$1000. Otherwise, several airlines fly to İstanbul via major European hubs. Winter fares from Montréal start at Can$1100 and summer ones at Can$1380, on British Airways via London.

A BETTER KIND OF TRAVEL

At Rough Guides we are passionately committed to travel. We feel that travelling is the best way to understand the world we live in and the people we share it with – plus tourism has brought a great deal of benefit to developing economies around the world over the last few decades. But the growth in tourism has also damaged some places irreparably, and climate change is exacerbated by most forms of transport, especially flying. All Rough Guides' trips are carbon-offset, and every year we donate money to a variety of charities devoted to combating the effects of climate change.

Flights from Australia, New Zealand and South Africa

There are no direct flights **from Australia or New Zealand** to Turkey. However, several weekly scheduled flights will get you there after either a plane change or short layover in the airline's hub city – typically Bahrain, Bangkok, Singapore or Milan – before the final leg of the journey. A marginally less expensive, but far more time-consuming strategy would involve taking a flight to London and then proceeding from there with, say, easyJet (Ⓦeasyjet.com).

Two-stop itineraries from Sydney are around Aus$1850 in low season to Aus$2700 high season, with Malaysian or Singapore airlines. **From Auckland**, Lufthansa (Ⓦlufthandsa.com), Singapore Airlines (Ⓦsingaporeair.com) and Emirates (Ⓦemirates.com) fly to İstanbul from NZ$2300 year-round.

Round-the-World (RTW) tickets including Turkey use combinations of airlines, and could be worth considering for a long trip taking in many destinations; generally, some free stopovers are allowed, with fares starting at Aus$2500.

From South Africa, Turkish Airlines (Ⓦturkish airlines.com) run flights five times a week **from Johannesburg** to İstanbul with starting prices around R7300 – early booking rather than time of year is the most important criterion for bagging a cheap seat. There are also flights **from Cape Town** with several airlines. South Africa Airways (Ⓦflysaa .com) flies daily via Frankfurt or Munich, but these are longer and more expensive.

By train

Travelling to Turkey **by train** is both slow and expensive, and only makes sense if you have plenty of time or are looking for an environmentally friendly way to travel. The best route **from the UK** begins with the Eurostar (Ⓦeurostar.com) service from London Pancras to Paris, then an overnight sleeper to Munich, followed by a daytime Euro-City departure to Budapest, and finally two more nights aboard a sleeper to İstanbul (including a change of engine in Bucharest), making a total journey of five days and four nights. As each leg is booked separately, you can stop off in any of the cities where you change trains, but the cost, a minimum of £350 one way, makes the purchase of an InterRail pass (see below) mandatory.

InterRail passes

The best train deal is provided by an **InterRail pass** (Ⓦinterrailnet.com), which offers unlimited travel (except for express train supplements and reservation fees) on a zonal basis within thirty European rail networks. These passes are only available to European residents, and you must provide proof of residency to purchase one. To reach Turkey via the route described above, you need a Global Pass. For under-26s, you're looking at €409 (£360) for a pass valid for one month's second-class travel covering thirty countries, including Turkey, €619 (£545) if you're over 26. A cheaper alternative is their five-days-travel-within-ten-days option – €169 (£149) for under-26s, or €259 (£228) for over-26s. It's possible to travel first class on an over-26s' pass at a considerably higher cost.

InterRail passes do not allow free travel between Britain and the Continent, although InterRail pass holders are eligible for discounts on rail travel in Britain and Northern Ireland, the cross-Channel ferries, and the London-to-Paris Eurostar service.

Packages and special-interest holidays

Although it's easy enough to sort out your own flight to, and accommodation in, İstanbul, many people still prefer to book a package, partly to avoid the hassle but also because they can actually work out cheaper than a DIY visit. A three- or four-night city break to İstanbul starts at around £160 for three-star B&B accommodation (excluding flights), while a seven-day stay in one of the city's classic luxury hotels can be as expensive as £3000. The determining price for city breaks is the departure airport – the cheapest options from the UK take advantage of easyJet's Luton– or Gatwick–İstanbul runs. **Specialist holidays** focusing on Byzantine art, Ottoman architecture and the like, which rely on the services of a guest lecturer, are much more expensive, costing from £1100 and up for a week.

AGENTS AND OPERATORS

Adventure World Australia ☎ 02/8913 0755 or ☎ 08/9226 4524, ⓦ adventureworld.com.au; New Zealand ☎ 09/524 5118, ⓦ adventureworld.co.nz. Tours of western and central Turkey, which include İstanbul and also the Gallipoli landing sites.

Anatolian Sky UK ☎ 0121/325 5500, ⓦ anatolian-sky.co.uk. Turkey specialist offering city breaks in classic hotels in İstanbul.

Andante Travels UK ☎ 01722/715 800, ⓦ andantetravels.co.uk. Relaxed but fascinating one-week guided tours of İstanbul's Byzantine and Ottoman heritage, with a specialist guide-lecturer, including all the sites you'd expect and a few surprises.

Cachet Travel UK ☎ 020/8847 3846, ⓦ cachet-travel.co.uk. Offers three-day breaks in a couple of decent hotels in Sultanahmet, with an additional nights' option.

Club Travel South Africa ☎ 0860/555 777, ⓦ clubtravel.co.za. City breaks to İstanbul and cheap flights.

Cultural Folk Tours US ☎ 1-800/935-TURK or ☎ 858/566-5951, ⓦ boraozkok.com. Up to nine annual departures by this 1978-established San Diego-based company, led (and musically accompanied) by Bora Özkök. Offer several bus tours that get off the beaten track, but will arrange private tours in İstanbul and environs for interested parties.

IAH UK ☎ 0870/027 2921, ⓦ iah-holidays.co.uk. City breaks in three-, four- and five-star accommodation, Formula 1 Grand Prix packages and ANZAC tours to Gallipoli.

Martin Randall UK ☎ 020/8742 3355, ⓦ martinrandall.com. Offers an interesting week-long art history-orientated itinerary visiting İstanbul, Bursa, Edirne and İznik, and another combining İstanbul with Cappadocia.

North South Travel UK ☎ 01245/608291, ⓦ northsouthtravel.co.uk. Flight agency offering discounted fares – profits are used to support projects in the developing world, especially the promotion of sustainable tourism.

Rosetta Travel Northern Ireland ☎ 028/9064 4996, ⓦ rosettatravel.com. Reliable flight and holiday agent, offering low flight prices out of Belfast, insurance, car hire etc.

STA Travel Canada ☎ 1-888/427-5639, Australia ☎ 134 782, New Zealand ☎ 0800 474 400, South Africa ☎ 086/178 1781, UK ☎ 0800 819 9339, US ☎ 1-800/781-4040; ⓦ statravel.com. Worldwide specialists in low-cost flights and tours for students and under-26s. Also student IDs, travel insurance, car rental, rail passes and more.

Sun Island Tours Australia ☎ 02/9283 3840, ⓦ sunislandtours.com.au. Specialize in eastern Mediterranean destinations, with several options in Turkey, the most pertinent of which combines İstanbul with ANZAC (Gallipoli).

Trailfinders UK ☎ 020/7628 7628, Republic of Ireland ☎ 01/677 7888, Australia ☎ 1300/780 212; ⓦ trailfinders.com. One of the best-informed and most efficient agents for independent travellers.

Travel Cuts US ☎ 1-800/592-2887, Canada ☎ 1-800/667-2887; ⓦ travelcuts.com. Canadian student-travel organization.

Tulip Holidays UK ☎ 020/8211 0001, ⓦ tulipholidays.com. Turkey and North Cyprus-only specialists, offering city breaks in a range of hotels in both Sultanahmet and Taksim. A good bet for combining the metropolis with a beach holiday on the Med or Aegean.

Wilderness Travel US ☎ 1-800/368-2794 or ☎ 510/558-2488, ⓦ wildernesstravel.com. Offers two eleven-day trips each including two days in İstanbul: one encompasses İstanbul, Cappadocia and the Aegean, the other a similar geography but the Aegean section is by yacht. Both allow three-day add-ons in İstanbul.

RAIL CONTACTS

Euro Railways ⓦ eurorailways.com. Really good all-in-one outlet for all sorts of passes and tickets, though you have to book tickets either stage by stage or buy a travel pass.

InterRail ⓦ interrailnet.com. You may save some money by booking your pass via the InterRail website.

The Man in Seat 61 ⓦ seat61.com. This non-commercial site is full of practical advice and planning on any train journey from the UK to just about anywhere in Eurasia (including Turkey). You can't buy tickets here, but all the necessary contacts are provided.

Arrival

İstanbul's main points of arrival are **Atatürk International airport on the European side of the city (used by the majority of scheduled airlines), and the less convenient Sabiha Gökçen, across the Bosphorus in Asia (used mainly by budget European carriers). Trains terminate at the centrally located Sirkeci station in Eminönü, just a short hop from lively Beyoğlu and Taksim, and the heart of the old city, Sultanahmet.**

By plane

İstanbul's **Atatürk International airport** (Atatürk Hava Limanı; ☎ 0212/465 3000, ⓦ ataturkairport.com) is 24km west of the centre at Yeşilköy, near the Sea of Marmara. It has two connected terminals, a ten-minute (covered) walk apart: international (*dışhatları*) and domestic (*içhatları*). The Havaş **bus service** runs from both terminals to the Turkish Airlines (THY) office on the north side of Taksim Square (every 30min; 3.30am–1.00am; 10TL); journey time into İstanbul is thirty minutes to an hour, depending on traffic. Stops include

Aksaray, 200m from Yenikapı station, from where you can take a municipal **train** to Cankurtaran station (for Sultanahmet) or walk up the hill north for five minutes to the T1 tramline (see p.24) for trams into Sultanahmet or across the Golden Horn to Galata. The other useful stop is Tepebaşı, for Beyoğlu and Galata.

The #96/T bus from the airport to Taksim Square costs only 3.5TL, but at the time of writing only accepted the İstanbulkart (see p.24) and the travel smartcard is not available at the airport – though this may change. Alternatively, a **taxi** from the airport costs around 35TL to Sultanahmet and 40TL to Taksim; consult the sign posted outside the arrivals hall for exact fares.

Many old-city hotels can arrange shuttle-bus airport collections for around €25, which saves any potential hassle (such as overcharging or deliberately travelling around the houses to run up the meter) with taxi drivers, or you can pre-book a shuttle bus for between €5 and €10 depending on the number of passengers (see ⓦistanbulairportshuttle.com for times). Leaving the city, set-time shuttle buses pick-up from most central hotels to take passengers to Atatürk International airport (10TL) or Sabiha Gökçen airport (30TL).

The M1 **Metro** (see p.25) runs from Atatürk International airport to the city centre (6am–12.30am; every 10min). To reach it, follow signs for "Hafif Metro/Rapid Transit"; you'll need to buy two *jetons* (small plastic tokens; 2TL each) from the kiosk. The metro connects with the tramway at Zeytinburnu, so get off here and head the short distance to the Zeytinburnu tram stop (this is where you need the second *jeton*). The tram runs to Sultanahmet (30–45min total travel time from the airport) and across the Golden Horn, via the Galata Bridge. You can alight at Karaköy for Galata and Beyoğlu (using the Tünel, the antique funicular; see p.25) or continue to Kabataş, from where you can take the modern funicular up to Taksim Square. If you miss the change at Zeytinburnu, it's possible to change from the Metro to the tramway from its terminus in Aksaray, but this requires a tricky walk beneath an underpass and over a bridge to the tram stop at Yusufpaşa – no fun if you've got luggage.

From the city's second airport, **Sabiha Gökçen** (ⓣ0216/585 5000, ⓦsgairport.com), used by easyJet and other low-cost European airlines, is out beyond the suburb of Pendik, in Asia. Shuttle buses run to Taksim Square (every half-hour; 5am–midnight; 12TL), taking at least an hour. Taxis are expensive (around 60TL to Taksim); the cheapest option is to take bus #E/3 to Levent Metro, then the M2 Metro to Taksim. More fun is to take the #E/10 to Kadıköy (every 30min; 5am–4am; 3TL; accepts cash). The bus stops right opposite the Türyol ferry terminal, which will whisk you across the Bosphorus (over fifty departures daily between 6.45am and 8.30pm; 2TL) to Eminönü.

By train

İstanbul has two main-line **train stations**, one at Sirkeci in Europe, the other at Haydarpaşa, across the Bosphorus in Asia. The two are linked by ferry.

Two daily trains from Western Europe arrive at **Sirkeci train station** (ⓣ0212/527 0051), located 250m above Eminönü ferry terminal: from Athens (23hr) via Thessaloniki (16hr) and Üzünköprü (6hr), and from Budapest (33hr) via Bucharest (20hr). The latter service connects with the rest of the European train network at Budapest. At Sirkeci, it's easy to find a taxi, or catch the tram from outside the station directly uphill to Sultanahmet or Aksaray. Alternatively, catch the tram across the Galata Bridge to Karaköy (for Galata/Beyoğlu) or Kabataş for Taksim via the funicular.

Trains from Asian Turkey arrive at **Haydarpaşa train station** (ⓣ0216/348 8020), 1km north of Kadıköy. For more information see the national railways (TCDD) website ⓦwww.tcdd.gov.tr. Ferries across the Bosphorus to Eminönü (for Sultanahmet) leave from in front of the station (daily 6.20am–12.10am; every 20min) and arrive directly below Sirkeci station. If you're staying on the Asian shore, buses, dolmuşes (both 2TL) and taxis (around 6TL) run from Haydarpaşa to Kadıköy and Üsküdar.

By bus

There are two major **otogars** (bus stations) in İstanbul: Esenler is 10km northwest of the centre on the E800 (İstanbul–Edirne toll road); Harem is on the Asian side between Üsküdar and Kadıköy. All national bus services stop at both, regardless of destination, and both are open 24 hours.

Esenler bus station (ⓣ0212/658 0505, ⓦotogar istanbul.com) is well organized, and some 150 companies have numbered ticket stands here. Most companies run free buses to and from Taksim, or can arrange for you to travel on one run by another company. To get to Sultanahmet from Esenler, take the M1 Metro (every 15min; 6am–midnight) from the station in the centre of the *otogar* to Aksaray and switch to the tram to Sultanahmet. Taxis into town cost around 18TL. Travelling from the city centre to Esenler by light railway, remember to get off at Otogar, not Esenler station. There's a (free) shuttle service from Taksim or Sultanahmet to Esenler (usually 1hr before departure) for tickets booked through a travel agent or bus company's city offices.

Arriving in İstanbul by bus from Asia, it's worth disembarking at **Harem bus station** (❶0216/333 3763), saving a tedious journey to Esenler through terrible traffic snarl-ups. From Harem, regular ferries cross the Bosphorus to Eminönü (hourly; daily 7am–10pm), while private operators run boats to Beşiktaş and Kabataş. Dolmuşes depart every few minutes for Kadıköy and Üsküdar, leaving from the south side of the complex, beyond the ticket offices. From either of these suburbs, ferries cross to Eminönü, and from Üsküdar to Beşiktaş as well (for Taksim), as do buses (try the #110) and dolmuşes. Taxis are available everywhere, but you must pay the bridge toll (3TL) on top of the fare.

By ferry

Car ferries, operated by IDO (İstanbul Deniz Otobüsleri; enquiries on ❶0212/444 4436, ⓦido .com.tr), cross the Bosphorus from Harem to Eminönü (hourly; daily 7.30am–9.30pm). **Sea bus**, car and passenger services from Yalova, Bandırma (on the İzmir–İstanbul route) and Güzelyalı (Bursa) arrive at the **Yenikapı ferry terminal**, off Kennedy Caddesi just south of Aksaray. From here, catch the suburban train from Yenikapı station, across the road from the ferry terminal; it's two stops to Sultanahmet (Cankurtaran station) or three to Sirkeci. Frequent buses depart Yenikapı for Taksim via Aksaray.

Cruise-ship arrivals will go through customs and immigration procedures at **Karaköy International Maritime Passenger Terminal**, across the Galata Bridge from Eminönü. From here (Karaköy-Galata) take the tram to Sultanahmet, or the Tünel up to Beyoğlu, or the tram to Kabataş then the modern funicular to Taksim; alternatively, take a taxi.

City transport

İstanbul has a wide choice of transport, from ferries and modern trams to an antique underground funicular and aged suburban trains. With over eleven million commuters a day, all public transport tends to be overcrowded, and pickpocketing is becoming a concern, so use your common sense when travelling.

The newly extended tramway links most parts of the city that you're likely to want to visit, and is by far the easiest way to negotiate certain sections of the city. The bus system is daunting, but manageable on certain routes; municipal trains are ramshackle but efficient; while taxis and dolmuşes (shared taxis) are very reasonably priced, with knowledgeable – if not necessarily good – drivers. Ferries across the Bosphorus and up the Golden Horn are also a great way of getting around – the year-round Bosphorus Tour is a favoured way of seeing the sights.

Traffic jams are unavoidable in İstanbul, though the historic Sultanahmet district is relatively traffic-free and easily explored on foot, as is most of Beyoğlu. Otherwise, expect to spend time in tailbacks as you travel to and from other areas of interest – it can take an hour by road from Sultanahmet to Ortaköy, for example. Where possible, travel by tram, metro, suburban train or ferry, though these can all be jam-packed at peak times. Kids under 6 travel free on city transport.

Buses

İstanbul's **buses** (*otobüs* in Turkish) come in a range of colours; the red-and-cream, green, and green/blue municipality buses all have "IETT" (İstanbul Elektrik Tramway ve Tünel) written on them. There are also a substantial number of privately run buses, mainly light blue. The main bus stops boast large route maps and lists of services. Most buses run daily from 6.30am to 11.30pm, though last buses depart from the outlying suburbs much earlier. For all municipal buses, either use an

JETONS

If you don't wish to purchase the İstanbulkart (see box, p.24) you'll need to purchase plastic tokens (*jetons*), which work on city buses, trams, metro, light rail, rail and ferries, from a *Jetonmatik* machine. The machines, located next to many stops – including Eminönü, Sultanahmet and Sirkeci – accept 5, 10 and 20TL notes as well as 25 kuruş, 50 kuruş and 1TL coins. The turnstiles at the entrance to tram, metro, train and ferry stops have a slot to accept the *jetons*. It makes sense to buy a handful of *jetons* before setting off on your city explorations, as some stops lack either a kiosk or machine to buy them, and in case the machine may be out of order.

İSTANBULKART – THE SMART-CARD WAY TO TRAVEL

An **İstanbulkart** (a credit-card-sized smartcard) is a must if you're staying for a few days and want to travel around the city using public transport. The card can be purchased for a refundable deposit of 10TL from kiosks in Eminönü, Sultanahmet, Sirkeci, Beyazit/Grand Bazaar, Aksaray and other major transport stops, and be "charged" to whatever value you require at the same places – or from machines with touch-screen instructions located close to major transport stops. The passes are accepted on all municipal and some private buses, sea buses, ferries, trains (for local journeys only), the metro and the tram.

At the entrance to tram, metro, train and ferry transport stops there are turnstiles; hold the İstanbulkart against the receptor and the journey cost (2TL) is deducted. The İstanbulkart is an updated version of the *akbil* system (which worked in the same way but used a metal disc held in a plastic key) and you'll see many locals using the old devices. It's important to know this as many places selling and charging the İstanbulkart advertise themselves only with a sign reading "Akbil dolum merkezi" or "Akbil dolum bayii". It's also possible at major transport hubs (outside Sirkeci station, for example) to top-up your İstanbulkart at a machine labelled "Elektronik bilet ve dolum cihazı" (electronic ticket top-up machine); there are on-screen instructions in English and German as well as Turkish.

İstanbulkart or buy a *jeton* (see boxes, p.24 and p.23, respectively) in advance from one of the white kiosks next to the main bus, tram or metro stops (2TL), which you deposit in the slot next to the driver on boarding. On privately run buses, the conductor will usually accept either a *jeton*, cash or the İstanbulkart.

On the European side, the **main bus terminals** are at Eminönü, Vezneciler (Beyazit), Taksim Square, Beşiktaş and Aksaray; and on the Asian side, at Üsküdar and Kadıköy. No buses pass through Sultanahmet, so walk, or catch the tram three stops, down the hill to the bus station at Eminönü (in front of the ferry terminal). **From Eminönü**, there are buses to Taksim, west-bound services to Aksaray and Topkapı, and services to the Bosphorus shore, through Beşiktaş, Ortaköy and Arnavutköy to Bebek, where you'll have to change to continue on through the suburbs as far as the village of Rumeli Kavağı. Buses **from Taksim Square** head through Mecidiyeköy to the northern suburbs, down along the Bosphorus through Beşiktaş, Ortaköy and Aranvutköy, and across the Horn to Topkapı and Aksaray. The **Metrobus** system, where buses use dedicated lanes, have speeded things up for commuters but the routes are of little interest to visitors.

Trains

The **municipal or suburban train network** (*banliyö treni*), operated by Türkiye Cumhuriyeti Devlet Demiryolları (TCDD), consists of one line on either side of the Bosphorus. It's hardly comprehensive, but elaborate plans exist to link the two via a tunnel under the Sea of Marmara (see p.26) by 2014.

Trains are frequent (daily 6am–midnight) and cheap, though crowded at morning and evening rush hours. One line runs **from Haydarpaşa** (enquiries on ☎0212/336 0475) out to Göztepe and Bostancı, and along the Gulf of İzmit to Gebze; the other, **from Sirkeci** (☎0212/527 0051), runs to Halkalı, along the shores of the Sea of Marmara, stopping at Kumkapı (known for its fish restaurants), Yenkapı (for the sea-bus ferry terminal), Yedikule (for the city walls and fortress) and Yeşilköy, not far from Atatürk International airport. Journeys cost the same flat **fare** (2TL) and İstanbulkarts are accepted on local lines.

Trams

The **main tram** service, or T1 *tramvay* (see box, p.27 for the **antique tram**) runs from Zeytinburnu via Topkapı to Aksaray (where it connects with the M1 Metro (or *hafif* metro), Laleli/Üniversite, Beyazit, Cemberlitaş, Sultanahmet, downhill to Eminönü, and across the Galata Bridge to Karaköy (Galata), Tophane, Fındıklı and Kabataş. It is the most useful mode of transport in the city for the majority of visitors, linking the old city (Sultanahmet and the Grand Bazaar) with the cultural and nightlife hub of Beyoğlu across the Golden Horn. Trams are frequent and operate from 6am to midnight. Approaching trams signal their arrival with a bell, and passengers must wait on the concrete platforms, placed at regular intervals along the tracks. Note that the tram stops are marked, confusingly, by the same "M" sign as the Metro.

Jetons (2TL) can be bought at *Jetonmatix* machines (see box, p.23) and are deposited in turnstiles on entry, or you can use an İstanbulkart.

The Metro

There are now several Metro lines in the city, though only the M1 and M2 lines (see transport map) will be of interest to the vast majority of visitors. The M1 Metro, or *hafif* metro, which runs west from Aksaray via the inter-city *otogar* near Esenler, to Atatürk International airport, is really a light railway, as only small sections of this line run underground. The M2 Metro, on the northern side of the Golden Horn, runs underground from Şişhane, at the Tünel end of İstiklal Caddesi, via Taksim Square, Omsmanbey, Şişli, Gayrettepe Levent, and right out to Haciosmanbey. The Metro systems either side of the Golden Horn will link up in the next few years, with a controversial bridge to connect them already under construction across the historic inlet. Trains leave every fifteen minutes (more frequently at peak periods) between 6am and 12.30am; *jetons* (2TL) are inserted in turnstiles on entry, or use the İstanbulkart. The M1 Metro, as well as being useful for getting to and from the airport, can also be used to reach the city walls, not far from the Kariye Museum.

Funiculars and the cable car

The **antique funicular** between Karaköy and İstiklal Caddesi in Beyoğlu is known as the **Tünel**, and connects with the antique tram (see p.27) on İstiklal Caddesi. A **modern funicular** (F1 on the transportation map) links Kabataş, at the northern end of the tramline, with Taksim Square (and the M2 Metro). The **cable car** linking the southern shore of the Golden Horn in Eyüp with the *Pierre Loti* café and Eyüp cemetery does not link with the rail or tram systems, but does save your legs. Use your İstanbulkart or buy a *jeton* (see p.24 and p.23 respectively) for all of these.

Dolmuşes

Dolmuşes are shared taxis (usually in the form of a minibus) running on fixed routes, departing only when full ("dolmuş" means "full"). Services on longer routes tend to run along main arteries and depart according to a schedule known only to their drivers. Dolmuşes display their destination in the window. A

USEFUL BUS ROUTES

If you can get the hang of it, buses are an okay way to travel around the city, and for some locations are the only feasible option, short of an expensive taxi ride. For information in English on all routes, check ⓦiett.gov.tr/en.

ASIAN SIDE
#12 and **#14** Kadıköy to Üsküdar.
#15/A Üsküdar up the Bosphorus to Beylerbeyi, Kanlıca and Anadolu Kavaği.

EUROPEAN SIDE
#22 Kabataş up the Bosphorus including Beşiktaş, Ortaköy, Kuruçeşme, Arnavutköy, Bebek, Emirgan and İstinye.
#25/A Haciosman Metro to Maslak, Tarabya, Sariyer and Rumeli Kavaği.
#28 Edirnekapı to Beşiktaş via Fatih, Eminönü, Karaköy, Tophane and Kabataş.
#28/T Topkapı to Beşiktaş via Fatih, Eminönü, Karaköy, Tophane and Kabataş.
#30/D Yenikapı to Ortaköy via Unkapanı/Atatürk Bridge, Karaköy and Beşiktaş.
#36/V and **#37Y** Vezneciler (Beyazit) to Edirnekapı via Fatih/Yavuz Selim Camii (city land walls and Kariye Museum).
#38/E Eminönü to Edirnekapı (city land walls) via Unkapanı/Atatürk Bridge and Fatih.
#40 Taksim up the Bosphorus including Beşiktaş, Kuruçeşme, Arnavutköy, Bebek, Emirgan, İstinye, Tarabya and Sariyer.
#43 Taksim to Beşiktaş via Nişantaşı and Maçka.
#54/HT Taksim to upper Golden Horn (for Miniaturk, Rami Koç Museum and Santralıstanbul).
#80T Taksim to Yedikule (city land walls).
#87 Taksim to Edirnekapı (city land walls and Kariye Museum).
#96T Taksim to Atatürk airport.
#151 Sariyer to Kiliyos (Black Sea) via Rumeli Fener.
#830 Otogar to Taksim via Fatih, Unkapanı and Tepebaşı.

THE MARMARAY PROJECT

In the autumn of 2008, the laying of sections of tubing forming a **tunnel under the Bosphorus** was completed and an underwater link between European and Asian İstanbul, an idea that first hit the drawing board back in the Ottoman period, finally became a reality. The tunnel will form part of a line stretching some 76km, from Halkalı on the European side to Gebze in Asia, and will link the city's two international airports, Atatürk and Sabiha Gökçen. The section from Yenikapı to Sirkeci will be underground, as will the new Sirkeci station and its counterpart across the Bosphorus in Üsküdar. The public opening was originally scheduled for 2011, but work has been delayed by the unearthing of many important archeological finds during construction, notably a massive Byzantine harbour, complete with more than thirty ships, at Yenikapı, and the opening has been rescheduled for 2014. The new rail link will integrate with the rest of the city's transport system, and should see some seventy thousand passengers per hour whizzing under the waters of the Bosphorus.

flat **fare** (fixed by the municipality) is levied: watch what Turkish passengers are paying – usually a little more than a municipality bus – shout your destination to the driver and pay accordingly, passing the money via other passengers. Dolmuş stands at points of origin are denoted with a signposted "D". Services can be hailed at any point along the route; they're most frequent during rush hour and operate later than the regular buses, sometimes until 2am. To get off, call: "*müsait bir yerde*" or "*inecek* (pronounced "inejek") *var*".

The only dolmuş routes of interest to most visitors are the yellow minibuses departing from the northern end of Tarlabaşı Bulvarı, just below Taksim Square, which run across into the old town and along the Sea of Marmara to the city land walls near Yedikule, or those running up the Asian side of the Bosphorus between Kadıköy and Üsküdar and beyond.

Taxis

Taxis are ubiquitous, with over nineteen thousand legal *taksici* (taxi drivers) in the city. They are invariably painted yellow. **Fares** are reasonable: a theoretical rate of just under 10TL per 5km, with an extra toll when crossing either of the Bosphorus bridges. All taxis are equipped with **meters**, but check that the driver switches it on to avoid arguments later. The rate flashes up alternately with the running cost. If there's any trouble, start discussing the *polis*, especially at any suggestion of a flat fare or if you think the driver has taken the longest possible route (both distinct possibilities), and if necessary note the registration number and call the Tourist Police (see p.33). Unregistered cabs are a major headache, with some ten thousand working the streets. If possible, arrange a taxi through your hotel as the staff should have some idea of the fare to your destination. Better still, persevere with the very efficient public transport system.

Ferries, sea buses and water taxis

The main **ferry** company is the efficient Sehir Hatları (City Lines; ☎444 1851, ⓦ.sehirhatlari.com. tr). A timetable, available from the ferry terminals and from tourist offices and their website, is essential so that you can be sure when the last ferry back departs, as timings do change. On the busiest routes – such as Karaköy to Haydarpaşa and Kadıköy, there are generally three to five ferries an hour between 6am and midnight; all have a flat fare of 2TL each way. For both ferries and the faster sea buses (see opposite), buy a *jeton* and deposit it at the turnstile on entry, or use your İstanbulkart (and save over 2TL per return trip). The busiest routes are a lso served by several other small, privately run ferries, many under the umbrella of the co-operative **Turyol**. Most Turyol boats leave from a terminal just west of the Galata Bridge in Eminönü, or over the water in Karaköy, again just west of the Galata Bridge, the destinations being Haydarpaşa and Kadıköy, respectively; tickets are sold at kiosks on the quayside.

At the main **City Ferry Terminal** at Eminönü – between Sirkeci station and the Galata Bridge – there's a line of ferry quays or terminals (*iskelesi* in Turkish). The reorganization and updating of the ferry terminals had almost been completed at the time of writing, but it's possible the authorities will change the destinations from the new departure terminals so be wary. On the west side of the Galata Bridge is Yemiş İskelesi, for ferries up the Golden Horn to Eyüp via Kasimpaşa, Fener and Balat (roughly hourly 7am–8pm). The ferry actually originates across the Bosphorus in Üsküdar so on the return journey make sure you get off at Eminönü. The terminal nearest to (the east side of) the Galata Bridge is Boğaz İskelesi, from where ferries run up the Bosphorus to Rumeli Kavaği (see box, p.147). Ferries from the terminal just east of this, the Hezarfen Ahmet Çelebi, cross to Üsküdar (daily 6.35am–9.30pm), while east of this the Evliya Çelebi terminal has boats crossing to Kadıköy (daily 7.30am–9pm). The Katıb Çelebi terminal had yet to be designated at the time of writing; east again of this is the terminal to IDO car ferry to Harem (daily 7am–8.40pm).

Regular Şehir Hatları ferries link Karaköy (on the other side of the Galata Bridge) to Haydarpaşa and Kadıköy (daily 6.30am–midnight). From Kabataş, ferries cross the Bosphorus to Kadıköy (Mon–Fri 7am–8pm), with a daily service (6.45am–9pm) from Beşiktaş to Kadıköy and Üsküdar. There are also regular ferries to the Princes' Islands from Kabataş (daily 6.50am–midnight, less frequent in winter; see p.159, for more details).

From Boğaz İskelesi, Şehir Hatları operates the popular daily **Bosphorus Cruise** (Boğaz Hatti; see box, p.147), a boat trip to Rumeli Kavağı and Anadolu Kavağı, the most distant villages up the Bosphorus on the European and Asian sides respectively (June–Oct daily 10.35am, noon, 1.35pm & 7pm).

Fast **sea buses** (deniz otobüsleri) run by İDO (İstanbul Deniz Otobüsleri; ☎0212/444 4436, ⓦido .com.tr), which run from Kabataş, at the eastern end of the tramway, across the Bosphorus and into the Sea of Marmara, though these run less frequently except at peak commuter times. Sea-bus fares are a flat 7.5TL for the Princes' Islands (6–12 daily) and 18TL to Yalova on the south shore of the Sea of Marmara. There are numerous other sea-bus routes, including Bakırköy to Bostancı via Kadıköy and Yenikapı (hourly 7.30am–10pm). **Timetables** are available from all sea-bus terminals. If you're heading for İznik via Yalova or Bursa, sea buses and the slightly quicker *hızlı feribot* (fast ferries) depart frequently from the terminal in Yenikapı, also a stop on the suburban train line from Sirkeci.

Water taxis (deniz taksi) are massively oversubscribed so, unless the fleet is considerably increased, don't bank on whizzing up and down the Bosphorus in one. Theoretically, you call ☎444 4498, give your name and your pick-up, drop-off points and a water taxi will collect you from one of the 27 designated docks, which include the Princes' Islands as well as numerous stops on both sides of the Bosphorus as far up as Rumeli Kavağı. Unless you are a Turkish speaker, the ⓦdeniztaksi.com website is of little use, so use your hotel to book one.

Driving

Driving in İstanbul is extremely hazardous – after South Korea, Turkey has the second highest fatality rate in the world (with 77 deaths per 100,000 vehicles on the road; by comparison, the UK has 13 deaths for the same number of vehicles) – and should be avoided unless you're a very experienced driver, and have the wherewithal to negotiate a strange, traffic-choked metropolis with poor signposting and few parking spaces. The only time it would make any sense is if you're circling the Sea of Marmara to take in Edirne, Gallipoli, Troy, Bursa and İznik. If you're still determined to drive in the city, you need to be at least 21 years old (27 for Groups E and above) to rent a car, with a **driving licence** held for at least one

TRAVEL NOSTALGIA: THE TÜNEL AND THE ANTIQUE TRAM

The easy way to make the long haul up the hill from the Golden Horn onto İstiklal Caddesi, İstanbul's premier shopping street, is via the **Tünel** (every 15min; Mon–Sat 7am–10pm, Sun 7.30am–10pm; 3TL). This one-stop funicular railway opened in 1875 and is the world's third-oldest passenger underground. The lower Tünel station is in Karaköy, just across the Galata Bridge, from where it takes a matter of minutes to whisk you to the upper station, at the bottom (southern) end of İstiklal Caddesi; use the İstanbulkart (see p.24) or purchase a ticket from the kiosk just inside the Tünel building before boarding. The Rahmi Koç Industrial Museum in Hasköy (see p.116) has a restored nineteenth-century Tünel car on display, worth seeking out if you're a period-transport or nostalgia buff.

The **antique tram** rattles its way along the 1.5-kilometre length of İstiklal Caddesi from the upper Tünel station in Karaköy to Taksim Square (every 15min; daily 9am–9pm; 3TL). Tickets can be purchased from kiosks at either end of the route or at the fixed-stop halfway, at Galatasaray School; the İstanbulkart is also accepted. With its turn-of-the-century look (drivers are adorned in vintage costumes) and smart red-and-cream livery, it lends pedestrianized İstiklal Caddesi a certain period charm – as well as saving your legs.

year. An **International Driving Permit**, from the RAC or AA in Britain/Australasia or the AAA/CAA in North America, is not essential – your own home licence will do at a pinch – but is very helpful, especially at traffic-control points (show the police your IDP, not your main home licence, in case they decide to keep it for any reason). **Rental rates** are quite high due to expensive vehicle prices in Turkey, and the high accident rate. The agencies below have pick-up points at Atatürk International airport and (bar Europcar) Sabiha Gökçen, and offices elsewhere in İstanbul – check their websites for working hours. Expect to pay 70–190TL a day for a week's hire (ten percent more for daily hire), depending on the car.

When checking a car out, agency staff should make a thorough diagrammatic notation of any **blemishes** on the vehicle – it's in your interest to make sure they do this, otherwise you might be blamed for something you didn't do. If you have an accident serious enough to immobilize you and/or cause major damage to other people's property, the traffic police will appear and administer alcohol tests to all drivers, results of which must also be submitted along with an official **accident report** (*kaza raporu*) in order to claim insurance cover. It's an offence to move a vehicle involved in a crash involving more than a minor bump before the police give the all-clear – leave it where it is, even if you're blocking traffic, otherwise all drivers involved risk an on-the-spot fine.

Fuel costs are very high (the second most expensive in the world after Japan) because of government taxes; diesel (*mazot* or *dizel*) is 3.9TL per litre, lead-free (*kurşunsuz*) around 4.5 TL per litre. Many of the major arteries around İstanbul are toll roads and you are required to buy a KGS card for €20 or 35TL from the rental agency, which will allow you to use the fast-booths at the toll points. There are plenty of filling stations on all major – and many minor – highways and at numerous points across İstanbul; the biggest have restaurants and mini-supermarkets, even the smallest a shop and toilets. **Credit and debit cards** (Visa Electron, Visa, Master-Card, American Express) are widely honoured for fuel purchases. As with most card transactions in Turkey, chip-and-PIN protocol is the norm. Car **repair workshops** and spare-part dealers are located in industrial zones called *sanayis* on the city's – and other town – outskirts.

CAR-RENTAL AGENCIES

Avis Ⓦ avis.com.
Budget Ⓦ drivebudget.com.
Europcar Ⓦ europcar.com.
Hertz Ⓦ hertz.com.

Tours

It's worth considering a **city tour** if you're pushed for time or just don't want to plan an itinerary yourself. The more specialist options offered by Fest (see below) take you to some little-known sites that you may struggle to find yourself, and provide an expert guide to interpret them for you.

TOUR AGENCIES

Backpackers Travel Yeni Akbıyık Cad 22, Sultanahmet ☎ 0212/638 6343, Ⓦ backpackerstravel.net. Conveniently located agency offering half- and one-day tours of the city.

City Sightseeing İstanbul Aya Sofya Karşısı 1, Sultanahmet ☎ 0212/234 7777, Ⓦ plantours.com. Hop-on, hop-off open-top bus tours departing opposite the Aya Sofya or Taksim Square, and allowing stops at the Dolmabahçe Palace, Old Pera, Edirnekapı (city walls) and Kumkapı.

Fest Travel Barbaros Bulvarı 74, Balmucu ☎ 0212/216 1036, Ⓦ festtravel.com.tr. Fest has been running a variety of cultural tours around the city for 22 years, and is the official operator for the Istanbul Foundation for Culture and Arts (IKSV). Their regular programme includes a half-day on the Bosphorus, an Islamic cultural tour, a Jewish heritage day and a hop-on, hop-off bus tour of the main sites. More interesting are the walking tours where the guides, usually specialist lecturers in their field, take you to out-of-the-way, little-known sites in various quarters of the city.

İstanbul Walks Eski Bağdat Cad 50/14, Küçükyalı ☎ 0216/489 6032, Ⓦ www.istanbulwalks.net. A limited programme of half-day walks from €20 to €55 per head, running most days of the year, with licensed guides. Separate walks include the classic sites on both sides of the Golden Horn.

Kirkit Voyage Amiral Tafdil Sok 12, Sultanahmet ☎ 0212/518 2282, Ⓦ kirkit.com. Very reliable company offering a variety of walking tours of the city – one concentrates on Byzantine İstanbul, another the palaces of the Bosphorus – using knowledgeable, professional guides. Also does tailor-made tours. The office is handily located if you're staying in Sultanahmet.

Turista Divan Yolu Cad 16, Sultanahmet ☎ 0212/518 6570, Ⓦ turistatravel.com. Very reliable, bustling general travel agency in the heart of the old city, for everything from daily İstanbul tours to plane and train tickets and car rental.

The media

Newspapers and magazines weren't even allowed in the country until the middle of the nineteenth century; since then, however, lost time has been made up for with a vengeance.

Nearly forty mastheads, representing the full gamut of public tastes from elevated to gutter, compete for readers' attention. The airwaves were controlled exclusively by the government until the late 1980s, but with satellite dishes and overseas transmitters widely available, a vast quantity of private, cable and digital stations now flourishes across Turkey.

Turkish-language publications

Around seventy percent of the **newspapers** sold nationally are produced by two giant media conglomerates, the Doğan and Sabah groups. Three titles – *Sabah*, *Hürriyet* and *Milliyet* – dominate the middle market; slightly to the left of these stands *Radikal*, the best paper to pick up in İstanbul for listings of cinema, exhibitions and concerts. *Taraf* is more radical than *Radikal* and incurs establishment ire on virtually a daily basis. The only high-end newspaper, *Cumhuriyet*, founded as the mouthpiece of the Turkish Republic in 1924, mixes conservative nationalism with old-style socialism. Turkey's Islamist papers generally give intelligent and thoughtful coverage – of the biggest sellers, *Yeni Şafak* and *Zaman*, the former is a strong supporter of the Justice and Development (AK) Party elected to power in 2002 and again in 2007, while the latter takes a more independent line. The principal weekly **magazines** are the picture-driven *Tempo* and *Aktüel*, which serve up a diet of showbiz gossip, news and features.

English-language publications

The longest-running English-language **newspaper**, widely available across central İstanbul, is the *Hürriyet Daily News*. The weekend edition, covering both Saturday and Sunday, has more features and less up-to-date news than the daily. Every edition has a listings page devoted, in the main, to İstanbul. *Today's Zaman*, the English-language offshoot of *Zaman*, is backed by the controversial figure of Fetullah Gülen, an Islamic scholar/businessman currently in exile in the US. It's glossier than the *TDN* and has more features written by expats than its rival. Broadly speaking, the *TDN* follows the secular/nationalist line and *Today's Zaman* is liberal/Islamic. Both cost 1.50TL and have online versions.

Glossy **magazines** include the bimonthly *Istanbul: The Guide*, sold at newsstands (7.50TL) or available free in many of the city's larger hotels. It's fine for listings of shops, restaurants, cafés and the like but poor on up-and-coming events and features. *TimeOut Istanbul*, the local imprint of the London listings magazine, is far superior and has an eighty-page English edition (6TL) of what's-on listings and useful coverage of new bars, clubs and restaurants. The bimonthly *Cornucopia*, an expensive (£10), glossy upmarket magazine, sometimes has interesting features on İstanbul, as well as general pieces on everything from carpets to property renovation. Its website (Ⓦcornucopia .net) has an online "what's on" İstanbul arts diary.

Easiest to find of the **international papers** are *The Guardian* (European edition), the *International Herald Tribune* and *USA Today*, though many other titles can be found in Sultanahmet and in Taksim/Beyoğlu.

Television

Turkish **TV** has come a long way since the early 1980s, when it was restricted to a single, closely controlled, state-run channel. There are now a plethora of national channels and many more regional ones.

Turkish channels include several state-owned TRT (Turkish Radio and Television) channels where programming veers between foreign historical drama and American films (both dubbed into Turkish) and talking-heads panel discussions, punctuated by classical Turkish music interludes, variety shows and soaps. TRT Müzik features traditional Turkish music, while TRT-6 made history in 2009, becoming the first state-run TV channel broadcasting in the Kurdish language, a tongue banned for political reasons until the 1990s. Private channels offering light entertainment, film reruns and current affairs, Show, Star, ATV and Kanal D are the most popular. Music-orientated channels devoting their time mainly to Turkish pop videos and short youth-related features include Kral and Power Turk.

There are several **English-language channels** shown on the nation's digital provider, Digiturk, which most mid-range-and-above İstanbul hotels offer. CNBC-e, a joint venture with America's NBC, devotes evenings and weekends to a mix of films and US TV comedy and drama shows. Its rival, E2, has a similar mix, and both are in English with Turkish subtitles. BBC Entertainment is anything but, with a tedious mix of home makeover, cooking programmes and mainstream comedies, though the post-10pm schedule is much better. Also available are CNN, BBC World, Euronews and Al-Jazeera, as well as Eurosport, National Geographic and the History Channel.

For football, Digiturk is the main provider and live Turkish Premier League football is exclusive to its Lig TV channel (look for the banners advertising it outside bars and cafés). English Premier League matches are shown on the pay-channel Premier League TV, available wherever Lig TV is showing; other matches, including the English Championship, are on a separate provider, D-Smart. If you really want to watch any major (and many minor) televised sporting event from around the world, the *North Shield* sports bar in Sultanahmet (see p.196) is the place to head for.

Radio

Frequency-crowding means even popular channels are almost impossible to pick up without interference. Of the four **public radio stations**, Radyo Üç (The Third Programme or TRT-3), most commonly found at 88.2, 94 and 99MHz, broadcasts the highest proportion of Western music. It also airs **news bulletins in English** at 9am, noon, 2pm, 5pm, 7pm and 10pm, though it is turgid stuff. NTV Radyo (102.8) has the news in English at 6pm daily.

For Western music, Açık Radyo (FM 94.9) provides a mixed diet of rock, jazz and soul, while Radyo Blue (94.5FM) specializes in dance, electronica and blues. Other big names offering Western music and production values include Capital FM (99.5), Kiss FM (90.3) and Metro FM (97.2). For Turkish music, the best stations are Kral (92.0) and, naturally enough, Best FM (98.4).

Festivals and cultural events

Despite the secular nature of the Turkish Republic, the nation's three major festivals are Muslim: Ramazan (Arabic Ramadan), Şeker Bayramı (Eid ul-fitr in Arabic) and Kurban Bayramı (Eid al-Adha), the latter two of which are major holidays as well. Otherwise, there's just a handful of festivals in and around İstanbul, notably the gypsy festival in Thrace and the oil-wrestling festival outside Edirne, though the city has an impressive cultural-events calendar.

Religious festivals

The religious festivals observed all over the Islamic world on dates determined by the Muslim Hijra calendar are celebrated in İstanbul, and two of the most important, the Şeker and Kurban bayrams, are public holidays. As the Islamic calendar is lunar, the dates of the four important religious festivals drift

backwards eleven days each year (twelve in a leap year), relative to the Gregorian calendar. However, future dates of festivals as given on Islamic websites are provisional, owing to factors such as when the moon is sighted and the international dateline, so expect variance of a day or so in the ranges in the lists below.

Ramazan, although it is not a public holiday, is arguably the most important Muslim festival, if you can call a month of daylight abstention from food, water, tobacco and sex a festival. It is not a public holiday, and working life carries on as normal despite the fact that much of the population, even in İstanbul, is fasting from sunrise to sunset. Try to avoid the roads during the hour leading up to the breaking of the fast (known as *iftar*), as tired, hungry and thirsty drivers rush home for much-needed refreshment. Few restaurants in İstanbul close for Ramazan, but particularly if you are in more conservative areas of the city such as Fatih, be discreet about eating, drinking and smoking in public during fasting hours. On the positive side, every night of Ramazan has become like a mini-holiday for many İstanbullus, with free meals doled out to the less well off from soup kitchens across the city, and a (very restrained) carnival-like atmosphere in places like the Hippodrome in Sultanahmet, where hundreds of stalls are set up for the entire month, selling everything from candy-floss and *gözleme* to Turkish coffee and *köfte*. It's very much a family occasion, and a great place to visit to see how the more conservative İstanbullus enjoy themselves – and to try some good-value, Turkish speciality foods. Also note that trying to find a seat in a restaurant at *iftar* can be tricky.

Kadir Gecesi (The Eve of Power) takes place between the 27th and 28th days of the month of Ramazan, the time when Mohammed is supposed to have received the Koran from Allah. The mosques – even more brilliantly illuminated than usual for the whole month – are full all night, as it's believed that prayers at this time have special efficacy; those who can't make it out tend to stay home reading the Koran and praying. On **Arife**, the last day of Ramazan, it is customary to visit the cemeteries and pay respects to departed ancestors; many rural restaurants are shut that evening.

The three-day **Şeker Bayramı (Sugar Holiday)** is held at the end of Ramazan, though it often stretches into a week-long break if the three crucial days fall in the middle of the working week. It is celebrated by family get-togethers and the giving of presents and sweets to children, and restrained general partying in the streets and restaurants; on the first night after Arife, you will have to book well in advance for tables at better restaurants.

The four-day **Kurban Bayramı (Festival of the Sacrifice)**, in which the sacrificial offering of a sheep represents Abraham's son Ishmael (a Koranic version of the Old Testament story) is marked by the slaughter of over 2.5 million sheep. It is even more important than Şeker Bayramı, with the head of the household beholden to sacrifice a sheep or goat on the main day of the festival.

During both Şeker and Kurban bayrams, which are also public holidays (see below), travel becomes almost impossible: from the afternoon leading up to the first evening of the holiday (a Muslim festival is reckoned from sunset) – and on the first and last days themselves – public transport is often completely booked up. If you're planning to head out of İstanbul, you'll struggle to get a seat on any long-distance coach, train, plane or ferry unless you book well in advance. Some shops and all banks, museums and government offices close during the holiday periods (although corner grocery stores stay open). The demographic balance of the city shifts, too, with millions departing the metropolis to visit relatives elsewhere in the country and visitors from all over Turkey and the Middle East heading into İstanbul.

PROVISIONAL ŞEKER AND KURBAN BAYRAMS DATES

2012 Şeker Aug 19–21; **Kurban** Oct 25–28
2013 Şeker Aug 8–10; **Kurban** Oct 14–20
2014 Şeker July 28–30; **Kurban** Oct 4–7
2015 Şeker July 17–19; **Kurban** Sept 23–26

Cultural festivals

The annual festival calendar is pretty full – at least between April and October, when most of the best events take place. The highlights are detailed below; for more information, consult the city tourist offices or the İstanbul Foundation for Culture and Arts (Ⓦ iksv.org). Tickets for most events can be bought online from Ⓦ biletix.com and Ⓦ pozitif-ist.com.

April

International Film Festival Ⓦ film.iksv.org/en. Turkish, European and Hollywood movies premiere at İstanbul's cinemas, mainly in Beyoğlu, plus the best of the non-English-speaking world's releases from the previous year and new prints of classic films – visiting celebrities add glitz and glamour. Midweek tickets are usually a bargain.

Tulip Festival Week-long festival honouring the national flower, including concerts, arts events and competitions at different locations

around the city, and a final showing of the hundred best tulips. Over three million bulbs flower across the city, planted by the municipality.

May

Chill-Out Ⓦ chilloutfest.com. Dance and electronica by the likes of Kruder & Dorfmeister and Bellaruche, held in the incongruous surroundings of the ultra-posh Kemer Golf and Country Club, out in the Belgrade Forest.

Conquest Celebrations Ⓦ ibb.gov.tr. Week-long celebration of the Ottoman conquest of old Constantinople (May 29, 1453) – concerts by the Ottoman Mehter military band, fancy-dress processions and fireworks.

Freshtival Held in Maçka's Küçükçiftlik Parkı, this festival mixes indie, dance and rock sounds. 2011 acts included the Crystal Fighters, Leftfield and assorted international and local DJs.

International Puppet Festival ☎ 0212/232 0224. A celebration of Turkish Shadow Theatre, or *karagöz* – silent puppets tell their tale behind a two-dimensional screen. One venue is the Kenter Theatre (see p.206).

International Theatre Festival Ⓦ iksv.org. Biennial event (next up in 2012), showcasing the best Turkish plays (by both local avant-garde and established theatre groups), and performances by leading foreign companies, which in the past have included the Royal Shakespeare Company. Some plays enacted at open-air venues such as the Rumeli Hisar, others in the Atatürk Cultural Centre and the Kenter Theatre.

Takva Festival Romany festival, generally lasting three days around the first weekend after May 6, held in Kırklareli, near Edirne, with bonfires, parades and music.

June/July

The İstanbul International Music Festival Ⓦ iksv.org. Concerts, recitals, dance and opera – this hugely successful festival was launched in 1973 to celebrate fifty years of independence and brings top-notch orchestras and soloists from all over the world to perform in such atmospheric venues as the church of Aya Irene. Organized by the İstanbul Foundation for Culture and Arts (IKSV), it lasts most of the month.

Kırkpınar Oil Wrestling Festival The premier festival for this still-popular traditional sport (see p.271), attracting big crowds to the fascinating border town of Edirne.

Sonisphere Ⓦ sonispherefestivals.com. Heavy Metal is popular among a swathe of Turkish youth and they come out in their black-clad droves to enjoy the likes of Metallica, Rammstein and Megadeth at this two-day festival.

July/August

International Jazz Festival Ⓦ iksv.org. Two weeks of gigs and jamming sessions from world-class performers. In the past this included luminaries like Dizzy Gillespie, more recently the likes of Marcus Miller and Norah Jones have taken the stage. The definition of jazz is stretched to include artists such as Nick Cave and Paul Simon. Outdoor venues include the Harbiye Açık Have Tiyatrosu.

Efes Pilsen One Love Ⓦ efespilsenonelove.com. Moderately alternative city-centre weekend-long festival generally held at trendy Santralıstanbul, with plenty of DJ-led dance sets and performances from international bands such as The Manic Street Preachers and Suede, plus home-grown acts like Baba Zula. Sometimes held in late June.

Rock N' Coke Ⓦ rockncoke.com. A weekend of Western and Turkish rock held on an airfield 50km to the west of the city; buses run from Taksim. Headliners in recent years have included Franz Ferdinand, The Cure, Korn, Limp Bizkit and Travis. The event was cancelled in 2008 and again in 2010, so check the web for details of future years.

September

International İstanbul Biennial Multimedia contemporary arts festival that usually runs mid-Sept to the first week in Nov (see box, p.208). Held odd years, next up in 2013.
İstanbul Arts Fair Ⓦ tuyap.com. A week-long fair selling the work of some fifty or so İstanbul galleries and visiting foreign artists – paintings, sculpture, pottery and fabrics. Held inconveniently at the Tüyap Centre, in the suburbs near Atatürk International airport.
Contemporary İstanbul Arts Fair Ⓦ contemporaryistanbul .com. Week-long exhibition in the Lütfi Kırdar Congress and Exhibition Centre, showcasing Turkish and international artists.

October

Akbank International Jazz Festival Ⓦ akbanksanat.com. Two-week festival concentrating on traditional jazz. Events include film screenings, informal jamming sessions and drum workshops. Varied venues include the Byzantine church of Aya Irene and the Babylon Performance Centre in Beyoğlu.

November

Efes Pilsen Blues Festival Two-day late-night blues festival – a showcase of new local talent and famous foreign bands, it's very popular with middle-class Turks, so book well in advance. Tours all of Turkey and abroad, so check the İstanbul dates do not fall in either Oct or Dec. Information can be found in listings magazines, usually a month or so in advance.

Travel essentials

Climate

İstanbul has a relatively damp **climate**, with hot, humid summers and cool, rainy winters. July and August are usually sweltering, while May, June, September and October offer the perfect combination of dry, warm weather and long daylight hours.

Winter – during January and February – can be very chilly in the city.

Costs

The Turkish **lira**, after years of rampant inflation, is relatively stable, with inflation now in single figures. At the time of going to press there were 2.5TL to the euro, 2.9TL to the pound and the dollar was 1.8TL. Despite a twenty to thirty percent devaluation of the lira over the course of 2011, the currency is a little over-valued, which, along with a fast-developing economy, means that it's no longer the cheap destination it was, with prices comparable to many places in Europe.

Stay in a hostel dormitory, eat in local workers' cafés or restaurants, avoid alcohol and the most expensive sites such as the Topkapı Palace and Aya Sofya and you could get by on 50TL a day. If that doesn't sound like much fun, double that and you could stay in a modest hotel, see the sights and have a beer or two with your evening meal. Equally, a night out on the town in the entertainment hub of Beyoğlu could easily set you back over 100TL, more if you head up to the chic rooftop bars or venture down to the swanky places on the Bosphorus.

Crime and personal safety

İstanbul is undoubtedly far safer than most large European or North American cities, and cases of mugging and assault against tourists are rare. Having said this, the crime rate is soaring, due in part to the increasing disparity between rich and poor. Take the same precautions you would in any European city and you should be okay. Bear in mind that all police are armed and, despite recent improvements in training and transparency, are generally feared by the locals.

Trouble

For the average visitor, **pickpocketing** is the main cause for concern: be particularly careful around Sirkeci station, the Eminönü waterfront, the Grand

AVERAGE MONTHLY TEMPERATURES AND RAINY DAYS											
	Jan	Feb	Mar	Apr	May	Jun	Jul	Aug	Sep	Oct	Nov	Dec
Max/min (°C)	8/3	8/3	11/4	15/7	21/12	25/17	28/21	82/21	23/16	19/13	14/8	9/5
Max/min (°F)	46/37	46/37	52/39	59/45	70/54	77/63	82/70	28/70	73/61	66/55	57/46	48/41
Rainy days	18	15	14	11	9	6	6	5.5	7	11	14	17

Bazaar, Aksaray, Taksim (especially at night) and the city land walls around dusk. You should also be careful on public transport, particularly when it is crowded. A daypack worn on your back is an easy target; either lock it with a small lock, or carry it on your front. Women should wear handbags across their bodies to make them more difficult to snatch, and keep a firm hold of your camera. Single women should be careful in Taksim and Beyoğlu at night, and both sexes should be aware of the bad reputation of Tarlabaşı (which parallels İstiklal Caddesi in Beyoğlu), where poverty and crime go hand in hand and sexual harassment (to women from men; to men from some transvestites and transsexuals) is a problem.

Lone males heading out for the night should be wary of **confidence tricksters**. The usual scenario is to be approached by a friendly Turkish male, who'll suggest a good club or bar to go to. In the bar, there are (surprise, surprise) some attractive females, who your "friend" suggests buying drinks for. When the bill comes (to you), it can run into hundreds of euros. Even if you don't have enough cash on you, you'll be forced to pay with your credit card. In cases like this, it is very difficult to prove criminal intent – use your common sense and avoid the situation arising. The **spiking of drinks** is also on the increase: make sure you buy your own drinks if you have any doubts at all about the person you're with.

To avoid the wrath of the local populace (and possibly the police as well) **never insult Atatürk or Turkey**, and don't deface, degrade, or tear up currency or the flag. Public drunkenness in general is frowned upon and will be considered an aggravating, not a mitigating factor should you run into trouble. Try not to be drawn into **serious disputes**, since while things rarely turn violent in Turkey, when they do they can turn *very* violent – if anybody seems to be insulting or provoking you, walk away.

Police

The police you're most likely to have any dealing with are the blue-uniformed **Polis**, the main force both in İstanbul and in towns and cities across the country. There's a tourist police centre at Yerebatan Cad 6 (❶0212/527 4503) in Sultanahmet with some English-speaking officers. The **Trafik Polis**, recognized by their white caps and two-toned vehicles, are a branch of this service and their main responsibility seems to be controlling intersections and doing spot-checks on vehicles at approaches to towns. İstanbul has a rapid-response squad of red-and-black-uniformed motorbike police known

as the **Yunus Polis**; they are generally courteous and helpful to tourists and may speak some English. In the towns, you're also likely to see the **Belediye Zabıtası**, the navy-clad market police, who patrol the markets and bazaars to ensure that tradesmen aren't ripping off customers – approach them directly if you have reason for complaint.

In general, Turkish police have had a bad reputation, but things are beginning to change. Once low-paid and ill-trained, their pay has risen substantially (reducing corruption) in recent years, and graduate-intake programmes have raised the overall level of education of the police force. The "glass-walls" policy (designed to make the police more accountable for their actions) was introduced, at least partially, to satisfy the Europeans as Turkey strives for full EU membership, and as a result, attitudes towards suspects have improved considerably. **If you are arrested** for any reason, stay polite and be patient – getting irate tends to be counterproductive. You have **the right to make a phone call** to a friend, hotelier or consul.

Note that it is obligatory to **carry ID** at all times – for locals and foreigners alike – so if you are concerned about having your passport stolen (or losing it) while out and about, at least carry a photocopy of the pages with your details and Turkish entry stamp on your person.

Electricity

Turkey operates on 220 volts, 50 HZ so most European appliances will work here. Plugs are European-style two-pin, so UK visitors should bring an adaptor. American appliances will need both an adaptor and a transformer.

Entry requirements

To enter Turkey, you'll need a full passport, and many countries require visas. For some, these are available only at the point of entry, for others from the Turkish consulate or embassy in their home country. Visa fees are collected in US dollars, euros and in some cases pounds sterling. Visas are required for citizens of the UK ($20, €15 or £10), Ireland ($20, €10 or £10), the US ($20 or €15), Canada ($60 or €45) and Australia ($20 or €15), among others. New Zealanders don't require one for a stay of up to 90 days, and South Africans should be able to obtain a thirty-day visa at the entry point to Turkey, but would be wise to enquire at a Turkish consulate before travelling. Everyone, regardless of nationality, should have at least six months' validity on their passport. Note that as entry requirements change from time to time, you should check what's required well before your intended departure date with the Turkish Ministry of Foreign Affairs at ⓦmfa.gov.tr.

Even though İstanbul's airports should be able to convert between different currencies (usually to your disadvantage) and give change for large notes, it's far better to arrive with the exact amount of money for your visa in the relevant currency. **Tourist visas** are multiple entry, and for most visitors, including citizens of the UK, Ireland, the US, Canada, Australia and New Zealand, are valid for three months from the date of issue – if you leave on a day-trip, to Greece or Bulgaria say, you should not have to pay for a new visa on re-entry. It is forbidden to take up employment during your three months.

Once inside the country, you can **extend your visa** once only, for a further three months, by applying to the Foreigners' Department (Yabancı Bürosu) of the Security Division (Emniyet Müdürlüğü) in İstanbul. Do this well before your visa expires, as it may take several weeks to process. If you know in advance that you want to stay longer, you should apply to the consulate in your own country for a **long-stay visa**. On arrival in Turkey, the Yabancı Bürosu will convert it to a residence permit (*ikamet tezkeresi*), valid initially for one year (two with a work permit). Further renewals will be for three or five years. In either case, you will be required to show means of support (savings, a regular income from abroad or legal work in Turkey) and relinquish your passport until the permit is issued. UK citizens pay €60 for a one-year residence permit.

TURKISH EMBASSIES AND CONSULATES ABROAD

Australia 60 Mugga Way, Red Hill, Canberra ACT 2603 ☎ 02/6234 0000.
Canada 197 Wurtemburg St, Ottawa, ON K1N 8L9 ☎ 613/244-2470.
Ireland 11 Clyde Rd, Ballsbridge, Dublin 4 ☎ 01/668 5240.
New Zealand 15–17 Murphy St, Level 8, Wellington ☎ 04/472 1290–92.
South Africa 1067 Church St, Hatfield 0181, Pretoria ☎ 012/342 5063.
UK 43 Belgrave Square, London SW1X 8PA ☎ 020/7393 0202.
US 2525 Massachusetts Ave NW, Washington, DC 20008 ☎ 202/612-6700.

CONSULATES IN İSTANBUL

Australia Asker Ocağı Cad 15, Elmadağ, Şişli ☎ 0212/243 1333.
Canada 16th Floor, Tekfen Tower, 209 Büyükdere Cad, Levent 4 ☎ 0212/385 9700.

New Zealand İnönü Cad 48/3, Taksim ☎ 0212/244 0272.
South Africa (Honorary Consul) Alarko Centre, Musallim Nacı Cad 113–115, Ortaköy ☎ 0212/260 378.
UK Meşrutiyet Cad 34, Tepebaşı, Beyoğlu ☎ 0212/334 6400.
US İstinye Mahallesi, Kaplıcalar Mevkii No.2, İstinye ☎ 0212/335 9000.

Customs and border inspections

Since Turkey's customs union with the EU in the year 2000, most European travellers are free to bring in valuable electronic gadgets without having them written into their passport. But since Turkey is not yet actually an EU member, **duty-free limits** – and sales – for alcohol and tobacco are still prevalent. Limits are posted clearly at İstanbul's airports, and apply for all frontiers. If you haven't exploited your allowance at your departure airport, you can usually buy duty-free goods at your Turkish port of arrival, at prices considerably cheaper than northern European airports.

Few people get stopped departing Turkey, but the guards may be on the lookout for **antiquities** and **fossils**. Penalties for trying to smuggle these out include long jail sentences, plus a large fine. What actually constitutes an antiquity is rather vague (see p.214), but it's best not to take any chances.

Health

Turkey does not have reciprocal heath arrangements with other countries, making health insurance mandatory. There are no vaccination requirements as such, though you should consult your doctor before travelling.

It's quite possible you'll suffer a mild bout of diarrhoea in İstanbul, particularly (though not only) if you eat from street stalls. **Tap water** is heavily chlorinated but best avoided – stick to bottled water. Lomotil or Imodium, trade names for the antiparastaltic diphenoxylate, are easily available in Turkey, though they block you up rather than kill the bug that ails you. Flagyll, on sale locally, is good if you go down with a more virulent stomach bug, but avoid drinking alcohol when taking it. In restaurants, avoid dishes that look as if they have been standing around and make sure meat and fish are well grilled. Don't, whatever you do, eat stuffed mussels in summer. If you're struck down, the best thing is to let the bug run its course and drink lots of fluids, including re-hydrating salts (Geo-Oral is a locally available brand). Eating plain white rice and yoghurt also helps. Stubborn cases will need a course of antibiotics – pharmacists are trained to recognize symptoms and you don't need a prescription for antibiotics. In theory, a state clinic (Develet Polykliniği) will treat foreigners for a very small fee.

Rabies is prevalent in Turkey, and İstanbul has its share of street dogs and cats. Be wary of any animal that bites, scratches or licks you, particularly if it's behaving erratically. First aid involves flushing a wound with soap and water after encouraging limited bleeding. Then go straight to a state clinic (within 72hr), where you should be given an injection (free of charge), the first of six, most of which you will probably need to have back in your home country.

Medical treatment

There are thousands of **pharmacies** (*eczane*) across İstanbul. Staff may know some English or German and are trained to diagnose simple complaints, take blood pressure, and the like. They also dispense medicines that normally require a prescription, such as antibiotics. Medication prices are low, but bring your prescription to find the (probably locally-produced) drug that best matches your needs. Pharmacies also sell **birth-control pills** (*doğum kontrol hapı*), **condoms** (*preservatif*; the slang term is *kılıf*) and **tampons** (Orkid is the best domestic brand). **Night-duty pharmacies**, often found near main hospitals, are known as *nöbet(ci)*; a list of the current rota is posted in Turkish in every chemist's front window, as "Nöbetçi Eczaneleri". For more serious ailments, you'll find well-trained **doctors** in İstanbul and the larger towns and cities. As the state sector hospitals are overcrowded and under-funded, it's preferable to go to an *Özel Hastane* or private hospital.

HOSPITALS

Alman Hastanesi (German Hospital) Sıraselviler Cad 119, Taksim ☎ 0212/293 2150, ⓦ almanhastanesi.com.tr. Reliable and well-run hospital, it also has a dental and eye clinic. Staff are proficient in English. Consultations around 160TL.
Amerikan Hastanesi (American Hospital) Güzelbahçe Sok 20, Nişantaşı ☎ 0212/311 2000, ⓦ www.amerikanhastanesi.org.

Very good reputation, long established and with good equipment and well-trained staff, it also has a dental clinic. Consultations around 140TL.
Cerrahpaşa Hastanesi Koca Mustafapaşa Caddesi, Cerrahpaşa ☎ 0212/414 3000, ⓦ ctf.edu.tr. A well-regarded teaching hospital in the old city.
Taksim İlkyardim Hastanesi (Taksim Emergency Hospital) Sıraselviler Cad 112, Taksim ☎ 0212/ 4300. State-run and deals with emergencies only; patients are often referred to another hospital.

DENTISTS

Alternatives to the practices in the German and American hospitals (see above), both with English-speaking staff, are:
Prodent-Can Ergene Valikonağı Cad 109/5, Nişantaşı ☎ 0212/230 4635.
Reha Sezgin Halaskargazi Cad 48/9, Harbiye ☎ 0212/240 3322.

Insurance

There are not yet any reciprocal health-care privileges between Turkey and the EU, so it's essential to take out an insurance policy before travelling, to cover against theft, loss, illness or injury. Before paying for a new policy, however, check whether you are already covered: some all-risks homeowners' or renters' insurance policies may cover your possessions when overseas, and many private medical schemes (such as BUPA and WPA) offer coverage extensions for abroad.

A specialist travel-insurance company can sell you a suitable policy, or consider the travel insurance deal we offer (see box below). A typical travel-insurance policy usually provides cover for the loss of baggage, tickets and – up to a certain limit – cash, cards or travellers' cheques, as well as cancellation or curtailment of your journey.

Many policies can be chopped and changed to eliminate coverage you don't need – for example, sickness and accident benefits can often be excluded or included at will. If you do take **medical coverage**, ascertain whether benefits will be paid as treatment proceeds or only after your return home, and whether there is a 24-hour medical emergency

---

ROUGH GUIDES TRAVEL INSURANCE

Rough Guides has teamed up with Columbus Direct to offer you tailor-made **travel insurance**. Products include a low-cost **backpacker** option for long stays; a **short break** option for city getaways; a typical **holiday package** option; and others. There are also annual **multi-trip** policies for those who travel regularly. Different sports and activities (trekking, skiing, etc) can usually be included.

See our website (ⓦ roughguides.com/website/shop) for eligibility and purchasing options. Alternatively, UK residents can call ☎ 0870/033 9988, Australians ☎ 1300/669 999 and New Zealanders ☎ 0800/559 911. All other nationalities should call ☎ +44 870/890 2843.

number. When securing baggage cover, make sure that the per-article limit – typically under £500/€750 – will cover your most valuable possession.

If you need to make a medical **claim**, you should keep receipts for medicines and treatment, and in the event you have anything **stolen or lost**, you must obtain an official statement from the police (or the airline that lost your bags). In the wake of growing numbers of fraudulent claims, most insurers won't even entertain a claim unless you have a police report.

Internet

The **internet** is part and parcel of life for millions of İstanbullus – even those who don't have their own computers or broadband mobile-phone access have access to myriad internet cafés, though there are frustratingly few in Sultanahmet. Virtually all hotels and hostels in the city have internet access – often both terminals and wireless, and wi-fi is invariably free apart from the top-end business hotels, where a steep charge is sometimes levied. Many of the trendier cafés, especially in Beyoğlu, also have wireless. Rates in internet cafés, most of which now have ADSL connections, tend to be 2TL per hour. The Turkish-character keyboard you'll probably be faced with may cause some frustration. Beware in particular of the dotless "ı" (confusingly enough found right where you'll be expecting the conventional "i") which, if entered by mistake, will make an email address invalid – the Western "i" is located second key from the right, middle row. The @ sign is usually on the "Q" key; press the "Alt Gr" key then "Q" to type.

Laundry

Most hotels have a laundry service, and some of the major hotels offer services to non-guests, at a price – the one at the *Ceylan Intercontinental* in Taksim (☎0212/368 4444) is 24-hour. There are no coin-operated laundries in the city, but there are plenty of dry cleaners, some of which will do your laundry.

Left luggage and lost property

There are left-luggage (*emanet*) facilities at Atatürk and Sabiha Gökçen international airports (15TL for 24 hours for a normal-sized bag). At Sirkeci station in Eminönü, there are left-luggage lockers charging 7TL for four hours, 50 kuruş per hour thereafter.

If you lose, or have something stolen, report it to the tourism police at Yerebatan Cad 6 (☎0212/527 4503) in Sultanahmet.

KDV: TURKISH VAT

The Turkish variety of VAT (*Katma Değer Vergisi* or **KDV**), ranging from 8 to 23 percent depending on the commodity, is included in the price of virtually all goods and services (except car rental, where the fifteen percent figure is usually quoted separately). Look for the notice *Fiyatlarımız KDV Dahildir* ("VAT included in our prices") if you think someone's trying to do you for it twice. There's a VAT refund scheme for large souvenir purchases made by those living outside Turkey, but it's such a rigmarole to get that it's probably not worth pursuing; if you insist, ask the shop to provide a *KDV Iade Özel Fatura* (Special VAT Refund Invoice), assuming that it participates – very few do, and they tend to be the most expensive shops.

Mail

The central post office on Büyük Postane Caddesi (☎0212/5261200; daily 8.30am–7pm for post, bank 8.30am–4.30pm, 24hr section for phone calls and buying stamps) in Eminönü, an imposing early twentieth-century building not far from Sirkeci station, is of most use to visitors staying in the old city. There's also a major post office at Yeniçarşı Caddesi, off İstiklal Caddesi and opposite Galatasaray Lycée (Mon–Fri & Sun 8.30am–5.30pm; ☎0212/251 5150). If you're staying in Taksim, the post office on Cumhüriyet Cad 2 (Mon–Sat 8.30am–5.30pm; ☎0212/243 0284) is the most convenient. Stamps are only available from the PTT.

Airmail (*uçakla*) rates to Europe are 1.10TL for postcards, 1.3TL for letters up to 20g. Delivery to Europe or North America can take seven to ten days. A pricier express (APG or *acele*) service is also available, which cuts delivery times for the EU to about three days. When sending items through post, it's best to leave the envelope or package unsealed as the post office staff may ask to see what's being sent.

Posting slots are clearly labelled – *yurtdışı* for overseas, *yurtiçi* for within Turkey, *şehiriçi* for local. To receive mail **poste restante** (general delivery), articles should be addressed to you, c/o "Postrestant, Merkez Postanesi, [city name], Turkey".

Alternatively for letters and parcels, private Turkish courier companies include Aras (☎444 2552, ⓦ araskargo.com.tr) and Yurtiçi (☎444 9999, ⓦ yurticikargo.com), both of which are very efficient, comparable in price to the PTT and have offices all around the city.

Maps

The maps included in this guide should be enough for most purposes, but there are a number of other decent maps available if you're looking for something to complement these. The cheapest option is the free city map dished out by the tourist offices in İstanbul; other maps can be bought from kiosks around the touristy parts of the city, including the clear and accurate (though it only covers a small part of the Asian side of the city) Keskin Colour's *İstanbul Street Plan 1*. A little dearer and better is Net Maps' *İstanbul* which shows more of the Asian side and has detailed maps of the Princes' Islands. Available from the better stationers and bookstores, *Sokak Sokak Avrupa* by İki Nokta is an A–Z-style atlas to the European side of the city; best of all, and worth considering if you want to explore the backstreets and find out-of-the-way sites and monuments, is Mepmedya's *İstanbul Avrupa Yakası*, the most detailed A–Z.

Money

In January 2005, in a bid to draw a line under the bad old days of hyperinflation, when millions of lira were needed to purchase the smallest everyday item, the government introduced the Yeni Türk Lirası (New Turkish Lira), abbreviated as YTL, and knocked all the zeros off. In January 2009, it was the turn of the "Y" to go, and the currency reverted to its old nomenclature, the **Türk Lirası** or **TL** for short. Despite the changes, many Turks still talk in millions, which can be confusing when you are asked "bir milyon" or one million lira for a glass of tea. **Coins** are in denominations of 1, 5, 10, 25 and 50 kuruş, as well as 1 lira, while **notes** come in denominations of 5, 10, 20, 50, 100 and 200 lira.

Rates for foreign currency are always better inside Turkey, so try not to buy much TL at home. It's wise to bring a fair wad of **hard currency** with you (euros are best, though dollars and sterling are often accepted), as you can often use it to pay directly for souvenirs or accommodation (prices for both are frequently quoted in euros), though make sure you know the current exchange rate. **Travellers' cheques** are, frankly, not worth the bother as exchange offices (see below) and some banks refuse them, while those that do accept them charge a hefty commission on transactions.

Banks and other exchange services

Unless things change dramatically, the lira's new-found stability means that you can change large amounts of cash in one go without worrying that inflation will erode its value. You should, though, try to keep all foreign-exchange slips with you until departure, if only to prove the value of purchases made in case of queries by customs.

Most Turkish banks, such as Yapıkredi and İşbank, change money. Best bet, though, is the state-owned Ziraat Bankası, open Monday to Friday, 8.30am to noon and 1.30 to 5pm, which gives a good rate, does not charge commission and usually has a dedicated currency exchange (*döviz*) counter. Queues, however, can be long. All banks now have an automated queuing system; take a ticket from the machine and wait for your number to appear on the digital display. It's also possible to change money at PTT (Post Offices), again commission-free. *Döviz*, or exchange houses, are common in the city, with several on Divan Yolu (old city) adjacent to the tram stop and İstiklal Caddesi (Beyoğlu). They buy and sell foreign currency of most sorts instantly, and have the convenience of long opening hours (usually Mon–Sat 9/10am–8/10pm, but some open daily) and short or nonexistent queues. Few now charge commission but the rate is less than banks or the PTT.

Credit/debit cards and ATMs

Credit cards are widely used in hotels, shops, restaurants and entertainment venues and with no commission (though many hotels offer discounts for cash payments). Don't expect, however, to use your card in basic eating-places or small corner shops. Swipe readers plus **chip-and-PIN** protocol are now the norm in most of Turkey.

The simplest way to get hold of money in Turkey is to use the widespread **ATM** network. Most bank ATMs will accept any debit cards that are part of the Cirrus, Maestro or Plus systems; you can also use Visa and MasterCard, but American Express holders are currently restricted to Akbank ATMs. Screen prompts

---

TIPPING

A service charge of ten to fifteen percent is levied at the fancier restaurants, but as this goes directly to the management, the waiters and busboys should be left five percent again if they deserve it. In some places, a mandatory tip (*garsoniye*) accompanies the service charge. Round odd taxi fares upwards (you may not have a choice, as the driver may genuinely not have small change); hotel porters should be tipped appropriately.

are given in English on request. The daily ATM withdrawal limit for most cards is about £250/€375 equivalent (or £80–200/€120–300 per transaction), depending on the bank or even individual ATM. You can also normally get cash advances (in TL only) at any bank displaying the appropriate sign.

Opening hours and public holidays

Shops are usually open daily from 9am to 6pm, though many open on a Sunday as well. **Grocers** open daily from 8am to 8pm (sometimes earlier or later) and supermarkets often stay open until 10pm. **Banks** and **government offices** open Monday to Friday 8.30am to noon and 1.30pm to 5pm. **Museum, site and gallery** opening hours also vary quite markedly. Most open from 8.30 or 9am until 5 or 6pm, though some close earlier and the biggest sights stay open until 7pm in summer. All sites and museums are closed on the mornings of public holidays, while İstanbul's palaces are generally closed on Mondays and Thursdays. **Mosques** are theoretically open from dawn (first call to prayer) until nightfall (last call to prayer) but in practice many only open at prayer times; at other times you'll have to seek out the caretaker (see box below). For more specific opening hours, refer to the relevant Guide chapters.

Public holidays

Banks, schools and government offices all close on five of the holidays listed below: New Year's Day, Independence/Children's Day, Youth and Sports Day, Victory Day and Republic Day.

January 1 Yılbaşı New Year's Day.

April 23 Ulusal Egemenlik ve Çocuk Bayramı Independence Day, celebrating the first meeting of the new Republican parliament in Ankara, and Children's Day.

May 19 Gençlik ve Spor Günü Youth and Sports Day, also Atatürk's birthday.

July 1 Denizcilik Günü Navy Day.

August 26 Silahlı Kuvvetler Günü Armed Forces Day.

August 30 Zafer Bayramı Celebration of the Turkish victory over the Greek forces at Dumlupınar in 1922.

October 29 Cumhuriyet Bayramı Republic Day commemorates the proclamation of the Republic by Atatürk in 1923. Parades through the streets, mainly by school kids banging drums and blowing trumpets.

November 10 The anniversary of Atatürk's death in 1938. Observed at 9.05am (the time of his death), when the whole country stops whatever it's doing and maintains a respectful silence for a minute. It's worth being on a Bosphorus ferry on this morning, when all the engines are turned off, and the boats drift and blow their foghorns mournfully.

Phones

Turkey uses a system of eleven-digit **phone numbers** nationwide, consisting of four-digit area or mobile-provider codes (all starting with "0") plus a seven-digit subscriber number. Numbers on the European side of İstanbul all begin with ☎0212, on the Asian side with ☎0216.

Given the Turkish penchant for chatting, **mobile phones** are essential accessories in İstanbul (and beyond). Assuming that you have a roaming facility, your home mobile will connect with one of the

---

MOSQUE MANNERS

Strolling around the tourist-thronged sites of Sultanahmet, or striding down the premier entertainment and shopping street of İstiklal Caddesi, it's sometimes hard to remember that you are in a Muslim city. İstanbul may be Turkey's most cosmopolitan, forward-looking urban centre, but a fair proportion of its inhabitants are both conservative and devout. Bear this in mind particularly when visiting a mosque. All those likely to be of interest to a foreign visitor (and many more besides) display some kind of "conduct" notice at the door outlining the **entry rules** – which are simple:

· Cover your head (women) and shoulders/upper arms (both sexes)
· No shorts or miniskirts
· Take off your shoes before entering. (Many mosques now provide a plastic bag for this – before entering, slip your shoes into the bag and carry them around with you. Alternatively, place your footwear on the shelves provided).

Especially if you are in a very devout area such as Fatih, try to avoid your visit coinciding with **noon prayers** – particularly those on a Friday – the most important prayer session of the week. Once inside the mosque, you're free to wander around, take photographs and admire the interior – but keep your voice down (there are often people praying or reciting the Koran outside of the five daily prayer times) and don't take pictures of worshippers unless they give their permission. Although the *imam* is a state-paid official, upkeep of the building is down to charity, so you may want to put a **donation** in the collection box.

local network providers – however, US mobiles won't work here. Charges, though, are high (up to £1.30/min to the UK), and you pay for incoming calls as well. Purchasing a **local SIM card** and pay-as-you-go package is worth considering if you intend making a lot of calls.

Turkcell SIM cards (which can take up to 24hr to activate) cost 35TL, including 5TL calling credit, or 45TL will get you the card and 20TL credit. Typically, calls cost 80 kuruş per minute to Europe and North America, an SMS message to the UK the same. To purchase a SIM card, you'll need to sign an agreement form and present your passport for photocopying at a major Turkcell, Avea or Vodafone outlet, where they'll fit the new card in your phone. All three companies have stands at arrivals in Atatürk and Sabiha Gökçen airports, with Turkcell having the widest coverage. If you buy from one of the many smaller mobile-phone stores and don't sign an agreement you run the risk of your phone not being registered for use in Turkey, and it will be blocked (usually within two weeks but sometimes much more quickly).

Calling home from Turkey

To call home from Turkey, dial ☎ 00 followed by the relevant international dialling code (see below), then the area code (without the initial zero if there is one), then the number.

Australia ☎ 61
Ireland ☎ 353
New Zealand ☎ 64
South Africa ☎ 27
UK ☎ 44
US & Canada ☎ 1

Smoking

The old saying "smokes like a Turk" is backed up by figures to prove it is a fairly accurate assessment, with over forty percent of the adult population (around 25 million) indulging the nicotine habit. Yet things are beginning to change. Smoking was banned on public transport and in airports, bus terminals and train stations back in 1997, and, much to everyone's surprise, the law is, more or less, adhered to. From July 2009, it was prohibited in all

public buildings, and all enclosed public spaces including bars, cafés, restaurants, clubs and the like.

Time

Turkey is two hours ahead of GMT, seven ahead of EST and ten ahead of PST. It is in the same time zone as South Africa, and seven hours behind Perth, nine behind Sydney and eleven behind Wellington. Daylight saving runs from the last Sunday in March to the last Sunday in October.

Toilets

In the majority of İstanbul homes, **Western-style toilets** are the norm – this is also true of those in most cafés, restaurants, bars, clubs, cinemas, tourist sites and so on. The only difference between them and the ones you're used to at home is the small pipe fitted at the rear rim of the basin – which serves the same purpose as a bidet. The tap to turn it on is usually awkwardly located, at low level, on the wall behind the loo. The waste bins provided are for "used" toilet paper – blockages are not uncommon.

In poorer, less visited neighbourhoods, however, **squat toilets** are still the norm. This is particularly true of those attached to mosques – in out-of-the-way parts of the city, the only "public" toilet you'll be able to find. There's always a tap and plastic jug right next to the toilet for washing the unmentionables but be warned that few provide paper, so carry some around with you. An attendant at the entrance will divest you of a lira (occasionally a little less) on your way out and, in return, give you a tissue and splash of cologne on your hands.

Note that cheaper bars and clubs around Beyoğlu sometimes have only one, unisex toilet.

Tourist information

İstanbul has six **tourist offices**. Most convenient for the majority of visitors is the one in Sultanahmet, near the Hippodrome at Divan Yolu 3 (daily 9am–5pm; ☎ 0212/518 8754), which has English-speaking staff and is moderately helpful. Other possibly useful offices are located in the *Hilton* on Cumhüriyet Caddesi near Taksim (daily 9am–5pm; ☎ 0212/233 0592) and on Beyazit Meydanı, just west of the Grand Bazaar (daily 9am–6pm; ☎ 0212/522 4902). If you can resist the temptation to get into the city centre as soon as possible, there's another in the arrivals terminal at Atatürk International airport (24hr; ☎ 0212/465 3151). The

ISTANBUL ON THE NET

There are many İstanbul related sites on the internet. A good general introduction to the country and İstanbul can be gained from the official **Ministry of Culture and Tourism** site (ⓦgoturkey.com).

GENERAL

ⓦ**turkeytravelplanner.com** Very informative site, regularly updated, dealing with travel in İstanbul and all over the country.
ⓦ**turkishculture.org** Not terribly innovative – but it does give a useful rundown on everything from architecture to ceramics, literature to music and lifestyles to cuisine – with plenty of photographs and illustrations.

ANTIQUITIES AND ARCHITECTURE

ⓦ**exploreturkey.com** Excellent background on the country's historical monuments, written by an archeologist, with much information on İstanbul, and some on İznik, Bursa, Troy and Edirne to boot, though last updated in 2004.
ⓦ**muze.gov.tr** Government website with information on the country's state-run museums, including the latest opening hours and admission fees.
ⓦ**patriarchate.org** Literate coverage of İstanbul's numerous Byzantine monuments, though you need broadband speeds to load the lavish illustrations quickly.

LISTINGS

ⓦ**iksv.org** Website for the İstanbul Foundation for Culture and Arts, with information on the city's major music, arts and theatre events, and an online booking service – an excellent site for arts lovers.
ⓦ**istanbulcityguide.com** Reasonable online listings site, though gives only the bare facts, plus features.
ⓦ**istanbuleats.com** Fascinating blog-cum-guide to the city's food scene – especially of the off-the-beaten-track, salt-of-the-earth places.
ⓦ**timeoutistanbul.com/english** This is the most informative listings site for finding out what's going on in the city.

---

tourist office in Karaköy Kemankeş Caddesi (daily 9am–5pm; ☎0212/249 5776) is really aimed at cruise-ship passengers disgorging from the nearby dock; the one in the entrance of Sirkeci station in Eminönü (daily 9am–5pm; ☎0212/511 5888) offers little except a few brochures.

TOURIST INFORMATION OFFICES ABROAD

ⓦ www.tourismturkey.org
Australia Room 17, Level 3, 428 George St, Sydney, NSW 2000 ☎02/9223 3055, ℮ turkish@ozemail.co.au.
Canada Constitution Square, 360 Albert St, Suite 801, Ottawa, ON K1R 7X7 ☎613/230-8654.
Ireland Refer to the embassy at 11 Clyde Rd, Ballsbridge, Dublin 4 ☎01/668 5240.
New Zealand Refer to the embassy at 15–17 Murphy St, Level 8, Wellington ☎04/472 1290.
UK First Floor, 170–173 Piccadilly, London W1V 9DD ☎020/7766 9300.
US 821 United Nations Plaza, New York, NY 10017 ☎212/687-2194; 2525 Massachusetts Ave NW, Washington, DC 20008 ☎202/612-6800.

Travellers with disabilities

Both Atatürk International and Sabiha Gökçen airports have wheelchairs and wheelchair-accessible toilets. **Getting around** İstanbul by the Metro and tram is possible, as they are, at least theoretically, wheelchair friendly, although at peak times the carriages are terribly crowded and getting access to some of the stations can be tricky. Some of the more modern buses have a ramp and low door but again can be very overcrowded and the drivers less than patient. The Metro running from Taksim Square north is the most wheelchair accessible, but of little interest to most visitors to the city. Public transport is theoretically free for disabled travellers but in practice, given the language barriers, may be difficult to obtain. Many of the city's pavements are broken and uneven, or cobbled, making things awkward – not to mention the number of steep hills.

The most **accessible sites** for the physically impaired are the Rahmi Koç Industrial Museum (see p.116), İstanbul Modern (see p.114) and the Pera Museum (see p.123). The Topkapı Palace (see pp.47–55) and Aya Sofya (see p.43) are partially accessible, the Blue Mosque (see p.60) and Yerebatan Cistern (see p.59) impossible.

Women and sexual harassment

Turkish women occupy all positions in society, from head-scarved housewives and devout Muslims robed head to toe in the all-enveloping çaşaf to secularized and "liberated" doctors living a single and independent life and high-school girls in short skirts and Converse baseball boots. Taking away the extremes, however, this is a socially conservative society and its women reflect this. Few go out to bars or clubs on their own, and though they may wear tight jeans and singlets, miniskirts and the like are still relatively rare. Wear jeans, trousers or sensible skirts, avoid eye contact with men, and try and look as confident and purposeful as possible. In conservative areas and when entering mosques or churches, make sure you're appropriately covered.

If you do get harassed, don't suffer it alone – make a public scene to elicit the support of bystanders. Using Turkish to get your message across, such as "Ayıp!" ("Shame!") or "Beni rahatsız ediyorsun" ("You're disturbing me"), or the stronger "Defol!" ("Piss off!") or "Bırak beni" ("Leave me alone") may help in theory, but only if you don't mangle the pronunciation. "İmdat!" ("Help!") is more straightforward and should enlist you some aid.

Working in İstanbul

Unemployment is high in Turkey, and jobs in all but the most specialist fields are hard to come by. The bureaucracy involved in getting work and residence permits is also onerous and relies on proof that the establishment or company cannot find someone to do the job from within the country – which is why most of the foreigners working in İstanbul are **teaching English** as a foreign language in a private school or college. There's a big demand for teachers in these schools, partly because of the high status accorded to learning English, and also because working conditions are not great and foreign-staff turnover tends to be high. Teaching posts for the bigger outfits are advertised in *The Guardian*'s educational section and the *Times Educational Supplement* in the UK, in the *International Herald Tribune* and the *Hürriyet Daily News* in Turkey, or check the expat website ⓦ mymerhaba.com. The pay is adequate (usually around 1800TL per month) but free accommodation is the norm, as is healthcare. The school or language school should also get, and pay for, your residence and work permits. In all but the top schools, students tend to be rather spoilt and lacking in motivation and the management dictatorial and far more concerned with keeping parents, rather than their staff, happy. In language schools it all depends on the motivation of your students.

It is worth getting a residence permit should you wish to stay in the city for a year or so and not work (perhaps to study, learn the language, etc). The once hefty fee has been reduced drastically to €60 for UK citizens and saves having to leave the country every three months, as you would have to if you were on a tourist visa (see p.34). Current requirements include a valid passport, a notarized translation of your passport, six passport-sized photographs, evidence that you can support yourself with the equivalent of $6000 (in a Turkish bank account), and the necessary form filled in in duplicate – and plenty of patience when visiting the Security Police (Emniyet Müdürlüğü) on Vatan Caddesi, A Blok, in Fatih, who issue the permit.

BENEATH THE DOME OF AYA SOFYA

Sultanahmet

The heart of old, imperial İstanbul, compact Sultanahmet is home to the city's best-known attractions. Here, commanding a magnificent position overlooking the Bosphorus and Sea of Marmara stands the Topkapı Palace complex, once the heart of the powerful Ottoman Empire. Nearby is another fabulous Ottoman relic, the monumental Sultanahmet Camii. Better known in English as the Blue Mosque, its name derives from the thousands of beautiful tiles adorning its airy interior. This working mosque, with its six slender minarets, mighty dome and cascade of semi-domes, proudly faces another monument, the former church of Haghia Sophia. This, the greatest legacy of the Byzantine Empire, is now the Aya Sofya Museum, home to a wonderful series of glittering figurative mosaics.

Further legacies of the Byzantine era lie just north of the Blue Mosque. The **Hippodrome**, where chariots raced and mobs rioted, is one of the oldest monuments in the city, while the **Yerebatan** and **Binbirdirek underground cisterns** were part of a superb water-supply system that ran right across the city. There are some excellent museums here, too, notably the **Archeology Museum**, featuring a superb array of finds from both Anatolia and former Ottoman domains, and the **Museum of Turkish and Islamic Art**, housed in the former palace of İbrahim Paşa.

South of the major sightseeing area, the steep, narrow streets running down from Cankurtaran to the Sea of Marmara are noteworthy for their surviving Ottoman houses, while a little to the southwest are a couple of minor architectural masterpieces: the mosques of **Küçük Aya Sofya Camii** and **Sokollu Mehmet Paşa Camii**.

Sultanahmet attracts millions of visitors annually and tourism is now its raison d'être. Parting visitors from their hard-earned cash has become something of an art form here – be prepared to fend off the subtle but persistent **hustlers** who gather around the Hippodrome and Divan Yolu, whose main aim is to draw you into one of the many carpet shops. Few locals still reside in Sultanahmet and virtually every business here caters to the tourist trade, so a meal or drink out here inevitably means sharing it with hordes of fellow visitors. For a more Turkish night-out, head across the Galata Bridge to Galata and Beyoğlu (see pp.119–126).

Aya Sofya

Sultanahmet Meydanı 1 • Tues–Sun: mid-April to end Sept 9am–7pm, last entry at 6pm; Oct to mid-April 9am–4.30pm • 20TL • Ⓦ www.ayasofyamuzesi.gov.tr

For almost a thousand years, **Aya Sofya**, or Haghia Sophia, was the largest enclosed space in the world, designed to impress the strength and wealth of the Byzantine emperors upon their own subjects and visiting foreign dignitaries alike. Built on the ancient acropolis, the first of Constantinople's seven hills, the church dominated the city skyline for a millennium. Following the Ottoman Turkish conquest of 1453, the domes and minarets of the city's mosques began to challenge its eminence.

Some history

Aya Sofya, "the Church of the Divine Wisdom", is the third church of this name to stand on the site. The first, a wooden basilica built in AD 360, was totally destroyed during a riot. The second, a grandiose marble structure of which fragments remain, was erected under Theodosius II in 415. Like its predecessor, this too was razed to the ground, in the Nika riots of 532 (see box, p.60). The iconic building you see today was commissioned in the sixth century by Emperor Justinian, who was determined his creation would exceed in size and splendour the Temple of Solomon in Jerusalem.

Prior to the pioneering work of the architects Justinian appointed to realize his dream, **Anthemius of Tralles** and **Isidore of Miletus**, most churches followed the pattern of the rectangular, pitch-roofed Roman basilica or meeting hall. Anthemius and Isidore were to create a building of a type and scale hitherto unknown in the Byzantine world, and no imitation was attempted until the sixteenth century. The vast thirty-one-metre-diameter dome, which seems to hover over a seemingly empty space rather than being supported by solid walls, was unprecedented. The work was completed in 537 and the Haghia Sophia was dedicated by Justinian on December 26th of that year.

In 558, part of the great dome collapsed in an earthquake. During reconstruction the height of the external buttresses and the dome was increased, and some of the windows blocked, resulting in an interior much gloomier than originally intended. The dome collapsed again in 989 and was rebuilt by an Armenian architect, Tridat. The worst desecration, however, was in 1204, when it was ransacked by Catholic soldiers during the **Fourth Crusade**. Mules were brought in to help carry off silver and gilt carvings and

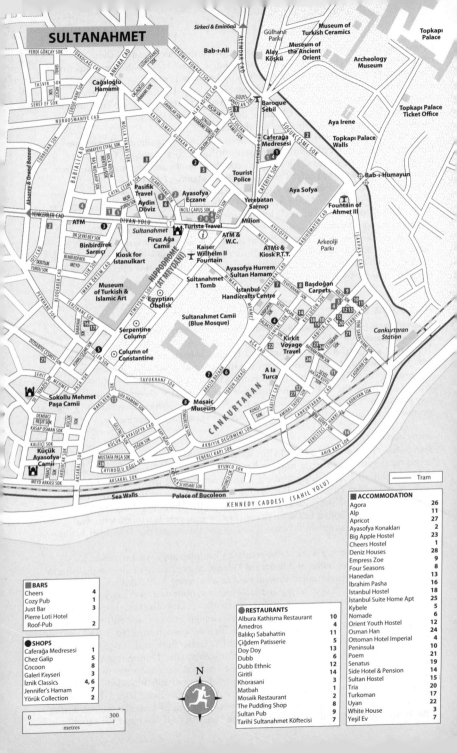

SULTANAHMET

Sirkeci & Eminönü
Gülhane Parkı
Museum of Turkish Ceramics
Topkapı Palace
Bab-ı-Ali
Museum of the Ancient Orient
Alay Köşkü
Archeology Museum
Baroque Sebil
Aya Irene
Topkapı Palace Ticket Office
Caferağa Medresesi
Topkapı Palace Walls
Bab-ı-Humayun
Tourist Police
Ayasofya Eczane
Aya Sofya
Yerebatan Sarnıcı
Fountain of Ahmet III
Milion
Turista Travel
Arkeolji Parkı
Firuz Ağa Camii
ATM & W.C.
ATMs & Kiosk P.T.T.
Kaiser Willhelm II Fountain
Ayasofya Hurrem Sultan Hamam
İstanbul Handicrafts Centre
Başdoğan Carpets
Sultanahmet 1 Tomb
Museum of Turkish & Islamic Art
Egyptian Obelisk
Sultanahmet Camii (Blue Mosque)
Serpentine Column
Kirkit Voyage Travel
Column of Constantine
Cankurtaran Station
A la Turca
Sokollu Mehmet Paşa Camii
Arasta Bazaar
Mosaic Museum
Küçük Ayasofya Camii
Sea Walls
Palace of Bucoleon
KENNEDY CADDESİ (SAHİL YOLU)

Binbirdirek Sarnıcı
Kiosk for İstanbulkart
Pasifik Travel Aydin Döviz
Cağaloğlu Hamamı

Roads listed: FERDİ GÖKÇAY SOK, TASVIR SOK, SEREF EF SOK, TÜRKOCAĞI CAD, ANKARA CAD, BABIALI CAD, NURUOSMANIYE CAD, CATAL ÇESME SOK, YENİÇERİLER CAD, DIVAN YOLU, İMRAN ÖKTEM CAD, TERZİHANE SOK, ŞEHİT MEHMET PAŞA SOK, TAVUKHANE SOK, CANKURTARAN, AKBIYIK CAD, KÜÇÜK AYASOFYA CAD, AKSAKAL SOK

--- Tram

N

0	300
metres	

a prostitute was seated on the throne of the patriarch. In 1452, far too late to save it, the Byzantine Church reluctantly accepted union with the Catholics in the hope that Western powers would come to the aid of Constantinople against the Turks. On May 29, 1453, those who said that they would rather see the turban of the Turk than the hat of a cardinal in the streets of Constantinople got their way when the city was captured. **Mehmet the Conqueror** rode to the church of Aya Sofya and stopped his troops looting the holy building. He then had it cleared of relics and said his first prayer there on the following Friday; this former bastion of the Byzantine Christian Empire was now a mosque.

Extensive restorations were carried out on the mosaics in the mid-nineteenth century by the Swiss **Fossati brothers**, but due to Muslim sensitivities the mosaics were later covered over again. The building continued to function as a **mosque** until 1932, when further renovations were carried out, and in 1934 Aya Sofya was opened as a **museum**.

INFORMATION   **AYA SOFYA**

Information and tickets The visitors' entrance is to the left (west) of the building as you look at it from Aya Sofya Meydanı, the large stretch of park between the Aya Sofya and the Blue Mosque. Queues can be substantial, especially when there are cruise ship and/or Turkish school groups visiting. The ticket office is just inside the entrance to the grounds of Aya Sofya, beyond which is a security check. The building itself is entered from the west, opposite which is a pleasant café and, north of it, the toilets. There's also a decent gift shop, inside the building off the outer narthex.

The courtyard

Before entering the building from the west, which has always been the main entrance to the church, it's worth remembering that where you are standing was once a great, enclosed forecourt to the church. Scattered around here are some interesting archeological fragments, including a carved-marble **ambo** (Byzantine pulpit) and many beautifully-carved capitals. Beyond the café is a collection of fallen masonry, with marble blocks elaborately carved in the late Roman style, once part of the classical temple-like facade of the second incarnation of the Haghia Sophia. In the sunken pit to the left of the doorways is the stepped base of this second church, along with a series of blocks with relief-carved sheep symbolizing the Twelve Apostles. The depth of the pit also gives a clear indication of how far the ground level has risen over the centuries.

The narthexes

Five large portals pierce the western wall of the building. The central one, known as the **Orea Porta** or "Beautiful Gate", was reserved for the imperial entourage. Beyond it is the **outer narthex** or vestibule, a long cross-vaulted corridor which today contains a series of display boards, running from left to right along the length of the narthex, outlining the history of the site from the early Byzantine period through to the Ottoman period and beyond. It's well worth looking at this display for the cross-sections, ground plans and reconstructions, which show how the building developed over the centuries. Also of interest here is a porphyry font to the left of the main portal and, to the right of it, the large marble sarcophagus of Empress Irene.

Five further doors lead through into the **inner narthex**, with a vaulted ceiling covered in gold mosaic and walls embellished with beautiful marble panels. The central portal to the nave is the **Imperial Gate**, again reserved for the Emperor and his entourage only. The Byzantines believed it was made with wood from Noah's Ark, but of more interest is the superb mosaic set in the half-moon-shaped recess (lunette) above the door. It depicts a seated **Christ Pantocrator** (the All Powerful) holding an open book showing a Greek inscription that reads "Peace be upon you, I am the light of the world". Grovelling to Christ's right is Emperor Leo IV, begging forgiveness for having married more times than was permitted under church law.

1

The nave

Entering the nave through the Imperial Gate, it is hard, even for the least spiritual of visitors, not to be awed by the sheer sense of space created by the heavenly dome, some 32m in diameter and 55m above floor-level. Pierced by forty windows, the scale of the dome is cleverly exaggerated by the addition of half-domes to west and east. The tympanum walls to the south and north of the central dome also emphasize the height of the building, especially as they are studded with rows of large, arched windows. At each corner of the nave are semicircular niches (*exedrae*). The galleries, which follow the line of these *exedrae* around the building, are supported by rows of columns and by four massive piers, which are the main support of the dome. The columns supporting the galleries are green antique marble, while those in the upper gallery are of Thessalian marble.

Worth noting in the northwest corner of the aisle is the **weeping column**. A legend dating from at least 1200 tells how St Gregory the Miracle-worker appeared here – the moisture subsequently seeping from the column has been believed to cure a wide range of conditions. Diagonally opposite, to the right of the apse, the circular marble-inlay panel in the floor is the **omphalos**, marking the spot where Byzantine emperors were crowned. The huge dome of the apse itself contains a ninth-century **mosaic of the Virgin Mary**, Christ seated on her lap.

Byzantine **mosaics** were designed to be seen by lamp- or candlelight, which shows off the workmanship to its best advantage: flickering light reflected in pieces of glass or gold, which had been carefully embedded at minutely disparate angles, give an appearance of movement and life to the mosaics. What remains of the **abstract**

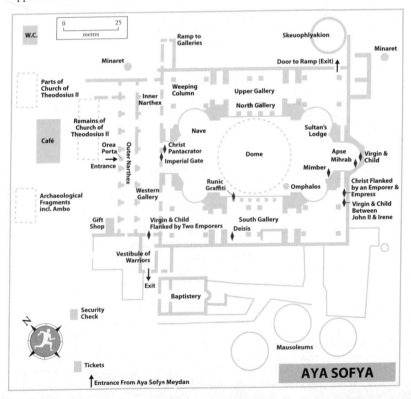

1

mosaics, and of the large areas of plain gold that covered the underside of the dome and other large expanses of wall and ceiling, dates from the sixth century.

Following the building's conversion to a mosque, several new features were added to suit its new purpose. Still visible today are the *mihrab*, slightly offset in the apse, a *mimber*, a sultan's loge, and the enormous wooden plaques that bear sacred Islamic names of God, the Prophet Mohammed, the first four caliphs and the prophet's grandchildren Hasan and Husayn. These and the inscription on the dome by the calligrapher Azzet Efendi all date from the time of the restoration by the Fossati brothers.

The upper galleries

To reach the galleries, head for the northern end of the inner narthex, from where a sloping ramp leads up to the upper gallery. The logical way to proceed is across the western gallery, stopping to note the circle of green Thessalian marble that marked the **throne of the empress**, before turning left and passing through the gap in a beautifully-carved marble screen into the south gallery. All the **figurative mosaics** in the Aya Sofya date from after the Iconoclastic era (726–843). One of the best is a **Deisis** scene to the right of the marble screen, depicting Christ, the Virgin and St John the Baptist. Although this mosaic is partly damaged, the three faces are all well preserved: that of John the Baptist is especially expressive, betraying great pain and suffering, while the Virgin has downcast eyes and an expression of modesty and humility. Opposite this, scratched into the balustrade running around the inside of the gallery, is some Viking **runic graffitti**. It was probably left by one of the members of the Varangian Guard, a unit which acted as personal bodyguards for later Byzantine emperors, recruited from Scandinavia.

On the east wall of the south gallery, contiguous with the apse, is a **mosaic of Christ flanked by an emperor and empress**. The inscriptions over their heads read "Zoë, the most pious Augusta" and "Constantine in Christ, the Lord Autocrat, faithful Emperor of the Romans, Monomachus". It is believed that the two figures are Constantine IX Monomachus and Empress Zoë, who ruled Byzantium in her own right with her sister Theodora before she married Constantine, her third husband.

The other mosaic in the south gallery, dating from 1118, depicts the **Virgin and Child between Emperor John II Comnenus and Empress Irene**, and their son Prince Alexius, added later. This is a livelier, less conventional work than that of Zoë and Constantine, with faces full of expression: Prince Alexius, who died soon after this portrait was executed, is depicted as a wan and sickly youth, his lined face presaging his premature death.

To exit the galleries, you must head to the northeast corner of the north gallery, from where a ramp leads back down into the nave.

The Vestibule of Warriors

Today's exit from the building is from the southern end of the inner narthex, through a door leading into the **Vestibule of Warriors**. In the Byzantine period, this provided an alternative imperial entrance to the church and was where the emperor left his sword and crown. As you pass from the inner narthex into the Vestibule of Warriors, a large mirror reminds you to turn around and look upwards to see the most impressive mosaic of all, a **Virgin and Child flanked by two emperors**. Dated to the last quarter of the tenth century, it shows Emperor Justinian, to the right of the Virgin, offering a model of Aya Sofya, while Emperor Constantine offers a model of the city of Constantinople.

The Topkapı Palace

Topkapı Sarayı Müzesi • Daily except Tues: mid-April to end Sept 9am–7pm, last entry 6pm; Oct to mid-April 9am–5pm • 20TL • Free to enter the first court • ⓦ www.topkapisarayi.gov.tr

The **Topkapı Palace** (Topkapı Sarayı) was both the symbolic and political centre of the Ottoman Empire for nearly four centuries, until the removal of the imperial retinue to Dolmabahçe, by Sultan Abdülmecid I in 1853. It's a beautiful setting in which to

1

wander and contemplate the majesty of the Ottoman sultanate, as well as the cruelty exemplified by institutions such as the Harem and "the Cage".

Originally known as *Sarayı Cedid*, or New Palace, Topkapı was built between 1459 and 1465 as the seat of government of the newly installed Ottoman regime. It was not at first a residence: Mehmet the Conqueror had already built what would become known as the Old Palace on the present site of İstanbul University (see p.84) and even after he himself moved, his harem stayed on at the old site.

In accordance with Islamic tradition, the palace consists of a collection of buildings arranged around a series of courtyards, similar to the Alhambra in Granada or a Moghul palace in India. Although this creates an initial impression of disorder, in fact the arrangement is meticulously logical. The **first court** was the service area of the palace and open to all, while most of the second court and its attendant buildings were devoted to the Divan, or Council of State, and to those who had business with it. The pavilions of judges were located at the **Ortakapı** (the entrance to the palace proper, between the first and second courts), in accordance with the tradition that justice should be dispensed at the gate of the palace.

The **third court** was mainly given over to the palace school, an important imperial institution devoted to the training of civil servants, and it is only in the **fourth court** that the serious business of state gives way to the more pleasurable aspects of life. Around the attractive **gardens** here are a number of pavilions erected by successive emperors in celebration of their victories. Here, the glorious views and sunsets could be enjoyed in privileged retreat from their four-thousand-member retinue.

The various adjustments made to the structure and function of the buildings were indicative of the power shifts in the Ottoman Empire over the centuries. During the "Rule of the Harem" in the sixteenth century, for example, a passageway was opened between the Harem and the Divan. In the eighteenth century, when the power of the sultan had declined, the offices of state were transferred away from the "Eye of the Sultan" (the window in the Divan through which a sultan could monitor proceedings) to the gateway that led to the palaces of the Grand Vizier, known as the Sublime Port.

INFORMATION   TOPKAPI PALACE

Tickets The ticket office for the Topkapı complex is situated to the right of the path as it approaches the second gate; that to the Harem, which charges a further admission, is in the second courtyard. Audioguides (10TL) for both Palace and Harem are available at the ticket office and at a kiosk just through the second gate.

Visiting tips Much of your time exploring (and you will need at least half a day) will be spent outside, either in the court gardens or walking between separate buildings, so

try to pick a dry day. Should your visit coincide with large parties of cruise-ship passengers, or mostly charming but always noisy groups of Turkish school children, the queues to some rooms, especially the Imperial Treasury and Room of the Relics of the Prophet in the third court, can be interminable.

Eating Apart from a small café in the second court, there's only the exorbitantly priced *Konyalı Café* for food, so it's best to eat before entering.

The first court and Aya Irene

Most visitors approach the palace by entering the first court through the great defensive imperial gate of Mehmet the Conqueror, the **Bab-ı Hümayün**. Before stepping through the gate it's worth admiring the delightful eighteenth-century Rococo **Fountain of Ahmet III**, just to the right of the gateway. The street here is inevitably busy with tour buses dropping their charges, but the crowds and general melee is entirely in keeping with the origins of the first courtyard, which, as the palace's service area, was always open to the general public. Once through the gateway, the long-defunct **palace bakeries** are behind a wall to the right of the courtyard and the buildings of the **imperial mint and outer treasury** (all currently closed) are behind the wall north of the church of Aya Irene. In front of Aya Irene were located the quarters of the straw-weavers and carriers of silver pitchers, around a central courtyard in which the palace firewood was stored. The church itself was variously employed as an armoury and storage space for archeological treasures.

Today, **Aya Irene**, "the Church of the Divine Peace", is generally closed to visitors. The best chance to see the interior is when it opens for occasional exhibitions or concerts, including the summer İstanbul International Music Festival (see p.31). The original church was one of the oldest in the city, but it was rebuilt along with Aya Sofya after being burnt down in the Nika riots of 532. Around the semicircular apse is the only **synthronon** (seating space for clergy in the apse of a church) in İstanbul to have survived the Byzantine era. It has six tiers of seats with an ambulatory running behind the fourth tier. Most of the interior is now plain, exposed brickwork, and even the plastered apse is decorated with nothing more than a crude cross.

Ortakapı, the second court and the Divan

To reach the second court you pass through the Bab-üs Selam, "the Gate of Salutations", otherwise known as the **Ortakapı**, or middle gate. In the Ottoman period, only the sultan was allowed to ride through here, everyone else had to dismount. Surmounted by attractive octagonal towers, it marks an imposing entrance to the main part of the complex. Today, the ticket turnstiles and security checks are located in this gateway.

Immediately to the right after passing through the security check are a couple of glass cases containing scale-models of the palace complex, which are very useful for orientation. To the left and hidden from view down a hill are the **Privy Stables of Mehmet II**, which are used for temporary exhibitions. Diagonally left are the buildings of the Divan and the Inner Treasury and the entrance to the Harem. Opposite the Divan, on the right side of the courtyard, is the kitchen area, while straight ahead is the gateway to the third court.

The gardens between the paths radiating from the Ortakapı are planted with ancient cypresses and plane trees, rose bushes and lawns. Originally, they would also have been resplendent with peacocks, gazelles and, most importantly, fountains. This **second court** was the scene of pageantry during state ceremonies, when the sultan occupied his

---

THE CAGE

The Cage was adopted by Ahmet I as an alternative to fratricide, which had become institutionalized in the Ottoman Empire since the days of Beyazit II. To avoid wars of succession, Beyazit ruled that a sultan should execute his brothers upon his accession to the throne. The Cage was introduced as a way around this practice, but in the event proved a less than satisfactory solution. After the death of their father, the younger princes would be incarcerated along with deaf mutes and a *harem* of concubines, while their eldest brother acceded to the throne. They remained in the suite of rooms of the Harem known in Turkish as **Kafes** (the Cage) until such time as they were called upon to take power themselves. The concubines never left the Cage unless they became pregnant, and great care was taken to prevent this, either by the removal of their ovaries or by the use of pessaries, since if it did occur they were immediately drowned.

The decline of the Ottoman Empire has in part been attributed to the institution of the Cage. The sultans who spent any length of time there emerged crazed, avaricious and debauched. Osman II, for example, enjoyed archery, but only when using live targets, including prisoners of war and his own pages. He was assassinated by the janissaries, to be replaced by Mustafa I, who had all but died of starvation in the Cage and was even madder than his predecessor. He, too, was assassinated. The worst affected of all, however, was İbrahim, better known as **Deli İbrahim** (İbrahim the Mad). He spent 22 years in the Cage, and when they came to take him out he was so sure he was about to be assassinated that he had to be removed forcibly. His reign was characterized by sexual excess and political misrule (his mother, Köşem, once complained that there was not enough wood for the Harem fires and he responded by having his grand vizier executed). Eventually, in response to a rumour of *harem* intrigue, İbrahim had all bar two of his 280 concubines bound in sacks and thrown into the Bosphorus. According to one version of events, only one survived; wriggling free of her bonds, she was rescued by a passing French ship and taken to Paris.

1

TOPKAPI PALACE

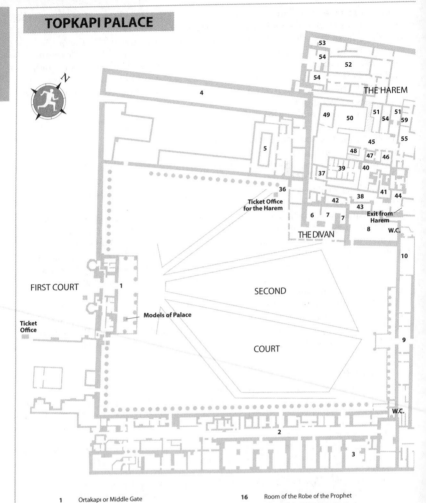

THE HAREM

THE DIVAN

FIRST COURT

SECOND

COURT

Ticket Office
for the Harem

Exit from
Harem

W.C.

Ticket
Office

Models of Palace

W.C.

1	Ortakapı or Middle Gate	16	Room of the Robe of the Prophet
2	Kitchens and Cooks' Quarters (Porcelain & Glass Collection)	17	Rooms of the Relics of the Prophet
3	Reconstructed Kitchen	18	Hall of the Treasury (Closed) (Sultans' Portraits & Miniature Collection)
4	Stables and Harness Rooms	19	Hall of the Pantry (Museum Directorate)
5	Barrack of the Halberdiers of the Long Tresses	20	Imperial Treasury (Pavilion of Mehmet II)
6	Hall of the Divan	21	Disrobing Chamber of Selim II Hamam
7	Offices of the Divan	22	Site of Selim II Hamam
8	Inner Treasury (Arms & armour collection)	23	Site of Selim II Hamam Boilers
9	Gate of Felicity (Bab-üs Saadet)	24	Hall of the Expeditionary Force
10	Quarters of the White Eunuchs (Costume collection)	25	Circumcision Köşkü
11	Throne Room	26	Terrace and Bower
12	Ahmet III Library	27	Pool
13	Library (Mosque of the School)	28	Baghdad Köşkü
14	Harem Mosque	29	Pool
15	Court of the Room of the Robe	30	Revan Köşkü
		31	Tulip Gardens of Ahmet III
		32	Mustafa Paşa Köşkü

33	Physician's Tower	51	Apartments of Senior women
34	Mecidiye Köşkü	52	Court of Women's hospital
35	Third Gate	53	Hospital Hamam
36	Entry to the Harem (Carriage Gate)	54	Hospital Kitchen Quarters
37	Mosque of the Black Eunuchs	55	Sultan Ahmet Kiosk
38	Court of the Black Eunuchs	56	Harem Garden
39	Barrack of the Black Eunuchs	57	Valide Sultan's Court
40	Princes' School	58	Valide Sultan's Dining Room
41	Quarters of the Chief Black Eunuchs	59	Valide Sultan's Bedroom
42	Quarters of the Treasurer	60	Valide Sultan's Hamam
43	Quarters of the Chamberlain	61	Kadin's Quarters
44	Aviary Gate (Kuşhane Kapisi)	62	Golden Road
45	Courtyard of the Women of the Harem	63	Ahmet III Dining Room
46	Kitchen of the Women	64	Throne Room Within
47	Hamam of the Women	65	The Sultan's Hamam
48	Stairs to Bedrooms	66	Osman III Terrace
49	Laundry	67	Terrace of Selâmlik Garden
50	Women's Dormitory	68	Apartment of the Selamlik (Sultan's Rooms)

1

throne beneath the Bab-üs Saadet. At all times, even on one of the three days of the week when the courtyard was filled with petitioners to the Divan, silence reigned here, as people obeyed the rules of conduct imposed in the presence – actual or potential – of the sultan.

As you enter the buildings of the **Divan** you'll see the metal grille in the Council Chamber (the first room on the left), called "the Eye of the Sultan". Through this he could observe the proceedings of the Divan, where the eminent imperial councillors sat in session, and which took its name from the couch running around the three walls of the room. The building dates essentially from the reign of Mehmet the Conqueror, and the Council Chamber was restored to its sixteenth-century appearance in 1945, with some of the original İznik tiles and arabesque painting. The other two rooms of the Divan have retained the Rococo decorations of Ahmet III. The **Divan tower**, rebuilt in incongruous Neoclassical style in 1825, rises above the council chamber, but is currently not open to visitors.

Next to the Divan is another building from Mehmet the Conqueror's original palace, the **Inner Treasury**, a six-domed hall preceded by a double-domed vestibule and supported internally by three piers. Reopened in late 2011 following major restoration, the former treasury houses an impressive collection of (mainly) Ottoman **arms and armour**. Look out for the curved sword of Mehmet the Conqueror inscribed with the words "may the necks of the enemies of Sheriat become the scabbards of this sword", and all the usual paraphernalia of late medieval warfare, from maces and axes to bows and shields. Kids may be intrigued by the hologram room, with flickering 3D representations of Ottoman janissaries and cavalry.

Across the courtyard from the Divan are the **palace kitchens and cooks' quarters**. Much of this complex was destroyed by fire in 1574, though the chimneys were stylishly reconstructed by Mimar Sinan, as were eight of the ten domes behind them (the two southernmost domes date back to the reign of Mehmet the Conqueror). The ten kitchens, which had a staff of 1500, all served different purposes. The kitchens were closed for restoration at the time of writing but should reopen in 2012.

The third court

As you pass through the **Bab-üs Saadet**, "the Gate of Felicity", the **Throne Room** is immediately in front of you. This building, mainly dating from the reign of Selim I, was where the sultan awaited the outcome of sessions of the Divan in order to give his assent or otherwise to their proposals. This courtyard was also home to the Enderun or Palace School, making it arguably the most important courtyard in the palace, as here the administrators, soldiers, artisans and artists, who formed the backbone of the whole imperial Ottoman edifice, were trained.

The grey marble building at the centre of the third courtyard, the **Ahmet III Library** is restrained and sombre compared to his highly decorative fountain outside the gates of the palace. To the right of the gate, behind the colonnade running around the southern edge of the courtyard, is the **Hall of the Expeditionary Force**, sometimes referred to as the Hall of the Campaign Pages (*Seferli Kouudu*), which houses a collection of embroidery and a very small selection from the imperial costume collection. The latter includes a charming little outfit of Selim I's – red with yellow circles – prompting the question of where he could have acquired his epithet "the Grim". Behind the hall is the *hamam* of Selim II, who fell there in a drunken stupor and died later of his injuries.

The Imperial Treasury

The **Imperial Treasury** is housed in the rooms that once functioned as the Pavilion of Mehmet II, which takes up most of the southeast side of the third courtyard, to the right of the entrance. The first two rooms – the right-hand one of which was used as the *camekan* or disrobing chamber of the *hamam* of Selim II – are beautifully proportioned and domed.

The first room contains a number of highly wrought and extremely beautiful objects, including a delicate silver model of a palace complete with tiny birds in the trees, a present to Abdül Hamid II from Japan. The big crowd-puller in room two is the **Topkapı Dagger**, which starred alongside Peter Ustinov in the Sunday-matinee classic *Topkapi*. A present from Mahmut I to Nadir Shah that was waylaid and brought back when news of the shah's death reached Topkapı, the dagger is decorated with three enormous emeralds, one of which conceals a watch. In the third room, the **Spoonmaker's Diamond**, the fifth-largest diamond in the world, is invariably surrounded by a gawping crowd, which perhaps gives some impression of the effect it must have had during its first public appearance, adorning Mehmet IV's turban at his coronation in 1648.

The fourth room boasts a bejewelled throne and the hand and occipital bone of John the Baptist, but otherwise it's a relative haven of restraint. Ivory and sandalwood objects predominate, refreshingly simple materials whose comparative worth is determined by craftsmanship rather than quantity.

Across the courtyard from the Imperial Treasury, the Pavilion of the Holy Mantle houses the **Rooms of the Relics of the Prophet**, holy relics brought home by Selim the Grim after his conquest of Egypt in 1517. The relics were originally viewed only by the sultan, his family and his immediate entourage on days of special religious significance, but were opened to the public in 1962. They include a footprint, hair and a tooth of the Prophet Mohammed, as well as his mantle and standard, swords of the first four caliphs and a letter from the Prophet to the leader of the Coptic tribe. The most precious of the relics are kept behind glass, attractively arranged and lit.

The fourth court

The **fourth court** consists of several gardens, each graced with pavilions. The **Baghdad Köşkü**, in the northeast corner of the tulip gardens laid out under Sultan Ahmet III, was built by Murat IV to celebrate the conquest of Baghdad in 1638. The exterior and cool, dark interior are tiled in blue, turquoise and white, and the shutters and cupboard doors are inlaid with tortoiseshell and mother-of-pearl. The **Circumcision Köşkü**, in the Portico of Columns, a short way west of the Baghdad Köşkü, also dates from the reign of İbrahim the Mad. Outside, it's covered in İznik tiles of the sixteenth and early seventeenth centuries. Any number of different patterns are represented in the eclectic design, but they include some of the most beautiful panels from the very best İznik period. Between these two beautiful *köşk*s is a terrace graced by a small gilt canopy, the İftariye, built by İbrahim the Mad in 1640 to celebrate the breaking of the fast during Ramadan. From here, the views up the Golden Horn, across to Galata and towards the Bosphorus, are superb. At the other end of the Portico of Columns is the **Revan Köşkü**, built to commemorate the capture of Erivan in the Caucasus by Mehmet IV.

The **Mecidiye Köşkü** – the last building to be erected at Topkapı – commands the best view of any of the Topkapı pavilions. It now houses the expensive *Konyalı Café* (see p.179), and on a clear day from its garden terrace you can identify most of the buildings on the Asian shore of the Bosphorus.

The Harem

Daily except Tues 10am–4pm • 15TL

The entrance to the Harem is in the second court. The word "harem" means "forbidden" in Arabic; in Turkish, it refers to a suite of apartments in a palace or private residence where the head of the household lived with his wives, odalisques (female slaves) and children. The Harem in Topkapı lies between the sultan's private apartments and the quarters of the Chief Black Eunuch. It consisted of over four hundred rooms, centred on the suites of the sultan and his mother, the valide sultan. Around these, in descending order of rank, were the apartments of the wives, favourites, sultan's daughters, princes, housekeepers, maids and odalisques.

1

The Carriage Gate

The Harem was connected to the outside world by means of the **Carriage Gate**, so called because the odalisques would have entered their carriages here when they went on outings. To the left of the Carriage Gate as you enter the Harem is the **Barracks of the Halberdiers of the Long Tresses**. Blinkered to ensure the privacy of the women, they carried logs and other loads into the Harem, as well as serving as imperial guardsmen. The Carriage Gate and the Aviary Gate were both guarded by black eunuchs, who were responsible for running the *harem*, but only allowed to enter in daylight hours. At night, the female housekeepers took charge and reported any unusual occurrences to the Chief Black Eunuch.

The rooms of the Harem

The *Altın Yol*, or **Golden Road**, ran the entire length of the Harem, from the quarters of the Black Eunuchs to the fourth courtyard. Strategically located at the beginning of this passageway were the **apartments of the Valide Sultan**, also rebuilt after 1665. They include a particularly lovely domed dining room. A passageway leads from her apartments to those of the women she controlled, the senior women of the court. These compact areas had an upper gallery, in which bedding was stored, windows and a hearth

Beyond the Valide Sultan's apartments, to the north, are some of the most attractive rooms of the palace. These were the apartments and reception rooms of the *selamlık*, the sultan's own rooms. The largest and grandest of them is the **Hünkar Sofrası**, the Imperial Hall, where the sultan entertained visitors. Another important room in this section is a masterwork of the architect Sinan: the **bedchamber of Murat III**, covered in

---

THE WOMEN OF THE HAREM

The concept of the *harem* has long held a grip on the western imagination. The most famous product of the Topkapı *harem* was Haseki Hürrem, or Roxelana, wife of Süleyman the Magnificent. Prior to their marriage, it was unusual for a sultan to marry at all, let alone to choose a wife from among his concubines. The marriage, and the subsequent installation of the *harem* women in the palace, established the women of the *harem*, and especially the **valide sultan** (the mother of the reigning sultan), in a position of unprecedented power and enabled women to take more control over affairs of state.

Roxelana began this new order in characteristic vein: she persuaded Süleyman to murder both his grand vizier, İbrahim Paşa, and his son, the heir apparent, Mustafa – the latter in order to make way for her own son, Selim the Sot. The favourite of Selim the Sot, **Nur Banu**, made a significant change to the layout of the Harem when she became valide sultan in her turn. She moved her suite of apartments from one end of the Golden Road to the other, so that it was located next to that of her son, Murat III. This also meant she was lodged near to the entrance of the Divan and could easily listen in on affairs of state. Nur Banu encouraged her son in debauchery (he fathered a total of 103 children, 54 of whom survived him) and persuaded him to murder his most able minister, the Grand Vizier Sokollu Mehmet Paşa.

The number of **odalisques** (female slaves) employed in the *harem* increased steadily with the decline of the Ottoman Empire, and by the reign of Abdülaziz (1861–76) there were 809 in Topkapı. Many were imported from Georgia and Caucasia for their looks, or were prisoners of war, captured in Hungary, Poland or Venice. Upon entering the *harem*, they would become the charges of the *haznedar usta*, who would teach them how to behave towards the sultan and the other palace inhabitants. The conditions in which the majority of these women lived were dangerously unhygienic and many of them died from vermin-carried and waterborne diseases, or from the cold of an İstanbul winter. The women who were chosen to enter the bedchamber of the sultan, however, were promoted to the rank of imperial odalisque, given slaves to serve them, and pleasant accommodation. If they bore him a child, they would be promoted to the rank of favourite or wife, with their own apartments. If the sultan subsequently lost affection for one of these women, he could give her in marriage to one of his courtiers.

1

sixteenth-century İznik tiles and kitted out with a marble fountain and, opposite, a bronze fireplace surrounded by a panel of tiling representing plum blossom.

The northernmost rooms of the Harem are supported by immense piers and vaults, providing capacious basements that were used as dormitories and storerooms. Below the bedchamber is a large indoor **swimming pool**, with taps for hot and cold water, where Murat is supposed to have thrown gold to women who pleased him. Next to the bedchamber is the light and airy **library of Ahmet I**, with windows overlooking both the Bosphorus and the Golden Horn; beyond this is the **dining room of Ahmet III**, whose walls are covered in wood panelling painted with bowls of fruit and flowers, typical of the extravagant tulip-loving sultan. To the southwest of the bedchamber are two rooms originally thought to be the notorious **Cage** (see box, p.49), though this is no longer believed to be the case – the Cage was actually situated in various rooms on the floor above.

The Aviary Gate

The exit from the Harem is the **Aviary Gate**, or Kudhane Kapısı, which brings visitors into the third court. One of the most infamous of all the valide sultans, Mahpeyker Sultan, also known as *Ködem*, "the leader", was assassinated here. She was the effective ruler of the Ottoman Empire during the reigns of her two sons, Murat IV and İbrahim the Mad, and since she was not banished to the old palace after the death of İbrahim (as was customary), she also ruled during the reign of her grandson Mehmet IV. She was eventually murdered on the orders of a jealous rival, the new Valide Sultan Turhan Hatice, by the Chief Black Eunuch. At the age of 80, the toothless old woman was stripped naked and strangled, after allegedly putting up a ferocious struggle.

Gülhane Parkı and around

Gülhane Parkı surrounds Topkapı Palace on all sides and was once the extended gardens of the sultans. It is now a public park with mature trees, home to nesting herons in spring; it's a good place for kids to run off steam, though there's little play equipment. For tea and sustenance, the *Set Üstü Çay Bahçesi* (see p.179) in the northeast corner of the park is excellent; from here you can admire the Goth's Column, erected in the third or fourth century to commemorate a victory over the Goths, and views over the Bosphorus. The park stays open until well after dusk during the summer months, though the security guards are vague about exact closing times. The entrance to the History of Science and Technology in Islam (see p.67) is inside the park, and one approach to the wonderful Archeology Museum complex is also through the park.

Bab-ı-Ali

Heading downhill along the line of the tram from Sultanahmet, past the entrance to Gülhane Parkı, you'll see on the left an ornamental gateway, the **Bab-ı-Ali** or Sublime Porte. It marked the entrance to the administrative centre of the Ottoman Empire where, from the mid-seventeenth century onwards, the vizier presided over the day-to-day running of the empire. The Baroque-style gate, only erected in 1843, seems rather grandiose for its present-day purpose, marking the back entrance to the **Vilayet Binası**, the headquarters for the province of İstanbul.

Alay Köşkü

Opposite the Bab-ı-Ali, built into the high stone walls of Gülhane Parkı, part of the outer defences of the Topkapı Palace built by Fatih Mehmet II around 1465, is the **Alay Köşkü**. From this raised gazebo, sultans could watch official parades pass by, or, as was the wont of the more suspicious rulers, keep an eye on who was passing in and out of the Bab-ı-Ali across the road. One, Murat IV, kept his subjects on their toes by firing crossbow bolts at them from up here. The *kösk* was undergoing renovation at

1

the time of writing and may well open to the public; the sloping ramp allowing sultans to reach the look-out on horseback is reached from inside Gülhane Parkı, a short way back up the hill.

The Archeology Museum complex

Osman Hamdi Bey Yokuşu, Gülhane • Enter either through Gülhane Parkı or from the first courtyard of the Topkapı Palace • Tues–Sun: mid-April to Sept 9am–7pm; Oct to mid-April 9am–5pm • 10TL • ✆ istanbularkeoloji.gov.tr

The **Archeology Museum** complex, comprised of three separate buildings, contains a stunning array of finds from Anatolia, the Middle East and İstanbul itself. One of the city's most underrated sights, it attracts none of the crowds of the Topkapı Palace or the Aya Sofya. The museum was established in 1875 in the **Çinili Köşk** (Tiled Pavilion), which still forms part of the museum complex. In 1891 a purpose-built Neoclassical pile, designed by the French architect Alexander Vallaury (also responsible for the *Pera Palace* hotel, see p.123), was completed opposite the Çinili Köşk to house the rapidly expanding collection. Today this is home to the majority of objects on display here, along with a smaller building, the **Museum of the Ancient Orient**, which houses the oldest finds. The museum was established as a direct response to the Western powers removing shiploads of antiquities from the Ottoman Empire to stock museums in London, Paris, Berlin and elsewhere. Given that the former Ottoman domains included lands home to some of the world's most exciting ancient civilizations, from the Assyrians to the Hittites, Egyptians to the Greeks and Romans to the Byzantines, it's hardly surprising that this museum complex contains so many world-class exhibits.

The Museum of the Ancient Orient

The entrance to the **Museum of the Ancient Orient** (Eski Dark Eserleri Müzesi) is just to the left as you pass through the complex's ticket barrier. Housed in a fine Neoclassical building built in 1883, which was formerly a fine arts school, it contains a small but dazzling collection of Anatolian, Egyptian and Mesopotamian artefacts. The superbly preserved, late Hittite basalt lions flanking the entrance date from the ninth century BC, and give a taste of the incredible state of preservation of some of the exhibits inside.

One of the most interesting exhibits is the oldest peace treaty known to mankind, the **Treaty of Kadesh** in Room 7, found at the Hittite capital Hattusa. Written in cuneiform script, it was signed in 1269 when a battle fought on the River Orontes (today's Ası Nehri in Anatolia), between Pharaoh Ramses II and the Hittite king Muvatellish, ended in stalemate. The treaty includes a ceasefire agreement and pledges of a mutual exchange of political refugees, and was originally engraved onto silver tablets. It is the world's first known peace treaty, and a copy has pride of place in the United Nations' headquarters in New York.

The blue-and-yellow **animal relief** in the corridor beyond Room 1 dates from the reign of Nebuchadnezzar (604–562 BC), the last hero-king of Babylonia, when it would have lined the processional way in Babylon. Other exhibits were taken from Nebuchadnezzar's palace-museum, located at the Ishtar Gate. Another massive relief, in Room 8, depicts the **Hittite king Urpalla** presenting gifts of grapes and grain to a vegetation god, who is three times his own size and wearing a rather attractive pair of curly-toed boots. This is a plaster copy of a relief found at İvriz Kaya near Konya, dating from the eighth century BC.

Other exhibits include a **Sumerian** love poem and a tablet of Sumerian proverbs dating from the eighteenth century BC. There's also a figure of a Babylonian duck in Room 7, with an inscription identifying it as a **standard weight** belonging to a priest called Musallim Marduk: it weighs about 30kg and dates from around 2000 BC, making it the oldest known standard measure.

1

The Archeology Museum

One of the catalysts for the construction of the main building of the complex was to provide a home for the stunning sarcophagi uncovered by Osman Hamdi Bey, the Director of Ancient Antiquities, during excavations at Sidon in 1887. There is much else to see, however, in this wonderful museum, making it a must for anyone interested in the history of this great city and the lands over which it once ruled.

The most exciting objects in the museum, the **Sidon Sarcophagi**, can be found in Rooms 9, 8 and 7 (to reach them turn left at the main entrance). Chief among them is the **Lycian Sarcophagus**, depicting centaurs, sphinxes and griffons, as well as scenes from Greek mythology. It is in the Lycian style, but the carvings show a Peloponnesian influence in the stocky bodies and broad faces of the human figures. In the same room are the anthropoid sarcophagi from Sidon, which illustrate the fifth-century BC fashion for Egyptian models in Greek sculpture. The **Tabnit Sarcophagus**, the oldest Sidon discovery, is in fact Egyptian in origin. A hieroglyphic inscription on the chest of this alabaster mummy-case states that it belonged to an Egyptian commander named Penephtah.

Dating from the end of the fourth century BC, the fabulous **Alexander Sarcophagus** is so-called because it is covered with scenes of Alexander the Great hunting and in battle. It is ascribed variously by different sources to a ruler of the Seleucid dynasty or to the Phoenician Prince Abdolonyme. The metal weapons originally held by warriors and huntsmen on the sarcophagi were stolen prior to the excavations of Hamdi Bey, presumably when the burial chambers were looted.

The Ionic architecture of another of the Sidon sarcophagi, the **Sarcophagus of the Mourning Women**, shows eighteen members of the *harem* of King Straton (who died in 360 BC) in various poses of distress and mourning. From Room 7 you can continue round into the northeast wing of the museum, where there are several rooms containing more funerary relics. Right of the entrance, Rooms 13–20 contain a comprehensive collection of statuary dating from the Archaic through to the Roman period, much of it of superb quality. Room 16 exhibits a vivid statue of a young Alexander the Great, carved in the stylized manner popular at Pergamon, on Turkey's Aegean coast, in the second century BC.

The new wing, to the rear of the main body of the museum, contains exhibits from the **Thracian and Bithynian civilizations**, but of most interest is the **Byzantine collection**. A small but beautifully lit collection of artefacts that highlights the successful transition between Classical Roman and Christian Byzantine art, it includes a relief-carved plinth decorated with Nike, the winged goddess of victory, once topped by Constantinople's greatest charioteer, Porphyrius, which once stood in the Hippodrome (see p.59).

On the first floor, **İstanbul through the Ages** gives a brilliant overview of the city's complex history. The actual exhibits are small scale but carefully chosen – don't miss the case containing the bronze serpent's head, knocked off of the fifth-century-BC Serpentine column (see p.60) in the Hippodrome, or the section of the chain used to block access to the Golden Horn to enemy ships during the Byzantine period.

The next level up is devoted to the **Anatolia and Troy through the Ages** collections, well worth seeing, especially if you have either been to or are planning to visit the legendary city of Troy (see pp.259–261). The exhibits include a range of artefacts unearthed by Heinrich Schliemann and his successor, Dorpfield, at Troy, including much gold jewellery. On the third floor, **Neighbouring Cultures of Anatolia** concentrates on the ancient civilizations of Syria, Cyprus and Palestine and includes the famous Siloam inscription, a votive tablet dating back to the eighth century BC written in Paleo-Hebraic.

The Museum of Turkish Ceramics

The graceful **Çinili Köşk** or Tiled Pavilion – a few metres north of the Museum of the Ancient Orient – was built in 1472 as a kind of grandstand, from which the sultan could watch sporting activities such as wrestling or polo. It now houses the

Museum of Turkish Ceramics, displaying tiles of equal quality to those in Topkapı Palace and İstanbul's older mosques, along with well-written explanations of the different periods in the history of Turkish ceramics. Look particularly for polychrome tiles of the mid-sixteenth to mid-seventeenth centuries, dating from the longest and most successful period of tile production. Interesting exhibits include a mosque lamp from the Sokollu Mehmet Paşa Camii (see p.62), a ceramic coffee-cooler in which beans were placed after roasting and before grinding, and Murat III's attractive little fountain in the wall of the last room of all, after the İznik collection.

Yerebatan Sarnıçı

Entrance on Caferiye Sok · Daily: mid-April to Sept 9am–6.30pm; Oct to mid-April 9am–5.30pm · 10TL

Yerebatan Sarnıçı, the "Sunken Cistern" (also known as the Basilica Cistern), is one of several underground cisterns, this one buried under the very core of Sultanahmet and the first to have been extensively excavated. Although generally crowded, it warrants a prolonged exploration.

Probably built by the Emperor Constantine in the fourth century, and enlarged by Justinian in the sixth, the cistern was supplied by aqueducts with water from the Belgrade Forest. In turn, it supplied the Great Palace and later Topkapı Palace. The cistern fell into disuse after the Ottoman conquest and its existence was only brought to public attention in 1545 by the Frenchman **Petrus Gyllius**. He had been led to it by local residents, whose houses were built over the cistern and who had sunk wells into it. They even kept boats on the water from which they could fish its depths – Gyllius' interest was first aroused when he found fresh fish being sold in the streets nearby.

In 1987, fifty thousand tonnes of mud and water were removed, the walls were covered to make them impermeable, and eight of the columns were sheathed in concrete to fortify the structure. The construction of raised pathways to replace the rowboats used by early tourists may seem a desecration, but they do facilitate a leisurely examination of interesting bits of masonry, as does the careful spotlighting. Despite the piped muzak, the cistern is deeply atmospheric, with carp swimming lazily through the floodlit waters and water dripping steadily from the vaults above.

The largest covered cistern in the city, Yerebatan held eighty thousand cubic metres of water. The small brick **domes** are supported by 336 columns, many of which have Corinthian capitals. The columns' varied styles probably indicate that they were made from the recycled remnants of earlier structures. One column, with a tear-drop relief-carved pattern, looks like it came from the triumphal Arch of Theodosius in Beyazit (see p.83). The two **Medusa-head capitals** supporting a couple of columns in the southwest corner, brought to light when the cistern was drained, are also clearly relics from an older building. Part of the 1963 James Bond classic *From Russia with Love* was filmed here.

The Hippodrome

The arena of the **Hippodrome**, formerly the cultural focus of the Byzantine Empire, is today the **At Meydanı** ("Square of Horses"). Completely repaved in 2011, it is flanked to the northwest by İbrahim Paşa Palace, now the Museum of Turkish and Islamic Art, and to the southeast by the Blue Mosque.

A stadium was first constructed here by the Roman Emperor Septimius Severus in 203 AD and later enlarged by Constantine the Great for the performance of court ceremonies and games. Estimated to have held up to 100,000 people, the original orientation and dimensions of the 480-metre-long arena have been more or less preserved by the present-day square. Even after the fall of Constantinople in 1453, the Hippodrome continued to be a focus of state ceremony for the Ottoman sultans.

Assuming entry from the northeast end of the square, where it opens out onto Divan Yolu/the tram line, the first point of interest is a pretty domed structure, the

1

CROWD TROUBLE IN CONSTANTINOPLE

The crowds who attended the chariot races and other events held at the Hippodrome were split into two factions, the **Blues** and the **Greens**. The former were generally upper class, politically conservative and orthodox regarding religion; while the latter were from the lower classes and more radical in their political and religious views. Rivalry between them was every bit as rabid as that between present-day UK football-team supporters, often bubbling over into hooliganism and riots.

In 532, the rivalry was forgotten when members of the Blue faction combined forces with the Greens against Emperor Justinian in protest at heavy taxation, and in the resulting **riots** – which derived their name from the battle cry *Nika* (Victory) – much of the city, including the church of Aya Sofya, was destroyed. It was the former courtesan, Empress Theodora, who eventually shamed Justinian into action and, as a result, thirty thousand Greens and a few hundred Blues were trapped and massacred by the forces of General Belisarius in the Hippodrome. Chariot racing was banned for some time after this, and it was a number of years before the Greens recovered to the extent that they could compete in either the sporting or the political arena.

Fountain of Kaiser Wilhelm II, a gift to Sultan Abdülhamid II from the German emperor, in town in 1898 to drum-up support for his grandiose Berlin–Baghdad railway scheme. The fountain is built on the line of the original gateway to the arena for chariots and spectators. Continuing southwest down the square, you'll reach the **Egyptian Obelisk**. Originally 60m tall, only the upper third survived shipment from Egypt in the fourth century. The obelisk was commissioned to commemorate the campaigns of Thutmos III in Egypt during the sixteenth century BC, but the scenes on its base commemorate its erection in Constantinople under the direction of Theodosius I. The northeast side depicts the Emperor watching from the imperial box as the obelisk is erected, on the northwest he watches vanquished foes parade past, on the southwest he is enjoying a chariot race, while on the southeast Theodosius wreathes the victors.

Continue down to the **Serpentine Column**, which comes from the Temple of Apollo at Delphi, where it was dedicated to the god by the 31 Greek cities that defeated the Persians at Plataea in 479 BC. The column was brought to Constantinople by Constantine the Great; the three intertwining bronze serpents originally had heads, which splayed out in three directions from the column itself. The jaw of one of the serpents was lopped off by Mehmet the Conqueror on his arrival in Constantinople as an act of defiance against such symbols of idolatry and the remaining heads were probably removed in an act of vandalism at the beginning of the eighteenth century – one of them is on display in the Archeology Museum (see p.56).

The third ancient monument on the *spina* is the so-called **Column of Constantine** a 32-metre-high column. In the tenth-century the Emperor Constantine Porphyrogenitus restored the pillar and sheathed it in gold-plated bronze – an ornamentation that was taken and melted down by the Crusaders during the sacking of Constantinople in 1204. These three monuments are the sole survivors of the array of obelisks, columns and statues that originally adorned the *spina*, the raised central axis of the arena, around which chariots raced.

The great curved-end of the chariot racing track, the **sphendrome**, has been subsumed by a neo-Ottoman building, but its massive retaining wall can be seen by exiting the southeast corner of the square and following Naklibent Sokak around to the right.

Sultanahmet Camii: the Blue Mosque

Sultanahmet Meydanı • Mon–Thurs, Sat & Sun 9am until one hour before dusk prayer call, Fri 9am–noon

On the southeastern side of the Hippodrome is the **Sultanahmet Camii**, or **Blue Mosque**. Its instantly recognizable six minarets, imposing bulk and prominent position on the İstanbul skyline, combine to make it one of the most famous and visited monuments in the city. Despite this, many architectural historians compare it unfavourably to the earlier works of the master architect, Mimar Sinan (see box, p.80). From the outside, the building is undeniably impressive, particularly on the all-important approach from the Topkapı Palace along Babıhümayün and Kabasakal *caddesis*. Above the level of the courtyard, the mosque is a mass of shallow domes and domed turrets, hardly broken by a single straight line.

Before construction began, in 1609, objections were raised to the plan of a six-minareted mosque. It was said to be unholy to rival the six minarets of the mosque at Mecca, and perhaps more pertinently it would be a great drain on state revenues. The true cause of the objections, however, probably had more to do with the need to destroy several palaces belonging to imperial ministers to make way for construction.

Inside the mosque, four **"elephant foot" pillars** (so called because of their size) of 5m in diameter impose their disproportionate dimensions on the interior, appearing squashed against the outer walls and obscuring parts of the building from every angle. But it's the predominantly blue colour of the internal decoration that is the biggest draw, from which the name "Blue Mosque" is derived. The **tiles** – over twenty thousand of them – constituted such a tall order that the İznik kilns were practically exhausted. Still in evidence are the clear bright colours of the best period of İznik ware, including flower and tree panels as well as more abstract designs. Exit opposite where you entered, via the northeast side door.

Outside, at the northeast corner of the complex, is the **royal pavilion**, approached by a ramp and giving access to the sultan's loge inside the mosque – the ramp meant that the sultan could ride his horse right up to the door of his chambers.

INFORMATION   SULTANAHMET CAMII

Entrance The mosque is best approached from the attractive and graceful northwest, Hippodrome-facing side, from where a graceful portal leads into the beautiful courtyard. This is surrounded by a portico of thirty small domes and has the same dimensions as the mosque itself. It's also possible to enter the courtyard from the Aya Sofya side of the mosque, through the northeast portal. Unless you are a practising Muslim, you are forbidden from entering the mosque itself via the main southwest facing door. Assuming that you are in the courtyard of the mosque, exit it via the southwest portal and bear left along the outside of the mosque to a side door, where there is often a sizeable queue. Here you must remove your shoes and put them in a plastic bag (provided).

The tomb of Sultan Ahmet I
Tues–Sat 9am–4pm • Free

Outside the precinct wall to the northwest of the mosque is the *türbe* or **tomb of Sultan Ahmet**, decorated, like the mosque, with seventeenth-century İznik tiles. Buried here along with the sultan are his wife and three of his sons, two of whom (Osman II and Murat IV) ruled in their turn. This successive rule of brothers was only possible because Sultan Ahmet had introduced the institution of the Cage (see box, p.49), thus relieving himself and his sons of the burden of fratricide upon accession to the throne. Unfortunately, Osman was completely mad and unfit to rule by the time he left the Cage to take up the reins of office. Murat IV only escaped this fate by succeeding to the throne at the age of 10, before the conditions in the Cage had affected him.

The Museum of Turkish and Islamic Art
Meydanı Sok 46 • Tues–Sun: mid-April to Sept 9am–7pm; Oct to mid-April 9am–5pm • 10TL

The **İbrahim Paşa Sarayı** (Palace of İbrahim Paşa), on the western side of the Hippodrome, is now the **Türk ve İslam Eserleri Müzesi** (Museum of Turkish and Islamic Art), an attractive, well-planned museum, containing one of the best-exhibited collections of Islamic artefacts in the world. The sixteenth-century setting of cool, darkened rooms around a central garden courtyard obviates the need for expensive technology to keep the

1

sun off the remarkable exhibits, which highlight the wealth and complexity of Islamic art and culture. The museum also boasts an excellent courtyard **café**.

The palace itself is one of the few private Ottoman residences to have survived – at least in part – the fires that periodically destroyed large areas of the city. Much of the building has, however, disappeared. What remains was rebuilt in stone – to the original plan – in 1843. Originally completed in 1524 as a wedding present for İbrahim Paşa, Süleyman the Magnificent's newly appointed grand vizier, the palace is a fitting memorial to one of the most able statesmen of his time, whose abilities were matched only by his accumulation of wealth and power. His status can be judged from the proportions of the palace's rooms and by its prominent position next to the Hippodrome: later sultans were to use its balconies to watch the festivities below. İbrahim controlled the affairs of war and state of the Ottoman Empire for thirteen years and fell from grace partly as a result of the schemings of Süleyman's wife, Roxelana. Even so, it doesn't seem unreasonable that Süleyman should distrust a servant who could say to a foreign ambassador: "If I command that something should be done, and he [the sultan] has commanded to the contrary, my wishes and not his are obeyed." The strangled body of İbrahim Paşa was found in a room of the Topkapı Palace. Süleyman the Magnificent ordered it to be buried in an unmarked grave and İbrahim Paşa's possessions, not least the palace, reverted to the Crown.

The museum exhibits

The main concentration of permanent exhibits deals with Selçuk, Mamluk and Ottoman Turkish art, though there are also several important Timurid and Persian works on display. Temporary exhibitions run in the downstairs hall. Labels are in English, but are rather brief, so be prepared to do some follow-up reading.

The **Selçuk Empire**, centred in Konya, preceded that of the Ottomans in Anatolia, and it is interesting to trace influences from one to the other. Ceramic techniques, for example, were obviously well developed by the Selçuks, judging from the wall tiles on display in the museum, and the woodcarvings from Konya also suggest a high level of craftsmanship and artistry, which may have influenced later Ottoman work.

Other impressive exhibits include sixteenth-century Persian miniatures, which like many Ottoman works defy the Islamic stricture against depicting human or animal forms. Pictures in lacquer and leather-bound Persian manuscripts feature a tiger ripping into an antelope and another of a dancing girl dated 1570. The tiny Sancak Korans were meant for hanging on the standard of the Ottoman imperial army in a jihad (holy war), so that the word of God would precede the troops into battle.

The **Great Hall** of the palace is occasionally devoted to special exhibitions about aspects of Islamic art, but more usually it houses a collection of **Turkish carpets** that is among the finest in the world. These range from tattered remains dating from the thirteenth century to carpets that once adorned İstanbul's palaces, some weighing thousands of kilograms. On the basement floor, there's an exhibition of the **folk art** of the *Yörük* tribes of Anatolia, which includes examples of a *kara çadır* (literally "black tent", a domicile woven from goat hair that can still be seen in central and eastern Anatolia) and a *topakev* (a tent constructed around a folding frame, used by nomads in Anatolia and Mongolia for over a thousand years). There is also a fascinating display of what life was like in a late-Ottoman wooden house in Bursa.

Sokollu Mehmet Paşa Camii

Mehmet Paşa Yokuşu, Kadirga • Theoretically open at prayer times only, but the caretaker is usually around to unlock it during the day

A pleasant couple of minutes' walk from the southwest corner of the Hippodrome leads down the steep Mehmet Paşa Yokuşu to **Sokollu Mehmet Paşa Camii**. This, one of Mimar Sinan's (see box, p.80) later buildings (1571), is a seldom-visited gem. Sokollu

Mehmet Paşa, who commissioned the mosque, was the last grand vizier of Süleyman the Magnificent and it was his military expertise that later saved the Ottoman Empire from the worst effects of the dissolute rule of Selim the Sot. He was eventually assassinated as a result of the intrigues of Nur Banu, the mother of Murat III, who was jealous of his power.

The large mosque **courtyard** is surrounded on three sides by the rooms of the medrese, now occupied by a boys' Koran school (the boys inhabit the dervish lodge at the back of the mosque and can be seen seated in the porch studying the Koran during term time). At the centre of the courtyard is a handsome fountain with a pretty up-curved parapet to its dome.

The **interior** of the mosque is distinguished by the height of its dome and the impressive display of İznik tiles on its east wall. These are from the best period of Turkish ceramics: the white is pure, the green vivid and the red intense. Calligraphic inscriptions are set against a jungle of enormous carnations and tulips, and the designs and colours are echoed all around the mosque and in the conical cap of the *mimber*, the tiling of which is unique in İstanbul. While the stained-glass windows are copies, some of the original, extremely delicate **paintwork** can be seen in the northwest corner below the gallery and over the entrance. Embedded in the wall over the entrance and above the *mihrab* are pieces of the Kaaba from Mecca.

Küçük Ayasofya Camii

Küçük Ayasofya Caddesi, Sultanahmet • Daily 7am–dusk • Donation

Located some 500m below the Blue Mosque is the often-overlooked but well-restored **Küçük Ayasofya Camii**, the "small mosque of Aya Sofya". Like Aya Sofya itself, it was built as a church between 527 and 536 to service the palace of Hormisdas, and is thought to precede its larger namesake. It was originally named after two Roman soldiers, **Sergius** and **Bacchus**, who were martyred for their faith and later became the patron saints of Christians in the Roman army, then was renamed because of its resemblance to Aya Sofya. The church was converted into a mosque comparatively early in the sixteenth century during the reign of Beyazit II.

Like most Byzantine churches of this era, its **exterior** is unprepossessing brick, and only inside can the satisfying proportions be properly appreciated. It is basically an octagon with semicircular niches at its diagonals, inscribed in a rectangle, but both these shapes are extremely irregular. This has been variously ascribed to a pragmatic solution to an awkward space at planning stage, or to shoddy workmanship. The original marble facing and gold leaf have vanished, but a frieze honouring Justinian, Theodora and St Sergius runs around the architrave under the gallery. Opposite the main entrance to the mosque is a medrese, the courtyard of which now serves as a shady tea garden.

The sea walls

At Küçük Ayasofya Camii, you're almost down at the Sea of Marmara and close to the best-preserved section of the **sea walls**, built in 439 by Cyrus, prefect of the East. They originally stretched from Saray Burnu to the city walls of Constantine the Great, and were later extended by Theodosius to meet his land walls, with thirteen gates piercing the eight-kilometre course. Theophilus, the last Iconoclast emperor, rebuilt the walls in the ninth century to hold off a possible Arab invasion.

Nowadays, the best way to see the walls is from the suburban train (see p.24), since the tracks run along their length and out of the city; indeed, parts were destroyed when the rail lines were built. The best-preserved remains are a stretch of a couple of kilometres between Ahır Kapı, near Cankurtaran train station, and Kumkapı, with a walkway along Kennedy Caddesi.

1

The Palace of Bucoleon and the Great Palace

About halfway between Küçük Ayasofya Camii and Cankurtaran train station, the facade of the Palace of Bucoleon, a seaside annexe to the **Great Palace of the Byzantine emperors**, is one of the most melancholy and moving survivors of Constantinople. The Great Palace was an immense complex of buildings, and included the Palace of Bucoleon and the Magnaura Palace, rather than a single structure, covering around five square kilometres from Sultanahmet to the sea walls.

Draped in beautiful red vine and set back from the road with a little park in front, it's easy to miss what's left of the **Palace of Bucoleon**, especially if you pass at speed along Kennedy Caddesi. Three enormous marble-framed windows set high in the wall offer glimpses of the remains of a vaulted room behind. Below the windows, marble corbels give evidence of a balcony that would have projected over a marble quay (the waters of the Marmara once reached almost as far as the palace walls). For the rest of the Great Palace, you'll need a lively imagination, though an impressive complex of vaulted basements can be reached via the **Başdoğan carpet centre** on Kutluğun Sokak, or the *Albura Kathisma* restaurant (see p.185) on Akbıyık Caddesi. Further down towards the coast fragments of wall and ancient palace, on streets or tucked away in backlots, are all that survive. Further sections of the palace exist under land belonging to the *Four Seasons Hotel* (see p.169). Excavated in 1998, these are said to contain a vaulted chapel with some frescoes still intact. At the time of writing this large area of land was undergoing excavation/renovation and will open as an "archeological park" when the work is complete – there is a display board about the park opposite the south corner of the Aya Sofya.

The Mosaic Museum

Torun Sokak 113 • Tues–Sun: mid-April to end Sept 9am–7pm, last entry 6pm; Oct to mid-April 9am–5pm • 8TL

The other substantial reminders of the Great Palace (see p.64) are the mosaics displayed in the **Büyüksaray Mozaik Müzesi** (Mosaic Museum), 500m inland from the Palace of Bucoleon. To reach it requires running the gauntlet of salespeople in the **Arasta Bazaar** – a renovated street-bazaar selling tourist gifts, whose seventeenth-century shops were originally built to pay for the upkeep of the nearby Blue Mosque.

Many of the mosaics in the museum are presented *in situ*, so that some idea of their original scale and purpose can be imagined. The building has been constructed so that some of the mosaics are viewed from a catwalk above, but can also be examined more closely by descending to their level. Smaller surviving sections of mosaic, each square metre of which contain some forty thousand tesserae, have been wall-mounted. All these remains were once part of a large mosaic decorating the palace's peristyle (an open courtyard surrounded by a portico). The scenes depicted by the mosaic artists, probably dating from Justinian's rebuilding programme of the sixth century, are extraordinarily vivid and give a valuable insight into everyday Byzantine life. On one, a man with a staff leads a camel surmounted by two riders; on another, a herdsman pulls an unwilling goat. In another fine scene, four boys drive hoops along with sticks – two of them have their tunics edged in blue, the other two in green, touching proof that rivalry between "the Greens" and "the Blues" in the Hippodrome did not preclude friendship. Despite the Christian nature of the Byzantine world, scenes from classical mythology also abound – check out the hero Bellerophon battling the fire-breathing monster known as the Chimera.

Divan Yolu

The main approach from Sultanahmet to Beyazit (see p.83) is **Divan Yolu**, a major thoroughfare that gained its name because it was the principal approach to the Divan from the Topkapı Gate. Hordes of people would pour along it three times a week to

1

THE "WORLD FAMOUS" PUDDING SHOP

Back in the heady days of the 1960s, when Flower Power ruled and kaftans, Afghan coats and Jesus sandals were seen as serious fashion statements, every right-thinking young person wanted to head east – to "India, maan". In those days that meant an arduous overland trip from Europe – via İstanbul. In folk memory at least, the so-called **Hippy Trail** was one long procession of VW campervans daubed with peace logos and spaced-out hitchhikers wondering whether they were in Brussels or Belgrade. **The Pudding Shop** (or, to give it its proper name, the *Lale* (*Tulip*) *Restaurant*; see p.179) became the gathering point for those travellers setting out on the most difficult leg of the trail – across Anatolian Turkey and into Iran, Afghanistan and Pakistan and on to the fabled land of India.

The **Çolpan brothers**, Idris and Namik, having established their restaurant on Sultanahmet's busy Divan Yolu in 1957, were surprised to find their eatery becoming *the* place where hippies met to swap stories and arrange onward transport. With typical İstanbullu business savvy, they put up a bulletin board where travellers could post a note offering a ride to Kathmandu, a message for a long-awaited travelling companion, or helpful advice for novice travellers. Business boomed and the sales of rice pudding (one of the desserts on offer that gave the *Lale* its "unofficial" moniker) soared.

The Hippy Trail may have gone the same way as the Afghan coat, but the Pudding Shop continues to thrive. It is still run by the Çolpan brothers and, many redecorations later, the hippies' bulletin board – the original travellers "blog" – is preserved as a reminder of a bygone era.

make their petitions to the court. In Roman and Byzantine times, this street was the Mese or "Middleway" and ran from a triumphal arch known as the **Milion**, a marked fragment of which remains at the eastern end of Divan Yolu, westwards through the city – eventually linking in with the great Roman road system to reach as far as the Adriatic. Today it remains a crucial part of the city's transport network, though it is now given over to the trams that rattle their way from Zeytinburnu, through old İstanbul and over the Golden Horn to Kabataş.

Off a narrow street running south from Divan Yolu Caddesi is the **Binbirdirek Sarnıçı** (Cistern of a Thousand and One Columns). At 64m by 56m, this is the second largest cistern in the city and is accessible via an entrance in its impressively thick retaining wall on İmran Ökten Sokak. The structure, now bone dry and half its former height due to a false floor, charges 10TL for entry when it is not being used as a function room for weddings, circumcision ceremonies and the like.

Originally, the hall was over 12m high, as can be seen from the small area of four columns excavated to the original floor. The cistern is thought to have been built under the palace of Philoxenus, one of the Roman senators who accompanied Emperor Constantine to the city. It dried up completely around the fifteenth century and was later used as a spinning mill until the early twentieth century.

SPICE BAZAAR VIEWED FROM *PANDELI'S*

Sirkeci, Eminönü and Tahtakale

Heading north, down from the tourist fleshpots of Sultanahmet towards the Golden Horn, there's a gradual change from tourism to commerce. Offices still fill the upper storeys of the fine buildings lining the bustling streets of lower Sirkeci and Eminönü, while shopkeepers selling everything from trainers to electrical appliances vie for business at street level. İstanbullus outnumber visitors and many of them depend on each other, not tourism, for their livelihoods, particularly in the bazaar quarter of Tahtakale. There are plenty of worthwhile attractions; Sirkeci station, once the eastern terminus of the *Orient Express*; the charming Ottoman-era Spice Bazaar; the Yeni Camii, a mosque as popular with hawkers and pigeons as it is with worshippers; and the Rüstem Paşa Camii, a mosque famed for its glorious İznik tiles.

GETTING THERE

By tram and train The tram from Sultanahmet stops in both Sirkeci and Eminönü before snaking its way across the Galata Bridge to Beyoğlu, while a useful suburban train line runs from Sirkeci station out along the shores of the Sea of Marmara to the city's land walls.

Sirkeci

Once-workman-like **Sirkeci** is gradually giving way to the demands of tourism; its northern fringes, abutting Sultanahmet, have been the first to succumb, with the streets either side of the tramline full of hotels, restaurants and cafés. Closer to the waterfront, however, approaching the once-opulent Sirkeci station, it remains largely a transport and commercial area. The area has, unsurprisingly, a largely transient population – its estimated permanent population of thirty thousand swells to some two million souls thronging the daytime streets and/or working in the multitude of local businesses. The city's seemingly unstoppable tourism boom will no doubt accelerate the gentrification of the area, as will the completion of the Marmaray Project (see box, p.26).

İstanbul History of Science and Technology in Islam Museum

Gülhane Parkı • Daily except Tues 9am–4.30pm • 5TL

In the old imperial stables in Gülhane Parkı, the **History of Science and Technology in Islam Museum** (İstanbul İslam Bilim ve Teknoloji Tarihi Müzesi) houses a series of replicas of inventions by Islamic scientists between the eighth and sixteenth centuries. Purists may deplore the absence of genuine artefacts but the models, produced at the Johann Wolfgang Goethe University in Frankfurt, are extremely well crafted and were based on genuine source material. They are beautifully displayed and certainly belie the West's often patronizing attitude towards science and technology in the Muslim world. Exhibits include a model of a planetarium based on the tenth-century works of the Islamic astronomer as-Siğzi, and a model based on a twelfth-century water-powered clock, shaped like an elephant.

Sirkeci station

Ankara Caddesi

World-famous **Sirkeci station** (see box, p.8), a stone's throw from the waters of the Golden Horn, is best reached by following the tramline down from Sultanahmet. Opened with great fanfare in 1888, right in the heart of imperial İstanbul, this grandiose temple to steam was once the eastern terminus for the famed *Orient Express*, the train that linked Paris and Vienna with İstanbul – and became a metaphor for style, opulence and, of course, intrigue. Designed by Prussian architect August Jachmund, the station was an Oriental fantasy, with a Parisian-style dome, minaret-like turrets and Moghul-influenced windows. The station retains a faded grandeur despite the passage of time – make sure you wander around to the building's north facade, facing the Golden Horn, as this was the original entrance – but the glamour days are long gone. Sirkeci now serves İstanbul commuters rather than the socialites and spies of its heyday, and may well be superseded altogether as plans to restructure the city's transport system (see box, p.26) appear not to include this venerable old station.

Eminönü

Eminönü fronts the ferry-choked waters of the Golden Horn, the curving inlet that cleaves the European shore. The historic Mısır Çardısı or **Spice Bazaar** is the district's major draw, though the **Yeni Camii** or "New Mosque" runs it a close second.

Given its role as one of the city's major transport hubs, it's no surprise that the area bustles with activity from dawn until the late evening. One almost obligatory rite here is to partake of a fish sandwich. They are best bought from the *Tarihi Eminönü Balık*

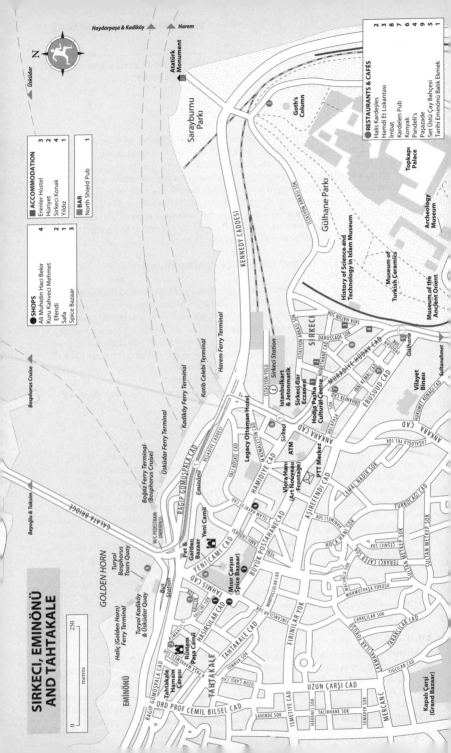

SIRKECI, EMINÖNÜ AND TAHTAKALE

0   250
metres

N

Haydarpaşa & Kadiköy   Harem

Üsküdar

GOLDEN HORN

Beyoğlu & Taksim

Bosphorus Cruise

Turyol Bosphorus Tours Quay

Haliç (Golden Horn) Ferry Terminal

Turyol Kadiköy & Üsküdar Quay

Bus Station

Boğaz Ferry Terminal

Üsküdar Ferry Terminal

Kadiköy Ferry Terminal

Katib Çelebi Terminal

Harem Ferry Terminal

Sarayburnu Parkı

Atatürk Monument

GALATA BRIDGE

RAGIP GÜMÜŞPALA CAD

KENNEDY CADDESI

İSTASYON YOLU

Sirkeci Station

Gülhane Parkı

Goth's Column

Topkapi Palace

Archeology Museum

Museum of the Ancient Orient

Museum of Turkish Ceramics

History of Science and Technology in Islam Museum

Legacy Ottoman Hotel

Istanbulkart & Jetonmatik

Sirkeci/Gar Eczanesi

Hodja Pasha Cultural Centre

Vlora Hanı (Art Nouveau Frontage)

PTT Merkez

ATM

Yeni Camii

Pet & Garden Bazaar

Mısır Çarşısı (Spice Bazaar)

Rüstem Paşa Camii

Tahtakale Hamam Çarşısı

Kapalı Çarşı (Grand Bazaar)

EMINÖNÜ

TAHTAKALE

WC PEDESTRIAN UNDERPASS

ORD PROF CEMIL BILSEL CAD

UZUN ÇARŞI CAD

TAHTAKALE CAD

HASIRCILAR CAD

YENİ CAMİ CAD

TAHMIS CAD

HAMIDIYE CAD

HALIL KÖSKÜ CAD

REŞADIYE CADDESI

BÜYÜK POSTAHANE CAD

AŞIREFENDI CAD

ANKARA CAD

EBUSUUD CAD

HÜKÜMET KONAĞI CAD

MURADIYE HÜDAV CAD

DARÜSSADE SOK

SIRKECI

STASYON ARKASI SOK

TAYA HATUN SOK

Vilayet Binası

Sultanahmet

Gülhane

SHOPS
Ali Muhidin Hacı Bekir	4
Kuru Kahveci Mehmet	2
Efendi	1
Safa	1
Spice Bazaar	3

ACCOMMODATION
Erenler Hostel	3
Hürriyet	2
Sirkeci Konak	4
Yıldız	1

BAR
North Shield Pub	1

RESTAURANTS & CAFÉS
Halis Kardeşleş	2
Hamdi Et Lokantası	3
İmbat	8
Kardelen Pub	7
Konyalı	6
Pandeli's	4
Paşazade	9
Set Üstü Çay Bahçesi	5
Tarihi Eminönü Balık Ekmek	1

Ekmek, just to the left of the Galata Bridge, where chefs in gilt-brocade faux-Ottoman waistcoats grill the fish in front of your eyes. To the north, small boats moored to the dockside bob up and down in the swell, hawkers whizz remote-controlled cars through the legs of potential punters, and *simit* (a sesame-coated bread ring) sellers are kept busy by those who don't fancy fish or the other Eminönü delicacy, a carton of pickled vegetables. If you can find a peaceful spot amongst the mayhem, the views north across the Golden Horn and the **Galata Bridge** to Galata, and west to the equally busy waters of the Bosphorus, are fabulous. Underground, the **subways** are home to hordes of shops selling fake designer clothing, cheap trainers, battery-operated dancing giraffes, and a lot more. Despite the hassle, however, they're a far better choice than trying to negotiate the road and tram track separating the quayside from the rest of the area – getting across these in one piece is not an easy task.

2

PTT Merkez
Büyük Postahane Caddesi

The **PTT Merkez** (Central Post Office) was designed by Vedat Tak and has been used as a post office since 1909. Tak, the first Turkish architect to study abroad, was a pioneer of the First National Architectural Movement, which, following the formation of the Turkish Republic in 1923, aimed to blend contemporary European architecture with traditional Turkish styles and create something fitting for the new, progressive country. The structure is certainly monumental, with a sweeping facade split by two towers that were originally planned to hold clocks – one Ottoman in style, the other European. The interior is cavernous, its rather gloomy atmosphere enlivened by neo-Ottoman floral murals, aged and nicotine-stained wooden counters and original 1920s light fittings.

Vlora Han
Corner Muhzirbadı Sokak and Büyük Postahane Caddesi

The wonderfully ornate Art Nouveau apartment building situated just across from PTT Merkez (see above) was formerly the **Vlora Han**. Stylized rosebud relief plasterwork and whiplash wrought-iron work make this one of the most obvious Art Nouveau buildings in the city – if not the most artistic (that accolade goes to the Botter House in Beyoğlu; see p.122). Unfortunately, it's looking rather neglected and the lower storeys are marred by billboards.

Legacy Ottoman Hotel (Vakıf Han)
Hamidiye Caddesi

Even more monumental than the PTT Merkez (see above), the **Legacy Ottoman Hotel** (originally the **Vakıf Han**) was built in 1912, a colossal office block that paid testament to the wealth of the area and its commercial importance in the early twentieth century. Another example of the First National Architectural Movement, its reinforced-steel frame and cut-stone facade show a European influence, the tiled panels and domes that of an Ottoman past.

The Galata Bridge

The vast majority of visitors to İstanbul cross the **Galata Bridge** at least once during their stay. It won't win any architectural prizes, but the link between the two sides of European İstanbul, separated by the waters of the Golden Horn, is undeniably a city landmark and has been immortalized in Geert Mak's wonderful book *The Bridge* (see p.310). The noise from the trams, cars, trucks and buses crossing over the bridge, the ferries docking beside and passing under it, and the gabble of the tidal wave of milling pedestrians is deafening. The views from here, however, down the Golden Horn and into the Bosphorus itself, are superb, particularly at sunset. The upper deck is always lined with anglers, their numbers swelling to ludicrous proportions on a Sunday, and you have to pick your way carefully through bait buckets and strands of tangled line, sinkers and hooks.

The current bridge, built in 1994, is its fifth incarnation – the first was constructed in 1845 during the reign of Sultan Abdülmecid. The bridge has always had a symbolic significance, linking as it did the old, imperial and Islamic part of the city with the largely Christian, "Europeanized" area of Beyoğlu – home to foreign traders, diplomats and the like. To some extent, this gulf persists, with the old city's (the area on the historic peninsula, contained by the city land walls) curious mix of foreign visitors and conservative Muslim inhabitants contrasting with the vibrant nightlife and upwardly mobile, progressive residents of Beyoğlu.

Yeni Camii
Yeni Camii Caddesi

The **Yeni Camii**, or "New Mosque", is a familiar city landmark, sited across the busy road from Eminönü's ferry terminal. An imposing building, most visitors admire it only from the outside, though the interior is open to all. The last of İstanbul's imperial mosques to be built it was, like all such mosques, part of a complex that included a hospital, *hamam*, fountains and a market.

The only imperial mosque to be built during the reign of Mehmet III, the site chosen by Safiye, the Queen Mother, was regarded as wholly inappropriate. It occupied a slum neighbourhood inhabited by a sect of Jews called the Karaites, who were relocated across the Horn to Hasköy; a synagogue and church had to be demolished to make room for it. The site was also dangerously close to the water's edge, and the building programme was constantly plagued by seepage from the Horn.

An even greater hindrance to its construction was court politics. The original architect was executed for heresy and the work was interrupted again by the death of Mehmet III and the banishment of his mother to the Old Palace. Construction had reached as far as the lower casements when it was halted, and the Karaites returned to camp out in the rubble. It was another sixty years before the Valide Sultan Turhan Hatice, mother of Sultan Mehmet IV, completed the building.

THE GOLDEN HORN

The derivation of the name **Golden Horn** is obscure (the Turkish name, *Haliç*, simply means "estuary"). One fanciful suggestion is that it was coined during the fifteenth-century siege of the city, when all the gold and precious objects the Byzantine citizens could collect were thrown into the inlet to save them being taken by the advancing Ottoman forces. Visitors in Ottoman times wrote about the area's perfumed waters, though by the 1950s the author Yaşar Kemal described it in *The Sea-Crossed Fisherman* (see p.312) as "a filthy sewer". Recent years have seen a huge improvement, though swimming is still not recommended.

Despite the pollution, the Golden Horn is one of the finest **natural harbours** in the world and its fortunes have been closely linked with those of the city. On two separate occasions, capture of the Horn proved to be the turning point of crucial military campaigns. In 1203–04, Crusaders took the Horn and proceeded to besiege Constantinople for ten months, until they breached the walls separating the inlet from the city. The second occasion was a spectacular *tour de force* by Mehmet the Conqueror, who was prevented from entering the Horn by a chain (links of which can be seen in both the Archeology Museum and the Military Museum) fastened across it and so carried his ships overland at night and launched them into the inlet from its northern shore. Mehmet then constructed a pontoon across the top of the Horn, over which he transported his army and cannon in preparation for the siege of the land walls, which were finally breached in 1453.

For the Ottoman Empire, the Horn was a vital harbour, supplying the Genoese, Venetian and Jewish trading colonies on its northern shore. It was also a site for **ship construction**, though most shipbuilding yards have moved east of İstanbul to Tuzla.

The mosque was designed by a pupil of Sinan (see box, p.80) and is generally considered to lack the grace of the great master's works. It is, nonetheless, an attractive mosque, built on a cruciform plan, with a large central dome surmounting four semi-domes. Entry is from a fine courtyard surrounded by porticoes, with an attractive octagonal *şadırvan* in the centre. As in most Ottoman mosques, the portico, running at right angles across the entry wall, has a raised platform used as an overspill prayer area when the mosque is full, or by late arrivals. Two attractive *mihrab*s puncture the wall either side of the main portal, embellished, like the doorway itself, with a finely carved stalactite design. The wooden doors are inlaid with mother-of-pearl, and the main *mihrab*, again with a stalactite design, is heavily gilded.

Mısır Çarşısı: the Spice Bazaar
Daily 9am–7pm

The most atmospheric part of the Yeni Camii complex is the **Mısır Çarşısı**, the "Egyptian Bazaar", which is better known as the **Spice Bazaar**. The origins of the name are uncertain. In the Byzantine era, the site of the bazaar was the corn-trading centre, and "Mısır" means both "corn" and "Egypt" in Turkish. On the other hand, the name may derive from the fact that many of the Ottoman Empire's spices were imported from Egypt and were flogged in the "new" spice bazaar, or from the fact that it was endowed with customs duties from Cairo. Completed a few years before the Yeni Camii, this L-shaped bazaar has 88 vaulted rooms and chambers above the entryways at the ends of the halls. One of these, over the main entrance opposite the ferry ports, now houses the Greek restaurant, *Pandeli's* (see p.186).

Despite its name, the range and quality of spices in the bazaar is not what it was and prices aren't cheap – the shops in the surrounding maze of alleys, whether they are selling pistachios fresh in from the southeast of the country to dried mulberries or figs from the Aegean, are much better value than what's on offer inside. Of more interest in the bazaar itself are the varieties of *lokum* (Turkish delight) and the many bizarre concoctions being passed off as aphrodisiacs.

Outside and to the right as you approach from the Yeni Camii is **Tahmis Caddesi**, lined by hole-in-the-wall shops stocking a wonderful array of cheeses, olives, dried fruit, spices, dried meats and all manner of delectable foodstuffs at bargain prices. Leading off east from this strip of shops is **Hasırcılar Caddesi** (Street of the Strawmakers) where there are yet more speciality shops, including, on the corner, *Kurukahveci Mehemet Efendi* (see p.217), a coffee emporium in a fine Art Deco building, with perpetual queues outside.

Another interesting place to explore is the **garden/pet bazaar** on the east side of the Spice Bazaar. It's not a place for the sentimental: chicks and ducklings cluck frantically in open-topped cardboard boxes, while goldfinches flit from side to side of their tiny bamboo cages. There's even a leech doctor, the tools of his trade wriggling uninvitingly in an enormous glass jar. More prosaic, though, are the bags of seeds and decorative bamboo plants on sale here.

Tahtakale

Tahtakale ("Wooden Castle"), the incredibly busy traditional bazaar quarter west of Sirkeci and northwest of Eminönü, is lifted from mundanity by the presence of one of the city's best small mosques, the **Rüstem Paşa Camii**. Mosque aside, there's little to do except wander the cobbled streets, watching the few surviving *hamals* (stevedores) bent double under their loads, or wonder at just who is going to buy the mountains of brushes, pans, coat hangers and other cheap plastic household paraphernalia on sale here. There are a few locally made items, such as hand-carved wooden spoons, on display, but the vast majority of stuff is imported from the Far East. One building of note is the **Tahtakale Hamam Çardısı** dating back to the early years of the Ottoman conquest of the city in the fifteenth century. Built as a *hamam*, it continues to serve the local community – but as yet another shopping centre rather than a bath-house.

Rüstem Paşa Camii
Hasırcılar Çarşısı

Rüstem Paşa Camii, opposite the Tahtakale Hamam Çarşısı, is one of the most attractive of İstanbul's smaller mosques and very welcoming to visitors. Built for Süleyman the Magnificent's grand vizier, Rüstem Paşa (who was responsible, along with Roxelana, for the murder of the heir apparent Mustafa), the mosque dates from the year he died, 1561, and was probably built in his memory by his widow Mihrimah, Roxelana's daughter.

Designed by Sinan (see box, p.80) on an awkward site, the mosque is easy to miss as you wander the streets below. At ground level on the Golden Horn side, an arcade of shops occupies the vaults, also home to the cheap and traditional workers' café, the *Halis Kardeşler* (see p.179). Pass east through a small courtyard below the level of the mosque and turn left to reach the steps leading up to the mosque's terrace. Through an attractive entrance portal is a wide courtyard and a tiled double-portico along the west wall. It's almost like entering a theatre, with the tiles of the portico as backdrop and the mosque interior, whose dimensions are not immediately apparent, backstage. The visitors entrance is on the left as you look at the mosque, just beyond a small stall selling guide books, along with İznik-tile fridge magnets and the like.

The **tiles**, inside and out, are among the best in any mosque in Turkey. They date from the finest period of İznik tile production, when techniques for producing tomato-red – slightly raised above the other colours – had been perfected. Designs covering the walls, piers and pillars, and decorating the *mihrab* and *mimber*, include famous panels of tulips and carnations and geometric patterns. Inside are galleries supported by pillars and marble columns and about as many windows as the structure of the mosque will allow.

The Grand Bazaar and around

The city's Kapılı Çarşı, known to most foreigners as the Grand Bazaar, was the prototype of today's shopping malls, and is the best-known and largest historic covered bazaar in the world. Understandably, most visitors to İstanbul opt to spend some time wandering its myriad alleyways and soaking up the atmosphere. The other major attraction in this sprawling district is İstanbul's finest mosque complex, the Süleymaniye, majestically situated atop the old city's third hill. Viewed from afar, it is one of the most distinctive silhouettes on the İstanbul skyline; up close, it still exudes an air of sanctity and learning. The areas around the Grand Bazaar and the Süleymaniye are well worth exploring, although few visitors venture beyond the key sights.

East of the bazaar, on either side of Divan Yolu, historically the main artery through the Byzantine and then Ottoman city, are the **Çemberlitaş**, the famed Column of Constantine, and the **Çemberlitaş Hamamı**, one of the city's most popular and atmospheric Turkish baths. To the north, below the Süleymaniye, is a wonderfully well-preserved stretch of the fourth-century **Aqueduct of Valens**, spanning one of the old city's busiest thoroughfares, Atatürk Bulvarı.

Just west of the bazaar, the **Beyazit Meydanı**, a busy square dominated by the Beyazit Camii, one of the city's earliest imperial mosques, attracts itinerant vendors and students streaming in and out of the main gates of İstanbul University. Further west are **Laleli** and **Aksaray**, adjacent districts that have acquired a certain notoriety in recent years but have an atmosphere all of their own and contain some worthwhile Byzantine and Ottoman monuments – as well as some interesting places to eat. Running steeply down to the Sea of Marmara south of the bazaar, the narrow streets of **Gedikpaşa** and **Kumkapı** are scattered with churches of various denominations and a notable Ottoman *hamam*.

GETTING THERE

It's easy enough to walk to all the areas covered in this chapter from the old city, but if you want to save your legs you can take the T1 tram from Sultanahmet and get off at either Çemberlitaş or Beyazit (for the Grand Bazaar or Süleymaniye complex), or Laleli (for the Şehzade and Laleli mosques). For Kumkapı, either walk down from the Grand Bazaar area or take the suburban *banliyo* **train** from Cankurtaran.

Kapalı Çarşı: the Grand Bazaar
Mon–Sat 9am–7pm

With 66 streets and alleys, over four thousand shops, numerous storehouses, moneychangers and banks, a mosque, post office, police station, private security guards and its own health centre, İstanbul's **Grand Bazaar**, or **Kapalı Çarşı** (Covered Bazaar), is said to be the largest enclosed bazaar in the world. Complementing the retail outlets, around the bazaar humming workshops produce some of the goods sold there.

The bazaar was built on the site of an earlier Byzantine trading area soon after the Ottoman conquest of the city in 1453. Originally, a particular type of shop was found in a certain area, with street names reflecting the nature of the businesses. Many of these distinctions are now blurred as the trade in certain goods has moved on, while that of others has expanded to meet new demands. In Ottoman times, bazaars throughout the empire consisted of both a covered and an open area centred on a *bedesten*, a domed building where foreign trade took place and valuable goods were stored. In İstanbul, the commercial centre was based around two *bedestens*, both inside the covered bazaar: the **İç Bedesten** (Old Bazaar) probably dates from the time of the Conquest, while the **Sandal Bedesteni** was added in the sixteenth century to cope with the quantity of trade in fine fabrics that the capital attracted. The bazaar actually extends well beyond the limits of the covered bazaar and the whole area was once controlled by strict laws laid down by the trade guilds. These rules reduced unhealthy competition between traders and similar unwritten laws control market forces among traders in the Grand Bazaar even today.

Whether you actually enjoy wandering around here is very much a matter of temperament and mood; you'll either find the hassle from traders intolerable – though the many **cafés** in the bazaar (see p.180) do offer a welcome respite – or you'll be flattered to be paid more attention in one afternoon than you've received in your entire life. Receiving the sales patter from a persuasive trader or three is part of the Grand Bazaar experience but remember one golden rule – once you have agreed a price for an item you are morally obliged to purchase it. The Society of Kapalı Çarşı Traders polices the area, issuing warnings to those deemed too intimidating, so if you find yourself uncomfortably targeted look around for one of the maroon-uniformed security guards.

THE GRAND BAZAAR & AROUND

0   100
metres

Aquaduct of Valens

Museum of Caricatures

Column of Marcian

Arkeoloji Parkı

Saraçhane Parkı

Şehzade Camii

Historia Mall

İstanbul Municipal Building

Kalenderhane Cami

AKSARAY

Aksaray (M)

Topkapı

LALELI

İstanbul Üniversitesi (Faculty of Science & Literatu

Valide Camii

Laleli Camii

Yusufpaşa

Aksaray

Laleli/Üniversite

Zeytinburnu

Mesipaşa Camii

Yenikapı Station

Havaş Airport Bus Stop

Yenikapı Waterfront Parkı

Yenikapı Ferry Terminal

● RESTAURANTS	
Ağa Kapısı	1
Akdeniz Hatay Sofrası	6, 11
Antakya Café Restaurant	10
Daruzzafiye	2
Erenler Çay Bahçesi	9
Fes Café	8
Kalamar	13
Kör Agop	12
Şeref Buryan	3
Tarihi Kuru Fasuliye Süleymaniye Erzincanlı Ali Baba	4
Van Kahvaltı Sofrası	7
Vefa Bozacısı	5

■ BAR	
Murat Bira Evi	2

■ CABARET	
Orient House	1

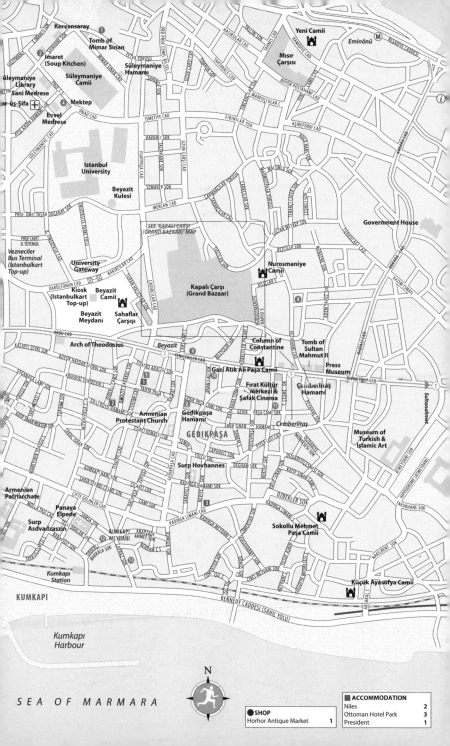

EXPLORING THE BAZAAR

The **best time to visit** is during the week, as Saturday sees the bazaar and its surroundings crowded with local shoppers. Expect to get lost, as although all streets are marked their signs are often hidden beneath goods hung up on display. However, try finding Kavaflar Sokak for shoes, Terlikçiler Sokak for slippers, Kalpakçılar Başı and Kuyumcular *caddesi* for gold, and Tavuk Pazarı Sokak, Kürkçüler Sokak, Perdahçılar Caddesi and Bodrum Hanı for leather clothing. Carpet-sellers are just about everywhere, with more expensive collector's pieces on sale on Halıcılar Çarşısı, Takkeciler and Keseciler *caddesi*, and cheaper ones in the İç Cebeci Hanı. Ceramics and leather and kilim bags can be found along Yaulıkçılar Caddesi, just off it in Çukur Han, and also along Keseciler Caddesi.

The **İç Bedesten**, located at the centre of the maze, was traditionally reserved for the most precious wares because it could be locked at night. You'll still find some silver and gold on sale, but these days it contains an eclectic mix of goods along with the jewellery. For a more authentic experience, check out **Kalcılar Han** where you will see silver being cast and worked with skills that have been handed down over the generations.

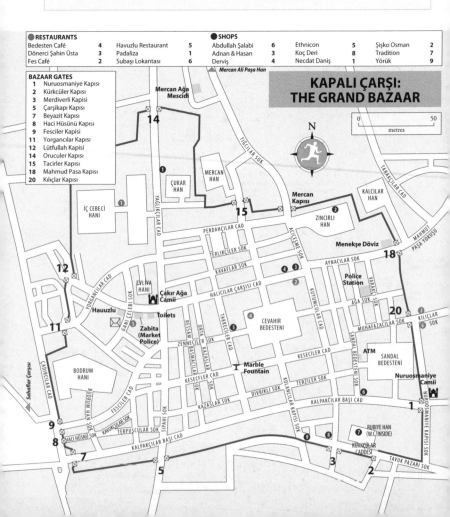

● RESTAURANTS				● SHOPS					
Bedesten Café	4	Havuzlu Restaurant	5	Abdullah Şalabi	6	Ethnicon	5	Şişko Osman	2
Dönerci Şahin Üsta	3	Padaliza	1	Adnan & Hasan	3	Koç Deri	8	Tradition	7
Fes Café	2	Subaşı Lokantası	6	Derviş	4	Necdat Daniş	1	Yörük	9

BAZAAR GATES
1 Nuruosmaniye Kapısı
2 Kürkçüler Kapısı
3 Merdiverli Kapısı
5 Çarşıkapı Kapısı
7 Beyazit Kapısı
8 Hacı Hüsünü Kapısı
9 Fesciler Kapısı
11 Yorgancılar Kapısı
12 Lütfullah Kapısı
14 Oruculer Kapısı
15 Tacirler Kapısı
18 Mahmud Paşa Kapısı
20 Kılıçlar Kapısı

KAPALI ÇARŞI: THE GRAND BAZAAR

Çemberlitaş (Column of Constantine)

A short way southeast of the Grand Bazaar, where Vezirhanı Caddesi intersects with Divan Yolu, is the **Çemberlitaş** ("the hooped stone"), a burnt column of masonry, also known as the **Column of Constantine**. It was erected by Constantine the Great in 330 AD, to commemorate the city's dedication as capital of the Roman Empire. For the next sixteen centuries, the city was known as Constantinople. The column consists of seven drums of porphyry and used to be surmounted by a statue of the emperor. The iron hoops from which it derives its Turkish name were bound around the joints in the porphyry after an earthquake in 416 damaged the column. The current scorched condition dates from the great fire of 1779, which destroyed much of the surrounding area. Opposite it to the east is the tourist-friendly Ottoman-era Çemberlitaş Hamamı (see p.227).

Tomb of Sultan Mahmut II

82 Divan Yolu, Sultanahmet • Daily 9am–5pm • Free

Just east of the Çemberlitaş tram stop lies a walled **cemetery**, dominated by the 1838 **Tomb of Sultan Mahmut II**, a large, ornate *türbe* containing the coffins of Mahmut and his son (Sultan Abdül Aziz) and grandson (Sultan Abdül Hamit), as well as some of his female relatives. The well-tended cemetery contains dozens of graves of lesser statesmen, and includes that of **Ziya Gökalp**, the architect of Turkish nationalism, who died in 1924.

3

Press Museum

Divan Yolu 84 • Mon–Sat 10am–6pm • Free

The rather run-down **Press Museum** (Basın Müzesi) offers a fascinating insight into the world of the Turkish press, dating back to the sixteenth century. Exhibits include copies of newspapers from the early Republican era, including one from 1928 in both Arabic and Roman scripts (Arabic was banned in 1928 as part of Atatürk's modernization programme), which features a cartoon where anthropomorphized Arabic letters are being chained up and led away into oblivion. Upstairs is a room devoted to the (depressingly numerous) number of Turkish journalists slain in the course of their work – the most recent addition being that of the İstanbul Armenian Hrant Dink, assassinated by an ultranationalist youth in January 2007.

Nuruosmaniye Camii

Vezirhanı Caddesi, Beyazit

From Divan Yolu, a north turn up Vezirhanı Caddesi leads to the **Nuruosmaniye Camii**, or Mosque of Sacred Light, opposite one of the main entries into the Grand Bazaar, the Çarşı Kapı. Begun by Mahmut I in 1748 and finished seven years later by Osman III, this mosque was the first and most impressive of the city's European-influenced, Baroque-style mosques, and set the fashion in Baroque and Rococo architecture for the following century. The square main prayer hall, dominated by a semicircular apse-like projection containing the mihrab, is surmounted by a lofty dome. The courtyard is of most architectural interest, however, as instead of the usual square or rectangle it is almost horseshoe-shaped. Neglected by most visitors, it is both attractive and, due to its proximity to the Grand Bazaar, always busy with worshippers.

Gazi Atık Ali Paşa Camii

Yeniçeriler Caddesi, the western extension of Divan Yolu

The **Gazi Atık Ali Paşa Camii** is one of the oldest mosques in the city. It was built in 1496 by Atık Ali Paşa, a eunuch who rose to the rank of grand vizier under Sultan Beyazit II. He was eventually deposed, but rose once again to high office before being killed in battle in 1511. The main dome over the prayer hall is a little over twelve metres in diameter, though the sense of space inside is heightened by the addition of a half-dome over the *mihrab* and smaller twin domes to either side. This design – essentially a rectangular room divided unequally by a huge arch – predates that of the city's larger, more famous mosques.

The Süleymaniye Külliyesi

Northwest of the Grand Bazaar, on the third hill of the old city, is the **Sülemaniye Külliyesi**, a complex of buildings including theological schools, a hospital, library, soup kitchen, caravanserai, shops and tombs. These buildings are clustered around the centrepiece of the entire complex, a magnificent mosque, the Süleymaniye Camii. Built by the renowned architect **Mimar Sinan** (see box, p.80) in honour of his most illustrious patron, Süleyman the Magnificent, the complex is arguably his greatest achievement. The complex stands on the grounds of the first palace built in the city by the conquering Ottomans. When, in 1465, the imperial entourage moved to the new palace at Topkapı, the grounds of the old one were given over to the construction of the new complex, in what must have been a superb location overlooking the Golden Horn and its waterside parks and gardens. Begun in 1550, the whole complex took just seven years to complete, with Sinan and his family living on site during the entire process.

Many visitors first view the Süleymaniye from the Eminönü waterfront area, from where its slender minarets and curvaceous dome are seen to their best advantage. It is generally approached, however, from the southwest, via the aptly named Süleymaniye Caddesi, which joins the pedestrian-street of Sıddık Samı Onal Caddesi right in front of the mosque. Formerly known as **Tıryakı Çarşısı**, "market of the addicts", the name derives from the fact that the coffeehouses in this street, whose rents augmented the upkeep of the foundation, also served opium. Today the same street is lined with

---

MIMAR SINAN: MASTER BUILDER

Many of the finest works of Ottoman civil and religious architecture are the product of a genius who had the good luck to come of age in a rich, expanding empire willing to put its considerable resources at his disposal. **Mimar Sinan** (1489–1588) served as court architect to three sultans – Süleyman the Magnificent, Selim II and Murat III – but principally to the first, who owed much of his reputation for "magnificence" to this gifted technician.

Sinan was born in a small village near Kayseri, the son of Christian parents. Conscripted into the janissaries in 1513, he served in all the major Ottoman campaigns of the early sixteenth century. Thus compelled to travel the length and breadth of southeastern Europe and the Middle East, Sinan become familiar with the best Islamic and Christian architecture and was immediately able to apply what he had learned in the role of military engineer, building bridges, siegeworks, harbours and even ships. This earned him the admiration of his superiors, including Sultan Süleyman, who in recognition of his abilities appointed him court architect in April 1536.

Sinan completed his first major religious commission, İstanbul's **Şehzade Camii** (see p.82) in 1548, and shortly thereafter embarked on a rapid succession of ambitious projects in and around the capital, including the **Süleymaniye Camii** (see p.81) and the waterworks leading from the Belgrade Forest. Sinan then turned his matured attention to the provinces, gracing Edirne with the **Selimiye Camii** between 1569 and 1575 (see p.270), and a decade later fulfilling a long-standing wish as a devout Muslim by overseeing the restoration of the **Harem-i-Zerif mosque** in Mecca.

Unusually for his time, Sinan could make an objective assessment of his talents: he regarded most of his pre-1550 works as apprentice pieces, and posterity has generally agreed with the self-evaluations in his memoirs, the *Tezkeret-ül-Bünyan*. Despite temptations to luxury, he lived and died equally modestly, being buried in a simple tomb he made for himself in his garden in the grounds of the Süleymaniye Camii – the last of more than five hundred constructions by Sinan, large and small, throughout the empire.

pleasant pavement-cafés selling traditional Turkish meals at reasonable prices, including the tasty beans at the *Erzincanlı Ali Baba* (see p.181) café.

Süleymaniye Camii

The **Süleymaniye Camii** reopened after several years of restoration work in November 2010, though at the time of writing the attractive *avlu* (courtyard) on the northwest of the mosque was still under renovation. Visitors enter through the southwest portal, where plastic bags are provided for footwear, just across from the cafés on the former Tıryakı Çarşısı. Once inside, the overwhelming impression is one of light and uncluttered space, with a central dome 53m high (twice its diameter), surmounting a perfect square of 26.5m. The sense of space is further emphasized by the addition of supporting semi-domes to the northwest and southeast of the dome, while the monumental arched spaces to the southwest and northeast are filled with great tympana walls, pierced by a series of windows through which the light pours. The four great rectangular piers supporting the dome have been cleverly masked on two sides by linking them in with the arched colonnade walls.

A rope prevents non-worshipping visitors from entering the main part of the prayer-hall, but it's easy enough to admire the restrained arabesques and Koranic calligraphy adorning the interior, along with the simple Proconnesian marble *mihrab*. The tiles here, used sparingly for effect, are top-notch İznik-ware, fired with flower motifs in blue, red and turquoise on a white ground. The interior always feels cool, partly because a clever air-flow system was incorporated into the original design to direct soot from the candles and oil lamps to a single point – where it was collected and used for ink.

Tombs of Süleyman and Roxelana
Daily 5.30am–8pm • Free

In the **cemetery** outside the southeast prayer-wall of the mosque are the tombs of Süleyman the Magnificent and Haseki Hürrem, better known to the West as Roxelana, his powerful wife. Süleyman's tomb is particularly impressive: its doors are inlaid with ebony, ivory, silver and jade, and his turban is huge. Above, the spectacular inner dome has been faithfully restored in red, black and gold, inlaid with glittering ceramic stars. Both here, and in the neighbouring tomb of Roxelana, original tiles and some fine stained glass have survived the centuries.

Süleymaniye Library
Süleymaniye Külliyesi • Mon–Sat 8.30am–5pm

Behind the line of cafés on Sıddık Samı Onal Caddesi lies the **Süleymaniye Library**, housed in the Evvel and Sani medreses (theological schools). These buildings, mirror images of each other, are situated around shady garden courtyards. Süleyman established the library in an effort to bring together collections of books scattered throughout the city: there are some eighty thousand manuscripts stored here, gathered from eleven palaces and dating from the reigns of six different sultans. In theory, the library is open to the public, though they don't seem too keen on visitors and you'll need to leave your passport at the gate and wear an identifier tag around your neck. However, unless you're a specialist, there's little to be seen inside.

Ancillary buildings

A *mektep* (primary school) stands on the corner of Sıddık Samı Onal Caddesi and Süleymaniye Caddesi, and there are Koran schools and a language school, which taught the proper pronunciation of Arabic for reading the Koran. At the southwest corner of Sıddık Samı Onal Caddesi is the domed building of the *dar-üş-şifa* or hospital, today a maternity unit. Around the corner, opposite the entrance to the courtyard of the Süleymaniye mosque is the *imaret* (soup kitchen), which, despite its ornate design, was constructed as a public kitchen supplying food for the local poor. Fittingly, it now houses a well-regarded restaurant, the *Darüzziyafe* (see p.188). Just beyond it and currently closed to the public is a *kervansaray* which, in the Ottoman era, provided accommodation for travellers.

Tomb of Mimar Sinan

Mimar Sinan Caddesi

The **Tomb of Mimar Sinan**, at the northwest corner of the complex, just beyond the *kervansaray*, is in a triangular garden, which was the location of the architect's house during construction work. At the corner of the triangle is an octagonal eaved fountain. Perhaps there is no nicer way of being remembered than by providing the gift of water to passing strangers, but in Sinan's case it nearly caused his downfall. The fountain, as well as Sinan's house and garden, were liberally supplied with water, but when the mosques further down the pipeline began to run short, Sinan was charged with diverting the water supply for his household needs. The tomb itself has a magnificent carved turban, a measure of the architect's high rank – the eulogy written on the south wall of the garden picks out the bridge at Büyükçekmece as Sinan's greatest achievement.

The road heading down the hill to the left of the tomb leads to the Eminönü waterfront/Galata Bridge and it makes for a fascinating twenty-minute stroll through a colourful bazaar neighbourhood. If you don't fancy the walk, pop into the *Ağa Kapısı* café (see p.180) for stunning views over the Golden Horn and the Bosphorus. Alternatively, walk along the street to the right of Sinan's tomb, past rows of shops that are still a part of the mosque complex and sell paraphernalia for prospective pilgrims to Mecca, to the wonderful **Süleymaniye Hammamı** (see p.228).

The Aqueduct of Valens

The magnificent **Aqueduct of Valens** was originally built during the late fourth-century waterworks programme carried out by Emperor Valens, part of a distribution network that included reservoirs in the Belgrade Forest and various cisterns located around the city centre. It was in use right up to the end of the nineteenth century, having been kept in good repair by successive rulers, who maintained a constant supply of water to the city in the face of both drought and siege. More than six hundred of its original thousand metres are still standing, though the best single viewpoint is where the aqueduct crosses Atatürk Bulvarı – here it is two storeys high, reaching a height of 18.5m.

Column of Marcian

The little-visited Column of Marcian (450–457 AD) stands a couple of hundred metres southwest of the Aqueduct of Valens, at the crossroads of Kıztaşı Caddesi and Dolap Sokak. Known to Turks as Kız Taşı (The Girl's Stone), it is one of only four surviving columns erected to honour Byzantine emperors in the city (the Column of Constantine is another; see p.79). Although the statue of the emperor has gone, the granite column still sports a Corinthian capital and an eagle-carved plinth, while at the base is an inscription and a relief-carved goddess of victory. It's now a traffic island at a quiet crossroads, but in many ways is more impressive than Constantine's column in Beyazit.

Şehzade Camii

Şehzadebaşı Caddesi

Constructed in 1548, the **Şehzade Camii** stands in a pleasant park area southeast of the Aqueduct of Valens (see above). This "Mosque of the Prince" is so called because Süleyman the Magnificent had it built (by the ubiquitous Sinan; see box, p.80) in honour of his son Mehmet, who died of the plague aged 21. It is neither as large nor as dramatically situated as the Süleymaniye Camii, and in terms of architectural innovation falls short of the master's greatest works. Unlike the Süleymaniye, here Sinan used four semi-domes to support the central dome; the massive piers needed to support this spoil the aesthetics of what is a rather plain interior. Outside, however, the architect let his imagination run free, especially on the twin minarets, which are ribbed and decorated with vertical bands of low-relief-carved geometric patterns.

The Kalenderhane Camii

16 Mart Şehitleri Caddesi

The Byzantine Church of Kyriotissa was probably built around the start of the thirteenth century, on the foundations of an earlier church. It was renamed **Kalenderhane Camii** after the Kalender dervishes who converted it into a *tekke* (Dervish monastery) after the Conquest. It has the cruciform ground plan typical of Byzantine churches of its time, with much of the marble revetment and sculpture still in place. In front of the mosque, excavations going down 38m, for a station on the metro line that will link Beyoğlu with Yenikapı on the Sea of Marmara, have revealed the remains of a Roman building, part of a Byzantine palace and an Ottoman *hamam*.

The area just north of the Kalenderhane, where one of the final arches of the aqueduct spans 16 Mart Şehitleri Cad, is now a bohemian student quarter, with a few cheap cafés. For a more traditional feel, follow the line of the aqueduct back west for a couple of hundred metres, to *Vefa Bozacısı* (see p.181). Established in 1876 and little changed since, this is the oldest surviving purveyor in the city of *boza*, a fermented millet drink once drunk throughout the Ottoman world. Atatürk (see p.294) himself frequented the place, and the glass he drank from is proudly on display.

Beyazit Meydanı

Just to the west of the Grand Bazaar, **Beyazit Meydanı**, the main square of bustling Beyazit, is the principal approach to İstanbul University. Just off the east of the square is the famous **Sahaflar Çarşısı**, the secondhand-booksellers' market (although most of the books on sale nowadays are new). The Ottoman book market dates back to the eighteenth century, but long before that there was a Byzantine book and paper market on the site. After the Conquest, it lost its original identity to the spoonmakers, though booksellers gradually moved back in once printing and publishing were legalized in the second half of the eighteenth century.

Heading west from Beyazit, on the south side of the tram line opposite the southwest corner of the meydanı are a jumble of fallen marble columns decorated with curious tear-drop patterns. These formed part of the famed triumphal **Arch of Theodosius** which once marked the entrance to the Forum of Theodosius. Rebuilt on the site of the Forum Tauri in 393 by Emperor Theodosius I and thus named after him, it was the largest public space in Constantinople.

Beyazit Camii

Beyazit Meydanı

Beyazit Camii, to the east of Beyazit Meydanı, was completed in 1506 and is the oldest surviving imperial mosque in the city. It has a sombre courtyard full of richly coloured marble, including twenty columns of verd antique, red granite and porphyry. Inside, the building is a perfect square of exactly the same proportions as the courtyard (although the aisles make it feel elongated). The sixteenth-century fittings, including the carvings of the balustrade, *mihrab* and *mimber*, are all highly crafted. There are plastic bags provided to carry your footwear around, and scarves for females to cover their heads.

İstanbul University

Enter through the ornate gateway on the north side of Beyazıt Meydanı · Daily 9am–3pm

İstanbul University commands an impressive position at the crown of one of the city's seven hills; indeed, the fire tower located in the grounds, **Beyazit Kulesi**, is a landmark all over the city. It was under restoration at the time of writing, but should be open to visitors on completion.

The university occupies the site of the Old Palace of Mehmet the Conqueror, the imperial residence from 1453 until it burned to the ground in 1541, after which it was rebuilt to serve as a residence for concubines who had been retired after the accession of a new sultan. What's now the main university building was constructed by the French architect Bourgeois, in 1866, to house the Ministry of War. This moved to Ankara in 1923, along with the other departments of state, when the university (which until then had been scattered around the city in various medreses of the imperial mosques) was relocated here.

3

Laleli and Aksaray

The noisy, ugly spaghetti junction where Atatürk Bulvarı crosses Ordu Caddesi is the main focus of the districts of **Aksaray** and **Laleli**, whose atmosphere is distinctly different from anywhere else in İstanbul. It is not immediately appealing but there are a number of worthwhile sights here that lie well off most visitors' radars.

Many of the people here are from Russia, Eastern Europe and the Turkic states of Central Asia. In the early years following the collapse of the Soviet Union, Aksaray and Laleli were the centre of the so-called "suitcase trade", as poor traders arrived with cases loaded with odds and sods to sell, bought up local goods and sold them back in their home country. It's not exactly a rich area today, but most people coming from the former Soviet states now are here to spend, spend, spend, and the shops are full of some of the most outrageously nouveau riche and designer (both fake and genuine) fashion items you're likely to see anywhere.

Turkish women avoid Aksaray and Laleli, as it still has a reputation (justly so) for prostitution, though this is now confined to the quarter southwest of the Atatürk Bulvarı/Ordu Caddesi crossroads, where shady clubs and importuners abound.

Laleli Camii

Ordu Caddesi

Built in the Ottoman Baroque tradition of Nuruosmaniye Camii (see p.79) and the Ayazma Camii in Üsküdar (see p.143), the attractive **Laleli Camii** is perched above busy Ordu Caddesi, a minute's walk from the Laleli/Üniversite T1 tram stop. This mosque nonetheless owes more to traditional Ottoman architecture than ideas imported from Europe. It was founded by Mustafa III, whose octagonal tomb is located at the southeast gate. Selim III, who was assassinated by his janissaries, is also buried there.

The main Baroque elements in the mosque complex are the use of ramps (including one that the reigning sultan would have used to ride up to his loge), the grand staircases and the exquisite detail, noticeable in the window grilles of the tomb and in the carved eaves of the *sebil* (drinking fountain). Inside, a mass of pillars dominates, especially to the west, where the columns beneath the main dome seem to crowd those supporting the galleries into the walls. Back outside, the foundations of the mosque are used as a covered **market**, selling the cheapest of clothes and acting as an inducement for the local populace to worship at the mosque.

İstanbul University Faculty of Science and Literature

Ordu Caddesi

The imposing building housing the **İstanbul University Faculty of Science and Literature** was completed in 1944, and was designed according to the precepts of the Second

National Architectural Movement, a nationalist style of architecture that took its inspiration from Fascist movements in Italy and Germany. Designed by two of the pioneering Turkish architects of the day, Sedad Hakki Eldem and Emin Haid Onat, it is essentially a modernist building that incorporates a few elements of traditional Turkish architecture. With its monumental but plain, almost brutal, facade it couldn't be more of a contrast to ornate Laleli Camii, just down the road (see opposite).

İstanbul Municipality Building
Şehzadebaşı Caddesi

The colossal **İstanbul Municipality Building**, designed by Nevzat Oral in 1953, was the first truly international-modern building in the city. It's well worth seeking out (you can hardly miss it even if you wanted to). A rectangular structure with a grid facade, mounted on a columnar base, it has a definite presence, though plans are afoot to sell off the building and turn it into a hotel.

Mesipaşa Camii
Mesipaşa Caddesi

3

The beautiful **Mesipaşa Camii**, situated more or less opposite the Laleli Camii, was once the monastery Church of Myrelaion, dating back to 922 AD, and was converted into a mosque in 1501. Although the northwest wall is marred by a modern pine porch, the remainder of the outside has been lovingly restored. Of typical "cross in square" plan, topped by a rotunda with a very shallow dome, it is all curves and grace, and the slim red bricks used in its construction are in better condition than most Byzantine churches of this type in the city.

Gedikpaşa and Kumkapı

The areas directly south of the Grand Bazaar, **Gedikpaşa** and **Kumkapı**, centred around three major streets – Gedikpaşa, Tiyatro and Mithatpaşa *caddesis* – that run at steep angles down to the Sea of Marmara, lack any sight of real note but are great places in which to wander. In addition to a scattering of small mosques, there are a number of nineteenth-century Armenian Apostolic (orthodox) and Greek Orthodox **churches**, attesting to the districts' cosmopolitan past. A handful of Greeks still live around here, rather more Armenians, and you're almost as likely to hear Kurdish spoken as Turkish, as more recent times have seen a wave of migrant workers from the impoverished southeast of Turkey arrive to set up homes and businesses in these narrow streets.

Armenian Protestant Church
Gedikpaşa Caddesi

The handsome rendered-stone **Armenian Protestant Church** dates back to 1914, when it was rebuilt on the site of an earlier wooden church (1850) that suffered the same fate as so many wood structures in the old city – destroyed by fire. The church serves as a community centre for the mainly impoverished local Armenians, many of whom only arrived here from the former Soviet Armenia post-1990.

Surp Hovhannes
Sarayıçi Sokak

The Armenian Apostolic church of **Surp Hovhannes** (St Joseph's) dates back to 1827, though the original wooden structure burnt down and was replaced by the current building in 1876. The door to the compound in which the church is set is usually open, an encouraging sign of increasing tolerance towards minority Armenians by the city's Muslim Turkish majority, though photography is forbidden inside the cradle-vaulted church.

FISH FRENZY

Cobbled Çaparız Street, which leads to the suburban railway line running parallel to the sea, is a dense mass of **fish restaurants** (over forty of them), which erupt, especially on Friday and Saturday evening: into a frenzy of eating, drinking (mainly *rakı*), smoking, dancing (to *fasıl* music) and more drinking. It's not exactly local (most of the area's inhabitants are too poor to dine out here) it's largely Turks from elsewhere in the city out to party.

Panaya Elpeda
Gerdanlık Sokak

The substantial domed Greek Orthodox church of Kumkapı's **Panaya Elpeda**, with its gated entrance, dates back to the fifteenth century but has been rebuilt many times – the current, attractive Neoclassical structure belongs firmly in the nineteenth century. It contains one of the city's many *ayazmas* (sacred springs), but the caretakers aren't keen on letting visitors in.

3

Surp Asdvadzadzin
Şarapnel Sokak, Kumkapı

If you have any interest at all in İstanbul's Christian minorities, the one unmissable site in Gedikpaşa/Kumkapı is the Armenian Apostolic church of **Surp Asdvadzadzin** (known in Turkish as the Meryem Ana Kilisesi or Church of the Virgin Mary), dating back to 1641 – though much of what you see today dates from a rebuilding in 1886. This is the one Armenian church where you're guaranteed to see a sizeable congregation at the Sunday service, as its position, opposite the Armenian Patriarchate, makes it the city's most important. With black-clad priests chanting in front of the gilt altar, shafts of light illuminating the nave, the smell of incense heavy in the air, and members of the soberly dressed congregation kneeling and genuflecting before taking their pew, it's a moving sight.

The northwest quarter

Bounded by the major thoroughfare of Fevzi Paşa Caddesi to the west, the land walls of Theodosius to the north, the Golden Horn to the east, and the traffic-choked highway of Atatürk Bulvarı to the south, the northwest quarter is one of the least visited yet most interesting areas of old İstanbul. The magnificent Kariye Museum (once the Byzantine Church of St Saviour in Chora) aside, none of the sights here are major draws. For the most part, the only people you will see are locals going about their daily business – which is, of course, one of the area's greatest attractions. Remember that few people here speak a foreign language, mosques are often locked except at prayer times and most churches only open for services once a week.

This was once a very cosmopolitan area, with **Muslims, Christians, Jews** and even gypsies living in close proximity to each other. Most (though not all) of the Christians and Jews have long since departed, and the Muslims that are left, particularly in Fatih, are noted for their orthodoxy. Men in skull caps, voluminous *şalvar* trousers, long shirts and bushy beards are more redolent of Pakistan than Turkey, as are some of the women, draped head to toe in black *chadors*. Many of the area's inhabitants are migrants from impoverished rural areas in Anatolia, and you may well hear Kurdish spoken in the streets.

GETTING THERE

THE NORTHWEST QUARTER

By ferry Perhaps the most pleasant way to reach the area is by ferry up the Golden Horn, from Eminönü to Fener or Ayvansaray (every hour at a quarter to the hour 7.45am–3.45pm, hourly at five to the hour 4.55pm–6.55pm).

By bus The #99 bus from Eminönü will drop you just beyond the Atatürk Bridge for Zeyrek, but it also continues up to Fener, Balat and Ayvansaray. The #38/E from Eminönü

will drop you on Atatürk Bulvarı, just below the Zeyrek Camii, or it continues onto Edirnekapı (for the Kariye Museum; see pp.92–95) via Fatih Camii and the Yavuz Selim Camii.

By tram If you find the buses off-putting, take the T1 tram to Aksaray and walk up to the Aqueduct of Valens, beyond which the "quarter" begins.

Zeyrek

Zeyrek, an attractive area notable for its steep, cobbled streets and ramshackle wooden houses interspersed with small mosques, has a couple of interesting sights and, on İtfaiye Caddesi, now re-branded Kadınları Pazarı (The Women's Market) is a lively area full of restaurants including *Siirt Şeref* (see p.188) and businesses largely owned and run by Kurds.

The Museum of Caricatures and Humour

Atatürk Bulvarı, right underneath the Aqueduct of Valens (see p.82) • Tues–Sun 9am–4.30pm • Free

The quirky **Museum of Caricatures and Humour** (Karikatür ve Mizah Müzesi) is housed in the rooms of Gazanfer Medrese (built in 1599) around a pretty garden courtyard with a marble fountain. Cartoons are an important popular art form in Turkey: most papers employ a number of cartoonists, and the weekly *Gırgır* was the third best-selling comic in the world before many of its employees left to set up the rival *Avni*. The collection includes pieces dating back to 1870, with many exhibits concentrating on political satire. The museum was closed for restoration at the time of writing.

Zeyrek Camii

İbadethane Arkası Sok 6–8; reached by turning left off İtfaiye Caddesi

In the heart of Zeyrek nestles **Zeyrek Camii**, the former Church of the Pantocrator, built in the twelfth century and converted into a mosque at the time of the Conquest. The building is officially open only at prayer times, though you may be able to persuade the *imam* to open up for you (his house is up the stone steps behind the wooden door, next to the mosque). It originally consisted of two churches and a connecting chapel, built between 1118 and 1136 by John II Comnenus and Empress Irene. The chapel was built as a mausoleum for the Comnenus dynasty and continued to be used as such by the Paleologus dynasty. Although the tombs have been removed, there is still evidence of the graves beneath the pavement. Empress Irene also founded a monastery nearby, which was to become one of the most renowned religious institutions in the empire and later the official residence of the Byzantine court, after the Great Palace had been reduced to ruins. No trace remains of the monastery, nor of its hospice, asylum or hospital. There are plans to restore the whole building to its former glory – hence the large number of "*Satılık*" ("For Sale") signs cropping up in anticipation of the area's "gentrification".

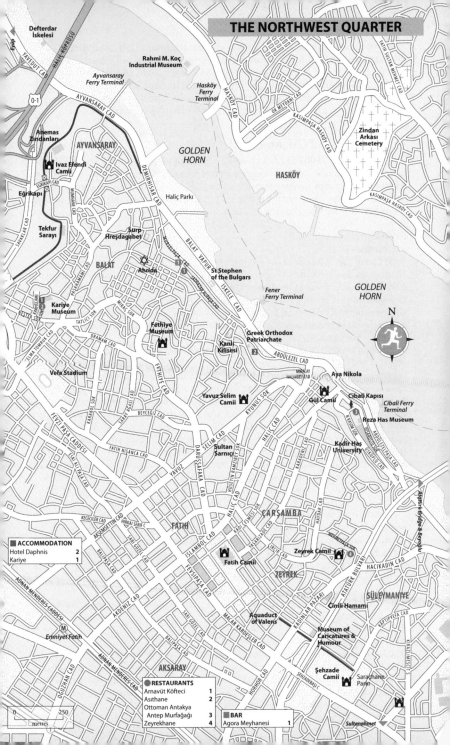

THE NORTHWEST QUARTER

Defterdar
İskelesi

Rahmi M. Koç
Industrial Museum

Ayvansaray
Ferry Terminal

Hasköy
Ferry
Terminal

GOLDEN
HORN

Zindan
Arkası
Cemetery

HASKÖY

Anemas
Zından
Zındanları

AYVANSARAY

Ivaz Efendi
Camii

Haliç Parkı

Egrikapı

Tekfur
Sarayı

Surp
Hreşdagabet

St Stephen
of the Bulgars

GOLDEN
HORN

Kariye
Museum

Ahrida

BALAT

Fener Ferry Terminal

Fethiye
Museum

Kanlı
Kilisesi

Greek Orthodox
Patriarchate

Aya Nikola

Vefa Stadium

Yavuz Selim
Camii

Gül Camii

Cibali Kapısı

Cibali Ferry
Terminal

Reza Has Museum

Sultan
Sarnıçı

Kadir Has
University

ÇARŞAMBA

FATİH

Zeyrek Camii

ACCOMMODATION
Hotel Daphnis 2
Kariye 1

Fatih Camii

ZEYREK

SÜLEYMANİYE

Çinili Hamamı

Aquaduct
of Valens

Museum of
Caricatures &
Humour

Emniyet Fatih

Şehzade
Camii

Saraçhane
Parkı

AKSARAY

RESTAURANTS
Arnavüt Köfteci 1
Asıthane 2
Ottoman Antakya 3
Antep Murfağağı 3
Zeyrekhane 4

BAR
Agora Meyhanesi 1

0 — 250
metres

Sultanahmet

The **mosque**, which occupies the south church, is also in an advanced state of dilapidation, and it's difficult to believe that it was once an imperial mausoleum. Among the surviving features are the revetments of the south apse and the original marble door frames. The floor, naturally, is covered in carpets but the *imam* may pull one of these back to give you a glimpse of the coloured marble underneath: an interlacing geometric pattern with figures of animals in its borders.

Upper Fatih and Çarşamba

The reputation of **Fatih** ("the Conqueror") and **Çarşamba** as conservative Islamic areas is deserved, though they're not associated with intolerance towards visitors of different religious and cultural persuasions – it's still worth bearing in mind, however, that locals here may be more likely to take exception to naked limbs and to having their picture taken without due warning than elsewhere in the city.

Fatih Camii
İslambol Caddesi

Fatih Camii, the "Mosque of the Conqueror", was begun ten years after the Conquest of İstanbul, in 1463, on the site of one of the most important Christian buildings in the city, the Church of the Holy Apostles, with much of the building material for the mosque complex coming from the demolished church. Completed in 1470, it was almost completely destroyed in an earthquake as early as 1766. At the time of writing, a long period of restoration work was almost complete, leaving the whole complex looking lighter and brighter than it has for decades.

The **outer precinct** of the mosque is large enough to accommodate the tents of a caravan. It is enclosed by a wall and, to north and south, by the medrese (theological academy) buildings, which accommodated the first Ottoman university. The **inner courtyard** of the mosque is one of the most beautiful in the city. Verd-antique and porphyry columns support a domed portico with polychrome edges, while an eighteenth-century fountain is surrounded by four enormous poplar trees. Over the windows outside the courtyard in the west wall, the first verse of the Koran is inscribed in white marble on verd-antique. At either end of the mosque portico there are inscriptions in the early İznik *cuerda seca* technique, whereby coloured glazes were prevented from running into each other by a dividing line of potassium permanganate, which outlined the design. The inscription over the mosque portal records the date and dedication of the mosque, and the name of the architect, **Atık Sinan**. He was supposedly executed the year after its completion on the orders of Mehmet, because the dome wasn't as large as that of Aya Sofya.

The **interior** is fairly dull, with less natural light than many mosques and little in the way of tile-work but it is often busy, even outside prayer times, acting as a social meeting place as well as a centre of serious Koranic study for both women and men.

The **tombs of Mehmet II** (Wed–Sun 9am–4.30pm; free) and of one of his wives, Gülbahar, are situated to the east of the mosque. The originals were destroyed in the earthquake, and while Gülbahar's tomb is probably a replica of the original, the *türbe* of the Conqueror is sumptuous Baroque. **Çorba Kapısı**, the "Soup Gate", to the southeast of the mosque, is original, inlaid in porphyry and verd-antique marble.

The Çarşamba Pazarı
Wednesday 9am–dusk

The **Çarşamba Pazarı** or **Wednesday Market** is the largest in the city. Its origins are uncertain, but it seems likely it was first established here in the Byzantine period, when this area was still rural. Eventually, as the city grew and engulfed the district, an entire neighbourhood was named Çarşamba after the market. The bazaar stretches for block after block in the streets to the northwest, southwest and southeast of the Fatih Camii complex, its awning, strung up between the narrow streets, providing welcome shade.

The goods on display here range from the usual cheap-and-cheerful household implements to fresh fruit and vegetables, and from cheap (and often even cheaper looking) clothing to bed linen and towels (rather better buys).

Yavuz Selim Camii
Yavuz Selim Caddesi, Fatih

The **Yavuz Selim Camii**, also called the Selimiye Camii, is one of the most attractive mosques in the city, and looking even more attractive after a long period of restoration. Built on a terrace on the crest of one of İstanbul's seven hills (the fifth, counting from Topkapı), it holds a commanding position over the surrounding suburbs. The mosque of Yavuz Selim, or Selim the Grim, was probably begun in the reign of Selim and completed by Süleyman the Magnificent. It is much more basic than the other imperial mosques, with just a single large dome atop a square room with a walled courtyard in front of it. The *avlu* (courtyard) in front of the prayer hall is quite beautiful, with a central fountain surrounded by tall cypress trees, the floor of the portico paved with a floral design and the columns a variety of marbles and granites.

The interior of the mosque is stunning in its simplicity, the shallower-than-usual dome emphasizing the sense of space. Light floods in through a series of windows in the tympanum arches and from the twenty-four stained-glass windows piercing the dome. The interior of the mosque falls well short of the austere, though, with gorgeous blue and white İznik tiles filling the lunettes above the lower windows and gilt-work highlighting the beautiful geometry of the stalactite carving above the *mihrab*.

The **tomb of Selim the Grim** (daily except Tues 9.30am–4.30pm; free), beside the mosque, has lost its original interior decoration but retains two beautiful tiled panels on either side of the door. Other tombs in the complex include that of four of Süleyman's children, probably the work of Sinan. The views from the northeast of the complex, looking out over the Golden Horn, are glorious.

Viewed on the approach down Yavuz Selim Caddesi, the mosque presents one of the most impressive facades to be seen in the city, in part because of its position next to the **Cistern of Aspar**, one of three open cisterns built during the fifth and sixth centuries in Constantinople. For centuries, this space housed market gardens and a village, but these were cleared years ago and sections are now in use as an attractive park, as well as basketball and tennis courts.

Sultan Sarnıçı
Ali Naki Sokak

This recently restored covered cistern, now known as the **Sultan Sarnıçı**, is around 29m by 19m. It has the usual brick-vaulted ceiling supported by 28 columns, some marble, others granite, each topped with beautifully carved Corinthian capitals. A few of the capitals bear the initials, in Greek, of the craftsmen who carved them, while others sport crosses. The cistern now serves as a function room, so don't be surprised to find the columns decked out with frills if there's a wedding celebration in the offing. There's neither official opening times nor an admission charge, but assuming there is no function on you're free to wander round and explore.

Fethiye Museum
Fethiye Caddesi, Katip Mustehattın Mah, Fatih • Daily except Wed 9am–4.30pm • 5TL

A major, but little visited, Byzantine gem, the **Fethiye Camii** was once the **Church of Theotokos Pammakaristos**. This medium-sized church, attractively set on a terrace overlooking the Golden Horn, was built in the twelfth century and conforms to the usual cross in a square design, its large central dome enhanced by four smaller, subsidiary domes. Despite the Ottoman conquest of Constantinople in 1453, it remained a Christian place of worship; indeed, between 1456 and 1587 it served as the seat of the **Greek Orthodox Patriarch** (now situated nearby, in the district of Fener). It was finally

A MULTI-FAITH CITY

As late as the early years of the twentieth century, the Ottoman lands that in 1923 became the new Republic of Turkey were home to a bewildering variety of **faiths** – Sunni Muslims, Alevis, Sufi dervish orders such as the Mevlevi and Nakşibendi, Jews, Yezidis, Greek, Syrian Orthodox and Armenian Apostolic Christians, Nestorians, plus converts from all these "native" branches of the Christian faith to Catholicism and Protestantism. During World War I and the War of Independence, however, all this was to change. Most Christians in Anatolia, seen as collaborators and potential fifth columnists by the Turkish Nationalists, either fled, were deported or killed. Non-Sunni Islam sects, also viewed with suspicion by the founders of the new, secular Turkish nation, were driven underground. Only in **İstanbul** did Christians remain in any numbers – over forty percent of the population – and despite the gradual emigration of most non-Muslims over the years since the formation of the Republic, İstanbul remains a multi-faith city.

In 1923, the **Greek Orthodox** population of the city was 100,000. It has now declined to some 3000, but the Orthodox Patriarchate is based in Fener (see p.98) and continues to serve the needs of the local Greek population, remaining, by tradition at least, the spiritual centre of the Eastern Orthodox Christian world. The **Armenian Apostolic (orthodox) Christians** have fared rather better, with a population of around 70,000. The community is spread across the city, though their religious focus is firmly in the old city, at Kumkapı (see p.85), where the Patriarchate building stands opposite a nineteenth-century church that attracts a full congregation every Sunday (see p.98). The Ottoman Empire was very welcoming to Sephardic Jews fleeing persecution in Spain in the fifteenth century and the community also prospered. Around 20,000 **Jews** now live in the city, with their most notable synagogues being in Balat (see p.98) and across the Golden Horn in Galata.

Of course, today's İstanbul is largely populated by **Sunni Muslims**. As elsewhere in the Islamic world, orthodoxy is finding a new voice – as you will discover if you wander the streets of neighbourhoods such as Fatih. Many İstanbullus, however, wear their religion very lightly (or take no heed at all), and for the average devout male, it's enough to attend the midday prayers on a Friday in one of the city's beautiful mosques and enjoy his Sunday off with his family. The Muslim population is not as homogenous as you might think, however. By some estimates, around twenty percent of Turkish citizens are **Alevi** – a curious (to the outsider) and mystical mix of Islam, shamanism and Shiism. While Sunni Islam is controlled by the state (religious officials such as *imams* are paid by the government, and sermons centrally checked), Alevis have led an "underground" existence beyond state sanction, worshipping in simple halls or private rooms known as *cemevi*. By tradition, they are staunch supporters of the secular regime (to avoid religious bigotry), even though they are neither recognized by, nor receive funding from, the state.

4

converted into a mosque in 1573, when it was renamed the Fethiye Camii or "Mosque of the Conquest". The main body of the building continues to function as a mosque and is usually only unlocked around prayer times. The southwest wing (originally a side chapel or parecclesion of the main church, added in 1310) was partitioned off during restoration work undertaken in 1949 and now serves as a **museum**. Helpful display boards in the entry to the chapel locate and give information on each of the mosaics, superb examples of the renaissance of Byzantine art, including, in the dome, Christ Pantocrator, encircled by the twelve prophets of the Old Testament. Other notable scenes show Christ with the Virgin Mary, the baptism of Christ and St John the Baptist.

The Kariye Museum

Kariye Mahallesi, Edirnekapı • Daily except Wed 9am–6pm • 15TL

Perched on a hill high above the old Jewish quarter of Balat, a stone's throw from the land walls of Theodosius, is the **Kariye Museum**. Formerly the church of St Saviour in Chora, its interior is decorated with a superbly preserved series of **frescoes and mosaics**. Among the most evocative of all the city's Byzantine treasures, it is thought to have been built in the early twelfth century on the site of a much older church far from the centre: hence "in Chora", meaning "in the country".

Between 1316 and 1321, the polymath statesman, scholar, philosopher and patron of the arts Theodore Metochites rebuilt the central dome and added the narthexes, the parecclesion (funerary chapel) and the stunning mosaics and frescoes that adorn both them and the nave. The unfortunate Metochites was stripped of his court position in 1328 following one of the all too common dynastic upheavals, and then imprisoned. He was eventually freed, though, and on his death in 1331 was buried in the funerary chapel of the magnificent church he left for posterity.

Turned into a mosque following the Ottoman conquest, the mosaics and frescoes were white-washed over until their restoration by the Byzantine Institute of America between 1948 (when it stopped functioning as a mosque) and its opening as a museum ten years later.

You should try to view the mosaics as they were originally intended by their (unknown) artists, as many of them fall into one of three narrative sequences, each telling a biblical story. This is not always easy as all the mosaics, bar the three in the nave, are spread confusingly over the walls, arches, pendentives and lunettes of the outer and inner narthexes. Use the plan (see p.94) to help you negotiate the museum and identify the scenes; numbers in the text below relate to their position on the plan.

INFORMATION   **KARIYE MUSEUM**

Arrival To reach the museum from the city centre, take the M1 metro to the Topkapı/Ulubatlı stop and follow the road on the inside of the land walls heading northeast before turning right onto Kariye Camii Sokak, a street containing a number of picturesquely renovated wooden houses, painted in pastel colours. Alternatively, and dropping you closer to the museum at Edirnekapı, take the #38/E bus from Eminönü.

Tickets and entrance The museum entrance is on the north side of the church; purchase your ticket before going through the automated turnstile. To enter the building itself follow the path (noting the prominent bulge of the apse, supported by buttresses) through the garden area to the door on the south side, which leads into the south bay of the inner narthex.

4

The Infancy of Christ

It makes sense to begin your explorations at the door in the west wall of the outer narthex, the exit from the museum, as when it was a church this was the main entrance. The Infancy of Christ narrative begins just north of here, on the north wall of the **outer narthex**, and the scenes are all conveniently located in the distinctive lunettes (semicircular recesses). Particularly impressive in this sequence are the **Enrolment for Taxation** (2), with an apprehensive-looking Mary standing before the tax officials, along with the **Massacre of the Innocents** (7). In this partially damaged scene, Herod's soldiers are shown taking children from their distraught mothers' arms, then butchering them.

Christ's Ministry

This is the most difficult series to follow as many of the scenes are damaged and, although most of the works of Christ are spread over the vaults of the outer narthex, they continue on into the inner narthex. Worth looking out for in the outer narthex is the **Miracle at Cana** (17) which depicts Christ, hand outstretched, turning water into wine. Nearby, in the only partially surviving scene of **Christ Healing a Leper** (19), the legs of the poor soul about to be healed are covered in almost comic-book spots. In an impressively complete scene in the inner narthex, **Christ Healing St Peter's Mother-in-Law** (22), St Peter is pictured alongside his bed ridden mother-in-law, with Jesus taking the poor woman's outstretched hand.

The Life of the Virgin Mary

Located in the inner narthex, these mosaics are based on the apocryphal gospel of St James, which gives an account of the birth and life of the Virgin and was very popular in the Middle Ages. They are remarkably complete and beautifully executed. One of the most delightful is the **First Seven Steps of the Virgin** (33), which shows the

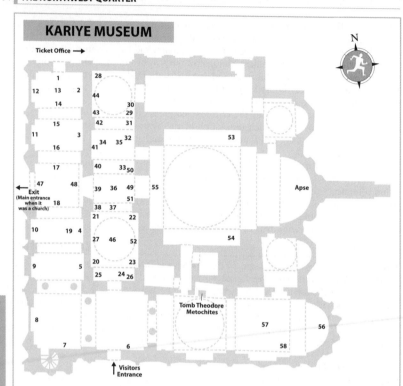

KARIYE MUSEUM

Ticket Office →

N

Visitors Entrance

Tomb Theodore Metochites

Apse

Exit
(Main entrance when it was a church)

THE INFANCY OF CHRIST

1   Joseph dreaming & the journey to Bethlehem
2   Enrolment for taxation
3   Nativity scene
4   The journey of the Magi & Magi appear before Herod
5   Herod enquires of the whereabouts of the new-born child
6   The flight into Egypt (partial)
7   Massacre of the innocents, ordered by Herod
8   Herod's soldiers continue slaying children
9   Mothers mourn their slain
10 Elizabeth flees with her baby son, John the Baptist
11 Joseph dreams of a return to Nazareth
12 Christ returns to Jerusalem

THE MINISTRY OF CHRIST

13 Christ with the doctors
14 John the Baptist bears witness to Christ
15 John the Baptist bears witness to Christ
16 Christ is tempted by the devil
17 Miracle at Cana, Christ turns water into wine
18 Multiplication of loaves
19 Christ healing a leper
20 Christ heals a blind and dumb man
21 The healing of two blind men
22 Christ healing St. Peter's mother-in-law
23 Christ heals the bleeding woman
24 Christ heals the withered hand
25 Christ heals a leper
26 Healing scene (inscription lost)
27 Christ heals assorted illnesses

THE LIFE OF THE VIRGIN MARY

28 Joachim has his offerings rejected
29 Joachim goes into the wilderness to pray
30 Anne's prayers are answered (Annunciation)
31 Meeting at the Golden Gate (Joachim and Anne)
32 Birth of the Virgin Mary
33 The first seven steps of the Virgin

THE LIFE OF THE VIRGIN MARY (CONTD.)

34 Priests bless the Virgin
35 The Virgin caressed by her parents
36 The Virgin is presented to the temple, aged three
37 An Angel gives bread to the Virgin
38 Instruction of the Virgin
39 The Virgin is given purple wool to weave
40 Zacharias praying before the rods of the suitors
41 The Virgin is awarded to Jospeh
42 Joseph takes the Virgin home
43 The Annunciation of the Virgin
44 Joseph goes away & returns to find Mary pregnant

THE GENEALOGY OF CHRIST

45 The Virgin and Child with Christ's ancestors
46 Christ Pantacrator with Christ's ancestors

THE DEDICATORY MOSAICS

47 The Virgin and Angels
48 Christ Pantacrator
49 Enthroned Christ and donor
50 St Peter
51 St Paul
52 The Deesis

THE NAVE MOSAICS

53 Jesus with Bible
54 The Virgin Hodegetria
55 Dormition of the Virgin

THE FRESCOES

56 The resurrection (Anastasis)
57 The Second Coming
58 Souls of the damned

4

infant Mary tottering between her mother, St Anne, and her father Joachim. Another warming family-scene, the **Virgin Caressed by her Parents** (35), depicts the infant Mary cradled between her mother and father. In **Zacharias praying before the Rods of the Suitors** (40), the Virgin Mary makes her marriage choice by selecting from the twelve sticks left by her suitors – she picks the one that is sprouting.

The inner narthex domes
In the northern dome of the inner narthex is a medallion of the **Virgin and Child**. In the sixteen upper ribs the kings of the house of David are depicted, below them a further eleven ancestors (45). A similar medallion in the southern dome of the inner narthex shows **Christ Pantocrator** in a medallion, while below him are ranged 24 of Jesus' ancestors, ranging from Adam to Jacob (46).

The dedicatory mosaics
These six large mosaic panels, placed in both the outer and inner narthexes, portray the dedication of the church to both Christ and the Virgin Mary. Above the main doorway into the outer narthex is **The Virgin and Angels** (47) depicting Mary, hands outstretched, with the infant Christ, shown here symbolizing the universe, on her bosom. Opposite, above the door through to the inner narthex, is **Christ Pantocrator** (48) bearing the inscription "Jesus Christ, the Land of the Living". Moving through into the inner narthex, straight ahead above the door into the nave is the **Enthroned Christ and Donor** (49). Perhaps the single most interesting mosaic of all, it depicts Theodore Metochites offering a model of the building to a seated Christ. The turban-like hat he is wearing is called a *skiadon* (sunshade). **St Peter** (50), the keys to heaven in his left hand, is portrayed on the left of the door to the nave, **St Paul** (51) on the right. Finally, right of St Paul is a large scene, **The Deesis** (52), showing Christ with his mother and two benefactors, Isaac (who built the original church) and a female figure, described in the inscription as "Lady of the Mongols, Melane the Nun".

The nave mosaics
Partially covered with revetment marble panels, the nave contains three striking mosaic panels. To the left of the apse, **Jesus** (53) holds an open bible in his hand. To the right of the apse **The Virgin Hodegetria** (54) cradles the infant Christ, while on the west wall above the door to the outer narthex is the **Dormition of the Virgin** (55), showing Mary on her death bier, Christ behind her holding a swaddled infant representing her soul.

The funerary chapel
In the north wall of the **funerary chapel** is the **tomb of Metochites**, the donor of the church, although the inscription has been lost. There are three other tombs in the walls here, as well as some finely-carved marble capitals, but the real glory is the frescoes. Contemporary with the work of the Italian painter Giotto, they seem to have much more in common with the early Renaissance than the stylized paintings of the earlier Byzantine period. There are over thirty different scenes depicted, all dealing, aptly for a funerary chapel, with death or resurrection.

The most spectacular is the **Resurrection** (56) also known as the Harrowing of Hell or, in Greek, the *anastasis*. This is a dramatic representation of Christ in action, trampling the gates of Hell underfoot and forcibly dragging Adam and Eve from their tombs. Satan lies among the broken fetters at his feet, bound at the ankles, wrists and neck, but still writhing around in a vital manner.

Along the Golden Horn
Most of the sights on the western bank of the Golden Horn lie more or less on the line of the old sea walls, which once ran right around the peninsula and linked into either

end of the great land walls of Theodosius – and thus completely encircled and protected first the Byzantine and then the Ottoman imperial capitals.

The best starting point is the **Atatürk Bridge** (Unkapanı Köprüsü), accessible by any Fatih- or Eyüp-bound bus from Eminönü. As you head northwest along the bank of the Horn, the narrow streets and jumbled houses of Fatih, Fener and Balat tumble down from the hills above, and traffic roars past on busy Ayvansaray Caddesi. Warm Sundays bring droves of picnicking families to the strip of park between the road and waterfront.

Reza Has Museum & Gallery
Kadir Has Üniversitesi, Çibali • Daily 9am–6pm • 3TL • ☎ 0212/533 6532, ⓦ rhm.org.truseum • Bus #99 from Eminönü

The intriguing **Reza Has Museum & Gallery** (Reza Has Müzesi) is housed in the **Kadir Has University**, an imposing, late nineteenth-century former tobacco factory. The museum and exhibition space are located on the north (right as you face it) of the university building. The museum, attractively laid-out in the bowels of the tobacco factory, itself built over a Byzantine cistern and Ottoman *hamam*, is a must for archeology buffs. A series of cases, set out chronologically from the Neolithic through to the Selçuk Turkish era, highlight the richness of Anatolian prehistory and history. Particularly fine is the case devoted to the metalwork of the first-millennium-BC Urartian civilization – look out for the beautifully-worked bronze belts depicting horses, chariots, warriors and mythological beasts. Also stunning is the collection of medical implements dating from the Hellenistic to the Byzantine periods and a collection of seals spanning the mid-fourth century BC to the Byzantine period. An exhibition space adjacent to this marvellous private collection hosts an eclectic but well-regarded series of temporary exhibitions, which have included everything from contemporary painting to the Ottoman fire service.

Çibali Kapısı and Aya Nikola
The **Çibali Kapısı** (Old Gateway), just beyond the Reza Has Museum (see above), pierces a surviving section of the old sea walls. Here, on May 29, 1453, the besieging Ottoman forces breached the Byzantine defences, a success that helped lead to the Muslim conquest of the imperial capital on the very same day. A little further along Abdülezel Caddesi, in a walled compound right next to the road, is the Greek Orthodox church of **Aya Nikola**. Although the current building dates from the mid-nineteenth century, it has a much longer history and was once a dependency of a monastery on Mount Athos, situated in what is now northern Greece. You'll need to ring the bell to gain entry. An Orthodox family live here and tend the building, which has a sacred spring, or *ayazma*, in the narthex. The interior of the church manages to be both garish and gloomy, but the iconostasis, in the form of the facade of a Classical-era Greek temple, is interesting.

Gül Camii
Gül Camii Sokak • Usually locked except for prayer times

The **Gül Camii**, once the Byzantine church of St Theodosia, is thought to have been built in the twelfth century. Reached by a flight of steps from the street below, it is a most attractive and well-preserved structure. Typical of the Byzantine style, it is made largely of courses of slim red bricks, alternating with narrower bands of pale limestone. More or less square in plan, it is topped with an elegant dome. The church was converted into a mosque soon after the Conquest, and its name, "Rose Mosque" in Turkish, is said to derive from the fact that when the Ottoman forces entered the church on May 29, it was still festooned with the roses put there by the Christians to mark the feast of St Theodosia that same day.

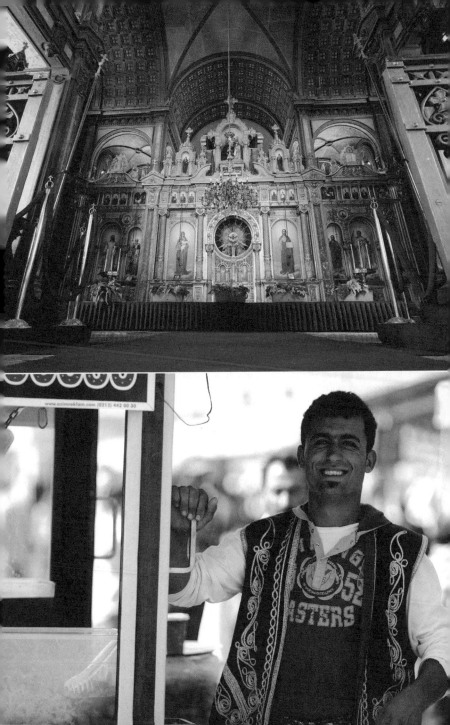

Greek Orthodox Patriarchate

Mursel Paşa Caddesi • Daily 9am–5pm • Free

The **Greek Orthodox Patriarchate**, known in Turkish as the *Fener Rum Patrikhanesi*, has been the spiritual centre of the Orthodox world since 1599 and remains so today – despite the fact that a Turkish court controversially ruled in 2007 that the spiritual authority of Patriarch Bartholomew I was confined solely to Turkey's few remaining Greek Orthodox Christians, rather than to the Orthodox Christian community worldwide. This appears to have little effect on the coachloads of tourists from Athens and elsewhere in Greece, who flock to the nineteenth-century **Church of St George** (which stands in the compound of the Patriarchate) on Sunday mornings in the tourist season – especially for the Easter Sunday Mass – or bring their offspring here to be christened. St George's is attractive enough, and watching the Orthodox pilgrims pay their respects is undoubtedly moving, but the church is architecturally undistinguished.

Kanlı Kilisesi

Tevki Cafer Mektebi Sokak

The thirteenth-century **church of St Mary of the Mongols** (in Greek, the *Panaghia Mouchliotissa*) is known in Turkish as the **Kanlı Kilisesi** or "Bloody Church". It's difficult to find in the backstreets above and behind the Patriarchate. The best landmark is the monumental red-brick Victorian Gothic-style **Fener Greek School for Boys**. Keep this to your left as you ascend the hill via the stepped street of Tevki Merdivenli Sokak until you reach the church. Rendered and painted an uninspiring red, this is the only Byzantine church in the city where Orthodox services have been carried out from before the Muslim conquest to the present day – the church contains a copy of the *firman* (decree) given by Mehmet the Conqueror that permitted worship to continue here. Ring the bell to gain admittance from the female Rum (as the minority Greek Orthodox population of the city is known to Turks) caretaker – the church is most interesting on a Sunday when services are still held here, though your arrival may well double the congregation.

St Stephen of the Bulgars

Mürsel Paşa Cad 85–8, Fener • Daily 8am–5pm • Free

St Stephen of the Bulgars is a curious, neo-Gothic white-painted church, stranded on a massive traffic-island-cum-park area. Built in 1896, it is made entirely from iron, cast in Vienna and carted all the way to İstanbul. That the Bulgarian branch of the Orthodox Church had the temerity to erect their church so close to the Greek Orthodox Patriarchate shows just how much rivalry there was between ethnic Bulgarians and Greeks in the late nineteenth and early twentieth centuries – a rivalry encouraged by the Ottomans and that was to lead to much bloodshed in the eastern Balkans. Signs of rust betray the chosen building material and if you want to attend one of the thrice-yearly services you will need to be here on Easter Sunday, December 27 or January 6.

Ahrida Synagogue

Kürkçu Çeşme Sokak, Balat • Contact the Chief Rabbinate the day before to arrange a visit ☎ 0212/243 5166

The **Ahrida Synagogue** is tucked inconspicuously away in the backstreets of the old Jewish neighbourhood of Balat. Sephardic Jews, expelled from Spain, were given sanctuary in the Muslim Ottoman Empire from 1492 (see p.285), and many naturally gravitated towards its capital, İstanbul – with large numbers ending up in Balat. The Jewish population has long since moved on, but the synagogue receives a remarkable number of visitors despite its out-of-the-way location and the fact that visits must be arranged the day before. Dating from the fifteenth century, it was rebuilt after a fire in the Ottoman Baroque style in 1694. The deceptively large interior can hold a congregation of 350, and its curved *tevah* (pulpit) is said to represent Noah's Ark.

Surp Hreşdagabet

Kamış Sok 2, Balat

The massive stone walls of the compound of **Surp Hreşdagabet** (Church of the Holy Archangels) are marred with graffiti and the chances of gaining admittance are slim – the Armenian family caretakers are suspicious of strangers and the heavy iron doors lack either a knocker or a bell (try on Thursday mornings when there is a service). It was built as a Greek Orthodox church in the thirteenth century but was later given to the local Armenian community following the conversion of their original church in Fatih into a mosque in 1627. The church's chief claim to fame today is the supposedly curative properties of its *ayazma* (holy spring) and the curious rite held on the second weekend of September each year, when Christians and Muslims alike come to have their ailments miraculously cured, and animals are sacrificed and the meat distributed to the needy.

4

TOMB OF EYÜP ENSARI, EYÜP CAMII

The land walls

If you enjoy exploring on foot, the walk alongside the six-and-a-half-
kilometre-long land walls of Theodosius II is one of the most interesting
things to do in the city. Despite the ravages of time and several earthquakes,
most recently in 1999, they have survived remarkably well. Some sections
have been completely rebuilt in newly dressed stone and cement bricks;
although some critics doubt the historical accuracy of some of this
restoration work, at least the casual visitor can gain a wonderful impression
of defensive fortifications that were un-breached for more than a thousand
years. A walk along the walls can take as little as two hours, though a full day
will allow time to fully enjoy them and the adjacent sites.

Most of the outer wall and its 96 towers are still standing; access is restricted on some of the restored sections, though elsewhere there's the chance to scramble along the crumbling edifice. The walls were built from limestone with contrasting bands of thin bricks, some of which were stamped with the name of the manufacturer or donor and bear the name of the emperor in whose reign they were made. Mortar mixed with brick dust was used liberally to bind the masonry; the towers had two levels, separated by brick barrel-vaults.

The number of run-down **slum dwellings** along the city walls has been reduced dramatically, but the towers and other nooks and crannies of the walls still attract vagrants and worse, making it a potentially risky area after dark. However, it's highly unlikely you'll encounter any problems in daytime. If time is limited, the two best **sites** to visit are the Yedikule fortifications and the Mihrimah Camii, a beautifully restored mosque designed by Mimar Sinan. The Kariye Museum, a former Byzantine church containing some of the best-preserved mosaics and frescoes in the world, also lies close to the walls (see pp.92–95).

GETTING THERE

By bus Buses from Eminönü include the #84 to Topkapı and #28 and #336E to Edirnekapı, or the #37Y from Vezneciler.

By tram and metro You can catch the T1 tram to the Pazartekte stop, or the M1 metro to Topkapı/Ulubatlı.

Reaching the north end of the walls The ferry from Eminönü to Ayvansaray İskelesi on the Golden Horn, just before the Haliç bridge.

Reaching the southern end of the walls A local (*banliyo*) train from Sirkeci or Cankurtaran to Yedikule station on the Marmara shore, from where it's a half-kilometre walk to the walls. Alternatively take the #80 bus from Eminönü to Yedikule, or the #80T to Yedikule. The Bakırköy dolmuş from the top of Tarlabaşı Bulvarı near Taksim Square should drop you right by the southern terminus of the walls.

Some history

The walls were named after **Theodosius II**, even though he was only 12 years old when their construction was started in 413 AD. Stretching from the Sea of Marmara to Tekfur Sarayı, 2km further out than the previous walls of Constantine, the walls were planned by Anthemius, Prefect of the East, to accommodate the city's expanding population. Along with the sea walls, which they join to the north above the Golden Horn at the Tekfur Sarayı and to the south on the shore of the Sea of Marmara, they formed a near impregnable defence for the city. The land walls were almost completely destroyed by an earthquake in 447 and had to be rebuilt in haste, since Attila's forces were on the point of attack. An ancient edict was brought into effect whereby all citizens, regardless of rank, were required to help in the rebuilding. The Hippodrome factions of Blues and Greens (see box, p.60) provided sixteen thousand labourers and finished the project in just two months. The completed construction consisted of the original wall, 5m thick and 12m-high, separated from an outer wall of 2m by 8.5m by a 20m strip of land, and a 20m wide moat. There were 96 towers of assorted shapes – square, round and polygonal – on the line of both the inner and outer walls, so many a visiting Crusader remarked that a child could toss an apple from one to another with ease. It's little wonder that even Attila's Huns, who numbered several thousand, decided against a siege.

Yedikule

The **Yedikule** neighbourhood, at the southern end of the land walls, around 5km from Sultanahmet, is an attractive if run-down quarter. Whether you reach the neighbourhood by suburban train, bus, dolmuş or taxi (see above), the natural starting point is the **Marble Tower**. Just over a half-kilometre walk from Yedikule station, at the extreme southern end of the land walls, today the tower is wedged uncomfortably between the shores of the Sea of Marmara and the traffic racing along the coastal highway that is Kennedy Caddesi. At the Marble Tower the land walls joined the sea walls; the tower itself was either a part of the defences or a small imperial pavilion.

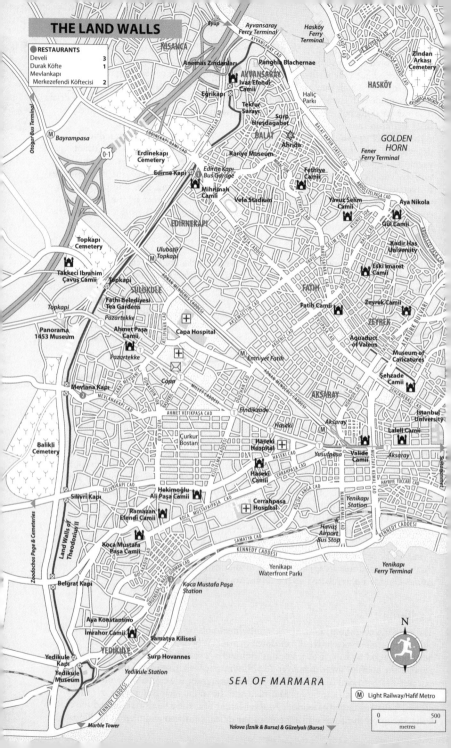

THE LAND WALLS

RESTAURANTS
Develi 3
Durak Köfte 1
Mevlankapı
Merkezefendi Köftecisi 2

Eyüp

Ayvansaray Ferry Terminal

Hasköy Ferry Terminal

NISANCA

Zindan Arkası Cemetery

Anemas Zındanları

Panghia Blachernae

HASKÖY

AYVANSARAY

İvaz Efendi Camii

Eğrikapı

Tekfur Sarayı

Haliç Parkı

Surp Breşdagabet

GOLDEN HORN

Bayrampaşa

Otogar Bus Terminal

0-1

Erdinekapı Cemetery

BALAT

Ahrida

Fener Ferry Terminal

Edirne Kapı

Kariye Museum

Edirne Kapı Bus Garage

Fethiye Camii

Mihrimah Camii

Vefa Stadium

Yavuz Selim Camii

Aya Nikola

EDIRNEKAPI

Gül Camii

Topkapı Cemetery

Ulubatlı/Topkapı

Kadir Has University

Eski İmaret Camii

Takkeci İbrahim Çavuş Camii

Topkapı

SULUKULE

Fatih Belediyesi Tea Gardens

FATIH

Zeyrek Camii

Topkapı

Pazartekke

Fatih Camii

ZEYREK

Panorama 1453 Museum

Ahmet Paşa Camii

Çapa Hospital

Aquaduct of Valens

Pazartekke

Museum of Caricatures

Çapa

Emniyet Fatih

Şehzade Camii

Mevlana Kapı

AKSARAY

İstanbul University

Fındıkzade

Aksaray

Laleli Camii

Balikli Cemetery

AHMET VEFİKPAŞA CAD

Çurkur Bostan

Haseki

Haseki Hospital

Yusufpaşa

Valide Camii

Aksaray

Hekimoğlu Ali Paşa Camii

Haseki Camii

Cerrahpaşa Hospital

Yenikapı Station

Silivri Kapı

Ramazan Efendi Camii

Havaş Airport Bus Stop

Koca Mustafa Paşa Camii

SAMATYA CAD

KENNEDY CADDESI

Yenikapı Ferry Terminal

Zfodochos Pege & Cemeteries

Land Walls of Theodosius II

Belgrat Kapı

Koca Mustafa Paşa Station

Yenikapı Waterfront Parkı

Aya Konstantino

İmrahor Camii

Samatya Kilisesi

YEDIKULE

Surp Hovannes

Yedikule Kapı

Yedikule Museum

Yedikule Station

SEA OF MARMARA

N

Marble Tower

Yalova (İznik & Bursa) & Güzelyalı (Bursa)

Ⓜ Light Railway/Hafif Metro

0   500
metres

Heading north across the highway, avoid walking along the inside of the walls as there is a city dog-pound here that seems to have far more canines outside it than in. Instead, wind through the pleasant park outside, exiting back onto the road and passing a cemetery behind which you can catch glimpses of the bricked-up triple arches of the **Golden Gate** (see below), incorporated into the land walls.

The Yedikule Museum

Kale Meydanı Caddesi, Yedikule • Tues–Sun 8.30am–6.30pm • 5TL

The **Yedikule Museum** comprises the substantial remains of fortifications added to the line of the Byzantine land walls by Mehmet the Conqueror in 1457–58, and with their twelve-metre-high curtain walls they form the castle-like structure that can be seen today. Despite its design, this was never actually used as a castle, but two of the towers served as prisons and others were used as treasuries and offices for the collection of revenue of the *Vakıf* (pious foundation). The two **prison towers** are those immediately to the left of the museum entrance. The inscriptions around the outside of the first of these were carved into the walls by prisoners, many of them foreign ambassadors on some hapless errand. The prison in the second tower doubled as an execution chamber: the wooden gallows and "well of blood", into which heads would roll, can still be seen, and the odd instrument of torture can be found lying about outside in the courtyard. The most famous victim of the execution chamber was Osman II, deposed and murdered in 1622 by his janissaries, and thus providing Ottoman history with its first case of regicide. The only structure in the great courtyard inside the fortification itself is a crumbling Ottoman mosque.

The so-called **Golden Gate** was a triumphal arch constructed where the outer, west-facing wall of the Yedikule fortifications would be built many centuries later. Built under Theodosius I in 390 and flanked by two marble towers, it originally stood alone and was used by important visitors of state and conquering emperors (generals were never permitted to pass through the gate, even after successful campaigns) making a grand entrance into Constantinople. When Theodosius II built the new line of walls, the Golden Gate was incorporated into them (and, of course, the section of land wall containing the gate was later incorporated into the Yedikule fortifications of Mehmet the Conqueror). The shape of the three arches is still visible on both sides of the wall, but it takes a degree of imagination to invest the structure with the glamour and dignity it must once have possessed. Michael Palaeologus was the last emperor to ride through in triumph, when the city was recaptured from occupying Crusaders (see p.283). After the empire went into decline, the gold-plated doors were removed and the entrance bricked up.

The walls between the Yedikule and Mevlana gates

Traffic wardens compete to direct traffic through the narrow entry of the Yedikule Kapı (Yedikule Gate), with its Byzantine eagle cut in the blackened marble overhead. To explore the walls running north from here, cut through the gate and follow them north, admiring the market gardens in the shadow of the ramparts, to **Belgrat Kapı**. This was a military gate, different from a public gateway in that there was no bridge crossing the moat beyond the outer walls. It was named for the captives who were settled in this area by Süleyman the Magnificent after his capture of Belgrade in 1521. Heading through the gate, you can ascend the renovated walls and walk north along the battlements for some three-hundred metres, descending again opposite an all-weather football pitch. North from Belgrat Kapı to Silivri Kapı, the walls are largely untouched, though the sections around **Silivri Kapı** itself have been extensively renovated. This gate was known to the Byzantines as Pege because of its proximity to a famous shrine, the Zoodochos Pege.

There is more restoration work at the **Mevlana Kapı**, and also some interesting inscriptions on the outer wall. The Theodosian walls reached completion at this gate,

5

since it was here that the Greens, building from the Marmara, met the Blues (see box, p.60), who were working southwards from the direction of the Golden Horn. A Latin inscription to the left of the gate celebrates this fact: "By the command of Theodosius, Constantine erected these strong fortifications in less than two months. Scarcely could Pallas [Athena] herself have built so strong a citadel in so short a time."

Zoodochos Pege

Silivrikapı Seyıt Nizam Cad 3 • Daily 8.30am–4.30pm • Free • To get here, cross the dual-carriageway via the pedestrian lights and walk a short way down Seyıt Nizam Caddesi; just past an Ottoman-era fountain, turn right onto Silivrikapı Caddesi and follow it around to reach Zoodochus Pege on your left

Known to the Turks as the *Balıklı Kilise* (Church with Fish), the shrine/church complex of **Zoodochos Pege** lies some 500m west of Silivri Kapı, in the midst of a sea of beautifully green and silent cemeteries. The well-kept shrine, dating back to the early Byzantine era, and the church built in 1833, are set in a walled compound dominated by a giant plane tree. The marble iconostasis resembles the facade of a classical temple, and the gloomy interior has maintained a certain sanctity. The focus, though, is very much on the *ayazma* (sacred spring) reached by steps leading down from the right of the church entrance. Fish swim lazily in a floodlit pool, and the row of taps above the basin, where pilgrims take the "holy" waters, are in the shape of crosses. According to legend, a hungry monk was frying some fish when he heard that Constantinople had fallen to the Turks. The disbelieving monk apparently said that was about as likely as the fish in his pan coming back to life, with which they leapt out of the pan and into the pool, where their descendants remain to this day. Visit on a Sunday, and the surrounding Muslim, Armenian and Greek Orthodox cemeteries are crowded with people paying their respects to the departed.

North along the walls to Topkapı

From Mevlana Kapı, follow the outside of the walls along a pleasant stretch of pavement that has been constructed on the line of the moat. Just south of Topkapı, the walls have been destroyed to make way for the enormous thoroughfare of Millet Caddesi. To cross (not easy, with the tramway running in the middle of a busy dual-carriageway) the road, use the pedestrian crossing a little to the east of the walls. Just outside of the walls are a couple of contrasting but worthwhile sights, the dramatic **Panorama 1453 History Museum** (see p.104) and the fascinating wooden mosque of **Takkeci İbrahim Çavuş** (see p.105).

Just north of Millet Caddesi are the pleasant Fatih Belediyesi tea gardens, with toilets. Continue walking on the inside of the walls until you reach the **Topkapı** ("Gate of the Cannonball"), named after the most powerful cannon of Mehmet the Conqueror, which in 1453 pounded the walls near here. Before huge sections of wall were demolished to make way for modern-day Millet and Adnan Menderes *caddesi* this was one of the main entries into the city and was known in the Byzantine era as the Gate of St Romanus.

Panorama 1453 History Museum

Topkapı Kültür Parkı, Merkez Efendi Mahallesi • Daily 9am–6.30pm • 10TL • ⓦ panoramikmuze.com • T1 tram from Sultanahmet to the Topkapı stop

Set in a pleasant park on the west side of the horrendously busy Topkapı/Edirnekapı Caddesi, the small **Panorama 1453 History Museum** pays homage to one of the landmark dates in Turkish history, the siege and capture of Constantinople by Sultan Mehmet (known after his historic victory as Fatih Sultan Mehmet or Mehmet the Conqueror. The centrepiece is a scene depicting the Ottoman army besieging the walls painted in a 360° sweep around the drum and shallow dome of the building, viewed from a central, circular platform. There are ten thousand painted human figures in the spectacular scene, with balls of Greek fire raining down on the besiegers, and the green banners of Islam held aloft by the attackers. Between the viewing platform and the

5

painted scene, the battlefield has been re-created with a realistic tableau of models and mannequins. The museum is cleverly lit and though serious historians may scoff at the overly dramatized scene, it's undeniably impressive, helping bring to life one of the most momentous events in world history. It's all the more powerful for being set in the shadow of the walls themselves, close to the point the Ottomans first breached them on May 29, 1453. Unfortunately all the sign boards are in Turkish, so you'll need an audio guide (5TL) to make the most of your visit.

Takkeci İbrahim Çavuş Camii
İbrahim Çavuş Sokak, Topkapı • Open prayer times only

The wooden **Takkeci İbrahim Çavuş Camii** was founded in 1592 by the eponymous *takkeci*, a maker of the distinctive felt hats (*takke*) worn by dervishes. Despite recent restoration work it retains much that is original, including its ribbed wooden dome and some fine tile panels from the best İznik period. There is gorgeous carved woodwork everywhere, making the interior look and feel quite different to the standard Ottoman mosque.

Sulukule to the Golden Horn

Between Topkapı and Edirnekapı, there's a pronounced valley, formerly the route of the Lycus River, now taken by Adnan Menderes (Vatan) Caddesi. This road is also difficult to cross – use the underpass marked by the metro sign a little to the east of the line of the wall. At this point, the walls are at their least defensible, since the higher ground outside gives the advantage to attackers. The famed **Orban cannon** of Mehmet the Conqueror was trained on this part of the walls during the siege of 1453, hence their ruinous state. It was here, too, that Constantine XI rode into the midst of the Turkish army after he realized that all hope of holding out was gone. **Sulukule** – the area inside the walls between Adnan Menderes Caddesi and Edirnekapı – was home to a gypsy community for close on a thousand years, but most of its traditional houses have already been bulldozed by the local municipality to make way for more upmarket residences, incurring a critical 2008 UNESCO report. For wall-walkers the consequence of this redevelopment is that once you have crossed Adnan Menderes Caddesi you need to head to the outside of the walls in order to continue north, past the new housing, before cutting inside again a couple of hundred metres or so south of the impressive **Mihrimah Camii**.

Mihrimah Camii
Edirnekapı • Daily dawn to dusk

One of many early Sinan works commissioned by Mihrimah, the favourite daughter of Süleyman the Magnificent, and her husband Rüstem Paşa, the beautiful **Mihrimah Camii** is situated on the sixth and highest of İstanbul's seven hills. Dating from somewhere around the middle of the sixteenth century, it has recently been restored to its former grandeur. Raised on a platform, it can be seen from all over the city, with the area beneath occupied by shops. The mosque and its dependencies have suffered in two earthquakes, the second of which brought the minaret tumbling down onto the mosque itself. The entry to the mosque today is from the north side.

Edirnekapı to Eğrikapı

Edirnekapı is so named because the road through it leads to modern Edirne. The wall around here has been well restored and you can explore the battlements and admire the views over the old city and the Golden Horn. Pass through the narrow gate from the city side and outside there's a plaque (in Turkish) proclaiming that this is where Mehmet the Conqueror made his triumphal entry into the city in 1453.

After crossing Fevzi Paşa Caddesi, continue north along the inner side of the walls for a couple of hundred metres to Kariye Bostancı Sokak (this street leads to the Kariye

5

Museum; see pp.92–95). Opposite this steps lead up to a renovated section wall, from where precipitous ladder-style steps (only for those with a head for heights) lead steeply up to the wall-top proper and thence to a tower boasting superb views over the Golden Horn, the Bosphorus and the Sea of Marmara. A little further along is the **Tekfur Sarayı** or Palace of the Porphyrogenitus. Built in the thirteenth or fourteenth century, this was a residence of the Byzantine royal family (possibly an annexe of the larger, but virtually vanished Blachernae Palace). It has a fine facade, with contrasting bands of red brick and pale stone, pierced by arched windows. Apparently, it was later used as a zoo, then a brothel, and, in the nineteenth century, as a poorhouse for down-on-their-luck Jews. It is usually padlocked, but a local youth may open up for you – for a tip.

Just beyond the palace, the nature of the walls changes. The original Theodosian walls, now lost, probably continued straight north and down to the Golden Horn. The remaining sections of surviving wall are later additions, built in the seventh century and bulging out to the west to enclose the expanding suburb of **Blachernae**, which had been left outside the original walls. They were rebuilt and massively strengthened in the reign of emperor Manuel Comnenus (1143–80) and later. The first gate in this newer section of walls is the narrow Eğrikapı, north of which are cobbled lanes winding through attractive cottage gardens and old houses.

Anemas Zindanları to the Golden Horn

Next to the prominent İvaz Efendi Camii is the **Anemas Zindanları** (closed for renovation at the time of writing), all that's left of the once magnificent Blachernae Palace, an imperial Byzantine palace of great importance from the twelfth century onwards. Only the vaults and corridors that ran beneath the palace remain, but there's a pleasant, shady tea-garden on site. A few minutes down from the Anemas Zindanları, reached from Dervişzade Sokak, is the unremarkable-looking **Greek Orthodox church of Panghia Blachernae**. The present structure dates only from 1867, but it was once one of Constantinople's most important churches, founded over a sacred spring (which still flows today) in the fifth century. The inhabitants believed that the robe and mantle of the Virgin Mary, brought here by pilgrims from Jerusalem, protected their city from harm. The church, which is usually open, also contained the Mandalyon, a piece of cloth bearing a miraculous imprint of Christ's face. This holy relic was looted by the Crusaders in the thirteenth century and the original church burnt to the ground in 1434.

From the church it is just a few minutes' walk down to the Golden Horn, from where you can get a bus or ferry from the Ayvansaray quay back to Eminönü.

Eyüp

Eyüp, around 1km north of the land walls and bordering the western bank of the Golden Horn, is one of the holiest places in Islam, its mosque being the site of the tomb of Eyüp Ensari, the Prophet Mohammed's standard-bearer. Muslims come here from all over the Islamic world on pilgrimage – try not to visit on Fridays, out of respect for conservative worshippers.

Eyüp Camii

Cami Kebir Sok 7, Eyüp • Daily dawn to dusk

The **Eyüp Camii** was built by Mehmet the Conqueror in honour of Eyüp Ensari, one of the small group of companions of the Prophet who was killed during the first Arab siege of Constantinople (674–678); a condition of the peace treaty signed following the siege was that his tomb be preserved. Later, the mosque hosted the investiture ceremonies of the Ottoman sultans: indeed, mosque and tomb face each other across the courtyard that was used for the ceremony. The exact site is marked by a raised platform surrounded by railings, from which two plane trees grow.

The original mosque was destroyed in the eighteenth century, probably by the same earthquake that put paid to Fatih Camii (see p.90). The present Baroque replacement, filled with light, gold, pale stone and white marble, was completed in 1800. The **tomb of Eyüp Ensari** (Tues–Sun 9.30am–4.30pm; free) is far more compelling, however (footwear should be removed and women should cover their heads before entering). Its facade and vestibule are covered in tile panels from many different periods and, although the effect is a bit overwhelming, the panels constitute a beautiful and varied display of the art form; you could spend weeks visiting individual buildings to see as many different designs and styles.

GETTING THERE EYÜP CAMII

The mosque is most easily reached up the Golden Horn from Eminönü – it's the last **ferry** stop before the Horn peters out into two small streams. The mosque and tomb are about a ten-minute walk from the Eyüp ferry terminal on Camii Kebir Caddesi; or catch the #99 or #39/A **bus** from Eminönü.

Tombs of Sokollu Mehmet Paşa and Siyavus Paşa
Camii Kebir Caddesi • Tues–Sun 9.30am–4.30pm

There are a number of other important tombs in the Eyüp district, as it was a popular place of burial for Ottoman dignitaries. Two of these, the **tombs of Sokollu Mehmet Paşa and Siyavus Paşa**, stand opposite each other on either side of Camii Kebir Caddesi, five minutes' walk from Eyüp Camii towards the Golden Horn. Five years before his assassination, Sokollu Mehmet Paşa commissioned Mimar Sinan to build his tomb, an elegantly proportioned, octagonal building of around 1574, notable for its stained glass, some of which is original; connected to the tomb by an elegant three-arched colonnade is a former Koran school. Siyavus Paşa's tomb, on the other hand, was probably actually built by Sinan for the children of Siyavus Paşa, who had died young. It's decorated with İznik tiles.

Eyüp cemetery
Eyüp is still a popular burial place, and the hills above the mosque are covered in plain modern stones interspersed with beautiful Ottoman tombs. To the north of the mosque, off Silahtarağa Caddesi, Karyağdı Sokak leads up into the **Eyüp cemetery**. Following the signs up this lane through the graveyard – most beautiful at sunset with an arresting view of the Golden Horn – it takes about twenty minutes from Eyüp Camii to reach the romantic **Pierre Loti Café** (daily 8am–midnight) made famous by the autobiographical novel of French officer-cum-author Pierre Loti (see p.312). The café has fine views over the Golden Horn and waiters in Ottoman costume serve up Turkish coffee.

If you've walked enough, there's a twin-cabin **cable car** (signed Telefrik in Turkish) linking the shores of the Golden Horn with the top of the hill (daily 8am–11pm; 2TL each way, or use your İstanbulkart). The cable-car lies some four-hundred metres north of the Eyüp ferry terminal.

VIEW TOWARDS THE OLD CITY FROM THE GALATA TOWER

Galata and the waterfront districts

Galata lies across the great curving inlet of the Golden Horn from the old city. In the late Byzantine period this district was a semi-independent Genoese colony and the great fortification-cum-look-out erected by the mercantile Italians, the Galata Tower, remains an İstanbul landmark. Today, the area is very much a part of vibrant, go-ahead İstanbul, as over the last decade or so the city's nightlife, shopping and arts scene, once centred on Beyoğlu's (see p.198) busy İstiklal Caddesi has spilled down the steep hillside into Galata. Nomenclature hereabouts is a little confusing, as sometimes Galata is seen merely as a part of the much bigger and vaguely defined area of Beyoğlu, but more confusingly is officially known in Turkish as Karaköy (literally "Black Village").

For the purposes of the description in this guide, the area comprising the waterfront between the Atatürk Bridge to the west and Kılıç Ali Paşa Camii to the east and bounded to the north by a line formed by Bankalar and Kemeraltı *caddesi* is Karaköy. North of this line, to the Tünel entrance at the southern end of İstiklal Caddesi, is Galata. The area around the **Galata Tower**, neglected and run-down for decades, is rapidly developing into a trendy, bohemian quarter, with a rash of arts and music venues, galleries, boutique hotels, cafés and bars springing up – plus a panoply of street art adorning shop-shutters and likely looking walls. It's worth strolling along the banking street of Bankalar Caddesi, admiring the intriguing Art Nouveau-style **Kamondo Steps** and watching the dervishes whirl at the **Galata Mevlevihanesi**. Also of interest is the **Arap Camii**, a large mosque converted from a fourteenth-century Catholic church.

Karaköy served as a port for both the Byzantines and the Ottomans, when it was enclosed within the walls of the Castle of Galata. The shipping industry has declined but massive cruise-ships dock a few hundred metres east of the Galata Bridge, ferries ply across to Asia from the terminal a little nearer to the bridge, and a number of private ferries run from a dock just west of it. Apart from the fine nineteenth-century commercial buildings, look out for the **Jewish Museum**, once the Zülfaris Synagogue, and the **Yeraltı Camii**.

Northeast from Karköy, parallel to the waterfront, is **Tophane**, a district that once housed an Ottoman cannon foundry. Two late-Ottoman-era mosques, the **Kılıç Ali Paşa** and **Nusretiye** camiis, are worth seeing, though the trendy **İstanbul Modern** gallery, superbly set on the Bosphorus waterfront, is the major draw.

Head west and north along the shore of the Golden Horn from Galata and things soon change, with run-down factories, off-limits military installations and neglected apartment blocks the order of the day. But even here urban regeneration is in full swing and, if you're looking for a break from the city's Byzantine and Ottoman past, there are three key sights spread along the Horn: the excellent **Rahmi M. Koç Industrial Museum**, with exhibits ranging from a penny farthing to a submarine; kids' favourite **Miniatürk**, with over a hundred scale models of Turkey's most famous sites; and the über-cool **Santralıstanbul**, an exhibition/museum/performance area centred on a refurbished power station on the campus of Bilgi University.

GETTING THERE AND AROUND

Arrival Visitors coming from the old city usually cross the Galata Bridge on foot (quite an experience) or ride the T1 tram across it and alight at the Karaköy stop.

Getting around The area is compact enough to enjoy on foot from here, though if you're heading for the İstanbul Modern it's worth riding the tram one stop on to Tophane or, to avoid the steep hill, you can ride the historic funicular, Tünel (see p.27), to the top and walk down in a few minutes to the Galata Tower.

Some history

During the early centuries of Ottoman rule, many Spanish Jews, Moorish traders, Greeks and Armenians settled in **Galata**, which became established as the city's **European quarter**. In time, foreign powers set up their embassies in the area, and it became a popular haunt of visiting merchants, traders, seamen and adventurers. The nightlife of the quarter was notoriously riotous even in the seventeenth century, when the Ottoman traveller Evliya Çelebi wrote "Whoever says Galata says taverns." Galata's development was hampered by the steep hill it is built on, and by the nineteenth century neighbouring Beyoğlu, on flatter land at the top of the hill, had superseded it as the location of choice for the city's European or Europeanized elite.

Galata

The fascinating district of **Galata** is dominated by the famous Galata Tower, but there's much else to see. Be prepared to explore it on foot though, as the narrow,

GALATA AND THE WATERFRONT DISTRICTS

BARS
Enginar	1
Ritim Galata	4

CLUBS & LIVE MUSIC
Atolye Kulebdibi	2
Nardis Jazz Club	3

ACCOMMODATION
Anemon Galata	5
Eklektik Guest House	1
Galata Life	2
Galata Residence	8
Rapunzel Guesthouse	6
Şimşek Han Apartment	7
Sumo Cat Hostel	4
World House Hostel	3

● RESTAURANTS
Fasuli	2
Galata House Restaurant	8
Galata Konak Patisserie	7
Güney	3
Istanbul Modern Café	4
Karaköy Güllüoğlu	10
Maya	9
Molly's Café	5
Roman's Culture Café	1
Tarihi Karaköy Balık Lokantası	11
Wisteria	6

● SHOPS
ArtEna	7
Berrin Akyuz	9
Binbavul Vintage	5
Crash	4
Dore Müzik	3
Felt in Love	8
Hammam	6
Lale Plak	1
Müzik Center	2

steep streets are impractical for public transport (except for the underground funicular, Tünel). Bankalar Caddesi (shown by its old name of Voyvoda Caddesi on some maps), reached by walking up the hill from the north end of the Galata Bridge along Karaköy Caddesi, is lined with superb nineteenth-century buildings that once housed (as the name "Bankalar" suggests) the city's major banks. Occupying a corner plot at the end of this street is a beautifully restored building, the **Minerva Han**, dating to 1911. The beige facade is enlivened by panels of pale-blue tiles, while a couple of Neoclassical stone statues, in the form of cherubs holding baskets of fruit, surmount the entrance. Formerly the Greek Bank of Athens, the building is now an annexe of the Sabancı University.

Ottoman Bank Museum and around

Bankalar Cad 35, Karaköy

Voyvoda Caddesi, more commonly and appropriately known today as Bankalar Caddesi (Street of Banks), is home to the former head office of the Ottoman Bank, designed by renowned French architect Vallaury in 1890. In late 2011 the building became a part of the Garanti Bank's SALT contemporary arts project, complete with a public library, rooms dedicated to research, and an exhibition space. It also contains the fascinating **Ottoman Bank Museum**, which relates the story of the bank's history through to the 1930s, as well as housing archive material from places as diverse as Beyoğlu's Italian Consulate and the nearby Church of St Peter and St Paul.

Close to the museum and running up from Bankalar Caddesi towards the Galata Tower are the sculptural **Kamondo Steps**. Gracefully curving twin staircases, they were commissioned and paid for by the wealthy Jewish Kamondo family, and photographed by Henri Cartier-Bresson in the 1960s. Further west, on Yanık Kapı ("Burned Gate") Sokak, is the only remaining Genoese **city gate**. Somewhat the worse for wear, it still boasts a marble slab bearing the Cross of St George.

Arap Camii and the Church of St Peter and St Paul

Of the many churches that once crowded the steep, narrow streets of Galata, few original structures now remain. One notable exception is the unusual building on Galata Mahkemesi Sokak, now a mosque known as the **Arap Camii**. With its tall square tower and pyramidal roof, it was, under the Genoese, the largest church in Galata but was later converted into a mosque to serve the needs of the Moorish community that settled here in the early sixteenth century following their expulsion from Spain. It stands on one side of an attractive closed courtyard, decorated with assorted pieces of ancient marble.

Further up the hill, on Galata Külesi Sokak, the Dominican **Church of St Peter and St Paul** dates back to the fifteenth century though the current building, designed by the Fossati brothers (who were also responsible for the restoration of the Aya Sofya) only dates back to 1841. Mass is held every day at 7.30am and on Sundays at 11am.

British prison

Galata Külesi Sok 61

The stone-built **British prison**, dating back to 1904, is tucked away on a narrow street below the Galata Tower. Today it houses the *Galata House* restaurant-café (see p.188) and the friendly owners will happily show you graffiti left by former inmates, including a sketch of the Rock of Gibraltar and the poignant words, "An unfavourable wind has brought the ship of my life to this shore." Under the capitulations granted by the Ottomans, Western powers had the right to try their citizens under their own law, rather than the draconian Ottoman code, so consulates possessed their own courthouses and prisons.

6

The Galata Tower

Daily 9am–8pm • 11TL

Built in 1349 by the Genoese, the **Galata Külesi** sits on the site of a former tower constructed by Justinian in 528. Originally known as the Tower of Christ, it stood at the apex of the several sets of fortifications that surrounded the Genoese city-state. It has had a number of functions over the centuries, including as a jail, a fire tower and even a springboard for early adventurers attempting to fly.

At 61m high, the tower's **viewing gallery** – reached by elevator – offers magnificent panoramas of the city and views across the Sea of Marmara and the Golden Horn. The view of Eminönü is particularly spectacular from here: the boats that nudge in and out of the ferry terminal form a foreground to the skyline of Beyazit and Sultanahmet, with the Yeni Camii directly below Nuruosmaniye, the Spice Bazaar beneath Beyazit Camii and the Beyazit fire tower rising above the Rüstem Paşa Camii. It's best to get here when it opens at 9am for the best morning light, or evening when the sun is at its lowest and the views most photogenic, though from 5pm the crowds begin to gather and there are queues stretching around the plaza. There's also a café on the top floor offering predictably overpriced drinks and snacks.

The area around the base of the tower has recently been refurbished and is now a pleasant plaza area where locals and tourists alike sit and watch the world go by from a park bench or one of the cafés opening onto the square.

The Galata Mevlevihanesi

Galipdede Caddesi • Daily except Tues 9.30am–5pm • 5TL • *Sema* dances second and last Sun of the month May–Sept 5pm, Oct–April 3pm

An unassuming doorway on Galipdede Caddesi (on the left if heading from the tower) leads to the courtyard of the **Galata Mevlevihanesi**, also referred to as the Divan Literature Museum. A former *tekke* (monastery) containing a *semahane* (ceremonial hall) of the whirling dervishes, the building now serves as a museum to the Mevlevi Sufi sect. Constructed in the late fifteenth century, this is the oldest surviving dervish monastery in İstanbul, though it has been rebuilt several times. It was closed for restoration at the time of writing, and it's uncertain what will be on display when it reopens, though hopefully the musical instruments that provided the sounds the dervishes whirled to will be back in place.

The Mevlevi Sufi order is one of the many mystical sects of Islam that were once rife across Anatolia, and were banned by Atatürk because of their supposed political affiliations and religious conservatism. The founder of the sect, Mevlana, was an iconclast who, in the thirteenth century, repudiated the strictures and hypocrisy of mainstream Sunni Islam. He preached love, charity and tolerance, and believed that

---

A CLASH OF CYMBALS, NOT CULTURES

İstanbul is often stereotyped as a place where the Christian West conflicts with the Islamic East. But clashes of a very different nature frequently take place on the city's "**Music Alley**" (Galipdede Caddesi; see p.222) – those of eager would-be buyers crash-testing a pair of cymbals. **Zildjian**, one of the best-known cymbal manufacturers in the world, originated back in 1618 when Armenian alchemist Avedis Zildjian, while seeking a way to turn base metals into gold, discovered the perfect metal to produce the perfect sound – an alloy of copper, silver and tin. The business prospered in the Ottoman centuries, supplying cymbals to the military Mehter Band (see p.128). In 1928 a new factory was established in Massachusetts in the US, though the original İstanbul workshop continued until 1978. Still going concerns in the city, however, are İstanbul Agop (Ⓦ istanbulcymbals.com) and İstanbul Mehmet (Ⓦ istanbulmehmet .com.tr), both set up by former craftsmen from the Zildjian workshop. The handmade wares of these two companies predominate in the shops on "Music Alley". Ironically, the Zildjian cymbals stocked by a few shops here are imported from the US.

union with God was possible through contemplation, meditation, dance and music (hence the "whirling" ceremonies the disciples engage in).

The whirling dervishes perform *sema* dances to Sufi music on the second and last Sunday of every month, with the main ceremony on December 17, the annual Mevlana holiday – though following restoration, this may be subject to change.

Karaköy

The port area of **Karaköy** is beginning to lose some – though not all – of its rough-and-ready character. Just west of the **Galata Bridge**, the vital link between the two sides of European İstanbul (see pp.147–153), is a small dock from where Türyol ferries run across the Golden Horn to Eminönü and across the Bosphorus to Üsküdar, Haydarpaşa and Kadıköy.

Karaköy's **port**, originally a Byzantine, then Ottoman shipyard, was once enclosed within the walls of the Castle of Galata and, from 1446 until the fall of the Byzantine city to the Ottomans in 1453, was further protected by a great chain stretched across the mouth of the Horn to prevent enemy ships from entering (see p.285). The waterfront west of the Galata Bridge is generally a run-down area of ships' chandlers (where you can purchase anchors and chains) and a few basic restaurants specializing in grilled fish and *köfte*. The views across to Eminönü are impressive, though it's an area best avoided at night. Things get smarter on the east side of the bridge, with a mix of good and distinctly average waterfront restaurants. Front-of-house hustlers abound, as this is where the cruise-ship passengers disembark after docking at the modernist Karaköy terminal, recognizable by its distinctive airport conning-style tower.

GETTING AROUND	**KARAKÖY**

Funicular Just inland from Galata Bridge is the Tünel underground funicular (see p.27), which will whisk you up to İstiklal Caddesi; the Tünel entrance is on Tersane Caddesi, just to the left of the first road junction beyond the bridge.

Azaz Kapı Camii

Atatürk Köprüsü yanı

The single most interesting sight in Karaköy is the **Azaz Kapı Camii**, situated below the level of traffic-choked Atatürk Bridge, a fine Sinan mosque, completed in 1578. Its style is reminiscent of the great Süleymaniye Camii, another Sinan masterpiece across the Golden Horn in the old city (see p.81), but on a much smaller scale. At its entrance is an ornate marble *sebil* (fountain) built in the Baroque style in 1733 for Valide Sultan Saliha Hatun, mother of Sultan Mahmut I.

Yeraltı Camii

Kemankeş Caddesi

Originally constructed around 580, the subterranean keep of the long-gone Castle of Galata is thought to be what is now the **Yeraltı Camii**, or "Underground Mosque". Inside is a forest of thick columns, supporting a low, vaulted ceiling. Two tombs in one corner purport to be those of Muslim martyrs killed in the first Arab siege of Byzantium (674–678 AD).

Turkish Orthodox Church of Panghia

There are a number of nineteenth-century churches lurking in streets behind the quay, including one belonging to the tiny **Turkish Orthodox Church of Panghia**, which split from the Greek Orthodox Patriarchate in Fener in 1921, when invading Greek forces were striving to wrest control of western Anatolia. The church has found itself embroiled in the Ergenekon gang case (see p.299) and has been accused of being a focal point for ultranationalist activities.

The Jewish Museum
Mon–Thurs 10am–4pm, Fri & Sun 10am–2pm • 10TL

The Ottoman Empire was long a safe haven for Jews fleeing persecution, pogroms and massacres in Christian Europe. They formed a very sizeable minority in the city and many prospered, taking advantage of Muslim strictures against usury and the Ottoman gentlemen's disdain of trade and playing a significant role in bringing prosperity to Galata and its environs. The origins of the Zülfaris Synagogue on Meydanı Perçemli Sokak, which houses the **Jewish Museum**, can be traced back to 1671, though the present building was erected in the nineteenth century. It was founded to celebrate the 500th anniversary of the arrival of the Jews following their expulsion from Spain and contains a small but fascinating amount of material, much of it donated by local Jewish families such as the Kamondos.

Although the ethnography section of the museum is interesting enough, with the expected display of torah, menorah, traditional costume and the like, it is the collection of photographs (and accompanying storyboards) outlining the successful relationship between Jews and Turks over the centuries that commands attention. Unlike the Ottoman Christian minorities, the Jews never agitated for their own state, and in 1920 there were Jewish deputies in the fledgling Republic's National Assembly. In 1933, Atatürk invited Jewish academics from Nazi Germany to help his modernization programme, thus saving them from almost certain death. The upstairs gallery shows Laurence Satzmann's photo documentary *Travels in Search of Turkey's Jews* and its accompanying film exploring the Sephardic Jewish population in mid-1980s Turkey.

Tophane

Approached from Karaköy along Kemeraltı Caddesi (a waterfront stroll may look an attractive option on a map but is, in practice, impossible) and a steep half-kilometre downhill from İstiklal Caddesi, **Tophane** is a mixed area of run-down dockland dotted with venerable Ottoman buildings.

Kılıç Ali Paşa Camii
Necatibey Caddesi

The most notable of Tophane's Ottoman buildings is the **Kılıç Ali Paşa Camii**, an attractive mosque dating from 1580, designed by the doyen of Ottoman architects, Sinan, towards the end of his life. Based on the Aya Sofya (see p.43), it was built to honour a former Italian slave who, when freed, became both an admiral and a Muslim and was the only Ottoman admiral to come up smelling of roses after their disastrous defeat in the Battle of Lepanto in 1571. Appropriately for a naval man, Kılıç Ali Paşa's mosque was placed on the banks of the Bosphorus. Though somewhat gloomy, the interior of the mosque is enlivened by a number of colourful stained-glass windows with arabesque designs. Originally part of a *külliye* complex, the octagonal tomb of the admiral stands in the small garden behind the mosque.

İstanbul Modern
Meclis-i Mebusan Caddesi • Tues–Sun 10am–6pm • 14TL; free Thurs 10am–8pm • ⓦ istanbulmodern.org • From Sultanahmet, take the T1 tramway to the Tophane stop just west of Nusretiye Camii, from where it's a three-minute walk

Tophane is home to the city's contemporary art collection, **İstanbul Modern**, set in a stylish revamped warehouse on the edge of the Bosphorus, just in front of the Nusretiye Camii and the *nargile* cafés. The museum's interior is all big, blank white walls and an exposed ventilation system, with views across the Bosphorus to the Topkapı Palace. A permanent exhibition in the upstairs gallery, to the right of the entrance, entitled "Modern Experiences – From Ottoman Empire to Turkish Republic", outlines the development of modern Turkish art and places it in its historical and social context. Beginning with the adoption of Western styles in the Tanzimat (reform) period between 1839 and 1876 (mainly formal oils) it moves on to showcase the twin strands of art in the early Republic – state-sponsored "heroic realism" and the private artists influenced by modern Western art movements. A section entitled "War and Art" deals mainly with the emerging Republic's struggle with the West in the War of Independence, another showcases the abstract art that began to influence Turkish painters from the 1950s. Also on this floor are an expensive but well-regarded **café-restaurant** (see p.183) with a terrace right on the edge of the Bosphorus, and a gift shop selling books, posters and tasteful souvenirs. Downstairs, there's a reference library, a cinema showing arts and independent films, plus plenty of space for the temporary exhibitions – an intriguing range of photographic and installation art by mainly Turkish artists – and an outside sculpture garden.

Up the Golden Horn

North along the shore of the Golden Horn from Beyoğlu and Karaköy lies the poor neighbourhood of **Kasımpaşa**. This industrial dockland area has the dubious distinction of being the cheapest property on the İstanbul Monopoly board. It is also the birthplace of Tayip Erdoğan, a working-class boy made good and now the charismatic if controversial leader of the ruling AKP (see p.298).

A couple of kilometres further up the Horn, **Hasköy** was for centuries a Jewish village, though most of İstanbul's approximately twenty thousand Jews have now moved further out of the city. It was also the location of an Ottoman naval shipyard and a royal park, which was cultivated as a fruit orchard throughout Ottoman rule and today is blessed with one unusual sight – the **Rahmi M. Koç Industrial Museum**.

Once a fetid stretch of virtually lifeless, polluted water (see box, p.70), the upper reaches of the Golden Horn have now been cleaned up. Fishermen now try their luck from the (shadeless) stretches of promenade that run along the water's edge – you can

NARGILE: HUBBLE-BUBBLE BUT NO TOIL OR TROUBLE

To most Westerners, the smoking device known (among other names) as the water pipe, hubble-bubble or hookah is associated with the hashish-toking counterculture of the 1960s. Either that or images of indolent, turbaned Muslims puffing away in some Eastern bazaar conjured up by romantic Orientalist painters such as Delacroix. In today's İstanbul, however, the **nargile** (as the water pipe is known here) is part and parcel of everyday life for an increasing number of Turks. After decades of declining popularity, *nargile* smoking is undergoing a major resurgence – mainly among the young, the affluent and students. *Nargile* cafés are booming, some decked out in faux-Ottoman style, others über-contemporary, and the largest concentration is in Tophane, right behind the Nusretiye Camii and en route to the İstanbul Modern.

The *nargile* first became popular in İstanbul in the seventeenth century, having spread there from India via Iran and Arabia. The spoilsport sultan of the time, Murat IV, leant on by the religious authorities, prohibited its use, but to no avail – *nargile* smoking became a popular (though male-only) pursuit and really only began to lose its popularity with the advent of the Turkish Republic, when all things Ottoman were deemed old-fashioned and reactionary.

In Ottoman times, opium was often the smoker's preference; today, it is strictly tobacco – albeit the strong stuff – and arguments rage in Turkey over which is more harmful, cigarette or *nargile*. Although *nargile* pipes are popular tourist buys, *nargile* smoking is very much a Turkish thing to do, and you may find it rather intimidating to try one for the first time surrounded by local "old hands". Don't be put off, though – the whole point of *nargile* cafés is for people to come together, loll around on floor cushions and smoke, chat and chill.

follow this from the model mania that is **Miniatürk**, in the district of **Sütlüce**, to the trendy **Santralıstanbul** cultural centre, a twenty-minute walk away to the north.

Rahmi M. Koç Industrial Museum

Hasköy Cad 27 • Tues–Fri 10am–5pm, Sat & Sun Oct 1–March 31 10am–6pm, April 1–Sept 30 10am–8pm • 12.50TL • ⦿ rmk-museum
.org.tr • Catch bus #47 from Eminönü, on the opposite side of the Horn, or the #54/HT from Taksim; alternatively, the ferry that runs
between Eminönü and Eyüp stops at Hasköy ferry terminal, from where it is a short walk

İstanbul's only industrial museum, the **Rahmi M. Koç Müzesi** is a gem, and makes a welcome change from the standard Byzantine and Ottoman sights. Constructed in the eighteenth century as a factory for anchors and their chains, the museum's arching brickwork and spacious halls have been authentically restored. The work was completed by Rahmi M. Koç in 2001, one of Turkey's most famous – and wealthiest – industrialists, to house his private collection of models, machines, vehicles and toys, originating from all over Turkey and Europe but mainly from Britain. The best time to visit is Saturday afternoon, when there are special exhibitions based around a collection of slot machines, the old Kadiköy–Moda tram and the history of flight.

On the first floor, the starboard main engine of the *Kalender* steam ferry, made in Newcastle upon Tyne in 1911 and decommissioned in the 1980s, is the main exhibit – press a button and you can see its pistons move. On the ground floor are a number of old bikes, from penny-farthings to an early Royal Enfield motorbike complete with basket chair for side carriage. The model railway is disappointing in terms of moving parts; far better is the ship's bridge, reconstructed from a number of Turkish and British vessels of the 1920s to 1940s. All the instruments are explained in English, with sound effects and working parts, including an echo sounder, an early dimmer switch and a very loud alarm bell. The museum's ongoing projects include raising the Australian navy's first submarine, sunk off Gallipoli in World War I.

The other section of the museum, across the main road by the Golden Horn, contains a moored submarine (6TL, though the sub had been taken away for maintenance at the time of writing) and a section of train track complete with a tiny old station. There's also a street of period shops, from a chemist's complete with a set of old jars labe lled "poison" to a ship's chandler's. Boy racers will love the selection of carefully restored cars covering the sublime (a 1965 Rolls Royce Silver Cloud) to the ridiculous (a 1985 Trabant).

The museum hosts a number of temporary exhibitions, so it's worth checking their website before your visit.

Miniatürk

Imrahor Caddesi • May–Oct Mon–Fri 9am–7pm, Sat & Sun 9am–8pm; Nov–April daily 9am–9pm • 10TL • ⦿ www.miniaturk.com.tr •
Bus #47, #47/C or #47/E from Eminönü or the #54/HT from Taksim

On the north side of the monumental Haliç Bridge, in dull Sütlüce, is one of those attractions you'll either love or hate: **Miniatürk**. Although it's set more or less on the banks of the Golden Horn, you could be anywhere, as the attraction is entirely surrounded by a high fence. On display here are over a hundred 1:25 scale models of some of Turkey's most impressive sights, spaced out along a 1.8-kilometre signed route. Forty-five of them are of attractions in İstanbul – from the relatively obscure (Sirkeci Post Office) through to the most famous (the Blue Mosque) – another 45 cover sights in Anatolia, including the Library of Celsius at Ephesus and Atatürk's mausoleum, the Anıtkabir, in Ankara, and there are also fifteen from former Ottoman dominions. Not all of the well-detailed models are buildings – if you've ever wanted to see Cappadocia's fairy chimneys or the travertine cascades of Pamukkale in miniature, then this is the place to come. Miniatürk's **Zafer Müzesi** (Victory Museum) celebrates Atatürk's military successes at Gallipoli in 1915 (see p.263) and during the Turkish War of Independence. Of interest to youngsters will be the giant chess set, maze and play area to the right of the entrance.

Santralıstanbul

Kazımkarabekir Cad 2 • Energy Museum and gallery Tues–Fri 10am–6pm, Sat & Sun 10am–8pm • 10TL combined entry • Ⓦ santralistanbul.org • A free shuttle-bus runs to and from outside the AKM building on Taksim Square half-hourly from 8am until 8.30pm (20min), and the #47 runs between Eminönü and Santralİstanbul; after 9.30pm you'll be reliant on a taxi

Set in the attractively landscaped campus of Bilgi University, built on reclaimed industrial land, **Santralıstanbul** is a museum/gallery/entertainment complex that has become a striking symbol of the new İstanbul. In the daytime, the major point of interest is the **Museum of Energy**, housed, appropriately enough, in an old power station. Between 1914 and its closure in 1983, this plant, the Silahtaraua, was the only electricity generating station in İstanbul. The interior is now a successful mix of the carefully preserved innards of the power plant and high-tech wizardry. Best of all is the gigantic control room with its banks of dials, gauges, switches and AEG metres, like the cockpit of some *Flash Gordon*-style 1930s spaceship. A walkway leads around the lower level of the cavernous interior and you can look down on the massive Sieman's engines. There's a thermal-imaging screen where you can gauge the heat of different parts of your body, while monitors set in the floor under metal grilles give a potted history of plants. The only drawback is that the explanations are in Turkish only.

To the left of the entrance is the **Contemporary Arts Gallery**, a major gallery/exhibition space, which has hosted events ranging from retrospectives of contemporary Turkish art to the headscarf issue. There are a couple of trendy café-bars here too, including *Tamirane* (see p.201) and *Otto-Santral*, both of which have live music and DJ sets.

6

Beyoğlu, Taksim and around

Vibrant Beyoğlu, across the Golden Horn from the old city, is centred on manic İstiklal Caddesi (Independence Street). İstanbullus come here in droves to shop, wine and dine, take in a film, club or gig, visit a gallery or the theatre, or simply promenade, and ever more visitors are basing themselves in this lively area to make the most of the nightlife and culture. Historic shopping arcades and elegant Art-Nouveau apartment blocks pepper the nineteenth-century streets, and the Catholic church of St Mary Draperis and the grander Franciscan church of St Antoine, both on İstiklal Caddesi, are well worth a visit. Nearby is an impressive museum-cum-gallery, the Pera Müzesi, and the grand nineteenth-century *Pera Palas Hotel*, once favoured by gentry arriving on the *Orient Express*.

İstiklal Caddesi runs for 1.5km from the **Tünel**, the recently restored funicular railway (see p.27), to **Taksim Square**, the focal point of the city and a symbol of the secular Turkish Republic. The square is undeniably impressive in scale, but as an imitation of a grand Western plaza, it's not a great success, lacking the essential monumental architecture to balance its broad expanse and robbed of any real atmosphere by its confusing traffic system. North of Taksim Square are the upmarket residential suburbs of **Nişantaşı** and **Teşvikiye**. Once the hunting grounds of the Ottoman nobility, the area was given over to residential development in the nineteenth century and became the preserve of the monied elite – including the family of Nobel Prize-winning novelist **Orhan Pamuk** (see box, p.128), who once lived in Nişantaşı. Apart from the impressive **Military Museum** in Harbiye, there are no obvious sights here, but if you want to shop for designer-label goods in trendy boutiques, then this is the place to do it.

GETTING THERE AND AROUND

By tram From the old city you can reach Taksim by taking the T1 tram to Karaköy, followed by the Tünel to the southern end of İstiklal Caddesi and then rattling up to the monumental square on the antique tram. Alternatively, take the tram to Kabataş and the modern funicular up to Taksim.

Getting around Broad İstiklal Caddesi, which links Galata with Taksim Square, has a period tram running its entire length but both it, and the surrounding side-streets, are best explored on foot. From Taksim Square there are frequent buses north to Harbiye and Nisantaşı, including the #43, or for Nisantaşı/Teşvikiye take the M2 Metro to the Osmanbey stop.

Beyoğlu

In the Ottoman era, **Beyoğlu**, then known as Pera (Greek for "beyond" or "across") was, along with Galata, the **European quarter** of the city. Home to merchants, businessmen and diplomats, one of the joys of the district are its fine nineteenth-century, Parisian-style apartment blocks – a complete contrast to the wooden buildings in the largely Muslim quarters of the old city across the Golden Horn. The area was also very popular with the city's non-Muslim minorities and the names of Armenian and Greek architects adorn the fronts of some of İstiklal Caddesi's grander buildings. Growth here was encouraged by the completion of the *Orient Express* railway in 1899, bringing tourists to the area and resulting in the construction of many grand hotels, including the famous *Pera Palas Hotel* (see p.123). Beyoğlu continued to prosper into the early years of the twentieth century, with music halls, opera houses, inns, cinemas and restaurants all packed to the rafters.

Although the Greek minority escaped the population exchange of 1923 (see p.294), many soon began to drift away, a situation exacerbated by the wealth tax imposed on Turkey's minorities in World War II and the anti-Greek riots of the 1950s. Other minority groups such as the Armenians and Jews followed suit, and Beyoğlu began to lose both its cosmopolitanism and its prosperity – and became positively sleazy. The revival of the area began in the late 1980s, and, in 1990, the pedestrianization of **İstiklal Caddesi** and the reinstallation of the old tramway heralded the transformation of the area. Today, Beyoğlu's old cosmopolitan nature is reasserting itself, partly owing to the increased number of tourists; indeed, so many foreigners were snapping up the district's atmospheric apartments that by 2010 the ten percent quota of properties that non-Turkish nationals could own in the district had been reached.

İstiklal Caddesi and around

Known as the "Grand Rue de Pera" prior to the foundation of the Turkish Republic in 1923, **İstiklal Caddesi** (Independence Street) is the city's most exciting street – but there is far more to this heaving thoroughfare than shopping and entertainment. It was widened and straightened following a fire in 1870 that destroyed over three thousand buildings: to fully appreciate its unspoilt and (largely) late nineteenth- and early twentieth-century architectural delights, you need to keep your eyes up, above the level

BEYOĞLU, TAKSIM & AROUND

N

● RESTAURANTS

Andon	17
Antiochia	28
Bar Bahçe	21
Canım Çiğerim	26
Cezayir	25
Changa	13
Çokçok	20
Cumhuriyet Meyhanesi	15
Ficcin	23
Hacı Abdullah	8
Imroz	9
Kafe Ara	18
Kallavi Nargile Café	22
Kallavi Taverna	1
Kenan Üsta	3
Leb-i-Derya Richmond	29
Munzur	12
Nizam Pide	10
Nizam Pide 2	14
Nature and Peace	11
Otherside	4
Pasific	27
Patisserie Mektup	5
Pia	6
Refik	30
Rejans	19
Rocinante	7
Saray	16
Sugar Café	24
Suheyla	10
Zencefil	2

■ ACCOMMODATION

Büyük Londra Oteli	5
Cihangir	4
Devman	11
Levanten Hostel	14
Marmara Pera	7
Monopol	12
Pera Palas	8
Richmond	13
Silviya	10
Suite Home İstiklal Apt	1
Tomtom Suites	9
Triada Residence	2
Vardar Palace	3
Villa Zurich	6

■ BARS

5 Kat	23
360	20
Badehane	32
Büyük Londra Oteli	18
Café Smyrna	30
James Joyce Irish Pub	3
Kaktüs	2
KV	34
Leb-i-Derya	33
Mikla	29
Nu Teras	27
Pano Şaraphanesi	15
Parsifal	1
Ritim Bar	8
Sahra Bar	14

■ CLUBS & LIVE MUSIC

Babylon	31
Bahçe	24
Bigudi	13
Bronx Pi	28
Dogzstar	17
Ghetto	12
Gizli	7
Hayal Kahvesi	5
Indigo	19
Jazz Café	10
Jolly Joker Balans	9
Minimuzikhol	22
Mojo	11
Peyote	4
Pixie Underground	21
Riddim	6
Roxy	16
Salon IKSV	35
Tek Yön	25
X-Large	26

● SHOPS

Ada Books	17
Ambar	13
Bershka	19
Bis	8
By Retro (Suriye Pasajı)	18
Demirören Mall	3
Denizler Kitapevi	14
D & R Books	1
Eren	20
Homer	11
Leyla	12
Librairie de Pera	21
Mavi Jeans	6
Mor Takı	9
Mudo Pera	16
Müstamel Eşya Evi	10
OXXO	5
Pandora	2
Paşabahçe	15
Roll	7
Vakko	4

KURTULUŞ DERESİ CAD
SİRKET SOK
FELTİÇMA SOK
DİLBAZ SOK
ÖMER
KALYONCU KULLUĞU CAD
AKKİRAZ SOK
KURDELA SOK
HAYYAM
HARMAN SOK
BİLGİN SOK
SİMİTÇİ SOK
ATMAN SOK
KERAMET SOK
TAKSİM CAD
EMİN KAM SOK
AYNALI ÇEŞME CAD
ASLAN SOK
BOCEK SOK
SAMANCI FERHAT CAD
TARLABAŞI CAD
HAMALBAŞI CAD
BALIK SOK

Photography Centre

British Consulate

Aurup Pasa

Aznavur Pasajı

Hazzopulo Pasajı

Yapı Kredi Cultural Centre

Galerist

Misir Apartment

St Antoine

KASIMPAŞA

GENERAL ASIM GUNDUZ CAD

KARAYSI SOK
MEŞRUTİYET CAD
KALLAVİ SOK

Pera Museum

Beyoğlu Is Merkezi

Palais Hollan

TEPEBAŞI CAD
REFİK SAYDAM CAD

Kasımpaşa Stadium

TEPEBAŞIAKARCA SOK
TEPEBAŞI CAD
BALYOZ CAD

TERKOS CAD

Mudo

MELEZ SOK

Hasanpaşa Parkı

TALLIŞ SOK

REFİK SAYDAM CAD
KUYU SOK

Markiz (Art Nouveau Interior)

İSMALİMESCIT SOK
POSTA CILAR CAD
CİTE DE SYRİE

Arter (Gallery)

Borusan Arts Cultural Cent

Hasanpaşa Park

Kasımpaşa İskelesi

SHISHANE CAD
AMBARLISOL SOK
HUZUR SOK
EVLİYAÇELEBİ CAD
EKÜ MUSA SOK

SCHERIBER SOK

Art Nouveau Facades

İSTİKLAL SOK
SİMAL SOK
MEŞRUTİYET CAD

St Mary Draperis

Botter House

Tünel

Metro Entrance

Tünel (İstiklal)

G YAZGAN SOK

İstiklal Eczanesi (Chemists)

Galata Mevlevihanesi

TERSANE CAD
ANKHURUROSTAN SOK

Eminönü & Sultanahmet

Crimea Memori Church

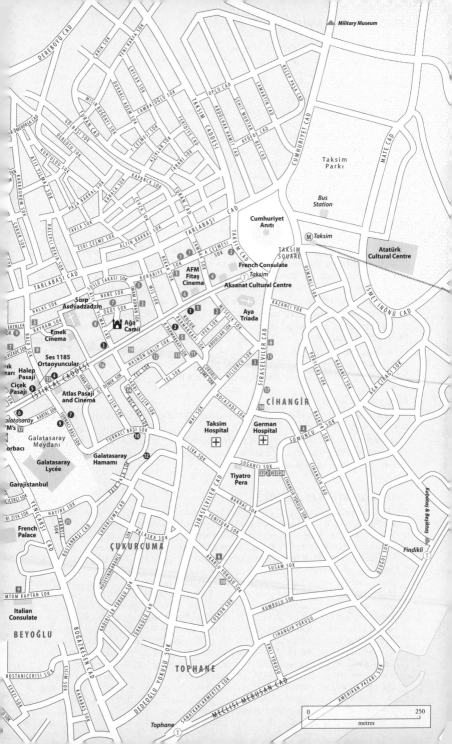

of the shops and eateries – which is easier said than done, given the number of milling shoppers, uneven paving stones, access vehicles and trams to contend with.

Crimean Memorial Church

Serden Ekrem Sokak • Service Sun from 9am

The incongruous Anglican **Crimean Memorial Church**, also known as Christ Church, was built in 1868 both to serve the city's British community and to remember the dead of the Crimean War. Designed by G.E. Street (the architect responsible for the Royal Courts of Justice in London), this fine church was constructed mainly with stone imported from Malta, and set in a walled compound-garden of chestnut, fig, oleander and palm. The compound is home to an Anglican chaplain; the best time to visit is during the Sunday service. Since 1991, over 2500 refugees from places as disparate as Nigeria and Sri Lanka have passed through here and they make up much of the congregation.

Botter House

457–477 İstiklal Cad

The first point of interest at the southern end of **İstiklal Caddesi** is the **Botter House**. Widely regarded as the finest building of its kind in the city, the apartment block boasts a stone facade decorated with stylized, relief-carved flowers and wrought-iron work executed in the "whiplash" style so typical of the curvilinear Art Nouveau movement. Commissioned in 1901 as a showroom, workshop and family house by Dutchman Jan Botter, tailor and couturier to Sultan Abdülhamid II, it is one of a number of structures around İstanbul designed by the Italian architect Raimondo D'Aronco. Unfortunately, the building is currently unoccupied and is in a disgraceful condition, with an ugly iron support beam, fly-posters and dusty, broken windows disfiguring its gorgeous exterior. There are plans, however, to turn it into a boutique hotel, which will at least salvage the gorgeous facade.

Asmalımescit Sokak

The many cafés, bars and restaurants of buzzing **Asmalımescit Sokak** and its ancillary alleys are virtually blocked by a plethora of tables, especially on weekend evenings, when the area is full of revellers. There are a couple of interesting **Art Nouveau facades** here, one fronting the Atlas Apartment building at Asmalımescit Sok 5/A, the other around the corner on Sofyalı Sok 5.

DIPLOMATIC RESIDENCES

The Turkish capital Ankara is now home to the country's major embassies, though this wasn't always the case. In the late Ottoman period, when İstanbul was the empire's capital, most foreign diplomats were based in palatial embassies on and around İstiklal Caddesi. Most still function as consulates and are some of the most attractive buildings in the district. The recently restored **Palais de Hollande** at İstiklal Cad 393 was built in 1858 on the site of the home of Cornelis Haga, the first Dutch diplomat in Constantinople during the fifteenth century. It now houses the Consulate to the Netherlands. Further along İstiklal Caddesi and off to the right on Nuri Ziya Sokak is the imposing **French Palace**, with its large central courtyard and formally laid-out gardens, the residence of ambassadors and consuls from 1831. Below the palace, on Tomtom Kaptan Sokak, stands the **Italian Consulate**, originally the Palazzo di Venezia, built in the seventeenth century and the earliest surviving diplomatic building in Beyoğlu. Casanova stayed here in 1744 and, according to his memoirs, didn't make a single conquest, although one İsmail Efendi claims to have been seduced by him. The **British Consulate**, a hundred metres or so north of İstiklal Caddesi on Hamalbaşı Caddesi, is the most impressive of all the consular buildings in Beyoğlu. Completed in 1855, it is set, following the 2003 terrorist attack that killed the then British Consul Roger Short, in a well-protected walled compound. It is a striking Renaissance-style structure, designed by Charles Barry, architect of the Houses of Parliament in Westminster, London.

St Mary Draperis

429 İstiklal Cad • Mon & Wed–Sat 10am–noon & 2–6pm, Tues & Sun 2–6pm • Mass Mon–Fri 8am, Sun 9am

The oldest church in the area, **St Mary Draperis** is set well below street level and reached by a steep flight of steps. Its origins on this site (the church was founded in the fifteenth century across the Golden Horn in Sirkeci) go back to 1678, but several fires over the centuries mean that the current building, designed by the Italian architect Semprini, dates only to 1904.

Patisserie Markiz

360–2 İstiklal Cad

The **Patisserie Markiz**, opposite St Mary Draperis (see above), boasts a beautiful Art-Nouveau interior. Pride of place is given to two faïence wall panels designed and executed in France, *Le Printemps* and *L'Automne*. Sadly the place is now a fast-food restaurant, but the listed interior is unchanged.

Pera Palas Hotel

Meşrutiyet Cad 52 • ☎ 0212/377 4000, ⓦ perapalace.com

For many of its well-heeled passengers, the palatial **Pera Palas Hotel** signified the real end of the line for the famous *Orient Express* (see box, p.8). Designed in the flamboyant Rococo style by the Turkish-French architect Alexander Vallaury and completed in 1892, this luxurious hotel ensured wealthy European visitors to the city enjoyed the levels of comfort they were accustomed to in London or Paris. Situated in the district of Pera (today's Beyoğlu), the European quarter of the city, the *Pera Palas* hosted an array of impressive and glamorous guests. The founder of the Turkish Republic, Kemal Atatürk, was a frequent visitor, and the room he used, 101, has been turned into a **museum** in his honour. Ernest Hemingway stayed here while reporting on the Turkish War of Independence in the early 1920s; actresses Zsa Zsa Gabor, Greta Garbo and Rita Hayworth brought a touch of Hollywood glamour, and the courtesan-turned-spy, Mata Hari, a frisson of decadent intrigue. Alfred Hitchcock checked into the *Pera Palas* when he was in İstanbul, while another master of suspense, Agatha Christie, was a regular guest and wrote part of *Murder on the Orient Express* in her favourite room, 411.

The hotel closed in 2006 and received a massive makeover before reopening in 2010 (see p.173); it has, rather inevitably, rocketed in price and lost some of its raffish charm. For a cheaper indulgence, head to the hotel's elegant ground-floor tea room, though it's not inexpensive – expect to pay 7TL for tea, and from 18TL for cake.

Pera Museum

Meşrutiyet Cad 25, Tepebaşı • Tues–Sat 10am–7pm & Sun noon–6pm • 10TL • ⓦ peramuzesi.org

By contrast to nearby Asmalımescit Sok (see opposite), the atmosphere on Meşrutiyet Caddesi, running parallel with İstiklal Caddesi to the south, is much more refined and businesslike. It is home to one of the city's premier galleries, the **Pera Museum** (Pera Müzesi), housed in a beautifully restored, late nineteenth-century building, once the prestigious Bristol Hotel. Most impressive of the permanent exhibits is a collection of European Orientalist paintings dating from the seventeenth to nineteenth centuries, including Osman Hamdi's *Tortoise Trainer*, which in 2004 the museum paid US$3.5 million to acquire. Other permanent exhibits include a collection of Anatolian weights and measures and a room devoted to ceramics (particularly tiles) from Küthaya. The museum also hosts major temporary exhibitions and has featured work from artists such as Joan Miró. Close-by is the legendary *Pera Palas Hotel* (see above).

St Antoine and around

İstiklal Caddesi • Daily 8am–7pm • Mass Sun 10am

The Franciscan **Church of St Antoine** is a fine example of red-brick neo-Gothic architecture, and the most visited church in the area. Originally founded in 1725 it was

HISTORIC ARCADES

Çiçek Pasajı (Flower Passage) is the most comprehensively restored of the many fine late nineteenth- and early twentieth-century arcades off İstiklal Caddesi. Originally known as the **Cité de Pera**, it takes its present name from the anti-Bolshevik Russian émigrés who set up flower shops in the arcade in the 1920s. Gradually, the flower shops were replaced by taverns, though the music and entertainment for these drinking dens was supplied courtesy of the same Russian émigrés. Today, it's home to a collection of attractive but rather overpriced and touristy restaurants.

In addition to Çiçek Pasajı, there are a number of other period arcades, which once housed primarily Armenian- and Greek-owned cafés, restaurants, shops and offices, dotted along the length of İstiklal Caddesi. The most southerly is **Suriye Pasajı**, once known as Cité de Syrie, an arcade with a fine facade designed by the Greek architect Bassiladis in 1908. Inside is the cornucopia-like vintage-clothes outlet By Retro (see p.220). Further north, near Galatasary tram stop, is the **Hazzopulo Pasajı**, dating from 1871; just beyond is the **Aznavur Pasajı** (1893), by the same Armenian architect responsible for the Mısır Apartment (see below). Reached from Sahne Sokak, just beyond Galatasaray Meydanı, the **Avrupa Pasajı** is one of the grandest arcades, with a barrel-vaulted roof and a line of Neoclassical statues; today, it's home to many gift shops. Just up from Çiçek Pasajı is **Halep (Aleppo) Pasajı**, housing a clutter of clothes and jewellery stores, the Ses 1185 theatre (see p.207) and a cinema. More or less opposite is **Atlas Pasajı** (1877), a beautiful four-storey arcade containing a decent cinema (see p.208) and a host of alternative-clothing stores (see p.220).

demolished to make way for a tramway at the beginning of the nineteenth century and rebuilt in 1913 by the İstanbul-born, Italian architect Mongeri. A shade further up on the right is the fine **Mısır Apartment**, built in 1910 by an Armenian architect, home to several art galleries (see p.207) and the trendy bar/restaurant *360* (see p.196).

Galatasaray Meydanı

The small square a little less than halfway along İstiklal Caddesi is known as **Galatasaray Meydanı** and is named after the famous school, the **Galatasaray Lycée**, set behind iron railings to the south of the square. The *lycée* was originally founded in the fifteenth century to complement the Palace School in the Topkapı Sarayı. The current school originated in 1868, when it was remodelled on French lines, though the building it is housed in dates back only to 1908. Many of Turkey's leading academics, politicians and civil servants were educated here. One of the by-products of the new, Western curriculum, was sport, and in 1905 the nation's leading football team, **Galatasaray** (see p.226), was born here. A small museum devoted to the club (Mon–Sat 9am–5pm; free) is now housed in the beautifully restored Neoclassical building opposite.

Aya Triada

İstiklal Caddesi

At the very end of İstiklal Caddesi, as it runs into Taksim Square, is the monumental Greek Orthodox Church of **Aya Triada**. Designed in 1880 by Vasili Ionnidi, it is built to a cruciform plan, with the main body of the church surmounted by a mighty dome. The interior is beautifully decorated, with the marble and gilt iconostasis particularly impressive. It's difficult to gain entry unless you coincide with a service, so Sunday mornings are the best bet.

Çukurcuma and Cihangir

Wander into the streets south and east of the most northerly section of İstiklal Caddesi and you immediately escape the hustle and bustle and enter a world of alternative-clothes stores and bric-a-brac shops. There are few genuine bargains to be had (unless you really know your stuff), but it's fun poking around. The best place to begin

CLOCKWISE FROM TOP TAKSIM SQUARE (P.126); BOTTER HOUSE (P.122); CHURCH OF ST ANTOINE (P.123)>

searching is **Turnacı Başı Sokak**, which is also home to the best *hamam* this side of the Golden Horn, the **Galatasaray Hamamı** (see p.228). The *hamam* underwent massive refurbishment in the 1960s, though it dates back to 1481. This neighbourhood is known as **Çukurcuma**, and although run-down at the moment, it looks certain to follow the lead of adjoining **Cihangir**, a trendy, arty district where well-heeled İstanbullus (and a growing number of foreigners) gaze down on the Bosphorus from stylish pavement cafés.

Taksim Square and around

Taksim Square takes its name from the low **stone reservoir** on its south side, constructed in 1732 to distribute water brought from the Belgrade Forest by aqueduct ("Taksim" in Turkish means "distribution"). It's a vast, open space with some park-like areas, but its main interest to visitors is as a travel-hub. From here buses and dolmuşes depart to various points of the city, it is a stop on the M2 Metro line to the northern suburbs and a modern funicular links it with the ferry terminal at Kabataş. A grandiose scheme fostered by the incumbent AKP government would see the whole area pedestrianized, all traffic go underground and the historic Topçu Barracks, demolished in 1940, rebuilt on their original location.

The monumental **Atatürk Kültür Merkezi** or **AKM**, to the east of the square, was one of the leading venues for İstanbul's various international festivals, and home to the State Opera and Ballet, the Symphony Orchestra and the State Theatre Company. Designed by architect Hayati Tabanioulu in 1956 it has, like so many concrete international-modern buildings, attracted a great deal of criticism, and at the time of writing it was closed, its future uncertain.

Military Museum

Valikonağı Caddesi, Harbiye • Wed–Sun 9am–5pm • 4TL • To get there, walk north along Cumhuriyet Caddesi from Taksim Square for fifteen minutes, or take the M2 Metro to Osmanbey

The **Military Museum** (Asker Müzesi), housed in the military academy where Atatürk (see p.294) received some of his education, is well worth visiting. The first objects of interest, in the pleasant garden area, include a massive nineteenth-century Krupp

---

TROUBLED TIMES IN TAKSIM SQUARE

Taksim Square's central location and scale make it ideal for **mass gatherings** and subsequent expressions of public feeling. The official Republic Day rallies held to celebrate important dates in Turkey's history (see p.294) convene here, as do hordes of chanting football fans following matches involving the national team or one of the city's big three club sides. On New Year's Eve, the plaza is thronged with revellers.

But when it comes to **political protests**, Taksim Square, a focus for left-wing and trade-union protests since the 1950s, has a bloody and violent history. In February 1969, over thirty thousand leftists, angry at Turkey's pro-American policies, marched on the square. Violence erupted when they were met by roving gangs of right-wing agitators, who allegedly attacked the demonstrators with knives and batons, resulting in the deaths of two protestors and the wounding of 150 more – an event now known as "**Bloody Sunday**". Worse was to come on May 1, 1977 when, during a Labour Day demonstration that attracted around half a million people, 36 of the predominantly left-wing demonstrators were killed. As in 1969, the perpetrators were allegedly right-wing extremists – shooting into the crowd from the roof of the *Intercontinental* (now the *Marmara*) *Hotel* and other buildings around the square – though no one was ever brought to justice for the attack.

Political and trade-union demonstrations were banned here for many years before the government finally relented in 2010, and the May 1 Labour Day demonstration that year passed without any major incidents.

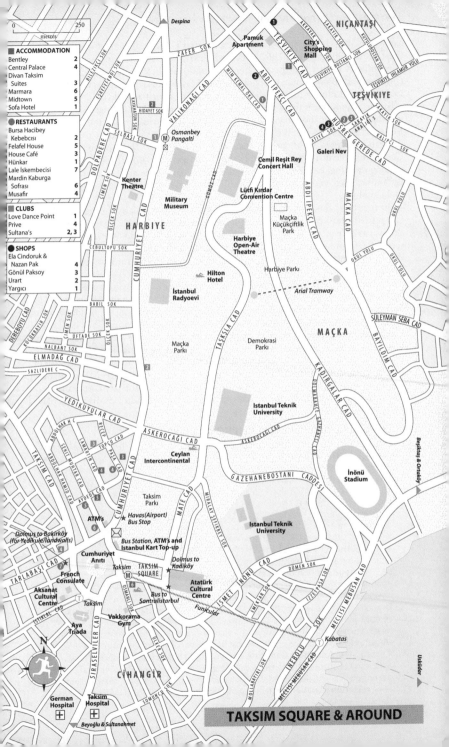

cannon used in the Gallipoli campaign, a Russian T-26B tank, one of the first used by the Turkish military, and a 1962 Lockheed CF-104 jet. The Turks take intense pride in their military history and there's a huge amount to see here in the labyrinthine maze of corridors and rooms, much of it housed in old-fashioned dark wood, glass-fronted cabinets – and most exhibits are labelled in English as well as Turkish.

The first room traces the origins of the Turks in Central Asia, the second has a wonderfully heroic diorama of the great Selçuk Turkish victory over the Byzantines at Malazgirt in 1071, while the third is devoted to the rise of the Ottomans, and includes the standard raised at the crucial Battle of Kosovo in 1389. The capture of Constantinople in 1453 is covered in the "Conquest of İstanbul" room, with another striking diorama. Near here, in an untidy pile, is part of the great chain which the Byzantines used so successfully for centuries to bar enemy ships from entering the Golden Horn.

The first floor concentrates largely on World War I, particularly the 1915 Gallipoli (see pp.261–266) campaign which is seen by Turks, quite rightly, as crucial to their survival as a sovereign power. The usual paraphernalia of World War I battles can be seen here, from heavy machine guns to canteens, medals to map cases. Also on the first floor is the **Mehter Band** (see box, p.128), which performs for museum visitors from Wednesday to Sunday (3–4pm).

Originating in 1289, **Mehter Band** members were janissaries who accompanied the sultan into battle. The band became an institution, symbolizing the power and independence of the Ottoman Empire. During public performances, band members sang songs about their hero ancestors and Ottoman battle victories. They had considerable influence in Europe, helping create new musical styles, such as the Spanish *a la turca*, and inspiring numerous composers (examples include Mozart's *Marcia Turca* and Beethoven's *Ruinen von Athens, Opus 113*). The kettledrum, *kös* in Turkish, was also introduced to the West as a result of interest in the Mehter Band. The band was abolished by Mahmut II in 1826, along with the janissary corps, and only re-established in 1914, when new instruments were added. Some of the pieces played

---

ORHAN PAMUK: UNLIKELY HERO OF CONSCIENCE

Most Turks just don't know what to make of their nation's first Nobel Prize-winner, Nişantaşı-born novelist **Orhan Pamuk**. To the liberal left, he's a talented writer who dares to challenge the Kemalist, nationalist-orientated establishment – who in turn accuse him of betraying his country. Moderates are happy to bask in the success of one of their nation's sons without questioning his beliefs too closely; many others are quick to condemn him whilst studiously avoiding actually reading any of his output.

The **controversy** surrounding Pamuk began in 2004, when the previously cautious novelist granted an interview to a Swiss newspaper and was reported as saying "I am the only one willing to say that one million Armenians and thirty thousand Kurds were murdered in Turkey". He was accused of "insulting Turkishness", a crime under article 301 of the Turkish Constitution. Although the accusation was subsequently dropped, in 2008 it emerged that Pamuk may have been the **assassination target** of an ultra-nationalist "deep-state" gang working within the establishment. As a result, he now spends most of his time abroad.

What is surprising is that such a storm has broken over the head of this benign-looking, fifty-something intellectual born into a wealthy family in respectable **Nişantaşı**. An urbane, cerebral author, his early works dealt with cultural and philosophical rather than political issues, and it wasn't until 2004's *Snow* that Pamuk engaged in any kind of political discourse. Many Turkish cynics, however, believe that by bringing up two of the nations "sacred cows" – the so-called **Armenian Genocide** and the "**Kurdish problem**" – in an interview with a European newspaper, he was deliberately courting what they saw as the anti-Turkish West in the hope of winning the Nobel Prize. Such machinations by Pamuk are unlikely, although his open rejection of nationalism in a country still in nation-building mode makes him an object of suspicion.

by today's band date back to the seventeenth and eighteenth centuries, others were written by Giuseppi Donizetti for Mahmut II's new army.

Nisantaşı and Teşvikiye

The area that today comprises the wealthy suburbs of **Nisantaşı** and **Teşvikiye**, a kilometre or so north of Taksim Square, was once the hunting grounds of the Ottoman nobility. The name Nişantaşı, or "target stone", derives from the custom of Ottoman soldiers setting up specially shaped stones to use for target practice here. The area began to be developed residentially in the nineteenth century and it soon became the preserve of the moneyed elite – including the family of Nobel Prize-winning novelist **Orhan Pamuk** (see box opposite), who once lived in Nisantaşı. There are no obvious sights here, but the City's Mall (see p.223) has some of İstanbul's most elite stores under one air-conditioned roof, and around it are a number of pleasant streets lined with fine, early twentieth-century apartments whose ground-floor shops boast equally exclusive outlets.

7

Beşiktaş and Ortaköy

Beşiktaş and Ortaköy, the two suburbs fronting the Bosphorus between the tram terminus at Kabataş and the Bosphorus Bridge, are firmly part of the city, despite Ortaköy's former status as a village. Beşiktaş boasted its own royal palace, a hippodrome and an important church (all now long gone) in the Byzantine era and developed into a major port under Ottoman rule; it remains an important ferry terminal today and is the first stop on the famous Bosphorus Cruise (see box, p.147). The area's real draw though, is its clutch of late nineteenth-century palaces and pavilions overlooking the strait – ornate, European-style residences for the last sultans of the decaying Ottoman Empire.

Palaces aside, until recently it was a little run-down, much frequented by students (Beşiktaş has the highest number of universities per square kilometre in the country) and other impecunious types, but the area's character is beginning to change, with a former tobacco warehouse being converted into a luxury hotel and a row of nineteenth-century houses transformed into a designer shopping street. **Ortaköy**, or the "Middle Village", a little further up the Bosphorus, with its picturesque setting on the waterfront, is crammed with upmarket cafés and bars packed with affluent young İstanbullus. The "village" is sandwiched between the horribly busy main coast road and the pretty waterfront, itself dominated by a splendidly ornate Ottoman Baroque mosque and the gigantic, yet sleek, bulk of the Bosphorus suspension bridge.

Beşiktaş

Northeast of Taksim Square, along the Bosphorus, the busy suburb of **Beşiktaş** is one of the best-served transport hubs in the city. Concrete shopping centres and a sprawling fruit-and-vegetable market cluster around the main shore road and ferry terminal, in front of which stands the bus station. Most visitors are here to see the **Dolmabahçe Palace**, successor to Topkapı as the residence of the Ottoman sultans. However, it's worth spending a few more hours in the neighbourhood if you can, to visit the city's excellent **Maritime Museum**, as well as leafy **Yıldız Parkı** and the **Çırağan Palace**. It's also home to one of İstanbul's three major football teams (see p.226).

GETTING THERE

BEŞIKTAŞ

By bus To get here by bus, take #25/T or #40 from Taksim.

By tram and funicular The T1 tram from Sultanahmet and Eminönü runs as far as Kabataş, as does the funicular down from Taksim Square, from where it's a little under 1km to the Dolmabahçe Palace.

By ferry Ferries run to and from the Asian side, to Kadıköy and Üsküdar (2TL).

The Dolmabahçe Palace

Dolmabahçe Caddesi • Tues, Wed & Fri–Sun: Nov–March 8.30am–4pm; April–Oct 8.30am–5pm • Selamlik/administrative section 15TL, Harem 10TL, combined ticket 20TL (no combined tickets sold after 3pm) • No cameras allowed inside

The **Dolmabahçe Sarayı** is the largest and most extravagant of all the palaces on the Bosphorus, with an impressive six-hundred-metre-long waterside frontage. Flanked by symmetrical flower-lined gardens with a magnificent clover-shaped pond and fountain at its heart, the exterior of the palace is arguably more beautiful than the interior, although if ostentatious displays of wealth and fittings dripping with gold are to your taste, you may disagree. Built in the mid-nineteenth century by Armenian architect Karabet Balian and his son Nikoğos, the palace's brazen riches suggest that good taste suffered along with the fortunes of the Ottoman Empire. The modern European stylings opt for flamboyance over flair, with crystal-lined staircases and chandeliers, dazzling upholstery and such profuse lashings of gold that the effect is a virtual assault on the senses. Indeed, critics see the palace's wholesale adoption of Western architectural forms as a last-ditch effort to muster some respect for a crumbling and defeated empire.

With groups of up to fifty people ushered through at a rapid pace, the tour experience (see p.133) is more akin to herding cattle, and the friendly, multilingual guides spend the majority of their time dealing with crowd control while dealing out choice snippets of information about the key rooms.

The first half of the tour consists of shuffling down corridors, sneaking a peek into the cordoned-off rooms and trundling single-file through exhibition rooms displaying semi-interesting collections of delicate tea cups and ornate household items. Thankfully, the second floor holds a few more impressive highlights – the **Sultan's reception room** is a Venetian-style boudoir with an outrageously decadent gold-plated ceiling; the antiquated **Abdul Medjid Library** offers an intriguing glimpse into the past

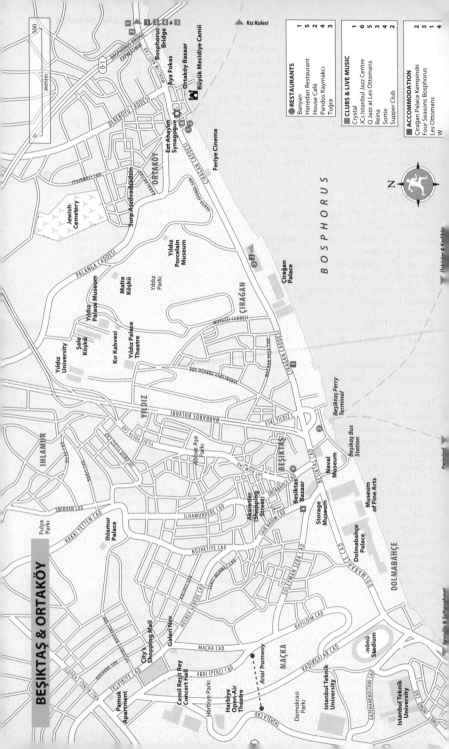

BEŞİKTAŞ & ORTAKÖY

RESTAURANTS

Banyan	1
Hanedan Restaurant	5
House Café	2
Pandos Kaymakcı	4
Tugra	3

CLUBS & LIVE MUSIC

Crystal	1
JCs Istanbul Jazz Centre	6
Q Jazz at Les Ottomans	5
Reina	3
Sortie	4
Supper Club	2

ACCOMMODATION

Çirağan Palace Kempinski	2
Four Seasons Bosphorus	3
Les Ottomans	1
W	4

Kız Kulesi

BOSPHORUS

N

Bosphorus Bridge

Ortaköy Bazaar

Aya Fokas

Büyük Mecidiye Camii

Est Ahayim Synagogue

Feriye Cinema

ORTAKÖY

Jewish Cemetery

Surp Asdvadzadzin

Yıldız Porcelain Museum

Malta Köşkü

Yıldız Parkı

Çirağan Palace

ÇİRAĞAN

Yıldız Palace Museum

Şale Köşkü

Yıldız University

Kır Kahvesi

Yıldız Palace Theatre

YILDIZ

Beşiktaş Ferry Terminal

Beşiktaş Bus Station

Abbas Ağa Parkı

BEŞİKTAŞ

Naval Museum

Beşiktaş Bazaar

Akaretler (Shopping Street)

Ihlamur Palace

İHLAMUR

Storage Museum

Museum of Fine Arts

Dolmabahçe Palace

DOLMABAHÇE

Fulya Parkı

Galeri New

City's Shopping Mall

Pamuk Apartment

Cemil Reşit Rey Concert Hall

Harbiye Open-Air Theatre

Harbiye Parkı

Demokrasi Parkı

Aria Tramway

MAÇKA

İnönü Stadium

Istanbul Teknik University

Istanbul Teknik University

500 metres

and the *hamam* and bathing quarters feature possibly the world's most luxurious squat toilet, made of exquisite marble. In the dining hall, the handmade parquet floors – an intricate puzzle design carved from ebony, rosewood and mahogany – are an incongruously delicate masterpiece hidden beneath the fancy furnishings.

The masterful 36-metre-high **ceremonial hall** (double the height of the rest of the rooms), held up by 56 elaborate columns, is the crown jewel of the tour and its centrepiece, a 4.5-tonne crystal chandelier glittering with 664 bulbs, is one of the largest ever made – a lavish present from Queen Victoria. The grand dome and pillars are actually made of wood and painted to create a 3D illusion that gives the impression of sculpted marble, an effect employed throughout much of the palace's ceilings. The ceremonies conducted in this hall were accompanied by an orchestra playing European marches and watched by the women of the *harem* through the *kafes*, grilles behind which women were kept hidden even in the days of Westernization and reform.

The *harem* section, reached along the waterfront, provides little stylistic deviation from the main building; its main attraction is Atatürk's bedroom, where the founder of the Turkish Republic died in 1938. The room itself, with its enormous Turkish flag adorning the bed, is a little disappointing, but it's none-the-less one of the most popular rooms of the palace with Atatürk-loving Turkish visitors. The clock in the room is still set at 9.05 – the hour of his death.

INFORMATION   THE DOLMABAHÇE PALACE

Tickets and tours On entering the grounds the ticket booth is to the left of the main entrance where you are obliged to join a tour (approx 2hr 30min for the combined tour) of the administrative and/or *harem* section – keep your entrance ticket handy as you'll need it to get into both. Aim to arrive early to avoid the crowds that amass from 10am onwards. Tours of the administrative section commence (follow the individual visitors signs) from the grand palace entrance, a looming feat of neo-Baroque architecture. English-speaking tours run every 15min so it's worth checking the times first before wandering the gardens.

Mimar Sinan Museum of Fine Arts

Barbaros Hayrettin Paşa İskelesi Sokak • Mon–Fri 10am–4.30pm • Free • Enter from the Kaymakamlık Building, around 300m northeast along the main road from the Dolmabahçe Palace entrance (see p.131)

The **Mimar Sinan Museum of Fine Arts** (Mimar Sinan Üniversitesi Resim ve Heykel Müzesi) is a seldom-visited but fine museum housing some fine, late nineteenth- and early twentieth-century works of art. The best of the collection gives an intriguing insight into the lifestyle and attitudes of the late Ottoman Turks. Highlights are the works of Osman Hamdi Bey (1842–1910) – the first Ottoman Muslim painter to have his work displayed abroad – including *Woman with Mimosas*, and the wonderful painting of a mosque doorway by Osman Hamdi's pupil, Devret Dad.

The Storage Museum

Entrance on Dolmabahçe Caddesi • Tues, Wed & Fri–Sun 9am–5pm • 2TL

Housed in the former kitchens of the Dolmabahçe Palace, the **Storage Museum** (Depo Müzesi) contains a staggering 42,000 different items, all of them from the palace. The mother-of-pearl-inlaid *hamam* slippers, Singer sewing machines, cast-iron AEG fans and delicate Limoges-ware tea sets are just some of the relatively mundane objects that help further our understanding of life in the palace during the late nineteenth and early twentieth centuries. The interior of the kitchens has been attractively restored and the objects well displayed – look out for the stereoscope made in London's Pall Mall and the most contemporary item on display, the 1930s Ericsson telephone switchboard that was so essential for communication in the gargantuan palace.

The Naval Museum

Barbaros Hayrettin Paşa İskelesi Sok, off Beşiktaş Caddesi • Wed, Thurs & Fri 9am–5pm, Sat & Sun 11am–7pm • 4TL

The worthwhile **Naval Museum** (Deniz Müzesi) is divided between two buildings: the one facing the water houses seagoing craft, while the other, on Cezayir Caddesi, is devoted to the maritime history of the Ottoman Empire and the Turkish Republic. Most of the labels are in Turkish, but the best of the exhibits – such as the enormous wooden figureheads depicting tigers and swans, and the display of items from Atatürk's yachts, the *Savarona* and *Ertugrul* – need little explanation. There's even a model of the ship that contributed to the Ottomans entering World War I – the *Sultan Osman I*. The ship was paid for by public subscription and built in Britain – but was never delivered, due to Britain's fear that the Ottomans were already committed to Germany. Instead, the British kept it, renaming it the HMS *Agincourt*, and the subsequent public outrage gave the "Young Turk" leadership just the excuse they needed for entering the war as Germany's allies.

In the adjacent building, the exhibition continues with a collection of caïques that were used to row the sultans to and from their homes along the Bosphorus. The oarsmen – the *Bostanci* – reputedly barked like dogs while they rowed so as not to overhear the sultans talking. The largest of these caïques, dating from 1648, needed an incredible 144 oarsmen to power it. The lovely mother-of-pearl inlay of the sultan's kiosk here can be viewed from above via a purpose-built walkway.

Çırağan Palace

Çırağan Caddesi

8

The sumptuous **Çırağan Palace** has a long history dating back to the seventeenth century, but today's European-style palace was first constructed in 1855 when Sultan Abdülmecid decided to move his official residence from Dolmabahçe. It was finally completed in 1874 during the reign of his brother Abdülaziz, who added a more Eastern flavour with Arabic touches, such as the honeycomb stalactites decorating the windows. It was here in the palace that, in 1876, Abdülaziz was either murdered or committed suicide (the cause of death was never established), and where Murat V was later imprisoned, until his death in 1904, after being deposed by his brother.

Abandoned until 1908, Çırağan housed the Turkish parliament until 1910, when a fire reduced it to a blackened shell. It was restored in 1990 to its present magnificence as one of İstanbul's most luxurious hotels, the *Çırağan Palace Kempinski* (see p.174) with a second renovation undertaken in 2006.

Visitors can enter the west side of the palace grounds to marvel at the ornate facade and take pictures, but entrance here is limited to guests of the imperial palace suites. The main hotel entrance is a good 200m further down Çırağan Caddesi; here non-guests may be admitted to eat or drink at one of the hotel's several swanky (and predictably pricey) restaurants (see p.191) or take a stroll around part of the spectacular gardens – known historically as the lush Kazancıoğlu Gardens.

Yıldız Parkı

Daily 8am–11pm

Yıldız Parkı, a vast wooded area opposite the Çırağan Palace (see above) and dotted with mansions, pavilions, lakes and gardens, was the centre of the Ottoman Empire for thirty years during the reign of Abdülhamid II. The buildings in and around the park constitute **Yıldız Palace**, a collection of structures in the old Ottoman style that are a total contrast to the Dolmabahçe Palace. Most of the pavilions date from the reign of Abdülaziz, but it was Abdülhamid – a reforming sultan whose downfall was brought about by his intense paranoia – who transformed Yıldız into a small city and powerbase.

Its superb hillside location makes the park one of the most popular places in İstanbul for city-dwellers thirsting for fresh air and open spaces, and on public holidays it's always crowded. Of the many buildings in the park, only the Yıldız Palace Museum and the Şale Köşkü are open to the public, though it's easy enough to wander around the outside of the other pavilions, each with marvellous terraces and panoramic views of the Bosphorus.

INFORMATION
YILDIZ PARKI

Getting there The palace buildings are a fifteen-minute walk up through the park from the southern entrance on Çırağan Caddesi. If you don't fancy the steep climb, you can take any bus or minibus from the main square in Beşiktaş by the ferry terminal and up Barbaros Bulvarı. Get off just after the former British Council building (opposite the *Conrad Hotel*) and follow the signs to "Yıldız Üniversitesi" and "Şehir Müzesi" to the right.

Eating A relaxing café, the *Kır Kahvesi* (9am–10pm) is a good spot for enjoying the shade provided by the towering chestnut, beech, linden and plane trees. Alternatively, the *Malta Köşkü*, built in 1870 and once used to imprison Sultan Abdülhamid's brother, Murat (on Abdülhamid's orders), is a reasonably priced restaurant/café (9am–10pm).

Şale Köşkü
Tues, Wed & Fri–Sun: March–Sept 9.30am–5pm; Oct–Feb 9.30am–4pm • 4TL

The most important surviving building in Yıldız Parkı is the **Şale Köşkü**. Like the Dolmabahçe Palace (see p.131), it was designed partly by the Armenian Balian brothers and partly by the Italian D'Aronco. The first of the pavilion's three separate sections was modelled on a Swiss chalet, while the other two were built to receive Kaiser Wilhelm II on his first and second state visits, in 1889 and 1898. The inside of the *köşk* belies its peeling exterior – the most impressive room, the **Ceremonial Hall**, takes up the greater part of the third section, with a Hereke carpet so big (approximately 400 square metres) that part of a wall was knocked down to install it. It was here, following the liberalizing Tanzimat reforms of 1839, that the sultan met his ministers to discuss matters of state. In the attractive dining room, at the top of the central stairway in the central section, the dining chairs were carved by the reclusive Abdülhamid himself.

Yıldız Palace Museum and Yıldız Porcelain Factory
The **Yıldız Palace Museum** (Yıldız Sarayı Müzesi; Tues–Sun 9.30pm–6pm; 5TL), situated below the Şale Köşkü, is housed in Abdülhamid's converted carpentry workshop, and exhibits items and furniture from throughout the palace. While not in their original setting, there are some exquisite porcelain pieces, giant vases and even some of the joinery produced by the sultan himself. Southeast of the museum is the **Yıldız Porcelain Factory** (Mon–Fri 9am–noon & 1–6pm), established here in 1890 to produce tableware for the palace. The pottery is still functioning, and the designs stick very closely to the ornate late nineteenth-century European styles favoured by the last Ottoman sultans. The attached gift shop stocks a range of the factory's produce, and there's an adjoining café with good views over the park.

Ortaköy

Once just a tiny fishing village, **Ortaköy** is now home to a burgeoning art scene with clusters of chic restaurants and cafés, upmarket theme bars and a bustling crafts market. Running north under the looming **Bouazıçı Köprüsü** – the transcontinental Bosphorus Bridge, completed in 1973 to celebrate the Turkish Republic's 50th anniversary – the suburb retains its allure in spite of its heavy renovation, with its cobbled pathways and quaint setting along the Bosphorus.

Heading north from the boardwalk area, just beyond the 1.5-kilometre-long Bosphorus Bridge, the neighbourhood plays host to some of the city's glitziest clubs (see p.201) where celebrity-spotting and cash-splashing takes place to a backdrop of the Bosphorus and a plethora of swanky restaurants.

GETTING THERE

ORTAKÖY

On foot Ortaköy is easily reached by foot from Beşiktaş – a pleasant 1km stroll down the road.

By bus You can take the #40 or #42/T bus from Taksim, or the #30 from Eminönü.

By tram and funicular Another possible route is to take the tram from Sultanahmet or the funicular from Taksim Square to Kabataş, then catch the #22, #22/RE or #25/E to Ortaköy.

Ortaköy waterfront

The charming waterfront in Ortaköy is the heart of the village, a lattice of paved streets on and around the Bosphorus, where debonair restaurants, tiny clothing boutiques and arty cafés have taken over even the tiniest of fishermen's cottages. Here a smattering of daily market stalls sell mostly jewellery and souvenirs but the main markets run at the weekends, when stalls line the waterfront square selling everything from handcrafted jewellery and accessories to piles of books (mostly in English, German and French). The Sunday *entel* (kicking off around midday) or "intellectual" **market** – so called as this area was once frequented by university students and teachers gathering to sip tea and discuss weighty topics – is a popular affair, with artists gathering to showcase their works and a wide array of colourful crafts on sale. A variety of cheap food stands offer everything from scrumptious fruit-filled waffles dripping with chocolate sauce to stuffed potatoes laden with cheese, yoghurt and olives. This is also the location of the distinctive Ottoman Baroque mosque **Büyük Mecidiye Camii**, built in 1855, a favourite photographers' subject with the Bosphorus Bridge in the background.

Running parallel to the Bosphorus, the main street, Muallim Naci Caddesi, boasts the attractive Greek Orthodox church of **Aya Fokas** (St Phocas) constructed in 1854, and the **Ezt Ahayim** synagogue; both are usually locked.

8

Surp Aszdvadzadzin

İlhan Caddesi • Services on Sun, or the caretaker may let you in

Ortaköy was, and to some extent remains, a cosmopolitan and tolerant area of the city, embracing numerous different religions. Perched high above the waterfront is the Armenian church of **Surp Aszdvadzadzin**, built between 1661 and 1684. Plain on the exterior, the barrel-vaulted, Neoclassical interior is lavishly decorated, and the gold-gilded altar is monumental.

HAYDARPAŞA STATION

Asian İstanbul

With so much to see and do in the historic old city and lively Beyoğlu, most
visitors put a trip across the Bosphorus to the Asian side of the city well
down their list of priorities. This is a shame, as even a quick visit will give you
a more rounded feel of how this great metropolis ticks. Kadıköy has a
sprinkling of minor sights and boasts a wonderfully compact shopping area,
some decent nightlife and one of the city's best restaurants (see p.191). Its
northern neighbour, Haydarpaşa, is worth a wander for its impressive early
twentieth-century station, the Crimean War Cemetery and the colossal
Selimiye Barracks, home to the Florence Nightingale Museum.

The choice of **Üsküdar** as the exit point of the Marmaray railway tunnel linking the European and Asian sides of the city (see box, p.26) should shortly wake it from its conservative slumber. In the meantime, there are a number of worthwhile **mosques** to visit (including a couple by the master architect Sinan), the landmark **Kız Kulesi** lies just offshore, and you can eat at one of İstanbul's best traditional restaurants (see p.191).

Despite appearances to the contrary, **Greek colonists** founded a city, Chalcedon, near present-day Kadıköy as early as 680 BC – some twenty years before the colony across the straits that became Byzantium, then Constantinople and finally İstanbul. Üsküdar was founded by that mercurial Athenian statesman-adventurer, Alcibiades, in 409 BC, and was known as Chrysopolis. The construction of the Marmaray tunnel in Üsküdar has revealed both **archaic** and **Byzantine**-era ruins – what else will turn up remains to be seen.

GETTING THERE

By ferry Regular ferries (daily 6am–midnight; around 20min) run to Kadıköy (from Eminönü and Karaköy), Haydarpaşa (Karaköy) and Üsküdar (Eminönü).

ASIAN İSTANBUL

By bus #12 and #12/A run at regular intervals between Üsküdar and Kadıköy, stopping at both Selimiye and Marmara University.

Kadıköy

The suburb of **Kadıköy** makes for a surprisingly enjoyable outing from the European side of the city. It's a lively place, with some great shops, restaurants, bars and cinemas. One of the area's charms is its local feel – hardly surprising as, unlike Sultanahmet or Beyoğlu, most of the people out and about here are residents. Towards the end of the nineteenth century, when the introduction of steam-driven ferries made commuting across the Bosphorus feasible, Kadıköy became a popular residential area for foreign businesspeople and wealthy Greeks and Armenians, whose most visible legacy is the **churches** southeast of the ferry terminal. There's a scattering of older constructions in amid the concrete; look out for the tall, narrow curves of the cream Art Deco-style **Kuru Kahveci Mehmet Efendi building**, home to the famous purveyor of Turkish coffee, and the beautifully restored **Süreya Opera House** on Bahariye Caddesi (see p.206); dating back to 1927, its ornate Neoclassical facade is adorned with relief-work pilasters, cherubs and Classical-style theatre masks.

Most things of interest in Kadıköy are to be found between the waterfront **Sahil Yolu** (coast road) and **Bahariye Caddesi**, a right turn off Söğütlüçeşme Caddesi, the steep, wide street leading uphill from the ferry terminal. The two latter streets have their own tram, a grittier version of İstiklal Caddesi's; indeed, the area bounded by Söğütlüçeşme Caddesi to the north, Bahariye and Emin Bey *caddesi*s to the east and south and the Bosphorus waterfront to the west is becoming a mini-Beyoğlu, with a similar mix of alternative-clothing stores, bookshops and bric-a-brac shops dotted among the cafés and restaurants spilling out onto jam-packed pedestrianized streets. It's also one of the best areas in the city for shopping, especially for spices, coffee, olives, dried fruit, nuts, Turkish delight and other goodies, in the colourful permanent market centred on **Guneşlibahçe Sokak**. A couple of nineteenth-century churches here, the Greek Orthodox Aya Eufemia and the Armenian church of Surp Takavor, opposite each other on Muvakkithane Sokak, attest to Kadıköy's non-Muslim past.

Kadıköy is home to Turkey's wealthiest football club, **Fenerbahçe** (see p.226), who reached the quarter-finals of the European Champions League in 2008. Their impressive stadium, the Rüştü Saraçoğlu, the largest club ground in the country, lies at the foot of the hill 400m east of Bahariye Caddesi. Running along its eastern side is the main drag known as **Bağdat Caddesi**, once part of the old Silk Route from China. It's of little interest today except as a place to pose, and as a place to buy the clothes to pose in.

KADIKÖY & HAYDARPAŞA

BARS
Isis	3
Karga	4
Viktor Levi	2

CLUB
Shaft	1

SHOPS
Ali Muhidin	3
Haci Bekir	4
Brezilya	2
Cafer Erol	
Kuru Kahveci	
Mehmet Efendi	1

RESTAURANTS
Baylan	1
Çiya Sofrası	4
Dicle Balik Lokantasi	3
Törek	5
Yanyali Fehmi Lokantasi	2

The Toy Museum
Dr. Zeki Zeren Sokak, Göztepe • Tues–Sun 9.30am–6pm • 8TL • Buses #GZ1, #GZ2, #10, #10/B or #10/S

Established in 2005 in a lovely nineteenth-century wooden villa – which, until the 1950s, housed one of the city's most famous toy shops – the **Toy Museum**, is the brainchild of poet Sunay Akin. It exhibits some four thousand toys on four floors, the oldest dating back two hundred years. Although there are some century-old German-made porcelain dolls on display, and a Barbie in her first employment role as an air stewardess, the exhibits are mainly male-orientated and themed, with rooms devoted to trains, space toys and soldiers among others. Much, but not all, of the collection is foreign, and there are examples of handmade dolls from Anatolia, a whirling-dervish puppet, and products of the Eyüp Sultan toy factory.

Haydarpaşa

North up the Bosphorus from Kadıköy, **Haydarpaşa** is dominated by the massive **Selimiye Barracks**, built in the early nineteenth century to house the new, Western-style army created to bring the power of the corrupt janissary corps to an end but today worth a visit for the **Florence Nightingale Museum**. Opposite, on Selimiye Camii Sokak, is the **Selimiye Camii**, constructed, along with the nearby *hamam*, for the use of the barracks' soldiers. Almost rivalling the barracks for sheer size is the main building of **Marmara University**, designed by Raimondo D'Aronco and notable for its quirky clock towers, though the **Karaca Ahmet Mezarlığı**, the largest Muslim graveyard in İstanbul, makes a more tangible destination. A sprawling place shadowed by ancient cypress trees, thought to have been founded in the mid-fourteenth century and now with an estimated one million graves, it's a ten-minute walk from the barracks on Tıbbiye Caddesi, in the direction of Üsküdar, or you can catch any number of buses, including the useful #12 and #12/A.

Haydarpaşa station

The waterfront area is adorned by the imposing, Germanic bulk of **Haydarpaşa station**, fronted by the attractive ferry terminal building designed by Vedat Tak, the architect responsible for the Central Post Office building near Sirkeci station (see p.67). **Haydarpaşa station** itself was designed by the German architects Otto Ritter and Helmuth Cuno; the historic mainline was completed in 1908 as part of Germany's grandiose plans for a Berlin-to-Baghdad railway and presented to Sultan Abdül Hamit II as a present by Kaiser Wilhelm II. Perched right on the edge of the Bosphorus (it was actually partially built on 1100 pillars sunk into the water), the palace-like building is an impressive sight as you cross from Europe to Asia by ferry.

A feature of the station is its multitude of beautiful stained-glass windows, which suffuse the cavernous interior with soft, pastel-coloured light. Germany's defeat in World War I ensured that the railway never served its intended purpose – linking Germany with the oil fields of the Persian Gulf and its African colonies. For the moment, the trains continue to roll into Haydarpaşa, bringing fresh batches of wide-eyed immigrants from rural Anatolia for a new start in the big city, but the transport system restructuring that threatens Sirkeci (see p.67) will also undoubtedly make Haydarpaşa redundant.

The British Crimean War Cemetery
Daily 7am–7pm • To get here, turn off Tıbbiye Caddesi into Burhan Felek Caddesi, between the university building and the emergency entrance to the GATA military hospital

Situated between the sea and Tıbbiye Caddesi, directly north of Haydarpaşa station, is the Marmara University and the **British Crimean War Cemetery**, a beautifully kept spot maintained by the Commonwealth War Graves Commission. Given as gift to Britain by the Ottoman authorities at the time of the Crimean War, it is shaded by cypress,

9

plane and ornamental firs and shelters the dead of the Crimean and the two world wars. The largest monument is an obelisk, with four wreath-holding angels at each corner, "raised by Queen Victoria and her people in 1857". The cemetery is in two parts, with the obelisk and various inscribed gravestones in the first, smaller part, and a more extensive graveyard in the larger landscaped area beyond. The war that caused the death of the soldiers and civilians interred here was pointless (less than sixty years later, Britain was fighting against, rather than with, the Ottoman Turks and alongside – at least until the Bolshevik Revolution – Russia), which makes the inscriptions on the gravestones and markers even more poignant.

The Florence Nightingale Museum

Kavak İskele Caddesi • By appointment only • Mon–Fri 9am–5pm • Free • Fax a photocopy of the identity page of your passport, plus desired visiting date and time, and telephone number to the museum's military guardians, at least 24hr before your intended visit • ☎ 0216/553 1009 or ☎ 0216/3107929

The imposing **Selimiye Barracks**, whose northwest wing was used as a hospital by the British during the Crimean War (1854–56), today houses the **Florence Nightingale Museum**. Florence Nightingale (see box below) lived and worked in the northern tower, where she reduced the death toll among patients from twenty percent to two percent, and established universally accepted principles of modern nursing. The museum contains two of her famous lamps, and you can see the rooms where she lived and worked. Whether you think it's worth the effort involved to gain access depends on your level of interest in the great woman. Most visitors find the monumental barracks and the whole rigmarole of dealing with the Turkish military (who lead the tour) at least as fascinating as the museum itself.

FLORENCE NIGHTINGALE: THE LADY OF THE LAMP

The **Crimean War**, fought between Russia and the ailing Ottoman Empire and its allies (Britain and France) between 1854 and 1856 was a particularly gruelling one. When news reports reached Britain of the appalling suffering of British troops in the campaign – caused largely by poor living conditions and totally inadequate medical care – public indignation led to a team of nurses, headed by **Florence Nightingale**, being sent to the military hospital at the Selimiye Barracks (see p.142) in Scutari (modern Üsküdar) on the Asian side of the Bosphorus. Although Nightingale had spotted the connection between hygiene and health and had concentrated mainly on cleaning the wards and medical equipment (such as it was), over four thousand soldiers died in her first winter. Despite her best efforts – she is said to have walked 6km of hospital ward each evening, her famous lamp in hand – her ministrations could not prevent **typhus**, **cholera**, **typhoid** and **dysentery** ripping through the hospital. The following year, the sewers of the hospital were overhauled and better ventilation introduced – massively reducing infection rates. Nonetheless, ten times more troops died from disease than battle wounds in the Crimean campaign.

A strict Unitarian, Nightingale saw herself on a God-given mission to alleviate suffering. Her dedication revolutionized health care and helped establish the universally accepted principles of modern nursing. She wrote a book on nursing, and in 1860 set up a training school for nurses at St Thomas' Hospital in London (now part of King's College London). She became a legend in Victorian Britain and was immortalized in Henry Longfellow's poem *Santa Filomena*:

Lo, in that hour of misery
A lady with a lamp I see
Pass through the shimmering gloom
And flit from room to room
Florence Nightingale

Üsküdar

9

Devout and conservative **Üsküdar** (a corruption of "Scutari" – the name used for what was a separate town in the late Byzantine era), has a completely different character to rowdy near-neighbour Kadıköy. Since the 1950s, the area has been characterized by wholesale migration from the more Islamic regions of Anatolia and has long been a centre of Islamic mystical sects. There are some fine imperial mosques in and around this (relatively) quiet suburb, plus a lively covered market. Secondhand furniture and ornaments are on offer at the **Üsküdar bit pazarı** (flea market) in Büyük Hamam Sokak, and there are also some reasonable jewellery and clothes shops. South along the quayside, in an area known as **Salacak**, are some good pavement cafés and bars, offering fantastic views across to Topkapı Palace and old İstanbul.

Mihrimah Camii
İskele Meydanı

The most obvious mosque in Üsküdar is **İskele** or **Mihrimah Camii**, opposite the ferry terminal. This sits on a high platform, fronted by an immense covered porch that is the perennial haunt of old men in knitted hats complaining about the changing times while they peruse the work on the Marmaray (see box, p.26) tunnel below. Designed by Mimar Sinan for Mihrimah, daughter of Süleyman the Magnificent, and built in 1547–48, this is the only Ottoman mosque with three semi-domes (rather than two or four), a result of the requirements of a difficult site against the hillside behind.

Yeni Valide Camii
Hakimiyet-i Milliye Caddesi

The **Yeni Valide Camii** was built between 1708 and 1710 by Ahmet III in honour of his mother. The mosque is most easily identified by the Valide Sultan's green, birdcage-like tomb, whose meshed roof was designed to keep birds out while allowing rain in to water the garden tomb below (now rather untidily overgrown). There's an attractive *şadırvan* (ablutions fountain) in the courtyard; the grilles of its cistern are highly wrought, their pattern echoed in the stone carvings above.

Çinili Camii and around
Cavuşdere Caddesi • Both mosque and *hamam* are best reached by a taxi from the waterfront (around 6TL)

One of the most attractive mosques in Üsküdar is the **Çinili Camii**, or Tiled Mosque. Dating from 1640, it's set in a pleasant, tree-shaded courtyard, but you will need to find the caretaker to open up the mosque itself. The tiles are mainly blues and turquoise, but there's a rare shade of green to be found in the *mihrab*. Below the mosque, in the same street, is the beautifully restored **Çinili Hamamı** (see p.227), which retains its original central marble stones for massage and acres of marble revetments.

Atık Valide Külliyesi
Valide Külliyesi Sokak

Dating from 1583, the **Atık Valide Külliyesi** complex is a work of the master architect Mimar Sinan (see box, p.80), built for Nur Banu, wife of Selim II and mother of Murat III. The mosque courtyard, surrounding an attractive *şadırvan*, is a colonnaded gem, unusual in that it contains a (very popular) teahouse. Worth inspecting inside are the underside of the wooden galleries that run around three sides of the prayer hall interior, which are beautifully painted, and the İznik tiles covering the *mihrab*.

Şemsi Paşa Camii
Paşa Lima Caddesi

The **Şemsi Paşa Camii**, beautifully situated on the waterfront looking across the Bosphorus to the skyline of the old city, rivals Örtaköy's Mecidiye Camii (see p.137) as the most picturesquely situated mosque in the city. It's considerably older, though

ÜSKÜDAR

RESTAURANTS
- Filizler Köftecisi 2
- Kanaat Lokantası 1

Büyük Çamlıca & Kısıklı Camii

Çinili Camii

Çinili Hamamı

Atik Valide Külliyesi

ÇAVUŞDERE

Bülbüldere Cemetery

Mihrimah Camii

Üsküdar Bit Pazar

Yeni Valide Camii

HAKIMIYETI MILLIYE CAD

Demokrasi Meydanı (Democracy Square)

Üsküdar Ferry Terminal

Şemsih Paşa Camii

Dolmuşes to Kadıköy

Bus Stop for Şile

ÜSKÜDAR

Salacak Ferry Terminal

DOĞANCILAR

Doğancılar Parkı

PAŞA LIMANI CAD

Kız Kulesi

BOSPHORUS

Beşiktaş

Kabataş

Eminönü & Haliç (Golden Horn)

Ankara

Mevlana, Haydarpaşa & Kadıköy

N

0   500
metres

(built in 1580 by the great Sinan), and its simple, domed structure looks glorious when seen from the water. It has been beautifully restored inside and out.

Kız Kulesi

Museum Tues–Sun noon–7pm • Free • **Restaurant** Daily 7.30pm–1am • **Kız** Boats from Salacak (on the main coast road between Üsküdar and Harem) 9am–6.45pm (5TL) • A private boat service operates for those who are eating and/or drinking at the tower from 8.30pm–12.30am; see ⓦ kizkulesi.com.tr

To the south of Üsküdar, on an island in the Bosphorus, is the small, white **Kız Kulesi** (Maiden's Tower) also known as Leander's Tower. The first tower was built by the Athenian commander Alcibiades in the fifth century BC to help control and tax ships passing through the Bosphorus. In the Byzantine period a chain was stretched between it and another tower on the historic peninsula, again to ensure passing ships paid their dues and it wasn't until the Ottoman era that it began to be used as a lighthouse. Several myths are associated with it: in one, a princess, who was prophesied to die from a snake bite, came here to escape her fate, only to succumb to it when a serpent was delivered to her retreat in a basket of fruit. The tower also featured in the 1999 James Bond film, *The World Is Not Enough*. It's worth visiting for the panoramic views up and down the Bosphorus and across to both the European and Asian sides of the city from the tower. In the evening the tower becomes an expensive restaurant.

The Bosphorus and the Black Sea resorts

One of the world's most eulogized stretches of water, the 31km-long Bosphorus Strait divides Europe from Asia and connects the Marmara and Black seas. Its width varies from 698m to 4.7km, and its depth from thirty to a hundred and ten metres. More interestingly, it has a powerful surface current flowing south from the Black Sea to the Sea of Marmara, while a sub-current flows in the opposite direction; this current, along with the strait's numerous twists and turns, make it particularly hazardous for shipping. The name derives from the Greek myth of Io, lover of Zeus, whom the god transformed into a cow to conceal her from his jealous wife Hera. She plunged into the strait to escape a gadfly, hence Bosphorus, or "Ford of the Cow".

Around 55,000 cargo ships, oil tankers and ocean liners pass through the strait each year; for residents and visitors alike the Bosphorus remains İstanbul's most important transport artery. The passenger ferries and sea buses that weave their way up and down from shore to shore provide one of the city's real highlights: along the way are imperial palaces and ancient fortresses interspersed with affluent waterfront suburbs, which become increasingly more like real villages the further north you head, and wooden *yalıs* (waterside mansions; see box, p.149).

Even further from the city are the beach resorts on the **Black Sea**. The former Greek fishing village of **Kılyos**, on the European side of the Bosphorus, has been overdeveloped and lost much of its former charm, but it does boast a thriving summer beach-bar/club scene. **Şile**, though equally built-up, is a little more laidback and enjoys a clifftop location and white sandy beaches. **Ağva**, some 50km along the coast from Şile, is the quietest and most attractive of the three, though given the extra travelling time from the city is really only worth considering for an overnight trip.

10

GETTING AROUND

You can take an independent tour of the strait by catching one of the **ferries** that ply the waters from Eminönü as far up as Anadolu Kavağı, or from Çengelköy up to İstinye – timetables (*vapur seferler*) are available from ferry terminals and tourist offices – though most visitors prefer the ease of the various **Bosphororus cruises** (see box below). To get more of a feel for the suburbs and villages themselves, hop on one of the **buses** that run back and forth on either side of the strait.

The European Shore

The **European Shore** is built up as far as Emirgan (and beyond), and the so-called Bosphorus villages of Kuruçeşme, Arnavutköy and Bebek are little more than suburbs

---

THE BOSPHORUS CRUISE

The boat trip up the Bosphorus from the bustling quays of Eminönü to the quiet fishing village of Anadolu Kavağı is one of the highlights of any visit to İstanbul. The long **Bosphorus Cruise**, run by the Şehir Hatları company (see p.26), leaves from the Boğaz ferry terminal just east of the Galata Bridge in Eminönü (daily 10.35am, May–Sept also noon & 1.35pm; one way 15TL; round trip 25TL).

In summer, especially at weekends, the queues to buy **tickets** can be very long, so give yourself at least half an hour to make your purchase – or, better, buy your ticket a day or two in advance. There are also often long queues to board, so late-comers will find themselves sat in the worst seats. The ferries are rather antiquated but comfortable enough, and you can buy snacks, sandwiches and drinks on board. The round trip, including a two-and-a-half-hour **lunch** stop at Anadolu Kavağı, takes about seven hours.

The boat **stops** at Beşiktaş, Kanlıca (Asia), Yeniköy, Sariyer and Rumeli Kavağı (all Europe) and, finally, Anadolu Kavağı (Asia); the only stop on the return is Beşiktaş. It's possible to leave the boat at any of the landings to explore the waterfront or hinterland, but most people do the return cruise. A shorter version is also available for 10TL, departing from the same ferry terminal and covering the same distance with no stops (bar at Üsküdar to pick up more passengers). The tour takes around two hours, departing Eminönü at 2.30pm (April–Oct daily; Nov–March Sun & public holidays).

Running between mid-June and mid-September only, a **night-time cruise** makes an alternative and attractive option, with the great suspension bridges lit-up like Christmas trees and the lights of Asia and Europe twinkling on either side. The boat departs Eminönü at 7pm, reaching Anadolu Kavağı at 8.30pm, where it moors for dinner, before arriving back in Eminönü around midnight.

The private Turyol company (see p.26) also runs tours up the Bosphorus, with departures every hour on the hour on weekdays, more frequently at weekends. Tickets cost 12TL for the one-and-a-half-hour round trip, which goes as far as the Fatih bridge.

of the city, whatever their predominantly wealthy residents may wish to believe. The former fishing villages of **Arnavutköy** and **Bebek** are still attractive, but the simple waterside *tavernas* and cafés of old have been replaced by swanky fish restaurants and bistros catering to the wealthy elite. Further north, **Emirgan** boasts the **Sakip Sabancı Museum**, which hosts major touring exhibitions of world-class art, and beautiful **Emirgan Parkı**. Beyond this, the major attractions are **Sadberk Hanım Museum**; the fishing village of **Rumeli Kavağı**, the furthest point of the Bosphorus Cruise; and, west of Sariyer, **Belgrade Forest**, a weekend haven for İstanbullus escaping the bustling city.

GETTING AROUND   THE EUROPEAN SHORE

By ferry Sehir Hatları (see p.26) ferries run between some of the Bosphorus suburbs, both on the European and Asian shores, but making the right connections is tricky. Consult their timetables.

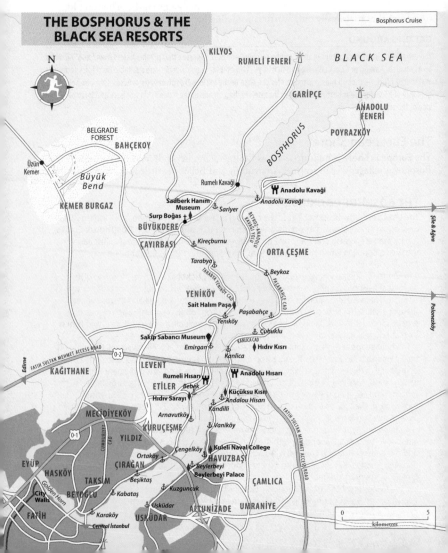

THE BOSPHORUS & THE BLACK SEA RESORTS

—— Bosphorus Cruise

By bus The very useful #25/E bus runs from the T1 tram terminus at Kabataş (or the #25/T and #40 from Taksim) to Sariyer, from where there are plenty of dolmuşes or the #25/A bus on to Rumeli Kavağı.

By metro You can also take the M2 Metro from Şişhane or Taksim to the Hacıosman Metro stop in Sariyer, then the #25/A bus to Rumeli Kavağı. The last #25/A back to Sariyer leaves at 9.30pm, from where you can catch the M2 Metro or a bus back to Taksim/Şişhane.

Kuruçeşme

10

From Ortaköy, the coast road runs north under the kilometre-long Bosphorus Bridge, the first of two intercontinental bridges that span the strait. **Kuruçeşme** (Dry Spring) is home to the Türkcell Kuruçeşme Arena (see p.202), a waterside venue hosting some of the biggest visiting acts, both Turkish and foreign. The **Cemil Topuzlu Parkı**, slightly to the south, is a small but pleasantly landscaped waterfront park, and location of the reliable, if expensive, *Parkfora* fish restaurant (see p.193). Further north and slightly inland are a couple of churches, both still in use and both – reflecting the affluence of the neighbourhood – far better maintained than the majority of those in the poorer quarters of old, walled İstanbul. The Armenian Orthodox **Surp Haç** (Church of the Holy Cross) on Kırbaç Sokak, dating back to 1681, has been recently restored; there's a service between 9am and noon on Sundays. Offshore is **Galatasaray Island**, a floating pontoon owned by the famous football club (see p.226) and boasting an Olympic-sized pool, restaurants, a nightclub and cafés.

Arnavutköy

Merging into Kuruçeşme, **ARNAVUTKÖY** is one of the most beautiful of the Bosphorus suburbs, especially when seen from the water, and is famous for its line of *yalıs*, wooden waterfront mansions with their boat moorings carved out beneath them (see box below). In the pretty backstreets above the main drag are the ruins of a synagogue, while a little to the east is the imposing bulk of the nineteenth-century Greek Orthodox **Ayos Taksiarchis** (Church of the Taxiarch), with an *ayazma* (sacred spring) in a nearby chapel. The monumental domed church shows how powerful the Greek community must have been here in the 1800s. Although Arnavutköy translates as the "Village of the Albanians", it was mainly inhabited by Armenians, Greeks and Jews.

YALIS

İstanbul's wealthy elite (and there are plenty of them – in 2007, the city was home to 27 of the country's top 30 taxpayers) may choose to live in luxury penthouse apartments, but in Ottoman times the place to be – at least in summer – was a wooden mansion, or *yalı*, right on the shores of the Bosphorus. These sumptuous two- or three-storey villas usually featured manicured lawns, peppered with rose beds and trees planted to provide shade, sloping down to the water's edge. Caïques bringing residents and guests to the *yalı* moored in an opening right under the house. Inside, the mansions were separated into the *haremlık*, used by women and family members only, and the *selamlık*, usually an all-male preserve where guests were entertained. There was also a *hamam*, a kitchen area and, of course, servants' quarters.

Most *yalıs* (from the Greek word for "coast") have not survived the vicissitudes of time, succumbing to fire, storm damage or wayward shipping. Those that remain are reminders of a more refined and leisured age when sailing boats rather than super-tankers drifted along the Bosphorus. There are some good examples on the European Shore in Arnavutköy and north of İstinye (look out for the **Ahmet Atıf Paşa Yalı**), but the best are on the Asian side, from slightly south of the Bosphorus Bridge right up to Beykoz – the dilapidated **Amcazade Hüseyin Paşa Yalısı**, just shy of the Fatih Bridge, is the oldest *yalı* on the Bosphorus. All are subject to preservation orders; and if you're tempted to buy one, be warned – the bureaucracy involved in restoration is positively (and perhaps appropriately) Byzantine. Those that persevere are amply rewarded, though: larger, restored *yalıs* can fetch millions.

Bebek and around

Bebek (Turkish for "baby") is the beginning of real wealth on the Bosphorus, and the suburbs from here to Sariyer encompass some of the most beautiful, priceless Bosphorus *yalıs*. The fifteen-minute walk from Arnavutköy follows an attractive park-fringed (but shadeless) promenade, popular with swimming children, fishermen and sunbathing pensioners. En route, before you reach the ferry terminal, you'll pass Bebek's most famous building, the waterfront **Hıdıv Sarayı** (Khedive's Palace), an Art Nouveau-style mansion belonging to the Egyptian consulate. Dishevelled for decades, it has recently been restored to its former glory.

Fortress of Rumeli Hisarı

Daily except Wed 9.30am–6pm • 3TL

The impressive fortress of **Rumeli Hisarı** is dramatically situated in the shadow of the first Bosphorus (Fatih) bridge. Grander than its counterpart, Anadolu Hisarı, across the strait (see p.154), this Ottoman fortress was constructed in four months in 1452. Its purpose, along with the smaller fortification opposite, was to block the strait and prevent besieged Constantinople receiving either military aid or supplies from the Black Sea – hence its original name of Boğaz-kesen or "the throat [strait] cutter". The two fortifications played an important role in the eventual fall of the city in May 1453 by cutting off the supply lines to the beleaguered Byzantine inhabitants.

Rumeli Hisarı is an extremely impressive fortification, comprising three major and three smaller towers, linked by curtain walls, and is spectacularly sited on twin hilltops. There's little to see inside but the views are grand and it houses a small open-air theatre, providing an atmospheric summer-evening venue for concerts and plays, particularly during the İstanbul International Music Festival (see p.31). Completed in 1988, the nearby Fatih Bridge is among the world's longest suspension bridges (1090m), and spans the Bosphorus at the point where King Darius of Persia crossed the straits by pontoon bridge in 512 BC (see box, p.278).

Emirgan

The leafy suburb of Emirgan, before the opening of the Sakip Sabancı Museum (see below), was best known for its beautiful park, the **Emirgan Parkı** (daily 8am–5pm). With its beautifully landscaped gardens and delightfully restored wooden *kösks*, it is the most appealing park in the city. Young kids will love it with its fairy-tale, Swiss chalet-style wooden *kösks* (one painted pink, one white, the other yellow and white), artificial lake and waterfall and decent play equipment; adults more for the swathe of green grass and stands of mature trees for shade. The *kösks* have decent, if not cheap, cafés; if you're on a budget, bring your own picnic or buy a *gözleme* (a cheese or spiced-potato, stuffed *paratha*-style bread) from the stand at the entrance.

Sakip Sabancı Museum

Tues, Fri, Sat & Sun 10am–6pm, Wed 10am–8pm • 10TL • ⓦ muze.sabanciuniv.edu • Buses #40, and #40/T from Taksim, and #22, #22/RE and #25/E from Kabataş run here; at weekends, a courtesy boat service runs here from Kabataş at 11am and 2.40pm, or from Beşiktaş quay at 11.15am and 3pm, returning to both at 1.30pm and 6pm

Set in gorgeous landscaped gardens just behind the waterfront, in a beautiful 1920s villa known as the Atlı Köşkü, **Sakip Sabancı Museum** plays host to major international exhibitions, which have included subjects as diverse as Picasso, Dalí and the Mongols. Permanently on display are some exquisite examples of Ottoman calligraphy, including some beautiful Korans, while a modern glass-and-steel extension features Turkish (and Turkish-based) artists of the late nineteenth and early twentieth centuries. The Sakip Sabancı is also the home of *Müzedechanga* (see p.193), the summer venue for the famed *Changa* restaurant in Beyoğlu.

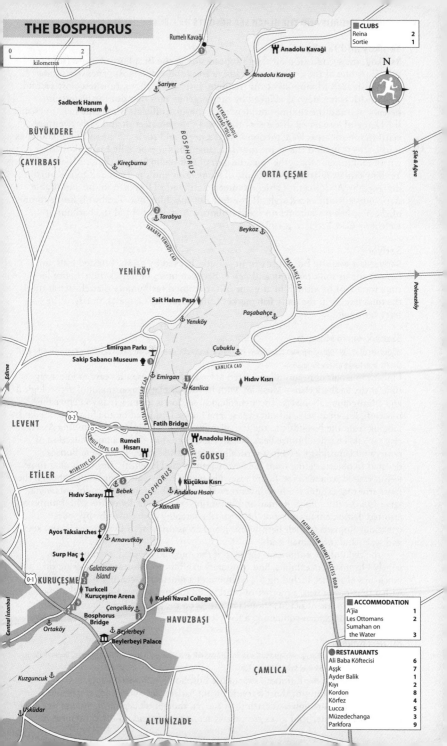

THE BOSPHORUS

0 — 2
kilometres

CLUBS
Reina 2
Sortie 1

Rumeli Kavaği 1

Anadolu Kavaği

Anadolu Kavaği

Sariyer

Sadberk Hanım Museum

BÜYÜKDERE

ÇAYIRBASI

Kireçburnu

BOSPHORUS

ORTA ÇEŞME

BEYKOZ-ANADOLU KAVAĞI YOLU

Şile & Ağva

Tarabya 2

Beykoz

TARABYA YENİKÖY CAD

YENİKÖY

PAŞABAHÇE CAD

Polonezköy

Sait Halım Paşa

Yeniköy

Paşabahçe

Emirgan Parkı
Sakip Sabancı Museum 3

Çubuklu

KANLICA CAD

Edirne

Emirgan 1

Kanlica

Hıdıv Kısrı

BALTALİMANİHİSAR CAD

Fatih Bridge

LEVENT

O-2

Rumeli Hısarı

Anadolu Hısarı

GÖKSU 4

ETİLER

CENGIZ TOPEL CAD

NISBETIYE CAD

KÜÇEL CAD

Küçüksu Kısrı

Hıdıv Sarayı

Bebek 5

Andalou Hısarı

BOSPHORUS

Kandilli

Ayos Taksiarches 6

Arnavutköy

FATIH SULTAN MEHMET ACCESS ROAD

Surp Haç

Vaniköy

Galatasaray Island

KURUÇEŞME

O-1

Turkcell Kuruçeşme Arena

8

Central Istanbul

Çengelköy

Kuleli Naval College

HAVUZBAŞI

9

Bosphorus Bridge

Ortaköy

Beylerbeyi

Beylerbeyi Palace

Kuzguncuk

ÇAMLICA

Üsküdar

ALTUNIZADE

ACCOMMODATION
A'jia 1
Les Ottomans 2
Sumahan on
  the Water 3

RESTAURANTS
Ali Baba Köftecisi 6
Aşşk 7
Ayder Balik 1
Kıyı 2
Kordon 8
Körfez 4
Lucca 5
Müzedechanga 3
Parkfora 9

N

Yeniköy and Tarabya

Yeniköy, the second stop on the European side of the Bosphorus Cruise (see box, p.147), is one of the city's most exclusive areas and is the most expensive property on the İstanbul Monopoly board. **Tarabya**, just up the shore, runs it a close second. The wealth is not new, as evinced by the gorgeous *yalıs* that dot the waterfront hereabouts, and the summer residences of consular officials who came here to escape the heat and associated diseases of the city. In the nineteenth and early twentieth centuries, both areas were predominately Greek, and there are a handful of **churches** in the streets behind the waterfront still functioning, especially in Yeniköy. Also worth looking out for is the splendid *yalı* of **Sait Halim Paşa** to the south of Yeniköy's quay, guarded by a couple of stone lions and the Twin Yalı to the north, designed by Abdülhamit's chief architect, Raimondo D'Aranco, in his inimitable, Art Nouveau-influenced style. If you feel like splashing out, Tarabya is home to one of the best **fish restaurants** on the Bosphorus, *Kıyı*, just behind the harbour at Kefeliköy Cad 126 (see p.192).

Sariyer

Sariyer is a wealthy Bosphorus-front suburb, backed by green, forested hills, and famous for its milk pudding and *börek*. Between buses or ferries there is ample time for a leisurely lunch in any one of the seafood **restaurants** that cluster around the quayside or in the daily **fish market** (one of the city's largest), north of the ferry terminal.

Sadberk Hanım Museum

Büyükdere Cad 27–29 • Daily except Wed 10am–5pm • 7TL • ⓦ www.sadberkhanimmuzesi.org.tr • Bus #25/E from Kabataş and the #25/T and #40 from Taksim pass by the museum

Housed in a pair of beautifully restored old waterfront houses, it's easy to idle away time at the **Sadberk Hanım Museum**, with its well-displayed assortment of archeological and ethnographical objects. The archeological section is to the left as you enter the museum, imaginatively laid-out over several floors. Displayed on the first floor are finds ranging from the Neolithic to the Phrygian periods, with highlights including Assyrian clay tablets, Urartian bronze belts, buckles and horse-bits – plus a fine collection of pottery oil lamps displayed in a vertically mounted wall case. The second floor is devoted to objects dating from the Mycenaean to the Hellenistic eras, including some well-executed Athenian red-figure vases and pretty Hellenistic scent bottles, though the most arresting exhibit is a fourth-century-BC candelabrum in the form of a dancing satyr. On the third floor, Roman and Byzantine-era exhibits dominate, with bronzes of assorted deities, a fine collection of *strigil* (the scraping device used by hygiene-conscious Romans in their bath-houses), and an assortment of Byzantine crosses, keys and scales and other small finds.

To the right of the entrance is the part of the museum devoted to ethnographic, largely Ottoman-era exhibits, and temporary exhibitions. Most interesting are the mock-ups of rooms, including the bedroom of a nineteenth-century home kitted out with a four-poster bed, a mother-of-pearl inlaid cabinet, a brass brazier and a wooden rocking horse. The museum's shop-cum-café is on the ground floor here, and gives onto a pleasant garden containing a few pieces of statuary.

Rumeli Kavağı

A local ferry connects Rumeli Kavağı with Anadolu Kavağı on the Asian side at 2.40pm and 6.10pm daily, returning at 7.20pm and 9pm. Four ferries run daily down to Sariyer from 9.30am–9.30pm

The last village on the European side of the Bosphorus is **Rumeli Kavağı**, a two-kilometre dolmuş or short ferry ride from Sariyer (see above). It's smaller, less developed and more down to earth than Sariyer, though it's beginning to lose its village feel. The quiet waterfront gives great views across to Asia and up the Bosphorus to where the strait merges with the Black Sea. There are some reasonable **fish restaurants** clustered around its ferry terminal, in particular the *Ayder Balık*, right next to the landing (see p.192). There's also a small private swimming **beach** here, one of the very few along the Bosphorus, though it is often restricted to women and children only.

Belgrade Forest

Most easily reached by car; by public transport, take #25/E bus from Kabataş to Büyükdere and then a dolmuş to the village of Bahçeköy, on the east side of the forest – from here it's a 1.5-kilometre walk to Büyük Bend reservoir

Several kilometres west of Büyükdere, an anonymous suburb astride the main road between Beşiktaş and Sariyer in the İstranca hills, **Belgrade Forest** (Belgrad Ormanları) was originally a hunting preserve of the Ottomans. The pine, oak and beech forest is now a popular retreat from the rigours of the city.

A sophisticated system of dams, reservoirs, water towers and aqueducts is still in evidence around the forest, which supplied İstanbul with most of its fresh water during the Byzantine and Ottoman eras. The most impressive of the aqueducts is the *Uzun* or **Long Aqueduct**, a one-kilometre walk south of Büyük Bend dam, one of seven dams in the forest. Its tiers of tall, pointed arches were built by Sinan for Süleyman the Magnificent in 1563. Close to the reservoir are the remains of Belgrade village, whose name came about after the capture of Belgrade in 1521, when a community of Serbian POWs were settled here to take over the upkeep of the water-supply system. In the seventeenth century, the forest was "discovered" by the city's foreign community, who came to seek refuge from a particularly nasty pestilence that was wiping out half of İstanbul, and for the next century or so many wealthy Christians had second homes here. In the 1890s, the village was evacuated by Abdülhamid II, who believed the inhabitants were polluting the city's water supply.

The Asian Shore

On the **Asian Shore**, a number of once-small villages have merged into a great suburb stretching all the way up from Üsküdar to the second Bosphorus bridge. Still quite attractive despite the urban sprawl, these former fishing villages hold a few surprises, from the waterfront nineteenth-century **Beylerbeyi Palace** and the Ottoman fortress

A SECOND BOSPHORUS

It may all turn out to have been a vote-garnering, pre-election gambit by ambitious Turkish PM Recep Tayip Erdogan, but in the spring of 2011 the Turkish news was full of a grandiose scheme to build a new Bosphorus channel to the west of the metropolis, Canal Istanbul. The PM, re-elected for a third term soon after his "magnificent and crazy plan" project announcement, wants the new canal to open in 2023 to coincide with the one hundredth anniversary of the foundation of the Turkish Republic. The advantages are obvious. The "original" Bosphorus would be freed of the dangerous tankers crowding the strait, leading to a safer city for residents and visitors alike, and enabling the waterway to become an even more integral part of the city's over-burdened transport infrastructure and thus a boon to tourism. Critics, however, point out that the project will be unfeasibly expensive, especially as by the terms of the Montreux Convention of 1936 merchant and passenger ships can use the Bosphorus both freely and without a toll, meaning the new mega-canal will almost certainly have to provide free passage. Conservationists point to the inevitable development of the banks of the new waterway, which they claim will push the limits of the city inexorably westward.

What seems almost certain to go ahead, however, is a third Bosphorus bridge north of the current pair. The government, who put the plan out to tender in November 2011, claim it is necessary to reduce traffic congestion, while opponents are convinced it will not only lead to more traffic in the city, but will also destroy the last major green area of the metropolis, as the forest and wetlands around the bridge will inevitably be developed for housing and industry.

Anadolu Hisarı, to the **Hıdıv Kısri**, a beautiful nineteenth-century villa set in a pleasant park, and the shell of a **Byzantine fortress** at Andolu Kavağı.

GETTING AROUND   THE ASIAN SHORE

By ferry Sehir Hatları (see p.26) ferries run between some of the Bosphorus suburbs, both on the European and Asian shores, but making the right connections is tricky. Consult their timetables.

By bus The #15 runs all along the Bosphorus shore from Üsküdar's main square as far as Beykoz; to reach Anadolu Kavağı from here, take the #15/A.

10

Beylerbeyi Palace
Tues, Wed & Fri–Sun 9.30am–6pm • 5TL • Bus #15 or #15/B from Üsküdar

The main attraction of **Beylerbeyi**, on the north side of the Bosphorus Bridge, is the **Beylerbeyi Palace**, a nineteenth-century white-marble summer residence and guesthouse of the Ottoman sultans. The palace was much admired by contemporary visitors from Europe – after her stay in 1869, Empress Eugénie had its windows copied in the Tuileries Palace in Paris. The interior decoration was designed by Sultan Abdülaziz himself, while some of the furniture, including the matching dining chairs in the *harem* and the *selamlık*, was carved by Sultan Abdülhamid II during his six years of imprisonment here, up to his death in 1918. The central staircase, with its fanciful twisting shape, is perhaps the highlight, but there are all kinds of details to savour, from the neo-Islamic patterns on the ceilings down to the beautiful Egyptian *hasır* (the reed matting on the floor). The pleasant café in the gardens is a very popular weekend breakfast spot.

Çengelköy
Bus #15 from Üsküdar

The pretty village suburb of **Çengelköy** is a short walk from Beylerbeyi. Its main landmark building, the **Kuleli Naval College**, once served as a hospital under the direction of Florence Nightingale in the Crimean War, though it's currently closed to the public. There's little of interest here apart from the boutique *Sumahan on the Water* hotel (see p.174), housed in an old *rakı* distillery, and its very stylish restaurant.

Küçüksu Kasrı
Tues, Wed & Fri–Sun 9.30am–4pm • 4TL • Bus #15 from Çengelköy – after passing a boatyard to your left, you'll cross a bridge over the Küçüksu Deresi; get off at the next stop, walk back to the sign saying "Küçük Saray Aile Bahçesi" and you'll find the palace at the end of a drive

Küçüksu Kasrı, sometimes known as Göksu Palace, takes both its names from the two nearby streams that empty into the Bosphorus. Built in 1857 by Nikoğos Balian, son of the architect of Dolmabahçe Palace, its exterior is highly ornate – the Rococo carving is best seen from the Bosphorus, the intended approach. The whole of the palace interior is decorated with lace and carpets from Hereke and lit by Bohemian crystal chandeliers. The floors are mahogany, inlaid with rose- and almond-wood and ebony; upstairs is an ebony table on which Sultan Abdülaziz was wont to arm-wrestle with visitors of state. The palace was constructed on the site of several earlier incarnations, and the fountain from one of these still stands, a fine example of Ottoman Baroque, built in 1796.

Anadolu Hisarı
Bus #15 from Üsküdar

The **Küçüksu Deresi** and the **Göksu** are the streams formerly known to Europeans as the "Sweet Waters of Asia", their banks once graced by picnicking parties of Ottoman nobility. On the north bank of the Göksu stands the Ottoman fortress of **Anadolu Hisarı** (open 24hr; free), beneath the towering Fatih Bridge. It was built by Beyazit I in 1397, when the Ottoman forces first reached the strait separating Asia from Europe. Along with the more recent Rumeli Hisarı fortress opposite (see p.150) the castle could effectively cut off the strait to unwanted shipping. The castle is best reached by the #15

bus from Üsküdar, though, its fine position apart, it's of no real interest except to castle-buffs. Near here, with fabulous views of the strait and the Fatih Bridge, is one of the city's best-regarded **fish restaurants**, *Körfez* (see p.193).

Kanlıca
Bus #15 from Üsküdar

Backed by verdant forest, the attractive suburb of **Kanlıca** is famed for its **yoghurt**, which can be eaten at any of the little quayside restaurants – try the cheap and cheerful *Asırlık*, by the ferry landing, housed in an old wooden building with a veranda giving right onto the Bosphorus. Alternatively, the *A'jia* **hotel**, in a delightful *yalı* at Çubuklu Cad 27 (see p.174), has a considerably more upmarket **restaurant** (see p.174).

On the top of a hill, a twenty-minute walk behind the waterfront, is the wonderful **Hıdıv Kısri** (Khedive's Villa) built for Abbas Hilmi Paşa, the last Khedive (the title given to governors of Egypt in Ottoman times), in 1900. It's an eclectic architectural mix, but look out for the Art Nouveau metalwork on the steam-powered lift and the beautiful stained-glass ceiling lights in the central tower. The building is now a restaurant and is surrounded by a beautifully maintained park with a café, both offering superb views over the Bosphorus.

Anadolu Kavağı
Bus #15 from Üsküdar to Beykoz; from here, take the #15/A

The last call on the Bosphorus Cruise from Eminönü (see box, p.147) is laidback **Anadolu Kavağı**. The village has a distinct, if dilapidated, charm – balconied houses with boat-mooring stations overlook the river, while the main street is lined with some reasonable **fish restaurants**. All offer fixed-menu meals aimed squarely at the Bosphorus cruisers, most of whom are captive prey for the two hours the boat docks here. A couple of decent options are the family-run *Ceneviz*, housed in an old building that once served as the village's *kahvehane* (teahouse), and the *Coskun Balıkçı*, set in an old wooden house, though neither are licensed.

Sprawling across an overgrown hilltop above the town is the Byzantine **fortress** (closed awaiting restoration at the time of writing) from which the village takes its name. With its typical Byzantine masonry of alternating bands of pale stone and red brick and D-shaped towers, it's an impressive sight and was once of supreme strategic importance as guardian of the strait. The views from the top over the Bosphorus are superb. Look out for various Greek inscriptions cut into the stonework, including the imperial logo of the Palaeologus dynasty (a cross with the letter "b" in each corner, which stands for "King of Kings, who Kings it over Kings"). To get to the fortress, follow Mirşah Hamam Sokak from the dock and walk uphill for half an hour.

The Black Sea resorts

The **Black Sea** is relatively accessible from İstanbul, and if you're staying in the city for any length of time over the summer, its seaside villages may exert a considerable pull. Bear in mind, however, that it takes up to two hours to reach Şile (not counting getting to the departure point, Üsküdar, on the Asian side of the Bosphorus), and not much less to reach Kılyos. Ağva, a good hour beyond Şile, is really only possible if you overnight. Summer weekends are extremely busy, as you would expect of seaside resorts so close to such a major conurbation, and the development of the resorts has been largely uncontrolled.

Kılyos

There's little of historical interest in **KİLYOS**, the nearest resort to İstanbul on the European side of the Bosphorus – the former Greek fishing village has sadly succumbed to a tide of holiday-home development, the beach is crowded, and the area's most imposing monument, a medieval Genoese castle, is occupied by the Turkish army and off-limits. If partying is your thing, however, there are a couple of private **beaches**, which offer assorted entertainment as well as loungers and umbrellas (see below).

GETTING THERE KILYOS

From the city centre, take the M2 Metro from Şişhane or Taksim to the Haciosman Metro stop. From here, bus #151 runs to Kılyos and Demirciköy from 6am to 9.30pm, with the last bus returning weekdays at 10.40, weekends at 10.20pm. The journey takes around 45min.

BEACHES

10

Dalia 2km from Kılyos in the village of Demirciköy ☏0212/204 0368, ⓦclubdalia.com. The low-key *Dalia* is a more relaxing option than *Solar Beach*, though it still offers various watersports. Mon–Fri 20TL, Sat & Sun 30TL. June–Sept daily 8am–6pm.

Solar Beach ☏0212/201 2101, ⓦsolarbeach.org. Offers activities ranging from beach volleyball tournaments and bungee jumping to skateboarding and hovercrafting; it also hosts the Electronica Festival every June. Mon–Fri 25TL, Sat & Sun 40TL. June–Sept daily 8am–7pm.

Şile

The construction of a major road linking the suburbs of Asian İstanbul to **ŞILE** has led to increased development; some İstanbullus live here and commute into town, or have a weekend summerhouse in the town. Out of season, it's easy to see Şile's attraction, perched on a clifftop overlooking a large bay and tiny island, with white sandy **beaches** stretching off to the west, but it gets very crowded in the summer season, especially at weekends when hordes of visitors pour in from stiflingly hot İstanbul. Beaches apart, there's little to occupy the visitor except to admire the pretty French-built black-and-white-striped **lighthouse** and the fourteenth-century **Genoese castle** on a nearby island – though neither are open to the public. To reach the seafront from the bus station head down attractively cobbled Üsküdar Caddesi, a street lined by cafés and bars. At the end of the street, with fine views over the harbour and pretty rock formations below, is the *Panorama Restaurant*, a good bet for a reasonably-priced fish meal.

Şile's main historical claim to fame is that it was visited by Xenophon and his Ten Thousand, the army that was left leaderless when its officers were all murdered by the Persians. They stayed in Şile, then known as Kalpe, and Xenophon wrote in his memoirs about how well the site suited the establishment of a city. Apart from tourism, the town's only other industry is the production of **Şile bezi**, a kind of cheesecloth that local women embroider by hand, which is sold both here and all over Turkey.

GETTING THERE ŞILE

By bus Several buses depart daily for Şile from a stop behind the waterfront Şemsih Paşa Camii in Üsküdar. The Şile Ekspres departs at 11.30am and 5.20pm, and follows the shortest and quickest route, returning at 5.40pm and 7.20pm.The slower #139 departs more than hourly from

7am, with the last bus back from Şile at 11pm. In summer, especially at weekends, seats are at a premium for late-afternoon/evening returns so it's best to book your seat back on arrival, otherwise you risk waiting around or, worse, getting stranded overnight.

Ağva

Some 97km from İstanbul, the village of **AĞVA** is a quieter, marginally less developed spot than Şile, 50km away, and more worthy of the journey from the city. The village is set in a beautiful location between two rivers, the Yeşilçay and the Göksü, both of which are fished to provide the livelihood of the local community. Ağva's **beach** has fine golden sand, but the currents here are notoriously strong so take care when swimming. There are several fish restaurants here, as well as a few boutique hotels (see p.174).

GETTING THERE AĞVA

By bus The #139/A bus from Üsküdar goes direct to Ağva via Şile, taking almost three and a half hours, otherwise take a bus to Şile, from where there are regular departures

on to Ağva. The last bus back to Üsküdar via Şile leaves at 8pm in summer.

BÜYÜKADA HARBOUR

The Princes' Islands

The Princes' Islands, situated in the Sea of Marmara some 15km southeast of the city and just a few kilometres off the Asian landmass, have always been a favourite retreat for İstanbullus. Four of the nine islands are easily accessible by ferry from İstanbul, the nearest taking only 35 minutes by sea bus. Predictably enough, this makes them very popular – the number of visitors annually has risen from six million in 2005 to a whopping ten million in 2010 – so they're hardly unspoilt island retreats. Most day-trippers, however, come to enjoy the bargain-priced boat ride out and back; once on the islands few do little more than mill around the cafés and restaurants at the ferry landing points.

Head out around the coast or, even better, inland, and you'll soon escape the crowds. Apart from the odd police or utility vehicle, no cars are allowed on the islands; their place is taken by four-person horse-drawn carriages known as *phaetons* (*fayton* in Turkish). Bicycling is very popular and an ideal way to get around these small islands, with rental bikes available at every ferry terminal – alternatively, as distances are generally short, you can explore on foot. There are plenty of (mainly stony) beaches, making them the city's best option for a day's sunbathing and swimming, though nearly all charge an admission fee. The islands' proximity makes them an easy day-trip from İstanbul, but to really appreciate their laidback charm, it's worth staying over (see p.175).

Some history

The islands have been inhabited since Classical times, but their first claim to fame derived from the copper mines of **Chalkitis** – modern Heybeliada – long since exhausted (but still visible near Çam Limanı). In the Byzantine era, numerous convents and monasteries were built on the islands and these became favoured – because of their proximity to the capital and ease of surveillance – as luxurious **prisons** for banished emperors, empresses and princes (often after they had been blinded). After the Conquest (see p.284), the islands were largely neglected by the Ottoman Turks and became a place of refuge for Greek, Armenian and Jewish communities.

In 1846, a ferry service was established and the islands became popular with Pera's wealthy merchants and bankers, mainly from the Christian and Jewish minorities, and it is their ornate wooden villas that give the islands their defining character. It wasn't until the early years of the Republic, however, that they became İstanbul's favourite **summer resort**. Mosques began to appear in the villages, and hotels and apartment buildings soon followed. A Turkish naval college was established on Heybeliada, and the islands received the rubber stamp of Republican respectability when Atatürk's private yacht was moored here as a training ship.

Not all of the islands have romantic connotations. Sivriada, which is uninhabited and cannot be visited, gained public notoriety in 1911 when all the stray dogs in İstanbul were rounded up, shipped out there and left to starve; while Yassıada is best known as a prison island, used for the detention of political dissenters. It was here that Adnan Menderes and two of his former ministers were hanged on September 16, 1961, after a military coup (see p.295).

GETTING THERE AND AROUND

The Princes' Islands are easy to reach, but get to the ferry at least an hour before departure in summer, especially on Sundays, as the queues can be massive. Having a topped-up İstanbulkart (see box, p.24) will save you having to queue for a ticket but won't guarantee you a seat, so it's still best to arrive early.

By ferry Şehir Hatları ferries run from the Adalar ferry terminal in Kabataş (handily placed beyond Beşiktaş at the end of the tram line) to the main islands of Kınalıada, Burgazada, Heybeliada and, lastly, Büyükada (June 20–Sept 18, 15 daily 6.50am–10.30pm; Sept 21–June 19, 9 daily 6.50am–10.30pm; 3.50TL, 2.75TL with an İstanbulkart). It takes around fifty minutes to reach Kınalıada, close on an hour and a half to Büyükada. Several smaller private companies also operate boats from Kabataş to the islands, including Mavi Marmara and Dentur Avrasya. They use smaller boats than Şehir Hatları, with pleasantly open decks to catch the summer breezes, and charge 5TL one way.

By sea bus The more expensive but much quicker sea bus (*deniz otobüs*) service also runs from Kabataş (June 20–Sept 18, Mon–Fri 8.15am–8.35pm, Sat & Sun 10.45am–8.50pm; Sept 21–June 19, Mon–Fri 1–2 daily; 7.50TL, 6TL with an İstanbulkart), taking as little as 35 minutes to Büyükada. Unlike the ferries, not all sea-bus departures visit all the islands – check before boarding. Also note that sea buses have no open deck, which is fine in dodgy weather but not so enjoyable on a warm summer's day.

Island-hopping Getting between the main islands is easy, but check ferry times at the docks and don't rely simply on a timetable; the service is notoriously changeable. An İstanbulkart or a handful of *jetons* (see box, p.23) makes island-hopping easier, but remember that each ferry "hop" will set you back 3.50TL.

11

Kabataş

Surp Krikor
Lusavoriç

Kınalıada
Turizm Plajı

Kınalıada

Yassıada & Sivriada

Kaşıkada

Aya Triada Mana

Değirmen Burnu Plajı

Green Beach Club

Sait Faik Museum

St John
the Baptist

Ertan Bike Hire

Kalpazankaya

Burgazada

Heybeliada

Çam Limanı

Ada Beach
Club

Aghios Spiridon

Heybelia
Sanitori

■ ACCOMMODATION	
Ayinikola Butik	
Pansiyon	9
Büyüada Princers	5
Mentap 45	1
Merit Halki Palace	3
Meziki	7
Naya Retreat	8
Özdemir Pansiyon	2
Prenset Pansiyon	4
Splendid Palas	6

SEA OF MARMARA

THE PRINCES' ISLANDS

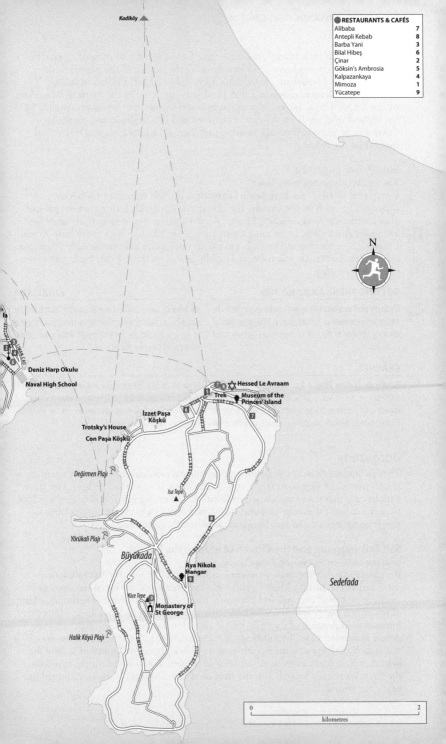

Kadiköy

N

Deniz Harp Okulu

Naval High School

Hessed Le Avraam

Trek

Museum of the Princes' Island

İzzet Paşa Köşkü

Trotsky's House

Con Paşa Köşkü

Değirmen Plajı

Isa Tepe

Yörükali Plajı

Büyükada

Aya Nikola Hangar

Sedefada

Yüce Tepe

Monastery of St George

Halik Köyü Plajı

0   2

kilometres

Kınalıada

Kınalıada, or "Henna Island", takes its name from the red colouring of its eastern cliffs; in Greek, it was known as *Proti*, since it's the nearest of the islands to the mainland. Like Heybeliada, Kınalıada's history is notable for exiles, including Romanus IV Diogenes, deposed after his disastrous defeat at the Battle of Manzikert by the Selçuk Turks. Today, its population is seventy percent Armenian, swelled by friends and relatives from the city in summer, and unless you have a particular interest in İstanbul's Armenian community, there is little of historical or cultural interest on the island.

Surp Krikor Lusavoriç
Three streets back and uphill from the ferry terminal

Completed in 1857, the **Surp Krikor Lusavoriç** is the sole Armenian Orthodox (Apostolic) church on the islands. The church's most notable features are the painted glass lunette windows depicting historic Armenian churches, mainly from lands now lost to the Armenians, in distant Eastern Turkey. On a hilltop high above Surp Krikor Lusavoriç, overlooking the town, is a monastery originally built in the early Byzantine era, though the church and associated buildings now on the site date back only to the nineteenth century.

11

GETTING THERE AND AROUND   KINALIADA

By ferry and sea bus Ferries and sea buses run from the Adalar ferry terminal in Kabataş (see p.159); they dock at the ferry terminal of the sole settlement on the east coast of the island.

By bike Cycling is the best way to tour the island, and the entire circuit should take an hour or so. There are a couple of shops just behind the ferry terminal renting out poorly-maintained bikes for 5TL an hour.

BEACHES

Kınalıada Turizm Plajı A free "people's" beach on the southeast of the island, a forty-minute walk or fifteen-minute cycle ride from the ferry terminal. Like virtually all Princes' Islands' beaches, it's stony, so you'll probably want to cough up 10TL for a lounger and umbrella. Next door to it is a posher pay-beach (20TL) with its own outdoor pool, and there are a few more pay beaches on the north and northeast shores of the island.

Burgazada

Though **Burgazada** lacks the quantity of late nineteenth- and early twentieth-century houses that make Büyükada (see p.164) so attractive, it more than makes up for this with its easy charm and narrow streets lined with palm, fig, bay and oleander. Much of the mature forest that once carpeted the island burnt in a forest fire in 2003, but is slowly being regenerated and Burgazada is pleasantly green once again.

Sait Faik Museum and the Church of St John the Baptist
Burgaz Çayırı Sok 15 · Tues–Fri 10am–noon & 2–5pm, Sat 10am–noon · Free

Burgazada's fascinating small **museum** is dedicated to the novelist **Sait Faik** (often described as the Turkish Mark Twain), who lived here, and the house has been so carefully preserved that you feel like you're trespassing. In the writer's bedroom, a pair of pyjamas is neatly folded on the bed, with a towel on the rack beside it. You get an immediate impression of the man, whose exceptional character is evidenced by the simple bohemian style of furnishings in his island home. A useful locator for the museum is the imposing nineteenth-century Greek Orthodox **Church of St John the Baptist**, whose dome dominates the main settlement as you approach the island on the ferry. It's usually locked, as is the associated sacred spring, or *ayazma*, located just below the church.

GETTING THERE AND AROUND

BURGAZADA

By ferry and sea bus Ferries and sea buses run from the Adalar ferry terminal in Kabataş (see p.159); they dock at the ferry terminal on the east coast of the island.

By bike Bikes are available for 15TL a day from Ertan

Bisiklet, some 400m south of the ferry terminal.

By phaeton *Phaetons* congregate just north of the ferry terminal, offering long tours of the island for 45TL, a shorter version for 35TL.

BEACHES

Alpazankaya For cheap swimming, head to Alpazankaya on the west coast of the island, a half-hour bicycle or 20TL *phaeton* ride from the ferry terminal. The small, rocky

swimming area has a fine restaurant of the same name in the pine trees above it. Mon–Fri 2.50TL, Sat & Sun 5TL. Daily 10am–midnight.

Heybeliada

Heybeliada, or the "Island of the Saddlebag", has managed to retain much of its village identity, and there's a strong community spirit among its permanent residents. It's a beautiful place, known for the beaches to which İstanbul residents flock in their hundreds at weekends. The family of the famous İstanbul writer Orhan Pamuk (see box, p.128) regularly spent the summer in one of the island's fine wooden Art Nouveau-style mansions.

Some buildings you might come across during a stroll around the island include the **Heybeliada Sanatorium**, a private home for TB sufferers located off Çam Limanı Yolu on the south side of the island, and the **Deniz Harp Okulu** (Naval High School), on the east side of the island, along the coast road from the main jetty, which was originally the Naval War Academy, situated here since 1852. The Greek Orthodox **Aya Nikola** church is a prominent red-and-cream building with a curious clock tower, just behind the waterfront in the town centre. On the south side of the island, on a pine-forested promontory, is the wooden monastery of **Agios Spiridon**. It's run-down and rather forlorn looking, but Orthodox visitors still light candles inside and admire the sea views from the outside.

Aya Triada Manastiri

Mon–Sat 10am–noon & 2–4pm · Free · By appointment only · ☎ 0216/351 8563

Heybeliada's main point of interest is the nineteenth-century **Aya Triada Manastiri**, the Greek Orthodox School of Theology, majestically situated on the peak of the island's northernmost hill. It's a pleasant fifteen-minute walk through pine forest (or take a *phaeton*; see below). You'll need to provide scholarship credentials to view the library of 230,000 books, including an important collection of Byzantine manuscripts. The building is set in beautiful grounds, and encloses a pretty, eight-hundred-year-old church, with a stunning gilt iconostasis. Orthodox priests were trained here until the government closed it in 1973 (attempts to reopen it are ongoing but continue to founder), and you can see the dusty classroom filled with age-blackened desks where the acolytes received instruction.

GETTING THERE AND AROUND

HEYBELIADA

By ferry and sea bus Ferries and sea buses run from the Adalar ferry terminal in Kabataş (see p.159); they dock at the ferry terminal on the main quayside of Rıhtım Caddesi, on the west coast of the island.

By bike Cycling is perhaps the best way to enjoy Heybeliada, its pine forests and hills making for scenic rides and rambles, with the added bonus of taking in one of the

beaches. There's bike rental near the quayside at İmralı Sok 3, and several other outlets nearby; all charge 5TL per hour, 15TL all day.

By phaeton Prices for *phaetons* from Ayyıldız Caddesi (which runs parallel to the front) to various destinations around the island are posted on a board in the street; tours of the island are also available by *phaeton* (20min 33TL, 40min 43TL).

BEACHES

Ada Beach Club ⓦadabeachclub.com. Attractively situated in a large bay on the island's south coast, and has a free shuttle-boat service from the ferry terminal area. There's a rather scruffy "people's" beach next door, where you can rent a sun lounger for 5TL. 20TL. Daily 9am–sunset.

Değirmen Burnu Plajı A good mid-range option, set in pretty pine forest on the south shore of a peninsula projecting from the northwest corner of the island. It's a small, shingly curve of beach at the foot of some small cliffs, and feels much wilder than the posher beach clubs.

It's a half-hour walk from the ferry terminal, and is best reached by *phaeton*. Mon–Fri 10.25TL, Sat & Sun 13.25TL. Daily 9am–sunset.

Green Beach Club ⓦgreenbeachclub.com. The smartest beach on the island, on the opposite side of the island from the ferry terminal – a free service boat departs from just north of the quay for beach-goers. There's thumping Turkish pop all day, but the on-site café is reasonably priced and the small, shallow sandy beach is ideal for kids. Mon–Fri 25TL, Sat & Sun 35TL. Late April to Sept 8am–sunset.

Büyükada

Büyükada (the "Great Island", the original *Prinkipo*, or "Princes' Island", in Greek) is the largest of the islands and has long been inhabited by minorities. It has traditionally been a place of retreat or exile, and Leon Trotsky lived here from 1929 to 1933, when he began to write his *History of the Russian Revolution*. Trotsky spent most of his time in a brick-built villa on Hamlacı Sokak, a steep street running down towards the sea off Çankaya Caddesi, below the attractive **Con Paşa Köşkü**, a fine *fin-de-siècle* mansion under restoration at the time of writing. To reach Trotsky's house (it is derelict, awaiting restoration as a museum) head southwest from the busy ferry-terminal area, along the main road used by the *phaetons* (Çankaya Caddesi) and turn right after the Con Paşa Konak – it's the second brick-built villa down the hill.

The large mansions of Büyükada tend to have beautiful gardens full of magnolia, mimosa and jasmine, and in the surrounding pine forests myrtle, lilac and rock roses grow wild, so the scents of the island on a summer's evening are one of its most memorable aspects, though often far stronger is the less desirable whiff of horse-dung.

After decades of ill-advised development, the island is beginning to take its past seriously. The open-air **Museum of the Princes' Islands** (ⓦadalarmuzesi.org) was due to open at the Çınar grounds at the time of writing, and will tell the history of the islands through Ottoman archive material, period photographs and oral history resources. Over on the east side of the island, the **Aya Nikola Hangar** (4TL; Tues–Sun 10am–5pm) has a permanent exhibition focusing on the island's writers and poets as well as hosting temporary exhibitions.

Yüce Tepe and İsa Tepe

The island consists of two hills, both surmounted by monasteries. The southernmost, **Yüce Tepe**, is the location of the **Monastery of St George**, which is probably on the site of a twelfth-century building. Close up, it consists of a series of chapels on three levels, with the oldest – containing a sacred spring – on the lowest level. In Byzantine times, the monastery functioned as an asylum – the iron rings set into the floor of the chapels were used for restraining the inmates. To reach St George, take a *phaeton* to the small park on the main road that runs over the hill, from where a steep cobbled path (plied by donkeys) leads up several hundred metres to the monastery. The cycle ride from the town to the monastery is a worthwhile alternative – cycle west from the central square behind the waterfront, past the *Splendid Palas* hotel and onto Çankaya Caddesi, with its succession of gorgeous wooden *fin-de-siècle* villas, before branching left and up into the forest; it takes around thirty minutes to cycle to the donkey stands at the foot of the hill.

The huge but decrepit building on the northern hill, **İsa Tepe**, is a late nineteenth-century Greek orphanage, closed down in 1964 and falling into wrack and ruin ever since. Said to be the second largest wooden building in the world, it has long been the subject of wrangling between Turkey and its ethnic Greek Orthodox minority. In 2010, a Strasbourg court ruled that the orphanage, appropriated by the Turkish authorities, should be returned to its original owners, the Fener Greek Patriarchate (see p.98).

GETTING THERE AND AROUND

BÜYÜKADA

By ferry and sea bus Ferries and sea buses run from the Adalar ferry terminal in Kabataş (see p.159); they dock at two adjacent terminals on Büyük İskele Caddesi in Büyükada's main town, from where the main square and most of the hotels, restaurants and shops are just a short walk away.

By bike With motor vehicles banned, there are bike rental shops (5TL/hr, 15TL/day) everywhere. Recommended is Trek, on Nisan Cad 23, just behind the clock tower, which has new, well-maintained bikes. Wherever you rent from, however, make sure you check that the brakes and gears work properly before setting off – if you're planning to

cycle inland, you'll need them. You'll also need to leave some ID as a guaranty. With swimming breaks and ascents to the high points there's plenty of scope to spend the whole day on two wheels, though you can comfortably whizz right around the island in an hour and a half.

By phaeton Horse-and-carriage tours (for up to four people; short tour 50TL, long tour 60TL) leave from the *phaeton* park off the main square on İsa Çelebi Sokak, 50m southwest of the ferry terminal.

By donkey Donkey rides up the hills (10TL) start from a little park just up Kadayoran Caddesi from the centre of town.

BEACHES

Değirmen Plajı Off Çankaya Caddesi, on the west coast. The cheapest (but tiniest) beach on the island, and the closest to the ferry terminal. 5TL. 10am–sunset.

Halik Köyü Plajı Heading south from the ferry terminal into remoter, forested terrain is the best of the islands' beaches, reached on a seven-minute stroll from the coast road, down a stepped path through typical Mediterranean trees and shrubs (or there's a free boat from the ferry terminal), with a cheap on-site café and showers. Although the beach itself is stony, looking not across the urban sprawl

of İstanbul but south across the sea to the green, southern shores of the Sea of Marmara, it's not hard here to imagine yourself on a remote Aegean or Mediterranean island. 10TL. Daily 8am–dusk.

Yörükali Plajı ⓦ yorukali.com. A little further south than Değirmen Plajı is this much bigger beach which offers a free boat transfer from the ferry terminal. Sunbathing is accompanied by loud Turkish pop, but the beach is sandy and good for kids. 20TL including lounger and umbrella. Mid-April to Sept 8am–sunset.

11

Accommodation

The number of visitors to İstanbul is rising sharply each year, but finding accommodation is rarely a problem. Needless to say, in a city of this size, every type of lodging is available, from multinational hotel chains and exclusive boutique establishments to basic city hotels and hostels for the budget-conscious. Apart from the most modest establishments (and even in many of these), en-suite bathrooms and breakfast are included in the price. Most also provide air-conditioning for the hot, humid summers and double-glazing and central heating to cope with the winter chills. All but a handful of the accommodation choices listed below provide free wi-fi access and most have a fixed terminal or two as well.

Budget and type of accommodation aside, the biggest decision you'll have to make is which part of the city to stay in. The **old city**, which includes Sultanahmet and other areas falling within the old Byzantine land walls, is by far the most popular choice, followed by the area across the Golden Horn: trendy **Beyoğlu** and environs, plus the business district of **Taksim** to the north. If you have the money and hanker after exclusivity, the hotels fronting **the Bosphorus** may be an attractive alternative. Spring and autumn are often busy and, particularly if you have your heart set on a special place, especially one of the more exclusive boutique hotels, it's advisable to book as far ahead as possible. Rooms with a sea view, or that look over landmark sites such as the Aya Sofya or Blue Mosque, carry a sometimes sizeable premium. Until recently all **hostel** accommodation was concentrated in the old city, but for those who are more interested in nightlife or contemporary culture, a rash of new places has opened up on the other side of the Golden Horn in Galata/Beyoğlu.

ESSENTIALS

Rates In this guide (including the Out of the City chapters), accommodation prices are, unless stated otherwise, quoted as the lowest price per double room in high season, though for backpacker hostels the rate for dorms is per person. Almost all prices below are given in euros, reflecting how most hotels advertise their rates. Note that walk-in rack prices can often be unrealistically high, having been fixed in a busy season or for the benefit of tour companies, and many hotels will be happy to bargain.

Seasons High season runs from mid-March to mid-November and Christmas and New Year, when prices are at their highest (though some establishments are a little cheaper in July and August). Most places offer discounts during the main low season, usually around 15 to 20 percent.

SULTANAHMET

12

The majority of first-time visitors to the city tend to stay in **Sultanahmet**, among the major attractions of the Blue Mosque, Topkapı Palace and Aya Sofya. The options around the **Hippodrome** are particularly good from a historical perspective, but the highest concentration of accommodation is to be found in and around **Akbıyık Caddesi**, an immensely popular backstreet with a package-resort atmosphere. There are plenty of quieter streets in nearby **Cankurtaran**, the area between Sultanahmet and the Sea of Marmara. The hotels off **Divan Yolu** have the advantage of being handy for the Topkapı–Eminönü–Kabataş tram.

AROUND THE HIPPODROME

Deniz Houses Çayıroğlu Sok 14 ☎0212/518 9595, ⓦdenizkonakhotel.com; map p.44. Set in a couple of adjacent townhouses on an interesting side street, this is a very friendly establishment. The front rooms in A Blok have sea views but some noise from the railway, and all of the smallish rooms have funky kilims and wooden floors. Rooms in B Blok are plusher, but lack sea views, though there's a great terrace with sea and city views, where guests can enjoy complimentary coffee. The owners also run the Backpackers Travel Agency, so are more helpful than most when it comes to organizing your stay. €75

★ **İbrahim Pasha** Terzihane Sok, 5 Adliye Yanı ☎0212/518 0394, ⓦibrahimpasha.com; map p.44. This lovingly-converted pair of early twentieth-century townhouses forms arguably the most tasteful boutique hotel in Sultanahmet, successfully blending a stylish modern interior with Ottoman antiques. The 24 uncluttered rooms are very comfortable and, owing to the side-street location, quiet. Views from the recently expanded roof terrace across the domes and minarets of Sultanahmet and down to the Sea of Marmara are superb, and the freshly prepared breakfast (with latte and espresso on tap) in the

cosy and charming downstairs breakfast room is a delight. Very friendly and well-run, with a useful guide to the city's best restaurants for all guests. Ten percent discount for cash. €99

Turkoman Asmalı Çeşme Sok, 2 Adliye Yanı ☎0212/516 2956, ⓦturkomanhotel.com; map p.44. Opened back when the term "boutique hotel" meant somewhere with period character and individuality, the friendly *Turkoman* continues to offer distinctive accommodation. Fashioned from a converted house done out in nineteenth-century Turkish style, right on the Hippodrome and opposite the Egyptian Obelisk, it boasts fine views of the Blue Mosque from the roof terrace. Each attractive room is named after one of the old Turkoman

---

TOP FIVE PERIOD HOTELS

A'jia Bosphorus, see p.174
Empress Zoe Cankurtaran, see p.169
İbrahim Pasha Sultanahmet, see p.167
Kariye Northwest Quarter, see p.171
Pera Palas İstiklal Caddesi and around, see p.173

tribes, and has a brass bed and wooden floors. Ask for one of the front, Hippodrome-facing rooms. Free airport transfers. **€129**

AROUND TOPKAPI PALACE

Ayasofya Konakları Soğukçeşme Sok ☎0212/513 3660, ⓦayasofyakonaklari.com; map p.44. Created from a series of ten nineteenth-century wooden houses on a cobbled street squeezed between the walls of the Topkapı Palace and the Aya Sofya, this is, without a doubt, one of the most atmospheric hotels in the city. The choice of rooms is bewildering, ranging from roomy suites (one with a Finnish sauna) to compact doubles. Staying in one of the rooms in the imposing Konuk Evi, a detached wooden mansion in its own garden opposite the main hotel, is about as close to period living as you can get, with original brass beds, parquet flooring adorned with Turkish carpets, and painted wooden ceilings. **€170**

★ **Cheers** Zeynepsultan Cami Sok 21 ☎0212/526 0200, ⓦcheershostel.com; map p.44. This hostel, set in an old house on a quiet side-street just off the tram line below the Aya Sofya, makes a refreshing change from the old-city options clustered around Akbıyık Caddesi. In addition to four- and ten-bed dorms, a/c doubles and twins are also available. Apart from the peaceful location, a real draw is the terrace bar, which looks over mature plane trees onto the west face of the Aya Sofya, a view few visitors ever see. Dorm **€15**, double **€60**

AROUND DIVAN YOLU

Kybele Yerebatan Cad 35 ☎0212/511 7766, ⓦkybelehotel.com; map p.44. Established over twenty years ago, this is a good choice if you're looking for somewhere a little quirky and oozing with retro charm. A late nineteenth-century rendered brick building, handily situated just behind busy Divan Yolu, it boasts over four thousand multi-hued antique-style light fittings. The sixteen spacious rooms have old wood flooring and brass and iron bedsteads. A rich breakfast, including olive oil from the Aegean-village home of the three friendly brothers who run it, is served in a shady courtyard full of candelabra, cushions, and retro knick-knacks, and there's a charming wooden outbuilding that serves as a lounge/library. **€110**

Nomade Ticarethane Sok 15 ☎0212/513 8172, ⓦhotelnomade.com; map p.44. Described as "ethnic trendy" by the French designer responsible for its chic interior, this hotel has white-floored rooms finished in bold colours, with rich coordinating fabrics and blonde-wood modernist furniture. The charming and sophisticated twin sisters who run it ensure excellent service. Rooms are a little on the small side, and some of the furniture is showing signs of wear, but it has one of the very best roof-terraces in the old city and the lavish breakfast includes the not always standard filter-coffee. **€100**

Ottoman Hotel Imperial Caferiye Sok 6/1 ☎0212/513 6151, ⓦottomanhotelimperial.com; map p.44. Hard to believe this wonderfully situated, lavishly refurbished hotel was once the *Yücelt Hostel*, springboard for India-bound overlanders in the 1970s. The best rooms (€240), have great views of the Aya Sofya, baths and plasma TVs; standard rooms face the main (tram) road, and all have tea- and coffee-making facilities. Attached is the very well regarded *Matbah* restaurant (see p.186). Good value for the location and level of comfort and style. **€150**

White House Çatalçeşme Sok ☎0212/526 0019, ⓦistanbulwhitehouse.com; map p.44. Immaculately presented rooms make this a popular choice for those seeking a touch of Ottoman style with all the mod cons. Think cream and gilt cornices, grained and painted wood furniture and sumptuous bedspreads and patterned wallpaper. It may be a touch ostentatious for some, but the lavish breakfasts, real coffee and roof terrace with commanding views of the Aya Sofya, Aya Irene and the Bosphorus more than compensate. **€109**

Yeşil Ev Kabasakal Cad 5 ☎0212/517 6785, ⓦistanbulyesilev.com; map p.44. On a leafy cobbled street between Aya Sofya and the Blue Mosque, and built in the style of the house that originally occupied the site, *Yeşil Ev* ("Green House") is furnished in period (mid-nineteenth-century) style, with wood-panelled ceilings and antique rugs. The rooms are good value for this quality and there's a fine garden restaurant with a central marble fountain open to non-residents. **€200**

CANKURTARAN

★ **Agora Guest House and Hostel** Amiral Tafdil Sok 6 ☎0212/458 5547, ⓦagoraguesthouse.com; map p.44. Blurring the lines between hotel and guesthouse, this is an excellent budget choice right in the heart of the old city. The tastefully furnished communal breakfast/lounge area has a massive flat-screen TV, a funky terrace and a great atmosphere. There are ten well-appointed doubles, and dorms range from four to ten beds. Highly recommended. Dorm **€15**, double **€70**

Alp Akbıyık Cad, Adliye Sok 4 ☎0212/517 9570, ⓦalpguesthouse.com; map p.44. Fine establishment, with a dark wood exterior, situated down a quiet lane. The smallish rooms, accessed from a winding marble staircase, are immaculately furnished, some with four-poster beds. Rooms 403 and 404 command a sea view. The pretty partially-covered breakfast terrace gives great views over the old city and Sea of Marmara. **€55**

Apricot Amiral Tafdil Sok 18 ☎0212/638 1658, ⓦapricothotel.com; map p.44. Set in a quiet backstreet running parallel to busy Akbıyık Cad and run by a Turkish/American business partnership, this recently made-over small hotel has an intimate atmosphere. Rooms vary in size and are painted in soothing apricot tones; some have

12

balconies. Bathrooms either have big baths, fancy showers or jacuzzis. When around, co-owner Hakan, a professional tour guide, is a font of knowledge about the city. They also have three stylish town house apartments nearby, with sea views. **€69**

Big Apple Bayram Fırını Sok 12 ☎0212/517 7931, ⓦhostelbigapple.com; map p.44. Dorms have laminate floors and metal bunk beds with new mattresses, and there are shared, clean, separate toilet and shower on each floor. For a substantial price hike, double, triple and family rooms are available – though a couple of these are windowless. There's a decent covered terrace with a cushioned area for lounging and a small roof terrace – both boast good views over the Sea of Marmara and Princes' Islands, and are the venue for the reasonable Turkish-style breakfast and cheap night-time drinking. Dorm **€13**, double **€55**

★ **Empress Zoe** Akbıyık Cad, Adliye Sok 10 ☎0212/518 2504, ⓦemzoe.com; map p.44. Comprised of several traditional townhouses, themselves built over the remains of an Ottoman bath-house, this is a friendly hotel with history. The 25 rooms are decorated throughout with the personal touch of American owner Ann Nevans. Most rooms are in dark wood with richly coloured textiles and attractive wall-paintings, all are individually decorated and furnished, and vary from standard doubles to a penthouse suite. You'll pay €20 or more for one with a balcony, a sea view or private garden. Part of the basement walls belong to the remains of the Great Byzantine Palace, and the sun terrace has panoramic views of the Blue Mosque and Aya Sofya. There's a lovely garden to one side, shaded by cypress, palm and bay trees where you can have breakfast or an evening aperitif. **€120**

Four Seasons Tevfikhane Sok 1 ☎0212/638 8200, ⓦfourseasons.com; map p.44. Until the early 1980s, this formidable Neoclassical building served as the Sultanahmet Prison before being completely renovated as one of the city's leading hotels. The watchtowers and exercise court are still evident beneath the flowers and vines, but the 54 beautiful high-ceilinged rooms are unrecognizable as former cells. The rooms are as sumptuous as you would expect, though the flat-screen TVs in the palatial bathrooms seem a little excessive. Excellent, attentive service, but suite prices run into the thousands. **€490**

★ **Hanedan** Akbıyık Cad, Adliye Sok 3 ☎0212/516 4869–418 1564, ⓦhanedanhotel.com; map p.44. Tucked away on a quiet side street off Akbıyık Cad, this friendly hotel, run by four friends, is great value for the quality of accommodation and service. The dark wood floors in the rooms are off-set by the pale plain walls, and the overall feel is one of unfussy comfort. There's a roof terrace with stunning views over the Aya Sofya and the Sea of Marmara, and a great spread for breakfast which includes filter coffee. Discount for long stays. **€65**

İstanbul Hostel Kutlugün Sok 35 ☎0212/516 9380, ⓦistanbulhostel.net; map p.44. Run by a friendly Romanian, Dan, this deservedly popular hostel has more of a family feel than its bigger rivals. It has a couple of double rooms (not en-suite), and dorms with anything from six to twenty beds, all with spotless, shared bathrooms. The beds are good quality and comfy. The cosy cellar-bar has big-screen satellite TV, video, fireplace and internet access, and there are more bars on the roof terrace. Dorm **€9**, double **€35**

Orient Youth Hostel Akbıyık Cad 13 ☎0212/517 9493, ⓦorienthostel.com; map p.44. This fine hostel boasts 152 beds, a rooftop terrace/bar with fine sea views, free wi-fi, safe boxes and internet access, and rates include a decent buffet breakfast. Dorms range from the cheapest – a cavernous room sleeping thirty – to a four-bed dorm for €17. There are also a variety of hotel-style rooms, including singles. Very well run and maintained, and excellently located for the major sights; with a very lively bar (including a happy hour from 5–7pm), it's a great choice if you want to party. Dorm **€11**, double **€40**

Osman Han Akbıyık Cad, Çetinkaya Sok 1 ☎0212/458 7702, ⓦosmanhotel.com; map p.44. Extremely well-run hotel fashioned from a 70-year-old building occupying a corner plot on a quiet side-street. Rooms are simply but tastefully furnished, and those on the third floor command sea views (€20 higher than the standard double rate). The buffet breakfast spread includes home-made jams, fresh fruit and pastries as well as muesli. **€75**

Peninsula Adliye Sok 6 ☎0212/458 6850, ⓦhotelpeninsula.com; map p.44. Comfortable budget accommodation on a quiet side-street, the simply furnished rooms (laminate floors and plain pastel walls) nonetheless boast a/c, central heating and double glazing as well as flat-screen TVs. The smallest doubles are cheaper than doubles in many of the hostels, and the place is spotlessly clean and well managed. Rooms and bathrooms are on the small side, but at these prices that's to be expected; there's also a roof terrace with great views. **€45**

★ **Poem** Terbıyık Sok 12 ☎0212/638 9744, ⓦhotelpoem.com; map p.44. This friendly and immaculately run establishment has been created from two adjoining nineteenth-century wooden mansion-houses, and rooms are named after famous Turkish poets or their poems. There's a twenty percent winter-season discount and a further five percent off for cash. Rooms with sea views and/or balconies are more expensive – the pick of the rooms, "Listening to İstanbul", is more than double the standard rate. The roof terrace has panoramic views of the Aya Sofya and the sea. **€75**

Senatus Akbıyık Cad 28 ☎0212/458 5866, ⓦsenatushotel.com; map p.44. Designer hotel of a very high standard, built on the site of the senate house of the Byzantine Magnaura Palace, which makes a bold statement

12

12

TOP FIVE HOSTELS

Agora Sultanahmet, see p.168
Cheers Sultanahmet, see p.168
İstanbul Hostel Sultanahmet, see p.169
Rapunzel Galata, see p.172
Sumo Cat Galata, see p.172

in an area where guests are more used to faux-Ottoman accommodation. There are 22 rooms, each tastefully decorated in rich browns and white, with big flat-screen TVs and tea- and coffee-making facilities. Prices vary according to size and whether they face the street or the somewhat gloomy rear. There's a very chic lobby bar and a la carte restaurant. **€180**

Side Hotel & Pension Utangaç Sok 20 ☎0212/517 2282, ⍟sidehotel.com; map p.44. Established back in 1989 and owned by three charismatic brothers, this bright, spacious and friendly hotel-cum-hostel offers immaculate service and traditional comfort for a reasonable price. The rooms on the hotel side are en suite and have a/c; those facing the rear have a small balcony. In the pension, six of the rooms on the upper floor share spotless bathrooms in the hall and have fans. There's a shared breakfast terrace that has great views of the Princes' Islands. Pension **€40**, hotel **€70**

Sultan Hostel Akbıyık Cad 21 ☎0212/516 9260, ⍟sultanhostel.com; map p.44. This large, well-established 160-bed hostel is very popular because of its convenient location, spotless rooms, comfy beds sporting gleaming white linen, and regularly cleaned, shared

bathrooms. Dorm prices vary according to the number of beds per room, ranging from the 26-bed basement "Harem" room to more pricey six-bed dorms (€16); some have en-suite showers and toilets. Doubles are also available, though don't work out cheaper than some of the budget hotels. The staff are very friendly and the restaurant (ten percent discount for guests), which spills out onto the street, is incredibly popular with both guests and passers-by. Dorm **€11**, double **€60**

Tria Terbıyık Sok 7 ☎0212/518 4518, ⍟triahotel istanbul.com; map p.44. This well-run, twenty-room hotel is situated in a quiet side-street just off bustling Akbıyık Caddesi. The deluxe rooms (401 and 402) command the best sea views, otherwise head up to the terrace breakfast room/bar/restaurant for stunning views of the Sea of Marmara to the south and the domes and minarets of Sultanahmet to the north. All rooms are traditional in feel, with dark wood and framed prints adorning the walls, but stylish and comfortable. **€79**

★ **Uyan** Utangaç Sok 25 ☎0212/518 9255, ⍟uyanhotel.com; map p.44. Atmospheric 29-room hotel set in a beautifully renovated, late 1920s corner-plot building in the heart of the old city. The ground-floor rooms are a little gloomy, but other rooms are light and airy, with light wood, oriental-rug-scattered floors, white walls and white bed linen. There are different sized rooms to choose from, from small doubles to a honeymoon suite. "Blue Mosque", room 405, has great views over the Blue Mosque and Aya Sofya, as well as Scandanavian-style furniture and a jacuzzi. An added bonus is the breathtaking view from the roof terrace. **€70**

SIRKECI

The area around Sirkeci station has much in its favour: Sultanahmet and the city's most famous sights are a short walk away up the hill; it's a stone's throw to the ferry terminals on the Golden Horn in Eminönü; and the nightspots on İstiklal Caddesi lie just across the Galata Bridge. Hotels in the lower part of this working, bustling neighbourhood tend to be better value than in Sultanahmet or Taksim, which may appeal to budget travellers keen to avoid the backpacker joints around Cankurtaran. On the downside, there's a paucity of decent eating places (with a few exceptions, see below), and it has the transitional feel common to areas around major stations the world over.

Erenler Hotel and Hostel Taya Hatun Sok 11 ☎0212/527 3468, ⍟hotelerenler.com; map p.68. A cross between an old-fashioned Anatolian hotel and a hostel, a stay here gives a much more authentic view of the city than the cluster of hostels in Cankurtaran. The rooms, including some dorms, are very basic but light and airy, some have a/c, other fans. The shared bathrooms (one squat and one western toilet) are clean. It's family run, has been going for twenty years, and is on a quiet street very convenient for the major sights and the tramway. Excellent value if you don't expect frills. Dorm **€10**, double **€35**

Hürriyet Nobethane Cad, Serdar Sok 19 ☎0212/520 3787, ⍟hurriyethotel.com; map p.68. A 35-room Kurdish-family-run hotel tucked away behind the station.

There are views over the domes of the roof of Sirkeci station to the Bosphorus from the breakfast terrace. The rooms in the most recently converted part of the building are better than the old ones, but all are clean and comfy, with laminate flooring and white painted wood furniture. The en-suite bathrooms are very clean, and there's 24-hour hot water. **€70**

Sirkeci Konak Taya Hatun Cad 5 ☎0212/528 4344, ⍟sirkecikonak.com; map p.68. The flagship of the *Sirkeci* group, this hotel was a nineteenth-century Ottoman *konak* (mansion) situated right next to the walls of Gülhane Parkı. Neither hip nor trendy, it is very professionally run and offers good old-fashioned comfort. There are tea- and coffee-making facilities in the rooms, palatial en-suite bathrooms and comfy beds. There's a fitness centre and small pool in the basement, and a decent fish restaurant on the roof terrace, which has commanding views over the park and Topkapı Palace. There's also free afternoon tea for guests and various demonstrations on offer, from Turkish cookery to Sufi culture. **€170**

Yıldız Hotel Nöbethane Cad 36 ☎0212/520 5254, ⓦhotelyildiz.com; map p.68. Old-school Anatolian-style hotel (rooms have mock-wood linoleum floors, metal-framed beds and rudimentary clothes-hanging facilities) offering no frills, but it's far better than the rather grotty exterior suggests, and has been going for over fifty years so it must be doing something right. If you're on a tight budget and want to avoid a hostel it's worth considering, as the staff are very friendly, you can make tea in the cavernous lobby, and the place is kept spotless. **60TL**

THE GRAND BAZAAR AND AROUND

The streets running down the hill to the Sea of Marmara south of the Grand Bazaar and Çemberlitaş remain workmanlike, with wholesale footwear outlets, leather workshops and the like, so make a refreshing change from the heavily touristed streets of Cankurtaran. The main sights are still within easily walking distance, however, and the tram stops Beyazit and Çemberlitaş very convenient.

★ **Niles** Dibekli Cami Sok 13 ☎0212/517 3239, ⓦhotelniles.com; map pp.76–77. Well-established hotel offering better value than most of its competitors in nearby Sultanahmet. The standard rooms are well appointed, with small but immaculately finished shower-bathrooms, while the suites (€130) are more elaborately furnished and decorated, in faux-Ottoman style, and boast marble, Turkish-bath-style bathrooms. There's a pretty ground-floor courtyard garden and a roof terrace with panoramic views over busy Yenikapı Harbour. Excellent value. **€70**

Ottoman Hotel Park Kadırga Liman Cad 85 ☎0212/516 0211, ⓦottomanhotelpark.com; map pp.76–77. Less ostentatious and located further from the major sights than its Sultanahmet sister, the *Ottoman Hotel Imperial* (see p.168), the *Park* makes an admirable choice for those seeking a less touristy part of the city to rest their bones after a day's sightseeing. Immaculately run, the comfortable rooms are well kitted out; some rooms have sea views. There's concierge service and a lovely breakfast rooftop terrace. **€89**

President (Best Western) Tiyatro Cad 25, Beyazit ☎0212/515 6980, ⓦthepresidenthotel.com; map pp.76–77. If you're looking for a centrally located hotel away from the crowds and street hawkers of Sultanahmet then you can't go far wrong with this place – a mere 100 yards from the Beyazit tram stop and a five-minute amble to the Grand Bazaar. The hotel earns its four-star rating with a stylish rooftop pool bar and terrace restaurant offering stunning panoramic views of the Mamara sea, Blue Mosque and the old town, there's also a chic British-style pub and a gym and spa on site. The standard rooms are modest yet elegant and the price includes a decadent buffet breakfast (Turkish and Continental) served on the rooftop. Free airport pick-up is available for direct bookings. **€139**

THE NORTHWEST QUARTER

There are only a couple of options worth considering in this atmospheric, traditional area of the old city, but their proximity to some of the city's most interesting yet little-visited sights is a major plus.

Daphnis Sadrazam Ali Paşa Cad 26 ☎0212/531 4858, ⓦhoteldaphnis.com; map p.89. This charming boutique hotel, contrived from a small terrace of century-old Greek townhouses, is situated close to the shore of the Golden Horn, just a short distance from Fener's Greek Orthodox Patriarchate – which means it gets its fair share of visitors from Greece. It's less messed about with than the majority of boutique conversions, though the front rooms, with views over the Golden Horn, are very noisy due to the busy main road. **€110**

Kariye Kariye Camii Sok 6, Erdirne Kapı ☎0212/534 8414, ⓦkariyeotel.com; map p.89. Situated right next door to arguably the finest Byzantine site in the city (the Kariye Museum; see pp.92–95) and a stone's throw from the Theodosian land walls, this nineteenth-century mansion has been restored with style and restraint. The rooms are done out in soft pastel colours, much of the furniture is ornate late-nineteenth century in style, and the polished honey-coloured parquet floor is enlivened by the odd tasteful kilim. There are ceiling fans rather than a/c, which is quite sufficient in this elevated, tree-shaded location. The reasonable prices reflect the rather small, shower-only bathrooms and the chipped paintwork. **€85**

12

GALATA, BEYOĞLU AND AROUND

The heart of Beyoğlu, the former European quarter, is undoubtedly İstiklal Caddesi, home to the city's densest concentration of restaurants, bars and clubs. Tepebaşı, a mixed commercial/tourist district just west of İstiklal Caddesi's southern end is home to a few trendy rooftop bars and restaurants and the impressive Pera Museum. Cihangir, on the northern side of Sıraselviler Caddesi, is an affluent yet bohemian backwater with splendid views of the Bosphorus. Taksim, the city's major business and shopping district, has a wide range of hotels aimed largely at business travellers and tour groups. To the north of Taksim Square, the posh neighbourhoods of Harbiye and, in particular, Nişantaşı, offer great shopping and a scattering of trendy places to eat and drink.

GALATA

Anemon Galata Büyükhendek Cad 11, ☎0212/293 2343, ⓦanemonhotels.com; map p.110. The sumptuous rooms in this rebuilt nineteenth-century townhouse near the Galata Tower aim squarely for comfort over style. Neo-Art Nouveau-style statuettes grace the lobby, stairs and bedside tables, while dark curtains, carpets and furniture contrast aesthetically with pastel and cream walls. The sizeable bathrooms have baths as well as showers, and the views from the incongruously designer-chic roof restaurant/bar are superb. €130

Eklektik Guest House Kadribey Çıkmaz 4 ☎0212/243 7446, ⓦeklektikgalata.com; map p.110. Seven individually decorated and furnished rooms (from cheerful retro to faux-Ottoman) in a converted period building with views over the imposing Galata Tower and Bosphorus – a great choice if you're looking for something a little different in this trendy area of the city. €140

Galata Life Galipdede Cad 75 ☎0212/245 2315, ⓦgalatalifeistanbul.com; map p.110. Light, spacious rooms with wooden floors and clinical white furnishings, opting for practicality over style. With only five rooms, there's a homely feel and the funky café downstairs adds a little panache to the equation, serving up a range of home-made breads, desserts, cookies and pastries. There's a bookshelf of English books available and a substantial Continental or Turkish breakfast served on the street-view roof terrace. €64

★ **Rapunzel Guesthouse** Bereketzade Camii Sok 3☎0212/292 5034, ⓦrapunzelistanbul.com; map p.110. This quirky hostel has bags of character with its original nineteenth-century stone walls, artistically scattered curiosities and colourful artwork. A little pricier than other backpackers' in the area, it's the small things here that make the difference – the roomy six-bed dorms with sparkling-clean en-suites, individual reading lights, hairdryers, a hearty breakfast and on-tap potable water. The team of young, attentive staff are keen to mingle with guests and always on hand with tips and recommendations for the area. Look out for the black-and-pink sign, as this place is easy to miss, and ring the doorbell. Dorm €18, double €55

★ **Sumo Cat** Ali Hoca Arkası, off Kalsıran Cad, Galata ☎0212/292 7866, ⓦsumocathostel.com; map p.110. A labour of love by its laidback and welcoming

English-speaking owners, this excellent conversion of a nineteenth-century Galata townhouse offers homely but stylish accommodation in three dorms (all en suite) and two en-suite doubles – all with a/c. Rooms are individually decorated with funky murals, and beds new and comfy. Space is at a premium in the dorms, but with the buzzing nightlife of the quarter on your doorstep nobody cares. There's a small downstairs kitchen and a ground-floor garden area. Dorm €14, double €60

World House Hostel Galipdede Cad 85 ☎0212/293 5520, ⓦworldhouseistanbul.com; map p.110. This colourful ninety-bed hostel ticks all the boxes for a budget traveller – clean, modern and in a great location. Bright, high-ceilinged rooms, coded security locks and friendly, enthusiastic staff lift this place a notch above the Sultanahmet hostel scene. Despite the nearby 24hr entertainment, it's quiet too – bar the prayer call from the adjacent mosque. The hostel also has a sister hostel *Liberta*, just off İstiklal Cad, as well as short/long-term apartments – check the website for details. Dorm €12, double €50

İSTIKLAL CADDESI AND AROUND

Büyük Londra Oteli Meşrutiyet Cad 117, Tepebaşı ☎0212/249 1025, ⓦlondrahotel.net; map pp.120–121. Palatial, mid-nineteenth-century townhouse; many of the rooms are time-worn and cluttered with battered period furniture, which gives the hotel its retro-bohemian charm. Others that have been modernized have inevitably lost their raffishness. Ernest Hemingway stayed here in 1922 when he was a journalist covering the Turkish War of Independence, as did Alexander Hacke when shooting the definitive film of the city's music scene, *İstanbul: Crossing the Bridge*. €50

★ **Devman** Asmalımescit Sok 52 ☎0212/245 6212, ⓦdevmanhotel.com; map pp.120–121. Modern, modest and well-run hotel at the bottom end of one of the city's liveliest night-time haunts. It is good value – all rooms are a/c and include a basic buffet breakfast. The street outside is a hive of activity until the early hours, especially at weekends, so it's not a great option for light sleepers. It's not going to win any design awards, but the spacious rooms have nicely coordinated furnishings and the blue-tiled bathrooms are spotless. €50

Levanten Hostel Kumbaracı Yokuşu 35 ☎0212/251 4755, ⓦlevantenhostel.com; map pp.120–121. Undersold by its non descript entrance that looks more like an internet café than a hostel (look out for the yellow hostel flag high up on the walls), this cheap and cheerful dwelling offers some of the cheapest out-of-season rooms in the area. Sparse, neutral interiors and cheap furnishings give this away as a budget option but it's none-the-less clean, light and spacious. The decidedly more elegant entrance hall, guest cooking facilities and included breakfast (albeit very basic) add to the appeal. Dorm €8, double €60

Marmara Pera Meşrutiyet Cad 21 ☎0212/251 4646, ⓦthemarmarahotels.com; map pp.120–121. Opulent yet stylish hotel housing the cool *Mikla* restaurant (see p.190), the *Marmara* claims to meld 1930s nostalgia with 1970s romanticism. A great feature of summer visits is the elegant rooftop pool and bar, with glorious vistas over the city. The rooms feature modish modular furniture, crisp white linen and flat-screen TVs, and the views from those on the upper storeys are stunning. €120

Monopol Meşrutiyet Cad 223, Tepebaşı ☎0212/251 7326, ⓦmonopolhotel.com; map pp.120–121. Opposite the old US Embassy building, the rooms at the *Monopol* are plain but comfortable. Not exactly brimming with style or character, it's nonetheless good value for such a prominent area, though the front rooms can get noisy at night when the Beyoğlu bars turn out. €70

Pera Palas Meşrutiyet Cad 52, Tepebaşı ☎0212/377 4000, ⓦperapalace.com; map pp.120–121. A contender for the most atmospheric hotel in İstanbul (see box, p.123), the *Pera* was built in the nineteenth century to accommodate *Orient Express* passengers – its rooms are marked with the names of famous occupants such as Agatha Christie and Graham Greene. It reopened in 2010 following a lengthy restoration and has managed to maintain much of its character, but prices are astronomical. €399

Richmond Hotel İstiklal Cad 445 ☎0212/252 5460, ⓦrichmondhotels.com.tr; map pp.120–121. Nowhere near as trendy as you might think given its central location on buzzing İstiklal Cad and the presence of one of Beyoğlu's coolest roof-bars, *Leb-i-Derya Richmond* (see p.190). The standard rooms are plain, with white walls and muted brown soft-furnishings, but do come with music systems. It's perennially popular with businessmen and travellers alike – and if you can stretch to a suite, they're considerably more stylish (and expensive at €349). Top-floor rooms at the back have Bosphorus views and a hefty €40 supplement. €130

Silviya Asmalımescit Sok 54 ☎0212/292 7749, ☎243 6115; map pp.120–121. Clean and friendly, the *Silviya* is timeworn but worth considering if you want a budget hotel in the thick of the nightlife action. Try to get a rear room as the ones fronting onto the street can be very noisy. The sizeable, carpeted rooms are painted a soothing green, with immaculate bathrooms. The meagre breakfast is taken in the small ground-floor TV room. €45

★ **TomTom Suites** Boğazkesen Caddesi, Tomtom Kaptan Sok 18 ☎0212/292 4949, ⓦtomtomsuites.com; map pp.120–121. A designer hotel fashioned from an early nineteenth-century Franciscan nunnery, virtually opposite the ornate and historic Italian Consulate (see box, p.122). The suites are spacious and soothingly decorated in soft whites and muted browns; bathrooms have underfloor heating, a jacuzzi and rain showers. For Beyoğlu, this is an extremely quiet location. €189

Triada Residence İstiklal Caddesi, Meşelik Sok 4 ☎0212/251 0101, ⓦtriada.com.tr; map pp.120–121. Small but very stylish rooms in a lovely turn-of-the-century townhouse on a quiet side-street opposite Aya Triada church. All rooms have boldly grained wood laminate floors, an American-style kitchen including a coffee-making machine and fridge – plus there's a shared sauna. One of the few genuine boutique-style hotels in this part of town, with fabulous views from the roof terrace over the domes of the Greek Orthodox Triada church. €120

Vardar Palace Hotel Sıraselviler Cad 54, Taksim ☎0212/252 2888, ⓦvardarhotel.com; map pp.120–121. Gothic-feeling apartment building dating from 1901, on an interesting street running southwest from Taksim Square. There are no views at the back, and rooms at the front are noisy, but it's a reasonable option for the area, with period mahogany furniture, spacious rooms and a friendly atmosphere. €99

CIHANGIR

Cihangir Arslan Yatağı Sok 33 ☎0212/251 5317, ⓦcihangirhotel.com; map pp.120–121. Offering old-fashioned comfort in a quiet backstreet in the affluent, rather arty suburb of Cihangir, with large, cosily lit rooms decorated with traditional dark-wood furniture. Service is excellent, and a huge buffet breakfast is served on a commanding terrace. You'll pay half as much again for a room with a Bosphorus view. Rates include airport transfer. €80

Villa Zurich Akarsu Yokuşu Cad 44–46 ☎0212/293 0604, ⓦhotelvillazurich.com; map pp.120–121. Delightful, good-value hotel situated on a trendy street in Cihangir, where well-heeled but slightly alternative locals mingle with a sizeable foreign community. It offers large, well-equipped doubles – some with stunning panoramas of the Bosphorus – and a baby-sitting service is available. The rooftop terrace has the best views of all, serving as the breakfast salon and, in the evening, the well-regarded roof-top *Doğa Balık* fish restaurant. €99

TAKSIM SQUARE, HARBIYE AND NIŞANTAŞI

Bentley Halaskargazı Cad 75, Harbiye ☎0212/291 7730, ⓦbentley-hotel.com; map p.127. One of the first wave of retro-modernist hotels in the city, the Italian-designed *Bentley* offers minimalist urban chic in a

12

convenient location between Taksim Square and upmarket Nişantaşı. White, beige and black are the tones of choice in the appealing rooms, each kitted out with flat-screen TV and wi-fi. There's also a gym and a sleek restaurant. **€240**

Central Palace Lamartin Cad 18 ☎0212/315 5500, ⓦthecentralpalace.com; map p.127. This hotel aims to offer a healthy lifestyle concept to its guests – which means no alcohol, organic steamed vegetables, an exercise bike in every room, jacuzzi in the bathroom and hypoallergenic bedding. All of this goodness will likely be undone by a day tramping the polluted streets of the city, but if you're looking for faux-Ottoman luxury a minute's walk from Taksim Square, it's a good choice. **€190**

Marmara Taksim Square ☎0212/251 4696, ⓦthemarmara.com.tr; map p.127. This premier five-star, twenty-storey hotel, right on Taksim Square, is one of İstanbul's landmark buildings. The spacious and luxurious rooms all have great views over Beyoğlu and mix functional chic with old-fashioned, faux-Ottoman flourishes. Facilities include a swimming pool, gym, Turkish bath and spa. **€190**

Midtown Lamartin Cad 13 ☎0212/361 6767, ⓦmidtown-hotel.com; map p.127. Stylish yet functional hotel with crisp linen, wall-mounted flat-screen TVs and tea- and coffee-making facilities in the sizeable rooms – some of which have Bosphorus views. It's not the city's most characterful hotel and is aimed at business people and groups rather than independent travellers, but there are good deals on offer and the attached restaurant (serving Turkish and international dishes) is pretty good. **€121**

Sofa Teşvikiye Cad 123 ☎0212/368 1818, ⓦthesofahotel.com; map p.127. Housed in an attractive turn-of-the-nineteenth-century block, the *Sofa* is one of those designer hotels that offer minimalist charm for maximum prices. That said, it's well located in the heart of chic Nişantaşı, the rooms are spacious, with natural-wood floors and restrained furnishings, the en-suite bathrooms feature rainshowers and herbal soaps, and there's a small fitness room and spa. **€220**

BEŞIKTAŞ AND ORTAKÖY

There are no budget options in Beşiktaş or Ortaköy – you pay a massive premium for the waterfront locations here, but if you are looking for distinctive Bosphorus-front accommodation close to the city centre and major sights it's worth considering.

Çırağan Palace Kempinski Çırağan Cad 32 ☎0212/326 4646, ⓦkempinski.com; map p.132. Unashamedly luxurious hotel, housed in an elaborately restored Ottoman palace right on the waterfront. Every possible extravagance is on offer here, from a selection of gourmet restaurants, an enormous outdoor pool and spa, an indoor art gallery, designer boutiques and even optional airport pick-up by helicopter. **€470**

Four Seasons at the Bosphorus Çırağan Cad 28 ☎0212/381 4000, ⓦfourseasons.com/bosphorus; map p.132. Set in a sprawling nineteenth-century palace on the Bosphorus and offering all the luxuries you'd expect of a *Four Seasons* hotel – high-end cuisine, innovative spa menu, lavish furnishings and astronomical prices. **€540**

WHotel Süleyman Seba Cad 22 ☎0212/381 2121, ⓦwhotels.com/istanbul; map p.132. Super-sleek boutique hotel that feels more like a nightclub than a hotel with its purple and green lighting, glittering pillars and mirrored ceilings. This place is all about the show so dress to impress and look important whether frequenting the indoor pool and spa or sipping a custom-made cocktail in the flashy lounge bar. Innovative rooms, most likely to appeal to the male psyche, range from the swish "Wonderful" room to the swish "wow" suite. **€215**

THE BOSPHORUS AND BLACK SEA RESORTS

Acqua Verde Kurfalı Yakuplu Caddesi, Kurfalı Köyü, Ağva ☎0216/721 7143, ⓦwww.acquaverde.com.tr. Set right on the banks of the river, 800m in from the beach, rustic charm is the order of the day in this boutique hotel. Rooms have exposed stonework and wrought-iron beds with decorative Ottoman-style soft furnishings. A favourite weekend retreat for wealthy İstanbullus, it doesn't come cheap. **360TL**

★ **A'jia** Çubuklu Cad 27, Kanlıca ☎0216/413 9300, ⓦajiahotel.com; map p.151. This sixteen-room hotel, converted from the beautiful Ahmet Rasim Paşa *yalı* (traditional wooden waterfront mansion) has managed to retain its period elegance despite having received a full minimalist-style makeover. The rooms on the top floor, built into the roof space, have delightful balconies with simply stunning Bosphorus views – and also offer the best value. Books up very quickly in season. **€300**

Les Ottomans Muallim Nacı Cad 68 ☎0212/359 1500, ⓦlesottomans.com; map p.151. The lovingly restored Muhsinzade Mehmet Pasha Mansion, famed for its magnificent Ottoman architecture, now houses one of İstanbul's most exclusive hotels. If you can make it past the indulgent display of celebrity guest photographs lining the entrance foyer, the hotel offers such delights as a private cinema and its own fleet of boats waiting to whisk guests down the Bosphorus. **€800**

★ **Sumahan on the Water** Kuleli Cad 51, Çengelköy ☎0216/422 8000, ⓦsumahan.com; map p.151. A late-Ottoman distillery converted into a wonderful hotel right on the Bosphorus in the pretty suburb of Çengelköy, this is one of the city's best boutique hotels, winning a number of prestigious awards. There's a range of stylishly decorated rooms blending the contemporary and the traditional, all with great views and some with fireplaces for those cool evenings. Like the *A'jia*, it has a modest number of rooms so book well in advance. **€295**

THE PRINCES' ISLANDS

By far the busiest night on the islands for accommodation is Saturday, when prices are usually fifty percent more than other nights. This does not prevent rooms filling up, so advance booking is definitely recommended for weekend stays. Accommodation on Büyükada is uniformly expensive, though the chance to stay in a grand restored mansion or boutique sea-front hotel may be appealing; accommodation is cheaper and more low-key on neighbouring Heybeliada.

BURGAZADA

Mehtap 45 On the northeast coast of the island ☎ 0216/381 2660; map pp.160–161. Though it's got all the mod cons, this is fairly spartan for a boutique hotel and might not seem incredibly good value, but the rooms are comfortable enough, the views northwest to the metropolis superb, and owner Abbas will proudly tell you how much England football legend Bobby Charlton enjoyed his four-day stay here. **180TL**

HEYBELIADA

Merit Halki Palas Refah Şehitler Cad 88 ☎ 0216/351 0025, ⓦ merithotels.com; map pp.160–161. A nineteenth-century villa, restored in dubious taste by the *Merit* hotel group as the only five-star hotel on the islands, incorporating a gym, jacuzzi and outdoor pool. Rooms are plainly decorated, enlivened with floral-pattern bedspreads and many have good views of either pine forest or the sea. **€150**

Özdemir Pansiyon Ayyıldız Cad 41 ☎ 0216/351 1866, ⓦ www.adalar-ozdemirpansiyon.net; map pp.160–161. The cheapest option on the island, offering tiny chalet-type en-suite rooms with a shower over squat toilets, plus larger rooms in the main block. No breakfast. **50TL**

Prenset Pansiyon Ayyıldız Cad 40–42/A ☎ 216/351 0039, ⓦ www.prensetpansiyon.com; map pp.160–161. This converted apartment building with a wood-trimmed exterior offers reasonable value, despite most rooms not having views. Friendly management, comfortable rooms with immaculate modern bathrooms, and central heating in winter. **100TL**

BÜYÜKADA

★ **Ayanikola Butik** Aya Nikola Mevki 104 ☎ 0126/382 4143, ⓦ ayanikolabutikpansiyon.com; map pp.160–161. Right on the waterfront in the former vineyard of the nearby Aya Nikola monastery, on the east coast of the island, this eleven-room boutique hotel is a gem. Each room has a sea view and is individually furnished with antique furniture and fittings, which contrast wonderfully with the plain white walls, stripped floors and exposed brickwork. The "special" rooms have a bed right next to the picture-window giving stunning views over to Asia. **230TL**

Büyükada Princess İskele Meydanı ☎ 0216/382 1628, ⓦ buyukadaprincess.com; map pp.160–161. Offers neatly furnished a/c rooms of various sizes with TV and mini bar in a well-restored late nineteenth-century building with pool. Prices may be negotiable. **160TL**

Meziki Malül Gazı Cad 24 ☎ 0216/382 3444, ⓦ mezikihotel.com; map pp.160–161. A gorgeous mansion on the eastern outskirts of the main settlement, not far from the ferry terminal, the *Meziki* is housed in an Italian-designed, *fin-de-siècle* villa liberally adorned with neo-Renaissance murals. Rooms are big, high-ceilinged and furnished with antique furniture, with those on the front boasting sea views. For period charm, it's hard to beat but note that to keep the rooms as original as possible there are shared bathrooms on the landings. **150TL**

Naya Retreat Maden, Yılmaz Türk Cad 96 ☎ 0216/382 4598, ⓦ nayaistanbul.com; map pp.160–161. A fine 105-year-old wooden mansion set in lush gardens on the island's east coast, the unusual *Naya* is a hybrid yoga/alternative therapy/meditation centre cum semi rural retreat. It is run by the well-travelled and laidback Ludwig, who offers rooms furnished in an upmarket ethnic-hippie style, in the house, or tents in the rambling garden. **€80**

★ **Splendid Palas** Nisan Cad 23 ☎ 0216/382 6950, ⓦ splendidhotel.net; map pp.160–161. A few minutes west of the ferry terminal, the *Splendid Palas*, dating from 1908, was once host to Edward VIII and Mrs Simpson. It has serious *fin-de-siècle* grandeur, with cupolas, balconies, a good restaurant, excellent service and a garden with a swimming pool out back. Closed Nov–March. **US$130**

APARTMENTS

Apartments are a good choice for many visitors, particularly if you are staying for a while or, in the case of the larger apartments, if you are a group or family. Even booked on a night by night basis, the price of a small apartment is often similar to that of a hotel of a similar standard and, of course, for stays of a week or more the cost can drop substantially. The prices quoted here are for a one-night stay. New apartments are coming onto the market all the time and the following websites are worth looking at to see what's available: ⓦ istanbul-flats.com, which has many apartments at bargain prices; and ⓦ thehouseapart.com which deals solely with upmarket properties and has prices to match. It's also worth checking ⓦapricothotel.com for apartments in Sultanahmet and ⓦperfectplaces.com for more possibilities across the city.

THE OLD CITY

★ **İstanbul Suite Home** Dizdariye Çeşmesi Sok 51 ⓣ0212/458 5255, ⓦistanbulsuitehome.com; map p.44. Situated a little way from the main tourist haunts, in a tall, narrow townhouse on a quiet backstreet south of Divan Yolu, the five apartments here are extremely stylish and very good value. Modish without being minimalist, all pale wood and white, three apartments have two bedrooms, two a single bedroom. All have a spacious dining area with attached kitchen. The appliances are all top quality (including flat-screen TVs), and there's a shared roof terrace with views over the Sea of Marmara. Free pick-up from Atatürk International Airport. €155

GALATA, BEYOĞLU AND TAKSIM

Divan Taksim Suites Cumhuriyet Cad 49 ⓣ0212/254 7777, ⓦdivan.com.tr; map p.127. White blinds, white rugs, white furnishings, blonde-wood floors: this is Scandinavian-style minimalism in the heart of Taksim. The suites all work on an open-plan scheme, with well-kitted-out kitchens off a spacious sleeping/dining/sitting area. The 110m-square Bosphorus penthouse suite offers great views over the waterway and as much light as you can handle through its roof windows. All suites have large workstations and wi-fi, plus music system and TV. €210

★ **Galata Residence** Bankalar Cad, Felek Sok 2, Galata ⓣ0212/292 4841, ⓦgalataresidence.com; map p.110. Spread over three buildings in close proximity, the *Galata Residence* offers a range of varying-size apartments for short- and long-term stays, all housed in beautifully restored late nineteenth-century buildings. The apartments aren't as designer-flash as some of the newer places around but they're extremely comfortable, well-located and fitted with a/c. Considerable discounts for weekly and monthly lets, as well as for cash payments. There's a wide range of rooms so it's worth checking out a few options before you decide. €81

Şimşek Han Apartment Yüksek Kaldıran Cad 14–24, Galata ⓦperfectplaces.com; map p.110. Just steps below the Galata Tower this beautifully renovated top-floor apartment has fabulous views over the Golden Horn to the old city and Sea of Marmara beyond. Sleeps up to six, and above is a roof terrace with cooking and dining facilities and an incredible panorama. US$190

Suite Home İstiklal İstiklal Cad 45 ⓣ0212/245 0772, ⓦistanbulsuite.com; map pp.120–121. In the heart of the action, near the Taksim end of buzzing İstiklal Cad, offering three standards of room: business class; business roof room, where you pay more for the view; and spacious family suites. Decor is simple and modern without being too minimalist, and the kitchens are well equipped and functional. Worth considering if you're here for a week or more, as prices drop considerably for longer stays. €99

NIZAM PIDE

Eating

Gourmets rank Turkish food, along with French and Chinese, as one of the three classic cuisines. This is great news for visitors to the nation's cultural capital, as the very best of it can be found here in İstanbul. The city's rich and varied cuisine derives from its multi ethnic Ottoman heritage, when it was capital of an empire stretching from the Middle East to the Balkans and the Caucasus to North Africa. İstanbullus, like all Turks, are demanding when it comes to food, and want the freshest ingredients, the best service and, if possible, a little something extra than the person on the next table – maybe a bigger shot of pomegranate syrup in the salad or a few extra chillies to spice up their kebab.

13

Fortunately for them, Turkey, with so many climatic zones and an important rural economy, produces a stunning array of **fresh fruit and vegetables** – the best of which find their way to the markets and shops of the metropolis. Fresh **fish** comes in from the nearby Black Sea, Sea of Marmara and Aegean, and the **lamb** is as succulent and the **yoghurt** as thick, creamy and delicious as you'd expect from a people who trace their origins back to Central Asian nomadic pastoralism.

İstanbul has eating places to suit every budget, though **prices** have risen across the board in recent years. A breakfast portion of the mouth watering, crumbly cheese-pie *peynirli boreğı* will cost around 4TL, a sesame-seed-coated bread ring or *simit* a quarter of that from a street vendor. A couple of lira will get you a tasty take-out chicken-filled *döner* wrap in parts less frequented by tourists, three more a hearty vegetable or pulse stew from a basic restaurant; fresh, oven-baked *pide* (Turkish-style pizza) will set you back between 6TL and 10TL depending on the location of the restaurant. By way of contrast, a latte will burn at least 6TL hole in your pocket, while a meal with drinks at a chic fusion-style joint in Beyoğlu or one of the upmarket Bosphorus fish restaurants will cost at least a 100TL a head.

Once there was a fairly firm line drawn between different kinds of eating establishments in Turkey, but this has broken down recently, particularly in İstanbul. The demarcation made here between the various eating places (and, indeed, the bars listed in "Nightlife" is far from precise, with many cafés serving full meals as well as snacks – by and large, if it's listed under restaurants, it's the kind of place where you'd sit down to an evening meal.

TRADITIONAL EATING PLACES

There are plenty of places to find good-value meals in the city, though these are often unlicensed. Nowadays it's quite common to find establishments that combine elements of everything, often concentrating on *hazır yemek* for the lunchtime trade and knocking out kebabs and *pide* in the evening. These kinds of eating places can be found all over the city, though they are at a premium in Sultanahmet. Street cart vendors fill the olfactory gaps.

Pastanes, the Turkish take on the patisserie, serve up all kinds of *baklava*, milk-based puddings and more familiar sweeties such as chocolate eclairs.

Börekçi dish up different kinds of pastries, both savoury and sweet, and are particularly popular at breakfast time.

Çorbacıs specialize in various kinds of soup, popular both for breakfast in winter, for lunch or after a night out on the town.

Lokanta are, traditionally, restaurants emphasizing *hazır yemek* (also known as *sulu yemek* or "watery food") – pre-cooked dishes kept warm in a steam tray, especially stews. The food at the best *lokantas* can be the most delicious you'll have in the city.

Kebapçıs and **köftecis** specialize in the preparation of *kebapçs* and *köfte* respectively, with a limited number of side dishes – usually just an array of salad, yoghurt and desserts. They vary enormously in quality but the best will make you realize why Turks are so passionate about bits of grilled meat.

Pidecis concentrate on flat-breads topped with cheese, meat, vegetables and various combinations of them all, baked to perfection in wood-fired ovens.

Meyhanes (taverns) have a long history in this city and are more popular now than ever, with hordes of İstanbullus going out on the town, especially at weekends, to eat their way through reams of *meze* (starters) and fish mains, downing copious amounts of *rakı* before singing and dancing along to roving bands of Roma musicians.

Restoran are less boisterous than *meyhane*. The simpler serve little more than grilled meats, salads and an array of *meze* to accompany the alcohol, while the more upmarket ones specialize in dishes with their origins in the finest Ottoman cuisine, or reflect the changing times and serve fine Mediterranean or Asian-influenced cuisine.

Ocakbaşı A twist on the *kebap* restaurant, where *kebaps* and other meats are grilled over charcoal. The vast majority serve alcohol and at their best the food is exquisite.

ESSENTIALS

13

Alcohol is forbidden in Islam so, even in a secularized Muslim country like Turkey, many restaurants do not serve alcohol. Of the traditional eating establishments only *meyhanes*, *restorans* and *ocakbaşıs* (see box, p.180) serve alcohol, but there are plenty of modern cafés, fusion and international-style restaurants that are licensed, and more than a few kebab places also serve alcohol. We have indicated in the listings which places are unlicensed.

CAFÉS, PATISSERIES AND CHEAP EATS

Café society in İstanbul is as wide ranging as in any other European capital, with everything from traditional male-only teahouses to stylish (and expensive) café-bars – and an ever increasing number of multinational coffee chains. Most of the trendy café-bars are to be found in Beyoğlu, though there are a few passable options in the tourist heartland of Sultanahmet.

SULTANAHMET

Çiğdem Patisserie Divan Yolu Cad 62 ☎0212/526 8859; map p.44. For over forty years, the *Çiğdem* has been offering a good selection of both Turkish and non-Turkish pastries and sweets. Try the crisp on the outside, chewy on the inside *acı badem*, a traditional almond-flavoured biscuit, or the reliable *baklava* (6TL a portion). Also does a decent range of coffees, from Turkish to latte, and of course tea. Unlicensed. Daily 8am–11pm.

Doy Doy Sıfa Hamamı Sok 13 ☎0212/517 1588, ⓦdoydoy-restaurant.com; map p.44. A backpacker's institution, with a well-deserved reputation for cheap and well-prepared kebabs and *pide* from 9TL, *sulu yemek* from 4TL. There are a few choices for vegetarians. Dining is on four floors, including a roof terrace with great views of the Sea of Marmara and, at night, the illuminated Blue Mosque. Unlicensed. Daily 8am–11pm.

The Pudding Shop (Lale Restaurant) Divan Yolu Cad 6 ☎0212/522 2970; map p.44. This Sultanahmet institution first opened its doors in 1957, and in the late 1960s became *the* meeting place for hippies and other travellers overlanding to India (see box, p.65). *The Pudding Shop* is still dishing up its signature rice pudding (6TL) along with a wide array of traditional Turkish dishes. Service is canteen-style, but the food's good, it's right near the major sights and serves alcohol. Daily 7am–11pm.

Sultan Pub Divan Yolu Cad 2 ☎0212/511 5638; map p.44. Long-established and touristy café-bar, set in a nineteenth-century building diagonally opposite the Aya Sofya. There are tables outside in summer, from where you can watch the endless processions of fellow visitors. The food is both Turkish and international (mains 18–25TL) and reasonably tasty for such a touristy establishment. Daily 9.30am–1am.

Tarihi Sultanahmet Köftesi Divan Yolu Cad ☎0212/511 3960; map p.44. The longest established of three *köfte* specialists at this end of Divan Yolu, and frequented by Turkish celebrities (check out the framed newspaper clippings and thank-you letters on the tiled walls). A plate of tasty meatballs, pickled peppers, fresh bread and a spicy tomato-sauce dip costs 10TL. Windows in the upstairs salons boast views across the Aya Sofya and Blue Mosque. Unlicensed. Daily 11am–11pm.

EMINÖNÜ AND SIRKECI

Halis Kardeşler Rüstem Paşa Camii Yanı ☎0212/528 1076; map p.68. A great lunchtime pit stop if you are visiting the gorgeous Rüstem Paşa Camii (see p.73). Set in a vaulted room in part of the mosque complex, it has a good range of unpretentious food designed to keep the local traders and artisans happy. The tasty lentil soup costs 1.50TL, *kadın budu köfte* (meatballs in a delicate batter) are 4TL and *Arnavut ciğeri* (Albanian-style liver) for the same bargain price. Unlicensed. Daily 7am–6pm.

Kardelen Pub Muradiye Cad 3 ☎0212/522 8393; map p.68. Unpretentious *meyhane* near Sirkeci station, with an ivy-covered facade and a rather zany tiled roof terrace. Female visitors may feel uncomfortable without male company among the mainly male clientele. Hearty *mezes* from 6TL and grills 10TL and up. Much beer and *rakı* are downed, especially when one of İstanbul's Big Three football teams is on the huge TV. Daily 10am–2am.

Konyalı Mimar Kemalettin Cad 5, Sirkeci ☎0212/513 9610; map p.68. Excellent pastry and cake shop opposite the station much frequented by the area's businesspeople, who eat their breakfast standing at the marble-topped counters. A hearty portion of cheese-filled *su böreği* makes an excellent breakfast, with a large tulip-shaped glass of tea for 2TL. Adjoining is the *Konyalı Lokanta*, a good-value bet for a traditional Turkish tradesman's lunch. Unlicensed. Mon–Sat 7am–8pm.

Set Üstü Çay Bahçesi Gülhane Parkı, Sirkeci ☎0212/513 9610; map p.68. This open-air café, tucked away at the southern end of the park near the Goth's Column, with great views over the Bosphorus and back up

> ## TOP FIVE SOUTHEAST TURKISH CUISINE
> **Akdeniz Hatay Sofrası** Grand Bazaar and around, see p.186
> **Çiya** Kadıköy, see p.191
> **Develi** Land walls, see p.188
> **Mardin Kaburga Sofrası** Taksim Square and around, see p.190
> **Siirt Şeref Büryan Kebap Salonu** Grand Bazaar and around, see p.188

13

AN A–Z OF TURKISH CUISINE

Appetizers (meze) Turkey is justly famous for its *meze*, in many ways the heart of the nation's cuisine. The best and most common include: *patlıcan salatası* (aubergine mash), *piyaz* (white haricot vinaigrette), *semizotu* (purslane weed, usually in yoghurt), *mücver* (courgette croquettes), *sigara böreği* (tightly rolled cheese pastries), *imam bayıldı* (cold baked aubergine with onion and tomato) and *dolma* (any stuffed vegetable, but typically peppers or tomatoes).

Baklava and pastry-based desserts There are a variety of different *baklava*-related desserts, all permutations of a sugar, flour, nut and butter mix. The best is *antep fıstıklı sarması* (pistachio-filled *baklava*); *cevizli* (walnut-filled) *baklava* is usually a little cheaper. Also worth trying is *künefe*, another southeastern Turkish treat made from mild goat's cheese, topped with shredded wheat soaked in syrup, and baked in the oven.

Bread (ekmek) The standard Turkish loaf, sold from glass-fronted cabinets outside grocery stores across the city, is good if an hour or two old, but soon goes spongy and stale. Flat, semi-leavened *pide* bread is served with soup, at *kebapcıs* and during Ramadan. Unleavened *durum*, like a tortilla, is the wrap of choice in cheap *döner* joints. *Mısır ekmeği* (corn bread), a Black Sea staple, sometimes makes an appearance, as does German-style rye bread.

Cheese (peynir) There's far more to Turkish cheese than *beyaz peynir* (like Greek feta), a ubiquitous element of the standard Turkish breakfast. *Dil peynir* ("tongue" cheese), a hard, salty cheese that breaks up into mozzarella-like filaments, and the plaited *oğru peynir*, can both be grilled or fried like Cypriot *halloúmi*. *Tulum peynir* is a strong, salty, almost granular goat's cheese cured in a goatskin. *Otlu peynir* from the Van area is cured with herbs and eaten at breakfast; cow's-milk *kaşar*, especially *eski* (aged) *kaşar* from the Kars region, is also highly esteemed.

Meat dishes (etli yemeği) *Karnıyarık*, aubergine halves stuffed with a rich mince-filling, is a delicious staple, as is *güveç*, a clay-pot fricassee. *Hunkar beğendi* (beef stew on a bed of puréed eggplant and cheese) has its origins in Ottoman times and is a must-try. *Saray kebap* (beef stew topped with bechamel sauce, and oven-browned), *macar kebap* (Hungarian-style stewed meat and vegetables topped with mashed potato and cheese, then baked) are both standards.

Grilled meats (ızgarı) Kebabs include the spicy *Adana*, with its sprinkling of purple sumac herb betraying Arab influence; *İskender kebap*, best sampled in the city of Bursa (see p.251), is heavy on the flat bread and yoghurt. *Köfte* (meatballs), *şiş* (stewed meat chunks, usually mutton or beef) and *çöp* (bits of lamb or offal) are other options. Chicken (*piliç* or *tavuk*) is widely available, usually either as a skewer-cooked *şiş* or a breast fillet. In some places, you can ask for a *durum*, when the meat and garnish are served in a flat-bread wrap. *Pirzola*, tiny lamb chops, are usually only available in *restoran*.

Fish (balık) Budget mainstays include *sardalya* (sardines – grilled fresh), *hamsi* (anchovies – usually fried) and *istavrit* (horse mackerel). *Mercan* (red bream), *lüfer* (bluefish), *kılıç* (swordfish)

---

to the walls of the Topkapı Palace, does excellent samovar-style Turkish tea and is a great place to rest-up after sightseeing. Also has a simple snack-menu with toasted sandwiches 5TL. Daily 9am–10pm.

AROUND THE GRAND BAZAAR

★ **Ağa Kapısı** Nazir Izzet Efendi Sok 11 ☎0212/519 5176; map pp.76–77. Tucked away on a dead-end street just below the Süleymaniye Camii and frequented mainly by local traders, conservative headscarved female students and their lecturers, the three-storey *Ağa Kapısı* has picture windows beyond compare, giving stunning panoramic views down over the Galata Bridge, the mouth of the Golden Horn and the Bosphorus beyond. The food is simple and cheap – try the *gözleme* (a kind of *paratha* stuffed with goat's cheese, 6TL) and a glass of tea, traditional Turkish style, or indulge in one of their Ottoman-style sherbet drinks (6TL). Smokers

may opt to simply puff away on a *nargile* (15TL) on the roof terrace. Unlicensed. Daily 8am–midnight.

Antakya Café Restaurant Divan i Ali Sok 16 ☎0212/518 0117, ⊛antakyarestaurant.com; map pp.76–77. Despite the overly ambitious menu and flashing neon sign, the Arab-influenced food at the *Antakya* (the Turkish name for ancient Antioch, by the Syrian border) is excellent. The baked hummus (7TL), the walnut-and-pomegranate-sauce-rich *gavurdağı* salad, or the *Antakya yoncası*, a chicken, cheese, pine-nut and pistachio kebab wrapped in thin bread (16TL), are particularly worth trying. Their *kabak tatlısı*, candied pumpkin served drenched in sweet tahini sauce, is delicious. Also serves pizzas, *pide* and standard kebabs. Unlicensed. Daily 10am–midnight.

Erenler Çay Bahçesi Ali Baba Türbe Sok Medressi, Yeniçeriler Cad 36/38 ☎0212/528 3785; map pp.76–77.

and *orfoz* (giant grouper) are highly prized and expensive. *Çipura* (gilt-head bream) and *levrek* (sea bass) are usually farmed and consequently good value – if less tasty. Fish, whatever its price, is usually simply prepared and grilled.

Ice cream (dondoruma) The genuine *Maraşlı döşme dondurma* (whipped in the Kahraman Maraş tradition – a bit like Italian *gelato*) is the ice cream of choice in İstanbul. That served with *baklava* in the better *pastanes* is usually Maraş.

Milk-based puddings (muhallebi) *Süpangile* ("*süp*" for short, a corruption of *soupe d'Anglais*) is an incredibly dense, rich chocolate pudding with sponge or a biscuit embedded inside. More modest dishes are *keşkül* (a vanilla and nut-crumble custard) and *sütlaç* (rice pudding) – one dessert that's consistently available in ordinary restaurants. The most complicated dish is *tavukgöğsü*, a cinnamon-topped morsel made from hyper-boiled and strained chicken breast, semolina starch and milk. *Kazandibi* (literally "bottom of the pot") is *tavukgöğsü* residue with a dark crust on the bottom – not to be confused with *fırın sütlaç*, which looks the same but is actually *sütlaç* pudding with a scorched top baked in a clay dish.

Offal (çöp) *Böbrek* (kidney), *yürek* (heart), *ciğer* (liver), and *koç yumurtası* (ram's egg) or *billur* (crystal) – the last two euphemisms for testicle, less commonly found of late – are just some of the more entertaining specialities, but far more readily available is *kokoreç*, seasoned lamb's intestines often cooked on a charcoal grill and available from street vendors.

Salad (salata) *Çoban* (shepherd's) *salatası* is the generic term for the widespread cucumber, tomato, onion, pepper and parsley salad (beware, the peppers are sometimes hot); *yeşil* (green) salad, usually just some *marul* (lettuce), is only seasonally available. M*evsim salatası* or seasonal salad – perhaps tomato slices, watercress, red cabbage and lettuce hearts, sprinkled with cheese and drenched in dressing – resembles a Western salad and often accompanies a kebab meal.

Soup (çorba) The most frequently encountered soups are *mercimek* (lentil), *ezo gelin* (rice and vegetable broth – thick enough to be an appetizing breakfast), *paça* (trotters) or *işkembe* (tripe) soup laced liberally with garlic oil, vinegar and red pepper flakes, an effective hangover antidote/preventative.

Steamtray dishes (hazır or sulu yemek) Dishes such as *kuru fasulye* (bean soup – rather like baked beans in tomato sauce), *taze fasulye* (French beans), *sebze turlu* (vegetable stew) and *nohut* (chickpeas) are usually found in *lokanta*s (and the home). Meaty favourites include *sebzeli köfte* (meatballs stewed with vegetables) and various types of chicken stew.

Turkish Delight (lokum) The best-known Turkish sweet, *lokum* is ubiquitous. In its basic form, it's just solidified sugar and pectin, flavoured (most commonly) with rosewater and sprinkled with powdered sugar. More expensive are versions liberally studded with nuts, usually either walnuts or pistachios. Although you might find a complimentary piece in your hotel room, it's not traditionally found in restaurants or even *pastanes*, but is for sale in virtually every souvenir shop and the Grand and Spice bazaars (see p.75 and p.72, respectively).

In the courtyard of a three-hundred-year-old *medrese* (religious school), this cheap and cheerful bazaar-worker-oriented *nargile* café has waterpipes for 12TL, tea for a lira and snacks like toasted sandwiches. Unlicensed. Daily: April–Oct 7am–3am; Nov–March 7am–midnight.

Fes Café Ali Baba Türbe Sok 25/7A, off Nuruosmaniye Cad, Kapalı Çarşı ☎ 0212/ 526 3071; map pp.76–77. A trendy mix of traditional and new, with designer tables spilling out onto a quiet cobbled street. There's a big flat-screen TV, mellow piped music and, despite its location, the majority of the clientele are mainly well-heeled Turks. Sandwiches are wholesome and filling and reasonable value at 12TL, and there's also a good selection of home-made cakes. A hole-in-the-wall branch can be found in the Grand Bazaar on Hacılar Cad 62, which keeps bazaar opening hours. Unlicensed. Daily 8am–9pm.

★ **Tarihi Kuru Fasuliye Süleymaniye Erzincanlı Ali Baba** Siddik Samı Onar Cad 11 ☎ 0212/513 6219; map pp.76–77. In the gorgeous Süleymaniye Camii complex, with tables set out on the precinct between the mosque and medrese behind, this simple place serves up some of the tastiest beans in town (and they're not out of a can) for a bargain 4TL – though beware of the hot chilli pepper draped innocently atop your steaming bowl of buttery, tomato-sauce-drenched pulses. Unlicensed. Daily 9am–7pm.

Vefa Bozacısı Katip Çelebi Cad 104/1 ☎ 0212/519 4922, ⓦ vefa.com.tr; map pp.76–77. Worth a look just to see the interior: old tiled floor, dark-wood shelves, ornate Victorian-style mirrors, 1920s light-fittings, and bottles of vinegar with label designs unchanged for decades (Atatürk was here in 1937). The *boza* (3TL), a cloudy, viscous drink made by fermenting bulgur wheat with sugar and water

13

and best drunk in the winter months, is an acquired taste but very healthy. Unlicensed. Daily 7am–midnight.

IN THE GRAND BAZAAR

★ **Bedesten Café** Cevahir Bedesteni 143–151, Kapalı Çarşı ☎0212/520 2250; map p.78. An oasis of peace and tranquillity in the Grand Bazaar, decorated with two giant *alem* – the brass crescent- and star-topped finials that adorn mosque domes and minarets – and an even bigger portrait of Atatürk. The food is prepared using quality ingredients with delicacies such as the scrambled tomato and pepper omelette *menemen* or a full Turkish breakfast for 11.50TL. Lunch mains include Turkish ravioli (*manti*) in garlic and yoghurt sauce (16.50TL), and there's a great selection of cakes. It even has its own toilets, a rarity among bazaar establishments. Unlicensed. Mon–Sat 8.30am–6.30pm.

★ **Dönerci Şahin Usta** Nuruosmaniye Kılıçlar Sok 7 ☎0212/526 5297; map p.78. One of the best places in the city to try a real kebab, conveniently situated right outside the Nuruosmaniye Gate of the Grand Bazaar. Succulent lamb freshly layered on the vertical spit each morning is dished up with sliced tomatoes, onions smothered in sumac, green peppers and an oven-fresh mini-*pide* bread. It's a hole in the wall place with no seats, and the long queues attest to its loyal clientele. It's the real deal (cheaper kebab joints use fatty meat and frozen, pre-prepared *döners*). 8TL for a kebab, best washed down with the frothy salted yoghurt drink *ayran* (2TL). Unlicensed. Mon–Sat 10am–3pm.

Havuzlu Ganı Çelebi Sok 3, Kapalı Çarşı ☎0212/527 3346; map p.78. Appealing Grand Bazaar restaurant, with Ottoman-style decor and white tablecloths on dark-wood tables laid out beneath a barrel-vaulted ceiling. Offers a good range of kebabs (the *İskender* is recommended) and *hazır yemek* dishes. Brisk service, tasty food and reasonable prices (kebabs around 10TL). Unlicensed. Mon–Sat 10am–5pm.

Padaliza Off Yağlıkcılar Cad, Kapalı Çarşı; map p.78. The best-value eating establishment in the Grand Bazaar itself (near the main entrance, at the entrance to İç Cebeci Hanı) in a beautifully restored, exposed-brick, barrel-vaulted *han*. The waiters are white-shirted and black-tied

but are friendly rather than formal, and dish up delicious stuffed vegetables (6TL) and a variety of kebabs, including *kağıt kebabı*, cubes of lamb and vegetables oven-baked in greased-paper for 10TL. There are some tables in the bustling alley outside. Unlicensed. Mon–Sat 10am–5pm.

Subaşı Lokantasi Nuruosmaniye Cad 48, Çarşı Kapı ☎0212/522 4762; map p.78. Behind Nuruosmaniye Camii, just outside the main entrance of the Grand Bazaar, this traditional *lokanta* serves excellent lunchtime food to the market traders. Highly rated by many Turkish newspapers (their restaurant reviews adorn the walls), you should go early (noon–1pm), as it gets packed and food may run out. Mains cost between 8 and 13TL a portion depending on the amount of meat in them – try the stuffed peppers or delicious *karnı yarık* (mince-topped aubergine). Unlicensed. Mon–Sat 9am–6pm.

THE NORTHWEST QUARTER

Arnavut Köfteci Mursel Paşa Cad 149; map p.89. Although not quite so long-established as the late nineteenth-century Greek building in which it's housed, this one-room café has been around for fifty years or more – the owner a fair bit longer. The motley array of vintage Formica-topped tables, each a different pastel hue, are usually packed with down-to-earth locals, though an occasional crop of trendy media types turns up from time to time. The *köfte* (8TL) are delicious, especially when washed down with a glass of *ayran*. Unlicensed. Mon–Sat 4.30am–6.30pm.

THE LAND WALLS

Durak Köfte Mihrimah Sultan Camii Altı 361, Edirnekapı ☎0212/532 5581; map p.102. Handily located right next to the entrance to the newly restored Mihrimah Camii, this workers' café dishes-up tasty Macedonian-style *köfte* for 7TL, *kuru fasuliye* (haricot beans in tomato sauce) for 2.50TL and several other unpretentious dishes, at a point where wall-walkers may well be in need of sustenance. Daily 10am–6.30pm.

Mevlanakapi Merkezefendi Köftecisi Mevlanakapi Cad 39 ☎0212/587 9868; map p.102. A real locals' joint, located a three-minute walk west from Mevlanakapi, just past the Hacı Evliya mosque, this makes a great lunch stop if you are exploring the land walls. Firm but tender *köfte* served with bulgur salad, tomatoes, onions and a spicy chilli sauce cost 8TL, while *piyaz* (a haricot bean salad) is 4TL; kebabs and lentil soup are also served. Mon–Sat 10am–6.30pm.

GALATA AND THE WATERFRONT DISTRICTS

★ **Fasuli** İskelesi Cad 10–12, Tophane ☎0212/243 6580; map p.110. Housed in an attractive nineteenth-century corner-plot building, this establishment turns the

---

TOP FIVE FISH RESTAURANTS

Balıkçı Sabahattın Sultanahmet, see p.185

Giritli Sultanahmet, see p.186

İmroz İstiklal Caddesi and around, see p.190

Kıyı Bosphorus, see p.192

Tarihi Karaköy Balık Lokantası Galata and waterfront, see p.189

humble haricot bean into an art form (7TL). Cooked in a creamy tomato and butter sauce, made with only the freshest ingredients, including butter imported from the owner's native Trabzon on the Black Sea and beans from the Pontic Alps. Other dishes include tender *pirzola* (lamb cutlets) for 15TL, and you can finish off with the unusual *Laz boreği*, an eastern Black Sea variation of *baklava*. Unlicensed. Daily 7am–11pm.

Galata Konak Patisserie Hacı Ali Sok 2, Galata ☎0212/252 5346, ✆galatakonakcafe.com; map p.110. Just down from the Galata Tower, this stylish café dishes up delicious lattes (with Amaretto biscuits) and a range of tempting cakes and desserts from 6TL. For something a little more substantial, head up the lantern-lit stairwell or take the antique lift to the rooftop terrace restaurant for a mix of Turkish and European fare and an expansive view over the Golden Horn. Popular with locals and tourists alike, it always seems to be packed. Unlicensed. Daily 9am–9pm.

İstanbul Modern Café Meclis-i-Mebusan Cad Antrepo 4, Karaköy ☎0212/292 2612; map p.110. A chic, fashion-conscious place, as you would expect from a café attached to the city's leading contemporary arts gallery (see p.114), with a spacious terrace overlooking the Bosphorus. A blend of international and Turkish food (mains from 20TL) but with the snail-pace service it's probably better to opt for a latte – it's worth the 8TL to sit on the terrace and watch the ships go by. Daily 10am–midnight.

★ **Karaköy Güllüoğlu** Rihtim Cad 17, off İskelesi Cad 10–12, Karaköy ☎0212/293 0910, ✆karakoygulluoglu .com; map p.110. Buttery, nut-filled *baklava*, often eaten with a generous dollop of chewy Maraş ice cream, takes pride of place here and draws in sweet-toothed families from across the city. This branch is the original of a popular countrywide chain, founded in 1949 by the Güllüoğlu family, *baklava* connoisseurs from Gaziantep, the nation's pistachio and *baklava* capital. Daily 10am–midnight.

★ **Molly's Café** Camekan Sok 1, Kuledibi, Galata ☎0212/245 1696; map p.110. Tucked down a narrow, trendy street of boutique shops just below the Galata Tower, this laidback café/reading room is patronized by an interesting and eclectic mix of educated locals, expats and visitors. Run by welcoming Canadian expat Molly, it's a great place to sample her vegetable lasagne (15TL), home-made cakes (from 6TL) and chat to clued-up İstanbullus. There's a small terrace out back for balmy summer evenings, and regular events including book readings and live music. Daily 9am–9pm.

ISTİKLAL CADDESI AND AROUND

Canım Ciğerim Minare Sok 1, Beyoğlu ☎0212/252 6060; map pp.120–121. Just off buzzing Asmaaltı Geçiti, this is a small, trendy and very popular place with set menus of chicken, lamb or liver *şiş* skewers served with

fresh flat *lavaş* bread and four varieties of salad, plus grilled vegetables (15TL). Daily 10am–midnight.

Çorbacı Galatasaray Lisesi Yanı, off İstiklal Caddesi ☎0212/244 5169; map pp.120–121. Next door to İstanbul's best bookshop, Homer (see p.216), all the standard Turkish soups are offered here, plus several more unusual ones. Try the *yuvarlama*, a yoghurt and rice base livened-up with spicy mini-*köfte* for 5.50TL, and there's a fixed menu of soup, pilaf rice and *ayran* for 9TL. Unlicensed. Mon–Fri 8am–2.30pm, Sat & Sun 9am–6pm.

Kafe Ara Tosbağa Sok 8/A, off Yeniçarşı Cad, Beyoğlu ☎0212/245 4105; map pp.120–121. A great place, tucked away just off Galatasaray Meydanı, with a raft of tables out in the alley and a lovely dark-wood bistro-style interior lined with black-and-white images of Ara Güler (see box, p.206). Choose from big bowls of salad from 12TL or more expensive dishes like steak cooked with a basil sauce for 25TL. The clientele are generally prosperous, but it's not overly posh and is the perfect spot to rest your feet after the rigours of shopping on İstiklal Cad. Unlicensed. Mon–Thurs 8am–11pm, Fri 8am–midnight, Sat & Sun 10am–11pm.

Kallavi Nargile Café Kallavi Sok 2, Beyoğlu ☎0212/245 9154; map pp.120–121. Take the elevator up to this calming, wood-walled and -floored café for a coffee (6TL), a puff on a *nargile* (15TL) or a simple snack (sandwiches, pastas and burgers as well as Turkish dishes) and enjoy fine views over the Bosphorus – *Kallavi Nargile* was one of the first rooftop venues. Unlicensed. Daily 11am–1am.

Nizam Pide Büyükparmakkapı Sok 13, off İstiklal Cad, Beyoğlu ☎0212/249 7918, ✆nizampide.com; map pp.120–121. Excellent *pide* (7TL and up), from the traditional *kuşbaşı pide*, topped with diced meat, to a more exotic mushroom-topped variety. Also serves great soups and beans in a rich tomato sauce. There's a second branch – *Nizam Pide 2* – on Kalyoncu Kulluk Cad, behind Nevizade Sok in the Fish Market, and both are regularly rated among the top ten *pide* outlets in Turkey. Unlicensed. Open 24hr.

★ **Pia** İstiklal Cad, Bekar Sok 6, Beyoğlu ☎0212/252 7100, ✆piasarikahve.com; map pp.120–121. Delightful split-level café favoured by elegant women. There are tables out on the street in summer, protected from passing pedestrians by potted plants, and the interior is cosy and welcoming, with a wrought-iron spiral staircase leading to the upstairs gallery. The food is well prepared and reasonable value, with salad bowls from 12TL and the popular *Pia* burger 16TL. The drinks are served in slim glasses and topped with lemon and a cherry. Daily 10am–2pm.

★ **Saray** İstiklal Cad 107, Beyoğlu ☎0212/292 3434; map pp.120–121. Best value of İstanbul's upmarket patisseries (5–9TL), serving mouthwatering profiteroles.

13

Established in 1935, the emphasis is on classic Turkish desserts such as fırın sütlaç (baked rice pudding), irmik helvası (semolina with nuts) and baklava-type sweets, including wonderful fıstık sarma (pistachios packed in a syrup-drenched pastry roll), though it also serves good Turkish food. Daily 6am–11pm.

TAKSIM SQUARE AND AROUND

Felafel House Şehit Muhtar Cad 19 ☎0212/253 7730, ⓦfelafelhouse.net; map p.127. Run by a Palestinian father and son, the felafel here are as tasty, and the hummus as rich, smooth and creamy, as you'd expect from such a partnership. A set felafel, hummus and salad meal costs 10TL. Expect Arab and Israeli neighbours while you eat at the street tables or inside the fluorescent-lit galley-like interior. Unlicensed. Daily 11am–1pm.

House Café Atiye Sok 10 ☎0212/259 2377, ⓦthehousecafé.com; map p.127. A large communal table dominates proceedings here, and despite the upscale neighbourhood, it's friendly and welcoming. The house burger is very popular, the coffee good and the bar prices not bad for this über-rich part of the city. There's also a branch in a charming domed Ottoman building attached to the Teşvikiye mosque, very popular in summer with its outside tables. Mains from 18TL. Daily 8am–midnight.

Lale İşkembecisi Tarlabaşı Bulvarı 3 ☎0212/252 6969; map p.127. Turks swear by İşkembe Çorbası (tripe soup) as a cure for hangovers, and there's plenty of need for that remedy in hedonistic Beyoğlu. This famous Taksim institution, established in 1960 and housed in a smart but historic building, specializes in the bits others disdain and if you fancy tripe (8TL), lamb's head, brain or trotter soup, this is the place to head for. Be wary, though, Tarlabaşı Bulvarı has a dodgy reputation at night for crime (see p.33). Unlicensed. Open 24hr.

BEŞIKTAŞ & ORTAKÖY

Banyan Muallim Naci Cad Salhane Sok 3 ☎0212/259 9060, ⓦbanyanrestaurant.com/en; map p.132. Inventive Asian fusion cuisine featuring jazzed-up versions of all the usual suspects – dim sum, tempura, wok-fried noodles – and throwing in a few surprises too. Everything from Vietnamese to Indian gets a nod, with a wide range of vegetarian options. The terrace views of Ortaköy mosque and the Bosphorus Bridge are stunning, but they'll cost you, with mains starting at 40TL. Daily noon–2am.

House Café Salhane Sok 1 ☎0212/227 2699, ⓦthehousecafé.com; map p.132. With ten branches scattered around İstanbul and a spanking-new boutique hotel opened up next door, this chain of modern eateries (see also above) is a hit with the young and affluent. Putting a posh spin on western classics, menu staples range from burgers and pizzas to a pricey but scrumptious Sunday

brunch (40TL). Elegant white and gold decor and a beautiful terrace showcase why this place is so popular. Mon, Thurs & Sun 8am–2am, Fri & Sat 8am–2am.

Pandos Kaynakcı Mumcu Bakkal Sokak, Beşiktaş ☎0212/258 2616; map p.132. A dilapidated hut, seemingly unrenovated since its opening in the early 1900s, this place is fast becoming one of the region's most popular breakfast haunts with platters of sumptuous kaymak (clotted cream made from buffalo milk), fresh honey and assorted mezes all for under 5TL. With its peeling paint and understated logo printed on the glass front, Pando is easily overlooked; head for the unmissable Beşiktaş fish market and ask one of the locals to point you in the right direction – the owner and namesake, now pushing 90, is something of a local institution. Get there early to nab a seat. Daily 7am–6pm.

ASIAN İSTANBUL

Baylan Muvakkithane Cad 19, Kadıköy ☎0216/336 2881; map p.140. This famous patisserie is a must for nostalgia buffs, with its 1950s dark-wood and chrome frontage. The trellis-shaded garden area is popular with mums and their offspring, many of whom tuck into traditional ice creams or plates of pastel-coloured macaroons for 7TL. Evidence of the Christian Armenian origins of the café can be seen in liqueur chocolates on sale here. Daily 10am–10pm.

Törek Dr Isat Işık Cad, Kadıköy ☎0216/347 1875, ⓦtorekmanti.com; map p.140. Family-orientated place specializing in mantı (Turkish ravioli) and çiğ böreği, a samosa-style pie stuffed with meat or cheese and deep-fried. They also serve lentil soup for a bargain 2.50TL, and there's a shady terrace out back. Unlicensed. Daily 7am–11pm.

THE BOSPHORUS

Ali Baba Köfteci Arnavutköy Cad 104, Arnavutköy ☎0212/265 3612; map p.151. Cheap-and-cheerful pine-clad place specializing in generous portions of köfte and fasuliye (haricot beans topped with sliced onion) for around 12TL. Many famous visitors have given their seal of approval to this modest Arnavutköy institution – just check out the signed photos of footballers, politicians and pop stars on the walls. Unlicensed. Daily 10am–11pm.

Aşşk Muallim Naci Cad 170/A, Kuruçeşme ☎0212/265 4734, ⓦasskkahve.com; map p.151. On the waterfront but hidden behind a delightful Art Deco-style building now housing a Makro supermarket, and at its best in summer when the tables in the cobbled courtyard afford fine vistas of the Bosphorus. Food is Mediterranean/international, organic and expensive, with paninis from 20TL and grilled chicken in lemon, honey and pepper sauce for 29TL, but the setting makes it worthwhile. Tues–Sun 9am–10pm.

VEGETARIAN FOOD

13

Given the quality and quantity of fresh fruit and vegetables (not to mention pulses) produced in Turkey, things should be pretty good for **vegetarians**. Unfortunately, those tasty-looking vegetable dishes on offer in the steamtrays in most *lokantis* are usually made with lamb- or chicken-based broth; even bulgur and rice may be cooked in meat stock, as can lentil soups. To check, ask "*İçinde et suyu var mı?*" ("Does it contain meat stock?"). In traditional restaurants, strict vegetarians should confine themselves to *mezes*, salads, omelettes, *böreks* and the cheese-topped varieties of *pide*.

Lucca Cevdet Paşa Cad 51/B, Bebek ☎ 0212/257 1255, ⓦ luccastyle.com; map p.151. This may be a casual café-bar but that's upmarket Bebek "casual", and unless you're fashionably dressed you may feel uncomfortable. That said, the interior's a fun mix of the genuinely old (check out the nineteenth-century ceiling reliefs), the retro (1950s-style prints) and the ethnic (African masks). Food ranges from tapas (6–22TL) to lemon sea-bass (35TL). Daily noon–2am.

RESTAURANTS

The restaurant scene in İstanbul is, as to be expected in such a huge and fast developing city, very varied. There are countless places offering **international cuisine**, and an increasing number of İstanbullus appear as fond of pasta, burgers, pizzas et al as they do their native cuisine. The liveliest restaurants and *meyhanes* (see p.180), catering largely to theatre/cinema-goers and young İstanbullus heading out on the town, are in **Beyoğlu** and **Taksim**, especially on Nevizade and Asmalımescit *sokaks*. **Kumkapı**, southwest of Sultanahmet and almost on the shores of the Sea of Marmara, is famed for its *meyhanes*, over fifty of them lined up either side of a narrow street running down from Kumkapı Meydanı. Many *meyhanes* offer fixed menu deals, with either a couple of home-produced drinks included or, more expensive, as many (local) drinks as you wish. Wandering gypsy musicians and the drunken carousing of hordes of İstanbullu revellers make for a fun meal out in either of these areas. Trendy **Ortaköy**, fronting the Bosphorus, is another option – especially if you're heading for one of the nearby waterfront clubs (see p.201). The eating places in **Sultanahmet** cannot compare in terms of quality or entertainment to those across the Golden Horn, but if you're looking for somewhere convenient after a heavy day's sightseeing, there are a few honourable exceptions. The well-heeled can combine dinner with an evening sea-taxi (see p.26) ride north along the Bosphorus to a fancy fish restaurant. Alternatively, cheap ferries run across the Bosphorus to the Asian suburb of **Üsküdar**, which has a couple of decent options, and to **Kadıköy**, with its lively bars, fish market and one of the city's most popular restaurants.

SULTANAHMET

Albura Kathisma Akbıyık Cad 26 ☎ 0212/518 9710; map p.44. Quite a few restaurants in the area now serve regional Anatolian-style dishes, but *Albura* was among the first and remains one of the best. Try the special Kathisma Palace, a lamb casserole with figs and almonds (50TL for two people). Angora wine is priced at a reasonable (for İstanbul) 48TL a bottle. The dining room is a cavernous but stylish bare-brick affair, and there are plenty of outside tables on this bustling tourist street. Daily 10am–11pm.

★ **Amedros** Hoca Rüstem Sok 7, Divan Yolu ☎ 0212/522 8356; map p.44. A sophisticated café-restaurant that's a world away in ambience to the tourist dives that dominate Sultanahmet's dining scene. It's best in summer, when the action moves to the white-clothed tables in the narrow pedestrian street. The interior manages to be both stylish and homely, and the food is good, too – a mixture of European (try the Flame Marmer steak) and traditional Anatolian (the *testi* kebab, a succulent lamb and vegetable stew slow-cooked in a sealed clay pot, is a good bet). The service is attentive

without being obsequious and the whole place is very professionally run. Mains from 20TL. Daily 11am–1am.

★ **Balıkçı Sabahattın** Seyit Hasan Koyu Sok 1, Cankurtan ☎ 0212/458 1824; map p.44. A fish restaurant in the refreshingly down-to-earth streets beside Cankurtaran station, just a five-minute walk from touristy Sultanahmet. It's not cheap (it's the in-place for monied locals), but is about as atmospheric as you can get, with vine-shaded tables set out in a narrow alley (in summer) or a wood-floored dining room in an old wooden house (winter). Starters begin at 6TL, mains from 30TL, with seasonal, locally caught fish on the menu. Daily 11am–1am.

Dubb İncili Çavuş Sok ☎ 0212/513 7308; map p.44. A funky spot with one Indian and two Turkish chefs serving up authentic Subcontinent dishes in a chic yet ethnic setting. The rooms, spread over several floors, are small, and there's a roof terrace and tables on the street. Delicious *samosas* and *pakoras* cost 8–10TL, vegetable curries 17TL, and meat curries 20–25TL. Reservations advised at weekends. Nearby in Cankurtaran, on Amiral Taftil Sok 25,

13

Dubb Ethnic (☎ 0212/517 6828), is run by the same people and offering a selection of Indian, Japanese, Korean and Thai dishes. Daily noon–midnight.

Giritli Keresteci Hakkı Sok, Ahırkapı ☎ 0212/458 2270, ⊛ giritlirestoran.com; map p.44. Atmospheric fish restaurant set in a historic building near the *Armada Hotel*, specializing in Cretan dishes (the owner/chef's great-grandfather was an immigrant from Crete). For a no-holds-barred evening out go for the fixed menu at 95TL, and enjoy a sea-food pilaf, 23 *meze* morsels and three hot starters, followed by a choice of four or five fish – and as much beer, wine or *rakı* as you can drink. Daily noon–midnight.

Khorasani Ticarethane Sok 39/41, Divan Yolu ☎ 0212/519 5959, ⊛ khorasanirestaurant.com; map p.44. If you are staying in Sultanahmet, this is the nearest place to sample authentic southeastern Turkish cuisine, including hummus and the spicy walnut and pepper dip, *muhamara* (8TL a portion). The wonderful kebabs are prepared *ocakbaşı* style over a charcoal grill – try the pistachio version (21TL). There are tables on the cobbled pedestrian street, with a stylish mezzanine-floored dining room for colder weather. Watch out for the ten percent service charge. Daily noon–1am.

Matbah Caféeriye Sok 6/1 ☎ 0212/514 6151, ⊛ matbahrestaurant.com; map p.44. Attached to the *Ottoman Imperial Hotel*, all dishes served here are based on those prepared in the Topkapı Palace kitchen in Ottoman times. The various menus, which took chef Necati a year and a half to prepare, are changed several times each year – if you're curious about the type of food favoured by the Ottoman sultans, give it a try. Garlicky lamb trotter served on rye bread (22TL), or goose baked with rice in a delicate pastry cover (38TL) are just a couple of dishes on offer. Great views over the Caféeriye Medresesi, too. Daily 11am–midnight.

★ **Mosaik Restaurant** Divan Yolu Cad, İncili Çavuş Sok 1 ☎ 0212/512 4177; map p.44. A well-established restaurant in a nicely restored, late nineteenth-century house, all wooden floors, kilims and subdued lighting. The tables out on the quiet side-street are great in the warmer months, and there's an atmospheric, separate downstairs bar (with small beers at 8TL). Serves a range of less common Turkish dishes, including Armenian, Greek and Kurdish specialities from 18TL. Daily 9am–midnight.

EMINÖNÜ AND SIRKECI

Hamdi Et Lokantası Kalçın Sok 17 Tahmis Cad, Eminönü ☎ 0212 528 0390; map p.68. The uninspiring facade of this five-storey joint fronting the square in Eminönü belies the quality and value of the food on offer inside. The best bet is to sit the terrace, which offers great views over the Golden Horn, Galata and the Bosphorus

beyond. Tender, charcoal-grilled kebabs of various kinds form the mainstay of the menu, but it's also a good place to try another southeastern Turkish speciality, *lahmacun*, a thin *chapati*-type bread smeared with spicy mincemeat. The *baklava* desserts are also top-notch. It's not cheap though, with kebabs from 18TL. Daily 11am–midnight.

İmbat Hudavendigar Cad 34 ☎ 0212/520 7161, ⊛ imbatrestaurant.com; map p.68. The rooftop restaurant of the *Orient Express* hotel offers a mixed menu, including new takes on Turkish classics, such as hot *tulum* (a goat's cheese cured in a goatskin bag) served in breadcrumbs. A *meze* plate, mainly Mediterranean vegetables in olive oil, is enough for two people (18TL), while grilled fish starts from 28TL and meat dishes are over 30TL. Great views over Gülhane Parkı to the Topkapı Palace and Aya Sofya, and across the Bosphorus. Daily noon–1am.

Pandeli's Mısır Çarşısı 51, Hamıdıye Cad ☎ 0212/527 3909; map p.68. Head through the main, waterfront-facing entrance of the Spice Bazaar and back towards the doorway; on your right is a staircase leading up to the restaurant. Over seventy years old, decorated throughout with blue and white tiling and run by Greek and Turkish owners, this atmospheric period restaurant is particularly known for its sea bass (mains from 22TL). Mon–Sat 11.30am–4pm.

★ **Paşazade** Sirkeci İbn-I Kemal Cad 13 ☎ 0212/513 3757, ⊛ pasazade.com; map p.68. Well-run faux-Ottoman place, one of a number of restaurants in the little streets to the west of Gülhane Parkı, all offering quite a different feel to the tourist places around Akbıyık Cad. The interior may verge on twee, but the service is good and the food (try the lamb blanquette with quince) tasty and good value (mains from 12TL). It's traditional Turkish cuisine with a twist, there's plenty of choice for vegetarians, and in warm weather the outside tables make for great people-watching. Daily noon–1am.

AROUND THE GRAND BAZAAR

★ **Akdeniz Hatay Sofrası** Ahmediye Cad 44/A, Aksaray ☎ 0212/531 3333, ⊛ akdenizhataysofrasi .com.tr; map pp.76–77. This cavernous, spotless emporium may not suit those in search of a romantic dinner, but it serves the very best southeastern Turkish food in the city. There's a strong Arab influence to the mind-bogglingly extensive menu (the Turkish province of Hatay, on the southeastern Mediterranean seaboard, is still claimed by Syria as its own). The hummus (6TL) is served warm and liberally sprinkled with pistachios, and the *bakla* (7TL), a broad bean purée drenched in tahini sauce, is delicious; the whole chicken roasted in salt (*tuzda tavuk*), 38TL, needs to be ordered a couple of hours ahead. There's

13

even a range of home-made delicacies to take away. Unlicensed. Mon–Sat 9am–midnight, Sun 8am–1pm.

Darüzzafiye Sifahane Sok 6, Beyazit ☎0212/511 8414, ⓦdaruzziyafe.com.tr; map pp.76–77. The most distinctive choice if you're looking for a sit-down lunch while exploring the Süleymaniye mosque and its environs – this was once the kitchen that formed part of the Süleymaniye: külliyesi (mosque complex). The long, narrow dining hall, with its domed roof, is a very atmospheric environment in which to tuck into traditional Ottoman-style Turkish cuisine. Try the hearty *tencere külbastı*, a stewed beef kebab with carrots and onions. It's not too pricy considering the surroundings, with cold *meze* dishes from 8TL and mains from 15TL. Unlicensed. Daily noon–11pm.

Kalamar Çapariz Sok 15, Kumkapı ☎0212/517 1849, ⓦkalamarcom.tr; map pp.76–77. Run by a Kurd from a village on the shores of distant Lake Van, the *Kalamar* is a decent choice on the main restaurant drag in Kumkapı. They do get groups but, on weekend nights at least, ninety percent of the revellers are Turkish. Cold *meze* start at 6TL, farmed-fish mains 18TL and fresh-caught fish (such as sole and bluefish) from 25TL. Service is efficient (it has to be with half the customers dancing around the tables, and serenading gypsy bands roaming at will) and (alcoholic) drinks reasonably priced. Daily 11am–2am.

Kör Agop Ördekli Bakkal 7–9, Kumkapı ☎0212/517 2334; map pp.76–77. Third-generation Armenian-owned fish restaurant, one of the oldest in town (since 1938) and hugely popular. Offers a standard selection of seasonal fish, *mezes* and salads, accompanied by a *fasil* band in the evening. The set menu, which includes *meze*, a fish or meat main, fruit and unlimited local drinks, is 50TL – good value for a reliable night out. Daily noon–2am.

★ **Siirt Şeref Büryan Kebap Salonu** İtfaye Cad 4, Fatih ☎0212/635 8085; map pp.76–77. Located in the shadow of the towering late-Roman Aqueduct of Valens, this great establishment has been dishing up regional dishes from the Arab/Kurdish southeast of Turkey for decades. Best is the *perde pilaf*, a tasty concoction of rice, shredded chicken, almonds, pine-nuts and various herbs cooked in a pot until the outside "burns" to a tasty crust (10TL). *Büryan* is spring lamb cooked in a deep clay *tandır* (tandoori) oven and served chopped on a bed of soft *pide* bread. The street on which it stands is a colourful area full of (mainly Kurdish) immigrants from the southeast. Unlicensed. Daily 11am–11pm.

THE NORTHWEST QUARTER

★ **Asithane** *Kariye Hotel*, Kariye Camii Sok 18 ☎0212/534 8414, ⓦasıthanerestaurant.com; map p.89. Garden restaurant next door to the Kariye Museum; it's expensive, but you may feel like splashing out for good service and food in such a peaceful location. The menu is described as nouvelle Ottoman cuisine, with plenty of

stews, or try the *hünkar beğendi* (tender lamb with aubergine purée) or *nıbaç*, a spiced-lamb, meatball and carrot stew flavoured with coriander, ginger, cinnamon and pomegranate syrup, topped with crushed walnuts. Meals are served on a lovely chestnut-shaded terrace swamped by roses, accompanied by classical Turkish music. Daily 11.30am–11.00pm.

Ottoman Antakya Antep Mutfağağı Kadır Has Cad 9, Çibali ☎0212/631 7567; map p.89. A little off the beaten track, overlooking the Golden Horn east of the Atatürk Bridge, this fine restaurant offers some unusual, Middle Eastern-style dishes from the southeast of Turkey. The mains tend to be kebabs (18TL), but the starters are more unusual: *bakla ezme*, a traditional Antakya dip of puréed broad beans with olive oil; *çokelek salatası*, a spicy cheese salad; and *abugannaç*, a dip of aubergine, tomato, pepper, garlic and sour pomegranate sauce. It's decent value, with wine by the glass at 7TL, and well worth seeking out for a break from mainstream Turkish or international cuisine. Daily noon–midnight.

Zeyrekhane İbadethane Arkası Sok 10 ☎0212/532 2778, ⓦzeyrekhane.com; map p.89. In a wonderful location in the shadow of the Zeyrek Camii, with great views down over the Golden Horn, *Zeyrekhane* is run by the wealthy Koç family, and is appropriately expensive and exclusive. The lamb fillet on mashed aubergine (*beğendili kusu heleosu*) or the *Osmanlı ğuveç*, an Ottoman-style chicken stew cooked in a clay pot and served with *pilaf* rice, are both good choices. Mains cost 20–30TL, and wine is an outrageous 18TL per glass, but these prices don't stop lots of Turks frequenting the place. Eat on the terrace in summer, inside under a vaulted brick roof at dark wood tables in winter. Daily 9am–11pm.

LAND WALLS

★ **Develi** Gumuş Yüzük Sok 7, Samatya ☎0212/529 0833, ⓦdevelikebap.com; map p.102. Established in 1912, this famous place is noted for its excellent kebabs, cooked Gaziantep style, and a range of southeastern Turkish speciality starters including hummus. A great attraction here is the traditional square the restaurant overlooks, the sea-views from the terrace and the fact it's licensed. Great *baklava* for the sweet-toothed, too. Best reached by taking the suburban train from Sirkeci or Cankurtaran stations and alighting at Kocamustafapaşa station, from where it's a three-minute walk. Daily noon–midnight.

GALATA AND THE WATERFRONT DISTRICTS

Galata House Galata Külesi Sok 61 ☎0212/245 1861, ⓦthegalatahouse.com; map p.110. This restaurant offers all the comfort of eating in your own living room with small, cosy rooms, an outdoor terrace lit by fairy-lights and a menu of hearty Georgian cuisine (mains around

20TL) – try the house speciality *Hindali* (meat-filled dumplings in a tomato sauce). English-speaking host Mete and his wife Nadire, both born and bred in Galata, converted the former British Prison into this restaurant eleven years ago and are happy to show you around and entertain you with their many stories of the area and times past. History buffs can ogle the original prison fittings and try to decipher graffiti etched into the wall by prisoners. With only fifty seats, it's best to book ahead. Tues–Sun 3pm–midnight.

Güney Kuledibi Sah Kapisi 6, opposite Galata Tower ✆0212/249 0393, ⓦguneyrestaurant.com.tr; map p.110. A characterful restaurant with a classy wooden interior and bustling outdoor seating area, this place is always busy. Friendly, English-speaking waiters serve up a range of delicious stone-oven *pides* (Turkish pizzas), *kebaps* and *sulu yemek* (stews) for reasonable prices – mains from 12TL. Unlicensed. Mon–Sat 7am–10pm.

Maya Kemankeş Cad 35/A, Karaköy ✆0212/252 6884, ⓦlokantamaya.com; map p.110. A modern and very stylish twist on a traditional *lokanta*, *Maya* is run by a Turkish woman, Didem, who studied at the French Culinary Institute in New York. Soups start from 6TL, a wonderful array of *meze* from just a little more. It's a block back from the waterfront hustle (and there's plenty here as this is where the behemoth cruise-ships dock) in a comparatively peaceful location. Tues–Sat noon–11pm, Mon noon–5pm.

Romans Culture Café Ali Paşa Mescidi Sokak 2, Tophane ✆0212/251 9221, ⓦromanshotels.com; map p.110. Bohemian luxury where ornate furnishings fuse with newspaper collages, funky artwork and an eclectic colour palette, this spanking-new café is the brainchild of a team of local fashion designers. There's a creative selection of non alcoholic drinks and food is a mix of international and Turkish (mains from 18TL) – try the meat-laden Ottoman pizza – and local musicians take to the small stage in the evenings. At the time of visiting the boutique hotel upstairs was still under construction and plans to turn the basement into a licensed nightclub were under way. Daily 8am–2am.

Tarihi Karaköy Balık Lokantası Tersane Caddesi, Kardeşim Sok 45/A, Karaköy ✆0212/251 1371; map p.110. The lunchtime café here is noted for its delicious soup (7TL), dished up in a couple of small rooms at the base of a historic *han* (warehouse). Evening meals are served in more spacious accommodation upstairs, where there's a nice terrace overlooking the Golden Horn and old city. There's no farmed fish here, so expect to pay upwards of 40TL for a decent meal, with all fish grilled on charcoal in the traditional way. It's hard to find, which is sufficient to keep most tourists away. Licensed in the evening. Café daily 9am–9pm; restaurant daily 7pm–midnight.

Wisteria Galata Kulesi Sok 20 ✆0212/252 7218, ⓦwisteriaistanbul.com; map p.110. A recently converted missionary school, this spacious restaurant offers an enchanted ambience away from the bustle of Galata and is already gaining popularity among those in the know. Purple decor and pretty floral details pay homage to its namesake and the giant, airy courtyard features an open fire and live nightly piano performances. The menu is international gourmet cuisine but you pay for the romantic setting – expect to pay 30–40TL for a main alone. Daily 8am–late.

İSTIKLAL CADDESI AND AROUND

Antochia Minare Sok 5 ✆0212/292 1100, ⓦantiochiaconcept.com; map pp.120–121. A welcome addition to the Beyoğlu dining scene, which had no decent restaurants specializing in tasty southeastern Turkish cuisine. Try the *zahter* (a tangy thyme salad) for 10TL, or the spicy walnut and pepper *muammara* dip, followed by a marinated kebab served with paper-thin *lavaş* bread (kebabs from 22TL). One of the owners, Jale Balcı, has written a book about Antakya (ancient Antioch) cuisine, available here. Mon–Sat 11am–4am.

Çezayir Hayriye Cad 16 ✆0212/245 9980; map pp.120–121. This stylish restaurant sprang up before the boom in minimalist chic, and is no worse for that. Set in a beautifully restored turn-of-the-twentieth-century townhouse, it is soothingly atmospheric, with stripped-pine doors, space-enhancing mirrors, chandeliers and other refreshingly anti-modernist features. The food (modern Mediterranean/Turkish) is generally good, too. Best bet for a reasonable night-out is one of the fixed menus – the cheapest option (45TL) includes two drinks. Mon–Thurs & Sun 9am–2am, Fri & Sat 9am–4am.

★ **Changa** Siraselviler Cad 47 ✆0212/251 7064; map pp.120–121. Opened in 1999, this was one of the pioneers of fusion food in the city. That it has survived is a testament to its quality; indeed, it has spawned the equally successful *Müzedechanga* out in Emirgan (see p.193), which takes over when *Changa* closes for the summer. You can watch the chefs prepare your food in the kitchen under the glass floor beneath you and admire the replica Eames chairs and original artworks by some of Turkey's leading contemporary artists. Don't expect anything too Turkish, though. Mains from 40TL. Nov–June Mon–Sat 6.30pm–2am.

Çokçok Meşrutiyet Cad 51 ✆0212/292 6496, ⓦcokcok .com.tr; map pp.120–121. Designer Thai restaurant with a well-deserved reputation for both style and quality. Relax in the cocktail lounge before your meal and try one of the unusual concoctions on offer – Rain Odaiba is flavoured with ginger and coriander. Ingredients are brought in from Thailand and the chef is Thai, so this is the real deal. The lunchtime special set menu (noon–6pm) costs 32TL, the

13

13

evening one 54TL; mains from 25TL. Tues–Sun noon–midnight.

★ **Cumhuriyet Meyhanesi** Sahne Sok 47, Balık Pazarı ☎0212/293 1977; map pp.120–121. Excellent selection of *mezes* and fish dishes from 19TL, in a restaurant located at the heart of the Fish Market. Sit upstairs for a bird's-eye view of the stalls below and try to avert your eyes from the offal shop across the alleyway while you're eating. Atatürk himself ate and drank here, and it still has plenty of atmosphere, especially when the *fasıl* band are doing their rounds. Daily 10am–2am.

★ **Ficcin** İstiklal Cad, Kallavı Sok 13 ☎0212/293 3786, ⓦficcin.com; map pp.120–121. Unpretentious and great-value place on this quiet (by Beyoğlu standards) side street offering some unusual and substantial dishes. Try the eponymous *ficcin*, a kind of hearty, Caucasian meat pie, or the *çerkez mantası*, a ravioli-style dish where the pasta is stuffed with tomato and served in a yoghurt sauce (mains from 7TL). Soups include a tasty rocket-based one, wine and beer are both reasonably priced, and there's plenty of choice for vegetarians. Tues–Sat 8am–10pm.

Hacı Abdullah İstiklal Cad, Sakızağacı Cad 17 ☎0212/293 8561; map pp.120–121. An İstanbul institution, this is one of the best traditional restaurants (established in 1188), though its a little over priced. Most main courses are around 25TL – try the *hunkar beğendili kebap* (beef stew on a bed of aubergine and cheese purée) and the *ayva tatlı* (stewed quince with clotted cream) for 9TL. Unlicensed. Daily 11am–10pm.

★ **İmroz** Nevizade Sok 24; map pp.120–121. This Greek-owned İstanbul legend has been dishing up reasonably-priced fish dishes (mains from 16TL) since 1941. Spread over three floors and both sides of the busy pedestrian thoroughfare, it is perhaps the liveliest of the fish restaurants in the Balık Pazarı area. You can choose from a bewildering array of *meze* brought around on a tray. Despite the excellence of the food, most locals come here to drink and talk, and volume levels rise alarmingly as the *rakı* kicks in, so don't bother if you're looking for a quiet tête-à-tête with a loved one. Daily 11am–2am.

★ **Kenan Üsta Ocakbaşı** Kurabiye Sok 18, ☎0212/293 5619, ⓦkenanustaocakbasi.com; map pp.120–121. Master grillsman Kenan has been preparing succulent meat on this street for forty years, the last eight of them as owner of his own place. Watch him cook *lavaş* (tortilla-style bread) over his basement charcoal grill, smear it with olive oil, sprinkle it with pepper flakes, thyme and salt, then pop it back on the grill to finish. This bread is used as the "plate" to serve an astonishing array of kebabs and grilled meat to a loyal and virtually one hundred percent Turkish clientele. All the *meze* (so often laid out ready-made in chiller cabinets), salads and kebabs are prepared fresh. Choose from a selection of *rakı*s and enjoy a superb Turkish meal. Starters are 5TL,

kebabs 20TL, a glass of wine or double *rakı* 10TL. Daily 10am–2pm.

Leb-i-Derya Richmond İstiklal Cad 227 ☎0212/252 5460, ⓦlebiderya.com; map pp.120–121. Designer restaurant-bar on the roof of the plush *Richmond Hotel*. It's all blonde-wood and white trim – the gleaming white central bar takes pride of place, though the stunning views down over the Bosphorus are even more impressive. Lunches include a range of grills from 18TL, pastas from 15TL and giant salad bowls in the same price range. Evening meals are rather more expensive. Booking advised, especially at weekends. Mon–Thurs & Sun 11am–2am, Fri & Sat 11am–3am.

Mikla *Marmara Pera Hotel*, Meşrutiyet Cad 167/185 ☎0212/293 5656; map pp.120–121. The food served here is as simple and elegant as the venue's Scandinavian-inspired interior (fittingly so, as the chef is Turkish/Swedish in origin). The food is a Turkish/Mediterranean fusion – try the succulent lamb shank with summer vegetables and parsley. Mains cost from 40TL, and good-quality local wine by the glass is 20TL. Dress "casually upscale" as their website advises, if only to ensure you don't encounter problems passing through the ground-floor hotel security. Daily noon–2am.

Nature and Peace İstiklal Cad, Büyükparmakkapı Sok 21 ☎0212/252 8609; map pp.120–121. Earthy vegetarian restaurant on a lively street, where specialities include green lentil balls, felafels and nettle soup, from around 9TL a dish. Some chicken dishes are served, too, and the only alcohol available is wine. The café can feel cramped when busy. Mon–Thurs 11am–11.30pm, Sun 1–11.30pm.

Parsifal Kurabiye Sok 13 ☎0212/245 2588, ⓦparsifalde .com; map pp.120–121. Sophisticated, inexpensive menu blending Turkish and international styles, with an imaginative range of non-meat dishes, such as leek and soya burgers, and mouthwatering spinach pie. It's been around since 1996, and proprietor Ayfer Oğulları knows her business, and has created a homely, bistro-style atmosphere from the long, narrow dining area. Daily 11am–11pm.

Refik Sofyalı Sok 10–12, Tünel ☎0212/245 7879; map pp.120–121. Modest *rakı*-infused Turkish joint, a meeting point for local intellectuals, specializing in Black Sea cuisine. *Kara lahana dolması* is an unusual (for İstanbul) stuffed cabbage dish, popular with the locals. Refik Baba, the good-natured owner, likes to chat in numerous languages, though he doesn't speak much of any. Set menu 70TL, including as many local alcoholic drinks as you desire. Mon–Sat noon–midnight, Sun 6.30pm–midnight.

Rejans Emir Nevruz Sok 17, off İstiklal Cad ☎0212/244 1610; map pp.120–121. This famous establishment was founded by White Russians in the 1930s and thrives on its nostalgic reputation. It's somewhat shabby and staid, but has earned a new lease of life due to the increasing number of nouveau-riche Russian visitors with cash to spare. Considering the

13

quality of the food, it's not too expensive. Main courses (barbecued salmon, grilled quail) start from 15TL, best eaten accompanied by the excellent lemon vodka. Mon–Sat noon–3pm, Sun 7pm–midnight.

Zencefil Kurabiye Sok 8 ☎ 0212/2444082; map pp.120–121. The ever-changing menu includes vegetarian versions of various Turkish dishes, and Western-style meals such as vegetarian lasagne and quiche – from as little as 8TL – plus some chicken and fish specials from 16TL, great salads, home-made breads, herbal teas, mint lemonade and local wines. The courtyard area is a particularly enticing place to relax and enjoy your food. Mon–Sat 11am–midnight.

TAKSIM SQUARE AND AROUND

Bursa Hacibey Kebacısı Teşvikiye Cad 156/B, Nişantaşı ☎ 0212/231 7134; map p.117. Nişantaşı's well-heeled inhabitants are not going to put up with second-rate food, and this is a prime example – it's *the* place to try Bursa's famous *İskender kebap*, tender slices of grilled lamb in a rich tomato sauce and served on a bed of unleavened *pide* bread, at 21TL only a fraction more than in Bursa itself. Also serves *peynir tatlısı* (7TL), a hard-to-come-by and delicious cheese-based dessert. Unlicensed. Daily 11.30am–10pm.

Hünkar Mim Kemal Öke Cad 21, Nişantaşı ☎ 0212/225 4665, ⓦ hunkar1950.com; map p.117. Classic Ottoman/Turkish cuisine at its best. Originally opened in 1950 in ultra-orthodox Fatih, across the Golden Horn in the old city, it (wisely, given Nişantaşı's prosperity) moved to its present location in 2000. The trademark dish is *hünkar beğindi* (25TL) – literally "admired by the sultan" – with tender lamb served on a bed of smoky, mashed aubergine. The *irmik helvası*, a deliciously sweet semolina and almond dessert, is done particularly well here. There's a decent wine list, with a glass ranging from 13–20TL, in addition to the extensive menu. Evening reservations recommended. Daily noon–midnight.

★ **Mardin Kaburga Sofrası** Şehit Muhtar Cad 9, Taksim ☎ 0212/225 9595, ⓦ kaburgasofrasi.com.tr; map p.117. Unassuming little place specializing in the cuisine of the Mardin region, right on the Syrian border in Turkey's southeast, where Arabic and Kurdish are more widely spoken than Turkish. The *kaburga* is the main attraction – tender rib of lamb stuffed with delicately spiced *pilaf* rice (50TL for two people). For *meze*, there's *içli köfte*, spiced meatballs wrapped in a bulgur-wheat casing, steamed to a mouthwatering tenderness (3TL), or for the same price try the *mumbar*, intestines stuffed with rice and meat. Unlicensed. Daily 12am–2pm.

Musafir Recepepaşa Cad 7, Taksim ☎ 0212/235 2741; map p.117. The long, narrow dining area of this Indian restaurant is decked out with the usual "Indian restaurant abroad" trimmings (prints of elephants, Hindu deities) but is

stylish enough, and in summer there are a few tables out on the street. Service can be slow, but the food is very well prepared and authentic tasting, and there are plenty of dishes to choose from – with the *biryanis* being particularly good. Mains from 20TL. Daily 11am–11pm.

BEŞİKTAŞ

Hanedan Çiğdem Sok 27, Beşiktaş ☎ 0212/259 4017, ⓦ hanedanrestaurant.com; map p.132. A modern establishment split into separate meat (downstairs) and fish (upstairs) restaurants. Fresh, seasonal fish are available for selection and charged by the kilo and there's an extensive wine list on offer. Somewhat uninspiring decor is soon forgotten as you admire the terrace view over the waterfront ferry jetty. Expect to pay 50TL upwards for a fish meal with drinks. Daily 11am–12.30am.

Tuğra *Çırağan Palace Kempinski Hotel*, Çıragan Cad 32 ☎ 0212/326 4646; map p.132. Set on the first floor of the *Çırağan Palace*, this Ottoman-inspired restaurant offers candlelit terrace seating, live classical Turkish music and spectacular vistas over the Bosphorus. Try the *testi kebap*, cooked in a specially designed pottery urn that you crack open with a small hammer, but be sure to save some room, as the laden dessert trolley will soon catch your eye. Dress smart and bring your credit card – prices run upwards of 50TL for a main course alone. Daily 7pm–midnight.

ASIAN İSTANBUL

★ **Çiya Sofrası & Kebapçi** Güneşlibahçe Sok 43, Kadıköy ☎ 0216/330 3190, ⓦ ciya.com.tr; map p.140. A very well regarded place on a pleasant pedestrianized street. "Çiya" means "mountain" in Kurdish, though the inspiration for the food here comes from many different corners of this vast country – and beyond to the Middle East and Balkans. There are actually three restaurants, the two on the right as you approach along Güneşlibahçe street are kebab-orientated (the house *Çiya* kebab is tender meat coated with crushed pistachio and walnut, rolled in a thin unleavened bread and then baked – delicious), the one on the left focuses on salads, *meze* and stews. Choose your own selection of *meze* and salads and have your plate weighed to learn the price (around 10TL for a substantial lunch). An institution with İstanbullus, expats and visitors alike. Daily 10am–midnight.

Dicle Balık Lokantası Muvakkithane Cad 31/A, Kadıköy ☎ 0216/233 8474, ⓦ diclebalikrestaurant .com; map p.140. Most people ship across to Kadıköy for the wonderful *Çiya Sofrası*. But this bustling, spotless fish restaurant in the heart of the suburb's busy fish market, is a great alternative. *Meze* range between 6 and 9TL, there's a tasty fish *pilaf* for 7.50TL, a hearty fish soup done in a clay pot for 12TL and a whole range of fresh fish (the owners have the most-esteemed stall nearby in the market). Wine is a reasonable 8TL a glass, a small beer 6TL. There's a

13

terrace above the busy street offering a window to the Bosphorus. Daily 11am–1am.

Filizler Köftecisi Öğdül Sok 41, Üsküdar ☎0216/343 4549, ⓦfilizler.com; map p.140. Great family-orientated *köfte* palace on the coast road in Üsküdar, with great views across to Kız Külesi. The meat for the *köfte* (9TL a portion) is produced from the restaurant's own farm, they also produce the salted yoghurt drink Turks normally choose to go with meatballs, *ayran*, themselves. Prices are reasonable for the upmarket surroundings and vistas, and it's packed out on summer weekends with locals. They also do a very popular brunch between 10am and 2pm on Sundays for 35TL, with eighty items on the menu. There are plenty of other dishes to choose from, including a vegetarian *köfte*. Unlicensed. Open 24hr.

Kanaat Lokantası Selmanipak Cad 25, Üsküdar ☎0216/341 5444, ⓦkanaatlokantasi.com.tr; map p.140. One of the city's more famous *lokantas*, established in 1931, featuring copies of İznik-tile panels from the Selimiye Camii in Edirne and a copper chimney-piece. This huge, absolutely spotless and bustling place is excellent value and offers a range of twenty cold starters for 6TL and the same number of hot for a little more – the *Çerkez tavuğu* (Circassian chicken in walnut sauce) is divine. Mains start from a bargain 12TL and include some of the best *pirzola* you'll find anywhere. The desserts are equally magnificent and include fruits such as fig, quince or apricot stuffed with nuts and topped with cream (6TL). Unlicensed. Daily 6am–11pm.

Yanyalı Fehmi Lokantası Yağlıka İsmail Sok 1, off Soğütlüçeşme Cad, Kadıköy ☎0216/336 3333; map p.140. Established back in 1919 by refugees from Greece, this well-run place serves up some of the best food on the Asian side of the Bosphorus – and there's an incredible variety to choose from, with twenty types of soup alone, including non-standards such as okra or spinach. The *çömlek* kebab – meat, aubergine, beans, peppers, onion and garlic oven-cooked in a clay pot – is delicious (10TL). Or try the Persian-style chicken, including a *pilaf* containing parsley, nuts and egg. Desserts include *kabak tatlısı* (candied courgette), delicious when, as here, it's done well. Unlicensed. Daily 9.30am–10.30pm.

THE BOSPHORUS

Ayder Balik Rumelikavak İskele Cad 2, Rumeli Kavağı ☎0212/218 3434; map p.151. An atmospheric place next to the landing, where you order fish specials off a big tray and eat on the terrace right by the water's edge. *Meze* starts from a very reasonable 5TL, farmed fish such as sea bream is 15TL a portion, while caught fish start at double that. Daily 11am–midnight.

★ **Kıyı** Kefeliköy Cad 126, Tarabya ☎02162/262 0002, ⓦkiyi.com.tr; map p.151. Restrained mix of old (wood-panelling) and new (exposed ventilation system) interior, enhanced with superb prints by Ara Güler (see box, p.206) and examples of contemporary Turkish art. Expect to pay around a 100TL a head for a full fish meal with alcohol. Daily noon–2am.

Kordon Kuleli Cad 51, Çengelköy ☎0216/321 0475; map p.151. Stylish fish restaurant in a restored distillery, attached to the equally chic *Sumahan on the Water* hotel (see p.174). The indoor dining area is atmospherically lit, and the views from the tables outside (summer only) over the Bosphorus are wonderful. The fish is carefully selected and lovingly prepared (there's everything, depending on season, from bonto and bluefish to swordfish and turbot), though not cheap at often over 100TL a kilo. The array of *meze* is less than in many places

---

COOK LIKE A LOCAL, EAT LIKE A LOCAL

Many visitors are so taken with this cosmopolitan city's culinary treasures that they are determined to learn how to prepare them back home.

Cooking Alaturka ☎0212/458 5919, ⓦcookingalaturka.com. A great place to start, Cooking Alaturka runs fun and informative Turkish cookery classes from Akbıyık Cad 72/A, right in the centre of Sultanahmet. The courses are the brainchild of Dutch İstanbul-resident Eveline Zoutendijk, who opened the city's first cookery school back in 2003. For 50TL per head, you can learn how to prepare a four-course Turkish meal, for either lunch or dinner, with Eveline and chef Feyzi Yıldırım – and then eat it. Once you've learned how to stuff an aubergine without scooping out its tasty innards first, there's no looking back.

İstanbul Eats ⓦistanbuleats.com. To get to grips with İstanbul's vibrant food scene in a very different

way, İstanbul Eats run backstreet culinary adventures for small groups (2–6 people) of foodies who want to avoid the usual tourist haunts. As well as trying a whole range of traditional Turkish fare (from tandoori-cooked lamb and *simit* to freshly baked *pide* and stuffed and grilled lamb intestines) in the most unpretentious of surroundings, there's the chance to see how *lokum* (Turkish delight) is made and buy Turkish herbs, spices and deli-style favourites at the same prices the locals do. The walking tours last up to six hours and give a fascinating insight not only into the city's food, but also the lives of its inhabitants. They also do a handy guidebook to the city's lesser-known places to eat entitled *İstanbul Eats: Exploring the Culinary Backstreets*.

– quality rather than quantity is the rule here. Daily noon–midnight.

Körfez Körfez Cad 78, Kanlıca ☎0216/413 4314; map p.151. The fish here is all seasonal and fresh caught, so expect to pay a hefty 100TL or so for a full meal with wine. The grouper baked in a casserole with olives is just one of the more unusual fish dishes served up in this excellent establishment. Daily 11am–midnight.

★ **Müzedechanga** Sakıp Sabancı Cad 22, Emirgan ☎0212/323 0901; map p.151. Designed by the Autobahn group, this funky restaurant is located inside the Sakıp Sabancı Museum. The summer-season offshoot of Beyoğlu's *Changa* (see p.189), it serves up Turkish/Mediterranean fusion cuisine in a stylish but unstuffy environment – goatskin-covered bar stools mix easily with stripped-wood floors and retro 1950s-esque light fittings. There's a nice terrace with the inevitable Bosphorus views. July–Sept Tues–Sun 10.30am–1am.

Parkfora Muallim Nacı Cad 134, Kuruçeşme ☎0212/265 5063, ⓦparkfora.com.tr; map p.151. Right on the Bosphorus in the grounds of immaculate Cemil Topuzlu Parkı, this sophisticated fish restaurant sports dark wood floors, white tablecloths and a glorious veranda giving onto the water; the roof terrace is equally impressive. The city's rich and sometimes famous arrive here in top-of-the-range motors, and consequently it's expensive, with freshly caught fish costing around 140TL per kilo, easily enough for two. Daily noon–midnight.

PRINCES' ISLANDS

The restaurants on Heybeliada cater to locals all year round, and consequently there are plenty to choose from – generally simple and cheap, offering standard fish, *lokanta*, kebab and *pide* fare; most are situated on Ayyıldız Caddesi. In Büyükada, there are lots of reasonable fish restaurants along the seafront to the left of the ferry terminal. One street back from the shore road, İskele Caddesi has a selection of cheaper cafés, selling all the usual Turkish dishes.

Alibaba Restaurant Gülistan Cad 20, Büyükada ☎0216/382 3733; map pp.160–161. To the left of the ferry terminal, this is a good choice among the several restaurants on the waterfront, all of which have similar prices and ambience. It's a friendly, atmospheric place in an old (1927) high-ceilinged building, with white tablecloths and pictures of Atatürk and his side-kick İsmet İnönü (both of whom ate here) on the wall. Farmed-fish mains from 15TL, sea-caught fish from 70TL a kilo (ample for two people), plus the usual selection of *meze*. Daily 11am–midnight.

Antepli Kebap House Recep Koç Cad 34, Büyükada ☎0216/382 1919; map pp.160–161. Extremely good value for the islands, the *Antepli* offers a wide range of kebabs from 11TL, *pide* from 8TL, vegetable stews from 5TL and meat options from 8TL – plus a wide range of *meze*. Upstairs is a family section with a terrace overlooking the harbour area. No alcohol. Daily 9am–11pm.

Barba Yani Yalı Cad 6, Burgazada ☎0216/381 2404; map pp.160–161. Some 50m to the left of the jetty as you land, this Greek-run restaurant serves reasonably-priced fish dishes and *meze* (expect to pay around 30TL per person, including an alcoholic drink). With its natty chequered tablecloths and harbourfront location, it's an atmospheric spot to while away the time waiting for the next ferry back to the city.

Bilal Hibeş Çiğ Köfte Close to the Aya Nikola church, Heybeliada; map pp.160–161. A good vegetarian option serving home-cooked Turkish food such as *melemen* (a scrambled, tomato and pepper-filled omelette), *mantı* (yoghurt-drenched ravioli) and lentil *köfte*. Daily 10am–8pm.

Yücetepe Kır Gazino Aya Yorgi, Yüce Tepe, Büyükada; map pp.160–161. Simple but excellent restaurant right on Yüce Tepe, the hilltop crowned by the Monastery of St George, offering superb views across the island and the Sea of Marmara. The food is basic but freshly prepared and hearty, with deep-fried, cheese-filled *börek* one of the highlights. The home-made chips are delicious, as is the yoghurt-drenched aubergine starter. A satisfying lunch with a beer will set you back 18–24TL. Daily 9am–11pm.

LEB-I-DERYA, BEYOĞLU

Nightlife

The vast majority of İstanbul's best bars, clubs and live-music venues are concentrated in and around Beyoğlu, particularly on bustling İstiklal Caddesi, where the gamut runs from studenty bars with tables on the pavement to chic roof terraces. The Bosphorus waterfront in Ortaköy and Kuruçeşme boasts some of the glitziest clubs around, places where you'll rub shoulders with the city's nouveau-riche and wannabe celebrities, dance to the "best" Euro and Turkish pop and stagger back to your hotel with a massive hole in your trip budget. Across the water, in the more unassuming Asian suburb of Kadıköy lurk yet more venues, but the last ferry back to Europe leaves just as the action is hotting up.

A night out in İstanbul can **cost** as much as in London or New York, particularly if you head up to exclusive rooftop joints or down to the Bosphorus waterfront clubs. Alcohol is taxed at an exorbitant eighty percent, and a large beer in even a modest bar here is likely to be 7TL, a small one double that in one of the upmarket clubs, and cocktails, imported spirits and the like even more prohibitively priced. Probably the best-value night-out is at a **meyhane**, or tavern, where you can listen to a gypsy *fasil* band and enjoy a multi-course meal (with free drinks if you go for the fixed menu), or a **Türkü bar**, where the beer is a little over the odds but there's no cover charge.

Beyoğlu is an increasingly popular home to foreigners seduced by the area's trendy vibe but, by and large, once you're out of Sultanahmet, the vast majority of the people you'll be talking to, drinking with and dancing alongside will be İstanbullus. Usually a friendly, outgoing and gregarious lot, part of the fun of a night on the town is discovering more about them and their city – not as impossible as you might think, as many speak excellent English.

14

BARS

İstanbul is far from dry; away from conservative Islamic areas such as Fatih, **bars** range from the downright seedy to the achingly chic. The majority of visitors staying in Sultanahmet prefer to drink near their hotel, where the bars are tourist-oriented and other drinkers either fellow visitors or locals who work in the tourist trade. The liveliest places to drink here are Akbıyık Caddesi, which resembles the main drag of a Mediterranean resort on summer evenings, and Divan Yolu. Across the Golden Horn, however, lies buzzing Beyoğlu, which is where you should head for a real night out: a variety of bars – including many of the rooftop drinking establishments that have become so popular of late – line the lively streets and alleys leading off İstiklal Caddesi. **Kadıköy**, on the Asian side of the Bosphorus, has a couple of atmospheric drinking holes. The line between İstanbul's bars and cafés is blurred, so many of the places listed below also serve food and coffee, often until late.

SULTANAHMET

Cheers Divan Akbıyık Cad 20; map p.44. It's been around on busy Akbıyık Cad long enough to know what it's doing – knocking out reasonably priced beer (6TL for a draught Efes) to a mixed bag of hostel and hotel residents and locals working in the many tourist establishments hereabouts. There's a soundtrack of rock and dance classics. Daily 10am–2am.

Cozy Pub Divan Yolu Cad 66 ☎0212/520 0990; map p.44. Situated on a prominent corner plot, this pleasant dark-wood bar has tables out on the street in the warmer months – great for people-watching on hectic Divan Yolu. A large beer is 7TL, not bad for the location, a glass of local wine 9TL. There's a very Western-slanted food menu, with salads, pastas for 13TL, and a big mixed *meze* plate, ample for two, for 15TL. Daily 10am–2am.

Just Bar Akbıyık Cad 26 ☎0532/387 5729; map p.44. Right next door to *Cheers* (see above), this bar is virtually identical to its neighbour except that it has succumbed to the tourist-led pressure to introduce low-cushioned seating areas for *nargile*-tokers. Beers 6TL, *nargile* 15TL. Daily 10am–2pm.

Pierre Loti Hotel Roof-Pub Piyer Loti Cad 5, Divan Yolu ☎0212/518 5700; map p.44. There are plenty of hotel roof-bars with views in the old city, but this has to be one of the best. Reached by the hotel elevator to the fourth floor, then a couple of flights of stairs, it's the perfect place to watch the sun go down over the domes, minarets and waterways – a virtually uninterrupted 360° view. A glass of wine costs 10TL, large beer the same, and both served with a bowl of *çerez* (mixed nuts and roasted salted pulses). Daily 11am–midnight.

TICKETS AND LISTINGS

Tickets for many events, sporting as well as music, are available from specialist booking agency **Biletix** (☎0216/454 1555, ⊛biletix.com), either online or from outlets across the city – most usefully for visitors, from the D & R bookshop on İstiklal Caddesi. Bigger venues such as *Babylon* have both an online and venue-based booking service; otherwise, buy your tickets at the door.

For **magazine listings**, the monthly *Time Out İstanbul* (6TL) is the best bet. Rather less useful is the bimonthly *İstanbul The Guide* (7.50TL), a glossy that's okay for listings details of bars but doesn't really cover events. Otherwise, check ⊛www.pozitif-ist.com or the posters and flyers on and around İstiklal Caddesi. *Cornucopia*, a glossy bimonthly covering the Ottoman arts scene, auctions, galleries and exhibitions, is available from bookshops that stock foreign-language newspapers and publications (see p.216).

14

SIRKECI

North Shield Pub Ebusuud Cad 2 ☎0212/527 0931; map p.68. Situated right opposite the Gülhane tram stop and just a short step downhill from the Aya Sofya, this mock-English pub, part of a chain, is usually packed with sports addicts taking in big-screen football, rugby and cricket matches from around the world. It's very efficiently run and big beers cost a not unreasonable 10TL, considering you get to watch the game for free, and there's a decent pub-grub menu. Daily 11.30am–1.30am.

GRAND BAZAAR AND AROUND

Murat Bira Evi Gedikpaşa Cad 77/A ☎0212/517 8228; map pp.76–77. The mainly male clientele here sit at high tables and work their way through cheap (4.50TL including complimentary salted snacks) Efes beer. There's a tiny menu of fried *hamsi* (anchovies) for 4.50TL, or stuffed mussels for a lira less. It's not pretty, but it's a real working-class drinkers den – and handy after a stressful shopping bout in the bazaar. Not really suitable for unaccompanied women. Daily 8am–2pm.

THE NORTHWEST QUARTER

Agora Meyahanesi Vodina Cad 128, Balat ☎0212/635 4891; map p.89. If you've been exploring the colourful old neighbourhood of Balat and are in need of a beer, the *Agora*, housed in a charming nineteenth-century building, is a great option, with large beers for 4TL. This traditional place has featured in more than one *dizi* (Turkish soap) and several famous Turkish singers have strutted their stuff here. Hit-and-miss excitement-wise in the evenings, but always cheap with mains from 8TL, including fish. Daily noon–midnight.

GALATA

Enginar Hacı Şah Kapısı Sok 4, Galata ☎0212/293 9697; map p.110. On the corner of the Galata Tower square, this bar-restaurant offers an atmospheric, if touristy, spot to watch the world go by. Dark wood and brick interiors make this place feel like a modern drinking tavern with the street-side courtyard offering an alfresco alternative; it's a good pit-stop for a reasonably priced beer (7.50TL). Daily 10.30am–12.30am.

★ **Ritim Galata** Galata Kulesi Sok 3/C ☎0212/292 4926; map p.110. Just up from *Nardis Jazz Club* and down from the Galata Tower, this mellow bar attracts a more sophisticated crowd than many of the places up in Beyoğlu. In summer a few tables spill out onto the street, and the cosy interior, with a mezzanine floor and exposed brick work, is great. Large beers cost 10TL, not bad considering there are soothing sounds from the DJ, and a Turkish-fusion food menu. Daily 11am–2pm.

BEYOĞLU

5.Kat Soğancı Sok 7, off Sıraselviler Cad ☎0212/293 3774, ⊛5kat.com; map pp.120–121. In fashionable Cihangir, this is a sumptuous bar/dinner/dance club with a great reputation and even better views over the Bosphorus through the floor-to-ceiling windows or from the rooftop terrace bar. The owner was a noted film actress and runs the place with her mum. It's that kind of slightly offbeat joint, with special evenings covering everything from ethnic-cuisine tasting to listening to after-dinner monologues by celebrity guests. Dining gives way to dancing as the evening progresses. Mon–Fri 10am–2am, Sat & Sun 10am–3am.

360 Mısır Apartmanı 311, İstiklal Cad ☎0212/251 1042, ⊛360istanbul.com; map pp.120–121. Set in one of İstiklal Cad's most attractive nineteenth-century apartment blocks, with a stunning interior of plate glass and bare brick, and panoramic views over the city, this rooftop bar/café/restaurant has commanded more than its fair share of attention. It is the venue of choice for cash-rich İstanbullus and foreigners alike. Wine by the glass costs 14TL, salads around 24TL. If they don't like the look of you, you won't get in. A new *360*, across the Bosphorus in Kadıköy, opened in the summer of 2011. Mon–Thurs noon–2am, Fri noon–4pm & 6pm–4am, Sat 6pm–4am, Sun 6pm–2.30am.

TURKISH BEER

Local brewery **Efes Pilsen** has a stranglehold on the Turkish beer (*bira*) market, sponsoring everything from a blues festival to one of the country's leading basketball teams, so it's fortunate they produce a generally well regarded pilsner-type brew. In most cafés and restaurants this comes in bottles, either 33cl in the more upmarket places, or 50cl in more down-to-earth joints; bars and clubs often have it on draught. In some places it can be brought to your table in glass "barrels" of assorted litreages, complete with a tap so you can serve yourself – ideal for a group of drinkers. **Efes Dark** is a sweeter, stronger stout-style beer, while **Efes-Xtra** is eight percent proof, though neither is widely available in bars or restaurants. **Tuborg**, of Danish origins, is the other major home-grown beer. It is less widely available than Efes, though some people swear by it. Their red label beer is stronger than the standard green. Foreign beers are now widely available in İstanbul, but you'll pay at least a third more for the dubious privilege of drinking Corona, Fosters, Heineken or Becks.

RAKI IS THE ANSWER

The Turkish national aperitif is **rakı**, with an estimated 61 million litres being sunk annually. An anise-flavoured spirit, it is found (under different names) throughout many of the former provinces of the Ottoman Empire. *Rakı* is usually drunk over ice and turns a milky white when topped-up, as it should be, with water – giving the drink its Turkish nickname Aslan Süt (Lion's Milk). The most ubiquitous brand is **Yeni**, but connoisseurs claim Burgaz, Efe and Tekirdağ are better. Between 45 and 48 percent proof, it's the favourite tipple for Turkish men (and many women) in *meyhanes* (see p.178) and is the ideal accompaniment to plates of *meze* and fish, and slips down very easily. Expect to pay between 8 and 14TL for a double, according to the salubriousness of your surroundings. A cheesy slogan on İstanbul T-shirts "*Rakı* is the answer: I don't remember the question" gives fair warning to those who overdo it.

14

★ **Badehane** General Yazgan Sok 5 ☎ 0212/249 0550; map pp.120–121. Long-established and very popular small winter venue that spills out onto the alley in a big way in the summer. Crowded with students and alternative types, it serves cheap beer; people-watching and occasional live bands (usually winter only) provide the entertainment. If you're not in the big-money, rooftop-drinking league, this is one of the best places in Beyoğlu. Daily 9am–2pm.

Büyük Londra Oteli Meşrutiyet Cad 117 ☎ 0212/245 0670; map pp.120–121. The bar of this unspoilt hotel has avoided the modernization programmes that ruined the interiors of so many of Beyoğlu's *fin-de-siècle* buildings in the 1970s and '80s, long before retro was cool in this part of the world. While many of them attempt to re-create the feel of distant times, the *Büyük Londra* doesn't have to – it's still all dark, ornate wood, brocade and velvet drapes. You wouldn't want to spend all evening here, but it's worth popping in for an early drink or two and absorbing the atmosphere before heading off to livelier places. Daily noon–11pm.

Café Smyrna Akarsu Cad 29, Cihangir ☎ 0212/244 2466; map pp.120–121. The clientele are a trendy, well-heeled set, enjoying the laidback feel of the long, narrow interior with its motley array of mirrors and retro collectibles. In summer, there are a few tables on the street. Like many of the city's café-bars, you'll feel equally at home here nursing a coffee or sinking a beer – plus there's some decent, if pricey, food on offer. Wine from 12TL a glass, beers from 7TL. Daily 9am–2am.

James Joyce Irish Pub Irish Centre, Balo Sok 26 ☎ 0212/224 2013; map pp.120–121. Housed in a wonderfully ornate and rambling nineteenth-century apartment block, the Irish Centre's focal point is this lively pub, but there's also a bar with big-screen sports TV that gets very crowded for big occasions and live bands play most nights of the week. An Irish breakfast is served all day. Beer is an expensive 9TL. Mon–Thurs & Sun 1pm–2am, Fri & Sat 1pm–4am.

Kaktüs Imam Adnan Sok 4, off İstiklal Cad ☎ 0212/249 5979; map pp.120–121. Favoured drinking, meeting and eating haunt of the TV and advertising crowd, and a prominent (but not exclusively) gay venue. There's a selection of domestic and imported beers ranging from 7TL

to 10TL and wine by the glass between 12TL and 16TL; plus good coffee, salads and pasta. Mon–Sat 9am–2pm, Sun 11am–2am.

★ **KV** Tünel Gecidi 6, off İstiklal Cad ☎ 0212/251 4338, ⓦ kv.com.tr; map pp.120–121. There's a distinctly Edwardian feel to this delightful café-bar: the interior's subtle lighting illuminates a clutter of antiques and bric-a-brac, quite a contrast to the clean, minimalist lines of many of the city's fashionable cafés. The wine is good value at 13TL to 15TL a glass, with beers from 7TL, and there's a small but well-planned food menu. In summer, there are tables outside in the lovely old passageway it fronts, and you'd never know bustling İstiklal Cad was a stone's throw away. Daily 8.30am–2am.

★ **Leb-i-Derya** Kumbaracı Yokuşu 57/6 ☎ 0212/293 4989; map pp.120–121. Funkier, with a younger clientele than its sister venue, the Richmond *Derya* (see p.190), it boasts a picture-windowed lounge, balcony and small roof terrace, all of which look out onto where the Golden Horn meets the Bosphorus. It's a fabulous (if pricey) place for an early or late evening drink, but also has an extensive menu if you're in the mood to eat. Daily 11am–4am.

Nu Teras Meşrutiyet Cad 149 ☎ 0212/245 6070, ⓦ nupera.com.tr; map pp.120–121. This was one of the earlier roof-bars in the city and is still going strong. It's a top spot for a pre-dinner drink, watching the sun set over the Golden Horn and the domes and minarets of the old city beyond. Later on, unwind to chilled-out dance music into the early hours. June–Oct Thurs & Sun 6.30pm–2am, Fri & Sat 6.30pm–4am.

Pano Şaraphanesi Hamalbaşı Cad 26, off İstiklal Cad, Galatasaray ☎ 0212/292 6664; map pp.120–121. Beautifully restored century-old Greek wine bar. Beer, local wine and good-value – if not particularly exciting – food available (*meze* from 6TL, pasta dishes from 13TL and steaks 28TL and up). Packed to the rafters on Thurs, Fri and Sat evenings – get here early if you want a seat. Daily 11am–1pm.

Pasific Sofyalı Sok, off Asmalımescit; map pp.120–121. Small, friendly bar with a good playlist of rock and indie music and well-priced beer (6TL for draught Efes), and early

14

evening shots for a bargain 4TL. It's a struggle to find a seat on the alleyway tables in summer, but it's great fun watching the world go by (and some nights it seems like most of it does) on this hedonistic street. Daily 11am–2pm.

Ritim Bar Sahane Sok 20, Balık Pazarı ☎0212/24 90252, ⓦritimbar.com; map pp.120–121. Run by the owner of the *World House Hostel* (see p.172), this down-to-earth multistorey bar is packed weekends (and other nights as well) with a real mixture of locals and guests from the hostel, attracted by the well-priced beer (9TL) and eclectic mix of DJ-spun sounds on the roof terrace. Daily 10am–2pm.

ASIAN İSTANBUL

Isis Kadife Sok 26, Caferağa Mah, Kadıköy ☎0216/349 7381; map p.140. Three-storey townhouse that's a café by day and bar-club at night. Cutting-edge alternative music and good food, plus a garden shaded by chestnut and fig trees, open during the summer months. A large beer will set you back 7TL. Daily 11am–2am.

Karga Kadife Sok 16, Kadıköy ☎0216/449 1725; map p.140. Self-consciously cool venue on the trendiest street in Asian İstanbul, this grungy/arty place is set in a tall, narrow nineteenth-century townhouse. Inside, it's all wood and wall, with plenty of gloomy nooks for young lovers. Part pub (the lower floors) and part art gallery (top floor), it also has a large, pleasant garden out back. Beer is reasonable (7TL) for a big Efes, and there's a snack-type menu. Daily 11am–2am.

Viktor Levi Damacı Sok 4, Caferağa Mah, Kadıköy ☎0216/449 9329; map p.140. If you're over in Kadıköy looking for something less arty and grungy than *Isis* or *Karaga* this historic bar-restaurant may just fit the bill. It's housed in a rambling nineteenth-century house, with a massive shady courtyard garden out back, and serves its own wines, which it has been producing since 1914 and sells for upwards of 26TL a bottle. There's a massive menu too, with *meze* starting from 4TL, grills from 18TL. Daily 11am–2am.

CLUBS AND LIVE-MUSIC VENUES

İstanbul is a major player in the **clubbing scene** – reflecting the rapid pace of modernization, rising living standards of living and the sheer number of young people around – half of Turkey's population is under 29. Most urban Turks stay up late so don't expect the real action until well after 11pm. Unless you look the part, you might not make it past the bouncers, particularly in the flashy Bosphorus-front clubs; Beyoğlu clubs are less exclusive. Some establishments shut down for the summer (anywhere from mid-June to mid-Sept) and relocate to out-of-town venues – check listings for details. **Live-music venues** vary widely. Many have "house" bands that play one or more regular nights per week, with the best bands/artists (and highest entry fees – usually 30TL, which often includes a free drink, though the Bosphorus-front clubs are more expensive) reserved for weekends. This is especially true of the rock-style venues, where bands play either Turkish **rock** or sing covers in English. **Jazz** has a hardcore following; the people who do like it are, by and large, affluent and influential, and this has enabled a number of clubs to flourish and attract the biggest names from the international scene. There are plenty of talented jazz musicians from İstanbul who have made the international stage, including Okay Temiz and İlhan Erşahin, but they still play locally as well.

BEYOĞLU

★ **Babylon** Şehbender Sok 3, Asmalımescit ☎0212/292 7368, ⓦbabylon.com.tr; map pp.120–121. Set in a modest-sized but atmospheric bare-brick

vault, this is İstanbul's premier live-music club with a regular programme of local and foreign groups playing jazz, world, indie and electronica. Ticket prices vary wildly according to the act (booking office across the street daily

---

TURKISH WINES

The third largest producer of grapes in the world, Turkey should be a major-league player in the wine business, and there are vineyards scattered across western Anatolia between Cappadocia, the Euphrates Valley, Thrace and the Aegean. As yet though, **Turkish wine** (*şarap*) is little known outside the country, and surprisingly expensive within it. It has, however, become the drink of choice for the middle classes, especially "modern" women. A drinkable wine bought from a supermarket starts from around 15TL. Expect to pay three times that for the same bottle with a meal in even a modest restaurant. A glass of wine in a cheaper café-bar will set you back upwards of 8TL. The safest bets are the wines manufactured by Doluca (try the Villa or more expensive Antik) and Kavaklıdere (Angora red and Çankaya white). Imported wines are affordable at supermarkets but prohibitively priced in restaurants.

14

TOP FIVE DRINKS WITH A VIEW
360 Beyoğlu, see p.196
Cheers Sultanahmet, see p.195
Leb-i Derya Beyoğlu, see p.197
Nu Teras Beyoğlu, see p.197
Pierre Loti Hotel roof-Pub Grand
  Bazaar and around, see p.195

noon–6pm, or from Biletix); performances usually start around 10pm. Adjoining and part of the set up is *Nublu Babylon*, a smaller venue to showcase new artists. In summer, the action moves to the Aegean coast near İzmir; see website for details. Tues–Thurs 9.30pm–2am, Fri & Sat 10pm–3am.

Bronx Pi Terkoz Çıkmazı 8/1, off İstiklal Cad ☎0532/384 8080, ⒲bronxpisahne.com; map pp.120–121. Intimate and trendy club staging alternative and indie live acts, both local and international. Very popular with university students and twenty-somethings because of its reasonable drink charges. Entry varies according to act, free when there's no live music. Mon–Sat 8pm–4am.

★ **Dogzstar** Kartal Sok 3, off İstiklal Cad ☎0532/244 9147, ⒲dogzstar.com; map pp.120–121. Run by dedicated alternative-music fanatic Taylan, this place has come on leaps and bounds since it moved from its tiny former home on nearby Toşbaşağa Sok. He aims to support Turkish bands of all kinds – from psychobilly to electro-punk, and you can see the results at the regular live gigs (entry fee varies). Spread over three floors, with great views from the terrace, it's free midweek, with a variable cover charge at weekends. On non-gig nights, the three resident DJs spin a variety of sounds from dub, drum'n'bass to old-school punk. Daily 6pm–5am.

★ **Ghetto** Kamer Hatun Cad 10 ☎0212/251 7501, ⒲ghettoist.com; map pp.120–121. A great venue offering an eclectic mix of contemporary music styles, from funk and indie to dance and jazz. A real bonus is the beautifully restored nineteenth-century Greek house in which it is set – complete with original frescoes on a long, barrel-vaulted ceiling. It also boasts a cool terrace, which is free if you are not interested in the act on offer. Entry price varies. Daily 9pm–4am.

Gizli Bahçe Nevizade Sok 27, off İstiklal Cad ☎0212/249 2192; map pp.120–121. The ideal place to extend your evening after the full-on *meyhane* experience of Nevizade Sok is this chilled club, spread over the second and third floors of an Ottoman townhouse – with sofas to lounge on, and a balcony to escape the smoke and sweat. The eclectic music – everything from jazz and blues to rock and dance – is loud but there are quiet nooks to continue conversation. Daily 9pm–2am.

Hayal Kahvesi Büyükparmakkapı Sok 19 ☎0212/244 2558, ⒲hayalkahvesi.com.tr; map pp.120–121.

Attractive brick-and-wood joint with occasionally good blues and rock every night from 11pm. Fridays see ageing but deservedly popular Turkish rockers Bulutsuz Özlemi take the stage. In summer, the scene moves to Çubuklu Hayal Kahvesi in Burunbahçe on the Asian side of the Bosphorus (☎0216/413 6880). There's a free boat service from İstinye across the strait. Admission varies. Daily 5pm–4am.

Indigo Akarsu Sok 1/2, off İstiklal Cad ☎0212/244 8567, ⒲livingindigo.com; map pp.120–121. This remains the venue of choice for electronica lovers, though it has now embraced a more inclusive policy with a wider range of musical styles on offer. Bigger-name DJ's and acts, many international, tend to play Fri and Sat. Mon–Thurs & Sun 10pm–4am, Fri & Sat 11pm–5am.

Jazz Café Hasnun Galip Sok 20, off Büyükparmakkapı Sok ☎0212/252 0694, ⒲jazzcafeistanbul.com; map pp.120–121. Established in 1982, this was one of the first jazz venues in the city, though blues sometimes takes centre-stage here, despite the name. An intimate club with high tables overlooking the tiny stage, it showcases a real mix of talent – from new bands to studio artists such as the famed Bulent Ortaçgil. Entry prices vary according to the act. Shows start at 10.30pm & 1am. Daily 4pm–2am.

★ **Jolly Joker Balans** Balo Sok 22 ☎0212/251 7020, ⒲balansmuzik.com; map pp.120–121. Sprawling venue with good, on-site microbrewed German-style beer available in the adjoining *Balans Brau* bar. The main performance hall is impressive, seating up to 1500, and many of the shows are by mainstream Turkish pop stars. Mon–Thurs 10pm–2am, Fri & Sat 10pm–4am.

Mini Muzikhol Soğancı Sok 7, off Sıraselviler Cad ☎0212/245 1996, ⒲minimuzikhol.com; map pp.120–121. In the same building as *5.Kat*, this trendy, arty yet intimate club aims to bring electronica, dubstep, DJ sets and live bands of varying genre and nationalities to the city's more discerning clubbers, along with themed evenings. Wed–Sat 10pm–4pm

Mojo Büyükparmakkapı Sok 26, off İstiklal Cad ☎0212/243 2927, ⒲mojomusic.org; map pp.120–121. Traditional basement club with live music most nights. It's very hit and miss – some of Turkey's best rock acts played here in their early days, but on an off-night expect a poor, mainstream rock-covers outfit. Entry 10TL, rising to 30TL on Sat. Daily 10pm–4am.

★ **Peyote** Kameriye Sok 4, Balık Pazarı ☎0212/251 4398, ⒲peyote.com.tr; map pp.120–121. This is the city's best place for alternative/indie types looking for an underground scene. The owners are in a band themselves, and they give stage space to upcoming rivals from across the metropolis. There's a lively roof terrace with an eclectic mix of music, live bands play on the second floor, while the first floor is given over to electronica. Beers are a reasonable 7TL and the (variable) entry charges start from 10TL. Daily 10pm–4am.

Pixie Underground Toşbaşağa Sok 12; map pp.120–121. This small venue is musically one of the most cutting-edge clubs in Beyoğlu. Music includes indie and punk but the emphasis is on drum'n'bass, dub step and electronica. Beers are a respectable price and entry is usually free. Daily 2pm–4am.

Riddim Sıraselviler Cad 69/1 ☎0212/251 2723, ⓦriddim.com.tr; map pp.120–121. A mainstream venue offering a mix of R&B, hip hop (in the basement) and rock to locals and the odd expat, with a mix of live acts and resident DJs. Free admission to Friday night's RNB & Hip Hop evening. There's a terrace with diner-style tables at the rear offering cool Bosphorus views. Mon–Sat 9pm–5am.

Roxy Arslan Yatağı Sok 113, off Sıraselviler Cad ☎0212/249 1283, ⓦroxy.com.tr; map pp.120–121. Popular club established back in 1994, attracting a wide range of good-time punters happy to part with the steep 50TL weekend entry fee. Music ranges from dance to blues and electronica to jazz, and there are live acts – see the website for details. Closed July and Aug. Fri & Sat 10pm–4am.

★ **Salon IKSV** Sadi Konuralp Cad 5, Şişhane ☎0212/334 0752, ⓦsaloniksv.com; map pp.120–121. Trendy multi-purpose venue backed by the İstanbul Foundation for Culture and Arts (IKSV) hosting contemporary and classical music concerts, plus some theatrical performances. Tickets are available from Biletix (see box, p.95), or commission-free from the venue. Opening hours vary according to the act.

GALATA AND WATERFRONT DISTRICTS

Atolye Kuledibi Galata Kulesi Sok 4 ☎0212/243 7656, ⓦatolyekuledibi.com; map p.110. Stylish café-bar run by a group of local artists, musicians and actors, punctuated with a rotating wall of local artwork and photography. An odd mix of Italian and Mexican dishes grace the menu, cooked up in an open kitchen and served alongside a wide array of creative cocktails. With live jazz at the weekends and plans for daily performances, workshops and exhibitions, this innovative venue is still finding its feet but is definitely one to watch. Mon, Tues & Thurs noon–midnight, Wed, Fri & Sat noon–4am.

★ **Nardis Jazz Club** Kuledibi Sok 14, Galata ☎0212/244 6327, ⓦnardisjazz.com; map p.110. Run by local jazz musicians, this small, intimate venue offers a great introduction to the local jazz scene and is a popular haunt among young locals. A blend of mainstream and modern jazz takes centre stage, with a little fusion and ethnic jazz thrown in for good measure. Bands are mostly Turkish but international solo artists are regularly invited to perform alongside them. 30TL entrance fee. Mon–Thurs 9.30pm, Fri & Sat 11.30pm.

Tamirane Kazım Karabekir Cad 2/8 ☎0212/311 7310, ⓦtamirane.com; map p.110. Housed in the repair-shop for the power station that is now Santralıstanbul (see p.117) this very trendy bar/restaurant has a rolling programme of live music and DJ events. Sessions take place in the mornings, afternoons and evenings, with emphasis on mellow jazz, electronica, trip-hop and the like. The food and drink are expensive but there's no entrance fee and the chance to observe the city's metropolitan set at close-quarters is illuminating. Daily 10am–2pm.

ORTAKÖY

Crystal Muallim Nacı Cad 65 ☎0212/261 1988; map p.132. Though the admission price is steep, it does include a free drink, and this is probably the best place in the city for techno, house and other assorted dance sounds, at least for the twenty- to thirty-something crowd who flock here. The well-scuffed dancefloor says it all about the quality of foreign and local DJs who spin their stuff here; a gallery, decked-out in black and chrome, surrounds the dancefloor, and there's a terrace out front with gorgeous views to the Bosphorus Bridge. Thurs free, Fri & Sat 35TL. Thurs–Sat midnight–5.30am.

JCs İstanbul Jazz Centre Second floor, *Radisson Hotel* complex, Muallim Çırağan Cad, Salhane Sok 10 ☎0212/327 5050, ⓦistanbuljazz.com; map p.132. World-class jazz with two performances each evening (a mixture of Turkish and foreign artists), European-style food and a summer terrace overlooking the Bosphorus. Performances start at 9.30pm, but book ahead as tables can fill up fast. Tuesday is ladies' night, with free entry for females. Entrance fees vary according to the act. Mon–Sat 6pm–late, Sun noon–5pm.

Q Jazz at Les Ottomans Muallim Nacı Cad 163 ☎0212/359 1500, ⓦlesottomans.com; map p.132. If you're not intimidated (or appalled) by the thought of listening to jazz in one of the city's most expensive hotels, this could be for you. The two-hundred-seat Bosphorus-front venue helps to compensate for the incongruity, along with an ever-changing line-up of international jazz artists. Live music starts at 11pm and there's a 30TL entrance fee. Daily except Wed 7pm–3am.

Reina Muallim Nacı Cad 44 ☎0212/259 5919, ⓦreina.com.tr; map p.132. This exclusive joint has been running for nine years now and has clocked up a fair few celebrity guests in its time – Oprah Winfrey, Sting, Uma Thurman, Paris Hilton, to name a few. With its waterfront location, several dancefloors blasting Euro-pop and selection of themed restaurants (6pm–11pm), this is where the city's bright young things come to splash their cash. Entry is 50TL at weekends, free weeknights. Cocktails will set you back a stiff 30TL and if you don't have a chauffeur-driven car to collect you in the small hours, you'll probably feel out of place. Daily 6pm–4am.

Sortie Muallim Nacı Cad 141/2 ☎0212/327 8585, ⓦsortie.com.tr; map p.132. Just up the waterfront

14

from the *Reina*, this club and restaurant complex offers a similar, if slightly more restrained, vibe. A smart-casual dress code is enforced and music is strictly pop and house. Expect to pay 30TL for a cocktail and 10TL for a beer, although the Fri & Sat 40TL admission includes a token drink. Free weeknights. May–Sept daily 6pm–4am.

Supper Club Muallim Nacı Cad 65 ☎0212/261 1988, Ⓦsupperclub.com; map p.132. In a great location, right next door to *Crystal* (see p.201), this self-consciously cool venue is part of an Amsterdam-based group with branches around the world. Whether you view it as free-spirited hedonism or downright pretentious, this place aims to tickle the five senses with a roster of art, performance,

video, dance and music. Thurs & Sun free, Fri & Sat 35TL including a free drink. Thurs–Sun 6pm–2am.

ASIAN İSTANBUL

Shaft Osmancık Sok 13, Kadıköy ☎0216/349 9956, Ⓦshaftclub.com.tr; map p.140. Situated on a lively street where bars spill out onto the pedestrianized thoroughfare in summer, and much frequented by vaguely alternative and student types, this is the best club on the Asian side of the Bosphorus. Entry is a reasonable 15TL on Sat & Sun, with sets from the (mainly) rock acts starting from 10.30pm. Midweek entry is free, and there's blues and jazz as well as rock on occasion. Daily 2pm–4am.

ARENAS AND OPEN-AIR VENUES

İstanbul is becoming an increasingly important destination on the international pop music circuit, attracting some top acts – particularly in the summer months when outdoor shows are feasible. The three venues listed below are the most popular and central. When really big bands are in town, the city's football stadiums are roped in to house them. Tickets can be bought online or from a number of outlets (see box, p.195).

Harbiye Açık Hava Tiyatrosu Darülbedayı Cad, Harbiye ☎0212/232 8603. Holding close to four thousand punters, this medium-sized outdoor venue has seen sets from home-grown favourites Duman and Sezen Aksu and is a venue for various music festivals. Completed back in 1947, it is sometimes listed as the Cemil Topuzlu Open Air Theatre (Cemil Topuzlu Açık Hava Tiyatrosu).

Maçka Küçükçiftlik Park Kadırgalar Cad 4, Maçka Ⓦkucukciftlikpark.com. Eight-thousand capacity open-air venue just north of Taksim Square, attracting major

international acts such as Elton John and Interpol. Several festivals are also held here, including the heavy-metal Sonisphere and dance/house festival Freshtival.

Türkcell Kuruçeşme Arena Muallim Nacı Cad 60, Kuruçeşme ☎0212/263 3963, Ⓦturkcellkurucesmearena .com. For bigger-name Western pop and rock acts (Rihanna and Jamiroquai, for example), this Bosphorus-front open-air stadium is, along with Küçükçiftlik Park, the city's premier venue. That said, much of the summer programme consists of Turkish music. May–Sept only.

TRADITIONAL TURKISH MUSIC

There are many different types of Turkish music and all may, initially at least, sound incongruous, off-key even, to the Western ear – largely because of the copious use of quarter-tones. If you really want to scratch beneath the surface of what makes this city tick, it's worth searching out a **traditional music** venue. The *Türkü* bar, where traditional Anatolian folk songs are played, tends to be drinking-and-music-orientated, though most serve food as well. The *meyhane* (see box, p.178) experience is as much about the endless courses of food served as it is about the *fasıl* music (see p.303) that is played. In the **Türkü bar**, the focus is on the *bağlama*, a kind of long-necked lute played with amazing dexterity by experts. On a typical evening, expect to sit around, beer in hand, listening to its plaintive sounds. As the evening progresses, the *bağlama* player, perhaps accompanied by fellow musicians playing the *deblek* (a kind of bongo-drum) and a *ney* (a type of flute) raises the tempo and the audience gets to their feet, links fingers and dances the *halay*, the country's national dance. It's great fun and very popular among young İstanbullus – the latest global club sounds and traditional Anatolian folk music are not mutually exclusive in this city of paradoxes. *Fasıl* music is quite different and played mainly by *Roma* (gypsy) bands. Visit virtually any **meyhane** (such as those on Nevizade Sokak or in Kumkapı) and you won't be able to escape it even if you wanted to, as the musicians serenade each and every table in search of tips.

BEYOĞLU

Andon Sıraselviler Cad 89 ☎0212/251 0222; map pp.120–121. Massively popular with İstanbul's fashionable set, with five overwhelming floors, each with their own personality: there's Western-style pop on the first floor, and dancing in the *Pera* bar to İstanbul's best DJs; on Fri and Sat, the 20TL admission charge to either of these

dance venues includes one drink. There are local and imported wines and cheese in the second-floor *Wine House*; live Turkish music and belly-dancing in *Müdavim Bar* on the third; and a good introduction to *fasıl* music and *rakı* in the fourth-floor *meyhane*, with 101 types of *meze*. A fixed-price menu of 70TL (includes unlimited local alcoholic drinks) applies to the *Müdavim Bar* and *meyhane*; booking advised. and stunning views from the fifth-floor roof-terrace restaurant.

Kallavi Taverna Kurabiye Sok 16, off İstiklal Cad ☎0212/245 1213, ⓦkallavi20.net; map pp.120–121. A small, traditional restaurant, recently moved to this location. The fixed menu (60TL) includes ten starters, four mains, a dessert and fruit, plus unlimited local drinks. With live *fasil* music every night, it's very popular with the locals. There's another branch at Şefik Bey Sok in Kadıköy. Mon–Sat 11am–2pm.

★ **Mektup** Imam Adnan Sok 20, off İstiklal Cad ☎0212/251 0110, ⓦmektup.com; map pp.120–121. The food on offer here is limited in range but perfectly passable. More importantly, the *Türkü* music is of a very high standard– it has seen sets by notable artists such as Ebru Destan and Tuğbay Özay. Voted the best *Türkü* bar in the country by the *Hüriyet* newspaper, so booking is advisable – especially at weekends. Daily noon–4am.

Munzur Hasnün Galip Sok 21/A, off İstiklal Cad ☎0212/245 4669; map pp.120–121. The Munzur mountains, away to the east in the heartland of Turkey's Kurdish Alevi population (the Alevi have spawned the nation's best *bağlama* players), are the inspiration for this no-frills but lively *Türkü* bar. The food is okay, the drinks not too pricey, and when things get going there are plenty of linked bodies dancing around the tables. Daily 6pm–4am.

Süheyla Kalyoncu Kulluğu Sok 19, off Nevizade Sok ☎0212/251 8757; map pp.120–121. Friendly late-night *lokanta* behind the Balık Pazarı. The house band members are a talented lot and have been knocking out both *fasil* and *Türkü* classics for the last fifteen years – the sets usually begin around 9.30pm. The fixed menu is reasonable at 70TL, including local drinks, and much merriment is assured when things get into full swing. Booking advised weekends. Daily 8pm–2am.

14

THE GRAND BAZAAR AND AROUND

Kör Agop Ördekli Bakkal 7–9, Kumkapı ☎0212/517 2334; map, pp.76–77. This down-to-earth *meyhane* has a good reputation for the quality of the *fasil* bands that pay court to its diners (see p.188) – especially on Fri and Sat nights. Daily noon–2am.

NORTH OF TAKSIM

Despina Açıkyol Sok 9 ☎0212/232 6720. Out in the wilderness of the business district of Şişli, the sub-district of Kurtuluş was once home to a wealthy Armenian and Greek community. The *meyhane's* Armenian founder, Madame Despina, died in 2006, but the spirit of the place lives on. Its *fasil* band is renowned and people come out of their way to enjoy both the music and the Armenian-style *meyhane* food on offer. Daily noon–midnight.

CABARET

Cabaret in İstanbul essentially constitutes floor shows where belly-dancers (usually from Russia or Eastern Europe) strut their stuff in gaudy costumes, interspersed with Turkish folk dancing and singing. The entry price usually includes a several-course-long meal. Stick to the more established venues, the best of which are reviewed below, as some places charge exorbitant entry fees and tack on lots of hidden extras. The cabaret venues below have daily **performances**, unless otherwise stated, with dinner served at 7.45pm, and the show running from 8.30pm to around midnight.

★ **Hodja Paşa Culture Centre** Hodjapaşa Hamam Sok 3/B, Sirkeci ☎0212/511 4626, ⓦhodjapasha.com. Housed in a beautifully restored Ottoman *hamam*, with the dance area and seats atmospherically set beneath an exposed brick dome, a seventy-minute show introduces the visitor to music and dances from all parts of the Ottoman Empire for 50TL, including an interval drink. There's also a more specialist whirling dervish ceremony put on by sufis from the Galata Mevlevihanesi.

Orient House *President Hotel*, Tiyatro Cad 27, Beyazit ☎0212/517 6163, ⓦorienthouseistanbul.com. Traditional Turkish folk music, plus whirling dervishes and belly-dancing. A four-course meal with wine and show costs 120TL a head, though if you forgo the meal it's 80TL.

Sultana's Cumhuriyet Cad 40/D, Harbiye ☎0212/219 3904, ⓦsultanas-nights.com. Belly-dancing and folklore show, costing €70 with dinner, unlimited local drinks plus free transport from any hotel (cheaper rates can be negotiated if you just turn up at the door). A deal without dinner but including one drink is €40.

Turkish Cultural Dance Theatre, Fırat Culture Centre, Divan Yolu, Sultanahmet ☎0554/797 2646, ⓦdancesof colours.com. Presents a whirling dervish music and dance show in a restored house that once belonged to a distinguished *dede* (leader). This is purely theatre, with no dinner or the other trappings of a club. 45TL. Tues, Thurs, Sat & Sun.

İSTANBUL MODERN

The arts

Vibrant İstanbul is the cultural hub of the country, and hosts an ever-increasing number of arts and cultural festivals, matching most other European cities for the breadth of its arts scene. In 2010 it was chosen as a European Capital of Culture, which provided a real boost to the city's arts scene. Unfortunately, major plans to remodel and pedestrianize Taksim Square (see p.126) have delayed the restoration of the landmark Atatürk Cultural Centre (AKM), previously the home of the state symphony orchestra, opera and ballet, and the future of this important International Modern-style building is uncertain.

In the meantime, the lovingly restored Süreyya Opera House in Kadıköy is a great place to see quality **opera** and **classical music** concerts which, along with **ballet**, form an important part of the city's cultural life. **Theatre** is popular, though most plays performed on the thirty or so stages in the city are in Turkish. The State Theatre Company puts on occasional plays in English, and foreign theatre groups such as the Royal Shakespeare Company perform during May's International İstanbul Theatre Festival. The main **annual event** is the İstanbul International Music Festival during June and July, which includes jazz, classical and world music concerts, as well as performances by the İstanbul State Symphony Orchestra.

İstanbul Modern, opened in 2004, has helped pave the way for a revival of the visual arts in the city, aided and abetted by the acclaimed International Biennial. The city has plenty of cinemas and film festivals, though outside of festival periods cinemas show Hollywood films in English with subtitles. The output of the fast-growing domestic **film industry** is screened in Turkish.

ESSENTIALS

Information on all music and theatre events, and on the various cultural festivals, is available from the İstanbul Foundation for Culture and Arts (IKSV), Sadı Konuralp Cad 5, Şişhane, Beyoğlu (☎0212/334 0700, ✇iksv.org).
Tickets for most events and performances can be purchased online from Biletix (✇biletix.com), whose website is in both Turkish and English. There are also several Biletix outlets around the city, the most useful of which is the D & R book and music store on İstiklal Caddesi. Otherwise, you can buy tickets from the relevant venue, either online or from their box office. For what's on, check *TimeOut İstanbul*.

CLASSICAL MUSIC, OPERA AND BALLET

As part of his great push to westernize the fledgling Turkish Republic and break from the Ottoman past, Atatürk tried to inculcate new values among the population, among them a love for Western classical music and opera. He was partially successful, and today most educated, middle- and upper-class Turks have at least a passing interest in **classical music**, **opera** and **ballet**. The İstanbul State Symphony Orchestra and İstanbul State Opera and Ballet Company are funded by the government, but there are several privately funded orchestras, including the renowned Borusan Philharmonic. The season runs from November to May, but in summer historic buildings like the former Byzantine church of Aya Irene and the Galata Mevlevihanesi provide prestigious venues for the international **İstanbul International Music Festival** (see p.31).

Akbank Culture and Arts Centre (Akbanksanat) İstiklal Cad 8/A, Beyoğlu (☎0212/252 3500, ✇akbanksanat.com. Multipurpose centre including a café, art gallery, dance studio, music room, library and theatre. The centre also hosts film festivals and organizes the annual Akbank Jazz Festival (see p.32). Tues–Sat 11am–7pm.

Atatürk Cultural Centre (AKM) Taksim Square; Theatre ☎0212/251 5600; Opera & Ballet ☎0212/243 2011; Symphony Orchestra ☎0212/243 1068; ✇idobale.com; map pp.120–121. This multi-purpose venue, shared by the state symphony orchestra, and theatre, opera and ballet companies, has apparently been reprieved from demolition; however, the AKM's future is far from certain, and at the time of writing restoration work, scheduled to finish in 2011, had ground to a halt.

Aya Irene Topkapı Palace, Sultanhmet. An atmospheric venue in the cavernous interior of the Byzantine Church of the Divine Peace staging classical music concerts at irregular intervals, usually in aid of charity, and features prominently as part of June's annual İstanbul International Music Festival. The seating may be reminiscent of a school assembly and the

acoustics are only moderate, but this is a special place.
Borusan Arts and Cultural Centre İstiklal Cad 213, Beyoğlu (☎0212/336 3280, ✇borusansanat.com; map pp.120–121. Home to the Borusan Philharmonic Orchestra, one of Turkey's most successful private orchestras, the complex also boasts one of the country's most extensive CD libraries and a decent art gallery.

Caddebostan Culture Centre Haldun Taner Sok 11, off Bağdat Cad, Kadıköy ☎0216/360 9095; map pp.120–121. This is the largest arts complex on İstanbul's Asian side, with a 650-seat auditorium as well as a smaller hall, cinemas, galleries and a bookshop. Some of the leading lights of the Turkish classical music scene play here.

Cemil Reşit Rey (CRR) Darülbedayi Cad 1, Harbiye ☎0212/231 5497, ✇crrks.org. The middle-class İstanbullu's venue of choice, this purpose-built concert hall features chamber, classical, jazz and Turkish music, plus regular performances by visiting international orchestras. It's also the venue for the İstanbul International Music Festival (June) and the CRR Piano Festival (Dec). Daily performances in season (Oct–May). It also has its own well-regarded symphony orchestra.

İş Arts Centre İş Sanat Kültür Merkezi, İş Kuleleri, Kule 17, Levent ☎0212/316 1083, ⓦissanat.com.tr. Out in the business district of Levent and best reached from the M2 Levent Metro stop, this multi-purpose venue, with an eight hundred-capacity main auditorium, is housed in a tower block. Classical music performances, jazz and world-music concerts are held here, plus plays – and there's an art gallery attached.

Lütfi Kırdar Congress and Exhibition Centre Darülbedayi Cad 60, Harbiye ☎0212/373 1100, ⓦicec.org. With a conference auditorium seating some 3500 and a performance hall, the Anadolu Auditorium, for over 2000, this is one of the city's premier spots for classical music and ballet – and for the best in traditional Turkish music. It also holds major art exhibitions, including the İstanbul Contemporary Arts Fair, in a new state-of-the-art exhibition hall.

Süreyya Opera Bahariye Cad 29, Kadıköy ☎0216/346 1531, ⓦsureyyaoperasi.org; tickets ⓦwww.dobgm.gov.tr; map p.140. Set in a gorgeous, beautifully restored opera house built in 1924, this is a delightfully intimate place to watch opera, ballet and classical music and a rare oasis of culture on the Asian side of the Bosphorus. The season runs from Oct to May.

Türker İnanoğlu Maslak Show Centre Büyükdere Cad, Derbent Mevki, Maslak ☎0212/286 6686, ⓦtimshowcenter.com. Located out in distant Maslak, and best reached by bus #25/T (Taksim–Sariyer), this is a populist venue, with everything from gypsy orchestras and Chinese acrobatic teams to ballet and Broadway shows. It's big, it's brash, and it's a long way from the old city, both in distance (15km from Taksim) and atmosphere – but it's certainly a part of İstanbul as it is today.

THEATRE AND PERFORMING ARTS

İstanbul has a thriving **theatre** scene, with venues in districts as diverse as ultra-orthodox Fatih and upmarket Harbiye, but unfortunately most productions are in Turkish. The best opportunity to see performances in English is during the **International İstanbul Theatre Festival** (see p.31), when many foreign companies hit town; ultra-cool Garajistanbul draws in international as well as home-grown artists, while the Kenter and Tiyatro Pera theatres stage occasional performances in English.

Garajistanbul Kaymakan Reşit Bey Sok 11, off Yeniciler Cad, Beyoğlu ☎0212/244 4499, ⓦgarajistanbul.org; map pp.120–121. Trendy, stripped-down performing arts venue in a former underground car park just off Galatasaray Meydanı, reached from Kaymakan Sok. This is as cutting edge as it gets in İstanbul, with workshops, films and art projects associated with modern dance, theatre and other performances. Its own company

performs at the venue and tours abroad, and it attracts quality performing artists from around the world. With seating limited to 250, it's worth booking for most things. Closed July & Aug.

Kenter Theatre Halaskargazi Cad 35, Harbiye ☎0212/246 3589, ⓦwww.kentersinematiyatro.com. Theatre founded by the famous Turkish actress Yıldız Kenter, who appears in most of the plays. There are some

ARA GÜLER: İSTANBUL'S HENRI CARTIER-BRESSON

Turkey's foremost photographer, **Ara Güler**, born in İstanbul in 1928, began his career in journalism in the same city in 1950. His prodigious talent eventually brought him to the attention of the international press and he worked for *Time-Life*, *Paris-Match* and *Der Sturm*. After making friends with Henri Cartier-Bresson, he joined the renowned Paris-based Magnum Agency.

Güler has taken pictures all around the world and interviewed and photographed such famous luminaries as Winston Churchill, Picasso and Salvador Dalí, but it is for the startling **black-and-white images** of his native city that Güler will be best remembered. It is no surprise that İstanbul's most famous literary son, Nobel Prize-winner Orhan Pamuk (see box, p.128), once a Beyoğlu neighbour of Güler, used a selection of his photographs to illustrate his 2005 memoir *İstanbul: Memories of a City*. Pamuk's melancholic text is enhanced by Güler's gritty images – ferries on the Golden Horn belching black smoke, washing strung across dank, narrow streets in the poor neighbourhood of Balat, or a ragged street urchin peeping out from behind an Ottoman tombstone in Eyüp.

For an idea of Güler's mastery of his craft – the small size and poor-quality reproduction of the photographs used in Pamuk's book do not do his images justice – check out the 1994 book *A Photographical Sketch on Lost İstanbul*, admire the images adorning his appropriately named *Kafe Ara* (see p.183) or check out his website ⓦaraguler.com.tr. You won't be disappointed by the man who has done more for İstanbul than Bresson did for Paris.

English-speaking performances, such as Shakespeare and Chekhov, and it's also the venue for the Turkish Shadow Play, performed on most weekend mornings. Season runs October to April.

Ses 1185 Ortaoyuncular İstiklal Cad 140, Beyoğlu ☎ 0212/251 186, ⊛ortaoyuncular.com; map pp.120–121. Set up in 1980 by multi-talented Ferhan Sensoy, who was educated at nearby Galatasaray Lycée but received much of his artistic training abroad, the Ses 1185 puts on an eclectic mix of local plays in this beautiful old theatre. Season runs October through May.

Tiyatro Pera Siraselviler Cad 70, Taksim ☎ 0212/245 4460, ⊛tiyatropera.com. Started in 2001 by the ambitious actress/director Nesrin Kazankaya, it stages a mix of Western (from Aristophanes and Shakespeare to Brecht) and Turkish productions, with some shows in English – usually Thurs–Sun, with performances starting at 8pm.

GALLERIES AND EXHIBITION SPACES

The visual arts scene in İstanbul is burgeoning, with new galleries opening with dizzying regularity. The inaugural **International İstanbul Biennial** (see box, p.208), first held in 1987, kick-started the current boom by giving a platform to both foreign and local artists. Corporate sponsors, particularly banks, have filled the void left by the absence of state funding and opened up a number of multi-purpose **exhibition venues** – mainly on İstiklal Caddesi.

15

Aksanat Culture and Arts Centre (Akbanksanat) İstiklal Cad 8/A, Beyoğlu ☎ 0212/252 3500, ⊛akbanksanat.com; map pp.120–121. Changing exhibitions of art and sculpture from a mix of well-known local artists, Turkish students and internationally acclaimed artists – plus an interesting selection of films of jazz and classical music concerts shown on a giant screen. Tues–Thurs 10.30am–7pm.

Arter İstiklal Cad 211, Beyoğlu ☎ 0212/243 7667, ⊛arter.org.tr; map pp.120–121. Five storeys of exhibition space for local and international contemporary artists, backed by the wealthy Vehbi Koç Foundation. Installations, performance art and more take centre-stage in this prominently located gallery. Tues–Thurs 11am–7pm, Fri–Sun noon–8pm.

Borusan Arts and Cultural Centre İstiklal Cad 213, Beyoğlu ☎ 0212/336 3280, ⊛borusansanat.com; map pp.120–121. A state-of-the-art exhibition space showcasing established Turkish artists as well as international names. Also home to the Borusan Philharmonic Orchestra (see p.205). Mon–Sat 9.30am–6pm.

Galeri Nev Maçka Cad 33, Maçka ☎ 0212/231 6763, ⊛galerinev.com. A small exhibition space in this prosperous suburb, featuring both Turkish and international artists. Mon–Sat 11am–6.30pm.

Galerist Mısır Apt, İstiklal Cad 165 ☎ 0212/244 8230, ⊛galerist.com.tr; map pp.120–121. Commercial gallery of considerable repute, showcasing some of the very best contemporary Turkish artists as well as international stars such as Andy Warhol. There are two further Galerist spaces, one nearby on Meşrutiyet Cad 67, the other on Süleyman Seba Cad 4–8 in Akaretler, Beşiktaş. Mon–Sat 10am–6pm.

Galeri Ziberman Mısır Apt, İstiklal Cad 163 ☎ 0212/251 4288. What used to be Casa dell' Arte, one of the city's best contemporary art galleries, is now the Ziberman. Showcases mainly home-grown contemporary artists in the landmark Mısır building. Tues–Fri 10am–7.30pm, Sat noon–7pm.

İstanbul Modern Meclis-I Mebusan Cad, Liman İşletmeleri Sahası Antropo 4, Karaköy ☎ 0212/334 7300, ⊛istanbulmodern.org. İstanbul's answer to Tate Modern in London, with regularly changing exhibits by contemporary Turkish and foreign artists, plus a cinema showing art-house movies, workshops (including ones for kids), a library, photography gallery and a chic café-restaurant. Admission is 14TL – an accompanying English audioguide will set you back 4TL. See p.114 for more information. Tues–Sun 10am–6pm, Thurs until 8pm.

Ottoman Bank Museum Voyvoda Cad 35/7, Karaköy ☎ 0212/245 5095, ⊛obmuze.com. Closed for a major overhaul at the time of writing, this fine nineteenth-century bank building owned by Garantı Bank will reopen as a contemporary arts centre, part of the SALT project. See p.111 for more information. Daily 10am–6pm.

Pera Museum Meşrutiyet Cad 141, Tepebaşı ☎ 0212/334 9900. Top three floors of a grand, wonderfully restored, nineteenth-century building exhibiting regularly changing works by contemporary artists, including a major Miró retrospective. See p.123 for more information. Entry 10TL. Tues–Sat 10am–7pm, Sun noon–6pm.

Proje 4L/Elgiz Museum of Contemporary Art Meydan Sok, Beybi Giz Plaza B Blok, Maslak ☎ 0212/290 2525 ⊛proje4l.org; map pp.120–121. Fine private collection of modern art by home-grown talent, with regular exhibitions of Turkish and international artists. Wed–Fri 10am–5pm, Sat 10am–4pm.

Sakıp Sabancı Museum İstinye Cad 22, Emirgan ☎ 0212/277 2200, ⊛muze.sabanciuniv.edu. Housed in a 1920s villa known as the Atlı Köşk, and owned by one of Turkey's wealthiest families, the Sabancıs, this welcome addition to the İstanbul arts scene held a major Picasso exhibition in 2006 – the first of its kind in Turkey – followed up in 2008 by a Dalí retrospective. See p.150 for more information. Entry 10TL. Tues–Sun 10am–6pm, Wed & Sat until 10pm.

SALT İstiklal Cad 136 ☎ 0212/292 7605. The noted Garantı Bank-backed Platform Garantı Contemporary Arts

Centre has reinvented itself as SALT, which promises to carry on the good work showcasing all kinds of contemporary art, with workshops, film screenings and lectures to boot. Tues–Sat noon–8pm, Sat 10.30am–6pm.

Santralİstanbul Kazım Karabekir Cad 1, off Sütlüce Cad 22 ☎ 0212/311 7000, ⓦ santralistanbul.org. Set in the grounds of Bilgi University, in space contrived from the outbuildings of a defunct early twentieth-century power station and next door to the Museum of Energy, Santralıstanbul has taken over from İstanbul Modern as the city's most innovative exhibition space. Features local and international artists, with an emphasis on video installations. Entry 10TL. Free shuttle bus from AKM, Taksim or Eyüp ferry. Tues–Fri 10am–6pm, Sat & Sun 10am–8pm.

Siemans Sanat Meclis Mebusan Cad 125, Fındıklı ☎ 0212/334 1104, ⓦ siemans.com.tr/seimansart. Founded in 2003, Siemans Sanat features regularly changing themed exhibitions showcasing predominantly young artists from both Turkey and abroad, with everything from drawings to video installations. Conveniently located near İstanbul Modern (see p.114). Daily 10am–7pm.

Yapı Kredi Cultural Centre İstiklal Cad 285, Beyoğlu ☎ 0212/334 1333, ⓦ ykykultur.com.tr; map pp.120–121. A real mixed bag of exhibitions at this prominent gallery, from photography to sculpture, modern art to ethnographia. Mon–Fri 10am–7pm, Sat 10am–6pm, Sun 1–6pm.

15 CINEMA

The Turkish **film industry** is booming, with internationally acclaimed directors such as **Nuri Bilge Ceylan**, **Fatih Akın** and **Ferzan Özpetek** leading the way (see p.307). As a result, an increasing amount of screen time is being taken up by home-grown films – until quite recently, Hollywood releases, with Turkish subtitles, dominated İstanbul's cinemas. The problem for the visitor is that unless you catch it at one of the film festivals (see p.31), it will be in Turkish with no subtitles. If you're thinking of taking your kids to a film while you're here (tempting given the paucity of child-orientated sights in the city), bear in mind that many of the imported films aimed at youngsters are dubbed into Turkish. Many of the modern multi-screen **cinemas** are situated in large shopping malls; a few old-style screens hang on in Beyoğlu, once the centre of domestic film production. The historic Emek, on Yeşilcam Sokak, was unfortunately closed at the time of writing, its future bleak. Most cinemas retain a fifteen-minute coffee and cigarette interval. Tickets cost from 8TL to 20TL, depending on the cinema, though most offer mid-week Halk Günü– or People's Day-discount nights. The annual **International Film Festival** (mid-April to May) takes place mainly at cinemas in Beyoğlu, while the excellent ten-day **AFM International Independent Film Festival** in February takes place in the AFM Fitaş in Beyoğlu.

AFM Fitaş İstiklal Cad 24–26, Beyoğlu ☎ 0212/292 1111, ⓦ afm.com.tr; map pp.120–121. A popular ten-screen cinema not far from Taksim Square, showing the newest films, with a cool pub upstairs. The smartest of the cinemas in Beyoğlu, but not the most atmospheric.

AFM Forum State-of-the-art ten-screen cinema in what claims to be Europe's biggest shopping centre, out in the suburb of Bayrampaşa but easily reached by the *hafif* metro. Mainstream fare but very comfortable.

Atlas İstiklal Cad 209, Atlas Pasajı ☎ 0212/252 8576; map pp.120–121. A three-screen cinema set above the shops of this historic arcade, showing the usual programme of Hollywood and home-grown products – with the

occasional, more arty film from time to time.

City Life City's Mall, Teşvikiy Cad 162, Nişantaşı ☎ 0212/373 3535, ⓦ citylifecinema.com. Seven-screen, state-of-the-art cinema housed in the retro-style City's Mall shopping centre in upmarket Nişantaşı, with trendy (and expensive) café-bars attached.

Feriye Çirağan Cad 124, Ortaköy ☎ 1212/236 2864, ⓦ umutsanat.com.tr. Three-screen cinema with a well-regarded attached café and seats either in the auditorium or (for a supplement) balcony. Handy if you're looking to kill some time before heading out to the bars and clubs in Ortaköy, though most releases are mainstream despite it being situated in a cultural complex.

ISTANBUL INTERNATIONAL BIENNIAL

Organized by IKSV, the İstanbul Foundation for Culture and Arts, the **İstanbul International Biennial** is a major showcase of contemporary art. From relatively humble beginnings back in 1987, it has grown incrementally and now rivals Venice, São Paulo and Sydney in the biennial stakes. Held on odd-numbered years, the biennials usually run September through November, are themed and use different venues across the city, from historic buildings such as the Topkapı Palace to urban-chic industrial warehouses. The 2011 Biennial, the twelfth, featured acclaimed Cuban artist Gonzalez Torres. Previous exhibitors include Turner Prize-winners Gillian Wearing and Gavin Turk. For more information, check out ⓦ iksv.org.

İstanbul Modern Meclis-I Mebusan Cad, Liman İşletmeleri Sahası Antropo 4, Karaköy ☎0212/334 7300, ⓦistanbulmodern.org. The best place for art-house, alternative and documentary films in the city, located on the lower floor of the Modern gallery (see p.114). Programme changes monthly.

Kanyon, Mars Kanyon Mall, Büydere Cad 185, Levent ☎0212/353 0814, ⓦwww.marssinema.com. Unsurprisingly, given its location in this ultramodern shopping mall, the ticket prices are above average, but probably worth it if you want the comfiest seats and best picture and sound quality in town.

Şafak Yeniçeriler Cad, Çemberlitaş ☎0212/516 2660, ⓦozenfilm.com.tr. The closest cinema to Sultanahmet, buried in the bowels of the Fırat Kültür Merkezi shopping mall, with seven screens showing the latest Western and Turkish releases.

Yeşilçam İmam Adnan Sok 10 ☎0212/249 8006, ⓦyesilcamsinemasi.com. This retro, bohemian, single-screen basement cinema is the best place to see Turkish and foreign art-house movies, and is the cheapest in the area, too. The walls of the gloomy café/foyer are papered with old cinema posters, and there's an antique projector on display. Unfortunately, they don't run the film if only a few people turn up – which happens quite regularly.

15

GAY PRIDE MARCH, İSTIKLAL CADDESI

Gay and lesbian İstanbul

İstanbul is the gay capital of Turkey, with the scene centred around Beyoğlu and Taksim, where most of the places reviewed in this section can be found. Although transvestite and transsexual singers and entertainers have been held in high esteem in Turkey since Ottoman times (see p.285), homosexuality remains a taboo, though consensual acts between 18-year-olds and over are legal. Advocating the lifestyle, however, is against the law and Lambda, Turkey's foremost gay-liberation group was closed by the courts for "moral impropriety". In 2011, however, it was running again and reported the eleventh Lesbian, Gay, Bisexual, Transvestite and Transsexual (LGBTT) day on its website (see opposite). Part of a series of marches held worldwide every June to celebrate Pride Week, over ten thousand people march down İstiklal Caddesi from Taksim Square, the only gay march held in a predominantly Muslim country.

The country as a whole, even the cultural capital of İstanbul, remains very **conservative**. Affection between males is part and parcel of society – straight males linking arms in public or resting their hand on a friend's thigh while chatting are common sights – but as a result of a tight-knit family life and the ensuing social pressure, Turkish gays usually feel obliged to keep their sexual orientation well under wraps. It's only in the moderately hedonistic atmosphere of the clubs of liberal Taksim that they feel free to express themselves – perhaps not surprisingly, as it's still technically possible to be arrested for cruising. Having said this, you'd be very unlucky to run into problems with the authorities, or be "gay-bashed", even though the word *"ibne"* (passive partner in a homosexual relationship) is a deadly insult here.

WEBSITES AND MEDIA

Lambda's premier gay website ⓦ lambdaistanbul.org is currently in Turkish only, so the best introduction to the İstanbul gay scene (in English) is the glossy ⓦ istanbulgay.com, which gives a run down of the best gay bars and clubs (including guided cruises of the best venues) and gay-friendly hotels, reviews the sauna cruising scene and has a section on lesbian İstanbul. Another good site in English is ⓦ absolutesultans.com, which gives a sound introduction to the realities of gay life in the city. The site is run commercially – gay tourism is their business – but even if you're not interested in their services, they do have some good tips. Alternatively, the weekly **TimeOut Istanbul** (see p.29) reviews gay and lesbian venues and has regular features on the city's gay scene. For accommodation, ⓦ turkey-gay-travel.com will help you find gay-friendly places to stay, and also has a few useful reviews of clubs and discos in the capital.

BARS AND CLUBS

Bigudi Mis Sok 5, Teras Kat, off İstiklal Cad, Beyoğlu ⓦ bigudiproject.com; map pp.120–121. The only dedicated lesbian venue in town – and that goes for all the staff, as well as the punters, situated on the roof terrace of an apartment building. Free. Fri & Sat 10pm–5am.

Love Dance Point Cumhuriyet Cad 349, Harbiye ☎0212/296 3358; map p.127. Glitzy, high-tech and spacious club opposite the Military Museum. DJs spin a wide range of sounds, from techno to Turkish pop. Its motto is "Love's here, where are you?" Wed free, Fri & Sat 25TL including one drink. Wed 11.30pm–4am, Fri & Sat 11.30pm–5am.

Otherside Zambak Sok 2/5, off İstiklal Cad, Beyoğlu ☎0212/235 7914; map pp.120–121. Small venue noted for its go-go boys, high prices and thumping house music. Daily 11.30pm–4am.

Prive Tarlabaşı Bul 28, Taksim ☎0212/235 7999; map p.127. Gay-only dance club, with a devoted following due to its reputation as a pick-up place. The city's oldest gay club, it plays mainly Turkish pop, and really gets going after 1am. This street has a bad reputation in the city for muggings and petty theft, so take care if you decide to venture out here. Sun–Thurs free, Fri & Sat 20TL including a drink. Daily 11pm–4am.

Rocinante Café Bar Oğut Sok 6/2, Sakızağcı Sok Cad, Beyoğlu ☎0212/244 8219; map pp.120–121. Behind the prominent Ağa Camii (mosque) on İstiklal Caddesi is this popular lesbian-friendly (the owner and many of her friends are lesbian) café-cum-meeting point. Daily 2pm–2am.

Sahra Bar Sadrı Alaşık Sok 40, off İstiklal Cad, Beyoğlu ☎0212/244 3306; map pp.120–121. For the super-confident only, this three-storey place caters to

16

BÜLENT ERSOY: THE NATION'S FAVOURITE DIVA

The rounded, smiling and heavily made-up face of **Bülent Ersoy** is a common sight on Turkey's TV screens and in the country's gossip magazines. Born in 1952, Ersoy became a popular singer before undergoing a sex change in 1981 – though she kept her male first name. Seen by the authorities, if not many of the general public, as a social deviant in a hard-line state still reeling from the effects of the 1980 military coup, she was banned from performing in public. After a period of exile in Germany, Ersoy returned to Turkey following a change in the law that allowed her to become a "legal" female. She went on to become even more popular than before, her public apparently adoring her flamboyant behaviour and outrageous dress sense as well as her singing and acting abilities. Despite the scandal caused when she married a man some twenty years her junior, Ersoy went on to co-host one of the nation's most popular TV shows, **Popstar Alaturca**. In 2008, she found herself in trouble again, when she publicly declared that were she a mother she would not send her son to fight in Iraq, where the Turkish military were conducting operations against the Kurdish Workers Party (PKK) – daring words in a country where it's forbidden to call conscription into question.

transsexuals, transvestites, queens and gays – with more than its fair share of heterosexual adventurers and rent boys. Daily 11am–2am.

Sugar Café Sakalsalim Çıkmazı 3/A, off İstiklal Cad, Beyoğlu ☎0212/245 0096, ⓦsugar-cafe.com; map pp.120–121. Low-key meeting and hangout joint off the busy main drag, somewhere to decide what you're going to do later on, with food on offer from 1pm–10pm. Daily 11am–1am.

Tek Yön Siraselviler Cad 63/1 Beyoğlu ☎0212/233 0654, ⓦwww.tekyonclub.com; map pp.120–121.

Very popular, long-standing mainstream club. The friendly staff perform occasional drag shows, and there's a garden out back to escape the noise. Daily 11.00pm–4am.

X-Large Kallavı Sok 12, off Meşrutiyet Cad, Tepebaşı ☎0212/788 737; map pp.120–121. Housed in a long-defunct historic Beyoğlu cinema, this mainstream but atmospheric venue features a popular drag revue and a massive bar. Locals claim it is the most European-style of the city's gay clubs. Wed–Sat 11pm–5am.

16

Shopping

Whether trawling through an Ottoman-era bazaar for carpets or kilims, sizing-up T-shirts in a retro-clothing shop, or mixing it with the middle classes in one of the city's myriad shopping malls, İstanbul has more than enough opportunities to keep the most dedicated shopaholic busy – there's even an annual forty-day shopping festival to entice buyers to the city with the lure of discounted prices. The Grand Bazaar may be a tourist trap, but it's nonetheless an unmissable experience. Known in Turkish as the Kapalı Çarşı, this hive of over four thousand shops has, for centuries, been performing the same function as modern malls – putting a host of different traders selling a welter of different goods under the same roof.

17

Far more manageable – and the place to head for spices and sweets, including the ubiquitous *lokum* (Turkish delight) – is the **Mısır Çarşısı**, or Spice Bazaar, on the crowded Golden Horn waterfront in Eminönü. In addition, there are dozens of street markets across the city, selling everything from fruit and vegetables to cheap household utensils and fake designer clothing; best is the Çarşamba Pazarı, held in the conservative Fatih district every Wednesday.

İstiklal Caddesi in Beyoğlu is İstanbul's main shopping thoroughfare, and is traffic-free save for an antique tram and service vehicles. Many major Turkish and international chains can be found along here, as well as the city's best bookshops. A number of arcades or **pasaj**, some of them dating back to the nineteenth century, run off İstiklal Caddesi, selling a mix of alternative and bargain secondhand clothing, interesting jewellery, retro cinema posters and quirky household items. Scattered around the city are a number of other shopping districts. Upmarket **Nişantaşı** and **Teşvikiye** are the places to head for international and Turkish designer fashion and accessories, with Cartier, Armani, Gucci et al displaying their wares in appropriately expensive shops – particularly on Abdi İpekçi and in the City's Mall. For foodstuffs, bric-a-brac and bargain clothing, the pedestrian streets behind the ferry terminal in **Kadıköy**, on the Asian side of the city, form a compact and atmospheric place to shop.

Malls are mushrooming across the city, with over eighty up and running in 2011 and more in the offing. Many are situated in distant and awkward-to-reach suburbs, but a few are easily accessible to visitors using public transport. One advantage of mall shopping is that prices are all marked up so you don't have to bargain.

ESSENTIALS

Opening hours Most shops are open Monday to Saturday from 9am to 7pm, though malls stay open daily until 10pm. Supermarkets and hypermarkets open daily from 9am to 10pm but smaller food shops close much earlier.

The Grand Bazaar is open Monday to Saturday from 9am to 7pm and is credit-card friendly, as are all shops bar the smallest of grocers (*bakkals*) or kiosks.

JEWELLERY

Dressing up and looking good is part and parcel of life to many İstanbullus, often taken to extremes by the well-heeled "ladies who lunch" of wealthy residential districts such as Nişantaşı. **Jewellery** is big business in Turkey, with gold and silver items sold by the gram. Traditionally, gold bangles and the like were purchased as hedges against inflation (earning interest is forbidden in Islam) and given as part of the "bride price" in traditional marriages. The Grand Bazaar and nearby Nuruosmaniye Caddesi are two good places to look for traditional and antique jewellery, Beyoğlu, Nişantaşı and the malls for modern designs.

Ela Cindoruk and Nazan Pak Atiye Sok 14/5, Teşvikiye ☎0212/232 2664, ⍟elacindoruknazanpak.com. A small and exclusive gallery-cum-shop run by a talented duo, one of whom studied jewellery design at Parsons School of Design in New York, the other under a master atelier in the Grand Bazaar. As well as their own designs, they also stock items by internationally renowned designers. Mon 2–7pm, Tues–Sat 10.30am–7pm.

Mor Takı Turnacı Başı Cad 10B, off İstiklal Cad, Beyoğlu ☎0212/292 8817, ⍟mortaki.com; map pp.120–121.

Cool, modern interior with an interesting range of handmade, chunky jewellery. Mon–Sat 10.30am–7.30pm.

Urart Abdi İpekçi Cad 18/1, Nişantaşı ☎0212/246 7194, ⍟urart.com.tr. This place has been going for well over thirty years, selling very upmarket jewellery, based on ancient Anatolian and Central Asian designs. They charge big bucks for their finely wrought stuff but at least pump some of it back into the arts in Turkey through sponsorship of events such as the Golden Orange Film Festival. Mon–Sat 9am–7pm.

ANTIQUES AND BRIC-A-BRAC

If you're expecting to find a real bargain, you'll probably be disappointed – the average İstanbullu may care little for the old and worn, but in a city of over fifteen million those who do are enough to ensure a buoyant price for the **antiques** available. Bear in mind that you're supposed to have clearance from the Museums Directorate to take anything out of the country that's over one hundred years old; in theory, the seller should already have an authorization certificate for the goods from the directorate – if not, don't buy. In practice, nobody is going to worry about a nineteenth-century biscuit tin,

CARPETS AND KILIMS

Turkish **carpets** and **kilims** are world famous, and with the best selection to be found in İstanbul, it's not surprising that buying one is high on many visitors' lists. Be warned, though, that they are no longer necessarily cheaper in Turkey than overseas. It's also worth knowing that if you are introduced to a carpet dealer by a tout (and there are plenty of those hanging around Sultanahmet and the Grand Bazaar) or tour operator, a hefty commission will be added. It's very easy to be drawn into buying something you don't really want at a price you can barely afford once you've been smooth-talked and drip-fed with copious quantities of apple tea. That said, it's still possible to get a good purchase here, and enjoy the process, providing you heed the following tips:

• Do some research, preferably before you leave home (check out some of the books reviewed in "Contexts").
• Avoid buying in the first shop you visit, and look around several. You can always go back – preferably the next day, when you've had time to think about it.
• Don't be embarrassed at how many carpets the dealer is laying out for you – that's his (or usually his lowly assistant's) job.
• Ask as many questions about the pieces that interest you as you can – this will test the dealer's worth, and could give you some interesting historical background should you make a purchase.
• Check the pieces for flaws, marks, density of weave, etc – this way, the dealer will know you're serious.
• Even in the most reputable shop, bargaining is essential. Whatever you do, don't engage in the process if you've no intention of buying.
• You'll probably get a better deal for cash.
• Most important of all, only buy the piece if you really like it and are sure it'll look the part back home – any other considerations such as future appreciation are mere distractions.

CARPET OR KILIM?

A **kilim** is a pile-less, flat-woven wool rug. The better-quality ones are double-sided (that is, the pattern should look much the same top or bottom). A *cicim* is a kilim with additional, raised designs stitched onto it; while the *sumak* technique, confined in Turkey to saddlebags, involves wrapping extra threads around the warp. By and large, kilims, traditionally woven by nomadic or transhumant Anatolian tribal groupings, are generally cheaper and more affordable than carpets. Turkish **carpets** are single-sided, with a pile, and can be wool, silk or a mixture of both. Needless to say, the higher the silk content, the more expensive the rug.

DEALERS

The following are all based in the Grand Bazaar (Mon–Sat 9am–7pm).

Adnan & Hasan Halıcılar Cad 89–92 ☎0212/527 9887, ⓦadnanandhasan.com; map p.78. A wide range of modern and antique kilims and carpets from a reputable dealership, established in 1978, with Ushak and Hereke carpets vying for shop space with Anatolian and Caucasian kilims.

Ethnicon Takkeciler Sok 58–60 ☎0212/527 6841, ⓦethnicon.com; map p.78. Fixed prices for kilims made in the traditional way (with natural dyes and no child labour) but with contemporary (often large, geometric blocks of colour) styling.

Şişko Osman Zincirli Han ☎0212/528 3548, ⓦsiskoosman.com; map p.78. Arguably the most knowledgeable dealer in the Grand Bazaar, reputable Şişko ("Fat") Osman's family origins are in the east of Turkey, but he has been flogging top-quality rugs to all-comers (including the rich and famous) here for many years. Over sixty percent of his clients are Turks, which

gives some idea of the quality of the (mainly) dowry pieces on offer here. His kilims range from €400 to €2500 and carpets €500 to €2500 – excluding the more expensive genuine period pieces, some dating back to the eighteenth century, stocked in one of his four adjacent shops.

Tradition Rubiye Han 11/12, Kürkçüler Sok ☎0212/520 7907; map p.78. Opened in 1988 and co-run by Frenchwoman Florence Heilbron, this fine establishment has a very good reputation, lots of repeat customers (including a whole coterie of French diplomats and politicians) and sells pieces from €50 to €10,000.

Yörük Kürkçüler Cad 17 ☎0212/527 3211; map p.78. Run by Ersoy, whose family came to the city from the Caucasus in 1864 via the Central Anatolian town of Kayseri. The stock runs from chemical-dyed pieces for as little as €80 to vintage dowry pieces up to €5000. Very reliable.

17

but a seventeenth-century Ottoman sword is a different matter. The best place for twentieth-century items (up to 1980s stuff) is the streets leading down from İstiklal Caddesi in Çukurcuma, or the Horhor Flea Market (see p.216).

Abdullah Sandal Bedestan 6, Kapılı Çarşısı ☎0212/522 8171; map p.78. Established in 1880 and run by the fluent-English-speaking Pol Şalabi, this small shop stocks a treasure-trove of icons, jewellery from 1800 to the 1950s and much else besides. Mon–Sat 9am–7pm.

Horhor Antique Market Yorum Kırık Tulumba Sok 13/22, Aksaray ☎0212/525 9977. Over two hundred bric-a-brac and antique shops in a multi-storey building in the drab suburb of Aksaray, a fifteen-minute walk from the Aksaray Metro station; there are bargains to be found. Daily 10am–8pm.

Kadıköy Antika Çarşısı Tellalzade Sok, Çakıroğlu İş Han, Kadıköy; map p.140. Tellalzade Sokak has a number of small shops selling all kinds of retro and bric-a-brac items, plus some genuine antiques and an excursion here

fits in well with food or souvenir shopping and the wonderful *Çiya* restaurant (see p.191).

Leyla Altıpatlar Sok 6, Çukurcuma ☎0212/293 7410. This well-established shop stocks all manner of antique clothing, from the late nineteenth century to the 1960s, plus a plethora of cloth-related items – including embroidered cushions and throws – collected by enthusiast Leyla Seyhanlı. Mon–Sat 10am–7pm.

Müstamel Eşya Evi Turancıbaşı Cad 38/1, off İstiklal Cad, Beyoğlu ☎0212/245 2110; map pp.120–121. Spread over two floors, this retro-orientated shop run by friendly, architect-trained Aslıhan Kendiroğlu, concentrates on the 1950s to the 1970s, from Bakelite phones to chrome light-fixtures and furniture to clothes. Mon–Sat 9am–7pm.

BOOKS

There are some good stockists of English-language **books** around the city, and it's also rewarding to browse through the secondhand-book markets and shops. The best-known is the Sahaflar Çarşısı (Old Book Market) at Beyazit, though it also sells new titles. Numerous secondhand bookshops cluster in Beyoğlu, especially in the backstreets off the east side of İstiklal Caddesi and down towards the Çukurcuma antique district. The annual **İstanbul Book Fair** (ⓦistanbulbookfair.com), held in late October or early November, is held in the İstanbul Sergi Sarayı on Meşrutiyet Caddesi, near the *Pera Palas Hotel*.

Ada Books İstiklal Cad 20 ☎0212//251 3878; map pp.120–121. Now as much a café as a bookshop, it remains a good source of glossy coffee-table books, and also sells Turkish and foreign CDs and DVDs. Mon–Fri 7am–10pm, Sat & Sun 9am–10pm.

Denizler Kitabevi İstiklal Cad 395, Beyoğlu ☎0212/249 8893; map pp.120–121. Specialists in nautical books and charts, plus an extensive range of collectors' books on Turkey and the Ottomans. Mon–Sat 9.30am–7.30pm.

Eren Sofyala Sok 34, Tünel, Beyoğlu ☎0212/251 2858, ⓦen.eren.com.tr; map pp.120–121. Art and history books, old maps and miniatures, with a comprehensive website (in English) for ordering specialist books. Mon–Sat 10am–7pm.

Galeri Kayseri Divan Yolu 58, Sultanahmet ☎0212/512 0456; map p.44. The biggest distributor of English-language books in Turkey, with a vast range of texts on Ottoman history and all other imaginable Turkish – and particularly İstanbul – topics. Daily 9am–8.30pm.

Greenhouse Bookshop Café Moda Cad 28, Kadıköy ☎0216/550 4961. Managed by an English woman and stocking an excellent range of books in English, including an extensive children's department. Mon & Wed–Sat 10am–6.30pm.

Homer Yeni Çarşı Cad 28, Beyoğlu ☎0212/249 5902, ⓦhomerbooks.com; map pp.120–121. Arguably the

best bookshop in the city, with a wonderful selection of everything archeological, historical and cultural written on Turkey. There's a good selection of English children's books, and the staff are very helpful. Mon–Sat 10am–7.30pm.

Librairie de Pera Galapdede Cad 22, Tünel, Beyoğlu ☎0212/243 3991; map pp.120–121. Excellent selection of antiquarian books, including English-language ones, plus maps of the Ottoman Empire, prints and photographs. Daily 9am–7pm.

Pandora Büyükparmakkapı Sok 3, off İstiklal Cad, Beyoğlu ☎0212/243 3503, ⓦpandora.com.tr; map pp.120–121. Split onto opposite sides of the road – with one side Turkish and the other containing an excellent selection of foreign-language books on three storeys; carries some gay literature and will order books on request. Now has branches in other parts of İstanbul, especially around the universities. Mon–Thurs 10am–8pm, Fri & Sat 10am–9pm, Sun 1–8pm.

Sahaflar Çarşısı Sahaflar Sok, Beyazit. Between the Grand Bazaar and the Beyazit Camii, this historic (it dates back to the early Ottoman period) collection of small bookshops now concentrates on textbooks for students from the nearby university but also has a reasonable selection of guides and other books about the city. Mon–Sat 9am–7pm.

17

SUPERMARKETS AND CORNER SHOPS

İstanbul has plenty of **supermarkets** if the thought of shopping for food at a street market sounds like too much hassle – although the fruit and vegetables are generally inferior in quality and much more expensive, it's easier to buy smaller quantities, and there's invariably a deli-type counter with a great array of different local cheeses, olives, pickles, salami-style meats and, sometimes, ready-prepared *meze*. The upmarket Macrocenter supermarkets at Abdi İpekçi Cad 24 in Nişantaşı and on Muallimnacı Caddesi down by the Bosphorus in Kuruçeşme are good bets; alternatively, all the malls listed have a supermarket (see p.222) – look out for the names Migros, Real, Tansaş and Corona. There are also smaller outlets, known as *market* or *bakkal*, all over the city, which are basically **corner shops** selling a limited range of fruit and vegetables, soft drinks (and sometimes alcoholic beverages), cheese, olives, packaged food, bread and the like – dearer than the supermarkets but often much more convenient.

FOOD AND SPICES

Turkey is a major producer and consumer of **herbs** and **spices**, and İstanbul is a great place to stock up on them, most obviously in the atmospheric **Mısır Çarşısı** (Spice Bazaar) – look out in particular for red *pul biber* (chilli flakes), *isot* (extra-hot chilli flakes, virtually black in colour), *kekik* (thyme), *nane* (mint) and *kimyon*. They're more than just a novelty, but the strings of dried peppers, aubergines and okra that Turks use over the winter when the fresh product is not available double as colourful kitchen decorations. *Nar ekşisi*, the viscous pomegranate **syrup** used so liberally in many Turkish salads, is cheaper here than your home country. A more unusual product is *pekmez*, a grape syrup usually made from either grapes or mulberries – it makes a sweet but healthy topping for yoghurt. Turkish **coffee** (*Türk kahvesi*) is about as traditional a Turkish product as you can get, though you'll need to buy a small pan known as a *kahve tenceresi* if you want to make it properly back home. Dried **fruits** are both great value and delicious – especially *kayısı* (apricots), *dut* (mulberries) and *incir* (figs) – as are pistachios (usually known as *Antep fıstığı*, after the town in southeast Turkey where they're grown), *fındık* (hazelnuts), which come from the Black Sea region, *ceviz* (walnuts) and *badem* (almonds). Then, of course, in all its glutinous splendour, there is *lokum*; known in the west as **Turkish delight**, there are in fact many varieties of this traditional favourite – and none of them chocolate covered.

Ali Muhidin Hacı Bekir Hamidiye Cad 83, Eminönü ⊕0212/522 0666; map p.68. Founded in 1777, this is a reliable place to buy top-quality Turkish delight (choose from over twenty varieties) and more unusual delicacies such as *fındıklı ezmesi* (hazelnut marzipan). The interior is a delight, with an eye-catching array of sugary treats displayed on period wooden shelves and in glass-fronted cabinets. It's tricky to find, set in the bustling narrow streets near the Spice Bazaar but well worth the effort. Or try the Kadıköy branch, opposite *Baylan* (see p.184) on Muvakkithane Caddesi. Mon–Sat 8am–9pm, Sun 9am–9pm.

Brezilya Güneşlibahçe Sok 42, Kadıköy ⊕0216/337 6317; map p.140. This place has been roasting and grinding coffee since 1920, but also stocks a good line of mulberry, grape, apricot and plum *pestil* (sheets of solidified molasses) and *cevizli sucuk* (a walnut-filled sausage of chewy molasses). Daily 9am–9pm.

Cafer Erol Yasa Cad 19, Kadıköy ⊕0216/337 1103; map p.140. A family confectionary business that began back in 1807, the Kadıköy branch, opened in 1945, is a work of art. Antique shop fittings, jars full of traditional *alkide* (boiled sweets), Turkish delight, *baklava* and, a real visual treat, exquisite *badem ezmesi* (marzipan) fruits. It's not cheap, but it is quality. Daily 9am–9pm.

Güllüoğlu Mumhane Cad 171, Karaköy ⊕0212/293 0910. Arguably the finest, and certainly the best-known, *baklava* in the city: delicious, buttery and nut-filled. If you're looking to take some home, this is a great place to buy it, but it's not cheap. Daily 10am–midnight.

Kurukahveci Mehmet Efendi Tamis Sok 66, Eminönü ⊕0212/511 4262. There are always big queues outside this wonderful paean to the aromatic coffee bean. Started in 1871, it's now housed in a rare impressive Art Deco building to the west of the Spice Bazaar. Sells beans and powder for Turkish and filter coffees, plus *sahlep*, the ground orchid-root drink so popular in İstanbul in the winter. There's another branch across in Kadıköy, a few minutes' walk back from the ferry terminal. Mon–Sat 9am–7pm.

Malatya Pazarı İstiklal Cad 375, Beyoğlu ⊕0212/245 7648, ⊛malatyapazari.com.tr. Malatya, in the far east of Turkey, is famous for its apricots, and you can sample the dried product here – some come in gift packs stuffed with pistachios and walnuts. There's also a wide range of nuts, sweets and spices. Daily 9am–7pm.

Mısır Çarşısı Eminönü; map p.68. To choose between the myriad purveyors of different spices, herbs, herbal teas, Turkish delight, nuts and dried fruit in the historic Mısır

17

Çarşısı (Spice Bazaar) would be meaningless. There're a number of stalls backing onto the outside of the walls selling fresh cheese, olives, dried fruits, nuts, etc and, both here and in the surrounding streets prices are cheaper than in the Mısır Çarşısı itself. Daily 9am–7pm.

Safa Hasırcılar Cad 10, Eminönü ☎ 0212/527 2277; map p.68. A small outlet in a fascinating street just west of the Spice Bazaar, offering a quality range of *baklava* and other nut-filled filo-pastry desserts for considerably less than more famous rivals. Well worth seeking out. Daily 9am–7pm.

HIGH-STREET, DESIGNER AND ALTERNATIVE FASHION

You'll find all the usual **high-street fashion shops** in İstanbul, as well as more upmarket places like Armani and Versace. **Turkish shops** (with multiple branches) to watch out for include: Beymen, Damat Tween, Homestore, Mavi, Mudo City, Mudo, OXXO, Silk and Cashmere, and Yargıcı. Vakko is one of the oldest and best-known fashion chains in İstanbul; Vakkorama is its youth-market offshoot. For **shoes**, look for Desa, Hotiç and Vetrina. **Designer clothing** outlets are mainly located in the shopping malls (see p.222) or in the streets around the districts of Nişantaşı, Osmanbey and Şişli (take any bus north from Taksim Square, from outside *McDonald's*). Many of the shops listed below also have branches in the shopping malls. **Turkish fashion** is beginning to compete on the catwalks, thanks to Rıfat Özbek, the darling of the European fashion world. Other names to watch out for in Turkish *haute couture* are Bahar Korçan, Gönül Paksoy, Ferruh Karakadlı and Murat Tadin, all of whom are working with the best Turkish fabrics: leather so fine that it is now processed for the Italian market, Bursa silk, and the universally famous Angora wool.

Berrin Akyüz Camekan Sok 5/b ☎ 0212/2523831 ⓦ berrinakyuz.com. Local designer Berrin splits her time between her Üsküdar outlet and here. This pint-sized boutique is overflowing with her quirky fashion pieces, including beautiful dresses, printed and beaded scarves, embroidered jewellery and cute knitted hats. There's a small men's range here too, but the main selection is at the Üsküdar branch (Dr Fahri Arabey Cad 98). Mon–Fri 10am–8pm, Sat & Sun 10am–5pm.

Beyman Akmerkez Mall, Nisbetiye Cad, Etiler ☎ 0212/282 0832. Quality chain shop for tailored men's and women's suits, dress shirts, silk ties and scarves, and other accessories. Daily 10am–10pm.

Bis Aznavur Pasajı, off İstiklal Cad, Beyoğlu ☎ 0212/292 9700; map pp.120–121. The two sisters who started this business hit on a new-found thirst for alternative street clothing among a small coterie of İstanbul youth. With unusual, retro-inspired designs and a host of accessories, it makes a welcome change from the high-street chains. Daily 9am–7pm.

Crash Galip Dede Cad 35, Galata ☎ 0212/252 7743; map p.110. A small, alternative outlet in up-and-coming Galata, with a good range of individually designed T-shirts, hoodies and shorts – plus some secondhand retro stuff as well. Mon–Sat 10am–9pm.

Gönül Paksoy Atiye Sok 6A, Teşvikiye ☎ 0212/216 9081. A one-of-a-kind designer, Gönül's clothing and accessories are mostly based on traditional Ottoman designs and motifs, using naturally woven and hand-dyed material. Mon–Sat 10am–7pm.

Mavi İstiklal Cad 195, Beyoğlu ☎ 0212/244 6255; map pp.120–121. Gap-inspired jeans label, selling good-quality denim wear, T-shirts, sweatshirts and funky bags – plus some trendy İstanbul T-shirts that make a welcome

alternative to the usual tourist tat. Mon–Sat 10am–10pm, Sun 11am–10pm.

OXXO İstiklal Cad 64A, Beyoğlu ☎ 0212/249 4263, ⓦ oxxo.com.tr; map pp.120–121. Trendy shop, offering up to twenty new items each week. Quirky and ever-changing gimmicks such as free lemonade and ice cream are a bonus. Mon–Sat 9.30am–9.30pm, Sun 1–9.30pm.

Roll Turnacıbaşı Sok 13/1, off İstiklal Cad, Beyoğlu ☎ 0212/244 9656, ⓦ rollist.com; map pp.120–121. The outlet of choice for indie types who want cutting-edge street fashion. Owner Hüseyin puts a defiantly Turkish twist on our obsession with the recent past, producing a range of tongue-in-cheek T-shirts emblazoned with "legendary" Turkish cars such as the Murat 124 and the Anadol, as well as favourite comic-book and film characters. Mon–Sat 10am–10pm, Sun noon–9.30pm.

Silk & Cashmere Akmerkez Mall, Nisbetiye Cad, Etiler ☎ 0212/282 0235. Scarves, hats, gloves, sweaters and shirts, using imported fabrics from China. Daily 10am–10pm.

Vakko İstiklal Cad 123–125, Beyoğlu ☎ 0212/282 2626, ⓦ vakko.com.tr; map pp.120–121. Classy 50-year-old Turkish fashion label renowned for its sense of style and use of fine fabrics. The clothes don't come cheap though, and you have to dress up a bit to get into the flagship shop on İstiklal Cad. At the Vakko Sales Store, on Yenicamii Cad 1 in Eminönü, items can be picked up for a quarter of the regular price. Daily 10am–10pm.

Yargıcı Vali Konağı Cad 30, Nişantaşı ☎ 0212/225 2912, ⓦ yargici.com.tr. Well-made and reasonably priced clothing, from work suits to sportswear and underwear. Mon–Sat 9.30am–7.30pm, Sun 1–6pm.

CLOCKWISE FROM TOP LEFT JEWELLERY FOR SALE; COFFEE AND TURKISH DELIGHT; TURKISH CARPETS, GRAND BAZAAR; SHOPPER ON ISTIKLAL CADDESI>

17

BUDGET AND SECONDHAND FASHION

Many Western high-street stores produce their clothes in Turkey, and a number of stalls and markets across the city specialize in seconds, production overruns and samples at bargain prices (10TL and up for T-shirts and tops, 25–50TL for jeans and trousers). Fakes abound, however, and manufacturers often insist labels are cutout, so it's not always easy to find a genuine bargain. The most convenient places to look for these items are the various arcades (some of them of historic interest; see box, p.124) off İstiklal Caddesi.

Atlas Pasajı Off İstiklal Cad 209, Beyoğlu; map pp.120–121. This historic arcade behind the Atlas Cinema, with its barrel-vaulted roof and Neoclassical columns, is youth-orientated, with alternative/street-style clothes outlets, cheap and cheerful jewellery shops, piercing places and CD/DVD shops, plus an amazing selection of original film posters in a couple of the basement shops. Daily 9.30–11pm.

Beyoğlu İş Merkezi İstiklal Cad 331–369, Beyoğlu; map pp.120–121. Three floors of end-of-line and seconds clothing, especially T-shirts, sweatshirts and jeans, with the occasional genuine bargain for the persistent. Daily 10am–10pm.

Binbavul Galipdede Cad 66, Galata ☎0212/243 7218; map p.110. *Binbavul* means "a thousand suitcases" in Turkish, and there's certainly enough vintage clothing,

theatrical costumes, retro-phones and the like in this rather gloomy emporium to fill that many and more. Sun–Thurs 11am–9pm, Fri & Sat 11am–11pm.

By Retro Suriye Pasajı, İstiklal Cad, Beyoğlu ☎0212/245 6420, ⓦbyretro.com; map pp.120–121. Set in the basement of this historic arcade is what claims to be Europe's largest secondhand-clothing shop. Owner Hakan Vardar scours Europe for vintage clothes and there are rails and rails of it here. Daily 10am–10.30pm.

Terkoz Çıkmaz İş Merkezi Beyoğlu; map pp.120–121. A side street off İstiklal Cad, next to the Paşabahçe glass shop, down towards Tünel, crammed with stalls of badly organized overruns bearing Western high-street names such as Next, River Island and Gap. Go right to the end and down the stairs for more organized bargain-bin action. Daily 10am–10pm.

MARKETS

Beşiktaş Pazarı Beşiktaş; map p.132. Saturday bazaar held in a warren of streets on either side of Şair Nedim Cad (about 10min from the ferry terminal). It's pot luck what you'll find, as just about any kind of clothing can turn up here. Daily 9am–dusk.

Çarşamba Pazarı Fatih. Occupying the narrow streets close to Fatih Camii, this is the most atmospheric of the city's markets, but better for fruit, vegetables and the like than bargain clothing. There are a few home-spun souvenirs like hand-made wooden spoons, rolling pins and bread-boards.

HANDICRAFTS AND GIFTS

You don't have to splash big money on a carpet or kilim to have something tangible and authentic to remember your visit by. Traditional **ceramics** from the western Anatolian town of Kütahya, including tiles, vases and plates, can be good purchases, as can embroidered tablecloths, cushion covers and towels. Meerschaum pipes, often carved into the shape of Ottoman dignitaries, make an unusual souvenir, as do *peştemals*, the cotton-wraps worn in the city's steamy *hamams*. **Copperware**, still spun (and traditionally tin-plated) in bazaars in far-away Turkish towns such as Gaziantep, is good value, as are the mother-of-pearl-in laidback gammon sets and other **wood** items from the same town. In their own way just as authentic as the traditional Ottoman crafts are the modern twists on old designs sold in upmarket household goods shops such as Padabahçe – especially **glassware**.

Ambar Kallavi Sok 12, off İstiklal Cad, Beyoğlu ☎0212/292 9277; map pp.120–121. This small, family-run shop sells a great range of organic and natural products from food to soap. Mon–Sat 9am–7.30pm, Sun 12.30–7.30pm.

ArtEna Camekan Sok 1, Galata ☎0212/243 5318, ⓦart-ena.com; map p.110. One of the longest-running of the many local designer boutiques along Camekan Sok, ArtEna is unmissable with its brightly painted shop-front, and crammed with handmade jewellery, clothing and bohemian accessories. Daily 10am–8pm.

Caferağa Medresesi Caferiye Sok, Soğukkuyu Çıkmazı 1 ☎0212/513 3601, ⓦcaferagamedresesi.com.

Built by the great Ottoman architect Sinan in the sixteenth century, this beautiful courtyard medrese is now an artists' workshop-cum-traditional handicrafts shopping centre. It's a charitable foundation and a rare low-key shopping opportunity in Sultanahmet, with traditional wares for sale, plus workshops where visitors can join in and learn about painting miniatures, marbling, calligraphy and other Turkish arts. Mon–Sat 8.30am–7pm.

Chez Galip At Meydan 78, Sultanahmet ☎0212/638 5180, ⓦchezgalip.com; map p.44. The pottery on sale at this prominent boutique overlooking the Hippodrome is made by hand in the Central Anatolian town of Avanos. Some of the pottery is based on traditional Ottoman wares, but more interesting is the range derived from Hittite and other ancient Anatolian peoples. It's not cheap, but the quality is excellent. Daily 9am–8pm.

Cocoon Küçük Aya Sofya Cad 13 ☎0212/638 6271; map p.44. Four floors showcasing gorgeously hued and patterned felt hats, bags, animals and even jewellery, plus a wide range of traditional Central Asian textiles, carpets and kilims. It's all very tastefully done and the prices not too unreasonable. There's a smaller shop in the Arasta Bazaar (same hours). Daily 9am–7pm.

Felt in Love Camekan Sok 2, Galata ☎0212/243 7574; map p.110. Adorable handmade figurines, hanging decorations, cards and accessories made entirely out of felt. They make a unique and beautifully crafted souvenir – the whirling dervish statuettes are an obvious eye-catcher and everyone from famous Turkish folk musicians to Santa Claus, and even Jesus have been immortalized in hand-sewn felt. Prices between 15TL and 45TL. Daily 9.30am–7pm.

Hammam Kule Çıkmazı, opposite the Galata Tower ☎0212/245 7075, ⓦhammam.com.tr; map p.110. Charmingly presented handmade soaps, essential oils, loofahs and lotions line the shelves here, providing everything necessary for an indulgent *hamam* experience. The ornate soap bowls and traditional Turkish towels would make great gifts, as would the beautiful hand-painted wooden soap boxes. There's also a sister stall operating out of *Molly's Café* (see p.183). Daily 11–7pm.

İstanbul Handicrafts Centre Kabasakal Cad 5, Sultanahmet ☎0212/517 6748; map p.44. Similar to but less laidback than the Caferağa Medresesi (see p.168), this is another restored medrese– an extension to the *Yeşil Ev Hotel* (see opposite) – where artists and craftsmen keep alive traditional skills such as *ebru* marbling, calligraphy, lace-making and embroidery. Daily 9am–8pm.

İznik Classics Arasta Çarşısı 67, Sultanahmet ☎0212/517 1705; map p.44. Some of the best examples of İznik tiles you'll see anywhere, beautifully displayed in this small shop in the Arasta Bazaar (there are other outlets in the Grand Bazaar and on nearby Utangaç Sokak). The tiles are handmade by different artists, and all reflect the high quality of the finest period of İznik pottery, and are consequently expensive, with prices from 120TL and up. Daily: summer 9am–9pm; winter 9am–7pm.

Mudo Pera İstiklal 401, Beyoğlu ☎0212/251 8682; map pp.120–121. Worth going in just to see the gorgeous Art-Nouveau interior, this long-established outlet has a range of upmarket giftware as well as quality clothing. Mon–Sat 10am–7.30pm.

Paşabahçe İstiklal Cad 314, Beyoğlu ☎0212/244 0544, ⓦpasabahce.com.tr; map pp.120–121. Sells a range of well-designed items that add the finishing touches to the homes of many middle- and upper-class İstanbullus – from cruet sets to juicers, dinner services to clocks. Some of its glass products, made up the Bosphorus in its Beykoz factory, are worth looking out for. Mon–Sat 10am–8pm, Sun 11am–7pm.

Yörük Collection Yerebatan Cad 35, Sultanahmet ☎0212/511 7766; map p.44. Run by the same team responsible for the charmingly eccentric *Kybele Hotel* (see p.168), this well-laid-out shop sells everything from beautiful silver and turquoise jewellery and contemporary-style kilims to cushion covers to framed Ottoman miniatures. Throw in hand-dyed silk scarves and Üzbek embroidery and the eclectic nature of this fine shop becomes apparent.

TEXTILES AND FABRICS

Turkey is famous for its textiles and fabrics – as well as producing reams of mass-produced cotton for Western and Turkish clothing manufacturers, it also has a small number of small-scale businesses and individuals who produce *peştemals* (*hamam* wraps), towels, tablecloths, runners and rolls of fabric.

Abdulla Halıcılar Cad 53, Kapalı Çarşı ☎0212/527 3684; map p.78. Restrained design is the key to this chic shop selling bath wraps (*peştemal*), bed linen, fluffy towels and the like – it tweaks traditional products to fit the tastes of the city's new elite and Western visitors alike. Also does a tasteful range of mohair rugs and handmade olive-oil-based soaps. Beautiful displays, helpful staff and fixed prices make it an oasis of peaceful browsing in the sometimes overwhelming Grand Bazaar. Mon–Sat 9am–7pm.

Derviş Keseciler Cad 51, Kapalı Çarşısı ☎0212/528 7883, ⓦdervis.com; map p.78. Another Grand Bazaar outlet stocking a lovely range of traditional handicrafts, including *peştemals* and towels. It also does a nice line in vintage kaftans imported from the Turkic republics of Central Asia, along with silk scarves. Mon–Sat 9am–7pm.

Jennifer's Hamam Arasta Bazaar, Sultanahmet ☎0212/518 0648; map p.44. All the textiles here are made from organic cotton, linen or silk and woven by hand on traditional looms. Prices are a little above average because of this, but the product is top-notch, with a fabulous range of *peştemals*, fluffy towels and scarves on offer. The owner is a knowledgeable Canadian. Daily 9am–8pm.

Necdat Danış Yağlıkçılar Sok, Kapalı Çarşısı ☎0212/526 7748; map p.78. This place has been selling hand-woven textiles for over forty years, and has an excellent reputation for its keen prices and wide range of scarves, *peştemals*, tablecloths and reams of gorgeous fabrics. They supplied the textiles used in the Hollywood film, *Troy*. Mon–Sat 9am–7pm.

17

LEATHER

Leather is big business in Turkey, and if you are after a belt, bag or jacket, it's worth hunting around – though prices aren't as low as they once were, except for poor-quality stuff, and unless you know your stuff it's easy to get ripped-off. Overall, it's probably better to buy from one of the outlets listed below.

Derimod Akmerkez Mall, Nisbetiye Cad, Etiler ☎0212/282 0668. Excellent-quality leather goods including coats, jackets, bags and shoes. Classic rather than cutting edge, but then most people don't want to make a short-lived fashion mistake at these prices. Daily 10am–10pm.

Koç Deri Kürküçüler Cad 22/46, Kapalı Çarşı ☎0212/527 5533; map p.78. Established in 1960, this specialist leather shop in the Grand Bazaar runs up stuff for the likes of Armani and Dolce&Gabbana. Needless to say, it's not cheap, but it does have a good reputation. Mon–Sat 9am–7pm.

Matraş Akmerkez Mall, Nisbetiye Cad, Etiler ☎0212/282 0215, ⓦwww.matras.com.tr. Everything in leather from this quality Turkish shop, including wallets, handbags, belts and briefcases. Mon–Sat 10am–8pm.

MUSIC AND MUSICAL INSTRUMENTS

Turkish **music** aside, you'll find a good general selection of world music, classical, pop and jazz in the music shops listed below and in the many outlets on İstiklal Caddesi and in the shopping malls. International CDs are often pricier than elsewhere in Europe, as there's no real discounting, but Turkish CDs are considerably cheaper. For **musical instruments**, traditional and otherwise, there's a myriad of instrument shops on and around Galipdede Caddesi (aka Music Alley), near the upper Tünel station in Beyoğlu. Many specialize in, or at least stock, top-quality home-produced cymbals (see box, p.112).

D & R Kanyon Mall ☎0212/353 0870, ⓦdr.com.tr. Chain that stocks a decent range of traditional and contemporary Turkish sounds, as well as foreign CDs, DVDs, computer accessories, books, magazines and games. There are other branches across the city; the branch on İstiklal Caddesi is a Biletix outlet (see box, p.195).

Dore Müzik Şahdeğirmeni Sok 3/B, just off Galipdede Cad, Tünel ☎0212/236 5713 ⓦdoremuzik.com.tr. One of several shops selling famed Turkish Zildjian cymbals (sadly now made in and imported from America), alongside various major drum brands and some traditional Turkish percussion items. Daily 10am–7pm.

Lale Plak Galipdede Cad 1, Tünel, Beyoğlu ☎0212/293 7739; map pp.120–121. A funky, old-style music shop, the best place for traditional Turkish music CDs but even more so for jazz. The staff know their stuff – aided, no doubt, by the continuity of a business that's been going for nigh on fifty years. Daily 9am–7pm.

Müzik Center Galipdede Cad 19, Tünel, Beyoğlu ☎0212/244 5885 ⓦistanbulmusic.net; map pp.120–121. This shop is one of many on a street jammed with musical instrument shops but stands out thanks to its wide range of Turkish folklore instruments. There's a mixture of cheaper beginner instruments and top-quality handmade items, all made in Turkey, plus some antique pieces on sale too. Music enthusiasts can purchase a *darbuka* (a goblet-shaped hand drum) for anywhere between 20TL and 600TL or a *bağlama* (a long-necked seven-string lute typically played with a plectrum) for upwards of 150TL and can then take part in one of the shop's many music workshops. Daily 9.30am–7pm.

SHOPPING MALLS

Although it's easy to view the US-style mall culture sweeping the city as a body blow to the traditional Turkish way of life, a mall is just a modern version of a bazaar.

Akaretler Şair Nadim Bey Cad 11, Akaretler, Beşiktaş; map p.132. Not a shopping mall, but a series of nineteenth-century houses once home to the workers at the nearby Dolmabahçe Palace, now given over to exclusive shops selling everything from luxury towels to international designer clothes by the likes of Jimmy Choo. It's near the trendy *W* hotel (see p.132) and makes an alternative to Nişantası for upmarket shopping opportunities. Daily 10am–7pm.

Akmerkez Nisbetiye Cad, Etiler ☎0212/282 0170. One of the first of the new Western-style shopping centres, with restaurants and a cinema, and shops carrying most top Turkish brands, plus quality European and American outlets. Daily 10am–10pm.

Cevahir Büyükdere Cad 22, Şişli ☎0212/380 0893, ⓦcevahir.com. With shops and food outlets spread over six storeys and a multiplex cinema, this was for several years the biggest mall in the city, and still very popular with İstanbullus. Daily 10am–10pm.

City's Mall Teşvikiye Cad 162, Nişantası ☎0212/373 3333, ⓦcitysnisantasi.com. An upmarket addition to the city's mall scene, well designed, with sleek Art Deco lines. It's exclusive and mainly fashion-orientated – think Louis

Vuitton, Dolce&Gabbana, Gaultier and the like. There's an attached luxury multi-screen cinema and a few posh places to eat. Daily 10am–10pm.

Demirören İstiklal Cad, Beyoğlu ⓦ demırorenistiklal .com; map pp.120–121. Opened to great fanfare in 2011 by Real Madrid and Portugal legend Cristiano Ronaldo, this controversial (İstiklal Caddesi is lined with historic buildings) mall is likely to be the most convenient for the majority of visitors, and includes a Vırgin Megastore, Mothercare and Gap among many other shops, as well as a cinema. Daily 10am–10pm.

Forum Paşa Cad, Bayrampaşa ⓣ 0212/443 1350, ⓦ forumistanbul.com. A fairly new mall, claiming to be Europe's biggest, As well as a host of shops it includes Turkuaz Zoo (see p.231) and a major multiplex cinema. Daily 10am–10pm.

Kanyon Büyükdere Cad 185, Levent ⓣ 0212/353 5300. An "open air" canyon-shaped, four-storey, state-of-the-art shopping mall featuring most popular Western consumer chains for clothes, food, gifts, etc, and an extremely plush cinema. Daily 10am–10pm.

Sports and activities

The most popular spectator sport in the country is football, and the heart of the game in Turkey is very much the metropolis of İstanbul and the city's so-called Big Three clubs – Beşiktaş, Fenerbahçe and Galatasaray – have massive support not only in İstanbul but throughout Anatolia. Basketball, a major component of the national sports curriculum in schools, is next favourite, its main league again dominated by teams from İstanbul. The majority of adult Turks confine their passion for sport to the passive act of watching football and basketball matches on TV, or gambling on the outcome of games.

Keeping fit is an alien concept for most in a city where most people simply work too long or just can't afford to regularly attend the gym. It's hardly surprising, then, that Turkey won only eight medals in the 2008 Olympics. One of those was for wrestling, and the traditional sport of **oil wrestling** remains popular – the place to see it is at the Kırkpınar Festival near Edirne (see p.271).

BASKETBALL

Basketball's roots in Turkey lie in prestigious Robert College, a school founded in İstanbul in 1863 by an American philanthropist and still going strong, with the first basketball game in Turkey being played there in 1904. The predominantly young and vociferous fan-base of the professional clubs still has its roots at high-school level, where the sport has great prominence and inter-school rivalry, fuelled by the usual pom-pom-girl-style razzamatazz, is fierce. Many club sides are affiliated with the big football teams, and this – combined with the sponsorship lifeblood of the sport here – throws up team names such as Beşiktaş Cola Turka and Galatasaray CafeCrown. Fenerbahçe–Ülker (a major confectionary manufacturer) won the sixteen-strong Turkish Basketball League (TBL) four out of five times between 2006 and 2011. The national team, known as the "12 Giant Men", finished second to the US in the 2010 FIBA World Championships, and ranked sixth in the FIBA world rankings the same year. A few Turkish players have transferred to the NBA, far more US players have come the other way, and many TBL teams have American, Russian and European players in their ranks. For further information on venues, matches and **tickets**, see ⓦtbf.org.tr or contact the clubs (see p.226). Tickets for many matches (10TL and up) are available from ⓦbiletix.com.

Beşiktaş Cola Turka BJK Akatlar Spor ve Kültür Kompleksi, Gazeteciler Sitesi, Beşiktaş ☎0212/283 6600, ⓦbjk.com.tr.
Fenerbahçe–Ülker Fenerbahçe Spor Külübü Tesisleri, Kızıltoprak ☎0216/347 8438, ⓦfenerbahce.org.
Galatasaray CafeCrown Metin Oktay Tesisleri, Florya ☎0212/574 2901, ⓦgalatasaray.org.

FOOTBALL

One of the whipping boys of **international football** in the 1980s, today Turkey is a side to be taken very seriously. In 2002 they reached the semifinals of the World Cup and in 2008 they reached the semifinals of the 2008 European Championship, though they failed to qualify for the 2010 World Cup. Several Turkish players now play in the best leagues in the world, notably Hamit Altıntop and Nuri Şahin for Real Madrid. When in İstanbul, the national team usually play in one of the Big Three's stadiums (see p.226). The **domestic league** is dominated by İstanbul's **Beşiktaş**, **Fenerbahçe** and **Galatasaray**, but teams from Anatolia have begun to challenge their metropolitan rivals, with Bursaspor (from the city of Bursa; see p.240) winning the title in 2010. The season runs from August to May, with a winter break from mid-December to mid-January. Despite supporters' fanaticism, only the derby matches sell out quickly, and tickets for other games are usually easy to come by. Televised league matches, invariably featuring one of the Big Three, take place on

---

A SPOT OF BOTHER

Turkish fans may be able to put their differences aside to give the national teams passionate and undivided support, but **inter-club rivalry** between the İstanbul clubs, whether it be basketball or football, is intense. In the play-off finals, the thrilling series of games that decide which basketball team will be league champion, away fans are banned to avoid trouble.

Football is much worse, and every week in the season sees incidents somewhere in the country. Opposition supporters' coaches are regularly pelted with stones, seats ripped-up and objects thrown onto the pitch. In May 2011, a match between Bursaspor (around İstanbul chapter) and Beşiktaş was cancelled because of rioting before the game. Violence took racist overtones in 2010 when some Bursaspor fans taunted Diyarbakırspor (from the predominantly Kurdish southeast of the country) supporters with Turkish nationalist chants and threw plastic seats and other objects at them. The return match in Diyarbakır was abandoned after the home fans attempted to wreak revenge.

More optimistically, in 2011 the Turkish Football Federation ruled that clubs, often condemned to play in front of an empty stadium as a punishment for the unruly behaviour of their fans, would be permitted to let in under-12s and women only, free of charge. Fanatical Fenerbahçe supporters seized on this unexpected offer with relish, and more than 41,000 women and kids roared on their favourites (to a disappointing draw with lowly Manisaspor).

18

Friday, Saturday and Sunday evenings. The celebrations following derby match or national team victories are a sight to behold, with carloads of cheering fans hanging out of windows, waving flags and blaring horns. **Tickets** for most major matches can be purchased from Biletix (⌨biletix.com) or from the ground on match day; remember that ticket prices increase substantially for derby and other big games; expect to pay upwards of 25TL.

Beşiktaş İnönü Stadium, Dolmabahçe Cad, Beşiktaş ☎0212/236 7202, ⌨bjk.com.tr. The İnönü Stadium is the most attractive and convenient of the city's stadiums, seating up to 32,000 and set into the hillside just above the Bosphorus, near the Dolmabahçe Palace. Beşiktaş, known as the Kara Kartal or Black Eagles, traditionally play in black-and-white-striped kit. They have a more working-class image than their rivals and are the least successful, with twelve domestic titles to their credit, the last one in 2009, and an appalling record in Europe. Constant changes of manager have not helped their cause, but in Çarşı, the supporters' organization, known for its leftist and anti-authoritarian leanings, they have the most effective and politicized fan group in the city. According to Beşiktaş fans, "*gerçek adam renkli takım tutmaz*" or "real men don't support teams playing in coloured strips" – a reference to the red and yellow of Galatasaray and the blue and yellow of Fenerbahçe.

Fenerbahçe Şükrü Saraçoğlu Stadium, Kadıköy ☎0216/449 5667, ⌨fenerbahce.org. The wealthiest club side in the country, nicknamed the *Sarı Kanarya* or Yellow Canaries, Fenerbahçe reached the quarter finals of the 2008 Champions League under the stewardship of Brazilian legend Zico, despite losing out on the domestic title to arch rivals Galatasaray. Their stadium is by far the largest (52,000 capacity) and best appointed in the city, set in a valley some twenty minutes' walk behind the waterfront in Kadıköy, in Asian İstanbul. Despite the club's origins in the district's expat (mainly British) and Christian minorities at the start of the twentieth century, it was the favourite of the nationalist Atatürk. Today's big-name supporters include Nobel Prize-winning author Orhan Pamuk.

Galatasaray Türkcell Arena Stadium, Aslantepe ☎0212/305 1925, ⌨www.galatasaray.org. Despite winning the league title in 2008 and achieving Turkey's only international success at club level by lifting the UEFA cup in 2000, Galatasaray's star has been somewhat eclipsed of late by Fenerbahçe. Known as *Aslan* (lion) *Cimbom* (why is a mystery, as *Cimbom* has no meaning in Turkish), Galatasaray was formed by a group of Muslim students from Beyoğlu's Galatasaray Lycée in 1905. In seemingly perpetual financial turmoil, they moved to the cavernous Atatürk Olympic Stadium for the 2003/4 season, then back to the Ali Sami Yen, but since 2010 have settled in the purpose-built Turk Telekom Arena, a 53,000-seat stadium in Şişli. Previous managers have included Graeme Souness (who caused an uproar when he planted a Galatasary banner in the centre circle of Fenerbahçe's pitch following a cup-final victory there in 1996), George Haji and Frank Rijkaard.

SWIMMING POOLS AND GYMS

Few Turks swim either seriously or well, which is hardly surprising given the paucity of public pools nationwide, even in booming İstanbul. The Bosphorus is both polluted and notorious for its treacherous currents, though that doesn't stop the annual cross-Bosphorus swim held each July, usually with eight-hundred or so participants. For safer, cleaner seas, head out to the Princes' Islands (see pp.158–165) or the Black Sea resorts (see p.156). A number of sports clubs and universities do have pools, but the hassle of reaching them, getting a pass (one requires proof of Hepatitis B and C injections) and paying the exorbitant fee makes them hardly worth considering unless you're training for the Olympics. This leaves the pools of the big hotels (or Park Orman; see p.231) as the only rational option. Most of the luxury hotels have attached **gyms** or fitness-suites, and if you can't keep away from an exercise-bike or weights machine then you should consider a day-pass.

Ceylan Intercontinental Asker Ocağı Cad 1, Taksim ☎0212/368 4444, ⌨istanbul.intercontinental.com.tr; map p.127. Has the great advantage of being centrally located in Taksim, with a large, heated outdoor pool and pool bar. Mon–Fri 80TL, Sat & Sun 130TL. Daily 7am–8pm.

Cırağan Palace Hotel Kempinski Cırağan Cad 32, Beşiktaş ☎0212/326 4646, ⌨kempinski.com; map p.132. Indoor and outdoor pools in one of the city's most expensive hotels. The outdoor one is right on the Bosphorus, so you can watch the tankers glide past as you do lengths. Mon–Fri €100, Sat & Sun €160. Daily 7am–11pm.

Hillside City Club İstinye Park Mall, İstinye ☎0212/276 2297; bus #40/B from Beşiktaş.

Better-value than most places, this sports club has a steep 50TL entrance fee on weekdays, and 85TL at weekends. Good pool, terrace and café. Mon–Fri 7am–11pm, Sat & Sun 8am–9.30pm.

Hilton İstanbul Cumhuriyet Cad, Harbiye ☎0212/315 6000. Big, curvaceous outdoor pool with decent café-bar attached, plus an indoor pool. Entry includes use of the fitness centre. Mon–Fri 80TL, Sat & Sun 130TL. Daily 8am–6pm.

The Marmara Taksim Taksim Square ☎0212/334 8300, ⌨themarmara.com; map p.127. Conveniently located right on Taksim Square and better value than most of the big hotel pools, with great poolside views of the city. Mon–Fri 60TL, Sat & Sun 75TL. Daily 7am–7pm.

RUNNING

An increasing minority of İstanbullus have taken to **running**, though the crowded and often semi-obstructed pavements, horrendous traffic and consequent pollution, plus legions of bemused passers-by are just some of the obstacles. Best bet if you are staying in Sultanahmet is the concrete **promenade** running along the shores of the Sea of Marmara, though it's tough on the feet. Better are **Yıldız** or **Emirgan** parks (see p.134 & p.150) but dedicated, need-a-fix runners should head out to the **Belgrade Forest** (see p.153), where there's a 6.5km dedicated trail, or even the motorized traffic-free **Princes' Islands** (see p.158) for a 14km jog around the biggest island, Büyükada. By far the best time to run in the city is early on a Sunday, with the streets much quieter than at any other time in the week. For really serious runners the **International Eurasia Marathon** (🕸 istanbulmarathon.org) gives entrants the opportunity to run from Asia to Europe, and there are shorter alternatives and a fun-run for the less committed. It's held every October and gives the ninety-thousand or so competitors the unique chance to cross the Bosphorus Bridge on foot. The **Maltepe Coastal Road Race** (🕸 maltepe.edu.tr), also held in October, is open to all-comers.

18

CYCLING

Things are difficult for would-be **cyclists**, as the traffic is dense, ill-disciplined and sees cyclists as annoyances to be forced out of the way. The only time you'll see serious local cyclists braving the roads is on a Sunday. There's a waterfront cycle lane in Kadıköy, otherwise any of the Princes' Islands makes a very appealing cycling destination (see p.158).

HAMAMS

The **hamam** (Turkish bath) once played a pivotal role in hygiene, social discourse and religious life (they were usually part of a mosque complex, and cleanliness is part and parcel of Islam) in Turkey, but as the standard of living has increased, its importance (and the number of establishments) has drastically declined. As an exercise in nostalgia, however, it's well worth visiting one, particularly as the historic *hamams* of İstanbul, Bursa and Edirne are architectural gems. Lounging around on warm marble slabs, your fellow bathers lost in the steam and light streaming in from tiny bottle-glass windows set in an ancient dome, is an experience few people can resist. The historic *hamams* of the old city promote themselves remorselessly, and their brochures decorate the foyers of most İstanbul pensions and hotels. If you're out wandering and fancy an impromptu session in one of the smaller, neighbourhood baths, they are usually signposted – if in doubt look for the distinctive roof domes. Some are very run down, though the Turkish for "cockroach" ("*hamam böceği*" or "*hamam bug*") more likely comes from the roaches' love of humid, rather than dirty, places.

Ayasofya Hürrem Sultan Hamamı Bab ı Humayan Cad 1, Sultanahmet ☎ 0212/517 3535, 🕸 ayasofya hurremsultanhamam.com; map p.44. The Rolls Royce of the city's *hamam* scene, which opened in 2011 following years of restoration. Built by Mimar Sinan in 1556, it replaced the Byzantine baths of Zeuxippus on the same site and was named in honour of Süleyman's wife, Roxelana (known as Haseki Hürrem to Turks). The building is exquisite, with most of the original features having been preserved – even the marble squat toilets. There are separate mens and women's sections and all staff are highly trained masseurs. It's expensive, but considering the building's historical significance and the quality of service this is to be expected. Bath packages from €86 to €180. Daily 7am–midnight.

Çağaloğlu Hamamı Prof Kazim İsmail Gürkhan Cad 34, Çağaloğlu ☎ 0212/522 2424, 🕸 cagalogluhamami .com.tr. The most popular baths this side of town, famous for their beautiful *hararets* (steam rooms) – open cruciform chambers with windowed domes supported on a circle of columns. The baths were built in 1741 by Mahmut I to pay for the upkeep of his library in Aya Sofya, and the arches, basins and taps of the hot room, as well as the entries to the private cubicles, are all magnificently Baroque. Florence

Nightingale is said to have bathed here and the *hamam* has appeared in several movies, including *Indiana Jones and the Temple of Doom*. 69TL for self-service bath, 80TL including scrub, 115TL scrub and massage. Daily 8am–10pm.

Çemberlitaş Vezirhan Cad 8, Çemberlitaş ☎ 0212/522 7974, 🕸 cemberlitashamami.com.tr. Across Vezirhanı Caddesi from the Çemberlitaş Column is the celebrated four-hundred-year-old Çemberlitaş Hamamı, founded in the sixteenth century by Nur Banu, one of the most powerful of the valide sultans. Its central location means that the masseurs are well used to foreigners, making it a good, if expensive, place to be initiated into the rites of the Turkish bath. 39TL; 59TL with scrub. Daily 6am–midnight.

Çinili Hamamı Çavuşdere Cad 204, Üsküdar ☎ 0216/553 1593. Set in the Asian suburb of Üsküdar (see pp.143–145) this is one of the best-value *hamams* in the city. It's clean, set in a historic domed building dating back to 1684 and is about as authentic an experience as you can get, with few foreign visitors having either the determination to get here or to cope with the non-English-speaking staff. 14TL for self-service bath, massage 5TL, scrub 5TL. Daily: men 6am–10pm; women 8am–8pm.

18

HAMAM PRACTICALITIES

Hamams are usually either for men or women, or sexually **segregated** on a schedule, with women usually allotted more restricted hours, though a few offer mixed-sex bathing. Bring soap and shampoo or buy it in the foyer (most tourist-frequented *hamams* have a shop and café). Men are supplied with a *peştemal*, a thin, wraparound sarong, women generally enter in knickers but not bra; both sexes get *takunya*, awkward wooden clogs (or more prosaic plastic slippers), and later a *havlu* (towel). Leave your clothes in the changing cubicle (*camekan* in Turkish), where there are generally lockers for valuables.

The *hararet* or **main bath chamber** ranges from plain to ornate, though any decent *hamam* will be marble-clad at least up to chest height. Two or more *halvets*, semi-private corner rooms with two or three *kurnas* (basins) each, lead off from the main chamber. The internal temperature varies from tryingly hot to barely lukewarm, depending on how well run the baths are. Unless with a friend, it's one customer to a set of taps and basin; refrain from making a big soapy mess in the basin, which is meant for mixing pure water to ideal temperature. Use the scoop-dishes provided to sluice yourself. It's considered good etiquette to clean your marble slab with a few scoopfuls of water before leaving.

At the heart of the *hamam* is the *göbek taşı* or "navel stone", a raised platform positioned over the furnaces that heat the premises. The *göbek taşı* will be piping hot and covered with prostrate figures absorbing the heat. It's also the venue for the (very) vigorous **massages** from the *tellak* or masseur. A *kese* (abrasive mitt) session from the same person, in which dead skin and grime are scrubbed away, will probably suit more people. Terms for the *tellaks'* services should be displayed in the foyer. Few *hamams* have a female masseur, so women visitors may want to think very carefully before accepting a massage from a male masseur – though many do.

Rates vary enormously depending on the location, history and architectural merit of the *hamam*, with those in the historic old city generally far dearer than those in outlying districts. Scrubs and massages cost extra, so make sure you know what you'll be paying in advance.

Galatasaray Hamamı Turnacıbaşı Sok 24, Beyoğlu ☎0212/249 4342 (women's section), ☎0212/252 4242 (men's section), ⓦgalatasarayhamami.com; map pp.120–121. The most user-friendly and historic (it dates back to 1481) *hamam* in Beyoğlu, conveniently situated just off İstiklal Caddesi. At 50TL for a self-service bath, 95TL including scrub and massage, it's not cheap and the men's section is far more impressive than the female, which only opened in 1963. Daily: men 7am–10pm; women 8.30am–8pm.

Gedikpaşa Hamamı Hamam Cad 61, Gedikpaşa ☎0212/517 8956, ⓦgedikpasahamami.com. A couple of hundred metres below Ordu Caddesi, the Gedikpaşa Hamamı was built in 1475 and is looking a little frayed round the edges but is a fine Ottoman bath-house, with a big white dome punctured by the usual, tiny bottle-glass windows that allow the light (on a sunny day) to come streaming in. The entrance is on Emin Sinan Hamamı Sokak. 55TL with massage and scrub. Daily: men 6am–midnight; women 9am–11pm.

★ **Süleymaniye Hamamı** Mimar Sinan Cad 20 ☎0212/519 5569, ⓦsuleymaniyehamami.com. Built by Sinan in 1557, legend has it that the great architect took all his baths here from 1557 to 1588, but today it doesn't accept single males or females, only couples and families, and the bathing is mixed sex. It has been beautifully restored and is atmospherically located near the incomparable mosque of the same name. Good value: €35 for bath, scrub and massage. Daily 10am–midnight, last entry 10pm.

MINIATÜRK MINIATURE PARK

Kids' İstanbul

Turks adore children in an uninhibited, Mediterranean manner and younger kids may sometimes receive rather more attention than either they or their parents expect, especially if they are blonde. It's common practice to pinch chubby kiddie cheeks as a sign of affection, an act often accompanied by the word *maşallah*, which serves both to praise your offspring and ward off the evil eye. Turkish families tend to take their children with them wherever they go and think nothing of letting them run around restaurants until the early hours. In this sense, İstanbul is a great place to visit with kids. Another bonus is that children under 6 travel free on city transport.

On the downside, being dragged around the Aya Sofya and Topkapı Palace for hours on end is unlikely to appeal to many children, and the sheer number of bodies rushing through areas such as the Eminönü waterfront, İstiklal Caddesi or the Grand Bazaar may intimidate some. So, be prepared to take a break from the city-centre hassle, from time to time. Gülhane Parkı in Sultanahmet (see p.55) is a handy, wide-open space for kids to run off some steam and there are more and better parks out by the Bosphorus. Alternatively, take a boat trip up the strait, across to Asia or out to the Princes' Islands (see p.158), or visit one of the handful of child-orientated venues scattered around the city and its environs. A ride on either the modern tram or the period tram rattling along İstiklal Caddesi is fun, and the underground Tünel funicular is also fascinating for kids, as is the cable car from the Golden Horn up to the *Pierre Loti* café in Eyüp (see p.195).

Turkish **food** is sure to appeal to all children – *köfte* is just a tasty type of burger, *pide* a pizza without the tomato paste, and *gözleme* a stuffed pancake – and there are plenty of familiar fast-food outlets dotted around the city. *Maraş* ice cream is just as delicious as Italian *gelato* and comes in myriad flavours, and Turkish chocolate is as good as anywhere else. In general, restaurants are relaxed and very welcoming to families – just don't expect highchairs or changing facilities in the toilets.

Toys sold in markets and cheaper stores (largely Far East imports) tend to be more expensive than the same thing would be back home. Nappies are widely available from all the supermarkets, most *eczane* (chemists) and many *bakkals* (general stores), and there are Mothercare branches at various locations across the city.

MUSEUMS, ATTRACTIONS AND GALLERIES

Archeology Museum (see p.56). Has a small area devoted to youngsters, with a miniature wooden horse of Troy and replica Neolithic dwellings among other stuff on show, though this was under reorganization at the time of writing. In any case, kids are just as likely to be enthralled by the museum's wonderful sarcophagi.

İstanbul Modern (see p.114). Runs summer programmes (for kids aged 4–13).

Military Museum (see p.126). Tanks, Ottoman-era weaponry and colourful dioramas will appeal to many children.

Miniatürk (see p.116). Bound to engage interest with its one-hundred plus pint-sized models of some of İstanbul's (and Turkey's) most impressive monuments and sights, from Atatürk International airport to the Aya Sofya.

Panorama 1453 Museum (see p.104). Built in sight of the walls besieged in 1453, this museum gives a stunning 360-degree artist's impression of the action.

Rahmi M. Koç Industrial Museum (see p.116). Far more to keep them entertained than, for instance, the Archeology Museum, with a submarine moored in the Golden Horn to explore, a cute railway station and length of track, a cornucopia of vintage cars, motorbikes and planes, plus regular special exhibitions and events aimed specifically at children.

Sakıp Sabancı Museum (see p.150). Usually has a child-friendly art/design workshop running alongside its latest exhibition.

Santralistanbul Energy Museum (see p.117). Allows kids to ride an electricity-producing bike, see the world through a snake's eyes and watch lightning bolts in a plasma globe. There are also summer art-based workshops here – though they're in Turkish.

Toy Museum (see p.141). Though inconveniently located out in Göztepe, this is as much for adults as kids, with its collection of toys, dolls and the like dating back to the nineteenth century. There are special activities at weekends, including a puppet show.

PARKS

To escape the urban hurly-burly, head for one of the city's parks – although providing little in the way of play equipment, there are normally plenty of grassy areas, trees for shade and, in the first three listed below, fabulous views down over the Bosphorus.

Emirgan Parkı Emirgan (see p.150). Combined with a trip to the Sakip Sabancı Museum (see p.150) and lunch at *Sütis* or one of the cafés in the park, this park in the posh Bosphorus suburb of Emirgan makes a great day's outing with kids. There's some decent play equipment for little ones, a delightful ornamental lake complete with waterfall and ducks, and the late-Ottoman wooden pavilions are like something out of *Heidi*. Daily 9am–6pm.

Gülhane Parkı Sirkeci (see pp.55–59). The opening hours of this park are not set in stone, so if there's no one else around you may be turfed-out earlier. There's a meagre amount of play equipment, but plenty of space to run around, and a nice tea-garden, the *Set Üstü* (see p.179) for snacks. Summer 7am–11pm, winter 9am–dusk.

Hıdıv Kısri Kanlıca (see p.154). The grounds of this gorgeous Art Nouveau(ish) villa are more compact than either Yıldız or Emirgan, but have the advantage of being on the Bosphorus Cruise (see p.147), meaning you can enjoy a boat journey up the river, then hop off and taxi-it or walk the short way up the wooded hillside, where the kids can enjoy the open space while you relax in the outdoor café and admire the stunning views. Daily 9am–11pm.

Park Orman Büyükdere Cad, Maslak ☎0212/328 2000. Large park with an impressive outdoor pool (mid-June to mid-Sept; Mon–Fri 35TL, Sat & Sun 50TL; under-12s free), and plenty of picnic areas, woodland trails and open spaces for wandering around in – plus an ice rink and restaurants. Take the #25/T bus from Taksim Square. Daily 9am–7pm.

Yıldız Parkı Çırağan Cad, Beşiktaş (see p.134). A lovely landscaped park full of mature trees for shade on hot summer days. There's a paltry amount of play equipment (for younger kids only), but it's a great place to run around in. There's a café or two, fine Bosphorus views, and the guided tour of the opulent Şale Köşkü is not too demanding for older kids. The park is set on a steep slope, so if you're pushing a buggy: beware. Summer 9am–6pm, winter 9am–5.30pm.

ACTIVITIES

Most children find boat rides across the Bosphorus (see box, p.147) as entertaining as the places listed below.

Aqua Club Dolphin Cemal Paşa Cad, Su Oyunları Merkezi, Bahçeşehir ☎0212/672 6161, ⓦwww .aquaclubdolphin.com. Impressive waterpark with all the usual slides, twister bowls and float rides in well-landscaped gardens, plus dolphin shows. Free shuttle buses depart from outside the Atatürk Kültür Merkezi on Taksim Square between 8.30am and 9.30am; alternatively, take bus #76/D or #76/E from Taksim. Mon–Fri 40TL, Sat & Sun 45TL, 8–12s half-price, under-7s free. May to mid-Sept 9am–6pm.

Bab Bowling Yeşilcam Sok 24, off İstiklal Cad, Beyoğlu ☎0212/251 1595, ⓦwww.babbowling.com.tr; map pp.120–121. For older kids, this conveniently situated café has a six-lane bowling alley and an (overpriced) fast-food café. Daily 10am–midnight.

Faruk Yalçın Zoo Tuzla Cad 15, Bayramoğlu, Darica, Gebze ☎0262/653 6666, ⓦwww.farukyalcinzoo.com .tr. A long way out of town on the Asian side of the city near Gebze, and you really need your own transport to get here. This park is beautifully landscaped and has over three thousand species on show, including lions, lemurs and zebras, plus some colourful birdlife. Adults 15TL, children 5–17 10TL, under-4s free. Daily 9am–5pm.

Turkuazoo Forum Mall, Paşa Caddesi, Bayrampaşa ☎0212/443 1350, ⓦforumistanbul.com.tr. Turkey's first giant aquarium has all the usual aquatic draws, from piranhas and sharks to stingrays and reef fish, drifting around in 29 tanks and an 80m-long acrylic tunnel. Set in Europe's largest mall (see p.222), so there's lots more to do here, including the ten-screen cinema. To get here, take Metro 1 to Kocatepe. Adults 25TL, children 2–16 18TL. Mon–Fri 10am–6pm, Sat & Sun 10am–8pm.

Galleria Büyükdere Cad 185, Ataköy ☎0212/559 9560, ⓦwww.galleriabowling.com. With a skating rink, ten-pin bowling alley and cinema, this now-venerable mall should provide a distraction for bored kids. To get here, take #71T or #72T bus from Taksim Square. Daily 10am–10pm.

Rainforest Café İstinyepark Mall, İstinye Bayırı Cad, İstinye ☎0212/345 6262, ⓦwww.rainforestcafe.com. Popular, jungle-themed restaurant that organizes kids' parties, has entertainment and diversions such as robot crocodiles, and serves up child-friendly meals. To get here, take bus #40 from Taksim Square. Daily 10am–9pm.

Sapphire Büyükdere Cad, Levent; Metro 4, Levent. This graceful, award-winning 261-metre-high tower, completed in 2011, claims to be the tallest building in Europe. The views from the top are stunning on a clear day. 15TL. Daily 10am–11pm.

DAY-TRIPS

Black Sea resorts A trip to Kiliyos or Şile (see p.156 & p.157) is another possibility, though it entails a long bus journey (up to 2hr each way depending on traffic) and there are dangerous currents; the beaches are fine, if very crowded in midsummer.

Bosphorus Cruises Most kids like boats and the Bosphorus Cruises (see p.147) are great fun and reasonable value. There are two impressive suspension bridges to cruise under, a medley of seaborne traffic of all shapes and sizes to gawp at, and an endless stream of vendors with refreshments ranging from fresh orange juice to yoghurt dusted with icing sugar.

Princes' Islands A trip to these islands in the Sea of Marmara (see p.158) provides a welcome break from the heat of the city. Best bet is probably Büyükada, where you can take a ride in a horse-drawn carriage, hire a bike or splash about in the sea from one of the (mainly) pay beaches. Bear in mind that both these trips can get very crowded, especially at weekends, so get there early to bag seats for everyone.

19

AYA SOFYA MUSEUM

İznik and Termal

The laidback lake-side retreat of İznik, set in a beautiful rural setting of rich agricultural land and forested hills, is easily reached from İstanbul by high-speed ferry across the Sea of Marmara, followed by an hour's bus ride southeast. Known as Nicaea in ancient times, it once played a key role in the development of Christianity and is still encircled by impressive city walls. Long on history and short on crowds, it makes a great introduction to rural Turkey. Even closer to İstanbul lies the delightful thermal-spa resort aptly known as Termal, oozing fin-de-siècle charm amid the lush, wooded hills surrounding it.

İznik

It's hard to believe that **İZNİK**, a somnolent farming community at the east end of the lake of the same name, was once the seat of empires and scene of desperate battles. But looking around the fertile olive-mantled valley, you can understand its attraction for imperial powers needing a fortified base near the sea-lanes of the Marmara. Today, İznik is a backwater, slumbering away among its orchards, with tourism playing a distinct second fiddle to agriculture. The town's famous sixteenth-century ceramics, the best ever produced in Turkey, are now all but absent from İznik's museums and mosques, but the art has been revived and numerous shops specializing in İznik pottery dot the town's streets. It's possible to visit İznik as a long day-trip from İstanbul and have sufficient time to sample its monuments, but you'd be rushed and would end up seeing the sites (in summer at least) in the heat and glare of the midday sun. Worse, you'd have no time to absorb the atmosphere of this out-of-the-way place, which is as far removed from the big city as you can imagine. The lake itself, backed by low, wooded mountains, is quite beautiful, with reed-fringed shores and snow-white egrets fishing in the shallows.

With its grid-plan streets, İznik is easy to navigate. The main north–south boulevard **Atatürk Caddesi** and its east–west counterpart **Kılıçaslan Caddesi** link four of the seven ancient gates, dividing the town into unequal quadrants. Only enthusiasts will want to walk the entire perimeter of the double **walls**, now missing most of their hundred original watchtowers, but three of the seven portals are worth some time. Heavy traffic has been rerouted through modern breaches in the fortifications to prevent vibration damage to the original openings, now restricted to tractors and pedestrians.

The **lake** is swimmable in summer, but the town beaches are scrappy, and weed, algae and litter can foul the lake edges; you really need a car to reach the more attractive spots. Both roads out of town along the lakeshore stay close to the water and offer swimming possibilities at various tiny beaches along the way.

Some history

Founded by Alexander the Great's general Antigonus in 316 BC, the city was seized and enlarged fifteen years later by his rival Lysimachus, who named it **Nicaea** after his late wife. He also gave Nicaea its first set of walls and the grid plan typical of Hellenistic towns; both are still evident. When the Bithynian kingdom succeeded Lysimachus, Nicaea alternated with nearby Nicomedia (modern İzmit) as its capital until bequeathed to Rome in 74 BC. Under the Roman emperors, the city prospered as capital of the province, and it continued to flourish during the Byzantine era.

Nicaea played a pivotal role in early Christianity, by virtue of hosting two important **ecumenical councils**. The first, convened by Constantine the Great in 325 AD, resulted

20

THE FIRST COUNCIL OF NICAEA – A DEFINING MOMENT IN CHRISTIANITY

In 325 AD, when Christianity was still very much in its infancy, the Emperor Constantine invited bishops from all over the empire to his lake-side palace in Nicaea to discuss the hot topic of the day – the **nature of Christ**. Was he, as the followers of the presbyter Arius of Alexandria were claiming, of "like nature" but basically made of lesser stuff than God? Or was he, as a majority of believers thought, divine? This was not just some arcane theological question; it was a controversy threatening the very fabric of the empire. Across the Near East, rabble-rousing rival bishops were spouting forth their rhetoric, their followers scrawling pro- or anti-Arian graffiti on city walls and inflamed mobs of both persuasions were rioting in the streets.

At Nicaea, Constantine managed to persuade a majority of the bishops present to vote for his compromise solution, which was that God and Christ were "consubstantial" (ie Christ was both divine and human). Christ (the Son) was now officially accepted as divine and a co-equal part of the Holy Trinity, along with the Father and the Holy Spirit. The **Nicaean Creed**, as it became known, is still central to Christian belief today.

in the condemnation of the Arian heresy (see box, p.233). The seventh council (the second to be held here) was presided over by Empress Irene in 787 AD; this time, the Iconoclast controversy was settled by the pronouncement, widely misunderstood in the West, that icons had their proper place in the church so long as they were revered and not worshipped.

Nicaea's much-repaired walls seldom repelled invaders, and in 1081 the Selçuks took the city, only to be evicted by a combined force of Byzantines and Crusaders sixteen years later. The fall of Constantinople to the Fourth Crusade in 1204 propelled Nicaea into the spotlight once more, when the Byzantine heir Theodore Lascaris retreated here and made this the base of the improbably successful **Nicaean Empire**. The Lascarid dynasty added a second circuit of walls before returning to Constantinople in 1261, but these again failed to deter the besieging Ottomans, who, led by Orhan Gazi, the victor of Bursa, broke through in March 1331.

Renamed İznik, the city embarked on a golden age of sorts, interrupted briefly by the pillaging of the Mongol warlord Tamerlane in 1402. Virtually all of the surviving monuments predate the Mongol sacking, but the most enduring contribution to art and architecture – the celebrated **İznik tiles and pottery** – first appeared during the reign of Çelebi Mehmet I, who brought skilled potters from Persia to begin the local industry. This received another boost in 1514 when Selim the Grim took Tabriz and sent more craftsmen west as war booty; by the end of the sixteenth century, ceramic production in İznik was at its height, with more than three hundred functioning kilns. It was to be a brief flowering, since within another hundred years war and politics had scattered most of the artisans. By the mid-eighteenth century, the local industry had packed up completely, with products from nearby Kütahya serving as inferior substitutes. İznik began a long, steady decline, hastened by near-total devastation during the War of Independence.

The southeast quadrant

The town's southeast quadrant is home to a number of interesting buildings. Chief among these is the **Süleyman Paşa Medresesi** on Gündem Caddesi. Built in 1332, it is the oldest such Ottoman structure in Turkey and the first example of a school with an open courtyard surrounded by eleven chambers and nineteen domes. Three blocks south of the *medresesi* is the fourteenth-century **Yakub Çelebi Zaviyesi** on Yakup Sokak, founded by the luckless prince slain by his brother Beyazit I at Kosovo in 1389. A block to the east, nothing but foundations remain of the **Kimisis Kilisesi** (Church of the Assumption), the presumed burial place of Theodore Lascaris, which was destroyed in 1922.

Aya Sofya Müzesi

Atatürk Caddesi • Tues–Sun 8.30am–noon & 1–5pm • 7TL

The **Aya Sofya Müzesi**, housed in the heavily restored Byzantine Church of Holy Wisdom, founded by Justinian, is today set in pleasant gardens full of white and pink blooming oleander and palms. The current structure was built after an earthquake in 1065 and, as the cathedral of the provisional Byzantine capital, hosted the coronations of the four Nicaean emperors. The Ottomans converted it to a mosque directly on taking the city and Mimar Sinan (see box, p.80) restored it, but the premises were already half-ruined when reduced to their present sorry condition following the War of Independence. There is little to see inside bar an impressive synthronon (the semicircular tier of seating for clergy) in the apse, some fragments of mosaic flooring, and a faint **fresco** of Christ, John and Mary, at ground level behind a glass panel to the left as you enter.

İznik Vakıf

Halı Saha Arkası • Daily: Sept–June 8am–6pm; July & Aug 6–11am • Free • ☎ 0224/757 6025, ⓦ iznik.com

The **İznik Vakıf**, or İznik Foundation, clearly signposted in the southwest quadrant, was established in 1995 with the dual intentions of researching the early techniques used to produce İznik tiles and restarting production using traditional methods. Today, tiles of

IZNIK TILES TODAY

The best tiles made in İznik today, both at the İznik Vakıf and various other workshops around town, are composed primarily of locally quarried, finely ground quartz. This gives them good acoustic properties, making them especially suitable for use in mosques.

The tiles, beautiful and expensive, are redolent of the Golden Age of the Ottoman Turks imperial past, and as such are much sought after to adorn high-profile Turkish company headquarters. In İstanbul you can see them decorating the stations on the Metro line from Taksim to Levant and in the newly refurbished Tünel, and at the new terminal buildings of Atatürk International Airport. They are also on display in the Montréal Peace Park in Canada.

extremely high quality are manufactured and sold on site, though prices are high, and exact replicas of original designs are not reproduced for fear of them being passed off as genuine. During a visit, you'll see different production stages and receive a brief history of the İznik *œuvre*.

IZNIK

N

İznik Gölü

Yeraltı Mezar, Termal, Yalova & İstanbul

İstanbul Kapısı

Walls

Topkapı

ATATÜRK CAD

HOXTAY SOK

Walls

GÖL SOK

ALAATTIN MISRI SOK

MEYDAN SOK

Nilüfer Hatun İmareti

SAHİLİ CAD

Tea Gardens

Hacı Özbek Camii

Şeyh Kubettin Camii

Yeşil Camii

Line of Aqueduct

Belediye

Police

KILIÇASLAN CAD

KILIÇASLAN CAD

Lefke Kapısı

Göl Kapısı (Ruined)

Aya Sofya

GÜNDEM SOK

@

Abdülvahap Hill

SELÇUK SOK

İkinci Murat Hamamı

Excavation of Kilns

Süleyman Paşa Medresesi

MAHMUT SOK

MALTEPE CAD

Roman Theatre

ÇELEBİ SOK

Kimisis Kilisesi

HALİ SALA ARKASI

Bus Station

YAKUP SOK

Walls

Saray Kapısı

Yakub Çelebi Zaviyesi

ATATÜRK CAD

İznik Vakfı

Horoz Kapısı

Yenişehir Kapısı

Bursa

0   200
metres

RESTAURANTS

Cumalıkızık Gözleme Evi	1
Çamlık Motel	4
Karadeniz Pide Salon	2
Köfteci Yusuf	3

ACCOMMODATION

Çamlık Motel	3
Cem Otel	1
İznik Vakfi Konukevi	4
Kaynarca Pansiyon	2

BARS

Artı	1
Muzo Hol	2

The northeast quadrant

Just north of Kılıçaslan Caddesi squats the **Hacı Özbek Camii**, the earliest known Ottoman mosque, built in 1333 but much adulterated. Further along the road you'll soon reach a vast landscaped park to the north, dotted with İznik's most famous monuments.

Yeşil Camii

Yeşil Camii Sokak

The **Yeşil Camii**, or Green Mosque, erected toward the end of the fourteenth century, is a small gem of a building, its highlight the fantastic marble relief on the portico. Tufted with a stubby minaret that harks back to Selçuk models, the mosque takes its name from the green İznik tiles that once adorned its minaret; they've long since been replaced by mediocre, tri-coloured Kütahya work.

İznik Museum and Nilüfer Hatun İmareti

Tues–Sun 9am–noon & 1.30–5pm • 3TL

The **İznik Museum** is housed in the **Nilüfer Hatun İmareti**, a T-form building that served originally as the meeting place of the Ahi brotherhood, a guild drawn from the ranks of skilled craftsmen that also acted as a community welfare and benevolent society. It was commissioned by Murat I in 1388 in honour of his mother, Nilüfer. Daughter of a Byzantine noble, Nilüfer Hatun was married off to Orhan Gazi to consolidate a Byzantine–Ottoman alliance. Her abilities as a ruler were soon recognized by Orhan, who appointed her regent during his frequent absences.

Although the museum houses painstakingly restored pieces of fourteenth-century İznik tiles, which were excavated from the town's kilns, they are all incomplete and there are few of the beautiful sixteenth-century mosque ornaments and massive plates that are commonplace in the museums of İstanbul and abroad. More interesting is an exhibition of **Selçuk tile fragments** found in the area around the Roman theatre and in local kilns. Whether these earlier tiles were produced locally or imported is uncertain, though some evidence suggests that İznik ware is in part descended from that of the Selçuk Turks. The museum also has a good selection of finds, dating back to 6000 BC, from excavations at a nearby *hüyük* (settlement mound) called Ilıpınar – including pottery, bone tools and a fine Bronze Age clay burial sarcophagus. There are plenty of Roman-era relics on display, including a bronze dancing Pan, some Byzantine gold jewellery and, standing out among the nondescript marble clutter, a sarcophagus in near-mint condition. The garden area boasts a couple of very impressive Roman-era sarcophagi, along with stelae, giant pithoi and Ottoman headstones complete with turbans or fezzes.

The walls and beyond

The eastern **Lefke Kapısı**, the closest gate to the Yedil Camii, is a three-ply affair including a triumphal arch dedicated to Hadrian between the two courses of walls. Just outside is a stretch of the ancient **aqueduct** that until recently supplied the town. It's possible to get up on the ramparts here for a stroll, as it is at the northerly **İstanbul Kapısı**, the best preserved of the gates, the outer part of which was constructed as a triumphal triple arch to celebrate the visit of the Roman Emperor Hadrian in 124. The inner gate is decorated by two stone-carved **masks**, probably taken from the nearby Roman theatre. The wall area to the east of this gate is packed with small workshops manufacturing wooden crates for the local fruit industry. Other traces of Roman Nicaea are evident in the southwestern quarter: a course of **ancient wall** delimits the so-called Senatus Court, extending from the surviving tower next to the **Saray Kapısı**. The sadly neglected, graffitied **theatre** lies just inside this gate, and has lost most of its seating, but on the exterior retaining wall of the seating area you'll find a slab carved with a round shield and sword – a gladiator symbol. The area between the town and the lake here is a mass of orchards, with olives, figs, apple, medlar, walnut and mulberry growing in profusion, along with cypress, linden and plane trees.

ARRIVAL AND DEPARTURE   IZNIK

By sea bus The best way to reach İznik from İstanbul is to take the sea bus from Yenikapı to Yalova (1hr 10min; 18TL), from where regular mini- and midi-buses run to İznik (1hr; 9TL).

By bus There's one daily bus to İstanbul, leaving the *otogar*

(bus station) in the southeast quadrant at 7.45am, arriving at first the Harem (see p.23) and then the Esenler (see p.22) terminals in İstanbul. If you're heading on to Bursa (see pp.240–252), minibuses depart from the *otogar* between 5.30am and 9pm.

INFORMATION

Tourist office On Kılıçaslan Caddesi, just east of the Aya Sofya, in the *belediye* (municipality) building. There's also

an information kiosk on Atatürk Caddesi, next to the Aya Sofya Museum, but it seems to function infrequently.

ACCOMMODATION

Rooms, singles in particular, are at a premium in İznik and reservations are recommended between mid-June and mid-September – especially at the weekends.

Çamlık Motel Sahili Cad 11 ❶ & ❷0224/757 1631. This spotless, well-run hotel has small but comfortable rooms with balconies overlooking the lake, and is surrounded on three sides by olive groves and mulberry trees; there's also an excellent attached restaurant (see below). **100TL**

★ **Cem Otel** Göl Sahili 34 ❶0224/757 1687, ⓦcemotel.com. Set back slightly from the foreshore, the *Cem* is a long-established and well-run place. Rooms are plain but soothingly toned, spotless and equipped with flat-screen TVs. Rear rooms make up for the lack of a lake view with baths, front rooms have showers. There's a handy roof-terrace and a decent attached restaurant (which doubles as the breakfast room) downstairs. **120TL**

İznik Vakıf Konukevi Sahil Yolu Sok 13 ❶0224/757 6025, ❸info@iznik.com. The guesthouse of the

foundation dedicated to reviving the town's tile-making heritage (see box, p.235) is, as you might expect, adorned with all manner of colourful, intricate wall decorations. The good-value rooms are gleaming white and very tasteful and comfortable – plus there's a lovely shady garden. Be warned, though, it fills up with groups of resident artists and students in the summer, so booking well in advance is essential. **80TL**

Kaynarca Pansiyon Gündem Sok 1 ❶0224/757 1753, ⓦkaynarca.s5.com. The most appealing midtown budget option, run by English-speaking Ali and his charming family, offering dorm beds as well as en-suite singles, doubles and triples – all rooms have satellite TV, though there's neither a/c nor fans. Breakfast (5TL) is served on the rooftop terrace, and there's a kitchen for guests' use. Dorm **25TL**, double **70TL**

EATING AND DRINKING

Eating by the lakeshore, where some of the restaurants are licensed, is particularly popular with visitors; it's worth trying grilled or fried *yayın*, the excellent local catfish. For snacks or dessert, there are plenty of tea gardens, cafés and ice-cream parlours overlooking the lake. The town centre has a number of decent places for an (unlicensed) meal.

Artı Göl Sahili Yolu. A lake-view bar with tables set out in a pleasant garden. Attracts a fairly young crowd, drawn by the cheap beer (4TL) and the chance to strum their guitars in the open air. Daily 11am–midnight.

Çamlık Motel Sahili Cad 11. The nicest of the waterside restaurants in a lovely shady setting, dishing up *meze* and kebabs, including their speciality fish kebab, for around 30TL a head with beer.

Cumalıkızık Gözleme Evi Kılıçaslan Caddesi. A low-key place with a garden out front rustling-up a decent breakfast spread of bread, olives, cheese, honey, jams and yoghurt for 7.50TL, *menemen* for 5TL and filling *gözleme* for 3TL. Daily 8am–7pm.

Karadeniz Pide Salon Kılıçaslan Cad. This tiny cafeteria set in a characterful 1930s building serves fresh and cheap

pides washed down with *ayran* – you can watch the food being pulled into shape in the kitchen at the back. Daily 9am–11pm.

★ **Köfteci Yusuf** İznik Lisesi Karşısı. Smart new glass palace of a place, with friendly black-and-orange-suited waiters, dishing up *köfte* as delicious as anywhere in the country. The large portions come accompanied by a spicy tomato dip and grilled pepper and tomato – all for 7TL. They do a range of kebabs and other grills as well. Daily 8am–11pm.

Muzo-Hol Balık Pazarı. A town-centre drinking den for cheap beer – and they'll send out for food. There's no outside tables so as not to offend İznik's more pious residents, but it's friendly and nicely done-out with pine cladding. Daily 11am–midnight.

20

DIRECTORY

Banks The banks and ATMs are on Atatürk Caddesi, close to the Aya Sofya.
Internet Next door to the *Kaynarca Pansiyon* on Gündem Sok.

Hamam Both men and women use the İkinci Murat Hamamı (daily: women 8am–2pm; men 4–10pm; 15TL) just southeast of İznik's central roundabout and the Aya Sofya Müzesi.

Termal

The famous hot springs at **TERMAL** are set in pleasantly forested hills 12km to the southwest of the scruffy port town of Yalova, on the southern shore of the Sea of Marmara, southeast of İstanbul. Taking the waters in the *fin-de-siècle* splendour of one of the bath-houses built around these springs at Kaplıcılar, a little higher up in the hills than Termal itself, perhaps after a stroll along some of the forest trails around them, is a real wind-down after the hectic pace of life in the city. Although visited by Byzantine and Roman emperors, Termal's springs only became fashionable again at the turn of the twentieth century, and most of the Ottoman buildings date from that era.

Atatürk Müzesi

Baltacı Çifliği • Tues–Sun 8.30am–noon & 1–5pm • 3TL

Atatürk had a house built in Termal, now open as **Atatürk Müzesi**. Designed in the modernist style by one of the leading architects of the new Republic (see p.275), Sedad Hakki Eldem, it was built in 1929 and took a mere 38 days to complete – in time to host the visiting Shah of Iran. The house is still furnished pretty much as it was in Atatürk's day and gives a real insight into the man and his times. The bedroom of his adopted daughter and the nation's first female pilot, Sabiha Gökçen, is kitted-out with typically curvaceous Art Deco furniture, while the RCA radio the great man sat glued to night after night is on display, as is a German-made piano and a sideboard hand-carved by a reminder of the pre-Republican era, Sultan Abdül Hamit. Atatürk visited the house each summer until his death in 1938.

20

Kurşunlu Hamamı

Daily 8am–11pm • 15TL

The biggest single draw in Kaplıcılar is the outdoor pool of the Art Nouveau **Kurşunlu Hamamı**, with its swirling roof and bits of Roman relief-carving set into the walls. Here you can wallow in the hot waters and admire the architecture and sun-dappled forest canopy around you. Water temperatures reach 65 degrees Celsius, so the best time to visit is in winter, when the hot water provides a haven from the seasonal chill. In summer, you'll find yourself jumping out to sunbathe in order to cool off. Several **hamams** here – popular for their beneficial effect on rheumatism and skin diseases – offer communal pools with separate compartments for tour groups.

ARRIVAL AND DEPARTURE   TERMAL

By bus and sea bus To reach Termal, take the sea bus (18TL) from İstanbul's Yenikapı terminal to Yalova, from where there are frequent dolmuşes from the bus station (adjacent to the ferry terminal) for the half-hour run up to Termal (2.50TL). The first sea bus departs Yenikapı at 8am, the last back leaves Yalova at 7.30pm, so a day-trip is very feasible. Don't make the mistake of getting off in the town of Termal, with its rash of pensions, hotels and basic eateries; instead, continue on to Kaplıcılar, where the major baths (including Kurşunlu) are located. There are also frequent buses from İznik to Yalova.

ACCOMMODATION

The spa resort is completely dominated by two luxury hotels, both owned by the *Yalova Termal Kapıcıları* hotel group. A cheaper alternative, *Dinana* (see opposite), can be found nearby in an idyllic location in the village of Üvezpınar, on one of the surrounding hills.

Çinar Otel Kaplıcı, Termal ☎0226/675 7400, ⓦyalovatermal.com. This hotel dates back to the late nineteenth century, though it was much reconstructed in the early 1980s. Rooms are plain, with white walls offset by dark-wood trim, and small balconies overlooking a courtyard shaded by a giant plane tree. 160TL

Dinana Üvezpınar Kaplıcı, Termal ☎0226/675 7668, ☏675 7293. Family-run and clean, with twenty pleasant rooms all with balconies overlooking the forested mountains, and a restaurant serving simple meals. Üvezpınar is a two-kilometre hike up the road from the hotel, leading from the *jandarma* (rural police) station to the left of the entrance to Termal, or up steps leading from within the resort itself, though several of the dolmuşes from Yalova run right up to the village.

20

Bursa and Uludağ

As the crow flies, the historic and beautifully situated city of Bursa is less than a hundred kilometres from İstanbul. It's a good city for walking around, whether through the hive of bazaars, the linear parks of the Hisar district or the anachronistic peace of the Muradiye quarter. Snow-addicts may be more interested in the resort of Uludağ, perched high above the city, Turkey's longest-established ski resort. It's possible to take in Bursa in an extremely long day-trip from İstanbul, but to make the most of it you should spend at least one night here, more if you want to ski on Uludağ.

Bursa

Draped ribbon-like along the leafy lower slopes of Mount Uludağ (Great Mountain), which towers more than 2000m above it, overlooking the fertile plain of the Nilüfer Çayı, **BURSA** does more justice to its setting than any other Turkish city apart from İstanbul. It was the first capital of the mighty Ottoman Empire and contains some of the finest early Ottoman monuments in the Balkans, set within neighbourhoods that, despite being marooned in masses of concrete, are among the most appealing in Turkey.

Industrialization over the last four decades and the rise in population to a couple of million people mean that the city has lost some of its former elegance. Silk and textile manufacture, plus patronage of the area's thermal baths by the elite, were for centuries the most important enterprises. Today manufacturing takes precedence, with Tofaş (Fiat), Renault and Bosch all having major plants here, supplemented by canneries and bottlers processing the rich harvest of the plain, and the presence of Uludağ University. Following the upheavals of the late nineteenth and early twentieth centuries, Bursa was flooded with immigrants from former Balkan possessions of the Ottoman Empire. The vast numbers of more recent migrants, however, attracted by job opportunities at the various factories, hail from rural, poverty-stricken eastern Anatolia. Students provide a necessary leavening in what might otherwise be a uniformly conservative community. Some of this atmosphere derives from Bursa's role as first capital of the Ottoman Empire and burial place of the first six sultans, their piety as well as authority emanating from the mosques, social-welfare foundations and tombs built at their command.

Relatively few Westerners visit Bursa, but Arabs, attracted by its Islamic sights, the bath-houses clustered round the hot springs and the green cool of Uludağ, come here in their droves.

Some history

Although the area had been settled at least a millennium previously, the first city here was founded early in the second century BC by Prusias I, a king of ancient Bithynia, who in typical Hellenistic fashion named the town **Proussa**, after himself. Legend claims that Hannibal helped him pick the location of the acropolis, today's Hisar.

Overshadowed by nearby Nicomedia (modern İzmit) and Nicaea (İznik), the city stagnated until the **Romans**, attracted by its natural hot springs, began spending lavish amounts on public baths and made it capital of their province of Mysia. Justinian introduced silkworm culture, and Byzantine Proussa flourished until Arab raids of the seventh and eighth centuries, and the subsequent tug of war for sovereignty between the Selçuks and the Greeks, precipitated decline. During and after the Latin interlude in Constantinople (1204–61), the Byzantines reconsolidated their hold on Proussa, but not for long.

The start of the fourteenth century saw a small band of nomadic Turks, led by one **Osman Gazi**, camped outside the walls of Proussa. The city capitulated in 1326, following a ten-year siege, to Osman's son, Orhan, and the **Ottomans** ceased to be a wandering tribe of marauders. Orhan marked the acquisition of a capital and the organization of an infant state by styling himself sultan, giving the city its present name and striking coinage. Bursa began to enjoy a second golden age: the silk industry was expanded and the city, outgrowing the confines of the citadel, graced with monuments.

In the years following Orhan's death in 1362, the imperial capital was gradually moved to Edirne, but Bursa's place in history, and in the hearts of the Ottomans, was ensured; succeeding sultans continued to add buildings, and to be laid to rest here, for another hundred years. Disastrous fires and earthquakes in the mid-nineteenth century, and the War of Independence, only slightly diminished the city's splendour.

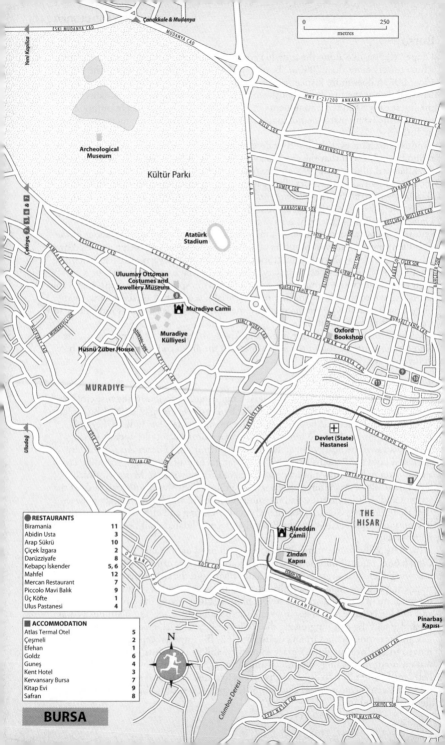

21

Orhan Gazi Camii
Orhan Gazi Meydanı

The 1336 foundation of the **Orhan Gazi Camii** makes it the second-oldest mosque in Bursa. Originally built as a *zaviye* for itinerant dervishes, this is the earliest example of the T-form mosque, with *eyvans* flanking the main prayer hall. The large central dome boasts eight windows which let light flood into the interior. The single minaret was not part of the original design, and wasn't erected until the nineteenth century, when the mosque was restored by a French architect. **Karagöz puppets**, the painted camel-leather props used in the Turkish national shadow-play, are supposed to represent workers who were involved in building the Orhan Gazi Camii. According to legend, the antics of Karagöz and his sidekick Hacıvat so entertained their fellow workmen that Orhan had them beheaded to end the distraction. Later, missing the comedians and repenting of his deed, he arranged to immortalize the pair in the art form that now bears the name of Karagöz.

Koza Parkı

Compact, paved **Koza Parkı**, with its fountains, benches and street-level cafés, is the real heart of Bursa. Though animated through the day and early evening, the plaza empties soon after dusk with the illuminated fountains dark and still, and the walkways deserted by 11pm – no doubt owing much to the fact that none of the places to eat around here are licensed.

Ulu Camii

On the far side of Koza Parkı looms the tawny limestone **Ulu Camii**, built between 1396 and 1399 by Yıldırım Beyazit I, from the proceeds of booty won from the Crusaders at Macedonian Nicopolis. Before the battle, Yıldırım ("Thunderbolt") had vowed to construct twenty mosques if victorious. The present building of twenty domes supported by twelve free-standing pillars was his rather loose interpretation of this promise, but it was still the largest and most ambitious Ottoman mosque of its time. The interior is dominated by a huge *şadırvan* pool in the centre, whose skylight was once open to the elements, and an intricate walnut *mimber* pieced together, it's claimed, without nails or glue. Its glass central dome allows light to flood in, illuminating the hordes of local and foreign Muslim pilgrims as they pray or sit and relax in the peaceful interior.

From the north porch of the mosque, you can descend stairs to the two-storey **Emir Bey Hanı**, originally a dependency of the Orhan Gazi Camii and now home to various offices and shops.

BURSA SILK AND THE COCOON AUCTION

The highlight of the year in Bursa is the **cocoon auction** of late June and early July, when silkworm breeders from around the province gather to hawk their valuable produce. At this time, Bursa's Koza Hanı becomes a lake of white torpedoes the size of a songbird's egg; the moth, when it hatches, is a beautiful, otherworldly creature with giant onyx eyes and feathery antennae. As long as you're careful, the merchants don't mind you walking the floor, or you can watch the melee from the upper arcades.

After being sent into a tailspin by French and Italian competition two hundred years ago, the Bursa silk trade has recently experienced a tentative revival. However, the quality of contemporary fabric cannot compare to museum pieces from the early Ottoman heyday and most of the better designs are made up in imported material, which is, however, still better quality than the Turkish. If you're buying silk in Bursa make sure the label says *ipek* (silk) and not *ithal ipek* (artificial silk).

The bazaar quarter

As befits a prominent settlement astride one of the many branches of the ancient silk route, trade and commerce have long been mainstays of the local economy. From the Ottoman period onwards, the heart of this commercial activity was a **complex of bazaars** to the north and east of Bursa's main mosque, the Ulu Camii (see opposite).

Koza Hanı

Daily 8am–8pm

The centrepiece of the bazaar quarter is the **Koza Hanı**, or "Silk-Cocoon Hall" (see box opposite), flanking Koza Parkı close to the Orhan Gazi Camii (see opposite). Built in 1491, when Bursa was the final stop on the Silk Route from China, it's still filled with silk and brocade merchants (plus a few jewellery stores), and prices are generally far cheaper than in İstanbul. On the lower level, in the middle of a cobbled courtyard, a miniscule *mescit* (small mosque) perches directly over its *şadırvan*, while a subsidiary court bulges asymmetrically to the east; there are teahouses and public benches in both.

Covered Bazaar and Bedesten

Mon–Sat 9am–7pm

The assorted galleries and lesser *hans* that comprise the covered bazaar are a delight for shoppers hunting for ready-to-wear clothing, silk goods, towels and bolts of cloth and furniture. The nearby *bedesten* is given over to the sale and warehousing of jewellery and precious metals.

Demirciler Çarşısı and beyond

Mon–Sat 9am–7pm

Despite quake and blaze, the **Demirciler Çarşısı**, or Ironmongers' Market, has kept its traditions intact. This market is on the east side of İnönü Caddesi, best crossed by the pedestrian underpass at Okcular Caddesi. Stall upon stall of blacksmiths and braziers attract photographers, but be advised that some expect a consideration for posing. From here, you can easily continue past a small mosque and some cabinet-makers' workshops to **Fırın Sokak**, which is lined with some of the finest old dwellings in town. At the end of this, the Irgandı Sanat Köprüsü bridge spans the **Gök Dere**, one of two streams that tumble through Bursa, forming an approximate eastern boundary for the centre. The bridge, an ill-advised copy of Florence's Ponte Vecchio, is lined with small shops and cafés, all struggling for business.

Yeşil Camii and Yeşil Türbe

Yeşil Türbe Daily 8am–noon & 1–5pm • Free

Situated a few minutes' walk east of the city centre, across the Gök Dere stream, the neighbourhood of Yeşil is built around its namesake mosque and tombs. Designed by the architect Hacı Ivaz atop a slight rise, the **Yeşil Camii** was begun in 1413 by Çelebi Mehmet I, victor of the civil war caused by the death of Beyazit I. Despite being unfinished – work ceased in 1424, three years after Mehmet himself died – and despite catastrophic damage from two nineteenth-century earth tremors, it's easily the most spectacular of Bursa's imperial mosques. The incomplete entrance, faced in a light marble, is all the more easy to examine for the lack of a portico; above the stalactite vaulting and relief calligraphy you can see the supports for arches never built.

Assuming that the restoration work in progress at the time of writing is complete, pass through a foyer supported by pilfered Byzantine columns to reach the **interior**, a variation on the T-plan usually reserved for dervish *zaviyes*. A fine *şadırvan* occupies the centre of the "T", but your eye is monopolized by the hundreds of polychrome **tiles** that line not just the *mihrab* but every available vertical surface up to 5m in height, particularly two recesses flanking the entryway. Green and blue pigments matching the carpets predominate, and praying amid this dimly lit majesty must feel something akin

21

to worshipping inside a leaf. Tucked above the foyer, and usually closed to visitors, is the **imperial loge**, the most extravagantly decorated chamber of all. Several artisans from Tabriz participated in the tiling of Yeşil Camii but the loge is attributed to Al-Majnun, which translates most accurately as "intoxicated on hashish".

On the same knoll as the mosque, and immediately across the pedestrian precinct separating them, the **Yeşil Türbe** contains the sarcophagus of Çelebi Mehmet I and his assorted offspring. Inside, the walls and Mehmet's tomb glisten with the glorious original Tabriz material.

Türk ve İslam Eserleri Müzesi
Yeşil Caddesi Tues–Sun 8am–noon & 1–5pm • Free

The medrese (theology academy) just east of the Yeşil Camii now houses Bursa's **Türk ve İslam Eserleri Müzesi** (Museum of Turkish and Islamic Art), set around a pleasant courtyard with fountain, trees and picnic tables. If the museum is short-staffed, certain rooms may be closed, but in theory you can view İznik ware, Çanakkale ceramics, kitchen utensils, inlaid wooden articles, weapons and a mock-up of an Ottoman *sünnet odası*, or circumcision chamber. There's also a case containing some fine Karagöz shadow-puppets, for which the city is famous.

Emir Sultan Camii

The **Emir Sultan Camii**, a 300m-walk east of Yeşil, is lost in extensive graveyards where every religious Bursan hopes to be buried. The mosque was originally endowed by a Bokharan dervish and trusted adviser to three sultans, beginning with Beyazit I, but it has just been restored again after enduring an Ottoman Baroque overhaul early last century, so you can only guess what's left of the original essence. The pious, however, seem to harbour no doubts, coming in strength to worship at the tombs of the saint and his family.

Yıldırım Beyazit Camii

Perched on a small hillock at the northeastern edge of the city, the **Yıldırım Beyazit Camii** is a substantial hike from downtown – you might want to take a dolmuş (marked "Heykel–Beyazit Yıldırım" or the more common "Heykel–Fakülte") from the dolmuş terminus behind the Atatürk statue on Cumhüriyet Alanı, which passes 200m below the mosque. Completed by Beyazit I between 1390 and 1395, the Beyazit Camii features a handsome, five-arched portico defined by square columns. The interior is unremarkable except for a gravity-defying arch bisecting the prayer hall, its lower supports apparently tapering away to end in stalactite moulding. The only other note of whimsy in this spare building is the use of elaborate niches out on the porch.

The associated **medrese**, exceptionally long and narrow because of its sloping site, huddles just downhill; today, it's used as a medical clinic. The **türbe** (tomb) of the luckless Beyazit, kept in an iron cage by the rampaging Tamerlane until his death in 1403, is usually locked. Perhaps the mosque custodians fear a revival of the Ottoman inclination to abuse the tomb of the most ignominiously defeated sultan.

The Hisar

The **Hisar**, the citadel area that was Bursa's original nucleus, nowadays retains just a few clusters of dilapidated Ottoman housing within its warren of narrow lanes and some courses of medieval wall along its perimeter. From where Atatürk Caddesi becomes Cemal Nadir Caddesi, just short of the distinctive glass pyramid marking the **Zafer Plaza** mall, it's possible to clamber up the pedestrian walkways to the summit of Hisar.

The view from the clifftop **park** at the summit, sprawling around the tombs and clock tower, is impressive, with reasonable cafés at the head of the walkways leading down to

Cemal Nadir and Altıparmak *caddesi*s. From either of these streets here you can follow signs west to Muradiye (see below), along the most direct route, or veer inland on a walk around the neighbourhood. At the southernmost extreme of the citadel, you exit at the **Pınarbaşı Kapısı**, the lowest point in the circuit of walls and the spot where Orhan's forces finally entered the city in 1326. From there you can stroll parallel to the walls, re-entering at the **Zindan Kapısı**, inside of which is the simple **Alaeddin Camii**, erected within a decade of the Conquest and so the earliest mosque in Bursa.

A more straightforward route follows Hasta Yurdu Caddesi until another generous swathe of park studded with teahouses opens out opposite the public hospital. The furthest teahouses have fine views of the Muradiye district and, from the final café and course of wall, obvious stairs descend to the **Cılımboz Deresi**, the second major stream to furrow the city.

Muradiye

Across Cılımboz Deresi from the Hisar lies medieval **Muradiye**, a green and pleasant suburb where Bursa's best-preserved Ottoman-era dwellings line quiet streets that spring into life for the Tuesday **street market**. The centrepiece of this tranquil district is the **Muradiye Külliyesi**, a mosque complex begun in 1424 by Murat II. It was the last imperial foundation in Bursa, though the tombs for which the mosque complex is famous were added piecemeal over the next century or so.

GETTING THERE **MURADIYE**

By bus and dolmuş If you're coming directly from the city centre, take one of the frequent dolmuşes from the stand behind Heykel (the Atatürk staue on Cumhüriyet Alanı), or a bus from the stop at the southern end of Cemal Nadir Caddesi (buses include the #2/A and #6/F2).

Muradiye Külliyesi Türbesı

Daily: May–Sept 8am–noon & 1–5pm; Oct–April 8am–5pm • Free

The ten royal tombs, **Muradiye Külliyesi Türbesı**, are set in tranquil gardens shaded by towering pine and plane trees. Should any of the tombs be locked, there are custodians on site who will open up for you. The first tomb encountered is that of **Şehzade Ahmet** and his brother Şehinşah, both murdered in 1513 by their cousin Selim I to preclude any succession disputes. The luxury of the İznik tiles within contrasts sharply with the adjacent austerity of **Murat II's tomb**, where Roman columns inside and a wooden awning out front are the only superfluities. Murat, as much contemplative mystic as warrior-sultan, was the only Ottoman ruler ever to abdicate voluntarily, though pressures of state forced him to leave the company of his dervishes and return to the throne after just two years. He was the last sultan to be interred at Bursa and one of the few lying here who died in his bed; in accordance with his wishes, both the coffin and the dome were originally open to the sky "so that the rain of heaven might wash my face like any pauper's".

Next along is the tomb of **Şehzade Mustafa**, Süleyman the Magnificent's unjustly murdered heir; perhaps a sign of his father's remorse, the tomb is done up in extravagantly floral İznik tiles, with a top border of calligraphy. Nearby stands the tomb of **Cem Sultan**, his elder brother Mustafa and two of Beyazit II's sons, decorated with a riot of abstract, botanical and calligraphic paint strokes up to the dome. Cem, the cultured and favourite son of Mehmet the Conqueror, was one of the Ottoman Empire's most interesting might-have-beens. Following the death of his father in 1481, he lost a brief dynastic struggle with the successful claimant, brother Beyazit II, and fled abroad. For fourteen years he wandered, seeking sponsorship of his cause from Christian benefactors who in all cases became his jailers: first the Knights of St John at Rhodes and Bodrum, later the papacy. At one point, it seemed that he would command a Crusader army organized to retake İstanbul, but all such plans came to grief for the simple reason that Beyazit

21

anticipated his opponents' moves and each time bribed them handsomely to desist, making Cem a lucrative prisoner indeed. His usefulness as a pawn exhausted, Cem was probably poisoned in Italy by the pope in 1495, leaving nothing but reams of poems aching with nostalgia and homesickness.

Hüsnü Züber House

Uzunyol Sok 3 • Tues–Sun 10am–noon & 1–5pm • 3TL

The **Hüsnü Züber House**, a former Ottoman guesthouse, was built in 1836 and sports a typically Ottoman overhanging upper storey, wooden roof and beams and a garden courtyard. It now houses a collection of carved wooden musical instruments, spoons and farming utensils, many of which were made by Hüsnü Züber himself, the present owner, who inhabits the house still. The main exhibit, however, is the house itself, one of the few of its era to have been well restored and opened to the public.

Uluumay Ottoman Costumes and Jewellery Museum

Murat Cad 2 • Daily 9am–6pm • 5TL

Housed in the cells of the former theological college of Dair Ahmet Paşa Medresesi, the **Uluumay Ottoman Costumes and Jewellery Museum** displays a range of original, traditional costumes from all over the former Ottoman domains – from Kosovo and Bursa to Bosnia and Zonguldak on Turkey's Black Sea. The mannequins the costumes are displayed on revolve in their glass cases when you enter the room and give a vivid impression of the ethnic hodge-podge that was the Ottoman Empire. There's a pleasant garden-café out back where local musicians sometimes hang out and play the flute and the *saz*, a long-necked lute-like instrument favoured by Turkish folk musicians.

Kültür Parkı

Token admission charge when entry booths are staffed

Sprawling **Kültür Parkı**, a kilometre or so from the city centre, is best reached from Çekirge Caddesi, through the southeast gate. Inside the park, there's a popular tea garden, a small boating lake, a mini-zoo, and a number of restaurants and *gazino*-style nightclubs. As you stroll, however, it quickly becomes obvious that there's no potential for solitude – though courting couples try their best – and no wild spots among the regimented plantations and too-broad driveways.

Arkeoloji Müzesi

Tues–Sun 8am–noon & 1–5pm • 2TL

At the west end of Kültür Parkı, just below Çekirge Caddesi, is the **Arkeoloji Müzesi** (Archeological Museum; closed for renovation at the time of writing). Exhibits in the Stone Room vary from the macabre (a Byzantine ossuary with a skull peeking out) to the homely (a Roman cavalryman figurine), but the adjacent hall featuring metal jewellery from all over Anatolia – watch chains, breastplates, belts, buckles, bracelets, anklets, chokers – steals the show. The west wing houses a modest coin gallery and miscellaneous, small ancient objects, the best of which are the Roman glass items and Byzantine and Roman bronzes. Oil lamps, pottery, a token amount of gold and far too many ceramic figurines complete these poorly labelled exhibits; while a garden of sarcophagi, stelae and other statuary fragments surrounds the building.

Çekirge

The thermal centre of **Çekirge** ("Grasshopper" – presumably a reference to the natural soundtrack of a summer evening) lies two kilometres northwest of the city centre. Most visitors come here to experience the Çekirge hot springs, which flow out of Uludağ's mountainside and are tapped into by the various hotels and bath-houses.

GETTING THERE

By bus Buses (including the #2/A), as well as dolmuşes, shuttle to and from the dolmuş stand near the tourist office on Atatürk Caddesi.

Yeni Kaplıca

Daily 6am–10pm • 5TL • Scrub 15TL, soap massage 25TL, oil massage 40TL

The male-only **Yeni Kaplıca** (New Baths) are accessible by a steep driveway beginning opposite the *Çelik Palas Oteli*, lying just beyond the Kültür Parkı (see opposite). In their present form, the baths date from the mid-sixteenth century. According to legend, Süleyman the Magnificent was cured of gout after a dip in the Byzantine baths here and had his vizier Rüstem Paşa overhaul the building. Fragments of mosaic paving stud the floor, and the walls are lined with once exquisite but now blurred İznik tiles.

Eski Kaplıca

Daily 7am–10.30pm • Men 28TL, women 24TL • Scrub 15TL, soap massage 15TL

The wonderful **Eski Kaplıca** (Old Baths), huddled at the far end of Çekirge Caddesi, next to the *Kervansaray Bursa Hotel*, are Bursa's most ancient baths (and much the nicest public bath for women). Byzantine rulers Justinian and Theodora first improved a Roman spa on the site, and Murat I in turn had a go at the structure in the late fourteenth century. Huge but shallow keyhole-shaped pools dominate the *hararetler*, or hot rooms, of the men's and women's sections, whose domes are supported by eight Byzantine columns. Scalding (45°C) water pours into the notch of the keyhole, the temperature still so taxing in the main basin that you'll soon be gasping out into the cool room, seeking relief at the fountain in the middle.

Hüdavendigar (Birinci) Murat Camii

On a hillock just west of the Çekirge thermal centre stands the **Hüdavendigar (Birinci) Murat Camii**, which, with its five-arched portico and alternating bands of brick and stone, seems more like a church teleported from Ravenna or Macedonia than a mosque. Indeed, tradition asserts that the architect and builders were Christians, who dallied twenty years at the task because Murat I, whose pompous epithet literally means "Creator of the Universe", was continually off at war and unable to supervise the work. The interior plan, consisting of a first-floor medrese above a highly modified, T-type *zaviye* at ground level, is unique in Islam. Unfortunately, the upper storey, wrapped around the courtyard that's the heart of the place, is rarely open to visitors.

Murat himself lies in the much-modified **türbe** across the street, complete apart from his entrails, which were removed by the embalmers before the body began its long journey back from Serbia in 1389. In June of that year, Murat was in the process of winning his greatest triumph over the Serbian king Lazarus and his allies at the **Battle of Kosovo**, in the former Yugoslavia, when he was stabbed to death in his tent by Milod Obiliç, a Serbian noble who had feigned desertion. Murat's son Beyazit, later better known as Yıldırım, immediately had his brother Yakub strangled and, once in sole command, decimated the Christian armies. Beyazit's acts had two far-reaching consequences: the Balkans remained under Ottoman control until early in the twentieth century, and a gruesome precedent of blood-letting was established for most subsequent Ottoman coronations.

ARRIVAL AND DEPARTURE

The best way to get to Bursa from İstanbul is either by bus or a combination of bus and ferry.

By bus Regular buses (20TL) depart from İstanbul's Harem and Esenler stations (see p.22), taking at least three hours from Harem, four or more from Esenler, depending on traffic. Buses arrive and depart from the bus station (☎0224/261 5400), 10km north of Bursa; to get there, catch the #38 opposite the town hall on Atatürk Caddesi. Çağlar, Kamil Koç, Pamukkale and several other companies run to İstanbul (with ferry transfer).

21

By sea bus The high-speed sea bus takes an hour and ten minutes (18TL) from Yenikapı ferry terminal to Yalova, from where buses and dolmuşes (9TL) run to Bursa (around 50min). Either way, you'll arrive at Bursa's bus station, 10km north of town on the Yalova road. To get to the city centre, take a yellow #38 bus, buying a ticket (2TL) from the kiosk before boarding. Alternatively, catch one of the (less frequent) crossings from Yenikapı to Güzelyalı (one and a half hours) and then a bus or dolmuş to the start of Bursa's metro system, at Organize Sanayı (around 30min). Once on the metro, travel to the Dehreküstü stop, from where it's a fifteen-minute walk south to the city centre.

GETTING AROUND

Bursa's position at the foot of the mountain has dictated an elongated layout, with most of the major boulevards running from east to west, changing their names several times as they go. Though Bursa is narrow, with many points of interest bunched together, it's sufficiently long enough for you to want to consider **public transport** to reach the outlying attractions.

By bus Only the #2/A (connecting Emir Sultan in the east of town with Çekirge to the west) and the #3/A (linking Heykel with the Uludağ *teleferik*) are of much use, and you need to buy tickets for them at the kiosks, which are handily located next to most central stops.

By dolmuş Dolmuşes are much simpler to use than the buses (fares start at 1.50TL); appearing in various colours, they all bear destination signs on their roofs, start from fixed points around the city, and pick up and let down passengers at places clearly marked with a large "D".

By metro The new and extensive metro system (daily 6am–midnight) is not as useful for visitors as it could be, as it doesn't connect the major points of interest, but is handy for travelling to and from the ferry terminal at Güzelyalı (see p.23).

Car rental There are a number of car hire firms in town, including Aktif, Çekirge Cad 139 (☎0224/233 0444); Avis, Çekirge Cad 143 (☎0224/236 5133); Budget, Çekirge Cad 39/1 (☎0224/223 4204); and Europcar, Çekirge Cad 41 (☎0224/223 2321).

INFORMATION

Tourist information In Koza Parkı, opposite Orhan Gazi Camii, in a row of shops under the north side of Atatürk Caddesi (Mon–Fri 8am–noon & 1–5pm; ☎0224/220 1848).

ACCOMMODATION

Reasonably priced hotels are generally plentiful in Bursa – it's a little off the backpackers' trail and often treated as a day-trip from İstanbul. Rich foreigners, particularly Arabs, gravitate toward the **luxury spa-hotels** in the western suburb of Çekirge (see p.248), 4km out of the centre, but there's also a cluster of modest establishments out here, around the **Birinci Murat Camii**. If you're interested in seeing monumental Bursa, then staying centrally, around Atatürk Caddesi, makes more sense.

CENTRAL BURSA

Çeşmeli Gümüşçeken Cad 6 ☎&☎0224/224 1511. Named after the *çeşme* (fountain) incorporated into the wall to the right of the front door, and much nicer than it looks from the outside, this immaculate, extremely welcoming hotel is run entirely by women. Rooms have minibars, TVs and fans, and a decent buffet breakfast is included. A real home from home. **120TL**

Efehan Gümüşçeken Cad 34 ☎0224/225 2260, ☻efehan.com.tr. Pleasant, three-star comfort in an old-looking but modern, centrally located hotel. Extras include minibar and satellite TV. Ask for one of the top rooms for mountain views. **110TL**

Guneş İnebey Cad 75 ☎0224/224 1404, ☻otelgunes @yahoo.com. Cheap, clean and friendly, in a much-restored old house with centrally heated rooms; squat toilets and showers are both on the landings. The singles (26TL) are tiny but good value. The backpackers' choice in Bursa, it is often full with Korean and Japanese travellers. **46TL**

Kent Atatürk Cad 69 ☎0224/223 5420, ☻kentotel .com. The town centre's most prominent hotel offers a high level of business-style comfort – large rooms with satellite TV and free tea- and coffee-making facilities – but with a packed *McDonald's* below it and the busy main street right in front, you'll probably want to keep the windows closed and the a/c on. Twenty percent discount for stays of more than one night. **€100**

★**Kitap Evi** Burç Üstü 21 ☎0224/225 4160, ☻kitapevi.com.tr. For those in search of something different, this boutique hotel on the citadel (Hisar) may well suit. There is a mixture of suites and standard doubles on offer, though all are individually furnished and decorated. Front rooms have fine views over Bursa but those facing the rear garden area are quieter. **€119**

Safran Arka Sok 4, off Ortapazar Cad ☎0224/224 7216, ☻safran_otel@yahoo.com. A beautifully restored wooden house, in the old part of town up on the Hisar. The nine rooms are modern, with a/c, minibar and TV, and are extremely comfortable. If you want a boutique hotel in a quiet, atmospheric location, this is the place. **€80**

21

ÇEKIRGE

Atlas Termal Hamamlar Cad 35 ☎0224/234 4100, ⓦatlasotel.com. The full thermal experience for a fraction of the usual price. The *Atlas* has two shiny marble *hamams* set in a mock Art Nouveau interior, as well as a reasonable restaurant, garden courtyard and terrace. The bedrooms are fussily traditional but have flat-screen TVs and boast excellent modern bathrooms. 120TL

Kervansaray Bursa Çekirge Meydanı ☎0224/233 9300, ⓦkervansarayhotels.com. A gargantuan and sumptuous hotel, next to the Eski Kaplıca (see p.249), with an assortment of swimming pools (the outdoor one is large enough for a proper swim), Turkish baths and saunas. There are five pricey restaurants and a baby-sitting service. 250TL

EATING AND DRINKING

Bursa's cuisine is solidly meat-oriented and served in a largely alcohol-free environment, reflecting the city's conservative nature. The best street to get a drink with your meal (or just a drink), is pedestrianized **Sakarya Caddesi**, between Altıparmak Caddesi and the walls of the Hisar above. This former fish market and the main street of the Jewish quarter has been reborn as an atmospheric place for an outdoor fish dinner or a drink on a summer's evening.

CAFÉS

Mahfel Namazgah Cad 2, Setbaşı Bridge, Heykel. Very popular café in a shady location above the river, dishing up Western- and Turkish-style snacks to a predominantly young set. Mains from 8TL and up. Live music weekend evenings. Daily 9am–11pm.

Ulus Pastanesi Öztat Apt 92, Atatürk Cad, Heykel. This tiny, old-fashioned shop/café has been going since 1920 and claims to be the oldest producer of *kestane şekeri* (chestnuts boiled and soaked in sugar) in Turkey, and uses no artificial ingredients. It also does a mean chocolate cake (6TL), wonderful Turkish coffee, speciality candied figs and orange peel served with a dollop of cream – plus a health-giving mulberry syrup (3TL).

RESTAURANTS

⭐ **Arap Sükrü** Kuruçeşme Mah, Sakarya Cad 6 & 29, Tophane. There are actually two rival establishments here owing to fraternal disputes: *Çetin* and *Ahmet*, with little to choose between them. Fish in all shapes and sizes (mains from 18TL, starters from 4TL), with beer, wine or *rakı* to wash it down, are served at tables on both sides of the cobbled street.

⭐ **Çiçek İzgara** Belediye Cad 5, Heykel. The best value centrally for lunch and dinner is this popular place on the upper of a period house behind the Belediye (Town Hall). Flawless service, tableclothed elegance and extremely reasonable prices – the house special and award-winning *izgara köfte* is 10TL, a cheese-stuffed version a lira more.

Great rice-pudding, too. Unlicensed. Mon–Sat 10am–11pm, Closed Sun.

Darüzziyafe İkinci Murat Cad 36, Muradiye. Housed in the beautifully restored *imaret* (kitchen) of the Muradiye Camii, you couldn't ask for more atmospheric surroundings to try *hunkar beğendi* (lamb stew served on a bed of mashed aubergine) or *mantarlı çoban kavurma* (sautéed meat, mushrooms, peppers and onions). Mains start from 12TL; for dessert try the delicate *keskülü fukara*, a kind of walnut and pistachio fool served with Maraş ice cream. Unlicensed. Daily noon–10pm.

Kebapcı İskender Atatürk Cad 60, Heykel. If you're in Bursa, you're beholden to sample *İskender* (see box below) – and this is the place to do it. The characterful 1930s building sees a steady stream of locals tucking into the only meal on offer – *İskender*. It's not cheap at 19TL but the meat is tender, the rich tomato sauce delicious, and the waiters even come around and drizzle melted butter on top to enrich it further. There's another branch on Unlu Cad 7.

Piccolo Mavı Balık Kuruçeşme Mah, Sakarya Cad 16, Tophane. This once-fashionable bar is now a decent fish restaurant, housed in an old Bursa building. Waiters are sharply dressed and attentive, essential when the place attracts the more moneyed locals. Mains around 20TL.

Üç Köfte İvaz Paşa Çarşısı 3. The name means "Three Meatballs", which is what you get, served up three times over so the food on your plate is always piping hot for 9TL. Unlicensed. Mon–Sat 11am–3pm.

BURSA SPECIALITIES

The most famous local recipes are *İskender kebap* (essentially *döner kebap* soaked in a rich butter, tomato and yoghurt sauce) – named after its supposed inventor, İskender (Alexander) Usta, a Bursan chef – and *İnegöl köftesi*, rich little pellets of mince often laced with cheese (when they're known as *kadarlı köfte*) and introduced by Balkan immigrants in the 1930s. *İskender kebap* is rich and extremely filling – think twice before going for the "*bir buçuk porsiyon*" (one and a half portion) on offer in most places. The city is also famous for its *kestane şekeri* (candied chestnuts) which are on sale everywhere – the chocolate-covered ones usually appeal most to the Western palate and make a great alternative to Turkish delight as a gift for friends or family.

21

ENTERTAINMENT

Bursa has relatively few nocturnal or weekend events, and the student contingent is responsible for any concerts that do occur. The **Kültür Merkezi** or Cultural Centre, on Atatürk Caddesi (☎ 0224/223 4461), hosts ever-changing art exhibitions and occasional concerts. The **open-air theatre** in the Kültür Parkı is the main venue for the touristy musical performances and folkloric presentations that form a big part of the annual **Bursa Festival** (June & July; ⊕ bursafestival.org). In early July there's the **Altın Karagöz** international folk dance competition (⊕ bursa.bel.tr), held in the open-air theatre (see above). It lasts a weekend and brings in teams of colourfully dressed troupes from Georgia and Greece to Taiwan and Mexico.

DIRECTORY

Banks and exchange There are plenty of banks with ATMs on Atatürk Cad, and exchange offices (Mon–Sat 8am–8pm) in the covered bazaar and on Altıparmak Cad.

Books Adım Kitapçılık, Altıparmak Cad 50.

Consulate UK (honorary consulate), Resam Şefik Bursalı Sok, off Başak Cad ☎ 0224/220 0436.

Hamams Çakır Ağa Hamamı, located just below the Hisar on Cemal Nadir Cad (men and women; daily 6am–midnight; 10TL); or head out to Eski Kaplıca (see p.249).

Hospitals Devlet (State) Hastanesi, Hasta Yurdu Cad, Hisar (☎ 0224/220 0020); Üniversite Hastanesi, P. Tezok Cad, Hastane Sok, Çekirge (☎ 0224/442 8400).

Internet access Bursa is well endowed with internet cafés – a reliable option is Bara Internet on Kocaoğlu Sok.

Left luggage At the bus station (daily 24hr).

Police Cemal Nadir Cad.

Post office Corner of Atatürk and Maksem *caddesis*.

Uludağ

Presiding over Bursa, the 2543-metre-high **Uludağ** is a dramatic, often cloud-cloaked massif, its northern reaches dropping dizzyingly into the city. In ancient times, it was known as the Olympos of Mysia, one of nearly twenty peaks around the Aegean so named (Olympos was possibly a generic Phoenician or Doric word for "mountain"), and it has a place in mythology as the seat from which the gods watched the battle of Troy (see p.259). Early in the Christian era, the range became a refuge for monks and hermits, who were replaced after the Ottoman Conquest by Muslim dervishes.

These days, the scent of grilling meat has displaced the odour of sanctity, since Bursa natives cram the alpine campsites and picnic grounds on any holiday or weekend. Getting there is definitely half the fun if you opt for the **cable car** (*teleferik*; see opposite) which stops at Kadı Yayla pastures (1231m), where shepherds still graze their flocks in a forest clearance. You can get off and wander around here before continuing up to the last stop at the **Sarıalan** picnic grounds (1635m), where a cluster of cafés and trinket shops await. Despite the weekend and holiday-period hordes, it's a pretty spot, with curious rock-outcrops, forest all around and the distant ridge line a marked contrast to the concrete of Bursa below.

Much of the dense middle-altitude forest has been designated a **national park**, and there are several marked hiking trails from Sarıalan. In fact, the best part of the mountain lies outside the park to the east, where a few hours' walking will bring you to some glacial **lakes** in a wild, rocky setting just below the highest summit. The prime months for a visit are May and June, when the wildflowers are blooming, or September and October, when the mist is less dense. However, due to its proximity to the Sea of Marmara, the high ridges trap moist marine air, and white-outs or violent storms can blow up during most months of the year.

SKIING ON ULUDAĞ

Skiing is possible on Uludağ from December to March (though it's better earlier in the season than later). There's a dense cluster of hotels, some with their own ski lift, at **Oteller** (1800m), where you can rent skis and ski clothes. There are thirteen different skiing areas around Oteller (around 30TL per day for a lift pass), which are served by eight chair lifts and seven T-bars. Prices and lift queues rise dramatically at weekends and in public holidays, especially New Year and the school mid-winter break (usually the last week in Jan and the first in Feb).

ARRIVAL AND DEPARTURE
ULUDAĞ

By cable car To reach the lower cable-car terminus from Bursa, take a dolmuş labelled "Teleferik" from the semi-underground rank behind the Atatürk statue (just south of Atatürk Cad). The wobbly *teleferik* gondolas (every 10–40min; daily: outward 8am–10pm; return 7.50am–10.20pm; 15TL return) stop first at Kadı Yayla before continuing up to Sarıalan every ten minutes or so in peak periods, but are cancelled in high winds. Long queues are the norm at weekends and in the summer school holidays (mid-June to mid-Sept). At Sarıalan, at the top, there's an army of dolmuşes waiting to take you to Oteller.

By dolmuş The alternative is to take a dolmuş all the way to Oteller (7TL), which winds the 32km of paved road up from Bursa's Orhangazi Caddesi, though it can occasionally be difficult to muster the necessary number of passengers (six).

By car It's possible to follow the same route as the dolmuşes in your own vehicle, the road veering off above Çekirge and climbing rapidly through successive vegetation zones. Staff at the Karabelen National Park gate, 20km into the park, charge 5TL per car when they're in the mood and sometimes have information to hand out. The final stretch of road, from just below the gate to the hotels at Oteller, is very rough cobble, designed to prevent drivers from skidding – or speeding – so allow an hour for the trip. In bad weather, you'll be advised to put chains on your wheels – and may not be allowed to make the journey without them.

ACCOMMODATION

There's little difference between the four- and five-star resort **hotels** at the road's end in Oteller. By far the best option is to check ⓦ uludaghotels.com for vacancies, rates and possible package deals. In the skiing season, you'll find rates of over 350TL per night with full board – and no shortage of people prepared to pay – though prices of the hotels that remain open can drop to half that out of season.

Çanakkale, Troy and Gallipoli

Two of history's bloodiest campaigns – one legendary, one all too real – were played out near the mouth of the Dardanelles, the narrow strait connecting the Aegean with the Sea of Marmara, some 310km southwest of İstanbul. The ancient city of Troy, scene of the epic conflict between heroes such as Achilles and Hector and immortalized by the father of Western literature, Homer, has long gripped the imaginations of people around the world. A much more recent conflict, the Allied forces' disastrous attempt to force the Dardanelles during World War I, also has great significance, particularly for Australians, New Zealanders and the Turks themselves, who all see it as marking the beginning of their "birth" as independent nations.

The obvious base from which to visit either or both of these sites is the modern town of **Çanakkale**, on the southern, Asian side of the Dardanelles; the World War I landing sites at **Gallipoli** (Gelibolu in Turkish) on the European side of the Dardanelles are a short ferry-ride away, and Troy lies just 30km to the south. For the pilgrimage to Gallipoli, some people chose **Eceabat**, at the southern end of the Gelibolu peninsula and opposite Çanakkale, as their base. Its only significance is as the major ferry terminal for the straits, but it's the nearest town to the battlefield and landing sites and takes on a character of its own around ANZAC Day (April 25).

Çanakkale

It's the **Dardanelles** (Çanakkale Boğazı in Turkish) that have defined **ÇANAKKALE**'s history and its place in myth. The area's Classical name, **Hellespont**, is owed to one Helle, who, while escaping from her wicked stepmother on the back of a winged ram, fell into the swift-moving channel and drowned. From Abydos, just northeast of modern Çanakkale, the youth Leander used to swim to Sestos on the European shore for trysts with his lover Hero, until one night he too perished in the currents; in despair, Hero drowned herself as well. Lord Byron narrowly escaped being added to the list of casualties on his swim in the opposite direction in 1810.

The name Çanakkale means "Pottery Castle", after the garish Çanakkale pottery that finds its way into the ethnographic section of every Turkish museum. An appealingly compact waterfront town, Çanakkale is enlivened by the presence of some thirty thousand students at the local university.

North of the ferry terminal, a broad, cafés lined esplanade leads to a replica of the Trojan **wooden horse** that featured in the 2004 Hollywood film *Troy*. The main focus of interest, however, is the cobbled streets running south of the ferry terminal. Here lies the ornate, late nineteenth century clock tower and the surviving European-style warehouses and houses, a reminder that before the horrors of World War I and the 1923 population exchanges (see p.294) this was a cosmopolitan town, with foreign consulates and Greeks, Jews and Armenians, as well as Turks, making up the local populace. Today, there's a string of lively bars and cafés in these narrow streets.

Some history

In 480 BC, **Xerxes**' Persian hordes crossed the waters on their way to Greece; and in 411 and 405 BC, the last two naval battles of the **Peloponnesian War** took place in these straits, the latter engagement ending in decisive defeat for the Athenian fleet. Twenty centuries later, **Mehmet the Conqueror** constructed the elaborate fortress of Kilitbahir directly opposite the Çimenlik Kale in Çanakkale (which he also built), to tighten the stranglehold being applied to doomed Constantinople. In March 1915, an **Allied** fleet attempting to force the Dardanelles and attack İstanbul was repulsed, with severe losses, by Turkish shore batteries, prompting the even bloodier land campaign usually known as Gallipoli. These days, the straits are still heavily militarized, and modern Çanakkale is very much a navy town.

Deniz Müzesi

Çimenlik Park • Tues, Wed, Fri–Sun 9am–noon & 1.30–5pm • 4TL

Situated in the pleasant Çimenlik Park, itself adorned with assorted field guns, torpedoes and other vintage weaponry, is the town's **Deniz Müzesi** (Military and Naval Museum), housed in the **Çimenlik fortress**, which dates back to 1461–62, constructed in the reign of Sultan Mehmet the Conqueror. Along with the fortress at Kilitbahir, clearly visible on the other side of the Dardanelles narrows, its purpose was to control the crucial straits. Much paraphernalia from the Gallipoli campaign is on show, including an unexploded 38cm shell fired from the British navy's premier battleship, the *Queen Elizabeth*. North of the fortress and moored to the quay is a replica of the mine-layer **Nusrat** (same hours and ticket as museum), which stymied the Allied fleet by re-mining at night, zones that the French and British had swept clean by day.

Arkeoloji Müzesi

Yüzüncü Yıl Caddesi, 2km from the centre of town • Tues, Wed, Fri–Sun 8.30am–noon & 1–5.30pm • 5TL • To get here, flag down any dolmuş along Atatürk Caddesi signed "Kepez" or "Güzelyalı" and get off at the museum.

An hour should be enough to take in the **Arkeoloji Müzesi** (Archeological Museum) – the collection is poorly labelled and the interior very gloomy, but some of the exhibits are quite stunning. Most impressive is the Polyxena Sarcophogus, the earliest relief-carved sarcophogus found in Asia Minor, dating back to the sixth century BC. One of the scenes carved on the side of the funerary monument depicts the sacrifice of Polyxena, a daughter of King Priam of Troy, by Achilles' son, Neoptolemus. Quite different but equally striking is a cabinet of terracotta figurines from ancient Assos. Dating from the fourth century BC, the quality of these grave goods, mainly depicting musicians, is superb. Also look out for the case of gold wreaths and diadems, and a lovely figurine of the goddess Aphrodite. The large garden area is littered with remnants from the classical-era sarcophagi – including columns, capitals, votive stelae and huge earthenware storage jars.

ARRIVAL AND DEPARTURE   ÇANAKKALE

By bus Regular buses, run by Çanakkale Truva, Metro and Kamil Koç companies, make the 310-kilometre trip to Çanakkale from İstanbul's Esenler bus station (5hr 30min; 40TL). The bus will drop you near the ferry terminal in the town centre, close to all the listed accommodation, before heading onto the new, out-of-town *otogar* (inter-city bus station). To return the same way, buy your ticket from the bus companies on the south side of Cumhüriyet Meydan near the tourist office, and along the western end of Cumhüriyet Bulvarı. You can either board near the ferry terminal or take a free service bus to the *otogar* and board there.

By sea bus Sea buses depart Yenikapı ferry terminal in İstanbul for Bandırma (2hrs; 30TL), from where frequent buses head on to Çanakkale (2hr 30min; 20TL).

GALLIPOLI AND TROY TOURS

The **World War I battlefields and Allied cemeteries** scattered along the Gelibolu peninsula are a moving sight, the past violence made all the more poignant by the present beauty of the landscape. The whole area is now either fertile rolling country, or cloaked in thick scrub and pine forest alive with birds, making it difficult to imagine the carnage of 1915. Much of the flatter land is still farmed, and ploughing often turns up pieces of rusting equipment, fragments of shrapnel, human bones and even unexploded munitions. **Troy** is set in an equally haunting landscape, and it's even harder to picture the legendary deeds of Achilles, Agamemnon, Odysseus and the like taking place here. A guided tour of either of these sites can enhance your visit significantly, though the plethora of explanatory panels at Troy, and the convenient local minibuses to the adjacent village of Tevfikiye, make it the easier of the two to do independently.

Hassle Free Tours, operated by the *Anzac House Hostel* (see p.258), offer a three-hour Troy tour (daily 8.30am; €32), which returns in time to join their Gallipoli tour that departs around 11.30am (7hr; €40); this includes lunch and a boat-trip off the ANZAC landing beaches. Over in Eceabat, *TJ's Hostel* (☎0286/814 3121, ⊛anzacgallipolitours.com) offers the same tours for a little cheaper, as does the *Crowded House* hostel's travel agency (see p.266). If there are a few of you, it might be worth hiring a car and your own guide for Gallipoli – TJ at *TJ's Hostel* is a mine of information, with an easy-going Aussie/Turkish demeanor, and Kenan Çelik (☎0532/738 6675, ⊛kcelik.com) is also renowned. Down at Troy, the local-born expert is Mustafa Aşkin (☎09 542/ 243 9359, ⊛thetroyguide.com), who speaks excellent English and has an engaging personality. Car hire is available in Çanakkale from Delta Rent a Car, Cumhuriyet Meydanı 21/1 (☎0286/814 1218).

Alternatively, you can book a **tour from İstanbul**. Hassle Free, at Yeni Akbıyık Cad 10 in Sultanahmet (☎0212/458 5500, ⊛anzachouse.com), run gruelling (6.30am–midnight), one-day guided tours visiting the battlefield sites for €99, or €119 for a more realistic two-day tour, including a night in their Çanakkale hostel (see p.258). Again *TJ's* and *Crowded House* offer the same kind of deal.

By plane Anadolu Jet (wanadolujet.com) and Bora Jet (wborajet.com) both fly from İstanbul Sabiha Gökçen (daily except Thursdays; 40min) with prices from 59TL; shuttle buses and taxis make the 7km journey from the airport into town (10TL and 25TL respectively).

To Troy and Gallipoli If you don't want to take a tour (see box opposite), catch a dolmuş to Troy from the minibus garage from just under the bridge on Atatürk Caddesi (daily 9.30am–8.00pm; April–Oct every 30min, Nov–March hourly; 5TL); but you'll need your own transport to reach the battlefield sites in Gallipoli.

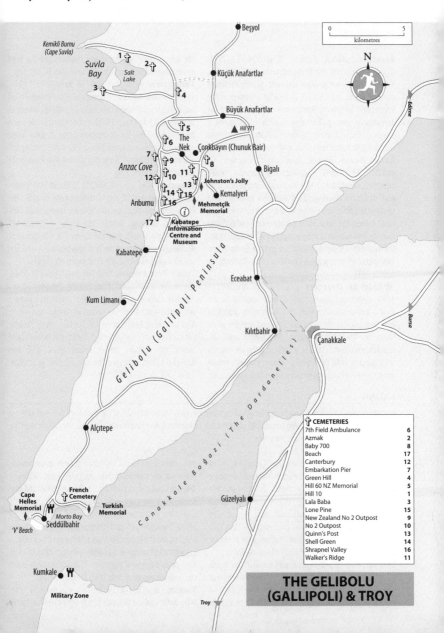

⚰ CEMETERIES	
7th Field Ambulance	6
Azmak	2
Baby 700	8
Beach	17
Canterbury	12
Embarkation Pier	7
Green Hill	4
Hill 60 NZ Memorial	5
Hill 10	1
Lala Baba	3
Lone Pine	15
New Zealand No 2 Outpost	9
No 2 Outpost	10
Quinn's Post	13
Shell Green	14
Shrapnel Valley	16
Walker's Ridge	11

THE GELIBOLU (GALLIPOLI) & TROY

INFORMATION

Tourist information On Cumhuriyet Meydanı, next to the main dock (May–Sept Mon–Fri 8.30am–7.30pm, Sat & Sun 10.30am–6pm; Oct–April Mon–Fri 8.30am–5.30pm; ☎0286/217 1187, ✉canakkaletourism@hotmail.com).

ACCOMMODATION

Other than around ANZAC Day (April 25), you'll have little trouble finding a room. Just south of the tourist office, the Saat Kulesi (clock tower) signals the entrance to a warren of alleys – Fetvane Sokak, Aralık Sokak, Yeni Sokak – that is home to various inexpensive hotels and *pansiyons*. Moving across Demircioğlu Caddesi, or closer to the water, you'll find the more upmarket hotels.

Anzac Saat Kulesi Meydanı 8 ☎0286/217 7777, ⓦanzachotel.com. Practically opposite the Saat Kulesi, this well-run two-star place has neat, plainly decorated en-suite rooms, plus a bath as well as a shower in the immaculate bathrooms. The owners of this hotel and the *Kervansaray* (see p.258) also run the slightly more expensive *Grand Anzac* (ⓦgrandanzachotel.com), around the corner on Kemal Yeri Sokak. **€40**

Anzac House Hostel Cumhuriyet Meydanı 61 ☎0286/213 5969, ⓦanzachouse.com. Well-equipped, clean backpackers' hostel offering basic dorms with laminate flooring, double-glazed windows and spotless bedding. There's free wi-fi and an upstairs video room (where the *Fatal Shore* documentary and *Gallipoli* starring Mel Gibson is shown nightly) while downstairs the Hassle Free travel agency office arrange Gallipoli and Troy tours (see box, p.256). Breakfast extra. Dorm **25TL**, double **70TL**

★ **Hotel des Etrangers** Yalı Cad 25–27 ☎0286/214 2424, ⓦyabancilarioteli.com. A great addition to the local accommodation scene, this eight-room boutique hotel is housed in the same building, and uses the same name, as its 1870's precursor. French-built and run, Heinrich Schliemann (see box, p.260) lodged in the original *Des Etrangers*. Solid stone walls, wooden shutters, ornate wood-carved ceilings and wooden floors help summon up the past without sacrificing any comfort, and the front rooms have balconies with partial sea-views (€100). **€80**

Kervansaray Fetvahane Sok 13 ☎0286/217 8192, ⓦotelkervansaray.com. A quiet, polite and friendly affair run by the same people as the *Anzac* (see above), housed in an unusual (for Turkey) red-brick mansion built a little over a hundred years ago for an Ottoman judge. It has a lovely courtyard garden and a new annexe with rooms that are just as comfy (and cheaper) if less characterful than those in the old part of the hotel. **€50**

Limani Yalı Cad 12 ☎0286/217 2908, ⓦhotellimani.com. Opened in 2010, this waterfront hotel straddles the divide between boutique and business hotels; think pale laminate flooring, white bed-linen, white-painted furniture, plain walls and flat-screen TVs. The economy doubles have no view so are best avoided, those with fine sea-views are, of course, the most expensive. **120TL**

Yellow Rose Pension Yeni Sok 5 ☎0286/217 3343, ⓦyellowrose.4mg.com. More relaxed, cheaper and less business orientated than rival *Anzac House* (see above), with basic – but en-suite – rooms of varying sizes dating back to an early 1980s conversion. The two private doubles out back are particularly popular. Breakfast is included, and there's also laundry service, video room, wi-fi and battlefield tours (arranged through *TJ's* over in Eceabat). Dorm **20TL**, double **60TL**

EATING

Restaurants and cafés line almost the full length of the quayside, both north and south of the main ferry terminal, offering a wide variety of dishes, including (inevitably) plenty of fish and seafood. As a simple rule of thumb, the further from the ferry terminal you go, the cheaper the prices.

Caféska Cumhuriyet Meydanı 28. Çanakkale's most stylish bistro with a funky yet elegant indoor dining space and a surprisingly affordable menu, including modern interpretations of traditional dishes, such as spiced meatballs with herb yoghurt, chilli salsa and sautéed potatoes. The big salad bowls are good value at 7TL to 15TL (one is enough for two people), and various pasta dishes are also on offer at the same price. Daily 10am–midnight.

Cevahir Fetvane Sok 15/A. A very popular and good-value spot serving home-cooked food. Choose a medium or large plate (6TL and 8TL respectively) and have it filled up with anything from chickpea stew to stewed okra, then help yourself to salad. A few tables dot the square outside in the warmer months. Unlicensed. Daily 10am–10pm.

Doyum Cumhuriyet Meydanı 13. The best kebab and *pide* restaurant in town, always packed with locals. It's spotlessly clean, the waitresses are attentive and the dishes well priced. The *kaşarlı pide* comes dripping with its tasty cheese topping, and the kebabs are tender. They even do *içli köfte*, spicy meatball wrapped in a bulgur-wheat coating. You'd be hard-pushed to spend more than 15TL, considerably less if you go for *lahmacun* or *pide*. Daily 8am–midnight.

Kahcevi Çarşı Cad 14. The best place in town for latte, filter coffee and the like, this trendy little place has tables set-out on a quiet pedestrianized street just down from the Yalı mosque. Daily 10am–11pm.

Özel İşkembe Salonu Saat Külesi Meydan. A busy place specializing in soups. Try the delicious *ezogelin* (spicy lentil and tomato) and a hangover-curing tripe soup, along with brain soup – which is hard to find outside İstanbul. The bread here is a rarity too, a dense brown, and *ayran* is served in little bottles. Very popular with locals. Daily 8am–midnight.

Yalova Eski Gümrükhane Sok 7. Established in the 1930s in the old fish market, *Yalova* has a lovely old tiled floor in the downstairs eating area, a stylish roof terrace with views over the sea, and offers a wide range of fish and seafood – the best in town. Farmed fish (sea bass or sea bream) cost around 20TL a portion, their "wild" brethren are sold per kilo – and work out much more expensive. Starters range from 5TL for vegetable-based dishes to 15TL for seafood *meze*. Daily 11am–midnight.

22

NIGHTLIFE

While nightlife for many locals tends to involve nothing more strenuous than a promenade and a meal along the front, the presence in town of a large student population means there's a burgeoning and surprisingly lively bar scene. Indeed, Fetvane Sokak, a narrow lane lined with some of the town's more attractive buildings, is now known locally as Barlar Sokak ("Bar Street"). Needless to say, things get even livelier around ANZAC Day, when Australians and New Zealanders make their presence felt. Several of the venues have **live music**, usually in an upstairs room, with a modest cover charge that includes a local drink.

Han Kahvesi Fetvane Sok. Set in the restored *Yalı Han*, a courtyarded Ottoman-era tradesman's hall, by day this is a favoured tea, coffee and *nargile* joint, while evenings, especially on weekends, see live music and much beer drinking from the local student population. Daily 10am–midnight.

Hayal Kahvesi Fetvane Sok. An offshoot of İstanbul's

famous *Hayal Kahvesi* club (see p.200), this is a cavernous bar set in a period building, with a courtyard café and live music upstairs most evenings. A 50cl beer will set you back 5TL, 3TL during Happy Hour (6–7pm). To see the band (usually rock covers) there's often a cover charge, especially at weekends. Sun–Thurs noon–Fri & Sat noon–2am.

DIRECTORY

Banks and exchange A number of banks (Mon–Fri 9am–12.30pm & 1.30–5pm) can be found on Cumhuriyet Bulvarı and, parallel to it, Kemal Yeri. There are also ATMs on these streets and next to the ferry terminal, and an exchange office next door to *Anzac House Hostel*.

Cinema The cinema below the Gima shopping centre, next door to the bus station, shows mainstream releases in English with Turkish subtitles.

Internet access Maxi Internet Café, Fetvane Sok. The Belediye İş Merkezi also has many smaller internet cafés, and access is available from most of the hotels and hostels, though these tend to be overpriced.

Hospital Hasan Mevsuf Sok (☎0286/217 1098).

Police Kayserili Ahmet Paşa Cad, just north of the ferry terminal.

Post office İnönü Cad (Mon–Sat 8am–11pm).

Troy

Daily: May–Sept 8am–7pm; Oct–April 8am–5pm • 15TL

Although by no means the most spectacular archeological site in Turkey, **Troy**, thanks to Homer, is a household name around the world. Known as Truva in Turkish, the remains of the ancient city lie around 37km south of Çanakkale, a few kilometres west of the main road. If you're expecting something on the scale of the city as re-created for the 2004 Brad Pitt epic *Troy* you are bound to be disappointed, as archeological excavations have revealed that the Troy of Homer (circa 1200 BC) would only have had a population of between five and ten thousand. The ruins are nonetheless impressive in the detail if not in scale, and modern scientific methods have managed to fill the gaps left by earlier excavations. Explanatory panels now dot the site, allowing laypeople to grasp the basic layout and gain a knowledge of the different settlement periods uncovered.

Some history

Until 1871, Troy was generally thought to have existed in legend only. The Troad plain, where the ruins lie, was known to be associated with the Troy that Homer wrote about in the *Iliad*, but all traces of the city had vanished completely. In 1868,

Heinrich Schliemann (1822–90), a German businessman who had made his fortune in America (see box below), obtained permission from the Ottoman government to start digging on a hill known to the Turks as Hisarlık, where earlier excavators had already found the remains of a Classical temple and signs of further, older ruins.

Schliemann's sloppy trenching work resulted in a certain amount of damage to the site, only rectified by the first professional archeologist to work at Troy, the respected Carl William Blegen, whose excavations began in 1932. Schliemann was also accountable for removing the so-called **Treasure of Priam**, a large cache of beautiful jewellery that was taken back to Berlin and subsequently displayed there until 1941, when it was squirrelled away for safety under the city's Zoo Station. The hoard disappeared during the Red Army's sacking of the city in May 1945; long suspected of having been spirited back to the USSR, it resurfaced spectacularly in Moscow in August 1993 and is now on display in the Pushkin Museum there. A legal tussle between Germany and the Russian Federation to determine ownership is now in progress – as well as careful forensic examination of the precious items to answer allegations that Schliemann fraudulently assembled the treasure from scattered sites in Asia Minor.

Whatever Schliemann's shortcomings, his initial, unsystematic excavations did uncover nine layers of remains, representing distinct and consecutive city developments that span four millennia. The oldest, **Troy I**, dates back to about 3600 BC and was followed by four similar settlements. Either Troy VI or VII is thought to have been **the city described by Homer**: the former is known to have been destroyed by an earthquake in about 1275 BC, while the latter shows signs of having been wiped out by fire about a quarter of a century later, around the time historians generally estimate the Trojan War to have taken place. **Troy VIII**, which thrived from 700 to 300 BC, was a Greek foundation, while much of the final layer of development, **Troy IX** (300 BC to 300 AD), was built during the heyday of the Roman Empire.

Although there's no way of being absolutely sure that the **Trojan War** did take place, there's a fair amount of circumstantial evidence suggesting that the city was the scene of some kind of armed conflict, even if it wasn't the ten-year struggle described in the *Iliad*. It's possible that Homer's epic is based on a number of wars fought between the Mycenaean Greeks and the inhabitants of Troy, who, it seems, were alternately trading partners and commercial rivals. Homer's version of events, however, dispensed with these pedestrian possibilities, turning the war into a full-scale heroic drama, complete with bit parts for the ancient Greek gods.

The site

Just right of the official entrance stands a 1970s reconstruction of the giant **wooden horse**; you can climb a ladder into the horse's belly and look out of windows cut into its flanks. The adjacent **excavation house** has a scale model of the site (when it's not out on loan) and an excellent video explaining the history of Troy and the excavations. Just beyond is the ruined city itself, on a small outcrop overlooking the Troad plain, which extends about 8km to the sea. The circular trail takes you around the site; the twenty or

---

HEINRICH SCHLIEMANN

German entrepreneur and archeologist **Heinrich Schliemann** was born into a poor Mecklenburg family in 1822. As a child he became obsessed with the myths of ancient Greece, a passion that would stay with him the rest of his life. Unable to pursue the interest professionally (although he did teach himself ancient Greek, in addition to several modern languages), he amassed a considerable fortune during the Californian Gold Rush of 1849, speculating on the stock market and as an arms contractor during the Crimean war. Always a larger than life character, he forsook commerce at the age of 46, then divorced his long-standing wife to marry a beautiful, seventeen-year old Greek girl, Sophia, before going on to become the world's most celebrated and successful amateur archeologist.

so panels enlisting the help of schematic diagrams are extremely helpful in bringing the ruins to life. Standing on what's left of the ramparts and looking across the plain that stretches out at your feet, it's not too difficult to imagine a besieging army, legendary or otherwise, camped below.

Most impressive of the extant remains are the **east wall and gate** (Panel 2) from Troy VI (1700–1275 BC), of which 330m remain, curving around the eastern and southern flanks of the city. The inward-leaning stone walls, 6m high and over 4m thick, would have been surmounted by a further three metres or so of mud-brick walling. The most important monument of Roman Troy IX, or Ilium, probably erected in the reign of Augustus (31 BC–14 AD), is the **Temple of Athena** (Panel 4). According to the Greek historian Strabo, an earlier temple on the same site was erected by one of Alexander the Great's generals, Lysimachus, after Alexander himself had visited the site and left his armour as a gift. Remains found by Schliemann proved the temple to be of the Doric order, and fragments of its coffered ceiling can still be seen dotted around. The partially reconstructed **Megaron Building** (Panel 5b; protected beneath a giant sail-shaped canopy, the top of which marks the height and shape of the mound under which the remains lay before Schliemann started his excavations) dates back to 2300 BC. The mud-brick masonry was turned a bright red when Troy II was destroyed by fire. Schliemann, erroneously as it turned out, used the evidence of this fire to draw the conclusion that this had been Homer's Troy and that the items he discovered here made up the Treasure of Priam. The burnt bricks you see today are re-creations – the originals lie underneath. From this panel you can also see the massive trench Schliemann drove through the mound in the hope of finding Homer's Troy. A little further on is a ramp (Panel 8), paved with flat stones from Troy II (2500–2300 BC), which would have led to the citadel entrance. Just to the left of this is where Schliemann claimed he found the horde of gold generally known as "The Treasure of Priam", some of which his wife Sophia (see box opposite) was photographed wearing, making the Schliemanns famous around the world.

There's little left standing of the **South Gate** (Panel 12) of Troy VI, but the stretch of paving leading through it is impressive. What interests most visitors here, however, is that this just could be Homer's Scaean Gate, scene of much of the dramatic action in the *Iliad* and portal through which the unwitting Trojans pulled the legendary wooden horse.

ARRIVAL AND DEPARTURE

TROY

By dolmuş From Çanakkale, dolmuşes depart from the minibus garage from just under the bridge on Atatürk Caddesi (daily 9.30am–8.00pm; April–Oct every 30min, Nov–March hourly).

Tours A number of companies offer tours from Çanakkale (see box, p.256).

INFORMATION

Entrance The site is signalled by the ticket office – marked "Gişe" – just opposite where the dolmuş from Çanakkale drops its passengers.

Books There are a few small shops here where you can pick up a copy of Troia/Wilusa by Dr Manfred Korfman (20TL), the archeologist who, between 1988 and his death in 2005, oversaw the site's excavation. The book is copiously illustrated and really helps bring Troy to life, especially as it contains a map that will guide you around and pages of information corresponding to numbers on the signs at the site.

Eating There's a reasonable self-service cafeteria that makes most of its profits serving hungry coach-parties.

Gallipoli (Gelibolu)

Burdened with a grim military history, but endowed with some fine scenery and beaches, the slender **Gelibolu (Gallipoli) peninsula** – roughly 60km in length and ranging between 4km and 18km wide – forms the northwest side of the **Dardanelles**, the narrow strait connecting the Aegean with the Sea of Marmara. Whether you approach the peninsula from Şarköy or (more likely) Keşan, the road there is pretty, swooping down in long arcs past the Saros gulf.

Site of the 1915 **Gallipoli landings** by the Allied troops, the peninsula contains a mind-numbing series of battlefields and cemeteries that tell of the tragic defeat by the Turkish forces. For Turks, the region also holds a great deal of significance, as the Gallipoli campaign made famous a previously unknown lieutenant-colonel, Mustafa Kemal, who later became Atatürk (see p.264). There's no public transport here so your best bet is a tour (see box, p.256) or to hire a car in Çanakkale.

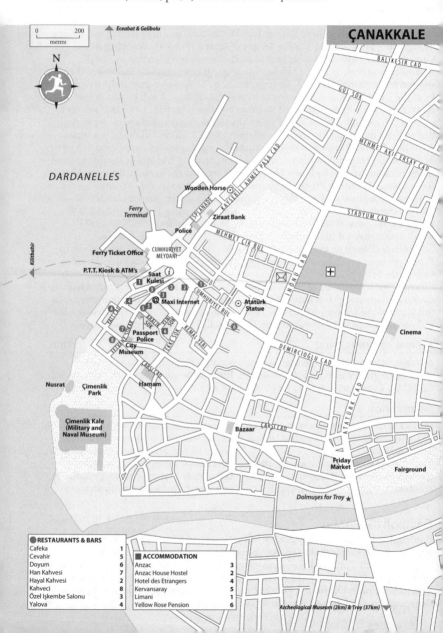

ÇANAKKALE

0 — 200 metres

N

Eceabat & Gelibolu

BALIKESIR CAD

GUL SOK

MEHMET AKIF ERSAY CAD

DARDANELLES

Wooden Horse

KAYSERILI AHMET PAŞA CAD

STADYUM CAD

Ferry Terminal

Ziraat Bank

ESPLANADE

Police

MEHMET ÇIK BUL

Killitbahir

Ferry Ticket Office

CUMHURIYET MEYDANI

P.T.T. Kiosk & ATM's

Saat Kulesi (i)

@ **Maxi Internet**

CUMHURIYET BUL

INÖNÜ CAD

Atatürk Statue

Cinema

Passport Police

City Museum

ÇARŞI CAD

KEMAL YERI

DEMIRCIOGLU CAD

ATATÜRK CAD

Nusrat

Çimenlik Park

Hamam

Çimenlik Kale (Military and Naval Museum)

Bazaar

ÇARŞI CAD

Friday Market

Fairground

Dolmuşes for Troy ★

RESTAURANTS & BARS
Cafeka	1
Cevahir	5
Doyum	6
Han Kahvesi	7
Hayal Kahvesi	2
Kahveci	8
Özel Işkembe Salonu	3
Yalova	4

ACCOMMODATION
Anzac	3
Anzac House Hostel	2
Hotel des Etrangers	4
Kervansaray	5
Limani	1
Yellow Rose Pension	6

Archeological Museum (2km) & Troy (37km) ▽

Some history

Soon after the start of World War I it became obvious to the Allies that Russia could not be supplied by sea, nor a Balkan front opened against the Central Powers, unless Ottoman Turkey was eliminated. **Winston Churchill**, in his earliest important post as First Lord of the Admiralty, reasoned that the quickest way to accomplish this would be to force the Dardanelles with a fleet and bombard İstanbul into submission. A combined Anglo-French armada made several attempts on the straits during November 1914, which were repulsed, but they returned in earnest on March 18, 1915. This time they managed to penetrate less than 10km up the waterway before striking numerous Turkish mines, losing half a dozen vessels and hundreds of men. The Allies retreated and command squabbles erupted over allocation of troops to the campaign. The generals saw the Western Front as paramount, whereas politicians – foremost among them, Churchill – wanted to knock Turkey out of the war first in order to weaken Germany, while at the same time exciting anti-Turkish feelings in Bulgaria and bringing it, too, into the war.

Regrouped at Mudros harbour on the Greek island of Limnos, the joint expeditionary forces took several months to prepare an amphibious assault on the Turkish positions along the peninsula. During this time, the British had no way of knowing that Turkish forces defending the straits were cripplingly under-supplied. Had they attempted it, another naval sprint down the Dardanelles might have succeeded, but instead the delay gave the Turks the chance to strengthen their own defences.

The plan eventually formulated by the British and French commanders called for an Anglo-French landing at Cape Helles, Seddülbahir and Morto Bay at the mouth of the straits, and a simultaneous **ANZAC** (Australia-New Zealand Army Corps) assault at Kabatepe beach 13km north. The two forces were to drive towards each other, link up and neutralize the Turkish shore batteries controlling the Dardanelles.

The landings

The Australians landed first at dawn on April 25, 1915, with the British and French making shore around an hour afterwards, followed by the New Zealanders later in the day. The rather hare-brained scheme ran into trouble from the start. Anglo-French brigades at the southernmost cape were pinned down by accurate Turkish fire, and the French contingent was virtually annihilated; after two days, they had only managed to penetrate 6.5km inland – and never managed to move any further. The fate of the ANZAC landing was even more horrific: owing to a drifting signal buoy, the Aussies and Kiwis disembarked not on the wide, flat sands of Kabatepe, but at a cramped and Turkish-dominated cove next to Arıburnu, 2km north. Despite heavy casualties (around two thousand on the first day alone), the ANZACs advanced inland in staggered parties, as the Turks initially retreated. The next day, goaded by their commanders, they managed to threaten the Turkish strongpoint of Çonkbayırı above. It was here that one Mustafa Kemal, a previously unknown lieutenant-colonel, rushed in reinforcements, telling his poorly equipped troops, "I do not order you to fight, I order you to die." Amazingly, it worked: the ANZAC force never made it further than 800m inland, despite a supplementary British landing at Cape Suvla to the north. With the exception of ferocious battles for the summit in early August, both sides settled into long-term trench warfare. Finally, around Christmas 1915, the Allies gave up, with the last troops leaving Seddülbahir on January 8, 1916. Churchill's career went into temporary eclipse, while that of Mustafa Kemal was only just beginning.

From carnage to nationhood

The reasons for the **Allied defeat** are many. In addition to the chanciness of the basic strategy, the callousness and incompetence of the Allied commanders – who often countermanded each other's orders or failed to press advantages with reinforcements – cannot be underestimated. With hindsight, you cannot help but wonder why the

22

ANZAC DAY

ANZAC Day, April 25, is the busiest day of the year for the Gelibolu peninsula, as thousands of Australians and New Zealanders arrive to commemorate the Allied defeat, providing a huge annual boost to the local economy. The day begins with the **Dawn Service** at 5.30am at ANZAC Cove, though most people arrive much earlier to camp out, as the police close all the roads around the grave sites to traffic from 3am. The service used to be a somewhat informal ceremony, but in recent years thousands have attended, and it now features official speeches, prayers and a representative from the Australian or New Zealand forces playing a poignant "Last Post" as the sun rises over ANZAC Cove. An hour's breakfast break follows before the rest of the morning's ceremonies resume – **wreath laying** at the British, French and Turkish memorials, and more services at the Australian memorial at Lone Pine and the New Zealand memorial at Chunuk Bair.

Allies didn't concentrate more on Cape Suvla and the flat, wide valley behind, skirting the fortified Ottoman heights to reach the Dardanelles' northwest shore. On the **Turkish side**, much of the credit for the successful resistance must go to Mustafa Kemal, then relatively obscure, but later better known as **Atatürk**. His role in the Turkish victory at Çonkbayırı is legendary. Mustafa Kemal seemed to enjoy a charmed life, narrowly escaping death on several occasions, and, aside from his tactical skills, is credited with various other extraordinary accomplishments, but primarily that of rekindling morale, by threats, persuasion or example, among often outgunned and outnumbered Ottoman infantrymen. Indeed, most Turks believe that their nation, salvaged from the crumbling wreckage of the Ottoman Empire, began its birth at Gallipoli, when they found the man (Atatürk) with the bravery and acumen to resist the Allies, and the Turkish soldier proved he was every bit as brave and able as his foes.

At various times, half a million men were deployed by defenders and attackers alike; of these, well over fifty percent were **killed, wounded or missing**. Allied deaths numbered around 52,000, while incomplete records have led to estimates of Turkish dead to be anywhere between 50,000 and 200,000. The carnage among the ANZACs, in particular, was especially severe compared to the island-nations' populations, but would in fact be dwarfed by the number of ANZACs killed on the Western Front later in the war – around 10,600 lost their lives in the Gallipoli campaign compared with some 60,000 for the entire war. Claims voiced in some quarters that the Allied top brass regarded the "colonials" as expendable cannon-fodder have never fully been borne out; indeed, more British and Irish troops died at Gallipoli than ANZACs, with two Irish battalions suffering over fifty percent casualties on the first day and the 42nd Manchester Division being almost completely wiped out. However, this baptism by blood had several long-term effects: a sense of Australia and New Zealand having come of age as sovereign countries; the designation of April 25 as ANZAC Day, a solemn holiday in Australia and New Zealand (see box above); and a healthy antipodean scepticism, pending an evaluation of actual national interest in the face of blandishments to join international adventures.

Kabatepe Information Centre and Museum

9km northwest of Eceabat • Daily 8.30am–5pm • 3TL

The first stop on most tours is at the recently refurbished **Kabatepe Information Centre and Museum**, which contains a well-labelled selection of war memorabilia, including touching letters home, photographs of the trenches, weapons and uniforms. The only sour note is the rather ghastly inclusion of some human, presumably Allied, remains.

The cemeteries, landing points and battlefields

The first points encountered along the coast road north of the centre are the **Beach**, **Shrapnel Valley** and **Shell Green** cemeteries – the latter 300m inland up a steep track, unsuitable for all but 4WD vehicles, and consequently missed out by most tours. These are followed by **ANZAC Cove** and **Arıburnu**, site of the first, bungled ANZAC landing and location of the dawn service on ANZAC Day. At ANZAC Cove, a memorial bears Atatürk's famous quotation concerning the Allied dead, which, translated into English, begins: "Those heroes that shed their blood and lost their lives … you are now lying in the soil of a friendly country." Looking inland, you'll see the murderous badlands that gave the defenders such an advantage. Beyond Arıburnu, the terrain flattens out and the four other **cemeteries** (Canterbury, No. 2 Outpost, New Zealand No. 2 Outpost and Embarkation Pier) are more dispersed.

A couple of kilometres north of Arıburnu are the beaches and salt lake at **Cape Suvla**, today renamed Kemikli Burnu ("The Bone-strewn Headland"), location of another six **cemeteries**: Hill 10, Azmak, 7th Field Ambulance, Green Hill, Lala Bala and Hill 60 (with its memorial to the New Zealand forces). All contain mainly English, Scottish, Welsh and Irish dead, with ANZAC graves also in Hill 10 and 7th Field Ambulance. The roads up here are little more than dirt tracks, and most tours don't make it this far.

From ANZAC Cove, tours go uphill along the road northeast that roughly follows what was the front line, to the strong points (now cemeteries) scattered around **Çonkbayırı** hill. To the left of this road is **Shrapnel Valley** – the single, perilous supply line that ran up-valley from the present location of Beach Cemetery to the trenches. First up is **Lone Pine** (Kanlı Sırt), lowest strategic position on the ridge and the largest graveyard-cum-memorial to those buried unmarked or at sea. Action here was considered a sideshow to the main August offensive further up Çonkbayırı; a total of 28,000 men died in four days at both points. Just up from Lone Pine is the **Mehmetçik Memorial** to the Turkish soldiers who perished, and at **Johnston's Jolly** (named after an officer who liked to "jolly the Turks up" with his gun) is a heavily eroded section of **trench**, peaceful now beneath the pine trees. **Quinn's Post**, the scene of some of the fiercest fighting of the entire campaign, is now "home" to 473 of the fallen, 294 of them unidentified.

From here the road forks: to the left is **The Nek** – where much of the action of Peter Weir's film *Gallipoli* takes place - and **Walker's Ridge** cemetery; to the right, the road continues uphill to **Baby 700** cemetery – the high-water mark of the Allied advance on April 25 – and to the massive New Zealand memorial obelisk and the five-monolith Turkish memorial on the crest of **Çonkbayırı** hill (Chunuk Bair). On the Turkish memorial are Atatürk's words and deeds – chief among the latter being his organization of successful resistance to the Allied attacks of August 6–10. The spot where the Turkish leader's pocket watch stopped a fragment of shrapnel is highlighted, as is the grave of a Turkish soldier discovered in 1990 when the trenches were reconstructed. On this part of the front, the trenches of the opposing forces lay within a few metres of each other, and the modern road corresponds to the no-man's-land.

To the southern cape

The harbour of **KABATEPE** village lies 2km south of the Kabatepe Information Centre. There's a good beach to the north of town – the intended site of the ANZAC landing – but if you're after a swim, wait until you reach **KUM LIMANI**, another 3km further south, where an even better strand fringes a warm, clean, calm sea, unusual this far north. There's been little development of this beautiful setting, but you probably won't be alone: a number of tour companies bring their clients here for a dip after battlefield sightseeing.

The British **Cape Helles Memorial** obelisk adorns the Turkish equivalent of Land's End, 16km beyond Kum Limanı and just past the village of Seddülbahir. From Cape Helles itself, the views south to Bozcaada (Tenedos), west to Gökçeada (Imvros) and east to Asia are magnificent, and abundant **Ottoman fortifications** hint at the age-old importance of the place. Tucked between the medieval bulwarks is an excellent beach, the **V Beach** of the Allied expedition, behind which is a **campsite** – and the biggest of five **British cemeteries** in the area. A turning just before Seddülbahir leads to the **French**

Cemetery above Morto Bay, one of the most striking of all the memorials, with its serried rows of named black crosses, and to the nearby **Turkish Memorial**, resembling a stark, tetrahedral footstool. Locally organized tours rarely venture this far, so if you're intent on seeing these two, you'll have to make your own arrangements (see box, p.256).

Eceabat

ECEABAT, smaller than Çanakkale (see p.255), is the closest base for visiting the battlefield sites, whether by yourself or on a tour. There is nothing much of interest – historical or otherwise – in the village itself and the only real reason to choose it over Çanakkale across the strait is to avoid the short ferry-hop.

ARRIVAL AND INFORMATION   ECEABAT

By bus and ferry Buses from İstanbul drop you near the ferry jetty, from where car ferries run across the Dardanelles to Çanakkale hourly (24hr; passengers 2TL, cars 25TL). The bus-company ticket offices are right in front of the jetty at Cumhuriyet Meydanı.

Information There's a PTT booth by the jetty, which can change money, and an ATM nearby.

ACCOMMODATION

Accommodation is plentiful, but you'll need to book well ahead if you want to stay in town for ANZAC Day.

Aqua İstiklal Cad 91 ☎ 0286/814 2458, ⓦ heyboss.com. A stone-faced hotel right on the waterfront near the jetty, with smart modern rooms, many with sea views. The open-buffet breakfast is taken in the rustic-looking dining room. **120TL**

Crowded House Hüseyin Avni Sok 4 ☎ 0286/814 1565, ⓦ crowdedhousegallipoli.com. A little way inland, more or less opposite the ferry terminal, this popular and well-run hostel has six-bed dorm rooms, doubles, a café and a book-swap service. Also the home of the Crowded House Travel Agency (see box, p.256). Dorm **€7**, double **€30**

TJ's To the right of the ferry terminal, looking inland from the waterfront ☎ 0286/814 3121, ⓦ anzacgallipolitours.com. At the time of writing, local character and guide TJ (married to an Australian) was in the process of turning his place into a boutique hotel-cum-hostel with something for everyone – including fully-equipped high-tech suite rooms for the film crews who visit fairly often from down under. He promises to be open by ANZAC Day 2012 (see website for details).

EATING AND DRINKING

There's a line of simple *pide* and *kebap* salons in front of the jetty, plus a smattering of antipodean-named **bars** around *TJ's Hostel*, easily spotted by the Australian and New Zealand flags hanging outside.

Hanimeli Feribot İskelesi. For home-cooked-style food, this slightly overpriced place is worth a look. The *mantı* is 9TL and *gözleme* 5TL, but it makes a change from the usual joints, and is female run. Unlicensed. Daily 10am–8pm.

Liman İskele Caddesi, around 400m south of the ferry terminal. By general consensus, the best food in town is served here at this well-priced fish restaurant with an attractive wooden interior. Wild-caught fish is seasonal and much more expensive than the fish-farmed staples of sea bream and sea bass (around 18TL a portion). Daily 11am–midnight.

22

OIL-WRESTLING FESTIVAL

Edirne

Out on the Thracian plain, some 230km northwest of İstanbul and only a short distance from the Greek and Bulgarian frontiers, lies the beautifully preserved Ottoman city of Edirne. Although tiny in comparison to İstanbul, with a population of around 130,000, Edirne once reigned as the capital city of the Ottoman Empire and has a clutch of impressive buildings to prove it. One of these, the Selimiye Camii, is arguably Turkey's finest Ottoman mosque, the crowning achievement of the imperial architect Mimar Sinan (see box, p.80). A delightfully relaxed and charming town, Edirne entertains a steady stream of day-tripping tourists, border hoppers and students from the town's university. The town's annual Kırkpınar oil-wrestling festival (see box, p.271), the most important in the country, not only attracts huge crowds but places Edirne firmly on the tourist map.

Some history

For all its humble beauty, Edirne is a town with a turbulent history – its strategic military setting has led to its repeated capture over the centuries. Founded as *Orestias* (if you believe the Greek mythology), Edirne has undergone numerous name changes throughout its varied history, first becoming the Thracian settlement of *Uscudama* and later, **Hadrianopolis**, designated the main centre of Roman Thrace by Emperor Hadrian.

Under the Byzantines it retained its significance as a strategic pit-stop for attempts on the capital or the Balkans, and time after time unsuccessful besiegers of Constantinople vented their frustrations on Hadrianopolis as they retreated. A fair few emperors met their ends here in pitched battles with Thracian "barbarians" of one sort or another.

By the mid-fourteenth century, the **Ottomans** had joined forces with the Byzantines in a web of mutual defence treaties and marriage links and in 1361 Hadrianopolis was surrendered to the besieging Murat I, making it the provisional Ottoman capital. It wasn't until 1458 that the Ottoman court was completely moved to the Bosphorus; a century later, Mehmet the Conqueror still trained troops and tested artillery here in preparation for the march on Constantinople.

Thanks to its excellent opportunities for hunting and falconry, Edirne, as the Turks renamed it, remained a favourite haunt of numerous sultans for three more centuries, earning the title *Der-I Saadet* or "Happiness Gate". It's said that there were enough victory celebrations, circumcision ceremonies and marriages held in Edirne to make even Constantinople jealous.

Decline set in during the eighteenth century, prompted largely by an **earthquake** in 1751. During each of the **Russo-Turkish wars** of 1829 and 1878–79, the city was occupied and pillaged by Tsarist troops; far worse were the Bulgarians, who in 1913 presided over a four-month spree of atrocities. The Greeks, as one of the victorious World War I Allies, **annexed Edirne** along with the rest of Turkish Thrace from 1920 to 1922, and Turkish sovereignty over the city was only confirmed by the 1923 Treaty of Lausanne.

Eski Camii

Talat Paşa Caddesi

The logical starting point for exploring Edirne is **Eski Camii**, the oldest mosque in town. This boxy structure, topped by nine vaults, is a more elaborate version of Bursa's Ulu Camii (see p.244). Emir Süleyman, son of the luckless Beyazit I, began it in 1403, but it was his younger brother Mehmet I – the only one of three brothers left alive after a bloody succession struggle – who completed it eleven years later. The mosque is famous for its giant works of **calligraphy**, the most celebrated being the large Arabic inscriptions on either side of the front door, one in the name of Allah, the other of Mohammed.

The Bedesten

Mimar Sinan Caddesi • Mon–Sat 9am–7pm

The **Bedesten**, Edirne's first covered market, was constructed by Mehmet I; a portion of its revenue went to the nearby Eski Camii (see above). The barn-like building, with its fourteen vaulted chambers – indebted to a Bursa prototype, as with Eski Camii – has been restored in the past decade, but modern shops and poor paintwork make the interior drab and unimpressive.

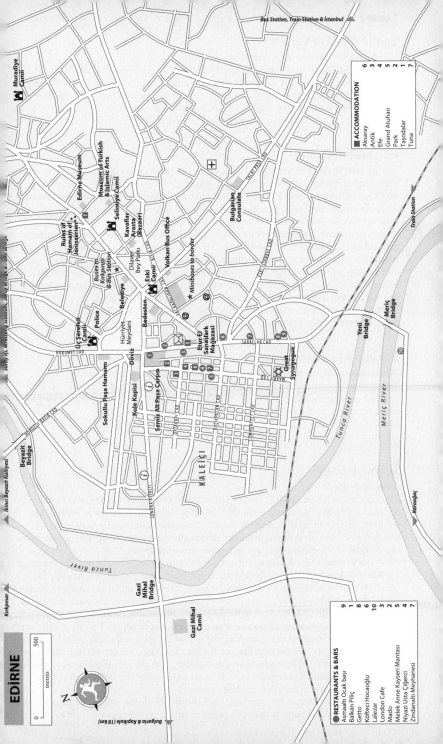

Semiz Ali Paşa Çarşısı

Corner of Londra Asfaltı and Saraçlar Caddesi · Mon–Sat 9am–7pm

The **Semiz Ali Paşa** bazaar was established by Mimar Sinan in 1568 at the behest of Semiz Ali, one of the most able and congenial of the Ottoman grand viziers. A massive fire in 1992 burned out many of its 130 shops, but renovations have been administered with care – particularly impressive is the beautiful multi-domed ceiling. Gold and silver jewellery and clothing are just some of the goods on offer here.

Üç Şerefeli Camii

The **Üç Şerefeli Camii** replaced the Eski Camii as Edirne's Friday mosque in 1447. Ten years in the making, its conceptual design represented the pinnacle of Ottoman religious architecture until overshadowed by the Selimiye Camii (see below) a short time later.

The mosque's name – "three-balconied" – derives from the presence of three galleries for the muezzin on the tallest of the four **minarets**, all of which are decorated with a different pattern – chequered, spiral, zigzag and fluted. Each of the three balconies is reached by a separate stairway within the minaret. The **courtyard**, too, was an innovation, centred on a *şadırvan* (ritual ablutions fountain) and ringed by porphyry and marble columns pilfered from Roman buildings. The experimental nature of the mosque is further confirmed by its **interior**, much wider than it is deep and covered by a dome 24m in diameter. It was the largest that the Turks had built at the time and, to impart a sense of space, the architect relied on just two free-standing columns, with the other four recessed into front and back walls to form a hexagon.

Sokullu Paşa Hamamı

Off Hükümet Caddesi · Daily 6am–10pm · 30TL including soap massage and scrub, obligatory 1TL tip for the towel boy

The sixteenth-century **Sokullu Paşa Hamamı**, across from Üç Şerefeli Camii, was built by Mimar Sinan. Locals rate it as the best *hamam* in town, and it's certainly a bargain when compared to the famous baths in İstanbul (see p.227), though it's not as well maintained as it might be. There are separate wings for men and women; the women's entrance is around the corner from the main street.

Selimiye Camii

Meydan, Babademirtaş Mah

The masterly **Selimiye Camii**, arguably Turkey's finest mosque, was designed by the 80-year-old Mimar Sinan (see box, p.80) in 1569 at the command of Selim II. The work of a confident craftsman at the height of his powers, it's visible from some distance away on the Thracian plain and is virtually the municipal symbol, reproduced on the sides of Edirne's buses, postcards and tourist brochures.

You can approach the Selimiye across Edirne's central park, Dilaver Bey, then through the **Kavaflar Arasta** (Cobbler's Arcade; Mon–Sat 9am–7pm), which was built by Sinan's pupil Davut and is still used as a covered market. Every day, under the market's prayer dome, the shopkeepers promise that they will do their business honestly. At the end of the market, a flight of stone steps will take you to the mosque **courtyard**, a visual spectacle with its surrounding portico made up of multiple domes, held up by ancient columns. At the centre of the courtyard, the delicately fashioned *şadırvan* (ablutions fountain) is the finest in the city. Each of the four identical, slender minarets has three balconies – Sinan's nod to his predecessors – and at 71m are the tallest in the world after those in Mecca. The detailed carved portal once graced the Ulu Camii in Birgi and was transported here in pieces, then reassembled.

It's the celestial **interior** (no cameras), specifically the dome, which impresses most. Planned expressly to surpass that of Aya Sofya in İstanbul (see p.43), it manages this

– at 31.5m in diameter – by a bare few centimetres, and Sinan thus achieved a lifetime's ambition. Supported by eight mammoth twelve-sided pillars, the cupola floats 44m above the floor, inscribed with calligraphy proclaiming the glory of Allah. Immediately below the dome, the muezzin's platform, supported on twelve columns, is an ideal place from which to contemplate the proportions of the mosque. The delicate painting on the platform's underside is a faithful restoration of the original and gives some idea of how the mosque dome must once have looked. The water of the small marble drinking fountain beneath symbolizes life, under the dome of eternity. The most ornate stone carving is reserved for the *mihrab* and *mimber*, backed by fine İznik faïence illuminated by sunlight streaming in through the many windows.

Türk ve İslam Eserleri Müzesi
Tues–Sun 8am–noon & 1–5pm • 3TL

An associated medrese, at the northeastern corner of the Selimiye Camii, is now the **Türk ve İslam Eserleri Müzesi** (Museum of Turkish and Islamic Arts), housing assorted wooden, ceramic and martial knick-knacks from the province. There are fifteen rooms including one dedicated to oil wrestling (see box below), with a portrait gallery of its stars, a pair of oil-wrestler's leather trousers and blow-ups of miniatures depicting this six-hundred-year-old sport through the ages.

OIL WRESTLING AND THE KIRKPINAR FESTIVAL

Oil wrestling (*yağlı güreş*) is popular throughout Turkey but reaches the pinnacle of its acclaim at the doyen of tournaments, the annual **Kırkpınar Festival**, staged early each summer on the Saray İçi islet outside Edirne. The preferred date is the first week of July, but the three-day event is moved back into June if it coincides with Ramadan or either of the two major *bayrams* (religious holidays) following it.

The wrestling matches have been held annually (except in times of war or Edirne's occupation) for over six centuries and, despite the rather sterile environment of the stadium that now hosts the wrestling, traditional routines still permeate the event. The contestants – up to a thousand per year – dress only in leather knickers called *kisbet* and are slicked from head to toe in diluted olive oil. Wrestlers are classed by height, not by weight, from toddlers up to the *pehlivan* (full-size) category. Warm-up exercises, the *peşrev*, are accompanied by the *davul* (deep-toned drum) and *zurna* (single-reed Islamic oboe), the music provided by the local Romany population. The competitors and the actual matches are solemnly introduced by the *cazgır* (master of ceremonies), usually himself a former champion.

The bouts, several of which take place simultaneously, can last anything from a few minutes to a couple of hours, until one competitor collapses or has his back pinned to the grass. Referees keep a lookout for the limited number of illegal moves or holds and victors advance more or less immediately to the next round until, after the second or third day, only the *başpehlivan* (champion) remains. Despite the small prize purse, donated by the Kırkpınar Ağaları – the local worthies who put on the whole show – a champion is usually well set-up in terms of appearance and endorsement fees and should derive ample benefit from the furious on- and off-site betting. On the whole, gladiators tend to be villagers from all over Turkey who have won regional titles, starry-eyed with the prospect of fame and escape from a rural rut.

FESTIVAL PRACTICALITIES

The wrestling itself spreads over three days, with the opening ceremony and children's bouts taking place from mid-afternoon Friday. Saturday's action lasts from midday until 5pm, with the final bouts and award/closing ceremonies between midday and 7pm on the Sunday. The best way to get tickets is through booking agent Biletix (see box, p.195).

Frequent free buses run from the Belediye building in the centre of Edirne to the stadium (around 10min). The Edirne municipality invariably organizes a series of ancillary events that prolong the festivities for another three days and include free Turkish music concerts in the park below the Selimiye Camii at 9pm each evening. For more information, see ⓦ kirkpinar.com.

23

Edirne Müzesi

Tues–Sun 8am–noon & 1–5pm • 5TL

The **Edirne Müzesi** (Edirne Museum), set in a modern building just northeast of the Selimiye Camii precincts, contains a predictable assortment of Greco-Roman fragments. Its ethnographic section focuses on carpet weaving and other local crafts, including colourful village bridal-wear, which preceded the bland white confectionery that's been adopted from the West.

Muradiye Camii

Mimar Sinan Caddesi • Admission only at prayer times

Northeast of the centre, the **Muradiye Camii** is an easy ten-minute, down-then-up, walk along Mimar Sinan Caddesi from the Selimiye Camii. According to legend, Celaleddin Rumi, founder of the Mevlevi dervish order, appeared in a dream to the pious Murat II in 1435, urging him to build a sanctuary for the Mevlevis in Edirne. The result is this pleasing, T-shaped *zaviye* (dervish convent) crouched on a hill looking north over vegetable patches and the Tunca River; the grassy entry court lends a final bucolic touch. The interior is distinguished by the best İznik tiles outside Bursa; the *mihrab* and walls up to eye level are solid with them. Higher surfaces once bore calligraphic frescoes, but these have probably been missing since the catastrophic earthquake of 1751. The dervishes initially congregated in the *eyvans* (transepts), which form the ends of the T's cross-stroke; Murat later housed them in a separate *tekke* (gathering place) in the garden.

The Great Synagogue

Edirne, along with İstanbul, İzmir and Salonica, was a major place of refuge for Jews fleeing persecution in sixteenth-century Europe – particularly Spain. The **synagogue** here, built in 1906, has twin stair-towers and a fine Neoclassical facade. It was once the largest in the Balkans, serving a population of some 22,000. Now abandoned, it is still worth strolling south down Maarif Caddesi from the city centre to have a look at it, though the old wooden houses that once housed the Jewish population have long been torn down to make way for apartment blocks.

Along the Tunca River

At Edirne, the **Tunca River** is crossed by the greatest concentration of historic bridges in Thrace, most of them now restored. The best way to see them is to take a stroll along the river parallel to the dykes and water meadows of the Tunca's right bank. Despite the litter, and the odd down-and-out who frequents the riverbanks in the evening, stretches of the river are charming – storks wade in the sluggish brown waters, frogs croak in the reeds and willows and poplars line the banks. A good place to start is at the pair of bridges furthest upstream, the fifteenth-century **Saray (Süleyman)** and **Fatih** bridges, which join the respective left and right banks of the Tunca with the river island of **Saray İçi**. The island once supported the **Edirne Sarayı**, a royal palace founded by Murat II, which was blown to bits by the Turks in 1877 to prevent the munitions stored inside from falling into Russian hands. Today, there's nothing much left except the rubble of some baths and a tower, next to which is a modern concrete stadium, venue for the Kırkpınar wrestling matches (see box, p.271).

Following the river bank west and downstream for half an hour brings you to the double-staged **Beyazit bridge**, which crosses another small island in the Tunca River. This seventeenth-century bridge is more commonly known as the Tek Gözü Köprüsü ("One-Eyed Bridge"). Across the bridge, on the left bank, is the **İkinci Beyazit Külliyesi** (see opposite).

Another twenty minutes' walk south along the river will bring you to the **Gazi Mihal bridge**, an Ottoman refurbishment of a thirteenth-century Byzantine span and hence the oldest around Edirne. Gazi Mihal was a Christian nobleman who became an enthusiastic convert to Islam – hence the epithet *Gazi*, "Warrior for the Faith". His namesake mosque is at the western end of the bridge, from where it's an easy five-hundred-metre stroll back into town.

İkinci Beyazit Külleyesi and Museum of Health
On the left bank of the river near the Tek Gözü Köprüsü bridge (see opposite) is the **İkinci Beyazit Külliyesi**, built between 1484 and 1488 by Hayrettin, court architect to Beyazit II. This is the largest Ottoman spiritual and physical-welfare complex ever constructed. Within a single irregular boundary wall and beneath a hundred-dome silhouette, are assembled a mosque, food storehouse, bakery, *imaret* (soup kitchen), dervish hostel, medical school and insane asylum. The restoration work, which has been going on for some years, is almost complete. Except for its handsome courtyard and the sultan's loge inside, the **mosque** itself is disappointing, and more interesting is the **medical school** in the furthest northwest corner of the complex. This was conveniently linked to the *timarhane*, or madhouse, built around an open garden, leading to the magnificent **darüşşifa** (therapy centre). This hexagonal, domed structure consists of a circular central space with six *eyvans* (side-chambers) opening onto it; the inmates were brought here regularly, where musicians would play to soothe the more intractable cases. Strange five-sided rooms with fireplaces open off three of the *eyvans*. The *darüşşifa* is now home to the well-intentioned but fairly dull **Trakya University Museum of Health** (Tues–Sun 9am–6pm; 5TL), boasting a collection of old medical equipment and photographs.

23

ARRIVAL AND DEPARTURE   EDIRNE

By bus Regular buses from İstanbul's Büyük Otogar (approx every 20min; 5am–midnight; 2hr 30min; 20TL) arrive at Edirne's bus station (☎0284/225 1979), just over 2km southeast of the centre. A free minibus service runs into town, stopping opposite the Belediye (town hall). This is the easiest place to buy your return ticket, with Volkan, Metro, Ulusoy and Nilüfer offices dotted around the bus stop. All companies run buses to İstanbul approximately

every hour from 8am till 8pm, with free minibus shuttles to the station leaving town 30min before departure.
By train Arriving by train is less appealing: the journey from İstanbul takes over six hours and the station is 1km beyond the bus station; from here, a taxi (15TL) is the easiest option into town. Trains depart İstanbul twice daily at 3.20pm and 10pm, and depart Edirne for İstanbul at 7.30am and 3am.

GETTING AROUND

You can tour the main sights of Edirne **on foot**, but as the Ottoman monuments are widely scattered you'll need a full day to do it. Walking, you can follow the willow-shaded banks of the Tunca River for some distance, but midsummer is hot and humid and what starts out as a pleasure can end up feeling more like a punishment. Public transport doesn't connect up the more far flung sites, but you could hire a **phaeton** (horse-drawn carriage) from the bottom of Saraçlar Cad (prices range from 7–12TL for a city tour but bargain hard) or take a taxi.

INFORMATION

Tourist office Londra Asfaltı 76 (Mon–Fri 9am–5pm; ☎0284/225 5260).

ACCOMMODATION

Accommodation can be tight in Edirne and advance bookings of at least a month are recommended during the main Turkish holidays and the Kırkpınar festival. Edirne's strategic location brings with it a price boost but there are still a few bargains to be found. If travelling in low season be sure to negotiate as the prices displayed in hotel lobbies can often be reduced up to a third.

Aksaray Alipaşa Ortakapı Cad 8 ☎0284/212 6035, ☎0284/225 6806. One of the best budget options around, this no-frills hotel housed in a nineteenth-century

wood-built mansion is as minimal as it gets. The cheapest rooms, with shared bathrooms, offer little more than a room with a bed, but are definitely a bargain. Despite the

lacklustre decor, rooms are clean and light and the affable, English-speaking staff add a homely vibe. There's no internet connection here, but *Melek Anne* down the road (see opposite) provides free wi-fi. Dorm 35TL, double 60TL
Antik Maarif Cad 6 ☎0284/225 1555, ⊛edirneantikhotel .com. From the gold-painted door frames to the ornate, mock-antique furniture, this place aims for lavish but falls slightly short thanks to its chintz linens and jarring hotel-logo carpet. The large rooms are comfortable, with high ceilings and moulded plasterwork, though the spacious bathrooms could do with a revamp. An acquired taste, perhaps, but there's nowhere else quite like it in town. 150TL
Efe Maarif Cad 13 ☎0284/213 6080, ⊛efehotel.com. Spirited, family-run hotel brimming with charm, *Efe* is nothing if not unique. It's the eccentric details that bring this place to life – vibrant photography collections throughout the hallways and traditional folk instruments dotted around reception. The stylish rooms are modern yet homely, there's an English-style pub (summer only) downstairs and a funky adjoining restaurant, *Patio*. 140TL
Grand Atunhan Saraçlar Cad, PTT Yanı ☎0284/213 2200, ⊛altunhanhotel.com. Teetering between retro cool and slightly passé, this glitzy abode offers good value for money, with sizeable, airy rooms equipped with flat-screen TVs, a/c and big, comfortable beds. Don't be put off by the bright lights of the disco-themed *Paparazi Bar*

adjacent to the foyer, as the rest of the joint is decidedly more restrained. 125TL
Park Maarif Cad 7 ☎0284/213 5276, ⊛edirneparkotel .com. Not quite as spruce as the nearby *Efe*, but a reliably clean and modern choice. Rooms are a little bland but a good size and in a great location for the (always negotiable) price. 100TL
Taşodalar Selimiye Camii Arkası No. 3 ☎0284/2123529, ⊛tasodalar.com.tr. Built in the Ottoman Palace mansion where Mehmet the Conqueror was born, this ten-room boutique hotel lives up to its history with luxurious interiors. Each room is named after a famous historical figure from Edirne and oozes style, with carefully selected mock-Ottoman furnishings, chandeliers and four-poster beds. Spotless en-suites add a modern touch and the exquisite tea garden and restaurant offer a magnificent view over the Selimiye Mosque. €110
Tuna Maarif Cad 17 ☎0284/214 3340, ⊛www .edirnetunahotel.com. Cheap wooden furnishings, rug-strewn floors and unsightly patterned linens make you feel like you're back in the 1980s, but this unassuming hotel is still good value for money and they may well accept a lower offer. The identical, medium-sized rooms are neat and cosy, and the friendly staff liven up an otherwise uninspiring building. 90TL

EATING AND DRINKING

Not one for the vegetarians, Edirne's speciality is *ciğar tava*, deep-fried slivers of calf's liver typically served with a hot chilli garnish. Many of Edirne's restaurants are unremarkable, with most of the more elegant fare confined to tourist-geared hotel restaurants and a smattering of lively cafés on Saraçlar Cad. Licensed places are scarce in the centre, while some of those along the river are as much about drinking (usually *rakı* or beer) as eating.

RESTAURANTS

Asmaaltı Ocakbaşı Saraçlar Cad No. 147 ☎0284/212 8712. The only licensed meat-grill downtown, with mains from 12TL, this is a popular haunt among locals. Don't be put off by the cluster of men smoking out the front – this is a family place inside. Daily 11am–midnight.

Balkan Piliç Saraçlar Cad 14. This nondescript little restaurant – look out for the chickens spit-roasting in the window – might not look up to much but it's packed with locals for good reason. There's plenty of wholesome *lokanta* fare on offer here, with a range of vegetable options and a hearty lamb roast. A plateful of various dishes will set you back around 15TL. Unlicensed. Daily 11am–10pm.

Köfteci Hocaoğlu Saraçlar Cad 73 ☎0284/214 7300, ⊛edirnekoftesi.com. With its hip orange colour scheme, minimalist-chic decor and outdoor seating, this joint has a fresh, modern feel and serves up the best *köfte* in town – charcoal grilled and served with heaps of crusty bread, chopped onion, parsley and a spicy tomato sauce. Mains from a very reasonable 9TL. Unlicensed. Daily 11.30am–9pm.

Lalezar Karaağaç Yolu Üzeri ☎0284/223 0600, ⊛lalezaredirne.com. 1.5km south of town on the Meriç River, this family-friendly restaurant has beautiful views of the Meriç River and its elegant, honey-coloured bridge. Food – kebabs and *meze* – is substantial and reasonably priced, served in waterfront gardens. One table is located in the branches of a tree. To get here, take the Karaağaç-bound minibus from in front of the PTT, or any red city bus heading south along Saraçlar Cad. Unlicensed. Daily noon–11pm.

Niyazi Usta Çiğerci Alipaşa Orta Kapı Cad 5. Regarded as the best place to sample local speciality, *ciğar tava* – strips of fried liver, best eaten with dried, fried red peppers and a bowl of *cacik* (yoghurt and garlic) – this humble eatery is popular with locals and tourists alike. Vegetarians should steer clear though, as there's little else on the menu. Mains around 10TL. Daily 11am–10pm.

Zindanaltı Meyhanesi Saraçlar Cad 127 ☎0284/212 2149. Decked out like an old drinking tavern with aged wooden panelling, dim lighting and a collection of curious antiquities hanging from the walls, this place is the epitome of laidback cool. The Turkish menu favours meat-heavy dishes such as *köfte*, grilled chicken or lamb chops – expect to pay around 15TL for a main course. For those preferring to eat in daylight, there's a peaceful rooftop terrace equipped with a gurgling water fountain. Daily 10am–midnight.

BARS & CAFÉS

Getto Saraçlar Cad 139 ☎0284/214 6050, ⊛gettocafe.com. Sleek and stylish bar and café with attractive outdoor seating – this is the only music-and-booze haunt you'll find downtown. There's an extensive cocktail and spirits menu, a menu of Turkish food and snacks, and free wi-fi. Daily 11am till late.

London Café Saraçlar Cad 74 ☎0284/213 8052, ⊛londoncafe.com.tr. An unexpected find, this two-storey affair is an approximation of a London pub, with dark-wood interiors and an old-fashioned bar. There's a

wide range of local and imported alcoholic drinks and a western-style menu of pastas, paninis and burgers. The outdoor seating is somewhat tainted by the noisy fountain right outside. Daily 10am–11pm.

Mado Saraçlar Cad 21 ☎0284/225 6236 ⊛mado.com.tr. This chain of cafés specializes in decadent desserts including *maraş* (a dense, sliced ice cream eaten with a knife and fork), waffles and a wide variety of *baklava*. There's a good range of gourmet sandwiches, Turkish pastries and breakfast *meze* plates on offer too. The Edirne branch is particularly appealing with its rooftop terrace and open-air seating right on the main street. Daily 8am–11pm.

Melek Anne Kayseri Mantası Maarif Cad 18. Friendly, female-run establishment serving up a rotating lunch menu of home-cooked specialities with prices ranging from 2TL to 6TL per dish. Try the delicious *karnıyarık* (meat-stuffed aubergine) or *gözleme* (a cheese-, potato- or mince-stuffed flatbread). A quiet, tree-shaded garden and free wi-fi add to the appeal. Daily 8am–9pm.

23

SHOPPING

There are a few covered bazaars in Edirne, of which the **Semiz Ali Paşa Çarşısı** (entrances on Londra Asfaltı or Saraçlar Cad; daily 9am–7pm) is arguably the most interesting and sells everything from pottery and souvenirs to cheap clothing, shoes, jewellery and household goods. Look out for Yaren Müsik and Müsik Aleteri, traditional music shops selling hand-crafted *baglamas* and *zithers*. The **Kavaflar Arasta** (Cobbler's Arcade; Mon–Sat 9am–7pm) near the Selimiye Camii is a good place to buy Edirne's traditional fruit-shaped soaps (the watermelon slice is particularly fetching), although there's little else on display here. A local speciality is *badem ezmesi* (marzipan), and a tiny but delightfully old-fashioned shop, Ezmecioğlu, Semiz Ali Paşa Çarşısı 1, sells the stuff for a fraction of the price you'll pay in the upmarket outlets in İstanbul's suburbs. Also look out for some of the best cheese in Turkey, *Edirne peyniri*, with a firmer texture and more delicate flavour than the standard white Turkish goat's cheese.

DIRECTORY

Banks and exchange There are several banks with ATMs along Londra Asfaltı and Saraçlar Cad as well as a number of *döviz* (exchange) offices on and around Hürriyet Cad, plus one at the entrance to the Semiz Ali Paşa Çarşısı.

Hospital Behind the Bulgarian consulate.

Internet access Eska Internet Café, Çilingirler Çarşısı; Nokta Internet Café, further down the same street opposite the dolmuş stand (both generally daily 9am–9pm).

Police Karanfiloğlu Cad, behind Şerefeli Camii.

Post office Saraçlar Cad (8am–8pm for letters, 9am–5.30pm for full postal services).

استانبولی
فتح ایدن غازی سلطان
محمد خان

OTTOMAN-ERA MINIATURE

Contexts

History

It may no longer be a capital, but İstanbul – the hub of two of history's greatest empires, the **Byzantine** and **Ottoman** – is one of the world's truly great cities. Given its long, glorious past, it is impossible to separate the history of the city from that of the lands it ruled, a territory which, at the height of the city's power, stretched from the Balkans to the Middle East and from the Russian steppes to the deserts of North Africa.

Prehistory

Until recently we knew very little about the prehistory of the area on which the modern metropolis of İstanbul now stands. In 2008, however, the excavation of the Yenikapı Metro station uncovered a **Neolithic burial site**, dating back to around 6500 BC. The skeletons and pottery grave-goods, taken for safe-keeping to the Archeology Museum in nearby Sultanahmet (see p.56), may have been buried beneath the homes of the deceased or formed part of a necropolis on the edge of a Neolithic settlement. This made the site at Yenikapı one of the earliest "villages" in Europe – part of a wider process whereby a sedentary, agricultural way of life spread from its source in Mesopotamia, through Anatolia and across the Bosphorus into Europe. A few finds from the **Chalcolithic period** (4500–3000 BC) have been made in the area around the Hippodrome, in the heart of Sultanahmet, along with some from the **Early Bronze Age** (3000–2000 BC) suggesting that settlement of the peninsula (the area that would be enclosed much later by the Byzantine land walls) was continuous since its **Neolithic** beginnings.

The city of the blind

What we know of the Bronze Age, Dark Age and early Greek Archaic periods comes from **myth** and **legend** rather than archeological or source evidence. The story of Jason and the Argonauts, in which the hero Jason sets off to the land of Colchis (in the eastern Black Sea) in search of the Golden Fleece, almost certainly derives from a **major historical movement** – Greek colonization. From the mid-eighth century BC onwards, Greeks sailed north and east from the Aegean, through the Hellespont, the Sea of Marmara and Bosphorus (probably the site of the so-called "clashing rocks" which almost crushed Jason's ship, the *Argo*) and up into the Black Sea, where they founded numerous colonies. The **Bosphorus**, a narrow, twenty-two-mile-long strait, became a crucial conduit linking the city-states of ancient Greece with their newly established colonies in the Black Sea, and a settlement was eventually founded in the early seventh century BC on the shores of the Bosphorus, controlling the trade route between the Black and Mediterranean seas.

The founders, seafarers from Megara, near Athens, built their settlement, known as **Chalcedon**, on the Asian side of the strait, on the site of the modern İstanbul suburb of Kadıköy. Some twenty years later, according to Greek tradition, an adventurer called Byzas, anxious to found a new city, consulted the Delphic Oracle.

The priestess told him to build his new city "opposite the land of the blind". It was a typically cryptic reply and Byzas set out for the Black Sea having no idea what was

6500 BC	800 BC	676 BC
The first traces of human settlement on the site of today's İstanbul	Greek colonists sail through the Bosphorus from the Aegean to the Black Sea	Seafarers from Megara in Greece establish a settlement in Chalcedon, today's Kadiköy (see p.139)

THE FIRST BOSPHORUS BRIDGE

In the late sixth century BC, the Persian king **Darius** ordered a bridge of boats to be built across the Bosphorus in order to facilitate troop movements and protect his supply lines in a campaign against the Scythians to the west and north of the Black Sea. According to the highly exaggerated figures of the ancient Greek historian Herodotus, some 700,000 Persian troops marched across this, the first Bosphorus bridge. Darius's expedition, which reached as far west as the Danube, is seen as the **first historic attack** by Asia on Europe, and was successful in stopping Scythian raids on the territory of the Persian Empire, which at that time spread from the banks of the Indus to the Bosphorus. Remarkably, the feat was not to be repeated until 1974, with the opening of the first Bosphorus suspension bridge.

meant. However, when he reached the Bosphorus he realized that the founders of Chalcedon had been "blind" not to notice that the peninsula opposite them, in Europe, was strategically a far better place for a settlement. Built on the top of a hill at the tip of the naturally defensible triangular peninsula, **Byzantium** commanded the passage both up and across the Bosphorus, had a natural deep-water harbour and defence in the inlet now known as the **Golden Horn** to the north, and only a narrow neck of land to defend against any possible enemy approaching from the west.

This location was coveted by the great powers of the day, and King Darius of **Persia** eventually absorbed Byzantium into his empire towards the end of the sixth century BC as part of his campaigns against the Scythians and the Greeks (see box above).

The classical era

By the end of the sixth century BC, the Greek cities of Asia Minor and the Hellespont region had become part of the Persian Empire. Usually they installed tyrants to keep control and this, allied with heavy taxation, caused increasing resentment among the independently minded inhabitants. When the powerful city-state of **Athens** was drawn into aiding the Greek cities of Asia Minor in their revolt against Persian rule at the beginning of the fifth century, the incensed Darius was determined to conquer mainland Greece. But following his defeat at Marathon in 490 BC and his successor Xerxes' reverses at Thermopylae and Salamis in 480 BC, then Plataea in 479 BC, the Persians abandoned efforts to push west. The **Spartan** general Pausanias, who had led the victorious Greeks at Plataea, was put in charge of a Greek fleet and in 478 BC captured Byzantium from the Persians.

Athens, Sparta and Alexander the Great

The inhabitants of the city, now free from the Persian yoke, were soon caught up in the conflict between the two superpowers of the Classical Greek world, **Athens** and **Sparta**. Byzantium soon became part of Athens' Delian League, its prosperity highlighted by the high tributes it paid to the league's coffers, a wealth based largely on its control of the grain trade from the Black Sea to the Mediterranean. Towards the end of the fifth century BC the city switched sides, cutting off the grain supply to Athens and helping ensure Sparta's victory in the long-running **Peloponnesian War**.

Opportunist Byzantium switched sides again in the fourth century BC, before rebelling in 356 BC and gaining its **independence**. In 340 BC, with Athens' star on the wane, the

667 BC	513 BC	478 BC
The foundation of Byzantium by Greek colonists from Megara, led by Byzas	Darius, King of Persia, captures Byzantium	The Spartan leader Pausanias liberates the city from Persian rule and it becomes a part of Athens' Delian League

newly emerging power of Macedonia threatened from the west. According to legend, the besieged city was saved when the forces of King Philip II of Macedon, attempting to force the city under cover of darkness, were illuminated by a miraculous waxing of the moon. The superstitious inhabitants praised the moon goddess **Hecate** for their salvation and began using her symbol, the star and crescent moon, on their **coinage** – a symbol adopted by Christian Byzantium many centuries later. When Philip's successor, **Alexander**, marched east to take on the mighty Persian Empire in 334 BC, rather than risk valuable men besieging Byzantium, he simply bypassed it and crossed the Hellespont (modern Dardanelles) into Asia. Following his famous victory against the Persians at the battle of Granicus, Byzantium threw open its gates. As a reward it was allowed to keep its independence, though it was compelled to acknowledge Macedonian overlordship.

The advent of Rome
During the early Hellenistic period the city suffered repeated **Scythian attacks** and, desperately needing to fund its war chest, raised the levy it charged on ships passing through the Bosphorus. In 220 BC this provoked a war with Rhodes, which Byzantium lost. Then, as the Romans moved eastward in the second century BC, first into Greece and then Asia Minor, the city negotiated terms with the Roman Republic, keeping its **autonomy** in return for payment of an annual tribute. By AD 79, the republic had become an **empire**, and Byzantium lost its privileges. Far worse was in store. Following the murder of the Emperor Pertinax in AD 193, a power struggle broke out between Pescennius Niger and Septimius Severus as to who would succeed him. Byzantium backed the loser and the victorious Severus laid siege to the city. After three years' resistance, Byzantium fell and a vengeful Severus razed the city to the ground and put most of its inhabitants to the sword.

The site of Byzantium was too strategically and commercially valuable to leave vacant and, within a few years, Severus ordered the city to be rebuilt. The new land walls followed a line west of the original, doubling the area of land occupied by the old Byzantium. Severus renamed the new city **Antoninia** and ordered the construction of three glorious temples to Apollo, Artemis and Aphrodite on the hilltop around where the Aya Sofya and Topkapı Palace now stand.

The new Byzantium prospered quietly, but during the early part of the fourth century it was well and truly thrust into the limelight. In AD 284 the Emperor **Diocletian**, in an effort to sort out the administrative problems of running a huge and unwieldy domain, divided the empire into two parts, each ruled by an emperor (or *Augustus*) and a junior ruler (or *Caesar*). This so-called **tetrarchy** was unworkable from the start, the idea of dynastic succession clashing with the merit-based system envisaged by Diocletian, and **civil war** ensued. The ruler of the western part of the empire, **Constantine**, defeated his rival **Licinius**, the emperor of the east, near Chrysopolis, on the Asian side of the Bosphorus in 324. Constantine, now sole ruler of the whole Roman Empire, was impressed with the superb location of Byzantium, just across the strait from the scene of the final battle, and commemorated his victory by founding it as his new imperial **capital**.

New Rome to Constantinople
Much work needed to be done to make the old city a worthy imperial capital. The **rebuilding** began in 326, with the city walls moved further westward yet again, enclosing an area some five times larger than the Antoninia of Septimius Severus. Work

340 BC	334 BC	195 AD
Philip of Macedon's night-time raid on the city fails	Byzantium surrenders to Philip of Macedon's son, Alexander the Great	Roman emperor Septimius Severus razes the city to the ground, only to rebuild it a few years later

continued for four years, during which time the **Hippodrome** (an arena used for games and court ceremonies) and Forum were enlarged, an imperial palace and large public baths were built. Constantine followed **tradition** and ordered works of art from around the empire to be brought to glorify the new capital, including the Serpentine Column from the Temple of Apollo at Delphi, now in the **Hippodrome**. Then, in May 330, during a grand ceremony in the Hippodrome, Constantine named the old Byzantium Nova Roma or the "New Rome", though it soon came to be known as Constantinopolis (Constantinople) or "The City of Constantine".

The Byzantine Empire

Under Constantine, Christianity moved from persecuted faith to official religion (see box below). In 392, Emperor **Theodosius I** took things a stage further, banning **paganism** and ordering the demolition of all pagan temples, a move effectively making the whole Roman Empire a Christian one. In 395, following the death of Theodosius I, the empire was divided by his two sons, with **Honorius** ruling the west from Rome and **Arcadius** the east from Constantinople. While the western part of the empire struggled to survive the invasion of the **Vandals** and **Goths**, Constantinople and the eastern half generally prospered. In 413, during the reign of Emperor Theodosius II, the land walls of the city were rebuilt a couple of kilometres further west again than those of Constantine. On a pragmatic level, the walls were needed to contain the growing population of the city and to withstand the threat of Attila the Hun; on a symbolic one they meant the city now incorporated seven hills, just like Rome. Although an **earthquake** caused the walls to tumble in 447, they were quickly rebuilt along the same lines. Theodosius II also ordered the construction of a monumental new church, the Hagia Sophia.

In 476, Rome fell to the Goths, and **Constantinople** became the sole capital of a much reduced empire. The collapse of the western part of the empire also marked a significant change in the nature of the eastern half, which developed an ever more distinct Greek and Christian – or Byzantine – character.

Imperial expansion, artistic expression

Six emperors ruled between the death of Theodosius in 450 and the accession of the greatest of all Byzantine emperors, **Justinian** (527–565) – a period that saw increased tension between Rome and Constantinople over papal supremacy. Justinian's prospects

---

CONSTANTINE AND CHRISTIANITY

Scholars still debate the date that Constantine fully embraced **Christianity**. In the **Edict of Milan**, issued in 313, he and his then co-ruler Licinius announced that this hitherto much persecuted faith was to be tolerated. His mother Helena, a devout Christian herself, no doubt exerted great influence over her son's beliefs and he was certainly attracted to the religion, though it seems he wasn't baptized until near his death in 337. Constantine had previously established his control of the Christian Church at the ecumenical **Council of Nicaea** in 325, when he ensured that the emperor was both head of state and head of the Church. Christianity, officially sanctioned and state controlled, became the dominant faith of the Roman Empire, and many churches were built within the confines of the new city walls.

324	330	337
Emperor Constantine declares the city will be the site of a new imperial capital and building commences	Constantine declares the newly rebuilt city Nova Roma or the "New Rome", though it soon becomes known as Constantinople	Constantine is baptized as a Christian

were, initially at least, rather dim. The Sassanid Persians threatened from the eastern borders of the empire and Justinian's great general, Belisarius, after some initial success, suffered an ignominious reversal in 531, after which the Byzantines were forced to pay a heavy tribute to ensure **peace**. Then, in 532, events at the heart of the empire almost led to disaster. Supporters of the two factions at the Hippodrome, the **Blues** and the **Greens**, named after the strip the rival charioteers wore, rioted in the streets of the capital. When Justinian ordered the execution of the ringleaders, the enraged mob turned its wrath on the emperor himself. Fortunately for him, the brilliant Belisarius was in the capital and not on campaign and he soon restored order, butchering thirty thousand of the most recalcitrant rioters in the process.

The damage caused in the so-called **Nika riots** gave Justinian a good excuse to glorify both himself and his imperial capital and, in the massive building spree that followed, the most magnificent structure erected was a third incarnation of the **Hagia Sophia**, the Church of the Holy Wisdom, since converted into a mosque and the name Turkicized to Aya Sofya (see p.43). Other ecclesiastical buildings included the exquisite **Church of Sergius and Bacchus** (today's Küçük Aya Sofya; see p.63) and the **Hagia İrini** (Aya İrene; see p.48), along with the rather more pragmatic **Basilica Cistern** (Yerebatan Sarnıçı; see p.59), which helped secure the capital's water supply.

Constantinople was now one of the greatest cities in the world. It sat at the centre of a revived empire, with Belisarius leading campaigns resulting in the re-conquest of much of the western part of the empire, including Italy, southern Spain and North Africa. The magnificence of Justinian's reign did not prevent his court historian, **Procopius**, from dishing up plenty of dirt on the emperor and his wife, a former prostitute who apparently danced publicly in the nude and encouraged geese to peck bread from her pubic hair.

Barbarians at the gate

In the centuries following the **death** of Justinian, the citizens of Constantinople had much cause to thank their city's natural defences and mighty walls. From the north came the Slavs and Avars, while the Serbs and Bulgars pressed from the northwest. The danger from the Sassanid Persians to the east, though, was even greater. Having taken Syria, Palestine, Egypt and much of North Africa from the Byzantines early in the reign of the Emperor **Heraclius** (610–641), they soon swept across Anatolia to reach the shores of the Bosphorus at Chalcedon, opposite Constantinople. Fortunately Heraclius was made of stern stuff and, taking command of a Byzantine army (the first emperor to do so since Theodosius I), he marched east and eventually defeated the Sassanians so thoroughly that they never recovered.

His work was soon undone. The armies of the new religion of **Islam** swept out of Arabia around 637 and all that Heraclius had won was lost to the Muslims. By 674, the **Arab armies** were at the gates of Constantinople, only to be repulsed by a formidable new weapon invented by the **Byzantines** and whose exact recipe is unknown to this day – Greek fire. This lethal substance could burn on water, and was used to great effect by the Byzantines, especially in naval battles. The Arab armies, however, kept coming and it wasn't until they were repulsed from the city in 718 that the threat finally ended.

Having saved themselves from the Muslim Arabs, the Christian inhabitants of the empire did their best to destroy themselves. Debates over **icon worship** (see box, p.282) resulted in vandalism and riots and destabilized Church and State for over a century. Yet

392	447	532
Paganism is banned by the Emperor Theodosius and the Roman Empire becomes an overtly Christian entity	The land walls are rebuilt and strengthened following a massive earthquake	Thirty thousand rioters, seeking to depose Emperor Justinian, are butchered in the Hippodrome

---

ICONOCLASM

Theological debate was very much a feature of the Byzantine Empire and in the eighth century a dispute arose over the use of images and icons. The **iconoclasts**, possibly influenced by similar prohibitions in Judaism and Islam, believed that figurative images, particularly of Christ and the saints, should not be venerated. Emperor **Leo III** (717–41) gave the movement official sanction when, in 726, he ordered the removal of a large gold icon of Christ from one of the doors of Justinian's palace. Opponents of the movement **rioted** in the streets, but this did not stop the iconoclasts, who ransacked churches and monasteries across the empire. Many wonderful works of religious art were destroyed during this period and Byzantine society was riven apart. The **Council of Nicaea** (see box, p.233) held in 787, ruled that icon worship was now permissible, but the dispute continued on until 847, further weakening an empire now beset by a new and more tangible threat, the Bulgars.

---

despite all these problems, the Byzantine Empire endured. The Bulgars were repulsed twice by the land walls of Theodosius in the ninth and tenth centuries and, within the walls, the capital enjoyed a brief **artistic revival**. In 1014, Emperor Basil II (976–1025), the "Bulgar Slayer", finally put an end to the **Bulgar menace** and incorporated their lands into the empire – though not before blinding fifteen thousand prisoners captured during the decisive battle. In 1054 the long-running disputes between Rome and Constantinople, stemming from doctrinal differences and competing claims as to who had authority over the Greek churches of southern Italy, resulted in a final schism between the **Catholic** and **Orthodox** churches. The Patriarch of Constantinople, despite being declared a heretic by the **pope**, was now more powerful than ever in the east.

The coming of the Turks

Having already lost land in the northwest to the Bulgars and much territory in the east of the empire to the Arabs, a new **Muslim** threat to the Byzantine Empire, the Turks, emerged in Anatolia. Originating from Central Asia, from the eighth century onwards these nomadic tribal peoples moved westwards in search of new pastures. Originally shamanists, by the end of the ninth century many had **converted** to Islam following their encounters with the Arabs. In 1071 one branch of these Turkic tribes, the **Selçuks**, met and decisively defeated the Byzantine army of Emperor Romanos IV Diogenes (1067–1071) at Manzikert, near **Lake Van** in eastern Anatolia. Diogenes was captured and the victors swept into Anatolia, finally establishing their capital at Konya in **Central Anatolia**. Although the Byzantines did manage to recapture some lost territory, the empire was much reduced.

The crusades

Luckily for the Byzantines, the Muslim Selçuk Turks seemed happy enough to leave the magnificent imperial capital alone. Instead it was fellow Christians, the **Crusaders**, who brought the city to its knees. The First Crusade passed through Anatolia en route to the Holy Land in 1097 without any problem, but in 1175, during the Second Crusade, Frederick Barbarossa encouraged the Selçuks to launch an attack against the Byzantines. The two armies met at **Myriokephalo** in 1176, with the Selçuks decisive victors. It was a

537	674	726
A magnificent new cathedral, the Hagia Sophia is completed on the site of the one burnt in the riots of 532	The defenders of Constantinople use lethal Greek fire against besieging Arab forces	Emperor Leo III declares icon veneration idolatry and many icons are destroyed, triggering rioting across the empire

disastrous defeat, quickly followed by the Balkan states, fed up with ever-increasing taxation, seceding from the Byzantine Empire. More alarmingly, in 1185 the **Normans** captured and sacked the empire's second city, **Salonica**. The writing was on the wall for Constantinople, despite the fact that the Normans were defeated before they reached the capital. On the Third Crusade in 1187, the invaders took Adrianople (modern Edirne), some 300km east of Constantinople, causing great alarm in the city.

Emperor **Alexius III** (1195–1203) came to power by deposing his brother, **Isaac II** (1185–1195). Isaac's son Alexius sought aid from the west to reinstate his father – a pretext to loot- and power-hungry Crusaders were only too happy to seize upon. The Fourth Crusade started in 1201, with the aim of capturing Constantinople – a plan backed by the **Doge of Venice**, who hoped to increase his city's trade by eliminating its eastern rival. In 1203 the Crusaders took **Galata**, on the north side of the Golden Horn. They now held a strategic position from which to attack the city without having to penetrate the mighty land walls. Alexius III fled the capital, taking the imperial treasury with him, and **Isaac II** regained the throne, though as he had been blinded on his deposition by Alexius III, Isaac's son and co-emperor **Alexius IV** (1203–1204) was the effective ruler. He was less than popular though, as his overtures to the west had resulted in the Crusaders turning their attention to **Constantinople** and, in January 1204 the populace revolted and deposed him.

It was left to the new emperor, **Alexius V** (1204), to face the Crusaders. On April 13, the besieging forces penetrated the less-formidable sea walls running along the south shore of the Golden Horn and poured into the capital. The Byzantines' wealth – accrued from their extensive domains – and culture – derived from a fusion of the glories of ancient Greece and Rome and the precepts of Christianity – had long been coveted by the Latin Crusaders. Motivated by resentment and greed, they ransacked the city. The artistic treasures and religious relics that had been amassed over the centuries were shipped west or simply destroyed and Alexius V was forced to jump to his death from atop the **column of Arcadius**.

Rule of what was left of the imperial capital was shared between **Count Baldwin** of Flanders and Dandolo, the **Doge of Venice**. The Byzantine Empire was not yet ready to fold, though. A new capital arose in **Nicaea** (modern İznik) on the south side of the Sea of Marmara. In 1261, its then emperor, **Michael VIII Palaeologos** (1261–1282), took Constantinople from the Latins and was crowned for a second time in the church of Hagia Sophia – effectively restoring the Byzantine Empire.

With the Latins no longer threatening from the west, and the Selçuk Turks' ambitions to expand westward thwarted by rampaging Mongol armies sweeping in from the northeast, the Byzantine Empire, despite its much-reduced size and status, underwent a mini-renaissance. This is seen most obviously in the wonderful early fourteenth-century frescoes and mosaics in the Church of **St Saviour** in Chora (now the Kariye Museum; see pp.92–95), out near the land walls.

The rise of the Ottomans

The **Ottomans**, like their **Selçuk kin**, hailed originally from Central Asia and were Muslim. By the late thirteenth century this semi-nomadic, Turkish tribal grouping had settled in Phrygia, in northwest **Anatolia**. Their leader was Osman, and his followers were known as Osmanlı, later westernized into "Ottoman". Within a few years, Gazi ("warrior of the

1054	**1071**	**1097**
The Orthodox and Catholic churches split over doctrinal and other disputes	The first Turks, the Selçuks, appear in Anatolia and defeat Emperor Romanos IV Diogenes at Manzikert	The First Crusade passes through Constantinople en route to the Holy Land

faith") Osman had extended the boundaries of his territory both to the east and the north. In 1326 his son and successor, Orhan, captured the important Byzantine city of Proussa (modern Bursa). Orhan took the title **sultan** and made Bursa capital of his mini-empire, marking the transition of the Ottomans from semi-nomadic pastoralists to a settled people with a state of their own. Orhan continued Ottoman expansion, largely at the expense of the Byzantines, taking Nicaea (İznik), Nicomedia (İzmit) and then Chrysopolis (Üsküdar), right opposite Constantinople on the Asian side of the Bosphorus.

The next sultan, **Murat I** (1360–1389), captured Adrianople (Edirne) in 1361. Later he took Ottoman arms into the heart of the Balkans, conquering Thrace, Macedonia, Bulgaria and Serbia. The Ottomans also battled with their Muslim and Turkish kin and, in a campaign against the Muslim Karaman dynasty in western Asia Minor, actually used Christian mercenaries in their army. By the time of Murat I's successor **Beyazit I** (1389–1403), the Byzantine Empire was little more than a rump state. Beyazit, known as Yıldırım or "Lightning" for the speed of his military campaigns, besieged Constantinople in 1394 but, thanks to its near-impregnable land walls, it survived. The inhabitants of the city could not, however, prevent the Ottomans building the fortress of **Anadolu Hisarı** on the Asian banks of the Bosphorus, just a few kilometres north of the city in 1397, giving them control of trade through the strait. The Ottoman conquest of the city had an air of inevitability about it, but the arrival in Anatolia of the Mongol warlord Tamerlane, who routed Beyazit's army at the Battle of Ankara in 1402, gave the **Byzantine Empire** a fifty-year reprieve. Beyazit was caged for a year before meeting his end and to make matters worse his four sons warred over the accession. Fortunately for the Ottomans, Tamerlane died in 1405 and **Mongol** power waned. The Ottoman Empire, reunited by **Mehmet I** (1413–21), resumed its expansion in the reign of his successor, **Murat II** (1421–51).

The fall of Constantinople

Weakened by the continual loss of territory and numerous sieges, the fall of **Constantinople**, known by the Byzantine Empire and many beyond simply as "The Polis" (City) – as if there were no other – was inevitable. Constantinople, both symbolically and strategically, was far too important not to be brought under Ottoman control. **Mehmet II** (1451–81) planned the siege meticulously. First he ordered the construction of the **Rumeli Hisarı**, a fortress on the European side of the Bosphorus directly opposite the Anadolu Hisarı fortress. The Ottomans now had control of traffic through the Bosphorus and completely blocked access to the city from the Black Sea. As the city was surrounded on three sides by water, he enlarged and outfitted a substantial fleet, which he placed in the

---

THE BYZANTINE LEGACY

The **Byzantine legacy** is a considerable one. For over a millennium this cosmopolitan, polyglot Christian empire kept the armies of Islam from Western Europe. Educated and civilized, its scholars and scribes copied and preserved Classical texts that might otherwise have been lost, arguably paving the way for the **Renaissance**. In terms of art and architecture its achievements were remarkable, particularly in the ecclesiastical field, with the innovative **Hagia Sophia** the inspiration for countless churches across the Orthodox world. Despite the various theological disputes that threatened to bring the empire to its knees on occasion, its capital, Constantinople, was a beacon of Christianity, and even today the city is the spiritual centre of Orthodox Christianity.

1204	**1261**	**1316**
Encouraged by the Doge of Venice, the army of the Fourth Crusade captures Constantinople and loots many of its treasures	Michael VIII Palaeologus recaptures the city from the Latins and the Byzantine Empire is restored	The Church of St Saviour in Chora is embellished with wonderful mosaics

Sea of Marmara to block access to the enemy from the south. Well aware of the number of times past sieges had foundered on the mighty land walls, he employed artillery and ballistics experts from Europe and then massed his land forces against the walls.

The defenders of Constantinople, led by the Emperor **Constantine XI** (1449–53), mobilized as best they could for the defence of their beleaguered city, manning the walls with troops, including their Italian allies, and stretching a huge chain across the mouth of the Golden Horn to prevent the entry of Ottoman ships. When the siege began, in February 1453, Mehmet II outsmarted the defenders by building a trail over the hills of **Galata** and rolling his ships down into the Golden Horn above the chain, causing great consternation in the city. Batteries of Ottoman artillery, including the mighty **Orban**, the largest cannon ever built, pounded the land walls mercilessly. For seven long weeks the seven thousand defenders held out against some sixty thousand Ottoman troops, but in vain. On May 29, Ottoman cannon breached the land walls between the Topkapı and Edirnekapı gates and the attackers poured in. Constantine XI, the last Byzantine emperor, perished in hand-to-hand combat on the walls, though his body remained unidentified among the slain. The Turks raced through the streets of the fallen city to the Haghia Sophia. Here, according to legend, the Patriarch, celebrating Mass, disappeared into the church walls and will not reappear until the city is back in **Greek hands**.

The Ottoman Empire

Sultan Mehmet was determined to make the city a worthy new hub for his already far-flung empire, though the city did not actually usurp **Edirne** as capital until the reign of **Selim I** (1512–20). Now entitled Fatih, or "Conqueror" Mehmet, he boosted the shattered population of the city by bringing in both Muslims and Christians (mainly Greeks and Armenians) from rural areas of the empire and instituting the long-lasting millet or "nation" system (see box, p.287). He then restored what had been neglected during the Byzantine Empire's years of decline, and rebuilding that which had been destroyed in the siege and subsequent sack of the city, especially the roads, the sewers and the water system. The **Topkapı Palace** (see pp.47–55) was completed in 1465, just to the south of the Hagia Sophia, which of course, was itself turned into a mosque, the **Aya Sofya**. The magnificent Fatih Camii or "Mosque of the Conqueror", with its associated hospital, theological school and soup kitchens, was typical of the many mosque complexes built across the city, where worship and philanthropy went hand in hand. The city walls were rebuilt, and the massive fortification of **Yedikule** added to them. The Genoese, pardoned by Fatih Mehmet for helping in the defence of Constantinople, were compelled to remove the walls surrounding their enclave in **Galata**.

Expansion

Mehmet was not content with rebuilding the city. The loyal janissary corps (see box opposite), ably supplemented by regular forces made up of conscripts rewarded with grants of land at the end of their service, made the Ottoman **military machine** the envy of the age. The empire expanded at a faster rate than ever, with the addition of most of what is now Greece, Albania, the majority of Serbia and Bosnia-Herzegovina in the west, the southern Black Sea coast to the northeast and Rhodes in the Aegean. **Toleration** of the customs and faiths of its subjects helped prevent rebellion, and effective **administration** meant the

1326	1361	1397
A Turkish tribal leader, Orhan Gazi, captures Proussa (today's Bursa) and makes it his capital	Murat I captures Adrianople (today's Edirne) from the Byzantines	The Ottomans build the fortress of Anadolu Hısar, on the Asian side of the Bosphorus, part of the plan to capture Constantinople

empire ran relatively smoothly, with the sultan's domains divided into a number of easily regulated districts, trade and industry encouraged (to the extent of granting trading rights to potential rivals such as the Venetians and Genoese) and taxes levied efficiently.

Beyazit II (1481–1512) improved the Ottoman fleet to such an extent that it was able to overtake Venice as the leading naval power in the Mediterranean, but was forced to abdicate by his own son, **Selim I** (1512–1520). An orthodox Sunni Muslim, Selim's immediate concern was his Shi'ite neighbour **Shah İsmail** of Persia. Islam had split into these two competing groups following a dispute over who was the rightful successor to the Prophet Mohammed, with the majority (later known as Sunnis) convinced the successor should be chosen from the community of Muslims, a minority (who became known as Shi'ites) believing he must come from Mohammed's family. İsmail was starting to promote Shi'ism both within and without his empire, encouraging the Shi'ite population of Anatolia to question Selim's rule. The sultan took no chances and butchered forty thousand Shi'ites in Anatolia before heading east to defeat the Shah in the battle of **Çaldıran** in 1514, a victory which sealed the eastern border of the Ottoman Empire – and still forms, more or less, the modern frontier between Turkey and Iran. Selim then turned south and conquered **Mesopotamia**, **Syria** and **Egypt**. Crucially, Mecca and Medina now fell under Ottoman control, as did the spiritual leader of the Islamic world, the **caliph**. From now on, Ottoman rulers saw themselves as both sultan and caliph and were able to promote themselves and their causes on both a temporal and a spiritual plane.

Selim I, known in the west as Selim "the Grim" for his severe manner and bigotry, was succeeded in 1520 by his son **Süleyman** (1520–66), a ruler with the rather more pleasing sobriquet "the Magnificent". Under his rule, the empire pushed its boundaries far into Europe. In 1529 the Turks caused the continent to quake by reaching the gates of **Vienna**, and until the failure of the siege of **Malta** in 1565 the Mediterranean was virtually an Ottoman lake. Arguably the leading world power of the sixteenth century, the Ottomans used the revenue raised from their military successes to glorify their great capital, **İstanbul**. Süleyman was blessed in having at his disposal the greatest architect of the Ottoman era, **Sinan**, who was equally blessed to be living and working at a time when the empire's coffers were overflowing. His İstanbul masterpiece, rivalled only by his **Selimiye Camii** (see p.270) in the former Ottoman capital of Edirne, was the **Süleymaniye** mosque complex (see p.81), which still dominates the skyline of the city, especially when viewed from across the Golden Horn in Galata.

The rot sets in

Süleyman's reign is rightly seen as a **golden age** – especially when compared to a Western Europe of small kingdoms engaged in petty squabbles. The empire stretched

---

İSTANBUL OR CONSTANTINOPLE?

The Ottomans were quite happy to keep the city's old name, **Constantinople**, albeit in the Turkicized form of "Konstantiniyye". This was, however, used alongside a new name, **İstanbul**, itself a corruption of the Greek *eis tin polin* or "to the city". The city was also known as **Islamboul** or "Full of Islam", a pious pun on the name İstanbul and, more rarely, **Dersaadet** or "Abode of Felicity". The name of the city wasn't changed officially until 1930, when the new Republic deemed "Constantinople" reactionary and imperialist.

1452	1453	1453
Mehmet II constructs Rumeli Hısar on the European side of the Bosphorus, opposite Anadolu Hısar, to control the strait	The two-month siege of the city ends with victory for the Ottomans and Mehmet II enters the city in triumph	The cathedral of Haghia Sophia becomes a mosque

INFIDELS IN THE EMPIRE

The Ottoman army had included **janissaries** in its ranks since the fourteenth century. This elite body was made up of Christian boys taken from their families, converted to Islam, and given the best military training. Other **non-Muslims** were barred from military service.

Indeed, the strict distinctions in the Ottoman world meant infidels were officially second-class citizens, known as "**rayah**" or cattle. This **millet** or "nation" system allowed the non-Muslim inhabitants of the empire (largely Armenian, Greek and Slav Christians and Jews), a fair degree of autonomy in return for paying their taxes. In spite of its apparent iniquities the system worked, with non-Muslim communities given a great deal of autonomy, and compared with the treatment of the Jews in Europe at the time, for example, the non-Muslim population of the empire was well off. Indeed, towards the end of the fifteenth century, the Ottomans sent "**mercy ships**" to the Iberian peninsula to collect and bring back to the empire the Jews persecuted and finally expelled by Spain and Portugal – many of whom eventually made their way to İstanbul and contributed greatly to the city's economic success. The Ottoman Empire may have been ruled by Muslims, but it was multiethnic, multi-faith and, for the period, very tolerant.

from the Balkans in the west to the Persian border in the east and from the steppes of Russia south into Lower Egypt, had an imperial treasury capable of funding magnificent works of architecture and was governed by an able administrator and legislator. Yet the seeds of decline were already taking root.

Although earlier Sultans had married, often expediently to princesses from neighbouring Muslim or Christian dynasties, **Süleyman** broke Ottoman precedent by wedding his favourite concubine, **Roxelana**, the daughter of a Ukrainian priest. The ambitious Roxelana ensured the succession of her first-born son, the weak and ineffectual **Selim II** (1566–74), and persuaded Süleyman to move the *harem* from the old palace grounds in Beyazit into the Topkapı Palace. Under Selim II, Topkapı became a pleasure palace and the sultan was happy to indulge himself – becoming known in the west as "Selim the Sot".

Selim II's rule set a precedent that successive sultans were to follow, and they became increasingly **detached** from the reality of ruling the empire. Isolated in the palace, manipulated by unscrupulous grand viziers and the mothers of sultans or favourite concubines, successive sultans seemed to lack the mental strength to efficiently manage the empire. The introduction of the **Kafes** or "Cage" under **Ahmet I** (1603–17), in which the heirs apparent were incarcerated in a suite of rooms in the Harem until it was their turn to take the throne (see box, p.49), may have been less brutal than the earlier custom of fratricide (**Murat III** had his five brothers put to death on his accession to the throne in 1574), but underlined the sultans' isolation.

Ahmet I was responsible for İstanbul's famous **Sultan Ahmet Camii**, better known in the west as the Blue Mosque (see p.60), but elsewhere the empire was stagnating. The **janissary corps** was becoming bloated, rising from some 12,000 under Mehmet II to 200,000 by the mid-seventeenth century. Rather than being an elite recruited from the empire's Christian population, membership was now handed down from father to son, effectively making the corps Muslim. Further easing of restrictions on membership allowed Muslims from outside the ranks of the janissaries to join the corps. Most had no military background and no intention of attaining one – their only interest was to collect their pay and extort cash from the defenceless peasantry, or even from the sultans themselves.

1459	**1481**	**1492**
Construction of the Topkapı Palace, the nerve-centre of the Ottoman Empire, begins	Beyazit II becomes Sultan, later named "the Just" for his tolerant rule	Beyazit sends an Ottoman fleet to Spain to save the expelled Jews

This corruption and nepotism was compounded by external pressures, with a Europe revitalized by the **Renaissance** now looking hungrily at Ottoman domains. In 1536 the **French** signed a treaty with the empire involving various trading advantages but, more worryingly, giving French nationals **exemption** from Ottoman taxes and the right to be judged by their own consuls under foreign law. The privileges offered to the French, and then to other European nations and even companies, became known as the **Capitulations**. They helped undermine Ottoman sovereignty and increased Muslim resentment against the empire's Christians, many of whom became employees of the European traders and were given the same rights and privileges as their foreign employers.

In 1571, a Christian force led by **Don John** of Austria, put together under the pope's auspices to reduce Ottoman power in the Mediterranean, defeated the Ottoman fleet at Lepanto. The battle proved that the Ottomans were not invincible and put paid to further expansion in Europe for some time. The late sixteenth and early seventeenth centuries saw the Ottomans battling the **Persians** on their eastern frontier, ending with the loss of Baghdad to Shah Abbas I in 1624. **Murat IV** (1623–40) proved more able than his predecessors and was the first ruler since Süleyman the Magnificent to personally lead his troops to war, culminating in the retaking of Baghdad in 1638. But Murat died at the age of 30 and the rate of decline began to accelerate. In 1656 the janissaries staged a major **rebellion**, hanging a number of leading officials outside the Blue Mosque in their anger at receiving their pay in copper, while in eastern Anatolia local warlords challenged Ottoman authority. The population of the empire more than doubled (from around 12 million to 25 or 30 million between 1525 and 1600) and landless **peasants** streamed into İstanbul and other urban centres, putting more pressure on the system.

Efforts to **expand** into Europe proved disastrous. Following several defeats at the hands of the Austrians, the Turks suffered a humiliating defeat while attempting to take Vienna in 1683, losing an entire army in the process. The empire lost Hungary and other territory in Eastern Europe, though the treaties of Carlowitz (1699) and Passarowitz (1718) did stabilize the **Balkan frontier**.

An era of reform

At the turn of the eighteenth century, the Ottoman Empire did what all empires do once they stop expanding – declined. Yet **İstanbul**, far from the troublesome frontiers and with a stranglehold over the empire's finances, remained a city of splendour. **Sultan Ahmet III** (1703–30) and his able grand vizier İbrahim Paşa, both much influenced by European (especially French) arts and culture, oversaw something of a **renaissance** in the capital during the so-called **Tulip Period**. The Fountain of Sultan Ahmet III, outside of the Topkapı Palace (see pp.47–55), is a good example of Baroque influence on Ottoman architecture in this period. More importantly, Ahmet set up the first press to print **books** in Ottoman Turkish. He also imported thousands of **tulip** bulbs from Holland and Persia, planting them in the palace gardens and illuminating them at night by roving tortoises with candles fixed to their shells.

Outside the capital, life was less frivolous. **Russia** had its eyes fixed firmly on Ottoman territory, especially the Bosphorus, control of which would give them crucial access from the Black Sea to the Mediterranean. The Ottomans suffered several reversals, notably off the **Aegean island** of Chios in 1771, and in 1779 they lost the **Crimea**. Russian interference in Ottoman affairs, often under the pretext of protecting the

1514	1517	1529
Selim I, known to the west as "the Grim", wins a crucial victory over the Persian Shah	Selim I captures Medina and takes the title of Caliph	The Ottomans reach the gates of Vienna under Süleyman the Magnificent

rights of the sultan's Greek Orthodox Christian subjects, would run until the Bolshevik Revolution of 1917 put a temporary end to Russian imperialism.

A much earlier **revolution**, that of France in 1789, was to have an enormous impact on the ailing Ottoman Empire. **Selim III** (1789–1807) came to the throne in the same year, and set out to reform the empire on Western, liberal lines. His efforts were, however, resisted by the janissaries, who forced him to dissolve his new, force before rebelling and finally **murdering** the sultan. His successor, **Mahmut II** (1808–39), realized he would have to take things more slowly if he were to succeed in reforming the near-moribund institutions of the Ottoman state. He had a lucky break in 1812, when Napoleon's invasion of Russia compelled the **Tsar** to sign a **peace treaty** favourable to the Ottomans; he was less lucky in 1821 when a full-scale **rebellion** broke out in Greece. The revolt, which ended in 1830 with the formation of an independent Greek state, marked the beginning of the end for the cosmopolitan Ottoman world, as ethnic groupings from the Balkans to the Middle East sought to break away from the empire – including **Egypt**, which seceded in 1838.

In the capital, Mahmut II fared rather better. Like Selim III, he founded a new, **Western-style army**, but unlike his predecessor he managed to suppress the inevitable janissary revolt in 1826. Appropriately, it was the new, professionally trained troops who crushed the ill-disciplined janissaries, bombarding their barracks and leaving the Hippodrome piled high with their dead. Not content with quelling the revolt, Mahmut disbanded the old elite corps and banned their supporters, the reactionary Bektaşi dervish order. Prussian and Austrian advisers were brought in to train his new army, and a military academy and medical school founded, with French as the language of instruction. In a further bid to catch up with Western Europe, Mahmut introduced formal **civil and foreign services**, insisted that all but clerics must wear Western-style clothing and replaced the "oriental" turban with the **fez**.

The sick man of Europe

Sultan Abdülmecid (1839–61) was quick to build on the modernization programme of his predecessor, heralding an era of change known as the **Tanzimat** (Reorganization or Reform in Turkish). The Tanzimat Fermanı (Reform Decree) set out the changes needed to revitalize the moribund empire. These included the devolving of some of the sultan's powers to advisers, attempts to end taxation irregularities and the reorganization of the finance system and Civil and Military code on the French model. Most important, and certainly far more controversial, was the declaration of full **equality** between the empire's Muslim and non-Muslim inhabitants, including Turks, Kurds, Armenians, Greeks, Jews and Circassians. The sultan further distanced himself from the past by moving his abode across the Golden Horn, from the Topkapı Palace to the grandiose European-style **Dolmabaçhe Palace** (see p.131).

The empire also began to experience something of an **economic revival** that continued through the nineteenth century and manifested itself in the capital by a wide variety of civic and commercial projects. Heading these, among many other positive developments, was the formation of the Ottoman Steamship Company in 1851, the construction of the Tünel underground funicular railway in Galata, the setting up of the British-funded Ottoman Bank, the construction of a bridge across the Golden Horn and the introduction of a postal service. Pera and Galata (today's Beyoğlu), inhabited

1558	1571	1616
Completion of the Süleymaniye Camii, the masterpiece of the finest Ottoman architect, Sinan	A Christian fleet led by Don John of Austria defeats the Ottoman navy at Lepanto	The monumental Sultanahmet Camii is completed after eight years

mainly by foreigners and the city's Christian and Jewish minorities, underwent a **building boom**. European-style apartment blocks, music halls, cafés, bars and restaurants lined the streets, especially the Grande Rue de Pera (today's İstiklal Caddesi). Modern hotels, notably the *Pera Palace* (see p.123), sprang up in what is now Beyoğlu, catering to the influx of tourists from Europe, a stream that became a flood when the **Orient Express** began disgorging its affluent passengers at newly built Sirkeci Station in 1888.

Unfortunately, Abdülmecid's extravagance plunged the Ottoman state into **debt**, and traditional bazaar craftsmen were decimated by the industrially produced goods that flooded in from Western Europe. The Tanzimat reforms also alienated many Muslims, who resented the new-found equality of the Christians and Jews, especially as the European traders had favoured the Greek, Armenian and Jewish minorities over the Muslim majority since the Capitulations that had begun back in the sixteenth century. To make matters worse for the Muslims, the empire's Christian minorities now had the right and the funds to build places of worship, and shiny new **churches**, largely Armenian Apostolic and Greek Orthodox, sprang up across the capital.

Had the Ottoman Empire been left alone to sort out its internal problems, things might have turned out differently. As it was, the empire became embroiled in the machinations of **Britain, France** and **Russia**. In 1853 **Tsar Nicholas I** said of the ailing empire "We have a sick man on our hands – a man gravely ill. It will be a grave misfortune if one of these days he slips through our hands", a clear indication of Russian designs on Ottoman territory. The **Crimean War** of 1853–56 began with an argument between Russia and France over the protection to be extended by each to, respectively, the Orthodox and Catholic churches in Ottoman **Palestine**. In the end Russia demanded the right to "protect" all the Ottoman Empire's Orthodox Christian subjects. Determined to prevent Russia getting its hands on Ottoman territory, Britain and France backed the sultan. The war ended, more or less, in a stalemate, though one side-effect was to bring **Florence Nightingale** to the massive Selimiye Barracks on the Asian side of the Bosphorus in Üsküdar. Her work in the hospital there, mainly looking after wounded and sick soldiers brought down from the Crimea, established the principles of modern nursing (see box, p.142).

Young Ottomans to Young Turks

Emboldened by the Tanzimat reforms, a new, liberal elite, the **Society of Young Ottomans**, sprang up in the reign of **Abdülaziz** (1861–76). Educated at the secular schools introduced in the reign of Abdülmecid and influenced by Western European political thought, this elite sought a constitutional monarchy. Less liberal than his predecessor, Abdülaziz was not amused and exiled the ringleaders. He proved a weak and ineffectual ruler, however. The genie of ethnic-nationalism, heralded by Greece's declaration of independence, was now well and truly out of the bottle, with revolts in Lebanon, Crete, Bosnia-Herzegovina, Montenegro and then Bulgaria to contend with. Abdülaziz's brutal suppression of these rebellions turned the European powers against the empire and, with the economy in freefall, the Young Ottomans, led by one Mithat Paşa, deposed the sultan.

The short-lived reign of Abdülaziz's nephew **Murat** gave way almost immediately to that of **Abdülhamid** (1876–1909) who, a few months into his rule, signed off a new **constitution** drawn up by Mithat Paşa and his associates. In theory this was a real step forward, confirming the equality of all Ottoman citizens, reducing the power of the grand vizier, introducing secular courts and establishing a parliamentary structure. The

1683	1729	1779
An Ottoman army is humiliatingly defeated while attempting to capture Vienna	Sultan Ahmet I sets up the Ottoman Empire's first printing press	The Ottomans lose the Crimea to Russia, who will remain a thorn in their side until 1917

sultan, though, was confirmed as both head of state and caliph of the Islamic world, and was able to use his position to subvert the new constitution.

The empire soon came under pressure from all sides. In 1877, the **Russians** attacked from the Caucasus and the Balkans, resulting in great territorial losses and ending with the enemy forces just a stone's throw from İstanbul. **Britain**, alarmed at the Russian advance, intervened and forced their withdrawal. As a reward Britain demanded, and was duly given, the right to govern **Cyprus** (to protect the sea link to India via Suez) in return for guaranteeing to defend the Ottomans if Russia attacked again. It also extracted a promise from the sultan to look after the empire's Christian minorities. Under the terms of the 1878 Conference of Berlin, the empire saw Romania, Montenegro and Serbia given **independence**, Bosnia-Herzegovina come under Austrian control, and Bulgaria gain autonomy.

In 1878, **Abdülhamid** dropped any pretence of consulting his ministers, and dissolved the chamber of deputies. He became increasingly paranoid, closeting himself away in a new palace, the **Yıldız Sarayı**, censoring the press and sending spies out across the empire. He began to emphasize the Islamic nature of the empire, seeing this as a bulwark against the designs of the Western powers, resulting in pogroms against the Christian Armenians in the east of **Anatolia** in 1895–96. At the same time, he cultivated Germany, which was then playing catch-up with the leading colonial powers, resulting in the construction of the famous **Berlin–Baghdad railway**, which ran through İstanbul. He also oversaw the introduction of an extensive **telegraph system** and tried to modernize the infrastructure of the state and to service its debts.

But, in 1889, a new movement arose to challenge the authority of the sultan. **The Committee for Union and Progress** (CUP) had its heart in the cosmopolitan city of Salonica in Macedonia, especially among the officers of the Third Army. Seeing the empire falling apart as ethnic group after ethnic group broke away to form states of their own, the CUP, nicknamed the Young Turks, began to see Turkish nationalism (as opposed to Pan-Islam or cosmopolitan Ottomanism) as a cure for the empire's ills. In July 1908 they demanded the **restoration** of the constitution of 1876 and, with feelings running high among the populace, the sultan had no choice but to accede.

In 1909 **Abdülhamid** was deposed for supporting a rebellion against the CUP and was replaced by a figurehead sultan **Mehmet V** (1909–18), who promised to respect the nation's will. Real power now lay with key officers within CUP and in 1913, enraged by what they saw as incompetence and cowardice in the war against an encroaching combined Bulgarian, Montenegran, Serbian and Greek army, the officers staged a coup and established a **military junta**. The unlikely alliance of Balkan states soon fell apart, allowing the Ottomans to retake parts of Thrace. This minor success was enough to make heroes of the junta, now effectively down to a triumvirate of Cemal Paşa, Talat Paşa and Enver Paşa.

World War I

The CUP was now firmly Turkish-nationalist, secular and technocrat in ideology, and authoritarian by nature. Ignoring public opinion and the counsel of other CUP members alike, the triumvirate signed an alliance with **Germany** on August 2, 1914. By November the country was at war with the Allied powers, getting off to a spectacularly bad start when Enver Paşa lost an entire army on the eastern front against Russia in 1914–15. On the southeast frontier the Arabs, with British support, rebelled and eventually gained their independence. The only bright spot was the successful resistance

1830	**1839**	**1853**
After a nine-year war, Greece breaks free of Ottoman control and becomes an independent state	The accession of Sultan Abdülmecid brings increased zeal to reform the empire along European lines	Tsar Nicholas I of Russia declares the Ottoman Empire the "sick man of Europe"

to Britain's attempts to force the Dardanelles, which guarded the sea approaches to the Bosphorus and İstanbul. The victory at **Gallipoli** (see pp.261–266) made a hero of **Mustafa Kemal**, later Atatürk, a young officer and CUP member, whose reward from an envious Enver was to be shunted off to various obscure fronts until the end of the war.

Following the 1917 Bolshevik Revolution, the Russians withdrew from the war and the Turks were able to secure their northeastern frontier. Despite this the Ottoman Empire, its cause hopeless from the outset of the war, surrendered to the Allies on October 30, 1918 and, on November 13, a British fleet sailed through the **Dardanelles** into the Bosphorus and occupied **İstanbul**.

An independent Turkey

At the end of World War I, Anatolia, the heartland of the Ottoman Empire, was shattered, its population drastically reduced by war, starvation and deportations. The victorious Allies immediately began their long-planned carve-up of the "sick man of Europe". The French occupied much of southeast Anatolia, the Italians parts of the Mediterranean and Aegean coast, the British İstanbul and Thrace, and the Greeks claimed İzmir, on the Aegean coast. Emboldened by the Ottoman Empire's humiliation and the backing of the Allies, particularly Britain, the Greeks were intent on reviving the idea of a **Greater Greece**, to include not only the Greek state that had emerged in 1830, but also much of the Aegean and Black Sea coastline of Anatolia, where millions of Greeks still lived. The sultan's abject capitulation to the Allies' demands, and the thought of the Ottoman Empire being totally dismembered and **Muslims** being made into second-class citizens, was too much for many Turks, who were now every bit as **nationalistic** as, for example, their former Balkan subjects.

The War of Independence

Mustafa Kemal, hero of Gallipoli, proved the catalyst for what would become known as the **War of Independence**. Foolishly commissioned by the collaborationist War Ministry to travel across Anatolia and halt the various bands of Turkish patriots who were refusing to lay down their arms, he set sail from İstanbul and landed at the Black Sea port of **Samsun** on May 19, 1919. Kemal succeeded in lighting the torch of revolt across Anatolia and soon the Turks were fighting the French in the southeast, the Italians in the southwest, the Armenians in the northeast, and the Greeks in the west. In 1920, the Nationalists claimed to be the rightful government and established a parliament in the dusty Central Anatolian town of **Ankara**. In the same year the **Treaty of Sèvres**, imposed on Sultan Mehmet VI (1918–22) by the Allies and promising, among other things, İzmir and Thrace to Greece, independence to Armenia and autonomy to Kurdistan, only served to fuel the determination of the Nationalists. In 1922 they routed the Greeks at the battle of Dumlupınar and the humiliated remnants of the Greek army were evacuated from İzmir.

The **Nationalists** were now in control, and in November 1922 they abolished the sultanate, forcing Mehmet VI to slip away from İstanbul on a British warship, bound for exile in Italy. The war-weary Allies were forced to come to terms with the new Turkish state, and the **Treaty of Lausanne**, signed on July 24, 1923, recognized the frontiers won in the War of Independence. In the internationally mediated population exchange of 1923, nearly all the Greek Orthodox Christians left in Turkey (some 1.3 million) were sent to Greece, and the Muslim Turkish population of Greece were sent

1854	1856	1888
Florence Nightingale arrives in İstanbul to tend the wounded	Abdülmecid abandons the Topkapı Palace and takes residence in the European-style Dolmabahçe Palace	Visitors from Europe arrive at newly built Sirkeci Station aboard the *Orient Express*

THE ARMENIAN QUESTION

World War I proved an unmitigated disaster for the empire's **Christian Armenians**. The traditional homeland of this ancient people was originally in what is now the far east of Turkey, but for many centuries they had lived in towns and cities right across Anatolia, with a huge population in **İstanbul**. At the start of the war, with Russia pressing from the east, they were seen by the Turkish authorities as the enemy within. Although some Armenians in the northeast border region did join the Russians following Enver's humiliating defeat at Sarıkamış in 1915, most did not. Nonetheless, virtually the entire Armenian population of Anatolia was rounded up and deported to the Syrian desert. Most did not make it and somewhere between 800,000 and 1.5 million Armenians perished in forced marches or were slain in massacres.

The issue is still very much alive today, with Armenians claiming their losses amounted to genocide, and the Turkish state denying any systematic slaughter. The Armenian lobby in the US continually presses the administration to recognize the massacres of World War I as **genocide**. The pressure has been resisted, largely because Turkey remains a vital US ally in the Middle East. While running for the presidency, Barack Obama confirmed his support for the Congressional passage of the Armenian Genocide Resolution, though once elected in 2009 he failed to fulfil his promise. France, however, with an Armenian community of some 300,000, passed a bill recognizing the genocide in 1998, while in Switzerland it is a criminal offence to deny it. The land border between Turkey and Armenia has been closed since 1992 following the Armenian occupation of Nagorno-Karabagh, territory belonging to Turkey's Turkic ally, Azerbaijan.

to Turkey. Although the Greek Orthodox population of İstanbul was exempted, along with the Muslims of western Thrace, it marked a sorry end for Ottoman cosmopolitanism and the ascendancy of virulent **ethnic nationalism**.

The Republic

The Turks, under the leadership of the charismatic **Mustafa Kemal**, had plucked victory from the jaws of defeat. A new, secular **Republic of Turkey** was declared on October 29, 1923. The old imperial capital of İstanbul was deliberately passed over in favour of the provincial town of Ankara, seat of the resistance in the War of Independence, and a new parliament created. **İstanbul**, brutally shorn of its political role, was forced to rely solely on its business and commercial acumen. Yet it was able to recover from the war more quickly than the rest of the country because its influential Christian minorities – forcibly ejected elsewhere – were permitted to stay in the former capital.

The new Republic, under Kemal's watchful eye, set about a drastic programme of **reforms**. The caliphate was abolished, religious schools (*medrese*) and dervish orders closed, and Islam brought under state control. The fez, seen as progressive when it replaced the turban in the Tanzimat reforms, was outlawed as reactionary. The Gregorian calendar replaced the Islamic lunar one, alcohol was legalized, streets were numbered and the Western Sunday, rather than the Islamic Friday, became the official day of rest. **Women** won greater rights, with divorce now a matter for civil rather than religious courts, polygamy was banned, and eventually full voting rights were established. A team of language experts was set up to purge Turkish of its many Arabic and Persian loan words and the **Arabic alphabet** was replaced by a Latin one. In 1934 the entire population was forced to adopt surnames (this was when Mustafa Kemal

1889	1909	1914
Foundation of The Committee for Union and Progress (CUP), better known in the West as the Young Turks	Sultan Abdülhamid is deposed by the CUP	Ottoman Turkey signs an alliance with Germany and enters World War I

THE KURDS: FROM THE MOUNTAINS TO THE CITY

An ancient people of Indo-European origin and language (unlike the Turks), the **Kurds** are a people without a country. Scattered over the difficult, mountainous lands where Turkey, Iraq, Iran and Syria meet, they form a sometimes restive minority in each. By far the largest number live in Turkey (somewhere between 12 and 25 million – the Kurds are not accepted as a minority group by Turkey and as such exact numbers are hard to estimate). The rural to urban migration that has characterized Turkey's development over the last sixty or so years has been exacerbated in the case of the Kurds by the often brutal conflict between the **Kurdish Workers Party** (PKK) and the Turkish security forces, especially during the 1980s and 1990s, which resulted in hundreds of thousands heading west as their villages were burned and pastures (Kurds are by tradition transhumant pastoralists) put off limits by the state. In fact today the largest Kurdish city in the world is neither Diyarbakır, the biggest Kurdish-dominated city in Turkey's southeast, nor Erbil, capital of the autonomous Kurdish enclave in northern Iraq, but İstanbul, with up to three million residents of Kurdish origin.

became "Atatürk" or "Father of the Turks"). The name Constantinople, which had been used in Ottoman times alongside İstanbul, was also banned (see box, p.286).

The reforms were radical and inevitably there was some opposition, notably in the **Kurdish revolts** of 1925, 1930 and 1938, as well as **assassination** attempts on the great man himself. These put a dampener on the development of real democracy, and attempts to go beyond the one-party rule of the founding **Republican People's Party** (CHP) quickly foundered. In 1926 **Sedad Hakki Eldem**, the young Republic's leading architect and a great admirer of Atatürk and his revolution, while standing in line to meet his hero in Bursa, commented "He (Atatürk) was born to be ruler and that is how they treat him. I don't like that kind of behaviour but it seems to be in our blood."

Understandably suspicious of the Western powers who had so recently attempted to carve up what was left of the Ottoman Empire, the Republic was determined to be self-sufficient, setting up its own banks and instituting a series of five-year plans to boost **agriculture**. State-controlled industries like mining, steel and cement did provide a certain amount of independence, but they were heavily subsidized and grossly inefficient.

Atatürk, his liver ravaged by a lifetime's devotion to the fiery aniseed drink *rakı*, died on November 10, 1938, aged 59. Ironically for a man so determined to excise his people's Ottoman past, he passed away not only in the old imperial capital, İstanbul, but in that symbol of late nineteenth-century royal excess, the **Dolmabahçe Palace**, on the banks of the Bosphorus in Beşiktaş.

World War II and beyond

Atatürk was succeeded as **president** by former right-hand man and architect of Turkey's diplomatic success at Lausanne, **İsmet İnönü** (1884–1973). Keen to avoid the mistakes of World War I, İnönü steered a skilful diplomatic course when World War II became inevitable, signing neutrality pacts with Britain and France in 1939 and a treaty of non-aggression with **Nazi Germany** in 1941. İnönü kept Turkey out of the war, but he couldn't stop the conflict affecting his country, and a **black market** economy developed; there were shortages of basic commodities, profiteering, and massive government budget deficits. To compensate, the state introduced the Varlık Vergisi or "**Wealth Tax**" applied

1915	1918	1919
The Turks, under Mustafa Kemal (later Atatürk) defeat the Allied landing forces at Gallipoli	Britain begins its occupation of İstanbul after the Allied forces' victory in World War I.	Mustafa Kemal lands at Samsun on the Black Sea, triggering the Turkish War of Independence

in a discriminatory fashion to extort money from the Armenian, Greek and Jewish population – most of whom lived in İstanbul. Defaulters had their property confiscated and/or were sent to **labour camps** in Anatolia, where many died. The country finally entered the war on the Allied side in early 1945, in order to qualify for **UN membership**.

Postwar democracy and two military coups

With Russia demanding territory in eastern Anatolia and joint control of the entrance to the Bosphorus, and the US promising aid to states threatened by communism, it was inevitable that Turkey would ally itself with the **Western powers**. The newly aligned Turkey, benefiting from **Marshall Plan aid**, was now under pressure to democratize. In the 1950 elections, a breakaway cell of the RPP, the **Democrat Party** (DP), led by **Adnan Menderes** (1899–1961), swept to victory. Flush with aid and loans, Menderes presided over an economic boom that saw the countryside flooded with shiny new imported tractors, and a new road system in **İstanbul** filled with equally shiny cars and trucks.

Of farming stock himself, Menderes was worshipped by the conservative **rural population** (one of his first acts was to rescind Atatürk's ban on using Arabic in the call to prayer) but distrusted by the bureaucratic and commercial elite in the cities, especially İstanbul and, crucially, also the staunchly secular military. When the economy began to falter in 1953, with a soaring **national debt**, huge trade deficit, and a massively over-valued lira, the DP became increasingly autocratic. Looking for a distraction from the country's economic woes, Menderes quickly found a suitable scapegoat, the İstanbul **Greek minority** population. In 1955, with tensions high over **Cyprus**, the DP-sponsored **demonstrations** soon got out of hand, with mobs ransacking Greek property. The police, apparently under orders not to intervene, stood and watched the mayhem. It was the beginning of the end for the city's **Greek Orthodox Christian minority**, many of whom left in the immediate aftermath of the riots.

With the country saved from bankruptcy only by an **International Monetary Fund loan**, an increasingly insecure Menderes became yet more authoritarian. Finally, their pay and social status diminished, the military snapped, and, on May 27, 1960, staged a coup. Menderes and two of his right-hand men were hanged for **treason** and many other ministers were jailed. A new constitution was unveiled, and in 1961 İsmet İnönü became prime minister of a coalition government with a leading general, Cemal Güreş, as president. The paradox of a **democracy** being "saved" by military intervention, a factor bedevilling Turkish politics to this day, was born.

Far from setting Turkey on the straight and narrow, the coup only served to further polarize and fragment the nation. During the 1960s, the number of political parties proliferated, with the mantle of the banned DP being taken up by the **Justice Party**. The RPP became an increasingly elitist party, drawing its support from the military, civil servants and business people owing their wealth to lucrative state contracts, and extremist parties emerged on both the left and right. **Street battles** between leftists and rightists, and violence on university campuses (not least in the nation's biggest city, İstanbul) eventually led the military to intervene again on March 12, 1971.

The 1980 military coup

After a few years of relative calm, the 1970s were to prove even more divisive for Turkey. Street fighting erupted once again between radicalized groups, pitching left against right

1922	1923	1936	1938
The Nationalists, led by Mustafa Kemal, abolish the Sultanate	The official establishment of the Republic of Turkey	Haghia Sophia, first a church, then a mosque, becomes a museum	Atatürk dies at Dolmabahçe Palace

and Alevi (see box, p.92) against Sunni – alongside a renewed national consciousness among the country's only large minority population, the **Kurds**, and the rise of an openly Islamic political party, the National Salvation Party. Right-wing gunmen opened fire on protestors attending a May Day rally in Taksim Square on May 1, 1977, resulting in 39 deaths. By 1980 there were, at one stage, over twenty tit-for-tat politically orientated murders a day in İstanbul, where followers of a particular group could be told apart by the shape of their moustache or what clothes they were wearing. A military takeover was inevitable and on September 12, 1980, the nation underwent a third **coup** – much, it has to be said, to the relief of ordinary Turks fed up with the escalating violence.

Rule by the new **military junta**, the National Security Council (NSC) lasted three years, with İstanbul and the rest of the country under **martial law**. Political parties were closed down, **trade unions** banned and their officials put on trial, universities purged of "radicals", and "seditious" literature burned. The new **constitution**, promulgated in 1982, was extremely restrictive in nature – banning, for example, the use of the Kurdish language – and continues to hamper true democracy in Turkey to this day.

Turkey reborn

The junta's restoration of civilian rule in 1983 marked a new beginning for Turkey, with the rise of a different breed of politician, less shackled to the restraints of the Kemalist revolution. Whether **US-educated technocrats** like Turgut Özal and Tansu Çiller or fiery **pro-Islamists** such as Necmettin Erbakan and Tayip Erdoğan, they began to see their country as part of, rather than isolated from, the world at large.

The Motherland Party and the Kurdish backlash

The first party to benefit from restored civilian rule was the newly formed **Motherland Party**, led by the charismatic half-Kurdish **Turgut Özal** (1927–93), which swept to power in the general elections – much to the chagrin of the military. Özal, a great orator and contradictory mix of pious Muslim and bon vivant, was in the mould of a **Thatcher** or **Reagan**, at least when it came to the country's finances, and he introduced sweeping reforms bringing Turkey in line with the **international economy**. This had mixed results, with a **tourism** boom boosting the nation's foreign currency reserves and spending on imported luxury goods decimating them. He angered the military-bureaucratic elite by easing restrictions on Islam, giving extra funding to the Department of Religious Affairs and allowing schools where religious instruction was a key component of the curriculum, inadvertently helping sow the seeds of **Islamic fundamentalism**.

Despite Özal's apparent liberalism, **human rights** abuses, which had peaked in the aftermath of the 1980 coup, continued. In the ethnically Kurdish southeast of the country, the military was engaged in a war of attrition with the **Kurdish Workers Party** (PKK). At a loss as to how deal with a people who refused to be assimilated, security forces sometimes resorted to less than legal methods to suppress the movement, further fuelling resentment in the economically backward southeast.

Özal died of a heart attack in 1993, depriving the country of a leader who, while far from perfect, was vigorous and reform-minded. Under Özal's successor and Turkey's first **female prime minister**, Tansu Çiller (b.1946), the early 1990s were dominated by corruption scandals, massive inflation and spiralling war in the southeast. This conflict

1939	1955	1960	1971
Turkey remains neutral for most of World War II	A weekend of rioting leads to the destruction of many Greek-minority-owned properties on İstiklal Caddesi	Turkey's first military coup	Turkey's second military coup

drove hundreds of thousands of villagers from their land, exacerbating a rural-urban migration that had been under way since the 1950s, and which had accelerated following Özal's market-orientated reforms. The **migrants**, bringing with them a different culture and a host of social problems for the future, settled in shanty towns on the outskirts of the big cities, particularly İstanbul, where a population of a little under three million in 1980 had risen fourfold by 2003.

The advent of political Islam

The loosening of restrictions on Islam by the secular **Atatürkist** state, begun under Menderes and reaching new levels under Özal, began to have a real effect in the political arena in the early 1990s. In the 1994 municipal elections, the overtly Islamic **Refah party** took İstanbul and many other cities across the land, including the capital, Ankara. İstanbul's Refah mayor was Tayip Erdoğan, who proved himself to be efficient, pragmatic and honest – rare attributes in the Turkish political scene. He addressed many of the most pressing problems plaguing the **metropolis**, laying on extra buses, improving the waste collection system, reducing pollution and providing facilities for the disabled. Secularist concerns that areas full of bars, clubs and restaurants such as Beyoğlu would be turned, overnight, into pious "dry" zones proved unfounded, and life went on much as before.

Following **Refah**'s success in the 1996 general elections, fears that the country would soon be subject to Iranian-style **Shariah rule** also proved groundless as Refah signed a **military treaty** with Israel, allowed the US continued use of airbases on Turkish soil, and party leader **Erbakan** laid a wreath at the mausoleum of that scourge of Islam, Atatürk. Despite this, in 1997 the nation's ultimate arbiters of power, the **National Security Council** (comprising Turkey's five top military commanders, the president, prime minister and three leading ministers) forced Erbakan to step down, in what has become known as the "silent coup", and Refah was dissolved.

In 1998 **Erdoğan**, then mayor of İstanbul for the newly formed pro-Islamic **Fazilet party**, was jailed for four months for "inciting armed fundamentalist rebellion" in a speech he gave in the southeast of the country. Ironically, the words he was prosecuted for ("the mosques are our barracks, the minarets our bayonets, the domes our helmets") were written by Ziya Gökalp, a leading idealogue of Turkish secular nationalism. In 1999 a massive quake rocked the environs of the city, with up to twenty thousand lives lost, mainly as a result of shoddy building. In the aftermath, the reputation of the military suffered, with soldiers more intent on preventing looting than helping the victims. In 2001, a major financial crisis saw the lira halve in value against the dollar and inflation rocket.

The rise and rise of the Justice and Development Party

In 2002, following the banning of Fazilet for anti-secular activities, its replacement, the **Justice and Development party** (AKP), swept to power with 34 percent of the vote and 363 out of 550 parliamentary seats. The first majority government for fifteen years, the election of a party composed of, and supported largely by, **conservative Muslims** sent shock-waves through the secular establishment. Five years later the same establishment was rocked even more severely. Objecting to the nomination of one of its own party, **Abdullah Gül**, as president (particularly as Gül's wife wore the traditional Muslim **headscarf**, seen as a symbol of political Islam) the military posted a warning on their website. The threatened coup, or "e coup" as it has become known, forced early

1977	**1980**	**1983**	**1993**
39 demonstrators shot by extremists at a May Day rally in Taksim Square	Turkey's third military coup	Charismatic Turgut Özal sweeps to power as leader of the Motherland Party	Özal dies, leaving a political vacuum

elections in July 2007. The voting public, reaffirming their belief in the policies of the current government, gave the **AKP** a whopping 47 percent of the vote nationwide – the first time for fifty years that a party had won a **second term** in office with an increased majority. Following this mandate, Gül was duly elected president. Then, in June 2011, the unprecedented happened when, for the first time in the history of the Turkish Republic, a party was elected for a **third consecutive term**. This time, although the AKP actually garnered a slightly higher number of votes (almost fifty percent), the number of seats they had in parliament dropped slightly, making it more difficult for the party to push through reforms without consulting the opposition.

Throughout this period the AKP's opposition, comprised of the military, academia, the civil service, powerful media groups and the party set up by Atatürk back in 1923 (the Republican People's Party or CHP), believed the secular nature of the state was under threat – as did many foreign observers. Indeed, many secular Turks, increasingly alarmed by the wave of popular support for the AKP were convinced the government were preparing the way for an **Islamic theocracy**, pointing to everything from the government's resolve to repeal the law forbidding women wearing the **headscarf** from working in state offices or entering university to the inordinately high taxes on **alcohol**.

The AKP years have been marked by a **murky conflict** between the secular establishment and the self-appointed guardians of the state, the military, and the democratically elected, **pro-Islamic government**. The AKP pushed through reform enabling military figures to be tried in civilian courts and many important generals and officers have been jailed pending trial in the **Ergenekon** (2008) and **Balyoz** (2010) conspiracy cases, accused of plotting provacateur attacks designed to create the impression that Turkey was under attack from revolutionary (eg Islamic) forces and thus justify a military coup. Although the conspiracy cases are likely to drag on for years, the AKP showed that it had the public backing and political will to curb the political influence of the military, and that the state's guardians were neither untouchable nor unaccountable.

Turkey's long-held ambition to be accepted as part of Europe had been boosted under the AKP in 2005, when accession talks formally opened, but by 2011 the process was mired in domestic indifference and outright hostility from EU member states France and Germany. Instead the government embarked on a "**zero problems with neighbours**" policy that, for example, saw Turkey and Syria (arch enemies back in the 1990s) begin a massive mine-clearing project along their long mutual frontier (2008) and the introduction of visa-free border crossings for each others' citizens to boost trade.

One of the chief reasons for the AKP's repeated electoral success was not its Islamic conservatism but the fact that the country began a period of sustained economic growth. In part this was because the AKP were prepared to do business with everyone, from pariah regimes such as Syria and Libya through to Saudi Arabia, Russia and China. Foreign capital flowed into the country, particularly from the rich Arab states – nowhere more so than to İstanbul, where property prices skyrocketed as a result. This rush of inward investment was only made possible because the AKP had provided a period of stable, majority government.

The "**Arab Spring**" of 2011 brought a more realistic appraisal of AKP's grandiose foreign policy, with PM Erdoğan forced to condemn Syria's leader Assad as ten thousand refugees flooded over the border into Turkey, and to evacuate thousands of

1994	1997	2002	2005
The pro-Islamic Refah party win İstanbul in municipal elections and Tayip Erdoğan becomes mayor	The Refah party is dissolved by the military in the "silent coup"	The pro-Islamic AKP, led by Tayip Erdoğan, sweep to power in the general elections	Accession talks for Turkey's membership of the EU formally open

Turks from Libya, where they were working in the drilling and construction industries. Relations with another Middle-East ally, already damaged in 2009 when Erdoğan stormed out of a meeting with Israeli president Peres in Davos, plummeted after Israeli commandoes stormed a Turkish ship taking aid to Gaza in 2010, killing nine Turkish citizens. In late 2011, after Israel refused to apologize for the deaths, Turkey downgraded its relations with Israel, expelled high-ranking diplomats and cut military ties. Actions like these made the tough, hard-talking and pious Erdoğan a well-known and popular figure to the Arab man in the street, although cynics at home saw his moves as cheap populism at best, dangerous neo-Ottomanism (ie an attempt to regain influence in lands once under Ottoman control) at worst.

To the present day

There is no doubt that Turkey has been transformed economically under the AKP. Major new highways lace the mountainous Anatolian interior, high-speed train links are being forged between major cities and cheap domestic air travel is booming. Along with Brazil, Russia, India and China, Turkey has become a major, emerging economy, ranking seventeenth in the world in 2010. Strolling down İstanbul's major shopping street, İstiklal Caddesi, or around one of the swish suburban malls, visitors soon realize just how much disposable income there is in this vibrant city.

With the AKP firmly in control until 2015 the economic future looks rosy. For İstanbul, this means that grandiose plans to build a **mega-canal** linking the Sea of Marmara with the Black Sea (see box, p.26) to relieve the dangerously congested Bosphorus could reach fruition. Other goals to span the famous strait with a third suspension bridge and build a couple of "satellite" cities north of the metropolis to avoid further overcrowding are realistic – if undesirable on environmental grounds.

However, on a national level the Kurdish question remains the most dangerous obstacle to Turkey's progress and future peace. The quest for what some Kurds term "democratic autonomy", led by the pro-Kurdish Peace and Democracy Party (BDP), has produced a virulently Turkish nationalist backlash which threatens the stability of the country. İstanbul itself faces other problems: its fabulous heritage is under threat from unbridled development (in 2010 it was close to being named and shamed on the UNESCO Endangered Heritage list), with the municipal authorities struggling to juggle the needs of the population with the preservation of its historic buildings. It continues to grow alarmingly quickly, meaning any improvements to infrastructure are only temporary – the population, twelve million according to the 2007 census, was in 2011 reckoned to be closer to seventeen million. The gap between rich and poor continues to widen, the social problems this engenders given a political twist by the city's substantial Kurdish population, the more radical of whom have been responsible for torching cars and fire-bombing municipal buses in the name of their nationalist cause (see box, p.292). Yet İstanbul will endure and ultimately prosper, as it has for millennia. Looking both East and West, blessed with a location both stunningly beautiful and strategically crucial, this will always be, as one inhabitant wrote of the city when it was Constantinople, a "city of the world's desire".

2007	2010	2011
The AKP wins the general elections with an increased majority	Nine Turkish citizens aboard a Gaza-bound relief ship are killed by Israeli commandoes and Turkey downgrades relations with Israel	The AKP wins a record third term in office, capturing almost fifty percent of the vote in general elections

Ottoman art and architecture

İstanbul was at least two millennia old when it fell to the **Ottomans** in 1453 (see p.285), but in the centuries that followed the former Byzantine capital was built anew. The cascading domes and soaring minarets of the imperial mosque complexes constructed under successive sultans still dominate the old city, but while religious buildings form the Ottomans' main architectural legacy, their palaces – and even the simple houses of ordinary citizens – are worthy reminders of a once-vibrant empire. Carpet weaving, pottery, calligraphy and miniature painting also flourished under Ottoman tutelage.

Religious architecture

The Ottoman Empire was Islamic, and İstanbul's imperial **mosques** and associated structures, known collectively as *külliye*, were given lavish treatment. The complexes usually included a *medrese* (school), a *hamam*, an *imaret* (soup kitchen), a hospital, accommodation for travellers and a cemetery. The ultimate *külliye*, magnificently positioned on the crest of İstanbul's third hill, is the **Süleymaniye** (see p.81), whose buildings are arranged with almost geometric precision around the mosque itself. Its architect, the incomparable Sinan (see box, p.80), is buried within its grounds. His finest achievement, however, is Edirne's **Selimiye Camii** (see p.270), where the mighty dome, cleverly supported by eight unobtrusive pillars, seems to float over the worshippers below.

Mosque features

Although there is no Islamic injunction for a mosque to have a **minaret**, most have at least one and many boast more; the Süleymaniye Camii (see p.81), atop İstanbul's third hill, has four, the Sultanahmet Camii, better known as the Blue Mosque (see p.60), boasts six. From the balconies of the minarets, pre-loudspeaker muezzins called believers to prayer. Their origin is ascribed variously to the fire watchtowers of pre-Islamic cities and early Christian ascetics, the Stylites, who dwelt atop pillars to bring them closer to God. While early Arab mosques derived from the simple, flat-roofed courtyard house of the prophet Mohammed, the later Ottoman style was based around domes and slender, cylindrical minarets.

Most mosques have a **courtyard** centred around the *şadırvan* or ritual-ablutions fountain, which worshippers use before prayer. A multi-domed **portico** on the northwest side of the mosque provides an "overspill" prayer area for busy times. Inside, the focus is the southeast, Mecca-facing **kibba** wall, punctured by a **mihrab** or prayer niche. Right of this is the **mimber**, a pulpit, from which the *imam* leads Friday prayers. As Islam forbids representation of the human form, Ottoman mosque interiors are enlivened by stylized geometric patterns and flowing Arabic calligraphy.

Secular buildings

The city's fifteenth-century conqueror, Sultan Mehmet II (see p.285), found its palaces already in ruins. Within five years a new palace, the **Topkapı** (see pp.47–55), rose on the splendid promontory overlooking the Bosphorus and Sea of Marmara. Following Islamic precepts, originating in the tented camps of nomadic warriors, Topkapı was a collection of low buildings set around a series of courtyards and gardens. By the nineteenth century the Ottoman Empire was busy reforming itself on European lines and the **Dolmabahçe Palace** (see p.131), built in 1853, was inspired by European royal dwellings such as Versailles, and revels in its ostentatiousness and gorgeous waterfront setting. By contrast, ordinary Ottoman citizens lived in humble wood, lath and plaster houses, crammed along narrow, atmospheric streets, their *cumbas* (projecting upper floors) often just a couple of metres from the home opposite. These dwellings coped much better with the earthquakes which are an ever-present fact of life for a city so close to a major fault line, but were subject to frequent fires, which is why so few remain today. The best places to see these homes are around Cankurtaran, Kumkapı and the northwest quarter (see pp.87–89).

Carpets and pottery

Whether providing comfort for the prostrated faithful or adding opulence to palaces or the *konak* (mansion) of a wealthy merchant, Ottoman-era Turkish **carpets** are real works of art. The best place to see examples – without getting smooth-talked in the Grand Bazaar – is the İbrahim Paşa Sarayı (see p.61).

The fourteenth-century arrival of blue-and-white Chinese porcelain inspired Ottoman **potters**. The very best wares were produced in pretty, lakeside İznik (see pp.233–238), with the form reaching its apogee in the late sixteenth century, when craftsmen added a rich, tomato-red raised relief to a palette that already included blue, turquoise, magenta, green and grey – best seen in the sumptuously tiled interior of the Rustem Paşa Camii (see p.72). Many other mosques throughout the old city are graced by İznik tiles, however, including the Blue and Sokollu Mehmet Paşa mosques.

Calligraphy

Arabic is the language of the Koran, and to Muslims **calligraphy** is the highest art form as it represents the word of God – you'll see quotations from the Koran and the *hadiths* (sayings of the Prophet) adorning the interior of any İstanbul mosque. The Ottomans also produced exquisite manuscript Korans, prayer books, framed artworks (*levha*) and decorative books of calligraphic exercises, not to mention the sultan's delightfully ornate imperial monogram, all visible at the Sakip Sabancı Museum (see p.150).

Miniatures

Miniature paintings were as much a part of illuminated Ottoman manuscripts as calligraphy, and a painting academy was established in the Topkapı Palace as early as the fifteenth century. As Ottoman power increased, so did the standard of the paintings, especially following the arrival of artists from Persia, Mesopotamia and Central Asia. Islamic convention was frequently ignored, with human figures, often the sultans themselves, figuring prominently, along with scenes from court ceremonies, legends and historical events such as the 1588 Siege of Vienna. Good examples can be seen at the İbrahim Paşa Sarayı (see p.61) and the Sakip Sabancı Museum (see p.150).

Music

İstanbul, following years of rural–urban migration, is now home to people from every part of Anatolia, and their musical heritage lives on in a metropolis often described as the nation's biggest village. **Traditional Turkish music**, its roots stretching back millennia to the different cultures and civilizations that have flourished here, is both complex and vibrant. Thankfully, it has managed to maintain both its creativity and popularity – even with the younger generation – though this has not prevented the rise of a lively, Western-influenced **rock**, **pop** and even **hip-hop** scene.

Traditional Turkish music

Traditional sounds have more than held their own in this fast-changing country. Channel-surf Turkish TV any evening and you're bound to hit upon a show or two devoted to native Turkish music, with the sight of a moustachioed bard coaxing melancholic Anatolian folk songs from his *saz* or *bağlama* (types of lute) or an orchestra of tuxedoed men and sombrely clad women solemnly accompanying a warbling *sanatçı* (singer of Turkish classical music). **Arabesk**, an Arab/Egyptian-influenced style of music invariably charting the singer's wretched lot in life, remains extremely popular, especially among the poor and dispossessed. Its most famous proponent, İbrahim Tatlıses, is a national institution, and until a drive-by shooting in İstanbul in 2010 left him paralysed, hosted his own enormously popular TV show. *Türkü* bars (see p.195) are devoted to the various lovelorn strands of **halk muziği** (best translated as people's or folk music) and are very popular with the younger generation.

Played mainly by Roma (gypsy) bands, **fasil**, a curious but lively hybrid of Ottoman classical and folk, with violins, clarinets, *darbuka* drums and powerful, emotive vocals to the fore, is the genre of İstanbul's vibrant **meyhane** scene (see p.178). The hypnotic, spiritual strains of **Sufi** music, most often associated with the Mevlevi or "whirling" dervish order, and popular among world-music aficionados, is very much a minority interest in its home country, though it can be heard in several places in the city, including the Mevlevihanesi in Galata (see p.112).

Turkish classical or **sanat** music is the most inaccessible home-grown style to foreign ears – and the least popular domestically despite the undoubted virtuosity of its leading musicians. Originating in the Ottoman court, this subtle, partly improvisational but often gloomy-sounding music is performed by chamber orchestras using a combination of traditional Turkish wind and string instruments backed by drums.

Music documentaries

The best introduction to a whole range of traditional Turkish music is Nezih Ezen's 2008 documentary, **Lost Songs of Anatolia** (ⓦ lostsongsofanatolia.com). A talented musician himself, Ezen's unsentimental but sensitive film is a labour of love some five years in the making. Travelling across Turkey's vast landscape, recording and filming in obscure towns and remote villages, he vividly captures the musical heritage of modern Turkey – one deeply rooted in the many ethnic and cultural identities that make up the nation. In the rain-soaked mountains of the eastern Black Sea, Laz (a Caucasian people who speak a language related to Georgian) dance the *horon* (a line dance) to the sound of the *kemençe* (upright fiddle) and *tulum* (bagpipe), while in the mountains of Bingöl a *dengbey* (Kurdish bard) uses only his voice to chart the history of his people. In an İstanbul apartment, a couple of elderly Armenian ladies sing a moving lament to an Anatolia long lost to them, while in the same city an ethnically Greek ensemble play a "Greek blues" *rebétika* number. A couple of rake-thin elderly bards in a smoky tea house in the Armenian border-town of Kars play the *saz* and battle out an instrument- and lyric-based duel; in the cotton fields of the Çukurova near Adana a group of young

SELECTED DISCOGRAPHY

The music reviewed below will provide a good introduction to the major strands of traditional Turkish music.

ARABESK

İbrahim Tatlıses *Fosforlu Cevriyem* (Emre). This live recording is a rare chance to hear what *arabesk* sounds like in the flesh, and gives a sense of Tatlıses' phenomenal vocal presence. Includes some of his all-time favourites, plus superb *uzun hava* semi-improvisations.

FOLK

Belkis Akkale *Türkü Türkü Türkiyem* (Sembol Plak). One of the greatest female *türkü* singers at her earthiest, carried along by driving *saz* rhythms – plus almost all of the traditional instruments of Turkey.

FASIL

Karşılama *Karşılama* (Green Goat, Canada/Kalan). İstanbul gypsy musicians led by Selim Sesler on G-clarinet, with locally trained Canadian vocalist Brenna MacCrimmon, interpret Roma music from western Turkey and the Balkans. Played with real panache, and it's good to have some of the vocal repertoire – gleaned from archival recordings and manuscripts – expertly showcased.

SUFI

Mevlana *Dede Efendi Saba Ayini* (Kalan). A benchmark recording of a complete Mevlevi suite (*ayin*) composed by Dede Efendi. The performers read like a who's who of early twentieth-century Turkish *sanat*, with Mesut Cemil on cello, Akagündüz Kutbay, Ulvi Erguner and Niyazi Sayın on the wind instrument known as a *ney*, Cüneyd Orhon on *kemençe* (a kind of violin) and Saadettin Heper on *küdüm* (kettle drum).

SANAT

Mesut Cemil *Early Recordings (Vol 1)* and *Instrumental and Vocal recordings (Vols 2–3)* (Golden Horn Records/US). Virtuoso musicianship and compositions from the man who ran the classical music section of TRT-İstanbul for decades.

women from Diyarbakir, poorly paid seasonal workers, find solace from their back-breaking labour in song. The DVD is easy to get hold of in İstanbul from any of the music shops listed on p.222, but you will have to rely on the power of the songs and fabulous scenery, as there are no English subtitles.

Although much of Fatih Akın's documentary **Crossing the Bridge** concentrates on contemporary music in İstanbul, there is plenty to keep traditional music buffs happy. The superb vocals and even better *saz* playing of Orhan Gençbay, a legend rivalled only by İbrahim Tatlıses in Arabesk music, feature, as does the heart-rending voice of the young Kurdish singer Aynur Doğan. The haunting sounds of Mercan Dede, a fusion of Sufi and modern electronica and big on the world music scene, get an airing, as do the Balkan sounds of Selim Sesler, playing with an unlikely (but very talented) singer of traditional Turkish songs, Canadian Brenna MacCrimmon. Difficult to buy for a sensible price in the UK, it's far cheaper in the US. The DVD is also widely available in İstanbul but you'll struggle to find a copy with English subtitles.

Contemporary music

Pop has a surprisingly long history in Turkey, from the Tango stars of the 1930s through to Presley imitators in the 1950s. It wasn't until the Seventies, though, that **rock** really took root, with the rise of the Anadolu (Anatolian) rock movement. Today, Western-style contemporary music is part and parcel of the diverse Turkish music scene – most of all in cosmopolitan İstanbul. The vast majority of these bands and singers perform in Turkish – which undermines their chances of achieving international success. But the best of them are worth a listen – and if you venture out into the city's labyrinthine **nightlife** scene you are bound, at some point, to have your ears assailed by familiar pop or hip-hop beats accompanied by unfamiliar Turkish vocals.

Rock

Duman are among the most accessible of the current crop of rock bands. Erroneously labelled punk in their early days (itself indicative of the relatively conservative nature of the scene here), the İstanbul-based group are in fact a straightforward rock band, mixing uptempo anthems with lighter ballads and traditional Turkish folk songs. *Bu akşam* ("This evening") and *Belki alısmam lazım* ("Maybe I'd better get used to it") are great songs by any standards.

Pinhani shot to fame in Turkey when some of their songs were used in the popular TV soap *Kavak Yelleri* ("Young and Carefree"), but don't let this put you off. Despite the number of disparate influences in their music – everything from Radiohead and the late, great Alevi troubadour Aşık Veysel to Greek *bouzouki* and Bach – their album *İnandığım Masallar* ("Fairy Tales You Can Believe In") is a wonderfully laidback, melodic and cohesive debut. Both bands have written paeans to their hometown, Duman's *İstanbul* an angry, punky thrash, while Pinhani's *In İstanbul* drips with urban melancholia.

Fellow "Stamboul" boys **Mor ve Ötesi** formed in 1995 and have built up a huge following in Turkey – in 2003 the indie four-piece played in front of 100,000 anti-Iraq war demonstrators in Ankara. Surprisingly, given their reputation for protest, they were chosen to represent Turkey in the 2008 **Eurovision Song Contest**, with *Deli* ("Crazy"), coming in seventh. Bear in mind that in Turkey the Eurovision Song Contest is not seen as the laughably kitsch endeavour it is across much of Europe – in this most patriotic of nations it is taken very seriously indeed.

Sertab Erener, the İstanbul-born belly-dancing diva who won the contest for Turkey in 2003 was, like Mor ve Ötesi, already a major star before the competition. She has recorded an album in English and appeared in **Fatih Akın's** *Crossing the Bridge* documentary (see opposite) singing an orientalized version of Madonna's *Music*.

Another couple of bands who feature in Akın's *Crossing the Bridge* are **Baba Zula** and **Replikas**. Prog-rockers Replikas take extended, experimental soloing to extremes but are talented musicians with a loyal following. **Baba Zula** may be wacky, but their self-styled "oriental-dub" or "psyche-belly" is mesmeric live and with their Sixties hippie throwback looks (big beards, long straggly hair, cowboy hats) and very un-PC belly-dancer they make an entertaining live act. Far more popular is **Şebnem Ferah**. Born in Yalova, near Bursa, she is of Balkan (Macedonian) ancestry. Her goth-metal looks, powerful voice and the helping hand of that doyenne of the Turkish music scene, **Sezen Aksu** (see p.306), have helped secure her fame – though her brand of soft rock and power ballads will not be to everyone's taste. İstanbul born and raised Hayko Çepkin mixes Anatolian rock with scream metal and lively stage act. **Nu-metallers Çileked** hail from Ankara, but frequently play in İstanbul. More radical are long-established punks **Rashit**, who have played with the likes of the Dead Kennedys and the Offspring and had their 2005 album *Herşeyin Bir Bedeli Var* released on Sony.

Hip-hop

The roots of the rap scene in Turkey lie among the Turkish community in Germany. Invariably urban, often poor, disenfranchised and discriminated against, hip-hop provided a natural outlet for their anger and frustration. The movement was kick-started by the suitably controversial **Cartel** in the mid-1990s. Their debut album was banned in Turkey and the group split soon after. The scene in İstanbul really got going with another star of *Crossing the Bridge* (see opposite), the city's very own Eminem – **Ceza**. Worshipped by multitudes of the city's disaffected youth, he was born on the Asian side of the Bosphorus in Üsküdar, taking his stage name (*ceza* means punishment) from one of his early jobs – handing out fines to people who failed to pay

---

MUSIC ON TV

Whether it's on a pint-sized hotel TV or a monster flat-screen in a café, restaurant, bar or club, you won't be able to escape the popular music channels. **Kral** and **Power Turk** are the most popular of the stations playing Turkish music – mainly pop, though Kral in particular mixes in some traditional stuff. **Dream** shows a blend of Turkish rock, indie, hip-hop and Western rock, while **MTV Türkiye** concentrates on non-Turkish artists. For traditional Turkish music try TRT Müzik.

---

their electricity bills. Ceza's success has bred envy, and in 2007 he was accused of lifting his beats straight from Eminem by rival İstanbul rapper **Ege Çubukçu**. Other names to look out for are **Sagopa Kajmer** and Ceza's sister, **Ayben**. Turkish vocals apart, what marks this home-grown hip-hop out from its US inspiration is the sampling of *arabesk* and other forms of traditional Turkish music rather than Western pop.

Pop

Pop music is huge in Turkey. It's also incredibly varied – though you might not think so on a first listen. Once a teen idol, now a housewives' favourite, **Tarkan** swivels his hips and belts out dance-orientated pop with apparent abandon, singing at the 2008 opening of the İstanbul Grand Prix. He's a big star in Germany as well as Turkey, and has produced one album in English.

Pop rockers/balladeers **Mustafa Sandal** and **Teoman** are firm fixtures on the TV music channels (see box above), as is the chanteuse **Yıldız Tilbe**. The multi-talented queen of the Turkish pop scene, **Sezen Aksu**, has helped to preserve and build upon the best of traditional Turkish urban music, both through skilfully updated covers of old songs and with new material incorporating their best elements. Nor is she afraid of controversy, tackling feminism, human rights and ethnic cleansing in Bosnia, and singing in Ladino (the language of Turkey's Jewish population) and Kurdish as well as her native Turkish. Her albums vary enormously in style but 1995's *Işık Doğudan Yükselir* ("The Light Rises from the East") is a good starting point. Another queen of the scene is the incredibly well-preserved, İstanbul-schooled Ajda Pekkan: born in 1946 and still touring, she has sold some thirty million albums worldwide and is a national icon.

Turkish cinema

Turkey has had a moderately successful **film industry** since the 1950s, when corny rural-boy-meets-rural-girl melodramas provided escapism for Anatolian villagers. The outside world took little notice until the 1970s, when a few maverick filmmakers took Turkish cinema in a more radical direction.

1971–99: Early successes

Yılmaz Güney, a popular actor turned director, was imprisoned several times during the Seventies and Eighties for his leftist leanings. He nonetheless produced a series of hard-hitting films in the years around the coups of 1971 and 1980. The best were *Sürü* ("The Herd"), which follows a Kurdish shepherd and his family taking their flock to sell in distant Ankara, and *Yol* ("The Road"). Written from the confines of his prison cell, with the outside directorial assistance of **Şerif Gören**, *Yol* takes an allegorical look at the state of the nation (then still under martial law) by following the fortunes of five prisoners who have been allowed a week's parole. The film was banned in Turkey, which only served to bring it to the notice of the international community, and in 1981 *Yol* was joint-winner of the Palme d'Or. The film finally made it onto the country's cinema screens in 1999, when it played to packed houses. Güney died of cancer in 1984, aged 46, the year after the release of his last film, *Duvar* ("Wall"), an unrelentingly gloomy critique of the country's overcrowded and brutal prison system.

With the exception of 1983's *Hakkâri'de Bir Mevsim* ("A Season in Hakkâri"), a visually stunning film examining the experiences of a young teacher sent to a remote Kurdish village to staff the local school, Turkish films in the 1980s made little impact on the outside world. Despite a lack of financial backing, the Nineties proved kinder, and in 1994 **Erden Kıral**'s *Mavi Sürgün* ("The Blue Exile") was nominated for an Academy Award. In 1995, **Mustafa Altıoklar**'s *İstanbul Kanatlarımın Altında* ("İstanbul Beneath My Wings"), set in the seventeenth century during the reign of tyrant **Murat IV**, drew critical acclaim and was a box-office hit. **Hamam**, made in 1998 by **Ferzan Özpetek**, sees an Italian star inherit a run-down Turkish bath in İstanbul. Through his efforts to restore it, he discovers his own sexuality, making this one of the few Turkish films dealing with gay relationships to have gone on general release.

2000 to the present: critical accolades

The new millennium has seen Turkish cinema hit new heights. Leading the way is **Nuri Bilgi Ceylan**, who won the prestigious Best Director Award at Cannes in 2008 for *Üç Maymun* ("Three Monkeys"), which tells a familiar story of how power corrupts. In it a powerful politician involved in a hit-and-run incident escapes justice by sending his driver to prison in his place – and then sexually abuses the driver's wife. Ceylan had come to prominence with *Uzak* ("Distant"), a beautifully crafted, İstanbul-set film of urban alienation which won the Grand Prix at Cannes. In between these two classics

---

TURKISH CINEMA – DOMESTIC REALITY

As in every country, what the critics adore the vast majority of the public ignore. Ceylan's arty **Uzak** attracted some 20,000 cinema-goers within Turkey, whereas 2008's **Recep İvedik**, director Şahan Gökbakar's tale of an uneducated burping, farting and spitting taxi driver let loose in a five-star hotel grossed $24 million domestically. Equally successful was 2006's ultra-nationalistic **Kurtlar Vadisi – Irak** ("Valley of the Wolves – Iraq") a huge box-office action-thriller hit, in which the Turks get their fictional revenge for the real-life arrest of some of their military boys by the Americans in northern Iraq in 2003. Both films have spawned equally popular formulaic sequels.

was the critically acclaimed but rather self-indulgent *Bklimler* ("Climates"), an existentialist tale of a failing relationship starring Ceylan and his wife, Ebru.

Fatih Akın, a German-born and -bred Turk, had both Turkey and Germany claiming his 2004 Golden Bear winner, *Duvar Karsısı* ("Head On"), as their own. Personalities and cultures clash in this sometimes brutal tale of ill-matched Turkish–German lovers. **Akın**'s 2005 documentary *Crossing the Bridge: The Sound of Istanbul*, made with **Alexander Hacke**, has won many recent plaudits and is an unparalleled introduction to this great city's music scene (see p.304). 2007's *Yadamın Kıyısında* ("Edge of Heaven") won the Best Screenplay Award at Cannes and five awards at Turkey's equivalent of the Oscars, Antalya's Golden Orange festival. Shot in Germany, İstanbul and the eastern Black Sea city of Trabzon, it traces the interconnecting lives of four Turks and two Germans, touching on issues of cultural estrangement, family relationships, lesbianism and political activism.

The first decade of the third millennium has seen a number of other Turkish films take their share of critical accolades. **Reha Erdem**'s 2006 *Bed Vaktı* ("Times and Winds") portrays the often grim realities of growing up in an idyllic-looking Turkish village and makes moving use both of the breathtakingly beautiful location of the village, which overlooks the Mediterranean from its cliff-edge eyrie, and the fresh-faced innocence of its child actors. 2007's *Yumurta* ("Egg"), the first part of a trilogy directed by **Semih Kaplanoulu**, won a fistful of awards at the Golden Orange. A typically Turkish tale, it traces the life of Yusuf, a struggling poet running a secondhand bookshop in İstanbul who returns to his hometown when his mother dies. The second part of the trilogy, *Süt* ("Milk"), winds back the clock to Yusuf's youth in his hometown, where he struggles financially trying to balance the family's milk business with writing poetry. 2010's *Bal* ("Honey"), the final part of the trilogy, won a Golden Bear at the Berlin International Film Festival and is set in the wild mountains of the eastern Black Sea. Based on a true story, 2008's *Gitmek* ("My Marlon, My Brando "), **Hüseyin Karabey**'s first feature (he is a respected documentary filmmaker) is a gripping story of a Turkish woman's search for her Kurdish lover, trapped in northern Iraq following the American invasion of 2003. The emotionally candid theatre actress Ayça leaves a rather grim looking Beyoğlu, crosses snowy Anatolia and enters Iran, hoping to meet her B-movie actor lover Hamal Ali on the Iran–Iraq border.

Iki Dil Bir Bavul ("On the Way to School") is a heart-warming documentary about the trials and tribulations of a Turkish teacher from the affluent west trying to teach in a dirt-poor village school in the ethnically-Kurdish southeast of the country, and won directors Orhan Eskiköy and Özgür Doğan the Best First Film award at Antalya's Golden Orange Film Festival. 2011's *Çoğunluk* ("Majority") showed a side of İstanbul few visitors are likely (or indeed want) to see. Set in unremittingly dull concrete suburbs, it tells the grubby but all too believable tale of a middle-class Turk, still living at home in his late twenties, attempting to subvert the brutal authority of his manipulative father by getting involved with the most "unsuitable" of women, an impoverished Kurdish waitress. 2011 also saw a return to top form for Nuri Bilge Ceylan, whose *Bir Zamanlar Anadolu'da* ("Once upon a time in Anatolia") was co-winner of the Grand Prix at Cannes. Set in small-town Anatolia, it's a murder-story of sorts but, as you would expect from Ceylan, is far stronger on atmosphere and mood than plot.

Books

Many of the books reviewed below are, inevitably, general works on the **Byzantine** and **Ottoman** periods that include, rather than focus specifically on, İstanbul. For information on the **latest books** available, try I.B. Tauris (ⓦibtauris.co.uk) or Saqi Books (ⓦwww.saqibooks.com). In the UK, it's possible to track down many of the books listed here through Turkey specialists Daunt Books, 83 Marylebone High St, London W1M 4DE (☎020/7224 2295, ⓦdauntbooks.co.uk). Most of the bookshops in İstanbul (see p.222) have a wide selection of books on Turkey, and much locally produced material (in English) which is hard to come by outside the city.

Note that "o/p" means **out of print**. Retail websites such as ⓦabebooks.com or ⓦbookfinder.com are excellent places to check for hard-to-find or out-of-print items; almost every book in this bibliography can be found secondhand or on a print-on-demand/special-order basis through these sources.

HISTORY

★ **Roger Crowley** Constantinople: The Last Great Siege: 1453. Brilliantly written account of the fall of the Byzantine city to the Ottoman Turks by an ex-İstanbul resident passionate about his chosen subject. If you're only going to read one history book on the city, make it this one.

★ **Caroline Finkel** Osman's Dream. A scholarly and meticulously researched yet engaging history of the Ottoman Empire, from its origins in the twelfth century through to its early twentieth-century collapse. For a single-volume work on such a vast topic it does a very commendable job.

★ **Jason Goodwin** Lords of the Horizons. A very readable account of the Ottoman Empire. Sceptics may decry its headlong pace and thematic approach, but if you've little or no prior knowledge of the Ottoman world, Goodwin's book helps bring a complex chunk of history to life.

Michael Hickey Gallipoli. The best single-volume history of the campaign.

Halil İnalcık The Ottoman Empire: The Classical Age, 1300–1600. As the title says; the standard work, not superseded since its first 1973 appearance.

Patrick Balfour Kinross The Ottoman Centuries. Readable and balanced summary of Ottoman history from the fourteenth to the twentieth century.

I. Metin Kunt & Christine Woodhead Süleyman the Magnificent and His Age. Concise summary of the reign of the greatest Ottoman sultan, and of the cultural renaissance over which he presided.

★ **Philip Mansel** Constantinople: City of the World's Desire, 1453–1924. Nostalgic, faintly anti-Turkish Republic popular history, focusing on the imperial capital and organized topically as well as chronologically. The best read on the city's Ottoman past.

Philip Mansel Sultans in Splendour – the Last Years of the Ottoman World. The illustrations – a collection of rare photos depicting unbelievable characters from the end of the Ottoman Empire – make this book. Well written, it contains much information not available elsewhere.

Cyril Mango (ed) Oxford History of Byzantium. An accessible introduction, taking in daily life, economic policy and scholarship among other topics.

★ **John Julius Norwich** Byzantium: The Early Centuries, The Apogee and The Decline. An astonishingly detailed, well-informed and readable trilogy. Norwich later compressed his great work into a single volume, the thorough and erudite A Short History of Byzantium.

Faik Ökte The Tragedy of the Turkish Capital Tax (o/p). Short, remorseful monograph on the discriminatory World War II tax, written by the İstanbul director of finance who was responsible for its implementation.

Procopius The Secret History. Often raunchy account of the murkier side of the reigns of Justinian and his ex-courtesan empress, Theodora, from no less an authority than the imperial general Belisarius's official war historian.

★ **Barry Rubin** İstanbul Intrigues. Unputdownable account of Allied/Axis activities in neutral Turkey during World War II, and their attempts to drag it into the conflict. Surprising revelations about the extent of Turkish aid for Britain, the US and the Greek resistance, and a wealth of detailed anecdote.

David Traill Schliemann of Troy: Treasure and Deceit. The man versus the myth of his self-publicity: if you're intending to visit the ruins of ancient Troy, this volume, portraying a crumbling edifice of Schliemann's reputation as an archeologist, will help bring the old walls to life.

Michael Wood In Search of the Trojan War. A very readable examination of the reality behind the legend that is Troy by Britain's best-known populist archeologist, and a companion to the BBC series of the same name.

★ **Erik J. Zürcher** Turkey, A Modern History. If you have time for only one volume covering the post-1800 period, make it this one; it's well written and breathes some revisionist fresh air over sacred cows and received truths. Also with an opinionated, annotated bibliography.

BIOGRAPHIES

Saime Göksu & Edward Timms *Romantic Communist: The Life and Works of Nazım Hikmet*. Turkey's most controversial modern poet, banned and imprisoned for seventeen years at home, Hikmet spent much of his life in the Soviet bloc and died in Moscow.

★ **M. Şükrü Hanioğlu** *Atatürk, an Intellectual Biography*. In exploring the ideas, ideologies and philosophies that influenced Atatürk, this relatively slim volume goes a long way to explaining why modern Turkey is the contradictory country it is.

★ **Patrick Balfour Kinross** *Atatürk, the Rebirth of a Nation*. Long considered the definitive English biography – as opposed to hagiography – of the father of the Republic

and still preferred by some to the newer Mango text (see below).

Andrew Mango *Atatürk*. Despite massive press acclamation, does not supersede Kinross's more readable tome as the best biography of the man, but merely complements it. Thorough and authoritative, but also steeped in military and conspiratorial minutiae.

Michael Strachan *Sir Thomas Roe 1581–1644: A Life*. Biography of an influential Elizabethan statesman who spent several years as ambassador to the Ottoman court and was head of the Levant Company. A fascinating insight into the perilous life and intrigues of Europeans in Constantinople.

MINORITIES AND RELIGION

★ **Taner Akçam** *From Empire to Republic: Turkish Nationalism and the Armenian Genocide*. Brilliant study by a Turkish academic resident in the US, which shows how the ethnic cleansing of the Armenian population from 1895 to 1923, and the subsequent suppression of any memory of these events, was crucial to incipient Turkish nationalism – and remains at the root of the Republic's modern problems.

Peter Balakian *The Burning Tigris: A History of the Armenian Genocide*. As partisan as one would expect from an Armenian-American, it is, nonetheless, a compelling and thorough analysis of the background to, and execution of, the massacres of the Armenians on Ottoman soil during

the late nineteenth and early twentieth centuries.

★ **Bruce Clark** *Twice a Stranger; How Mass Expulsion Forged Modern Greece and Turkey*. The Greeks of İstanbul initially avoided the fate of their kin elsewhere in Anatolia, but the forced population exchanges of 1923 made their eventual departure inevitable. A very readable study of a cataclysmic event.

Speros Vryonis *The Mechanism of Catastrophe*. Definitive study of the state-condoned anti-Greek riots of 1955, which left İstanbul's İstiklal Caddesi and Greek properties across the city in ruins and marked the start of the end for the city's Greek community.

VIEWS OF CONTEMPORARY TURKEY

★ **Stephen Kinzer** *Crescent and Star*. Engaging account of modern Turkey from the İstanbul-based correspondent of the *New York Times*. Whether *rakı*-drinking and *nargile*-toking with ordinary Turks, interviewing leading political figures, swimming across the Bosphorus or broadcasting the blues on his own show on Turkish radio, Kinzer has a gift for bringing the country to life.

Andrew Mango *The Turks Today*. This overview by a long-standing observer usefully concentrates on the period from the demise of Atatürk to 2004. By no means a rose-tinted view, but he gives the country an easy ride in too many

areas, and the chapter on Kurdish issues is highly disposable.

Chris Morris *The New Turkey Today*. More up to date than Mango's book, Morris (BBC correspondent in Turkey for four years) writes in a very readable manner on the usual topics, from political Islam to the Greeks and Armenians, and from the Kurdish question to Turkey's EU accession quest.

★ **Nicole & Hugh Pope** *Turkey Unveiled: Atatürk and After* (UK); also published as *Turkey Unveiled: A History of Modern Turkey* (US). A series of interlinked essays by two foreign correspondents who, after more than two decades in harness, understand Turkey better than most outsiders.

TRAVEL AND MEMOIRS

Shirin Devrim *A Turkish Tapestry: The Shakirs of İstanbul*. Turbulent chronicle of an eccentric, dysfunctional and talented aristocratic Ottoman family whose exploits, if anything, became even more colourful after 1923.

Laurence Kelly (ed) *İstanbul: A Traveller's Companion*. Well-selected historical writing and fascinating eyewitness accounts of historical events such as the Crusaders' sack of Constantinople.

★ **Geert Mak** *The Bridge*. Brilliant travelogue weaving the compelling tales of the petty traders, hustlers, pickpockets and fishermen who crowd İstanbul's iconic

Galata Bridge with a wonderfully succinct and evocative history of one of the world's great cities.

Mary Wortley Montagu *Letters* and *Turkish Embassy Letters*. Impressions of an eccentric but perceptive traveller, resident in İstanbul during 1716–18, whose disregard for convention and popular prejudice gave her the edge over contemporary historians.

★ **İrfan Orga** *Portrait of a Turkish Family*. Heartbreaking story following the Orga family from an idyllic existence in late Ottoman İstanbul through grim survival in the early Republican era.

★**Orhan Pamuk** İstanbul: Memories of a City. A thoughtful and sometimes moving memoir by Turkey's most famous novelist, reflecting on the author's troubled relationship with himself, his parents and the city he was born and raised in. The book's overriding theme is melancholy and decline from imperial greatness – reinforced by the copious black-and-white illustrations by Turkey's leading photographer, Ara Güler.

Mary Seacole The Wonderful Adventures of Mrs Seacole in Many Lands. This alternative Florence Nightingale was a black Jamaican who, unlike her paler-skinned compatriot, ministered to Crimean War casualties in İstanbul at her own expense.

★**Daniel de Souza** Under a Crescent Moon. Turkish society seen from the bottom looking up: an excellent volume of prison vignettes by a jailed Brit, who despite having only been in the country a matter of minutes before his arrest, now resides in Turkey.

ARCHITECTURE AND ARTS

Metin And Turkish Miniature Painting – the Ottoman Period (Dost Yayınları, İstanbul). Attractive, interesting account of the most important Ottoman art form. Loads of colour plates and well laid out.

Diana Barillari & Ezio Godoli İstanbul 1900: Art Nouveau Architecture and Interiors. Superbly researched and illustrated account of İstanbul's rich but neglected legacy of Art Nouveau architecture, in particular the works of Italian architect and longtime resident Raimondo D'Aronco. A nice corrective to the axiom that the city consists only of palaces, concrete towerblocks and crumbled wood terraces.

John Freely John Freely's İstanbul. Freely is the doyen of modern writers on the city. In this copiously illustrated book he combines descriptions of many of its monuments, much of its history and a wealth of personal musings on a lifetime's wandering through its streets to great effect.

★**Godfrey Goodwin** A History of Ottoman Architecture. The most comprehensive guide to Ottoman architecture, covering the whole of Turkey and providing a sound historical and ethno geographical context for any Ottoman construction you care to name. Far too heavy to cart around, though. Goodwin's Sinan: Ottoman Architecture and Its Values Today provides fascinating insights into the architect, his life and influences.

Richard Krautheimer Early Christian and Byzantine Architecture. An excellent survey from the Pelican "History of Art" series.

R.J. Mainstone Hagia Sophia: Architecture, Structure and Liturgy of Justinian's Great Church. A detailed study of one of the world's most important structures. A little technical and the illustrations are black and white only, but about as exhaustive as you can get on the subject.

Neville, Beck, Forsting and Moberly İstanbul: A Guide to Recent Architecture. The guide to get if your interest in architecture extends as far as the city's often overlooked nineteenth- and twentieth century buildings.

★**David Talbot Rice** Art of the Byzantine Era. A copiously illustrated general account of Byzantine art from the age of Justinian to the fall of Constantinople, with a lengthy (85 pages) chapter on the latter. An excellent introduction to the wonders of Byzantine architecture, frescoes, mosaics and other works of art.

J.M. Rogers Sinan: Makers of Islamic Civilisation. An eminently readable and well-illustrated introduction to the greatest architect of the Ottoman period.

Steven Runciman Byzantine Style and Civilisation (o/p). Excellent introduction to the world of Byzantium. His The Fall of Constantinople, 1453 remains a classic study of the event, vying with the reader's attention from the equally well-written book by Crowley (see p.309).

★**Hilary Sumner-Boyd & John Freely** Strolling through İstanbul. First published in 1972; indispensable if you love history and even more so if you like to conduct your researches on foot. The authors' knowledge of, and love for, this incredible city shine through on every page. Copious sketch-maps and ground plans of monuments complement the informative text. Definitive.

Jane Taylor Imperial İstanbul. Excellent, stone-by-stone guide, complete with site plans, of the major Ottoman monuments in Bursa and Edirne as well as İstanbul.

CRAFTS

Alastair Hull Kilims: The Complete Guide. Comprehensive and thoroughly illustrated survey of Turkish kilims. His Living with Kilims is an excellent manual on how to use and care for (as opposed to museum-ize) kilims in interior-decoration situations.

James Opie Tribal Rugs. Contains examples of Turkish and Kurdish rugs as part of a general Central Asian survey.

Kurt Zipper & Claudia Fritzsche Oriental Rugs: Turkish. Extensive discussions of weaving techniques, symbols, rug categories and the weavers themselves, along with a regional survey of distinctive patterns.

TURKISH FICTION IN TRANSLATION

Selçuk Altun *Songs My Mother Never Taught Me*. As different from the populist works of Barbara Nadel (see below) as it's possible to get, this celebral İstanbul-set thriller is cold and clinical yet strangely compelling.

Moris Farhi *Young Turk*. Ankara-born Farhi conjures up thirteen interwoven short stories in this delightful and moving evocation of İstanbul in the Thirties, Forties and Fifties. The cast of characters, whether they be Armenian, Greek, gypsy, Levantine or Turkish, are lovingly drawn, though the early coming-of-age tales are the most convincing.

Yadar Kemal Until the advent of Orhan Pamuk (see below), the best-known Turkish novelist in the West. His earlier works, the most famous of which is *Mehmed My Hawk*, are set in the foothills of the Toros mountains, but some of his later (and better) novels, are set in and around İstanbul, including *The Sea-Crossed Fishermen* (o/p) a psychological drama set against the background of an İstanbul sea-fishing village, contrasting an old man's struggle to save the dolphins in the Sea of Marmara with the fortunes of a desperate hoodlum at bay in the city.

Orhan Pamuk Internationally acclaimed, İstanbul-born writer and Turkey's first-ever Nobel Prize winner. His first work, *The White Castle*, is an excellent historical meditation in which a seventeenth-century Italian scholar is enslaved in the service of an Ottoman astronomer. The 1994-translated *The Black Book*, a mystery set in modern İstanbul, was more convoluted and surreal, and did well in

Turkey. But Pamuk's 1998 *The New Life* is, with nearly 750,000 copies sold, the most successful Turkish novel ever, and had foreign critics in raptures. His subsequent *My Name is Red*, a late sixteenth-century Ottoman-set murder whodunnit, is marred by poor characterization and clunky translation. 2004's ★ *Snow*, Pamuk's most controversial and political novel, is arguably his best. Set in the bleak, lonely northeastern outpost of Kars, it examines once-taboo topics such as political Islam and Kurdish.

Elif Shafak *The Flea Palace*. An engaging account, in the mould of Armistead Maupin, of the interwoven, tragicomic lives of the residents of a once-grand İstanbul apartment block. The author, of Turkish origin but born in Strasbourg, raised in Spain and now living in İstanbul, found herself, like Pamuk, drawing the ire of the establishment for her 2007 ★ *The Bastard of İstanbul*. In the book an exuberant, if dysfunctional, Turkish family play host to an Armenian-American girl in search of her identity. Well-drawn female characters drive a narrative which inevitably delves into the dirty linen basket of pre-Republican Turkey. Prosecuted under article 301 for "insulting Turkishness", the charges against her were eventually dropped..

Latife Tekin *Berji Kristin: Tales from the Garbage Hills*. The hard underbelly of Turkish life is shown in this surreal allegory set in a shantytown founded on an İstanbul rubbish dump. By the same author, *Dear Shameless Death* examines how rural families cope with the move to the big city.

FOREIGN LITERATURE SET IN TURKEY

Maureen Freely *The Life of the Party*. Salacious, desperate cavortings of Bosphorus University faculty and their families during the 1960s, including a thinly disguised amalgam of the author's father, John Freely, and others. An excellent read.

★ **Jason Goodwin** *The Janissary Tree*. Racy historical thriller with all kinds of skulduggery being uncovered by Yashin, a eunuch detective. A very palatable entry into a nineteenth-century İstanbul on the verge of the Tanzimat reforms, and a successful formula that has spawned three sequels: *The Snake Stone*, *The Bellini Card* and 2011's *An Evil Eye*.

Pierre Loti *Aziyade*. For what's essentially romantic twaddle set in nineteenth-century Ottoman İstanbul, this

is surprisingly racy, with good insights into Ottoman life and Western attitudes to the Orient.

Barbara Nadel *Her* İstanbul-set Inspector İkmen mysteries include *A Chemical Prison*, *Arabesque* and *Harem*. Some people love the tales of doughty, chain-smoking Inspector İkrem and various associates trawling through the city's underworld, others find them a tad unconvincing. They're well worth a try, though, conjuring up a side of the city barely imaginable to the average visitor.

Barry Unsworth *The Rage of the Vulture*. Set in the twilight of the Ottoman Empire, with the paranoid Sultan Abdülhamid during the last year of his reign observed by a troubled British officer-with-a-past stationed in İstanbul.

POETRY

Coleman Barks (trans.) *Selected Poems* Great introduction to the words of Rumi, though the translations are not literal.

Yunus Emre *The City of the Heart: Verses of Wisdom and Love*. Along with Rumi, the most highly regarded Turkish medieval Sufi poet; translated by Süha Faiz.

Talit Sait Halman *Living Poets of Turkey* (Dost Yayınları, İstanbul). A wide selection of modern Turkish poetry, with an introduction giving the socio political context. Halman also edited *Yunus Emre and His Mystical Poetry* (o/p), the

works of the medieval Islamic folk poet, with explanatory essays.

Nazım Hikmet *Poems of Nazım Hikmet*. The newest (2002), most easily available and most reasonably priced anthology by the internationally renowned Turkish communist poet, who died in exile in 1963.

Geoffrey L. Lewis (trans.) *The Book of Dede Korkut*. The Turkish national epic, set in the age of the Oğuz Turks: by turns racy, formulaic, elegant and redundant.

Language

English is widely studied in **Turkish** schools and has a great cachet, but away from tourist-dominated Sultanahmet or, to a lesser extent, sophisticated Beyoğlu, you won't come across many people who speak very much of it. It pays to learn as much Turkish as you can; even cosmopolitan İstanbullus greatly appreciate foreigners who show enough interest and courtesy to learn at least **basic greetings**. The main advantages of the language from the learner's point of view are that it's phonetically spelt and (almost always) grammatically regular. The disadvantages are that the vocabulary is unrelated to any language you're likely to have encountered (unless you're conversant in Arabic or Persian), and the grammar, relying heavily on suffixes, gets more alien the further you delve into it. Concepts like vowel harmony further complicate matters; trying to grasp at least the basics, though, is well worth the effort.

Phrasebooks and dictionaries

For a straightforward **phrasebook**, look no further than *The Rough Guide Phrasebook: Turkish*, with useful two-way glossaries and a brief and simple grammar section. To learn more, David Pollard and Asuman Çelen-Pollard's *Teach Yourself Turkish* is very good, and has an accompanying CD. Alternatively, there's the slimmer and cheaper *Turkish in Three Months*. The best series published in Turkey is a set of three textbooks and tapes, *Türkçe Öğreniyoruz (Engin Yayınevi)*, available in good bookshops in İstanbul.

Among widely available Turkish **dictionaries**, the best are probably the Langenscheidt/Lilliput miniature or coat-pocket sizes, or the *Concise Oxford Turkish Dictionary*, a hardback suitable for serious students. In Turkey, locally produced Redhouse dictionaries are the best value, though their fine print can be hard to read.

Pronunciation

Pronunciation in Turkish is worth mastering, since once you've got it the phonetic spelling helps you progress fast. The following letters differ significantly from English pronunciation.

Aa short a similar to that in f**a**r.

Ee as in b**e**t.

Iı unstressed vowel similar to the vestigial sound between the **b** and **l** of probable.

İi as in sk**i**.

Oo as in n**o**te.

Öö like ur in b**ur**n.

Uu as in bl**u**e.

Üü like ew in f**ew**.

Cc like j in **j**elly.

Çç like ch in **ch**at.

Gg hard g as in **g**et.

Ğğ generally silent, but either lengthens the preceding vowel or, when between two vowels approximates a **y** sound.

Hh as in **h**en, never silent.

Jj like the s in plea**s**ure.

Şş like sh in **sh**ape.

Vv soft, somewhere between **v** and **w**.

Vowel harmony

Turkish generally tries to adhere to the principle of **vowel harmony**, whereby words contain either the so-called "back" vowels a, ı, o and u, or the "front" vowels e, i, ö and ü, but rarely mix the two types. A small number of native Turkish words (eg *anne*, mother; *kardeş*, brother) violate the norms of vowel harmony, as do compound words, eg *bugün*, "today", formed from *bu* (this) and *gün* (day), and foreign (mainly from Arabic, Persian and French) loan words.

Words and phrases

BASICS

Mr (follows first name)	Bey	I'm English/Scottish/	İngilizim/İskoçyalım/
Miss (precedes first)	Bayanname	Welsh/Irish/	Gallerliyim/İrlandalıyım/
Mrs (literally lady; polite	Hanım	American/Australian/	Amerikalıyım/Avustralyalım/
Ottoman title; follows		from New Zealand	Yeni Zelandlıyım
first name)		I live in …	… 'de/da oturuyorum
Good morning	Günaydın	Today	Bugün
Good afternoon	İyi günler	Tomorrow	Yarın
Good evening	İyi akşamlar	The day after tomorrow	Öbür gün/Ertesi gün
Good night	İyi geceler	Yesterday	Dün
Hello	Merhaba	Now	Şimdi
Goodbye	Allahaısmarladık	Later	Sonra
Yes	Evet	Wait a minute!	Bir dakika bekle!
No	Hayır	In the morning	Sabahleyin
No (there isn't any)	Yok	In the afternoon	Öğle'den sonra
Please	Lütfen	In the evening	Akşamleyin
Thank you	Teşekkür ederim/Mersi/	Here/there/over there	Bur(a)da/Şur(a)da/Or(a)da
	Sağol	Good/bad	İyi/Kötü, Fena
You're welcome/that's OK	Bir şey değil	Big/small	Büyük/Küçük
How are you?	Nasılsınız? Nasılsın?	Cheap/expensive	Ucuz/Pahalı
	Ne haber?	Early/late	Erken/Geç
I'm fine (thank you)	(Sağol) İyiyim/İyilik sağlık	Hot/cold	Sıcak/Soğuk
Do you speak English?	İngilizce biliyormusunuz?	Near/far	Yakın/Uzak
I don't understand	Anlamadım/Türkçe	Vacant/occupied	Boş/Dolu
(Turkish)	anlamıyorum	Quickly/slowly	Hızlı/Yavaş
I don't know	Bilmiyorum	With/without (milk)	(Süt)lü/(Süt)süz
I beg your pardon, sorry	Affedersiniz	With/without (meat)	(Et)li/(Et)siz
Excuse me (in a crowd)	Pardon	Enough	Yeter

SOME COMMON SIGNS

Entrance/exit	Giriş/Çıkış	Foreign exchange	Kambiyo
Free/paid entrance	Giriş ücretsiz/Ücretlidir	Beware	Dikkat
Gentlemen	Bay(lar)	First aid	İlk yardım
Ladies	Bayanlar	No smoking	Sigara içilmez
WC	WC/Tuvalet/Umumî	Stop, halt	Dur
Open/closed	Açık/Kapalı	Military Area	Askeri bölge
Arrivals/departures	Varış/Kalkış	Entry Forbidden	Girmek yasaktır
Pull/push	Çekiniz/İtiniz	No entry without a woman	Damsız girilmez
Drinking water	İçilebilir su	Please take off	Lütfen ayakkabılarınızı
To let/for hire	Kiralık	your shoes	çıkartınız

ACCOMMODATION

Hotel	Hotel/otel	With a double bed	Fransiz yataklı
Pension/inn	Pansiyon	With a shower	Duşlu
Do you have a room?	Boş odanız var mı?	Hot water	Sıcak su
Single/double/triple	Tek/çift/üç kişilik	Can I see it?	Bakabilirmiyim?
Do you have a double	Bir/iki/üç gecelik çift	I have a booking	Reservasyonum var
room for one/two/	yataklı odanızvar mı?		
three nights?			

QUESTIONS AND DIRECTIONS

Where is the … ?	… nerede?	**How far is it to … ?**	… 'a/e ne kadar uzak?
When?	Ne zaman?	**What time does it open?**	Kaçta açılıcak?
What/What is it?	Ne/Ne dir?	**What time does it close?**	Kaçta kapanacak?
How much (does it cost)?	Ne kadar?	**What's it called in Turkish?**	Türkcesi ne dir?/Turkin
How many?	Kaç tane?		Turkçe nasıl söylersiniz?
Why?	Niye?	**Left**	Sol
What time is it?	Saat kaç?	**Right**	Sağ
How do I get to … ?	… 'a/e nasıl giderim?	**Straight ahead**	Doğru, direk

TRAVELLING

Aeroplane	Uçak	**Return**	Gidiş-dönüş
Bus	Otobus	**What time does it leave?**	Kaçta kalkıyor?
Train	Tren	**Can I book a seat?**	Reservasyon
Car	Araba		yapabılırmıyım?
Taxi	Taksi	**How many kilometres is it?**	Kaç kilome tredir?
Bicycle	Bisiklet	**How long does it take?**	Ne kadar sürer?
Ferry	Feribot, vapur	**Which bus goes to …?**	Hangi otobus … 'a gider?
Catamaran, sea bus	Deniz otobüsü	**Which road leads to …?**	Hangi yol … 'a çıkar?
Hitchhiking	Otostop	**Can I get out at a**	Müsait bir yerde
On foot	Yaya	**convenient place?**	inebilirmiyim?
Airport	Havalimani/havaalanı	**Parking/No parking**	Park yapılır/Park yapılmaz
Bus station	Otogar	**One-way street**	Tek yön
Train station	Gar, tren ıstasyonu	**No entry**	Araç giremez
Ferry terminal/jetty	İskele	**No through road**	Çıkmaz sokak
Harbour	Liman	**Slow down**	Yavaşla
A ticket to …	… 'a bir bilet	**Road closed**	Yol kapalı
One-way	Gidiş, sadece		

DAYS OF THE WEEK, MONTHS AND SEASONS

Sunday	Pazar	**June**	Haziran
Monday	Pazartesi	**July**	Temmuz
Tuesday	Salı	**August**	Ağustos
Wednesday	Çarşamba	**September**	Eylül
Thursday	Perşembe	**October**	Ekim
Friday	Cuma	**November**	Kasım
Saturday	Cumartesi	**December**	Aralık
January	Ocak	**Spring**	İlkbahar
February	Subat	**Summer**	Yaz
March	Mart	**Autumn**	Sonbahar
April	Nisan	**Winter**	Kış
May	Mayıs		

NUMBERS

1	Bir	**11**	On bir
2	İki	**12**	On iki
3	Üç	**13**	On üç
4	Dört	**20**	Yirmi
5	Beş	**30**	Otuz
6	Altı	**40**	Kırk
7	Yedi	**50**	Elli
8	Sekiz	**60**	Altmış
9	Dokuz	**70**	Yetmiş
10	On	**80**	Seksen

90	Doksan	500,000	Beşyüz bin
100	Yüz	1,000,000	Bir milyon
140	Yüz kırk	The most important ordinals, as in class of train,	
200	İki yüz	restaurant, etc, are:	
700	Yedi yüz	First	Birinci
1000	Bin	Second	İkinci
100,000	Yüz bin	Third	Üçüncü

TIME CONVENTIONS

(At) 3 o'clock	Saat üç(ta)	It's 8.10	Sekizi on geçiyor
2 hours (duration)	İki saat	It's 10.45	On bire çeyrek var
Half-hour (duration)	Yarım saat	At 8.10	Sekizi on geçe
5.30	Beş buçuk	At 10.45	On bire çeyrek kala

Food and drink

BASICS

Bal	Honey	Şeker	Sugar
Bulgur	Cracked wheat	Sirke	Vinegar
Buz	Ice	Su	Water
Dereotu	Dill	Süt	Milk
Ekmek	Bread	Tereyağı	Butter
Karabiber	Black pepper	Tuz	Salt
Makarna	Pasta (noodles)	Yağ	Oil
Mısır	Corn	Yoğurt	Yoghurt
Nane	Mint	Yumurta	Eggs
Pilav, pirinç	Rice		

USEFUL WORDS

Bakarmısınız!	Polite way of getting the	Garsoniye	"Waiter's" charge
	waiter's attention	Hesap	Bill, check
Bardak	Glass	Kaşık	Spoon
Başka bir...	Another...	Peçete	Napkin
Bıçak	Knife	Servis ücreti	Service charge
Çatal	Fork	Tabak	Plate

COOKING TERMS

Acı	Hot, spicy	Peynirli, kaşarlı	With cheese
Etli	Containing meat	Pilaki	Vinaigrette, marinated
Etli mi?	Does it contain meat?	Pişmemiş	Raw
Etsiz yemek var mı?	Do you have any meatless	Sıcak/soğuk	Hot/cold
	food?	Soslu, salçalı	In red sauce
Ezme	Paste; any mashed or	Sucuklu	With sausage
	crushed dip	Tava, sahanda	Deep-fried, fried
Fırında(n)	Baked	Yoğurtlu	In yoghurt sauce
Haşlama	Meat stew without oil,	Yumurtalı	With egg (eg *pide*)
	sometimes with vegetables	Zeytinyağlı	Vegetables cooked in their
Izgarada(n), ızgarası	Grilled		own juices, spices and
Kıymalı	With minced meat		olive oil (*zeytin yağı*), then
Kızartma	Fried then chilled		allowed to steep and chill

SOUP (ÇORBA)

Düğün	"Wedding": egg and lemon	Tarhana	Yoghurt, soured grain and spice
Ezo gelin	Rice and vegetable broth		
İşkembe	Tripe	Tavuk	Chicken
Mercimek	Lentils	Yayla	Similar to *tarhana*, with mint
Paça	Trotters	Yoğurt	Yoghurt, rice and celery greens

APPETIZERS (MEZE OR ZEYTINYAĞLI)

Antep/acılı ezmesi	Hot chilli mash with garlic, parsley, lettuce, onion	Mantar sote	Sautéed mushrooms
		Mücver	Courgette fritters
Barbunya	Red kidney beans, marinated	Patlıcan ezmesi	Aubergine pâté
Beyin salatası	Lamb-brains salad	Piyaz	White haricots, onions and parsley vinaigrette
Börülce	Black-eyed peas, in the pod		
Cacık	Yoghurt, grated cucumber and herb dip	Rus salatası	"Russian" salad – potatoes, peas and gherkins in mayonnaise
Çoban salatası	Chopped tomato, cucumber, parsley, pepper and onion salad		
		Semizotu	Purslane, usually mixed into yoghurt
Deniz börülce	Sea samphire	Sigara böreği	Cheese-filled pastry "cigarettes"
Deniz otu	Rock samphire		
Haydarı	Dense yoghurt and garlic dip	Tarama	Pink fish-roe
		Turşu	Pickled vegetables
İçli köfte	Usually meat in a spicy bulgur crust	Yaprak dolması/yılancı dolması	Stuffed vine-leaves
İmam bayıldı	Cold baked aubergine, onion and tomato	Yeşil salata	Green salad
		Zeytin	Olives

MEAT (ET) AND POULTRY (BEYAZ ET)

Adana kebap	Spicy Arab-style kebab	Kanat	Chicken wing
Beyti	Minced kebab wrapped in pitta	Karışık ızgara	Mixed grill
Billur/koç yumurtası	Testicle	Keçi	Goat
Böbrek	Kidney	Kiremit kebap	Meat served on a hot ceramic tray (*kiremit* = tile)
Bonfile	Small steak		
Ciğer	Liver	Köfte	Meatballs
Çöp kebap	Literally, "rubbish kebab" – tiny chunks of offal or lamb	Koyun	Mutton
		Kuzu	Lamb
Dana eti	Veal	Pastırma	Cured, spicy meat
Dil	Tongue	Piliç	Roasting chicken
Döner kebap	Fatty lamb from a rotisseried cone of meat slabs	Pirzola	Lamb chop, cutlet
		Saray kebap	Rissoles baked with vegetables
İnegöl köfte	Mince rissoles	Sığır	Beef
İskender or Bursa kebap	*Döner* drenched in yoghurt and sauce	Şiş kebab	Shish kebab
		Tandır kebap	Side of tender, boneless lamb baked in an outdoor oven
Kaburga	Spare ribs, or ribs stuffed with *pilaf* rice		
		Tavuk	Boiling chicken
Kağıt kebap	Meat and vegetables baked in wax paper	Yürek	Heart

FISH (BALIK) AND SEAFOOD

Ahtapod	Octopus	Çineköp	Baby bluefish; not very esteemed
Alabalık	Trout		
Barbunya, tekir	Red mullet, small and large respectively	Çipura	Gilt-head bream
		Hamsi	Anchovy (Black Sea)

İsparoz	Annular bream	Levrek	Bass; usually farmed
İstakoz	Aegean lobster	Lüfer	Bluefish
İstavrit	Horse mackerel	Mercan	Pandora or red bream; wild
Kalamar	Squid	Mezgit	Whitebait
Kalkan	Turbot	Midye	Mussel
Karagöz	Two-banded bream	Orfoz	Giant grouper
Karides	Prawns	Palamut, torik	Small/large bonito
Kefal	Grey mullet (Aegean)		respectively
Kılıç	Swordfish	Sardalya	Sardine
Kolyoz	Club mackerel	Yengeç	Crab

VEGETABLES (SEBZE)

Acı biber	Hot chillis	Marul	Lettuce
Bakla	Broad beans	Maydanoz	Parsley
Bamya	Okra or lady's finger	Nohut	Chickpeas
Bezelye	Peas	Patates	Potato
Domates	Tomato	Patlıcan	Aubergine, eggplant
Enginar	Artichoke	Roka, tere	Rocket greens
Havuç	Carrot	Salatalık	Cucumber
Ispanak	Spinach	Sarımsak, sarmısak	Garlic
Kabak	Courgette, zucchini	Sivri biber	Skinny peppers, hot or mild
Karnabahar	Cauliflower	Soğan	Onion
Kuru fasulye	White haricots	Taze fasulye	French beans
Kuşkonmaz	Asparagus	Tere	Similar to, but hotter than,
Lahana	Cabbage (usually stuffed)		rocket
Mantar	Mushrooms	Turp	Radish

SNACKS

Badem	Almonds	Lavaş	Flat bread, usually served hot
Börek	Rich layered pastry with		and "puffed-up" with dips as
	varied fillings		a starter
Çerez	Bar nibbles	Leblebi	Roasted chickpeas
Çeviz	Walnuts	Midye dolması	Mussels stuffed with rice,
Cezer(i)ye	Carrot, honey and nut bar		allspice and pine nuts
Çiğ börek	"Inflated" hollow turnovers	Mısır	Roasted and spiced corn
Dürüm	Pitta-like dough roll used to	Pestil	Sheet-pressed dried fruit
	wrap meat for takeaway	Pide	Elongated Turkish "pizza"
Fındık	Hazelnuts	Poğaça	Soft bread, plain or stuffed
Gözleme	Village flat-bread with various		with cheese or spicy potato
	savoury fillings	Antep/Şam fıstık	Pistachios
Kestane	Chestnuts	Simit	Bread rings studded with
Kokoreç	Mixed innard roulade		sesame seeds
Kuru üzüm	Raisins	Su börek	"Water *börek*" – steamed,
Lahmacun	Round Arabic "pizza"		lasagne-like cheese pie
		Yer fıstığı	Peanuts

TYPICAL DISHES

Güveç	Meat and vegetable clay-pot	Lahana sarma	Black-Sea version of stuffed vine-
	casserole		leaves, with baby cabbage
İç pilav	Spicy rice		leaves
Karnıyarık	Aubergine and meat dish, firmer	Mantı	Mince-stuffed "ravioli" topped
	than *mussaka*		with yoghurt and chilli oil

Menemen	Stir-fried omelette with tomatoes and peppers	Sebze turlu	Vegetable stew
		Tas kebap	Meat and vegetable stew
Saç kavurma	"Wok"-fried medley	Türlü sebze	Another name for *tas kebap*
Şakşuka	Aubergine, tomato and other vegetable fry-up		

CHEESE (PEYNIR)

Beyaz	White; like Greek feta	Otlu peynir	Herb-flavoured cheese
Çerkez	Like Edam	Tulum	Dry, crumbly cheese made in a goatskin
Dil	Like mozzarella		
Kaşar	Kasseri, variably aged		

FRUIT (MEYVE)

Ahududu	Raspberry	Kavun	Persian melon
Armut	Pear	Kayısı	Apricot
Ayva	Quince	Kiraz	Sweet cherry
Böğürtlen	Blackberry	Limon	Lemon
Çilek	Strawberry	Mandalin	Tangerine
Dut	Mulberry	Muz	Banana
Elma	Apple	Nar	Pomegranate
Erik	Plum	Portakal	Orange
Hurma	Persimmon or date	Şeftali	Peach
İncir	Figs	Üzüm	Grape
Karpuz	Watermelon	Vişne	Sour cherry

SWEETS (TATLI)

Acı badem	Giant almond biscuit	Kurabiye	Generic term for dry, shortbread-type biscuit
Aşure	Pulse, wheat, fruit and nut "soup"		
Baklava	Layered honey-and-nut pie	Lokum	Turkish delight
Dondurma	Ice cream	Muhallebi	Rice flour and rosewater pudding
Fırın sütlaç	Baked rice pudding	Mustafakemalpaşa	Syrup-soaked dumpling
İrmik helvası	Semolina and nut *helva*	Pasta	Any pastry or cake
Kabak tatlısı	Baked orange-fleshed squash topped with nuts and *kaymak*	Süpangile	Ultra-rich chocolate pudding, with sponge or a biscuit embedded
Kadayıf	"Shredded wheat" in syrup	Sütlaç	Rice pudding
Kadın göbeği	Doughnut in syrup	Tahin helvası	Sesame-paste *helva*
Kaymak	Clotted cream	Tavukgöğsü	Chicken fibre, milk and semolina toffee
Kazandibi	Browned residue of *tavukgöğsü*		
Keşkül	Vanilla-almond custard	Yaz helvası	Semolina-based *helva*, often chocolate-flavoured
Komposto	Stewed fruit		
Krem karamel	Crème caramel		

DRINKS

Ada çayı	Sage tea	Memba suyu	Spring water (non-fizzy)
Ayran	Salted yoghurt drink	Musluk su	Tap water
Bira	Beer	Meyva suyu	Fruit juice
Boza	Fermented millet drink	Papatya çayı	Camomile tea
Çay	Tea	Rakı	Aniseed-flavoured spirit
Kahve	Coffee	Sahlep	Orchid-root-powder drink
Maden suyu	Mineral water (fizzy), often called soda	Şarap	Wine

Glossary

Many of the **Turkish terms** below will change their form according to their grammatical declension (eg *ada*, island, but *Edek Adası*, Donkey Island); the genitive suffix is displayed in brackets, or the form written separately when appropriate.

GENERAL MEDIEVAL AND MODERN TURKISH TERMS

Ada(sı) Island.

Ağa A minor rank of nobility in the Ottoman Empire, and still a term of respect applied to a local worthy; follows the name (eg Ismail Ağa).

Ayazma Sacred spring.

Bahçe(si) Garden.

Bekçi Caretaker or warden at an archeological site or monument.

Belediye(si) Municipality – both the corporation and the actual town hall, for a community of over 2000 inhabitants.

Bey Another minor Ottoman title, like *ağa*, still in use; follows the first name.

Cami(i) Mosque.

Çarşaf A bedsheet – or the full-length, baggy dress-with-hood worn by religious Turkish women.

Çarşı(sı) Bazaar, market.

Çay(ı) 1) Tea, the national drink; 2) a stream or small river.

Çeşme(si) Street-corner fountain.

Dağlar(ı) Mountains.

Dolmuş Literally "filled" – the shared-taxi system; (see p.25).

Eski Old (frequent modifier of place names).

Ezan The Muslim call to prayer.

Gazı Warrior for the (Islamic) faith; also a common epithet of Atatürk.

Gazino Open-air nightclub, usually adorned with coloured lights and featuring live or taped *arabesk* or taverna music.

Gecekondu Literally "founded-by-night" – a reference to the Ottoman law whereby houses begun in darkness that had acquired a roof and four walls by dawn were inviolable.

Gişe Ticket window or booth.

Göl(ü) Lake.

Hacı Honorific of someone who has made the pilgrimage to Mecca; precedes the name, though rarely used conversationally as a term of address.

Hamam(ı) Turkish bath.

Han(ı) Traditionally a tradesmen's hall, or an urban inn; now can also mean an office block.

Harem The women's quarters in Ottoman residences.

Hastane(si) Hospital.

Hicrî The Muslim dating system, beginning with Mohammed's flight to Medina in 622 AD, and based on the thirteen-month lunar calendar; approximately six centuries behind the Miladî calendar. Abbreviated "H." on monuments and inscriptions.

Hittite First great civilization (c.1800–1200 BC) to emerge in Anatolia.

Hoca Teacher in charge of religious instruction for children.

İmam Usually just the prayer leader at a mosque, though it can mean a more important spiritual authority.

Irmak River, eg Yeşilırmak (Green River).

İl(i) Province, the largest administrative division in Turkey, subdivided into *ilçes* (counties or districts).

İskele(si) Jetty, dock.

Janissary One of the sultan's praetorian guard, levied exclusively from the Christian communities of the Balkans between the fifteenth and eighteenth centuries; *yeniceri* in Turkish. Famous for their devotion to the Bektaşi order, outlandish headgear and marching music.

Kaplıca Developed hot springs, spa.

Kilim Flat-weave rug without a pile.

Kilise(si) Church.

Konak Large private residence, also the main government building of a province or city; genitive form *konağı*.

Lokanta Restaurant; rendition of the Italian *locanda*.

Mahalle(si) District or neighbourhood.

Meydan(ı) Public square or plaza.

Meyhane Tavern where alcohol and *meze*-type food are served together.

Miladî The Christian year-numbering system; abbreviated "M." on inscriptions and monuments.

Muezzin Man who pronounces call to prayer (*ezan*) from the minaret of a mosque.

Namaz The Muslim rite of prayer, performed five times daily.

Nehir (Nehri) River.

Otogar Bus station.

Ramazan The Muslim month of fasting and prayer.

Saz Long-necked, fretted stringed instrument central to Turkish folk ballads and Alevi/Bektaşi devotional music.

Sema A dervish ceremony; thus *semahane*, a hall where such ceremonies are conducted.

Sufi Dervish – more properly an adherent of one of the heterodox mystical branches of Islam. In Turkey the most important sects were (and to some extent still are) the Bektaşi, Mevlevî, Helveti, Nakşibendi, Cerrahi and Kadiri orders.

Sultan valide The Sultan's mother.

Şehzade Prince, heir apparent.

Şeyh Head of a Sufi order.

Tuğra Monogram or seal of a sultan.

Ulema The corps of Islamic scholars and authorities in Ottoman times.

Vezir Vizier The principal Ottoman minister of state, responsible for the day-to-day running of the empire.

Vilayet(ı) Formal word for province; also a common term for the provincial headquarters building itself.

ARCHITECTURAL/ARTISTIC TERMS

Apse Curved or polygonal recess at the altar end of a church.

Arasta Marketplace built into the foundations of a mosque, a portion of whose revenues goes to the upkeep of the latter.

Bedesten(ı) Covered market hall for valuable goods, often lockable.

Camekân Changing rooms in a *hamam*.

Eyvan Domed side-chamber of an Ottoman religious building; also applies to three-sided alcoves in secular mansions.

Göbek taşı Literally "navel stone" – the hot central platform of a *hamam*.

Hararet The hottest room of a *hamam*.

Hisar Castle, fort.

İmaret(ı) Soup kitchen and hostel for dervishes and wayfarers, usually attached to a *medrese*.

Kale(si) Castle, fort.

Kapı(sı) Gate, door.

Kemer Series of vaults, or an aqueduct.

Köşk(ü) Kiosk, pavilion, gazebo, folly.

Kubbe Dome, cupola.

Kule(si) Tower, turret.

Kurna Hewn stone basin in a *hamam*.

Külliye(si) Building complex – term for a mosque and dependent buildings taken as a whole.

Medrese(si) Islamic theological academy.

Mescit Small mosque with no *mimber*; Islamic equivalent of a chapel; genitive *mescidi*.

Mezar(ı) Grave, tomb; thus *mezarlık*, cemetery.

Mihrab Niche in a mosque indicating the direction of Mecca, and prayer.

Mimber Pulpit in a mosque, from where the *imam* delivers homilies; often beautifully carved in wood or stone.

Minare(si) Turkish for "minaret", the tower from which the call to prayer is delivered.

Pendentive Curved, triangular surface, by means of which a dome can be supported over a square ground plan.

Pier A mass of supportive masonry.

Porphyry A hard red or purple rock containing mineral crystals.

Revetment Facing of stone, marble or tile on a wall.

Saray(ı) Palace.

Sebil Public drinking fountain, either free standing or built into the wall of an Ottoman structure.

Selamlık Area where men receive guests in any sort of dwelling.

Son cemaat yeri Literally "Place of the last congregation" – a mosque porch where latecomers pray.

Synthronon Semicircular seating for clergy, usually in the apse of a Byzantine church.

Şadırvan Ritual ablutions fountain of a mosque.

Şerefe Balcony of a minaret.

Tabhane Hospice for travelling dervishes or *ahis*, often housed in an *eyvan*.

Tekke(si) Gathering place of a Sufi order.

Türbe(si) Free-standing, usually domed, tomb.

Tympanum The surface, often adorned, enclosed by the top of an arch; found in churches or more ancient ruins.

Verd-antique Type of green marble.

Yalı Ornate wooden residence along the Bosphorus.

Zaviye Mosque built specifically as a hospice for dervishes, usually along a T-plan.

ACRONYMS AND ABBREVIATIONS

AKP *Adalet ve Kalkınma Partisi* or Justice and Development Party; Islamist movement headed by Recep Tayyip Erdoğan, which currently dominates parliament with a two-thirds majority (see p.298).

Bul Standard abbreviation for *bulvar(ı)* (boulevard).

Cad Standard abbreviation for *cadde(si)* (avenue).

CHP *Cumhuriyetçi Halk Partisi* or Republican People's Party (RPP).

IDO *İstanbul Deniz Ötöbüsleri*; company running İstanbul's car ferry and sea bus services.

KDV Acronym of the Turkish VAT.

MHP *Milliyet Hareket Partisi* or National Action.

PKK *Partia Karkaris Kurdistan* or Kurdish Workers' Party.

PTT *Post Telefon ve Telegraf*; the joint postal, telegraph and (formerly) phone service in Turkey.

Sok Abbreviation for *sokak (sokağı)* or street.

THY *Türk Hava Yolları*; Turkish Airways.

TRT Acronym of *Türk Radyo ve Televizyon*; the Turkish public-broadcasting corporation.

Small print and index

A ROUGH GUIDE TO ROUGH GUIDES

Published in 1982, the first Rough Guide – to Greece – was a student scheme that became a publishing phenomenon. Mark Ellingham, a recent graduate in English from Bristol University, had been travelling in Greece the previous summer and couldn't find the right guidebook. With a small group of friends he wrote his own guide, combining a highly contemporary, journalistic style with a thoroughly practical approach to travellers' needs.

The immediate success of the book spawned a series that rapidly covered dozens of destinations. And, in addition to impecunious backpackers, Rough Guides soon acquired a much broader readership that relished the guides' wit and inquisitiveness as much as their enthusiastic, critical approach and value-for-money ethos.

These days, Rough Guides include recommendations from budget to luxury and cover more than 200 destinations around the globe, as well as producing an ever-growing range of eBooks and apps.

Visit **roughguides.com** to see our latest publications.

Rough Guide credits

Editor: Emma Gibbs
Layout: Jessica Subramanian
Cartography: Ashutosh Bharti
Picture editor: Nicole Newman
Proofreader: Diane Margolis
Managing editor: Kathryn Lane
Assistant editor: Jalpreen Chhatwal
Production: Rebecca Short
Cover design: Nicole Newman
Photographers: Roger Mapp
Editorial assistant: Eleanor Aldridge

Senior pre-press designer: Dan May
Marketing, Publicity & roughguides.com: Liz Statham
Design director: Scott Stickland
Travel publisher: Joanna Kirby
Digital travel publisher: Peter Buckley
Reference director: Andrew Lockett
Operations coordinator: Becky Doyle
Operations assistant: Johanna Wurm
Publishing director (Travel): Clare Currie
Commercial manager: Gino Magnotta
Managing director: John Duhigg

Publishing information

This second edition published May 2012 by
Rough Guides Ltd,
80 Strand, London WC2R 0RL
11, Community Centre, Panchsheel Park,
New Delhi 110017, India
Distributed by the Penguin Group
Penguin Books Ltd,
80 Strand, London WC2R 0RL
Penguin Group (USA)
375 Hudson Street, NY 10014, USA
Penguin Group (Australia)
250 Camberwell Road, Camberwell,
Victoria 3124, Australia
Penguin Group (NZ)
67 Apollo Drive, Mairangi Bay, Auckland 1310,
New Zealand
Rough Guides is represented in Canada by Tourmaline
Editions Inc. 662 King Street West, Suite 304, Toronto,
Ontario M5V 1M7
Printed in Singapore by Toppan Security Printing Pte. Ltd.
© Terry Richardson 2012

Maps © Rough Guides
No part of this book may be reproduced in any form
without permission from the publisher except for the
quotation of brief passages in reviews.
344pp includes index
A catalogue record for this book is available from the
British Library
ISBN: 978-1-40539-003-3
The publishers and authors have done their best to
ensure the accuracy and currency of all the information in
The Rough Guide to İstanbul, however, they can accept
no responsibility for any loss, injury, or inconvenience sustained by any traveller as a result of information or advice
contained in the guide.
1 3 5 7 9 8 6 4 2

MIX
Paper from
responsible sources
FSC
www.fsc.org
FSC™ C018179

Help us update

We've gone to a lot of effort to ensure that the second
edition of **The Rough Guide to İstanbul** is accurate and
up-to-date. However, things change – places get
"discovered", opening hours are notoriously fickle,
restaurants and rooms raise prices or lower standards. If
you feel we've got it wrong or left something out, we'd like
to know, and if you can remember the address, the price,
the hours, the phone number, so much the better.

Please send your comments with the subject line
"Rough Guide İstanbul Update" to ✉ mail@uk
.roughguides.com. We'll credit all contributions and send a
copy of the next edition (or any other Rough Guide if you
prefer) for the very best emails.

Find more travel information, connect with fellow
travellers and book your trip on ✇ roughguides.com.

SMALL PRINT 323

ABOUT THE AUTHOR

Terry Richardson is based in the Mediterranean Turkish city of Antalya. He first visited İstanbul back in 1978 and has been an author of *The Rough Guide to Turkey* for over a decade. He leads history and archeology tours in İstanbul and elsewhere in Turkey, writes regular travel features for an English-language Turkish newspaper and occasional articles for the UK press. He was also involved in setting up Turkey's first two long-distance walking trails. When not researching, travelling or climbing the snow-capped Toros Mountains he's likely to be listening to punk/alternative music or following the fluctuating fortunes of Middlesbrough FC.

Acknowledgements

Many thanks to the talented Zoë Smith, winner of the Rough Guide/World Nomads travel writing competition. She ably aided and abetted me in part of the research for this guide and enabled to me view the great city of İstanbul through different eyes. Once again I'm indebted to Erkan of Talisman for hospitality and information, to the brilliant Turkish tour guide Seyhun Aktoprak for invaluable insights into the history of the city, and to another great guide, Berkant Topal, for insider tips on the very best places to eat. And whilst we're on food, here's to the wacky but inimitable Angelis of İstanbul Eats, who really knows how to bring

İstanbul's street food scene to life. My eldest son, Doug, did some sterling research and kindly double-checked (at his father's expense) a slew of Beyoğlu bars and clubs. Rhi and Jimi Davies both provided invaluable feedback on İstanbul hostels and nightlife. Dr Andrew Macek helped tighten-up the history section, whilst Prof. Trevor Watkins provided me with much useful information on the archaeology of the city. And many thanks to Emma Gibbs, who proved to be a fair but firm, supportive and effective editor. Finally, once again to the lovely Lem, this time for forgiving my absences and keeping me sane through the whole updating process.

Readers' letters

Thanks to all the readers who have taken the time to write in with comments and suggestions (and apologies if we've inadvertently omitted or misspelt anyone's name):

Adrienne, Stefanie Breinesberger, Jeff, David Loveday, Simon Nicholls, Nurten Özkoray, Neil Paknadel, Richard Sanger, Peter and Mary Siani-Davies, Jeremy Thomas, Mattias Thoren, Steve Vickers, Michael Wace, Elin Waxin.

Photo credits

Index

Maps are marked in grey.

Maps

Index

Listings key

■ Accommodation
● Restaurant
■ Bar/club/live music/cabaret
● Shop

City plan

The **city plan** on the pages that follow is divided as shown:

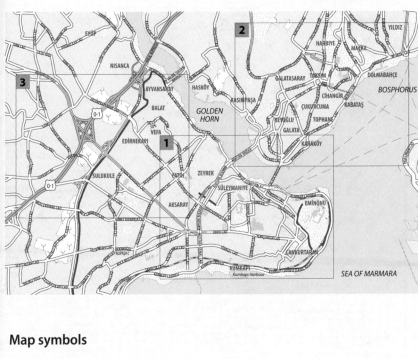

Map symbols

Ⓜ	Light railway/metro	◆	Point of interest	⁙	Ruins	⚘ Church (regional maps)
⊤	Tram	ⓘ	Tourist office	♥	Museum	Church (town maps)
⚓	Ferry terminal (regional maps)	⏛	Fountain	⊙	Statue	Building
★	Bus/Dolmuş stop	🗼	Lighthouse	🕌	Mosque	◯ Stadium
---	Cable car	✚	Hospital	✡	Synagogue	Christian cemetery
⋯⋯	Funicular	✉	Post office	🏛	Monument	Jewish cemetery
▲	Hill	@	Internet access	⚓	Swimming pool	Park/forest
⊠	Gate	♜	Castle	—	Wall	Beach

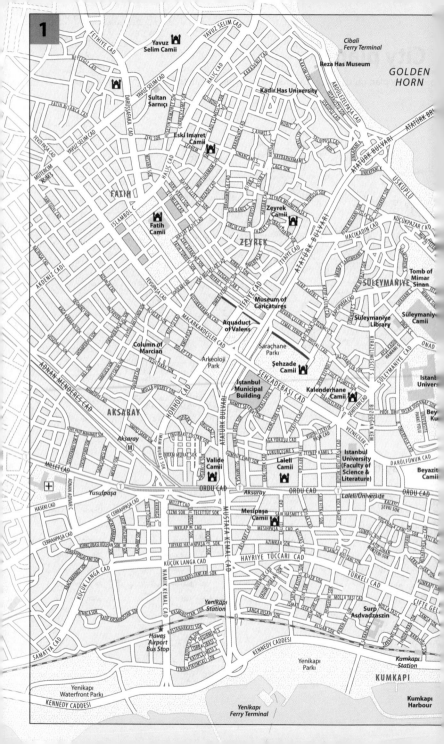

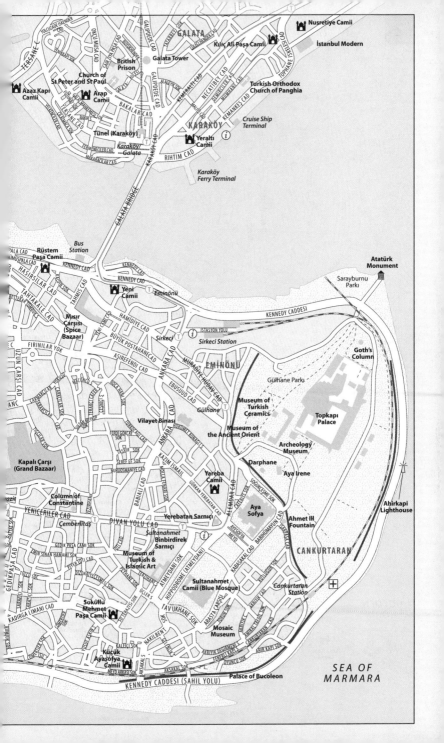

2

GOLDEN HORN

KASIMPAŞA

Hasanpaşa Parkı

Kasımpaşa İskelesi

Kasımpaşa Stadium

GALATASARAY

British Consulate

Hazzopulo Pasajı
Galerist
St Antoine
Pera Museum

Balık Pazarı
Emek Cinema
Çiçek Pasajı

Galatasaray
Galatasaray Meydanı
Galatasaray Lycée
Garajistanbul

Palais de Hollande
Mudo

Cité de Syrie

St Mary Draperis

BEYOĞLU

Italian Consulate

Metro Entrance

Tünel (İstiklal)

Galata Mevlevihanesi

Crimean Memorial Church

GALATA

Galata Tower

British Prison

Church of St Peter and St Paul

Azaz Kapı Camii

Arap Camii

Tünel (Karaköy)

Karaköy/ Galata

Minerva Building

Yeraltı Camii

Turkish Orthodox Church of Panghia

Kılıç Ali Paşa Camii

Tophane

TOPHANE

Nusretiye Camii

İstanbul Modern

KARAKÖY

Cruise Ship Terminal

Karaköy Ferry Terminal

TAKSIM

Cumhuriyet Anıtı

French Consulate

Aya Triada

Ağa Camii

İSTİKLÂL CADDESİ

Taksim Hospital

Germ Hosp

Tiyat Per

ÇUKURCUMA

PUBLIC TRANSPORT

BOSPHORUS

SEA OF MARMARA

GOLDEN HORN

M2
- Hacıosman
- Darüşşafaka
- Atatürk Oto Sanayi
- İTÜ Ayazağa
- Sanayi Mahallesi
- Seyrantepe
- 4 Levent
- 1 Levent
- Gayrettepe
- Şişli-Mecidiyeköy
- Osmanbey-Pangaltı

M1
- Aksaray
- Emniyet-Fatih
- Topkapı-Ulubatlı
- Bayrampaşa Maltepe
- Sağmalcılar
- Kartaltepe-Kocatepe
- Terazidere
- Davutpaşa
- Merter
- Zeytinburnu
- Bakırköy İncirli
- Bahçelievler
- Ataköy Şirinevler
- Yenibosna
- DTM-İstanbul Fuar Merkezi
- Havalimanı (Airport)

T1
- Kabataş
- Fındıklı
- Tophane
- Karaköy
- Eminönü
- Sirkeci
- Gülhane
- Sultanahmet
- Çemberlitaş
- Beyazıt Kapalı Çarşı
- Laleli/Üniversite
- Aksaray
- Yusufpaşa
- Haseki
- Fındıkzade
- Çapa Şehremini
- Pazartekke
- Topkapı
- Cevizlibağ AÖY
- Merkezefendi
- Akşemsettin
- Seyitnizam
- Mithatpaşa
- Zeytinburnu

M2 (top right)
- Gebze
- Osmangazi
- Fatih
- İçme
- Tuzla
- Aydıntepe
- Güzelyalı
- Tersane
- Kaynarca
- Pendik
- Yunus
- Kartal
- Atalar
- Cevizli
- Maltepe
- Süreyya Plajı
- İdealtepe
- Küçükyalı
- Bostancı
- Suadiye
- Erenköy
- Göztepe
- Feneryolu
- Kızıltoprak
- Söğütlüçeşme

T3 Kadıköy-Moda Tramway
- Kadıköy
- Haydarpaşa
- Üsküdar
- Harem

T4
- Habibler
- Mecid-i Selam
- Cebeci
- Sultançiftliği
- Hacı Şükrü
- Yeni Mahalle
- 50 Yıl-Baştabya
- Cumhuriyet
- Metris
- Karadeniz
- Taşköprü
- Ali Fuat Başgil
- Sağmalcılar
- Bosna-Çukurçeşme
- Uluyol-Bereç
- Rami
- Topçular
- Demirkapı
- Edirnekapı

T2
- Bağcılar
- Güneştepe
- Yavuz Selim
- Soğanlı
- Akıncılar
- Güngören
- Keresteciler
- Mehmet Akif

B1
- Halkalı
- Kanarya
- Soğuksu
- Küçükçekmece
- Florya
- Menekşe
- Yeşilyurt
- Yeşilköy
- Bakırköy
- Yeni Mahalle
- Kazlıçeşme
- Yedikule
- Koca Mustafa Paşa
- Yenikapı
- Kumkapı
- Cankurtaran

- Maçka Parkı
- Harbiye Parkı
- Beşiktaş
- Taksim
- Ağa Camii
- Galatasaray
- Odakule
- Tünel
- Beyoğlu

- Piyer Loti
- Eyüp

Legend
- M1 Aksaray - Havalimani Metro
- M2 Taksim - 4 Levent Metro
- T1 Zeytinburnu - Kabataş Tramway
- T2 Zeytinburnu - Bağcılar Tramway
- T3 Kadıköy - Moda Tramway
- T4 Edirnekapı - Sultançiftliği Tramway
- Taksim - Tünel
- B1 Sirkeci - Halkalı Suburban Railway
- B2 Haydarpaşa - Gebze Suburban Railway
- Karaköy - Beyoğlu Tunnel
- Funicular Railway
- Passenger Ferry
- Interchange Station

ROUGH GUIDES

WE GET AROUND

ONLINE start your journey at roughguides.com

EBOOKS & MOBILE APPS

GUIDEBOOKS from Amsterdam to Zanzibar

PHRASEBOOKS learn the lingo

MAPS so you don't get lost

GIFTBOOKS inspiration is our middle name

LIFESTYLE from iPads to climate change

...SO YOU CAN TOO

BOOKS | EBOOKS | APPS

Start your journey at **roughguides.com**
MAKE THE MOST OF YOUR TIME ON EARTH™